AMSCO®

New York

United States
History & Government

Cover Image: Statue of Liberty (Dedicated October 28, 1886) **Source:** Getty Images

PERFECTION LEARNING®

Reviewers and Consultants

Pui Lam Chan (Jack)
Assistant Principal, Social Studies
New Utrecht High School
New York City, New York

Rich Pyszczek
Coordinator of Social Studies
Buffalo Public Schools
Buffalo, New York

Jay Corcoran
Social Studies Chair
Walt Whitman High School
Huntington Station, New York

Greg Roos
Social Studies Teacher
Remsen Central School District
Remsen, New York

Doreen Gordon
Director of Social Studies and Business
Hauppauge Public Schools
Hauppauge, New York

Gloria Sesso
Director of Humanities
Patchogue Medford Schools
Patchogue, New York

Terrance M. McCarthy
K-12 Director of Humanities
Webster Central School District
Webster, New York

Nick Stamoulacatos
Supervisor for Social Studies
Syracuse City School District
Syracuse, New York

Contents

Introduction   vi

Preparing for the United States History and Government Exam   vi

Applying the Task Models   xvi

Chapter 1: Colonial Foundations (1607–1763) *Key Idea 11.1*   4

Civic Literacy Essay: Overview   5

Lesson 1: Europeans Invade the Americas *11.1a*   6

Lesson 2: Factors Influencing Colonial Development *11.1b*   14

Lesson 3: Colonial Political Developments *11.1c*   22

Chapter 1 Review   28

    Multiple-Choice Questions   28

    Short-Essay Questions   31

Chapter 2: Constitutional Foundations (1763–1824) *Key Idea 11.2*   34

Civic Literacy Essay: Close Reading   35

Lesson 1: Tensions Between Britain and the Colonies *11.2a*   36

Lesson 2: Rebellion and Independence *11.2b*   42

Lesson 3: Development of the Constitution *11.2c*   50

Lesson 4: The Constitution in Practice *11.2d*   58

Chapter 2 Review   66

    Multiple-Choice Questions   66

    Short-Essay Questions   70

Chapter 3: Expansion, Nationalism, and Sectionalism *Key Idea 11.3*   72

Civic Literacy Essay: Analyze the Documents   73

Lesson 1: Nationalism Strengthened and Challenged *11.3a*   74

Lesson 2: The Growth of Sectionalism *11.3b*   82

Lesson 3: The Civil War *11.3c*   90

Chapter 3 Review   98

    Multiple-Choice Questions   98

    Short-Essay Questions   103

Period 1 Civic Literacy Document-Based Essay   106

Chapter 4: The Post–Civil War Era (1865–1900) *Key Idea 11.4*   112

    Civic Literacy Essay: Describe Historical Circumstances   113

    Lesson 1: Reconstruction and Repression *11.4a*   114

    Lesson 2: Exclusion of Women Continues *11.4b*   122

    Lesson 3: Destiny and Destruction in the West *11.4c*   128

    Lesson 4: Immigrants in the West *11.4d*   134

    Chapter 4 Review   140

        Multiple-Choice Questions   140

        Short-Essay Questions   144

Chapter 5: Industrialization and Urbanization (1870–1920) *Key Idea 11.5*   148

    Civic Literacy Essay: Gather Evidence to Explain   149

    Lesson 1: Industrialization Transforms Economy *11.5a*   150

    Lesson 2: Consequences of Transformation *11.5b*   156

    Lesson 3: The Progressive Era *11.5b*   166

    Chapter 5 Review   174

        Multiple-Choice Questions   174

        Short-Essay Questions   178

Chapter 6: The Rise of U.S. Power (1890–1920) *Key Idea 11.6*   182

    Civic Literacy Essay: Organize Your Evidence   183

    Lesson 1: Shedding Isolation *11.6a*   184

    Lesson 2: World War I *11.6b*   192

    Lesson 3: The Home Front *11.6c*   202

    Chapter 6 Review   208

        Multiple-Choice Questions   208

        Short-Essay Questions   212

    Period 2 Civic Literacy Document-Based Essay   216

Chapter 7: Prosperity and Depression (1920–1939) *Key Idea 11.7*   222

    Civic Literacy Essay: Develop a Thesis   223

    Lesson 1: The 1920s: Social Change and Continuity *11.7a*   224

    Lesson 2: African American Culture Blossoms *11.7b*   230

    Lesson 3: Prosperity Then Depression *11.7c*   236

    Chapter 7 Review   245

        Multiple-Choice Questions   245

        Short-Essay Questions   249

Chapter 8: World War II (1935–1945) *Key Idea 11.8*   252

    Civic Literacy Essay: Write the Introduction   253

    Lesson 1: War Comes to Europe and Beyond *11.8a*   254

    Lesson 2: The United States at War *11.8a*   260

    Lesson 3: The Domestic Impacts of World War II *11.8b*   268

    Lesson 4: The Holocaust *11.8c*   274

    Chapter 8 Review   280

        Multiple-Choice Questions   280

        Short-Essay Questions   284

Chapter 9: The Cold War (1945–1990) *Key Idea 11.9*   288

    Civic Literacy Essay: Write the Supporting Paragraph   289

    Lesson 1: The Struggle for Influence *11.9a*   290

    Lesson 2: The World on the Edge *11.9b*   298

    Lesson 3: The Troubled Middle East *11.9c*   304

    Lesson 4: The End of the Cold War *11.9d*   310

    Chapter 9 Review   316

        Multiple-Choice Questions   316

        Short-Essay Questions   320

    Period 3 Civic Literacy Document-Based Essay   324

Chapter 10: U.S. Social and Economic Change (1945–Present)
    Key Idea 11.10   330

    Civic Literacy Essay: Write the Conclusion   331

    Lesson 1: The Civil Rights Movement *11.10a*   332

    Lesson 2: Diverse Groups Fight for Rights *11.10b*   340

    Lesson 3: The Federal Government's Role Debated *11.10c*   348

    Chapter 10 Review   356

        Multiple-Choice Questions   356

        Short-Essay Questions   360

Chapter 11: The United States in a Changing World (1990–Present)
    Key Idea 11.11   364

    Civic Literacy Essay: Reread and Evaluate   365

    Lesson 1: Military Action and Inaction in the 1990s *11.11a*   366

    Lesson 2: The War on Terror *11.11b*   372

    Lesson 3: Technology and Globalization *11.11c*   379

    Chapter 11 Review   387

        Multiple-Choice Questions   387

        Short-Essay Questions   391

    Period 4 Civic Literacy Document-Based Essay   395

Practice Regents Examination   401

Index   423

Introduction

Preparing for the United States History & Government Exam

This book prepares students for the New York Regents Exam that they will take at the end of 11th grade. The exam covers the United States History and Government course. It emphasizes the history practices and reasoning skills used by historians, with a strong focus on

- interpretion and use of evidence
- chronological reasoning and causation
- comparison and contextualization

Overview of the Exam

The exam is designed to test the knowledge and skills identified in the New York Social Studies Framework.

Types of Questions

All questions on the United States History Regents Exam will refer to a stimulus, such as an excerpt from a written document, a map, a photo, or a chart. The exam will be divided into three parts based on question type.

Format of the Exam	
Part and Question Type	**Number of Questions**
I. Multiple Choice	28 questions
II. Short Essay	Two sets of three questions
III. Civic Literacy Essay	One set of eight documents used to write one essay

Multiple-Choice Questions

Each question will be based on a stimulus. Each stimulus will be used to answer two questions. Students will need to both interpret the stimulus and use their knowledge of U.S. history and government to identify the best answer.

Short-Essay Questions

This part will consist of two sets of essay questions. Each set will include prompts based on two documents. Each prompt will ask students to write a short essay. The prompt will follow this pattern.

Context prompt will ask about the **context** in which the document(s) were created. It will ask about

- the historical context, the circumstances in time in which a historical development occurred
- the geographic context, the location in which the development took place

Source prompt will ask about the **source** that created the document(s). Students should

- identify the bias, point of view, audience, or purpose of the person (or people) who created the document, OR
- explain how the factor identified affects the reliability of the document as a source of evidence

Relationship prompt will ask about the **relationship** between the documents. The relationship will be one of three types. Students will

- identify and explain a cause-and-effect relationship between the events or ideas in the documents
- identify a turning point—a significant idea or historical event that brings about a change—associated with the events or ideas in the documents and explain why it is a turning point
- identify a similarity or difference between the ideas presented in the two documents

Civic Literacy Essay

Students will write a document-based civic literacy essay that is designed to test their ability to work with historical documents. The test will provide six documents pertaining to a certain constitutional or civic issue. In their essays, students should use evidence from the documents and from their own knowledge of U.S. history and government, including what they learn in this book, to

- describe the historical circumstances surrounding the constitutional or civic issue
- explain efforts to address this constitutional or civic issue by individuals, groups, and/or governments
- discuss the extent to which these efforts were successful or the impact they had on American society

Content Coverage

The exam focuses on certain events and facts in U.S. history. However, the inclusion of some other events and facts is necessary to supply proper historical context and coverage. Likewise, while the exam focuses on events and ideas in the United States, it reflects the growing importance of the United States' interaction with the rest of the world.

Thinking Skills and Task Models

The exam questions use a number of action verbs that indicate what the student is supposed to do. These form the foundation of the task models—the thinking skills students use and the activities they complete as part of their assessment. Some of the most commonly used verbs are listed in the following chart.

Responding to Verbs Used in Questions		
Action Verb	**Definition**	**Expectation**
Compare	To consider or describe as similar or equal	Provide and explain the ways in which two or more things are similar
Contrast	To set in opposition to show or emphasize difference	Provide and explain the ways in which two or more things differ from each other
Define	To give the precise meaning or the basic qualities of something	Provide a concrete, real-world example to strengthen a definition
Describe	To provide a representation in words	Note the attributes or characteristics of a place, idea, or person
Discuss	To offer a considered review	Give factors, definitions, descriptions, explanations, examples, etc., of something
Explain	To give an account or add details	Offer reasons or examples to make an idea plainly understood
Identify	To state a clear, concise, specific answer	Often, a single, well-written sentence is sufficient, but you can add clarifying details. However, do not contradict or add confusion to your original answer

Features of This Book

This book presents the core knowledge and skills that students need to learn as they study United States history and government. The features of the book are described below.

Introduction

In the Introduction, students will learn about the following:

- **Elements of the New York Regents Exam** Reveals the types of questions, the number of each type of question, time allotment, and how questions are structured
- **Features of *New York United States History & Government*** Explains the elements of the book such as the Introduction, the Chapter Openers, Lessons, Chapter Reviews, and Practice Exams
- **New York Social Studies Framework** Summarizes the New York Social Studies Practices, Common Core Reading Standards for Literacy in History/Social Studies, Unifying Themes, and Course Content for United States History and Government

Chapter Openers

In *New York United States History & Government*, each chapter begins with a two-page chapter feature. These openers are divided into four sections.

- **Chapter Overview** This provides a short introduction to the chapter content by examining its overarching themes.
- **New York Framework Standard Key Idea** Each chapter is organized around a single Key Idea from the New York Framework, beginning with a snapshot colonial America and continuing chronologically through to the modern issues of globalization and the movement for human rights.
- **Civic Literacy** This activity introduces students to civic and constitutional issues that may be the focus of the extended essay on the Regents Exam.
- **Civic Literacy Essay Features** These activities prepare students to contextualize, draw together evidence, and evaluate impact, key tasks on the civic literacy document-based essays.
- **Key Terms by Theme** The chapter's Key Terms are listed thematically, with page numbers included.

Lessons

Each lesson has a number of elements that help students learn important content and practice skills.

- **Conceptual Understanding** Lessons begin with a more focused standard from the New York Framework, indicating to students specifically what they will learn in the pages to come.
- **Skill: Analyze a Primary Source** Before students dig into the lesson narrative, they begin with instruction on analyzing a primary source. A source related directly to the key content for the lesson is accompanied by several marginal notes that provide tips to help students interpret the source.
- **Narrative** The core content described in the New York Framework is presented in clear, concise language.
- **Read Closely** Throughout the narrative, notes in the margin help students develop their skill at reading history. Most notes include a question for students to answer so they can immediately apply that skill to the text they are reading.
- **Application: Interpret a Primary Source** Finally, each lesson ends with another primary source for students to read and respond to questions about.

Chapter Review

Chapters end with a series of activities to help students analyze the chapter content and practice the sort of questions they will face on the Regents Exam. Tips for answering questions are offered where appropriate.

- **Multiple-Choice Questions** Students answer several sets of multiple-choice questions, each of which is based on one or more pieces of stimulus.
- **Short-Essay Questions** Students write short-essay responses to questions that refer to one or more documents.

Civic Literacy Document-Based Essays

Four chapters end with a prompt for a civic literacy document-based essay directing students to analyze six documents and use several to practice writing essays.

Practice Exam

This book concludes with a practice exam modeled on the Regents Exam.

New York Social Studies Framework

The state of New York provides guidance in what content and skills students should study. Some of this guidance is described below.

Social Studies Practices

Students are expected to learn a number of approaches, or practices, that will help them think like historians.

1. **Gathering, Interpreting, and Using Evidence** Students should learn to
   - use evidence to create and answer questions, but they should also learn to consider alternative hypotheses and answers
   - gather evidence from a wide range of sources and analyze its point of view, bias, purpose, and other important criteria
   - analyze the arguments of others, effectively make inferences and draw conclusions, and use disparate sources of evidence to create meaningful understandings of the past

2. **Chronological Reasoning and Causation** Students should learn
   - how events are related in time—that earlier ideas and events can influence those that come later
   - that events and ideas can have short- or long-term effects
   - the importance of historical continuity and change
   - to relate patterns of continuity and change to larger historical processes and themes

3. **Comparison and Contextualization** Students should learn to
   - compare multiple aspects of historical periods and/or events and geographic regions
   - analyze multiple historical developments within, across, and between societies and in a range of times and places
   - recognize the relationships between geography, economics, and history and see how these relationships function as a context for events and movements

4. **Geographic Reasoning** Students should learn to
   - ask geographic questions about the importance of place and use geographic tools to assess the relationships between people, places, and environments
   - assess the relationship between human activities and the environment
   - recognize how societies are influenced by place and region

5. **Economics and Economic Systems** Students should understand the impacts of such economic concepts as
   - marginal benefits/marginal costs, incentives, competition
   - property rights and the rule of law in a market economy
   - how government economic policies affect the economy

6. **Civic Participation** Students should learn to

- interact respectfully with others when participating in activities with their communities

- get involved, when necessary, in social and political issues both as an individual and with groups

- recognize that the protection of peoples' freedoms and rights in a democratic society depends on their taking responsibility to work to influence those in positions of power

Common Core Reading Standards for Literacy in History/Social Studies

Key Ideas and Details When analyzing sources, students should learn to cite textual evidence, determine central ideas and provide an accurate summary, and determine the difference between correlation and causation in a series of events.

Craft and Structure Students should learn to determine the meanings of history/social studies-focused words and phrases and analyze how key points in a text are highlighted by differing text structures.

Integration of Knowledge and Ideas Students should be able to use charts and graphs in conjunction with text, as well as analyze the extent to which text supports an author's claim.

Range of Reading and Level of Text Complexity By the end of grade 11, students should be able to read and comprehend history/social studies texts in the grades 11–12 text complexity band.

Common Core Writing Standards for Literacy in History/Social Studies

Text Types and Purposes Students should learn to

- introduce a topic and organize ideas using headings, tables and charts, and multimedia, when appropriate

- use linking words and phrases to create a cohesive text

- write arguments that focus on discipline-specific content, introducing claims and counterclaims fairly and supporting each with data and evidence

- develop the topic using solid and relevant facts, details, quotations, and other appropriate information

- using precise, domain-specific language and discipline-appropriate style, while maintaining an objective tone

- provide a concluding section that supports the argument

Production and Distribution of Writing Students should be able to improve their writing through revision, editing, rewriting, or refocusing their approach to suit a specific audience or purpose. They should also be able to use technology to publish, update, and distribute writing projects.

Research to Build and Present Knowledge Students should learn to conduct short and extended research projects, gathering and synthesizing information from multiple authoritative sources while avoiding plagiarism and using a standard citation format.

Range of Writing Students should be able to write over extended and shorter time frames for a variety of tasks, purposes, and audiences.

Unifying Themes

The 10 Unifying Themes for social studies represent different viewpoints that teachers and students can use when approaching the Key Ideas and Conceptual Understandings found in the New York Social Studies Framework.

1. **Individual Development and Cultural Identity (ID)** The development of personal and cultural identity occurs within the broader framework of a person's geography, era, social and economic class, experiences, politics, and more.

2. **Development, Movement, and Interaction of Cultures (MOV)** Cultural elements such as politics, religion, and race strongly affect things like literature, film, and music. Cultural diffusion and change over time strongly affect these and other cultural elements.

3. **Time, Continuity, and Change (TCC)** The formal research methods that historians apply help them reconstruct and interpret events, analyze historical cause and effect, and weigh the validity of competing theories of events.

4. **Geography, Humans, and the Environment (GEO)** Human populations and their activities have a profound effect on the natural environment. Interactions between people, places, regions, and environments are important aspects of history.

5. **Development and Transformation of Social Structures (SOC)** Social structures, such as economic and social classes and political and social institutions, are affected and often defined by gender, race, ethnicity, age, and other similar factors. This fact can promote social and political inequalities.

6. **Power, Authority, and Governance (GOV)** Different forms of government have differing characteristics and functions. In each form, power has different origins and is used in different ways (and sometimes abused). Diplomacy, conflict, and war are major aspects of governmental power and authority and major subjects of historical study.

7. **Civic Ideas and Practices (CIV)** In a democratic republic, citizens have certain freedoms, rights, and responsibilities (including civic participation and engagement). But in the modern, globalized world, do people have certain responsibilities toward the global community? In nondemocratic countries, people often struggle to achieve and keep basic freedoms and rights.

8. **Creation, Expansion, and Interaction of Economic Systems (ECO)** The study of history includes such economic topics as production, consumption, resource scarcity, supply and demand, trade, globalization, and the role of the government in the economy.

9. **Science, Technology, and Innovation (TECH)** Scientific, technological, and intellectual theories and discoveries directly influence social, economic, and cultural change.

10. **Global Connections and Exchange (EXCH)** Human societies have interacted from the very beginning, exchanging goods, ideas, and technologies. This has accelerated over time as technology has facilitated even greater cultural diffusion. Globalization has many social, political, and economic benefits and consequences.

Course Content

The New York Framework divides the content into 11 chapters.

1. **Colonial Foundations (1607–1763)** European colonization in North America resulted in cultural contact and exchange among diverse peoples. These interactions at times led to conflict. Regional differences—social and racial—developed for a variety of reasons in colonial America.

2. **Constitutional Foundations (1763–1824)** Growing political and economic tensions with Great Britain led the American colonists to declare their independence. Once independent, the new nation confronted the challenge of creating a stable federal republic.

3. **Expansion, Nationalism, and Sectionalism (1824–1865)** As the nation expanded, growing sectional tensions, especially over slavery, resulted in political and constitutional crises that culminated in the Civil War.

4. **The Post-Civil War Era (1865–1900)** The country was politically reunited after the war and constitutional rights were expanded. But during Reconstruction, those rights were undermined and issues of inequality continued for African Americans, women, Native Americans, Mexican Americans, and Chinese immigrants.

5. **Industrialization and Urbanization (1870–1920)** The United States transformed from an agrarian to an increasingly industrial and urbanized society. This created new economic opportunities, but it also resulted in societal problems that were addressed by a variety of reform efforts.

6. **The Rise of U.S. Power (1890–1920)** Many factors contributed to the United States' rise as a world power. Debates over the country's role in world affairs increased in response to overseas expansion and involvement in World War I. The United States' participation in the war had important effects on American society.

7. **Prosperity and Depression (1920–1939)** The 1920s and 1930s were a time of cultural and economic changes. The nation also faced significant domestic challenges, including the Great Depression.

8. **World War II (1935–1945)** The participation of the United States in World War II was a transformative event for the nation and its role in the world.

9. **The Cold War (1945–1990)** After World War II, the United States entered into the Cold War, an extended era of international conflict that influenced foreign and domestic policy for more than 40 years.

10. **U.S. Social and Economic Change (1945–Present)** Racial, gender, and socioeconomic inequalities were addressed by individuals, groups, and organizations. Political philosophies prompted debates over the role of the federal government in regulating the economy and providing a social safety net.

11. **The United States in a Changing World (1990–Present)** The political and economic status of the United States in the world has faced external and internal challenges related to international conflicts, economic competition, and globalization. Throughout this time period, the nation has continued to debate and define its role in the world.

Eleven Key Ideas

Each Key Idea in the New York Framework is the starting point for one chapter in *New York United States History & Government*. That Key Idea is stated on the first page of the chapter. Within each Key Idea are Conceptual Understandings, and each of these is the starting point for a lesson within the 11 chapters.

1. **Colonial Foundations**
2. **Constitutional Foundations**
3. **Expansion, Nationalism, and Sectionalism**
4. **Post-Civil War and Reconstruction**
5. **Industrialization and Urbanization**
6. **The Rise of U.S. Power and World War I**
7. **Prosperity and the Great Depression**
8. **World War II**
9. **The Cold War**
10. **U.S. Social and Economic Change**
11. **The United States in a Changing World**

Civic Literacy Issues

Throughout United States history, individuals, groups, and governments at the local, state, and federal levels have confronted important constitutional or civic issues. Understanding these efforts is part of civic literacy, knowledge a person needs to fully and successfully participate in public life. The chart below lists a few of the broad categories of constitutional or civic issues. Many of these are based on rights specified in the U.S. Constitution, particularly in the Bill of Rights. Also listed are examples of how people have responded to these issues.

Addressing Constitutional or Civic Issues

Constitutional or Civic Issue	Effort to Address the Issue	Discussion
Freedom of Speech and of the Press	**1788:** Mercy Otis Warren of Massachusetts published an essay calling for a protection for the freedom of the press in the newly proposed Constitution. See page 53. **1965:** Students wore black armbands to a school in Des Moines, Iowa, to protest the War in Vietnam. See page 346.	What limts should government place on the right to the free expression of ideas?
Freedom of Religion	**1681:** The colony of Pennsylvania was founded as a place where people could escape religious persecution. See page 33.	How should courts balance the freedom of religion with other rights?
The Rights of People Accused of Crimes	**1961:** A Florida inmate named Clarence Gideon wrote a letter to the Supreme Court saying he needed a lawyer so he could receive a fair trial. See page 344.	What limits should be placed on government in proscecuting people accused of crimes?
The Right to Vote	**1828:** By this time, most states had ended the requirement to own land in order to vote. See page 80. **1965:** Opponents of laws that made voting by African Americans difficult used protest marches and lobbying to win passage of a Voting Rights Act. See page 338.	How much responsibility does government have to make voting convenient?
Equality for Racial and Ethnic Groups	**1867:** Chinese workers in the western United States who were building a railroad went on strike for equal pay with White workers. See page 137. **1951:** Poet Langston Hughes attacked segregation in his poem "Harlem (Dream Deferred)." See page 231.	How does the country guarantee that everyone is treated fairly regardless of their race or ethnicity?
Equality for Women	**1848:** Reformers met at Seneca Falls, New York, to organize a drive for equal rights for women. See page 126. **1966:** The National Organization for Women organized people to demand equal pay for women and men who did the same work. See page 341.	When, if ever, should people be treated differently because of their gender?

Applying the Task Models

1. Best Use for a Source

Historians rely on primary sources to understand the past. Primary sources include any firsthand account of an event. They can be either a written or an artistic account by either participants or observers. However, each type of source has both strengths and weaknesses that influence how historians can use them best. The chart below lists some of the common types of primary sources and their strengths and weaknesses.

Evaluating Types of Primary Sources		
Type	**Strengths**	**Weaknesses**
Diary	Often reflects insight into how a person felt	Sometimes lacks context of how others thought or felt
Memoir	Often expresses an insider's view of events	Sometimes written to flatter a leader or attack an opponent
Speech	Often indicates what a leader believes or what the leader thinks listeners want to hear	Sometimes deliberately misleading in order to make the speaker popular
Newspaper reports	Often provides objective information	Sometimes sensationalized to sell copies
Government report	Often presents detailed, neutral, information	Sometimes reflects a government's bias
Religious artifacts	Often shows what people believed and held valuable	Sometimes open to several interpretations

For each source listed below, write a question that it could help answer.

1. The diary of a Pilgrim writing about his initial encounters with Native Americans

   _____

   _____

2. A letter home from an English merchant living in Colonial Virginia

   _____

   _____

3. A painting of Pennsylvania Quakers agreeing to a treaty with Native Americans

   _____

   _____

4. Ship records listing cargo on voyages between England and Boston Harbor in 1700

   _____

   _____

2. Identify the Author's Intention

Interpreting a source accurately requires understanding why the author wrote it. The table below summarizes issues to identify in order to recognize what an author is trying to communicate.

Influences Shaping an Author's Intention		
Type of Influence	**Description**	**Examples**
Point of View	The author's role in an event	• The author's level of wealth or race
Purpose	The reason the source was created	• A desire to persuade or to entertain
Context	The general historical conditions	• A time of economic prosperity or religious conflict
Bias	The values of the author	• A supporter of gender equality or slavery
Form of the Source	The nature of the source	• A long book or a short newspaper advertisement
Time the Source Was Created	The chronological period	• During the Mayflower landing or Colonial era
Place the Source Was Created	The geographic location	• A large coastal city or a small village in the mountains
Intended Audience	The people the author created the source for	• A few experts or all potential voters

For each source listed below, identify two influences that might shape how the author might write the item identified.

1. The diary of a French general commenting on the French colonies in Canada in the 1750s

   _____

   _____

2. A journalist writing in 1765 in a Massachusetts newspaper describing the effects of England's Stamp Act on the colonies

   _____

   _____

3. A letter from an indentured servant in 1653 to his parents describing the conditions in which he works and lives in Pennsylvania

   _____

   _____

4. A speech by Patrick Henry to the Virginia House of Burgesses in 1775 arguing for the creation of a state militia

   _____

   _____

3. Identify Support for a Claim

A claim is a statement asserted to be true. A well-written claim is not simply a personal preference. Rather, it can be supported—or opposed—with facts, reasons, or informed opinions.

Statement	Is this a good example of a claim?
In *Federalist Paper #51*, James Madison says that "if men were angels, no government would be necessary." I like this idea because it explains a complex idea in a simple way.	No: it is a personal preference. Other people cannot use evidence to prove or disprove it.
Madison's idea that government wouldn't be needed if men acted in the best interest of society is useful because it identifies self-interest as a problematic but genuine human instinct.	Yes: people can provide facts and informed opinions to support or oppose it.

The table below evaluates how well statements support a claim about the usefulness of Madison's idea of government being unnecessary "if men were angels."

Statement	Is this a good example of support?
Madison's statement explains how human nature makes government necessary.	No: it simply rewords the claim.
Madison wrote the original draft of the Constitution our government was founded on.	No: it is a true statement, but it's not relevant to whether his idea was useful.
If people didn't try to harm or cheat other people, whether in commerce or personal interaction, there wouldn't be a need for government entities to serve as the arbiter of fairness and justice.	Yes: it provides a concrete example to support the general statement.

Evaluate whether each sentence is a good example of a well-written claim.

1. I believe history is my favorite subject to study in school.

_____

_____

2. Madison's impression of how people interact as a society and the need for a governing body to serve as an arbitrator remains to this day one of the most insightful tenets of democratic theory.

_____

_____

Evaluate whether each sentence is a good example of support for this claim.

3. Studying the history of the United States prepares people to understand current events.

_____

_____

4. History classes usually require more reading than do mathematics courses.

_____

_____

4. Select a Plausible Claim

Historians build an interpretation about the past based on primary sources. Based on the sources, they make plausible claims that they think logically follow from the source.

However, not all claims based on a primary source are equally plausible. Following is a primary source written by George Hewes, one of the "Indians" who dumped the British tea into the harbor during the Boston Tea Party. Read it and consider the claims stated in the table after it.

> We were immediately ordered by the respective commanders to board all the ships at the same time, which we promptly obeyed. The commander of the division to which I belonged, as soon as we were on board the ship, appointed me boatswain, and ordered me to go to the [ship's] captain and demand of him the keys to the hatches and a dozen candles. I made the demand accordingly, and the captain promptly replied, and delivered the articles; but requested me at the same time to do no damage to the ship or rigging. We then were ordered by our commander to open the hatches and take out all the chests of tea and throw them overboard, and we immediately proceeded to execute his orders, first cutting and splitting the chests with our tomahawks, so as thoroughly to expose them to the effects of the water.
>
> **Source:** "The Boston Tea Party, 1773," EyeWitness to History, 2002

Claims and Plausibility

Claim	How plausible or logical is the claim?
The "Indians" wanted to make sure the tea was unusable.	Very plausible: Hewes clearly states the intention in breaking open the chests.
The ship's captain understood he couldn't stop the colonists and didn't want the situation to become violent.	Plausible: The captain willingly gives Hewes the keys and asks him not to damage the ship.
Hewes's commander felt he was capable of leading the revolutionaries on the ship.	Somewhat: The commander tasks Hewes with the important job of getting the keys from the ship's captain.
The ship's captain is sympathetic to the colonists' cause and willingly allows them to throw the tea overboard.	Not logical: Hewes says nothing about the captain's feelings about the situation. It is more likely the captain knows he's been overpowered and doesn't want to risk unnecessary violence or damage to the ship.

Evaluate the plausibility of each claim listed below.

1. The Townshend Acts of 1767 were a set of British laws that ultimately angered the colonists to political action.

_____

_____

2. Because the Stamp Act affected daily household goods, it resulted in turning every colonist against British rule.

_____

_____

3. In the early drafts of the Declaration of Independence, Jefferson included language ending the slave trade, even though he knew the idea would be met with fierce opposition from many of his fellow delegates gathered in Philadelphia.

_____

_____

4. The Revolution had a great impact on colonial women because they were needed to keep the colonies' economies running.

_____

_____

5. Identify Turning Points in History

A **turning point** is an event in history that led to lasting change. For example, the following excerpt demonstrates how a single battle can lead to crucial and lasting change in historical events. Near the end of the Civil War in April 1865, the Confederate Army attempted to make a stand against the advancing Union forces at Petersburg, Virginia. General Robert E. Lee was awaiting reinforcement troops from North Carolina. Lee knew stopping the Union army here was going to determine the progress of the war. The reinforcements didn't make it in time, and at the junction called Five Forks, the Union army overtook the Confederates and forced Lee and his dwindling army to retreat from Petersburg. Eight days later, Lee and the Confederate army surrendered, effectively ending the Civil War. In an address seven years after the war ended, Confederate General Jubal Early described the effect of the overwhelming loss at the Battle of Five Forks.

> The retreat from the lines of Richmond and Petersburg began in the early days of April, and the remnant of the Army of Northern Virginia fell back, more than one hundred miles, before its overpowering antagonists, repeatedly presenting front to the latter and giving battle so as to check his progress. Finally, from mere exhaustion, less than eight thousand men with arms in their hands, of the noblest army that ever fought . . . were surrendered at Appomattox to an army of 150,000 men; the sword of Robert E. Lee, without a blemish on it, was sheathed forever.
>
> **Source:** http://www.sonofthesouth.net/leefoundation/chapter8.htm

Understanding the Battle of Five Forks	
What does Early suggest hastened the surrender and end of the Civil War?	He suggests an overpowering antagonist and sheer exhaustion hastened the surrender.
Why was the retreat after this battle so important?	Lee realized he couldn't defeat the Union army and tried to save the troops he had by moving back more than 100 miles.
How does the Battle of Five Forks represent a turning point in history?	It was a final overwhelming blow to Lee's army and left the Confederacy no option but to surrender.

Describe how each of the following represented a turning point.

1. The Louisiana Purchase, 1803

_____

_____

2. The Seneca Falls Convention, 1848

_____

_____

3. The election of Abraham Lincoln, 1860

_____

_____

4. The 13th Amendment, 1865

_____

_____

6. Identify Change and Continuity in History

Continuity, an uninterrupted succession, and change are vital lenses through which historians attempt to analyze historical events and trends. Change is different from a turning point in that it is much less sudden. Historians often identify change by comparing two distinct historical moments to see how circumstances differ between them—for example, the United States before and after the Civil War. It is usually the case that when comparing two points in time such as these, while change is often apparent, there is also continuity. The following chart identifies examples of both change and continuity before and after the Civil War.

United States Before and After the Civil War	
Change	**Continuity**
Slavery was abolished.	Jim Crow laws continued to limit rights and freedoms for African Americans.
Freed slaves gained the right to vote with the 15th Amendment.	Poll taxes and other voter suppression laws in states prevented African Americans from voting.
Northern and Southern states unified with a stronger federal government.	Southern states remained primarily agrarian, while Northern states embraced innovations of the industrial revolution.
More women moved into the workplace and began exerting political power.	Women remained primarily homemakers and still did not have the right to vote.

Select an important event from history. Write it in the top bar. Then list three changes from before and after the event and three continuities.

Name	
Changes	**Continuities**
1.	1.
2.	2.
3.	3.

7. Identify Central Causes

In order to explain and understand historical events accurately, historians try to determine their central causes. Most historical events do not have a single, central cause. Rather, events take place in a framework with many variables. For example, some causes arise from long-term circumstances and some arise from short-term circumstances. Most arise from a combination of both. The chart below lists multiple causes of the reservation system for Native Americans in the United States.

Short-Term and Long-Term Causes of the Resevation System I	
Long-Term Causes	• Since Colonial times, Native Americans had their lands taken over by the growing settler population • Expansion of the American population westward included the Louisiana Purchase (1803) and the Mexican War (1846–1848)
Short-Term Causes	• The Transcontinental Railroad (1863–1869) • The United States government granting western land to settlers and sending U.S. troops to fight Native American tribes trying to defend their lands

Label each of the following as a long-term cause or a short-term cause of the reservation system and briefly describe its significance.

1. The Homestead Act of 1862

_____

_____

_____

_____

2. Broken treaties between tribes and the United States

_____

_____

_____

_____

3. The Native American wars

_____

_____

_____

4. The massacre at Wounded Knee

_____

_____

_____

8. Identify Central Effects

In their attempts to make sense of historical events, historians also try to determine their central effects. As is true with the causes of historical events, most do not have a single, central effect, and the effects manifest themselves over a continuum, with some being short term and others being long term. The chart below shows a number of effects of the Civil War.

Short-Term and Long-Term Effects of the Civil War	
Long-Term Effects	• The abolition of slavery • The preservation of the Union • The persistence of racial animus
Short-Term Effects	• Enslaved people were freed • Spike in migration of people from the South to Northern cities • Occupation of Southern states by federal troops

Label each of the following as a short-term or a long-term effect of the Civil War, and briefly describe its significance.

1. Political debate over states' rights versus federal rights

_____

_____

_____

2. The Freedman's Bureau

_____

_____

_____

3. The 15th Amendment

_____

_____

_____

4. The election of African Americans to Congress

_____

_____

_____

9. *Identify the Impact of Time and Place*

When and where a historical event occurred affects why it occurred. As a result, historians think about the importance of time and place on events and issues.

- What people or movements had impacts on other people or movements?
- Did an area's topography play a role?
- Did the involvement of another actor contribute to the outcome?

In the timeline below, note how time and place shaped events during the second Industrial Revolution in the United States.

Date	Events
1856	The Bessemer Process of mass-producing steel is invented, revolutionizing steel production.
1863–1869	The Transcontinental Railroad is begun and completed at Promontory Summit, Utah.
1878	Alexander Graham Bell invents the telephone; within 22 years, 1.3 million were in homes and businesses.
1878	Thomas Edison invents the first successful light bulb.
1890	The Sherman Antitrust Act restrains growth of monopolies in many industries (rail, steel, energy, etc.).
1913	Henry Ford perfects the assembly line production of cars, building one car every 93 minutes.
1913	The 16th Amendment establishes a progressive federal income tax based on total annual income.
1914	American Federation of Labor grows to over 2 million members and fights for higher wages, shorter weekly hours, and better working conditions.

Explain how either time or place influenced each event.

1. By 1880, John D. Rockefeller had cornered the oil business in the United States.

_____

_____

2. The late 19th century saw a large migration of people moving from rural areas to cities.

_____

_____

3. The number of possible voters in the U.S. nearly doubled with the ratification of the 19th Amendment in 1920.

_____

_____

4. An estimated 23 million European immigrants came to the United States between 1870 and 1920.

_____

10. Identify a Similarity

Historians closely study different documents or other evidence to make note of similarities and differences between them. Similarities in sources can help historians notice where a consensus exists or realize the strength of a certain theory. Differences can help show where bias might exist in a certain source or where further research is necessary. The following chart offers examples of ways that certain pieces of evidence might show similarities.

Types of Sources	Similarities
Two news reports of the same event	Statements that appear in both reports are likely to be accurate.
Two maps of the same region but from different periods	Boundaries that are the same show continuity in history.
Memoirs by two participants in an event	Recollections that are shared might suggest similarities in the outlook of the two writers.

Read the passage below. Identify three facts stated by the author. In the chart below, write three sentences stating similar facts to those given in the passage.

> Women of all classes risked their health, jobs, and reputations by continuing their protests. One historian estimated that approximately 2,000 women spent time on the picket lines between 1917 and 1919, and that 500 women were arrested. . . . The NWP made heroes of the suffrage prisoners, held ceremonies in their honor, and presented them with commemorative pins. Women went on publicity tours dressed in prison garb and talked about their experiences in prison in order to win public support for their cause. . . . Government officials found it increasingly difficult to refuse the vote to women who were contributing so much to the war effort. Anti-suffragist arguments about women's mental and physical inferiority were difficult to sustain as women took over jobs vacated by men drafted into military service.
>
> **Source:** https://socialwelfare.library.vcu.edu/woman-suffrage/national-womans-party/

Similarities
1.
2.
3.

11. Identify a Difference

Historians study documents and other evidence to locate and analyze differences. Differences often indicate turning points or change over time. The following chart offers examples of ways that certain pieces of evidence might show differences.

Types of Sources	Differences
Two news reports of the same event	Statements that appear in only one report reflect the reporter's point of view.
Two maps of the same region but from different periods	Elements that differ might show changes in population distribution or boundaries.
Memoirs by two participants in an event	Recollections that differ might reflect the participants' differing roles or viewpoints.

After reading these two sources on why the United States entered World War I, summarize the differences.

Germany's Gamble

The Germans were well aware that the U.S. could not and would not accept unrestricted submarine warfare, but launched it anyway. . . . The U.S. declaration of war was thus already taken into account when the final decision for unrestricted submarine warfare was made in January 1917. Indeed, [Field Marshall] Hindenburg explicitly admitted the day before "We count upon war with America." . . .[The Germans] thought the gamble would open up a window of opportunity in which they could defeat the British. If they defeated the British, then they could prevent Americans from coming to the mainland and they would have a victorious end to the war.

Source: https://www.rochester.edu/newscenter/looking-back-100-years-u-s-enters-world-war-i-on-april-6-1917/

A War of Choice?

Historians will debate forever whether the Great War could have been prevented. But for the United States, it was indisputably a war of choice. Germany neither threatened a trans-Atlantic attack, nor had the ability to mount one. And while Woodrow Wilson and the government's propaganda agency, the Committee on Public Information, portrayed the Kaiser's regime as a cruel autocracy, it could not raise an army without the approval of the Reichstag, an elected legislature. And was Imperial Germany so morally inferior to the three empires it was fighting—the British, the French, and, until March of 1917, the realm of the Tsar?

Source: https://newrepublic.com/article/118435/world-war-i-debate-should-us-have-entered.

12. Identify an Informed Action

The process of taking an informed action begins with education. In a democratic society, it is critical for citizens—individually or as part of a group or organization—to seek out and use important information about issues that affect their lives and the lives of their fellow citizens. (This highlights the absolutely crucial role that a free and independent press plays in a democratic society.) Once a citizen or group of citizens has identified an issue and formulated a viewpoint based on accurate information, one result can be civic activism—activities designed to improve people's communities, environments, and/or governments. A wide range of activities falls under the umbrella of civic activism:

- helping clean up a neighborhood park
- volunteering at a school or community center
- advocating for poor or homeless citizens
- raising money for a local library
- running for public office

Read the following article and answer the questions that follow it.

[Ida B. Wells] hired detectives from the Pinkerton Agency to investigate lynchings on her behalf; she then described them in articles in the *New York Age* for which she was then writing. At the same time, she was also speaking against lynching to groups around the country. . . . She was one of 60 prominent people nationwide who gathered in Chicago's Orchestra Hall to plan the formation of the National Association for the Advancement of Colored People [NAACP], although, believing it too passive an organization, she never participated in it. Instead, she spent time passionately fighting segregation in Chicago schools. . . . Ida was also a regular visitor of prisons, interviewing young Black inmates to discover why they had run afoul of the law. Her conclusion was joblessness. In 1910, she opened the Negro Fellowship League Reading Room and Social Center on Chicago's South State Street. In it, there was a large dorm for the homeless to sleep and a reading room stocked with Chicago newspapers, for job advertisements, and Southern papers for news of home. . . . When private funding for the Center ended, Ida moved it to a storefront and took a job as a probation officer to support it. When the Center closed in 1920, 1,000 men had found jobs through it and many others had found shelter there. During her Chicago years, Ida also . . . wrote articles for the *Chicago Defender*, founded the Alpha Suffrage Club and ran unsuccessfully for the Illinois state senate.

Source: https://www.classicchicagomagazine.com/ida-b-wells-the-drive-in-her-name/.

1. Explain Wells's primary focus in her social and political activities.

_____

_____

2. Describe why Wells might believe the NAACP was "too passive" an organization.

_____

_____

13. Answer Questions About Visuals

In the study of history, visual evidence, such as maps, graphs and charts, timelines, cartoons, and photographs, can be a source of critical evidence. Sources such as these need to be analyzed thoroughly. The following chart gives some suggestions on how to effectively analyze visual sources.

Types	Methods for Analyzing
Maps	• Study the map legend to understand what each dot, line, shading, and color, represents. • Use the map's compass and scale. • Note when the map was made, who made it, and for whom it was made to understand the point of view it represents.
Graphs and Charts	• Use the title to identify the graph's or chart's main idea. • Note how the headings, axes, and any types of lines or shading help organize the information. • Identify details that support the main idea.
Timelines	• Determine the time period covered in the timeline. • Identify how the timeline has been divided and why it was done in this way. • Identify patterns, such as cause and effect, continuity, and change.
Cartoons	• Look for signs of the cartoonist's political leanings and experiences that might represent bias. • Evaluate the cartoon in the context of the era it was created.
Photographs	• Analyze the details in the photograph. • Consider whether the photograph became a symbol of a historical era or event.

Find an example of a visual used in a recent news story. Answer the following questions about it.

1. What is the main point of the visual?

_____

_____

_____

2. What important details does the visual provide?

_____

_____

_____

3. What is the point of view of the person who created the visual?

_____

_____

_____

14. Identify Stakeholders and Issues

A stakeholder is anyone who has a share or an interest in an issue or enterprise. A stakeholder issue is the issue or enterprise in which the stakeholder is engaged. For example, imagine that in a state, a group wanted to pass a law by referendum removing an animal from a protected list and allowing people to hunt the animal in limited amounts. This would be the stakeholder issue. The stakeholders in this scenario are, broadly, the voters of the state and the legislators who introduced the referendum. But there are also more specific stakeholders, including

- members of conservation groups dedicated to wildlife preservation
- members of groups that support the right to hunt
- lobbying groups on both sides
- people who run outdoor-related tourism businesses such as hunting lodges

Read the following speech excerpt from Alabama Representative Richard Hobson arguing for prohibition in 1914, and answer the questions that follow.

A Case for Prohibition

Slaves in Shackles
When the drinking begins young the power of the habit becomes overwhelming, and the victim might as well have shackles. It is estimated that there are 5,000,000 heavy drinkers and drunkards in America, and these men might as well have a ball and chain on their ankles, for they are more abject slaves than those Black men who were driven by slave drivers.

Liquor Degenerates the Character
The first finding of science that alcohol is a protoplasmic poison and the second finding that it is an insidious, habit-forming drug. . . . the third finding [is] that alcohol degenerates the character of men and tears down their spiritual nature. Like the other members of the group of oxide derivatives of hydrocarbons, alcohol is not only a general poison, but it has a chemical affinity or deadly appetite for certain particular tissues. Strychnine tears down the spinal cord. Alcohol tears down the top part of the brain in a man, attacks certain tissues in an animal, certain cells in a flower. . . . Every type and every species is evolving in building from generation to generation along some particular line. Man is evolving in the top part of the brain, the seat of the will power, the seat of the moral senses, and of the spiritual nature, the recognition of right and wrong, the consciousness of God and of duty and of brotherly love and of self-sacrifice.

Source: https://prohibition.osu.edu/hobson

1. How is Hobson arguing his case for Prohibition?

_____

_____

2. Who are the stakeholders in the issue described in the passage?

_____

_____

15. Identify a Course of Action

Throughout history, issues have presented themselves, and a course of action—often recommended by a person, a group, or a government—is needed to address the issue.

Read the following 1940 fireside chat by President Franklin D. Roosevelt, addressing the nation about national defense and the ongoing German hostilities in Europe. Then answer the questions that follow.

Franklin Roosevelt on the Growing German Threat in Europe

There are many among us who in the past closed their eyes to events abroad—because they believed in utter good faith what some of their fellow Americans told them—that what was taking place in Europe was none of our business; that no matter what happened over there, the United States could always pursue its peaceful and unique course in the world. There are many among us who closed their eyes, from lack of interest or lack of knowledge; honestly and sincerely thinking that the many hundreds of miles of salt water made the American Hemisphere so remote that the people of North and Central and South America could go on living in the midst of their vast resources without reference to, or danger from, other Continents of the world. . . .

In the past two or three weeks all kinds of stories have been handed out to the American public about our lack of [military] preparedness. . . .The development of our defense program makes it essential that each and every one of us, men and women, feel that we have some contribution to make toward the security of our nation.

At this time, when the world—and the world includes our own American Hemisphere—when the world is threatened by forces of destruction, it is my resolve and yours to build up our armed defenses.

We shall build them to whatever heights the future may require.

We shall rebuild them swiftly, as the methods of warfare swiftly change.

For more than three centuries we Americans have been building on this continent a free society, a society in which the promise of the human spirit may find fulfillment. . . . We are continuing our efforts to bring the blessings of a free society, of a free and productive economic system, to every family in the land. This is the promise of America.

It is this that we must continue to build—this that we must continue to defend.

Source: https://millercenter.org/the-presidency/presidential-speeches/may-26-1940-fireside-chat-15-national-defense

1. What is the issue Roosevelt is addressing in this passage?

_____

_____

2. What course of action is Roosevelt suggesting to the American public?

_____

_____

3. What does Roosevelt say will be the ultimate reward for this course of action?

_____

_____

16. Identify Relationships in Time

Historians note the chronological order in which events happen. This can help them identify how one event might have caused a later one. Creating a timeline is one effective way of organizing historical events chronologically. The following timeline lists events after World War II at the dawn of the Cold War.

Date	Event
February 9, 1946	Stalin gives election speech asserting that communism and capitalism are not compatible.
March 5, 1946	Churchill gives his famous speech declaring an Iron Curtain has descended on Europe.
March 12, 1947	Truman Doctrine declares the U.S. role in stopping the spread of communism.
June 1947	Marshall Plan begins, providing financial aid to rebuild European countries devastated by the war.
June 24, 1948	Soviet Union begins the 11-month Berlin Blockade, cutting off Western Alliance supplies and aid to Berlin.
April 4, 1949	North Atlantic Treaty Organization (NATO) is established between the United States and Western European allies.
June 24, 1950	The Korean War begins. The United States supports South Korea, and the Soviet Union supports North Korea.

Historians are cautious about making claims of causation. To make a claim that one event caused another, historians need to do more than simply show that one event happened before another. Soviet action and aggression in Eastern Europe certainly contributed to the formation of NATO, but it's difficult to clearly assert that NATO caused the Soviets to back the North Koreans in the Korean War.

Number these events in chronological order. Then explain a likely cause-and-effect relationship between two or more of them.

Event	Order
A. The Yalta Conference between the U.S., England, and the U.S.S.R.	
B. Communist takeover of Czechoslovakia.	
C. Germany is defeated, ending World War II.	
D. Soviets test their first nuclear bomb.	
E. United States drops atomic bomb on Nagasaki.	
F. Berlin is divided into four zones of occupation.	

_____

_____

_____

_____

17. Identify a Problem

In history, a problem is a condition or event that causes difficulties for people. However, problems for some people are often opportunities for others. For example, weak regulations on air pollution might lead to problems such as lung disease for some people, but benefit those who own or work in factories.

The following chart shows the annual median household income by race/ethnicity in the United States. The data shows a consistent disparity between median incomes between the races over 40 years. The difference between White household income and African American remains a steady gap of about 20,000 throughout each decade. The largest growth of median income over the decades is in African American households—an $11,000 increase between 1980 and 2000. From 1970 through 2000, incomes for all households increase modestly every decade; however, all median incomes fell during the early 2000s—the largest drop occurred in African American households.

Median Household Incomes by Race/Ethnicity					
	1970	1980	1990	2000	2010
White	$51,380	$51,180	$55,194	$61,715	$58,185
Hispanic	$38,229	$36,743	$38,581	$44,867	$40,205
African American	$29,569	$28,972	$32,268	$40,131	$34,321

Source: https://www.epi.org/blog/real-median-household-incomes-racial-groups/

Identify the opportunities and problems that arose from the changes in the United States for the following between 1960 and 2010.

Changes from 1960 to 2010	
Women	
African Americans	
Asians	
Hispanics	
Muslims	
Immigrants	
LGBT Community	
Disabled Community	

1. Opportunities

_____

_____

2. Problems

_____

_____

18. Identify a Response to a Problem

When a problem exists, how can people, organizations, or governments respond to them? The following article describes a problem. This problem and a response to it are listed in the chart below.

September 11, 2001

On September 11, 2001, 19 militants associated with the Islamic extremist group al-Qaeda hijacked four airplanes and carried out suicide attacks against targets in the United States. Two of the planes were flown into the twin towers of the World Trade Center in New York City, a third plane hit the Pentagon just outside Washington, D.C., and the fourth plane crashed in a field in Pennsylvania. Almost 3,000 people were killed during the 9/11 terrorist attacks.

Operation Enduring Freedom, the American-led international effort to oust the Taliban regime in Afghanistan and destroy Osama bin Laden's terrorist network based there, began on October 7. Within two months, U.S. forces had effectively removed the Taliban from operational power, but the war continued, as U.S. and coalition forces attempted to defeat a Taliban insurgency campaign based in neighboring Pakistan.

Source: https://www.history.com/topics/21st-century/9-11-attacks

Problem	Response
Al_Qaeda terrorists hijacked four planes and crashed them into icon U.S. buildings and in a field in Pennsylvania, killing nearly 3,000 people.	The United States launched Operation Enduring Freedom against the Taliban in Afghanistan, targeting the terrorist network controlled by Saudi national Osama Bin Laden.

Read the following excerpt. Identify the problem and the response outlined in the piece.

Opioid Overdose Crisis, January 2019

Every day, more than 130 people in the United States die after overdosing on opioids. The misuse of and addiction to opioids—including prescription pain relievers, heroin, and synthetic opioids such as fentanyl—is a serious national crisis that affects public health as well as social and economic welfare. The Centers for Disease Control and Prevention estimates that the total "economic burden" of prescription opioid misuse alone in the United States is $78.5 billion a year, including the costs of healthcare, lost productivity, addiction treatment, and criminal justice involvement.

   The U.S. Department of Health and Human Services (HHS) is focusing its efforts on five major priorities: improving access to treatment and recovery services; promoting use of overdose-reversing drugs; strengthening our understanding of the epidemic through better public health surveillance; providing support for cutting-edge research on pain and addiction; advancing better practices for pain management. The National Institutes of Health (NIH), a component of HHS, is the nation's leading medical research agency helping solve the opioid crisis via discovering new and better ways to prevent opioid misuse.

Source: https://www.drugabuse.gov/drugs-abuse/opioids/opioid-overdose-crisis

Problem	Response

CHAPTER 1

Colonial Foundations (1607–1763)

Chapter Overview

At the tail end of the 15th century, European countries began to actively pursue colonial holdings abroad. Portugal and Spain began colonization first, but before long, northern European rivals joined in.

Europeans Invade the Americas In 1492, Christopher Columbus sailed west to find an alternative route to Asia. He instead happened upon the Americas. As a result, his Spanish employers began a mission of colonization that eventually encompassed much of the Americas. Millions of Native Americans died from European diseases, mistreatment, and warfare.

English colonization started slowly, but eventually it took root in Virginia and New England. As in the Spanish colonies, European diseases and aggression took a great toll. Dutch traders established a colony in and around the Hudson River Valley of what is today New York. Dutch activity focused on trade. Eventually, the English claimed the colony and renamed it New York. The French and the English both claimed the territory between the Appalachian Mountains and the Mississippi. War came as a result, and its outcome was momentous for Native Americans.

Society and Economy in the Colonies The developing American colonies had varied geography and different economic systems, and varying social and political hierarchies emerged in each. Landowners, members of the middle class, women, servants, and slaves all had positions on the social ladder. In some colonies, thousands of enslaved people worked on tobacco, cotton, and rice plantations. However, even colonies that had relatively few enslaved people depended on the wealth these people generated.

Colonies Develop Democratic Institutions Although the colonists were far from Europe, ideas from the European intellectual movement called the Enlightenment affected how they chose to govern themselves. Some of the most difficult questions included who would be allowed to vote and how much control colonists would have over how the government spent their tax money.

Civic Literacy: Inclusion Throughout the colonial period, new settlements wrestled with questions of who would be included or excluded. Religion was the main determinant, but what religions were acceptable often depended on what country started the colony.

New York Social Studies Framework

Key Idea 11.1: Colonial Foundations

European colonization in North America prompted cultural contact and exchange among diverse peoples; cultural differences and misunderstandings at times led to conflict. A variety of factors contributed to the development of regional differences, including social and racial hierarchies, in colonial America.

Source: *New York State Grades 9–12 Social Studies Framework*

Civic Literacy Essay: Overview

The civic literacy document-based essay, the final task on the Regents Exam, will require you to pull together a variety of information culminating in an argument that you support with evidence. The New York Board of Regents explains the elements in this final task this way (the key words that indicate tasks have been printed in bold type):

Civic Literacy Document-Based Essay Task

Short-response questions based on a set of six documents

Extended essay based on the set of six documents and focused on constitutional and civic issues

Essay Task: *Students will be instructed to* **read** *and* **analyze** *the documents. Using information from the documents and their knowledge of United States history and government, students will* **write an essay** *in which they are instructed to:*

- **Describe** the historical circumstances surrounding a constitutional or civic issue

- **Explain** efforts by individuals, groups, and/or governments to address this constitutional or civic issue

- **Discuss** the extent to which the efforts were successful,
  OR
  Discuss the impact of the efforts on the United States and/or American society

Source: *New York State Board of Regents*

At the beginning of each chapter, you will have a chance to learn more about each part of the civic literacy essay. Throughout the chapters, you will also have opportunities to practice the tasks.

Key Terms by Theme

Economics
joint-stock company (p. 8)
Virginia Company (p. 8)
subsistence farming (p. 15)
cash crop (p. 15)

Exchange
transatlantic slave trade (p. 17)
triangle trade (p. 19)

Geography
Jamestown (p. 8)
New England (p. 9)

Plymouth (p. 9)
Massachusetts Bay Colony (p. 10)
New Netherland (p. 11)

Governance
Powhatan (p. 8)
King Philip's War (p. 10)
French and Indian War (p. 12)
Enlightenment (p. 23)
Magna Carta (p. 23)
common law (p. 24)
direct government (p. 25)

Identity
Puritan (p. 9)
Pilgrim (p. 9)
Pequot (p. 10)

Movement
colonize (p. 7)

Social Structures
indentured servant (p. 17)

Conceptual Understanding
11.1a Contact between Native American groups and Europeans occurred through cultural exchanges, resistance efforts, and conflict.

Source: *New York State Grades 9–12 Social Studies Framework.*

Contact between European colonizers and Native Americans had been established for about 150 years when New France's former leader, Roland-Michel Barrin, put down his theories about the French colonial venture in America. He described the importance of both the French relationship with Native Americans and the French hold on their American possessions.

Analyze a Primary Source

Roland-Michel Barrin, Praise for the French Colonies, 1750

Read Closely: Claims
Writers often begin with a claim that is later reinforced by evidence. Underline the passage in which the writer makes a claim about France's warring accomplishments in the Americas.

Read Closely: Contradiction
Be aware that even the most accomplished writers sometimes contradict themselves. Here, the writer first states that Native Americans "hardly act except from instinct," but later, he describes how they strategically play the French and English against each other..

Read Closely: Evidence
The writer spells out one of the causes for his claim regarding French military success. Circle what factor he thinks is to the advantage of the French.

[The French should] make a more energetic and generous effort to increase and strengthen Canada and Louisiana, than the English are making in favor of their Colonies; since the French Colonies, despite their destitute condition, have always waged war against the English of the [American] Continent with some advantage, though the latter are, and always have been, more numerous; it is necessary to explain here the causes to which this has been owing.

The first is the great number of alliances that French keep up with the Indian Nations. These people, who hardly act except from instinct, love us hitherto a little and fear us a great deal, more than they do the English; but their interest, which some among them begin to understand, is that the strength of the English and French remain nearly equal, so that through the jealousy of these two nations those tribes may live independent of, and draw presents from, both.

The second reason of our superiority over the English is, the number of French Canadians who are accustomed to live in the woods like the Indians, and become thereby not only qualified to lead them to fight the English, but to wage war even against these same Indians when necessity obliges.

Hence `twill be seen that this superiority of the French in America is in some sort accidental, and if they neglect to maintain it, whilst the English are making every effort to destroy it, `twill pass into the hands of the latter. There is no doubt but such an event would be followed by the entire destruction of our settlements in that part of the Globe. This, however serious it may seem, would not be our only loss; it would drag after it that of the superiority which France must claim over England.

Source: Roland-Michel Barrin, *Memoir on the French Colonies in North America*, 1750.

The Spanish Arrive

Through much of the 15th century, Portugal sponsored numerous voyages of discovery and commerce into the Atlantic and along the West African coast. It claimed and **colonized** the unoccupied Madeira and Azores island groups, which became important producers of sugar and other agricultural goods for the Portuguese, and established trading posts and colonies on the African continent. Their ultimate goal was to open and dominate the spice trade by sailing east to India. Portugal's Iberian neighbors, Spain, could well see the benefits of exploration and colonization, and soon joined in.

Colonizing the Caribbean

In 1492, Christopher Columbus began the European colonization of the Americas. He landed first on the island of Hispaniola, which today includes the countries of Haiti and the Dominican Republic. The Spanish began to exploit the labor of the people, the Taino (a subgroup among the Arawaks), and the island's resources. This relentlessly forced labor, along with general maltreatment and the effects of European diseases (to which the Taino had no immunity) took a terrible toll. Between 300,000 and 1 million people lived in Hispaniola before Europeans arrived. The Taino died on Hispaniola at a staggering rate. By 1514, only 32,000 Taino remained. By 1548, there were only 500.

This pattern of depopulation repeated on successive Caribbean islands as Spanish dominion spread. To replace the native peoples as a source of labor, African people were abducted, enslaved, and brought to the Americas.

The North American Mainland

The Spanish used their bases in the Caribbean as a jumping-off point to invade the land that would one day become the United States.

- In 1513, Juan Ponce de Léon landed in what is today northeastern Florida, near St. Augustine, and explored south through the Florida Keys, which lie off Florida's southwestern coast. However, he failed to establish a colony.

- In 1528, Panfilo de Narváez and 400 Spaniards landed near Tampa Bay, on with 400 people. After battling Native American groups along the coast, the group attempted to sail along the coast toward Mexico. One by one, the boats were lost, and in the end, only four men made it to Spanish territory.

- In 1538, Hernando de Soto and a force of 700 people also landed near Tampa Bay. They explored as far west as what is today Louisiana. Hundreds, including De Soto died from disease and battles against Native Americans.

The Spanish explorations brought disease and warfare that weakened many Native American societies of the Southeast. In 1565, the Spanish finally established a permanent base at St. Augustine, Florida.

> **Read Closely:**
> **Cause and Effect**
> Notice when one process or event influences or directly causes future outcomes. Identify an important cause and effect related to the Spanish domination of islands of the Caribbean.

The English in America

In 1590, England's first attempt at establishing a toehold in America ended in failure and mystery. They settled a colony at Roanoke Island in what is today North Carolina. However, a supply ship from England was delayed for three years by war between England and Spain. When it finally arrived, the sailors found no trace of the more than 100 colonists in Roanoke.

Virginia

In late 1607, three ships left England for the Chesapeake Bay area to establish a new colony. To fund the venture, King James I authorized the establishment of the **Virginia Company**, a **joint-stock company** in which investors purchased shares in hopes of making a profit upon the colony's success. By spreading the risk among many people, the joint-stock method of ownership encouraged more people to become investors The investors hoped settlers would discover gold, silver, and a water route to the Pacific.

The settlers arrived in late-April 1608 and by mid-May had established **Jamestown** on an easily defended, but swampy and mosquito-ridden, peninsula 50 miles inland on the James River. The colony faced multiple serious issues:

- It had too many gentlemen looking for gold but too few farmers raising food.
- It suffered from power struggles among its leaders.
- Colonists found neither gold nor silver, nor a water route to Asia.

The Powhatans and the Colonists However, troubles with the many local Native American tribes were probably the most pressing problem for the settlers. Together, these tribes were known by the name of their leader, **Powhatan**. Although the Powhatans occasionally gave or traded food to the often-desperate settlers, they ultimately did not trust or want these newcomers in their lands.

The colonists' inability to store provisions, in spite of the natural bounty that surrounded them, and their reliance on spotty supply ships from England made them dependent on the Powhatans. In the winter of 1609, the Powhatans tried to rid themselves of the colonists. The natives refused to provide or trade food to the settlers and attacked hunting parties. The resulting winter-long famine, known as the Starving Time, reduced colonists to eating literally anything they could find—even resorting to cannibalism for survival. Of the more than 500 autumn residents of Jamestown, fewer than 100 made it to spring.

Rescue The arrival of ships carrying a new governor, provisions, and new colonists saved the colony from collapse. However, fighting with the Powhatans continued. Peace came in 1614 when Powhatan's kidnapped daughter Pocahontas married the English planter John Rolfe and converted to Christianity.

The arrival of Rolfe also began the colony's journey toward economic stability. From the West Indies, he brought with him a new, more marketable strain of tobacco than the one that was native to Virginia. The increasingly lucrative tobacco plantations began to multiply and the colony's population grew. But the Powhatans were not willing to idly watch as their lands were taken away.

Continuing Conflict In the first half of the 17th century, anger at English territorial expansion, cultural superiority, and attempts at Christian conversion led to two wars. In each, an initial surprise attack by the Powhatans and their allies, called a massacre by the English, led to a drawn-out war in which the English successfully focused on depriving their enemies of their food supplies. And at the end of each war, the English found themselves in a stronger position. The treaty that ended the Third Anglo-Powhatan War in 1646 displaced great numbers of Native Americans, opening great areas of fertile land to still more colonists.

English–Native American relations followed the pattern set in the early years for the remainder of the 17th century. The English colony grew in territory, population, and overall strength, at the expense of the Powhatans. By the late 1600s, most of the Native Americans of Virginia had been forced to sign treaties that placed them under the control of the English colonial government.

Read Closely: Turning Point
Look for ideas and actions that make a crucial difference in the course of history. In what ways did John Rolfe play a central role in keeping the Virginia colony going?

Read Closely: Unintended Consequences
Identify instances where figures or groups took a course of action that led to unforeseen outcomes. What were the long-term, unintended consequences of the Wampanoag desire to gain allies against the Narragansett?

POWHATAN
Held this state & fashion when Capt. Smith
was delivered to him prisoner.
1607

CAPTAIN SMITH BEFORE POWHATAN. (*From Smith's "Virginia."*)

Source: Getty Images
Powhatan led a coalition of about 30 tribes in eastern Virginia. He was wary of the settlers, but he also thought they could be his allies against his traditional rivals.

New England

The Jamestown colony of the Virginia Company was founded mostly as a commercial venture. It also had strategic value for England as a check on the colonial ambitions of Spain and France. In contrast, the colonies established in **New England** had another motivation: religious freedom. Members of the **Puritan** movement, so called because of their desire to purify the Church of England of Roman Catholic influences, faced persecution, and even imprisonment in England. They came to America to found communities where they would be free to practice their brand of Christianity.

Plymouth While most Puritans wanted to reform the Church of England, a few, known as **Pilgrims,** wanted to separate from it altogether. About 100 Pilgrims sailed for Virginia in September 1620. But their ship, the *Mayflower,* landed more than 400 miles north, in what is today Plymouth, Massachusetts. Desperately short of provisions, the Pilgrims decided to settle where they were. The population of Native Americans who had lived in the region had declined sharply in the decades before the Pilgrims arrived because of diseases attributed to European contact.

During their first winter in **Plymouth**, about half of the colonists died. Those who survived did so in part because of their contacts with the Native Americans remaining in the region, the Wampanoags. The two groups could help each other. The Pilgims wanted to learn to provide themselves with food in a new land. The Wampanoags wanted allies against their rivals, the Narragansett. A treaty, signed in 1621, cemented good relations between the two groups and laid the foundation for the Plymouth colony to quickly achieve stability.

The Plymouth colonists did not always have good relations with other Native Americans. In 1623, for example, Plymouth military leader Myles Standish responded to stories of an upcoming attack by Massachusetts warriors by luring them into an ambush disguised as a meeting to resolve tensions. Every last warrior was killed and their leader's head was mounted on the fort wall at Plymouth. The peace between the colonists and the Wampanoag, though, would last, for the lifetime of the Wampanoag leader Massasoit, who died in 1661. But relations between the Wampanoag and the growing English colonies eventually would sour and turn to open conflict.

> **Read Closely:**
> **Listing Distinctions**
> One way to help yourself understand distinctions between groups of people, individuals, or ideas is to make a diagram or list showing distinctions. Identify one similarity and one difference between Puritans and Pilgrims.
>
> _____
> _____
> _____
> _____
> _____
> _____

Massachusetts Bay Colony In 1630, a larger group of Puritans, about 1,000 people, founded the **Massachusetts Bay Colony**, just north of Plymouth. They were less radical than the Pilgrims. They wanted to reform, but not separate from, the Church of England. They believed that through their pious example, they could inspire reform by serving as a model for all peoples and communities.

However, the Puritan's example did not include tolerating other forms of religious worship. All members the Massachusetts Bay Colony were required to attend religious services and accept Puritan views. In spite of its narrow viewpoint and authoritarian ways, the colony grew to more than 20,000 inhabitants by the mid-1640s. These later settlers, part of what became known as the Great Migration, left England not just to escape religious persecution. They also came because the colony's economy—based largely on agriculture, lumber, shipping, and fishing—continued to grow and prosper.

Connecticut The rapid growth of Massachusetts Bay did not mean that all residents were content there. In 1636, one minister, Thomas Hooker and 100 followers migrated southwest where they established what would become Hartford along the Connecticut River. To free themselves of the domination of Massachusetts Bay, these settlers declared they were a separate colony. They drafted a document, Fundamental Orders of Connecticut, to govern themselves.

The arrival of permanent English settlements in Connecticut caused conflicts with Native Americans called the **Pequot**. The Pequot controlled regional trade in fur and wampum, valuable beads made from shells. The English threatened this control. The result was the Pequot War (1636–1638), which the English won.

By 1670, about 50,000 Europeans lived in New England. As occurred in the 1630s, tensions between Native Americans and Europeans led to a war—this one known as **King Philip's War**. It was named as such after the leader of the Wampanoag, Metacom, whom the English called King Philip.

> **Civic Literacy: Change**
> The Puritans set up prosperous, tight-knit communities based on shared religious values. However, their success attracted new colonists who did not share their religious beliefs. For these communities and others, success almost always brings new challenges.

War Between Colonists and Native Americans in New England		
Feature	**Pequot War (1636–1638)**	**King Philip's War (1675–1676)**
Alliances	• The Pequot and several other tribes • Massachusetts Bay and several other colonies, and some Native American tribes	• The Narragansett, Wampanoag, and other tribes • Massachsetts Bay, other colonies, and the Mohawk
Long-Term Cause	• The expansion of English settlements	• The expansion of English settlement
Immediate Cause	• The Pequot killed a party of English traders	• The Wampanoags killed a Christianized Native American accused of spying for the English
Results	• The English won. • The Pequots were claimed as slaves by other Native Americans or sold into slavery abroad by English.	• The English won. • Many Native Americans were sold into slavery in the Caribbean and Spain

As a result of these two wars, the power of the majority of New England's Native Americans was permanently broken. As the 17th century progressed, English colonies spread all along the Atlantic coast, to what would become Rhode Island, Maryland, Pennsylvania, and the Carolinas. As they spread out, colonists' hunger for land and resources threatened the very existence of every Native American society they encountered.

New Netherland

About 30 years after King Philip's War, Henry Hudson, an English explorer hired by the Dutch, founded the colony that later became New York. Hudson, like Columbus, was searching for a westerly passage to Asia. Further, like Columbus, Hudson instead found land Europeans settled on. In 1609, Hudson sailed up the river that today bears his name, as far as modern-day Albany before turning back. He claimed the river and its surroundings for the Netherlands.

However, colonization did not take hold right away. In 1624, the Dutch West India Company, a joint-stock company, sent 30 families to settle on Manhattan. Two years later, a company agent famously gave the equivalent of $24 in goods to the Native Americans in exchange for what the settlers thought was the right to own the island of Manhattan. The colony became known as **New Netherland**.

The Fur Trade Between 1624 and 1664, the Dutch West India Company established forts, settlements, plantations, and trading posts in Connecticut, on Long Island, and in Delaware. Its main focus, though, was north along the Hudson River Valley. These river valley settlements engaged in agriculture, but the real driver of the New Netherlands economy was trade. Particularly early on, this was dominated by the fur trade, largely in beaver pelts, which were highly sought after and very profitable in Europe. Between 1626 and 1632 alone, more than 60,000 animal pelts were shipped back to Europe where they were used in making coats and hats. By the mid-1650s, nearly 80,000 beaver pelts were exported each year.

The trade in fur greatly enriched the Dutch West Indies Company. But it also benefited the Native Americans who supplied the pelts. They were able to acquire valuable and useful goods in exchange for the furs, such as cloth, glassware, needles, axes, and knives. But the fur trade caused significant changes to their ways of life. Over time, they were forced to range farther and farther to hunt and trap increasingly scarce animals, and they did it for longer periods each year. This altered traditional roles within the societies and made Native Americans increasingly dependent on the Europeans.

English Control In the end, the colony was undone by the Netherlands maritime rivalry with England. As a result of each seafaring nation's attempts to dominate trade in several parts of the world, a series of Anglo-Dutch wars took place. In 1664, as part of these conflicts, the English sent a small fleet and army to New Netherland. Without any real army, the director general of the Dutch West Indies Company in New Netherland was forced to surrender. The English colony was renamed New York, for the Duke of York, brother of King Charles.

France's Colonial Venture

Like the Dutch, the French were eager to join the fur trade. After generally unsuccessful attempts to establish a colony by Jacques Cartier and others, in 1608, Samuel de Champlain established Quebec on the St. Lawrence River in what is today eastern Canada.

Read Closely: Patterns
When you are reading, keep an eye out for actions or events that repeatedly seem to take a similar path. Can you identify a general pattern for how relations between English settlers and Native Americans played out?

Read Closely: Central Effect
Look for ways to use information to focus on why things happen the way they do. What central effect do you think the differences in settlement patterns between the English and the French had on their American empires?

Making Alliances

Read Closely:
Transitional Words
Words and phrases such as *consequently* and *in contrast* clarify the relationships between ideas. Note them as you read so that you recognize the flow of ideas in a text. Identify three examples in the first two paragraphs of words that express the realtionship between ideas.

Champlain and others used their alliances with Native Americans to promote trade. In response, Native Americans used these trade alliances to involve Europeans in miltiary conflicts with each other. Most importantly, French setttlers fought alongside the Huron and their Algonquin allies against their Iroquois enemies. This established a pattern for the French of friendship with the Huron and Algonquin and hostility with the Iroquois.

In addition, alliances between the French and Native Americans were also forged in another way—through the marriage of Indian women to French men. There were several reasons for this situation.

- Native Americans in this region use marriage as a unifying force—a concept and practice that was also common in Europe.

- The ongoing and deadly nature of Native American warfare at the time meant that there were more women than men in many societies.

- The nature of French activity in early New France, more mobile and entrepreneurial than settled and agrarian, meant that few French women were among the initial settlers.

Alliances thus forged, the French extensively explored the American interior, establishing trading posts and missions and claiming territory for France. They explored the Great Lakes region, reached and navigated the Mississippi River, and by the late-17th to early-18th century, French forts and settlements had taken root in what would later be the states from Michigan and Wisconsin in the north to Louisiana in the south.

The French were able to establish themselves so widely, in part, because their footprint was so shallow. The British sought to claim and expand territory for more and more settlers, angering Native Americans and challenging their very existence. However the numbers of French settlers never approached that of the British. The French was less intrested in occupying land for agriculture and more interested in setting up posts to trade with Native Americans for furs.

The French and Indian War

Read Closely:
Long-Term Result
Look for decisive events that had long-lasting consequences. What results of the long battle between the British and the French in North America can still be seen today ?

In 1754, tensions between France and Britain led to a war that decided who would control North America. In the main, the **French and Indian War** (1754–1763) broke out over control of the lands west of the English colonies along the Atlantic seaboard. Both France and England claimed them, and the French fortification of the Ohio River Valley lit the fuse of war. The French and Indian War was the American part of the broader Seven Years' War (1756–1763), which pitted France, Austria, Sweden, and Russia against Great Britain and the powerful German states of Prussia and Hanover. The two sides battled not only across Europe and in North America, but in the Caribbean and India, too.

In North America, although the French and their Native American allies had the upper hand early on, British sea power and economic strength eventually proved decisive. In the treaty that ended the war, the British took Canada and claimed all of the territory west of their colonies up to the Mississippi River. This result was a disaster for Native Americans, as it opened a massive area for British settlement. Even though the British government forbade settlement west of the Appalachian Mountains with the Proclamation of 1763, settlers ignored the proclamation and occupied Native American lands in increasing numbers.

Application: Interpret a Primary Source

Read the excerpt and answer the questions that follow it.

The Dutch West India Company on the
Benefits it Provides the Dutch, 1633

First:. . . The Company hath . . . employed over six thousand, as well soldiers as seamen, and over eight or nine thousand during the last year. . . .

Secondly: Regarding duties

The company imported an excessively large amount of costly wares, such as Cochineal [red dye], Silk, Indigo, an innumerable quantity of Sugars, Hides, Ginger and other spices, Cotton, Elephants teeth, Tobacco, Brazil and other woods, Salt , Gums, etc., from the exportation of which to other countries the State had the benefit of large duties.

Thirdly: By the increase of the Trade and Wealth of the Commonalty

The said Company brought into the country a very large amount of gold and silver, both coined and uncoined; exported a vast quantity of all sorts of manufactures, most of which were made here; for the trade to Guinea alone requires, for all descriptions of manufactures, an annual outlay of above five tons of gold, and returns yearly into the country over ten tons of gold.

In like manner, a large quantity of goods was shipped to other parts of Africa and America, in return for which many other goods were imported, whereby the inhabitants of this country obtained trade and employment.

Fourthly: By strengthening the Country

The Company hath, at present, about one hundred and twenty well built ships, . . . all as well supplied with metal and iron pieces [weapons], and suitable ammunition, as any of the enemy's best and largest vessels.

One-third, or in case of need, fully one-half of those can almost always be employed in the public service.

Source: babel.hathitrust.org.

1. Summarize what the writer of this document believes the Dutch West Indies Company provides to the Dutch Commonwealth.

   _____

   _____

2. In what way does this document express the common political and economic belief of European powers at the time of its writing?

   _____

   _____

3. What information not appearing in this document might illustrate the difference between the overall approach and execution of the Dutch West India Company and that of the Virginia Company?

   _____

   _____

Factors Influencing Colonial Development

Conceptual Understanding 11.1b A number of factors influenced colonial economic development, social structures, and labor systems, causing variation by region.

At the time Richard Frethorne wrote this letter, some poor people in Europe were trying to improve their lives by coming to the British colonies in North America as indentured servants. In exchange for the trip to the colonies, they agreed to be servants for a certain number of years. Frethorne arrived in Jamestown in 1623 and worked on a tobacco plantation. He wrote this letter about three months after arriving, and records indicate he died in early 1624. "Loblollie" is boiled grains or beans. To "redeem" means to buy out of servitude or slavery.

Analyze a Primary Source

Richard Frethorne, Letter from an Indentured Servant, 1623

Read Closely: Intended Audience
When you analyze a primary source, think about the person or people the writer intended to read it. To whom did Frethorne write this letter? Circle the part of the letter that gives you this information.

Read Closely: Claim and Evidence
One way to engage with a history text is to think about whether the writer is making a claim and, if so, what evidence he or she provides to support that claim. Frethorne claims there is much sickness in the colony. Underline the evidence he provides to support that claim.

Read Closely: Specific Details
Note how the use of details adds legitimacy to a story. Frethorne uses vivid, compelling, and emotionally affecting language to enhance the impact of his description in hopes of motivating his parents to help him.

Loving and kind father and mother:

. . . This is to let you understand that I your child am in a most heavy case by reason of the country, [which] is such that it causeth much sickness, [such] as the scurvy and the bloody flux and diverse other diseases, which maketh the body very poor and weak. And when we are sick there is nothing to comfort us; for since I came out of the ship I never ate anything but peas, and loblollie [boiled grain]. As for deer or venison I never saw any since I came into this land. There is indeed some fowl, but we are not allowed to go and get it, but must work hard both early and late for a mess of water gruel and a mouthful of bread and beef. A mouthful of bread for a penny loaf must serve for four men which is most pitiful. . . . For we live in fear of the enemy every hour, yet we have had a combat with them . . . and we took two alive and made slaves of them. But it was by policy, for we are in great danger; for our plantation is very weak by reason of the death and sickness of our company. . . .

And I have nothing to comfort me, nor is there nothing to be gotten here but sickness and death. . . .

Goodman Jackson pitied me and made me a cabin to lie in always when I [would] come up, and he would give me some poor jacks [fish] [to take] home with me. . . . And he much marvelled that you would send me a servant to the Company; he saith I had been better knocked on the head. And indeed so I find it now, to my great grief and misery; and [I] saith that if you love me you will redeem [buy out of servitude] me suddenly, for which I do entreat and beg. . . .

Source: Richard Frethorne, letter to his father and mother, March 20, April 2 & 3, 1623, in Susan Kingsbury, ed., *The Records of the Virginia Company of London* (Washington, D.C.: Government Printing Office, 1935), 4: 58–62.

Factors Influencing Colonial Development

Where colonists landed and settled had profound effects on what their lives were like. Geography, economics, and social structures combined to shape the 13 colonies.

The Impact of Geography

Generally speaking, geography is the study of Earth and its inhabitants. More specifically, it is the study of a given area's physical features, its biological makeup, and the culture of the people who live there. The climate, natural resources, and terrain of the 13 colonies affected how people lived, what kind of work they did, and what kinds of societies they lived in.

Geographic Factors Colonists who arrived in different parts of what is now the United States faced different climates and weather conditions.

American Colonies

- The Northern, New England, colonies had a colder climate than the Middle or Southern colonies. The Northern colonies had lots of valleys, hills, and mountains. Because of the varied terrain, farms tended to be smaller there than in the South. Many New Englanders were engaged in **subsistence farming**, which means they generally planted enough crops or raised enough animals to feed themselves and their families. Northern farms were often small and required few workers. A farm of about 50 acres was big enough to support one family, but some New England farms were larger. The North also had rich fishing areas and abundant timber, which allowed settlers to make a living in other ways.

- The Southern colonies had a humid subtropical climate. Summers were hot, and winters were mild, with frequent rain. The growing season was longer than in the north. Southerners grew tobacco, rice, and indigo, which is a plant used to dye clothes. (Indigo dye was part of the first American flag, and people still use it today to dye blue jeans.) These were **cash crops**, which means that farmers sold them instead of growing just enough for their own use. Some Southern plantations had hundreds of acres and required thousands of workers.

Read Closely: Prediction
One way to engage with a history text is to think about what may happen next. Based on what you have read so far, what can you predict about how differences among these colonies may affect their economies?

• The Middle colonies had a geography that was between the extremes of the North and South. It had lots of fertile farmland. People there grew wheat and corn and raised livestock, meaning cattle, sheep, and pigs. People called the Middle colonies the "breadbasket colonies" because they were able to sell so much food to others.

Patterns of Settlement The first European settlers of what would become the 13 colonies knew almost nothing about the land that they were moving into. There were Spanish settlements in parts of today's United States, in Florida and the Southwest, but the first permanent settlement of English colonists was in Jamestown, Virginia. Settlers there hoped that they would find gold, but they found rich farmland instead. Those who sailed on the *Mayflower* hoped to settle near Jamestown but were blown off course and ended up on the rocky shores of what is now Massachusetts.

Early settlers in Virginia and Massachusetts nearly starved to death but received corn from local Native American tribes. Over the years, colonists began to understand which crops would grow in which regions. They also found other ways to make money.

Development of Colonial Economic Systems Jamestown and some other southern areas became centers of tobacco farming. This type of farming quickly exhausted the land, so there was a constant demand for new farmland. Tobacco was difficult to grow and required a large workforce. Rice and indigo plantations were also labor intensive. European demand for tobacco grew, keeping the Southern colonies afloat financially in the early stages of settlement.

Source: National Park Service / Wikimedia Commons

Tobacco farming in colonial America

**Read Closely:
Impact of Place**
It is crucial to consider how people's physical and economic surroundings can affect their actions and outcomes. What advantages might there be in having the Northern colonies' diversified economy?

Colonists in New England usually had small farms and grew a variety of crops to eat and sell. The climate and soil were not good for growing wheat or tobacco, but colonists were able to grow corn, pumpkins, squash, and beans. Colonists on the New England coast made money from fishing, whaling, and shipbuilding. Some colonists made their money from fur trading or from cutting timber. The variety of crops and occupations meant that New England's economic systems were more diversified than the South's were. In other words, New Englanders were much less likely to depend on one crop than Southerners were.

Many farmers in the Middle colonies were extremely prosperous. They kept some of their wheat and livestock to eat but exported much of the rest.

Colonial Social Structures and Labor Systems

Geography and economics affected the ways in which colonial society developed. These factors also affected what kinds of labor systems came into being. Race, too, played a role in the development of labor systems in the colonies—almost from the start.

Social Structures in the Colonies Almost every society has a hierarchy, which means that some groups have more power and are more respected than others. Landowners were members of the highest social classes in the colonies. In general, the more land someone had, the higher he or she was in the social hierarchy.

In the 1700s, the "middle class" emerged. These were people who were not as rich as the large landowners but not as poor as servants or enslaved people. The vast majority of early colonists were small freeholder farmers. They owned a modest amount of land that they and their families farmed. Many were part of this middle class. Various types of merchants and skilled artisans—blacksmiths, silversmiths, and the like— were, too, part of this middle class. White laborers and servants were beneath this group of businesspeople and artisans.

Women and the Social Structure Women were at every level in the social hierarchy of the colonies, but none had the same rights as men. Women in the upper and middle classes learned to read. A woman's land, possessions, children, and body belonged to her husband. Unmarried women could own property, but once a woman married, those rights passed to her husband. For this reason, some women chose not to remarry after the death of a husband. A few property-owning women were allowed to vote in some areas, but that was rare. (It would take roughly 300 more years until women gained the right to vote across the United States in 1920.)

Indentured Servants, Free Black People, and Slaves An **indentured servant** was a laborer whose passage to the colonies was paid for by an employer. In return for passage and food and shelter in the colony, the laborer was bound to work for the employer for an agreed-upon period—typically between four and seven years.

Free Black people were also part of the social hierarchy, below the middle class but above enslaved people. Some free Black people worked in skilled trades such as carpentry or barrel making.

Lower in the social hierarchy were enslaved Black people who served in households. And lowest of all were the enslaved people who worked in fields. They performed backbreaking work with little hope of ever being freed.

Clearly, labor systems in the colonies were complex. Landowners, farmers, craftspeople, servants, and Black people, both free and enslaved, were all part of the economy. Enslaved people were a significant part of the Northern economy, but they were in many ways the backbone of the colonial economy in the South.

Slavery Takes Hold

The **transatlantic slave trade**, in which Africans were abducted and forced into servitude by Europeans, began in the late 15th century. The Portuguese brought enslaved Africans to work on plantations on the Madeira and Cape Verde Islands by the 1480s. By 1502, the Spanish had begun to transport enslaved Africans to work in the Caribbean Islands. Over time, the practice broadened, with other Europeans in other areas adopting it as well. Over the course of the transatlantic trade in enslaved Africans, over 90 percent went to the Caribbean and South America. About 400,000 arrived in the North American colonies and, later, the United States. The overwhelming majority landed in ports from the Chesapeake Bay, south.

> **Read Closely: Visuals**
> Creating a visual can help you to summarize and recall what you have read. What kind of visual would you create to represent colonial society?

Slavery and the Colonial Economic System Slavery in the British North American colonies began in 1619, with the first transfer of captive Africans to the Jamestown colony in Virginia. Through the 1600s, the slave trade continued to grow.

Slavery in the colonies first developed in an area known as the Chesapeake that included present-day Virginia and Maryland. The region's major crop was tobacco, which had become popular in England and Europe. Slavery grew as the demand for tobacco grew. The production of tobacco, based on a system of enslavement, eventually allowed Maryland and Virginia to become the leading states of the South. Enslaved Africans showed their White owners better ways to grow indigo—a secondary crop for Southern planters, but one that became even more profitable than sugar or cotton.

Colonists in what are now South Carolina and Georgia built a slave society based on producing and exporting rice. Georgia, which had originally banned slavery, reversed itself in the mid-1700s. As rice production soared, the city of Charleston, South Carolina, with about 12,000 residents by the early 1770s, became one of the most populous cities in the British colonies.

The Triangle Trade Slavery in the northern British colonies developed on a much smaller scale than in the South, since there were fewer large farms and plantations in the North. The large farms that did exist often used slaves to grow and harvest wheat. So-called "provisioning plantations" in the North produced food and lumber destined for sugar plantations in the West Indies. Ships regularly sailed to the West Indies with meat, wheat, barrels, and lumber and returned with molasses to make rum. Much of this rum was then shipped to Africa and traded for enslaved people who would be sent to the West Indies and the Southern colonies. This **triangle trade** meant that people in the Northern and Middle

Speak and Listen: Previous Knowledge
Share with a partner what you already know about the triangular trade and about the conditions on the ships carrying enslaved people. Explain how you learned that.

Triangular Trade

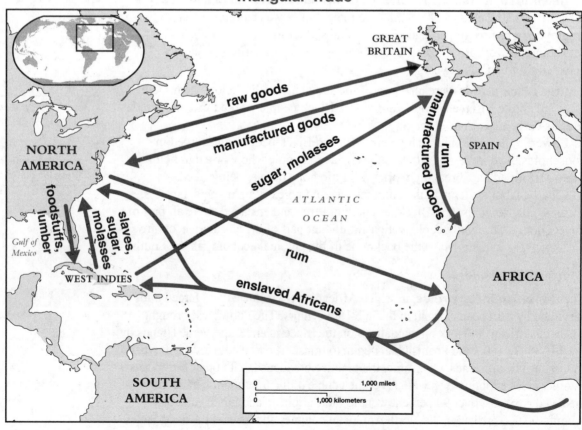

colonies who never saw the slaves on the West Indian plantations still profited from their labor.

The economics of slavery did not provide enough rewards to use on small farms and in small towns. For this reason, slavery did not became a significant factor in the Northern colonies. Still, the Northern colonies had a significant number of enslaved people. It is estimated that in 1756, on the eve of the French and Indian War, enslaved people were 25 percent of the population in and around New York City. Many of these enslaved people were laborers and skilled artisans.

Indentured Servitude vs. Slavery Indentured servants often worked for years under harsh conditions. However, once their time of servitude was up, they were able to earn wages. Some started businesses. Others married into families in their community. Slaves had no such opportunities. They, their children, and their children's children could be bought and sold.

Development of Slavery as a Racial Institution A single indentured servant might cost a Southern planter a thousand pounds of tobacco or more to hire. If he or she died or ran away, then the planter had lost a substantial investment. Capturing and enslaving Native Americans rarely worked because they knew the local land well, so they often escaped. But Africans were thousands of miles from familiar people or places. Escaping was much more difficult for them.

Planters in the Caribbean were already using enslaved Africans to work on plantations. When England's King Charles II established the colony of Carolina in 1660, he entered into the slave trade. Many of the first landowners in Carolina brought enslaved Africans with them. Slave traders began bringing enslaved Africans to colonial ports in ever larger numbers.

American legislatures also changed laws related to slaves. Under English common law, the child of an enslaved woman and a free man had the rights of the free man. But in 1662 the Virginia Assembly passed a law that children "borne in this country shall be held bond or free only according to the condition of the mother." In the colonies, slavery was for African people, it was lifelong, and it was the fate of children as well as parents.

> **Civic Literacy:**
> **The Impact of Slavery**
> The Southern colonies, Middle colonies, and New England colonies depended on slave labor in different ways. These differences would continue to affect the regions up to, during, and after the Civil War.

> **Read Closely: Turning Point**
> Some historical events have consequences that last for decades or even centuries. In what way was the Virginia Assembly's 1662 decision a turning point?

Application: Interpret a Primary Source

Read the excerpt and answer the questions that follow it.

Discovery that Ayuba Suleiman Diallo, a Runaway Slave Known as Job, Was a Literate Muslim, 1731

He was brought into the Tavern to us, but could not speak one Word of English. Upon our Talking and making Signs to him, he wrote a Line or two before us, and when he read it, pronounced the Words Allah and Mohammed; by which, and his refusing a Glass of Wine we offered him, we perceived he was a Mohammedan [Muslim], but could not imagine of what Country he was, or how he got thither; for by his affable Carriage, and the easy Composure of his Countenance, we could perceive he was no common Slave.

When Job had been some time confined, an old Negro Man, who lived in that Neighborhood, and could speak the Jolloff Language, which Job also understood, went to him, and conversed with him. By this Negro the Keeper was informed to whom Job belonged, and what was the Cause of his leaving his Master. The Keeper thereupon wrote to his Master, who soon after fetched him home, and was much kinder to him than before; allowing him a Place to pray in, and some other Conveniences, in order to make his Slavery as easy as possible. Yet Slavery and Confinement was by no means agreeable to Job, who had never been used to it; he therefore wrote a Letter in Arabic to his Father, acquainting him with his Misfortunes, hoping he might yet find Means to redeem him. . . . Mr. Denton . . . purchased him again of his Master for the same Money which Mr. Denton had formerly received for him; his Master being very willing to part with him, as finding him no ways fit for his Business.

Source: Thomas Bluett, *Some Memoirs of the Life of Job, the Son of Solomon, the High Priest of Boonda in Africa; Who was a Slave About Two Years in Maryland; and Afterwards Being Brought to England, was Set Free, and Sent to His Native Land in the Year 1734.*
London: Printed for R. Ford, 1734. Reprinted in Documenting the American South

1. With the broader context of the transatlantic trade in enslaved peoples in mind, do you think it was odd for a man such as Diallo to end up enslaved in the American colonies? Why or why not?

   _____

   _____

   _____

   _____

   _____

2. What evidence in the text points to the fact that Diallo was, in fact, different from other enslaved people whom the writer had encountered?

_____

_____

_____

_____

_____

3. What maybe not-so-obvious problem faced by enslaved people in the colonies does this excerpt point out?

_____

_____

_____

_____

_____

Source: Wikimedia Commons

This portrait shows formerly enslaved man Yarrow Mamout. Like Ayuba Suleiman Diallo, he was an educated Muslim from West Africa who eventually gained his freedom.

Conceptual Understanding 11.1c Colonial political developments were influenced by British political traditions, Enlightenment ideas, and the colonial experience. Self-governing structures were common, and yet varied across the colonies.

How do people govern themselves when they arrive in a new place? Who decides what the rules will be? Forty-one men signed this agreement describing what the new British colony of Plymouth would be. They wrote and signed the document on board a ship called the *Mayflower*.

Analyze a Primary Source

The Mayflower Compact, 1620

Read Closely: Connections
Primary sources often show connections among different groups of people. The first paragraph reveals that the authors of this agreement are religious and are subjects of King James.

Read Closely: Purpose
When analyzing a primary source, try to decide what purpose the creator of the document has in mind. What goals do the signers of this agreement have? Underline them.

Read Closely: Evidence
Circle two pieces of evidence that support the idea that the creators of this document did not consider themselves to be founders of an independent nation.

In the name of God, Amen. We whose names are under-written, the loyal subjects of our dread sovereign Lord, King James, by the grace of God, of Great Britain, France, and Ireland King, Defender of the Faith, etc.

Having undertaken, for the glory of God, and advancement of the Christian faith, and honor of our King and Country, a voyage to plant the first colony in the northern parts of Virginia, do by these presents solemnly and mutually, in the presence of God, and one of another, covenant and combine our selves together into a civil body politic, for our better ordering and preservation and furtherance of the ends aforesaid; and by virtue hereof to enact, constitute, and frame such just and equal laws, ordinances, acts, constitutions and offices, from time to time, as shall be thought most meet [fitting] and convenient for the general good of the Colony, unto which we promise all due submission and obedience. In witness whereof we have hereunder subscribed our names at Cape Cod, the eleventh of November, in the year of the reign of our sovereign lord, King James, of England, France, and Ireland, . . . and of Scotland. . . . Anno Dom. [The year of our Lord] 1620.

Source "Text of the Mayflower Compact," Pilgrim Hall Museum, Plymouth, MA
http://www.pilgrimhallmuseum.org/mayflower_compact_text.htm

European Influences

Although the colonists traveled far, they continued to be influenced by the ideas from their home countries. As they established their colonies, they and their descendants held onto and expanded upon many of the traditions of their homelands. Longstanding beliefs guided them, but new ideas and influences made their mark as well.

Enlightenment Ideas Affect the Colonies For hundreds of years, Christianity shaped Europeans' thoughts and beliefs. It continues to influence people in North America and around the world. However, beginning in the 1600s, ideas from a European intellectual movement called the **Enlightenment** changed how many people saw the world.

Enlightenment views conflicted with Christian views in significant ways. Each of these important worldviews supplied very different answers to some of life's most important questions.

Christianity	Enlightenment
What is human nature?	
Christians believed that people were born sinful. "In Adam's Fall / We sinned all," taught the *New England Primer*. For millions of colonists and early Americans, the *Primer* was their first textbook and the way they learned to read.	Enlightenment thinker John Locke taught that the human mind is a blank slate at birth. To Locke, the experiences a person goes through shapes his or her character.
What is the ideal society?	
Christians believed that the ideal society was a reflection of the kingdom of heaven. Even if life on Earth was cruel and unfair, they believed, believers would get their reward in heaven.	Enlightenment thinkers believed that the ideal society was one in which people worked together to protect their own rights and interests. People influenced by the Enlightenment were willing to change society to make it fairer and better. They would fight for change even if that meant rebellions or revolutions.
Which is more important: faith or reason?	
Many Christians worked hard to develop their powers of reason. However, Christians considered faith in God to be the most important quality a person could have.	People influenced by the Enlightenment saw the ability to reason as the highest goal of humans. "The way to see by faith is to shut the eye of reason," Benjamin Franklin wrote in 1758.

British Traditions Affect the Colonies In the British colonies, it made sense that they based their laws on Britain's laws and traditions. A key document of British law is the **Magna Carta**, which means Great Charter. This document, originally signed in 1215 by King John of England, states that the king or queen is not above the law. It is the basis of individual rights in both the British and the American legal systems. British colonists derived many of the principles that supported their grievances against the crown (and many foundations of the Constitution) from the Magna Carta, including:

- The right to trial by a jury of one's peers
- Freedom from taxation without representation

Read Closely: Turning Point As you read, look for ideas and actions that make a crucial difference in the course of history. How would the idea that a ruler is subject to the laws of the land change a political system?

• The right to due process of the law

• The right to a speedy and unbiased trial

• Freedom from cruel or unusual punishment

The Magna Carta lies at the center of many other countries' legal systems, too—particularly those, like the United States, that were former British colonies.

One important way that British and U.S. laws differ from the laws of many other countries is that Britain and the United States follow **common law**. Many countries in Europe and their former colonies follow civil law. As in Britain, judges in the colonies had more freedom to decide what laws meant that they would have under a civil law system.

Differences between Common Law and Civil Law		
	Common Law	**Civil Law**
What is it based on?	precedent (judges' decisions made in previous cases)	a legal code, parts of which go back to Roman times
What does it allow?	Generally, everything that is not expressly forbidden by law is allowed.	Civil law often has stricter and more specific rules than common law does.
What are some countries that use this structure as the basis for their laws?	• United States • Britain • Canada • Australia • Malaysia	• France • Holland • Germany • Spain • Portugal

The Colonial Experience Affects Colonial Institutions The colonies were isolated from their home countries back in Europe and from one another. In some regions and times, colonists were able to trade with local Native Americans. In other regions and times, colonists waged war against them. Natural resources varied greatly by region, which meant that each colony's economy was different.

Colonial Democratic Institutions

From New England to the Southern colonies, colonists struggled over how to govern themselves. Isolation and variations in populations and economic modes meant that North American colonies developed different forms of democracy.

People in every colony wanted control over their lives. They wanted what they considered fair treatment from their rulers back in Europe. Also, they were willing to pay taxes, but they wanted some control over how taxes were levied and how governments spent that money. Even though colonists throughout North America had many of the same desires, the democracies they built differed based on each colony's circumstances.

Mayflower Compact A compact is an agreement between at least two parties. The Mayflower Compact was signed on board the *Mayflower* in 1620. It was the first framework of government written in what is now the United States.

Because the *Mayflower* had been blown off course, away from its original destination in Virginia, the agreement that the passengers had previously signed no longer had any power. Forty-one men, almost all the adult male passengers on the ship, signed the compact. The 19 women and 33 young adults and children on board were not invited to sign it.

The Mayflower Compact stopped a brewing conflict on board the ship, which threatened the unity of the group. It was law until 1691, when the Plymouth colony it helped establish became part of the Massachusetts Bay colony. The compact provided the social structure for the early years of colonization in the area. It stated that the settlers were still loyal to the English king, but they would create their own "just and equal laws" as needed to govern themselves.

The compact also stated that the colonists were creating this colony for the "advancement of the Christian faith." It offered no protections for non-Christians.

Maryland Toleration Act of 1649 Americans today enjoy freedom of religious beliefs because of the U.S. Constitution's First Amendment, which took effect in 1791. Long before that, the colony of Maryland had the Maryland Toleration Act. It was one of the first laws in the Americas to protect people's right to believe and worship as they chose.

The act had harsh penalties for blaspheming. That means talking about God or religion in a disrespectful way. However, it also stated that people were not allowed to "wrong, disturb, trouble, or molest any person whatsoever within this province professing to believe in Jesus Christ for or in respect of his or her religion or the free exercise thereof within this province." Catholics and Protestants were allowed to freely practice their religions. This was no small achievement in an era with no shortage of wars that stemmed from religious differences. During the 17th century alone, European wars between Catholic and Protestant forces took the lives of millions of combatants and civilians. It is important to note, however, the Toleration Act did not apply to people who followed other (non-Christian) religions.

The colonial legislature repealed the act in 1654 and banned Catholics from living in the colony. In 1658 it reenacted the Toleration Act. These events show that religious toleration in the 1600s had some limitations that people today would not generally accept.

New England Town Meetings When the New England colonies began, their members needed to decide how to govern themselves and make decisions about religious freedom and taxation. The colonists developed town meetings.

At these meetings, any free, White, adult male citizen could publicly discuss issues, vote on laws, and help pass budgets. Only property owners who were White and male could vote in elections. In many parts of New England, these meetings took place in specially built meeting halls funded by taxpayers.

Town Meetings and Direct Government Town meetings are an example of **direct government** rather than representative government. Instead of electing someone to create and vote on policy and laws on their behalf, citizens undertook these tasks themselves.

Some experts consider direct government the purest form of democracy because there is no "middleman" making decisions for others. However, direct democracy has had little success in communities larger than a few hundred people. Town meetings still exist in parts of New England.

Today, people would not consider such a limited form of government to be truly representative. However, at the time, town meetings gave a voice to a relatively large number of people. Many individuals felt directly responsible for the success of their government. Eventually, leaders of the American Revolution took part in town meetings.

Read Closely: Distinctions
One way to help understand distinctions among groups of people, individuals, or ideas is to identify ways in which they are similar and different. Identify one similarity and one difference between the Mayflower Compact and the Maryland Toleration Act.

Virginia House of Burgesses In Britain, a burgess was a representative who took part in government. Virginia's House of Burgesses had democratically elected members—the first governing body in a British colony to do so.

Each settlement in Virginia could send two burgesses to the House. Originally there were 22 burgesses. Only White men who owned property could vote. Wealthy planters won almost all the burgess elections.

George Washington served in the Virginia House of Burgesses for 15 years before the Revolutionary War. Thomas Jefferson and Patrick Henry also won elections as burgesses. The experience they gained writing laws and working for voters helped them after the revolution. By the time of the Revolutionary War, more than 60 percent of White male adults in Virginia had experience as voters in local elections.

Read Closely: Patterns
When reading a text, keep an eye out for actions or events that repeatedly seem to take a similar path. Can you identify a general pattern of complaints that the colonists had about their home countries?

Source: Getty Images

Patrick Henry addresses the Virginia House of Burgesses.

Read Closely: Comparison
Read the quotation from Peter Stuyvesant. How might most people react to such a statement today?

Right of Petition in New Netherland One of the most important qualities of any government is whether it tolerates criticism. In the Dutch colony of New Netherland, colonists did not want to pay taxes unless they had a say in how the colony was governed. For this reason, the colony's director general, Peter Stuyvesant, created a citizens' board called the Nine Men.

In 1649, the Nine Men sent two protest documents to the Dutch government. Ironically, these protests criticized Stuyvesant and complained he did not listen to them. They asked for improved trading rights, a check on Stuyvesant's power, and more control over the spending of public money. Stuyvesant fought back, saying, "We derive our authority from God and the company, not from a few ignorant subjects."

The Dutch government improved trading rights soon after. However, Stuyvesant kept his high level of power until 1652. That year, the Amsterdam Chamber told him to set up a government with increased citizen control. Today the New York City Council traces its origins to that time period. By the time Stuyvesant handed over New Netherland to the British in 1664, its citizens had experience with representative government.

Application: Interpret a Primary Source

Read the excerpt and answer the questions that follow it.

Law Passed by the Council of New Netherland, 1648

Great complaints are daily made to the Director General and Council by the Indians or natives, that some inhabitants of New Netherland set the natives to work and use them in their service, but let them go unrewarded after the work is done and refuse, contrary to all international law, to pay [them] for their labors. These Indians threaten, that if they are not satisfied and paid, they will make themselves paid or recover their remunerations by other improper means.

Therefore, to prevent all trouble as much as possible, the Director General and Council warn all inhabitants, who owe anything to an Indian for wages or otherwise, to pay it without dispute and if in the future they employ [natives], they shall be held liable to pay upon the evidence and complaint of Indians, (who for good reason shall be considered credible witnesses in such cases), under the penalty of such a fine, as the circumstances shall indicate as proper.

Done at the meeting and published September 28, 1648, at New Amsterdam . . .

Source: "Ordinance of the Director General and Council of New Netherland, and of the Burgomasters and Schepens of New Amsterdam, September 28, 1648," *The Records of New Amsterdam from 1653 to 1674 anno Domini,* ed. Berthold Fernow (Baltimore: Geological Publishing Co, 1976). New York Historical Society Library.

1. How does this law fit in the broader context of colonial dealings with Native Americans during this era?

_____

_____

2. What about the mission of the colony of New Netherland might explain why it wanted "to avoid trouble as much as possible" in its dealings with Native Americans?

_____

_____

3. Paragraph two of the law states that the Native Americans "shall be considered credible witnesses in such cases." What does that say about how serious the Council of New Netherland was about limiting disputes in the colony? What does it say about the more general treatment of Native Americans in the colony?

_____

_____

Multiple-Choice Questions

Questions 1 and 2 refer to the excerpt below.

A. Robert Beverly, Virginia plantation owner and member of the House of Burgesses, on the Colonists of Virginia, 1705

> I can easily imagine . . . that this as well as the rest of the plantations, was for the most part at first peopled by persons of low circumstances, and by such as were willing to seek their fortunes in a foreign country. Nor was it hardly possible it should be otherwise; for 'tis not likely that any man of a plentiful estate should voluntarily abandon a happy certainty to roam after imaginary advantages in a New World. Besides which uncertainty, must have proposed to himself to encounter the infinite difficulties and dangers that attend a new settlement. These discouragements were sufficient to terrify any man that could live easy in England from going to provoke his fortune in a strange land.
>
> Those that went over to that country first, were chiefly single men, who had not the encumbrance of wives and children in England; and if they had they did not expose them to the fatigue and hazard of so long a voyage, until they saw how it should fare with themselves.
>
> **Source:** Robert Beverly, *The History and Present State of Virginia*, 1705

1. Which of the following best describes the historical reliability of this source?

   1. This is a government report, so it may reflect the government's political bias.
   2. This is a memoir by a wealthy politician, so the view it presents is likely to be biased.
   3. This is a history written by someone who personally witnessed events it describes, so it can be considered reliable.
   4. This is a history written nearly 100 years after the events it describes, so its claims should be verified using first-hand accounts.

2. Which of the following best describes the author's intention in writing this document?

   1. He was trying to describe the origins of the plantation system.
   2. He wanted to produce a written history of the colony of Virginia.
   3. He wanted to justify the colonists' use of slave labor.
   4. He wanted to justify England's colonization of Virginia by describing the Native Americans who originally lived there as persons of low circumstances.

B. Maryland Toleration Act, 1649

Be it therefore ordered and enacted. . . . That whatsoever person or persons within this Province…shall henceforth blaspheme God, that is, curse Him or shall deny our Savior Jesus Christ to be the Son of God, or shall deny the Holy Trinity . . . or the Godhead of any of the said Three persons of the Trinity or the Unity of the Godhead . . . shall be punished with death and confiscation or forfeiture of all his or her lands. . . . And whereas . . . that no person or persons whatsoever within this province, or the islands, ports, harbors, creeks, or havens thereunto belonging professing to believe in Jesus Christ, shall from henceforth be any way troubled, molested or discountenanced for or in respect of his or her religion nor in free exercise thereof within this province or the islands thereunto belonging nor any way compelled to the belief or exercise of any other Religion against his or her consent.

Source: Cecil Calvert, Lord Baltimore, "An Act Concerning Religion," 1649. Adapted from *Proceedings and Acts of the General Assembly*, Archives of Maryland Online

3. What was the writer's intention in this excerpt?

    1. To establish the principle of complete religious freedom

    2. To recognize that religion was a personal matter

    3. To allow all Christians to practice their faith without fear of persecution

    4. To reserve the colony for some but not all types of Christianity

4. What is the context in which this excerpt was written?

    1. Toleration of religious minorities was growing in England.

    2. Discrimination against Roman Catholics was common in Europe.

    3. Colonies such as Pennsylvania were becoming less tolerant of religious diversity.

    4. Puritans in Massachusetts had already established the principle of religious toleration.

5. Which of the following problems is addressed in the Maryland Toleration Act?

    1. Gender discrimination

    2. Discrimination against Jews and Muslims

    3. Discrimination against racial minorities

    4. Discrimination against any denomination of Christians

C. Canassateego, Speech at the Treaty with the Six Nations in Philadelphia

We know our Lands are now become more valuable. The White People think we do not know their Value; but we are sensible that the Land is everlasting, and the few Goods we receive for it are soon worn out and gone. For the future, we will sell no Lands but . . . we will know beforehand, the Quantity of the Goods we are to receive. Besides, we are not well used [fairly treated] with respect to the Lands still unsold by us. Your People daily settle on these Lands, and spoil our Hunting. We must insist on your removing them, as you know they have no Right to settle to the Northward of Kittochtinny-Hills. In particular, we renew our Complaints against some People who are settled . . . and we desire they may be forthwith made to go off the Land, for they do great Damage to our Cousins the Delawares [Lenni Lenape].

Source: Speech by Chief Canassateego of the Onondaga Nation of the Iroquois League, 1742

6. Which of the following describes the best use of Canassateego's speech?

   1. As an objective account of the relations between early White settlers and Native Americans

   2. As a contemporary account of the relations between White settlers and Native Americans from the point of view of a Native American, and therefore possibly biased

   3. As an example of an early treaty between White settlers and Native Americans

   4. As a declaration of war against White settlers who had stolen Native American lands

7. Which of the following best describes the purpose of Canassateego's speech?

   1. To request that the terms of the treaty be honored

   2. To request better quality goods in exchange for land in the future

   3. To tell White settlers that Native Americans would not sell them any more land

   4. To demand that White settlers move off the lands that they had paid for with poor-quality goods

8. How does Canassateego support his claim that Native Americans were not fairly treated?

   1. He says that White people think the Native Americans do not know the value of their land.

   2. He says that the goods they receive in exchange for the land are soon gone.

   3. He says that White settlers have moved into lands where they are prohibited and spoiled the Native Americans' hunting.

   4. He does not say anything to support the claim.

Short-Essay Questions

Study the two documents and answer the question that follows.

D. Christopher Columbus, Log Entry for October 13, 1492

They came loaded with balls of cotton, parrots, javelins, and other things too numerous to mention; these they exchanged for whatever we chose to give them. I was very attentive to them [the Arawaks], and strove to learn if they had any gold. Seeing some of them with little bits of this metal hanging at their noses, I gathered from them by signs that by going southward or steering round the island in that direction, there would be found a king who possessed large vessels of gold, and in great quantities. I endeavored to procure them to lead the way thither, but found they were unacquainted with the route. I determined to stay here till the evening of the next day, and then sail for the southwest; for according to what I could learn from them, there was land at the south as well as at the southwest and northwest and those from the northwest came many times and fought with them and proceeded on to the southwest in search of gold and precious stones. . . . I am determined to proceed onward and ascertain whether I can reach Cipango [Japan].

Source: Christopher Columbus, *Journal*, 1492. Edited by Bartolomé de Las Casas, c. 1530

E. Bartolomé de Las Casas on the Conquest of Hispaniola

Yet, those Spaniards to whom the Indians were given were themselves for the most part idiotic, cruel, avaricious, and infected with all sorts of vices. And this was the great care they had of [the Indians]: they sent the men to the mines to dig for gold, which is an intolerable labor; the women they turned to tilling and manuring the ground, which is drudgery even to men of the strongest and most robust constitutions. They gave them nothing else to eat but wild grasses and other such insubstantial nutriment, so that the milk of nursing women dried up, which meant that recently born infants all died. Since the females were separated from and did not live with the men, there were no new births among them. The men died in the mines, starved and oppressed with labor, and the women perished in the fields, broken from the same evils and calamities. Thus, the infinite number of inhabitants that formerly peopled this island were exterminated and dwindled away to nothing.

Source: Bartolomé de Las Casas, *A Short Description of the Destruction of the Indies*, 1542

1. In a short essay, describe the historical context surrounding the two documents above. Then identify and explain the cause-and-effect relationship between the events described in these documents.

Study the two documents and answer the question that follows.

F. William Penn, Letter to the Colonists of Pennsylvania

Source: Appletons' Cyclopaedia of
American Biography, 1888 /
Wikimedia Commons

William Penn

I hope you will not be troubled at your change and the king's choice. You are
not at the mercy of a governor that comes to make his fortune great. You will
be governed by laws of your own making, and live as a free, and, if you will,
serious and industrious people. I will not take the rights of any, or oppress his
person. In short, whatever serious and reasonable men can reasonably desire
for the security and improvement of their own happiness, I shall heartily
agree to.

Source: William Penn, Letter to the Colonists of Pennsylvania, 1681

G. William Penn Signing the Treaty with the Lenni Lanape (Delaware)

Source: Benjamin West, *Penn's Treaty with the Indians*, 1771–72

In 1681, King Charles II gave William Penn (1644–1718) a large tract of land between New York and Maryland. There Penn founded the colony of Pennsylvania, where he hoped that his fellow Quakers and members of other persecuted religions would be able to live in peace. He spent most of his life in England, only visiting Pennsylvania once, from late 1682 to 1684. During that time he established good relations with the Native Americans who lived there.

2. In a short essay, describe the historical context surrounding the two documents on page 32. Then analyze and explain how the purpose of the painting of Penn and the Lenni Lanape affects its reliability as a source of evidence.

Source: *The Graphic*, 1884. Getty Images

This engraving from the late 19th century shows the Quakers being expelled from Massachusetts in 1660. It was this sort of religious intolerance that led to the foundation of Pennsylvania, which was much more inclusive, although not entirely so.

CHAPTER 2

Constitutional Foundations (1763–1824)

Chapter Overview

In the late 1700s and early 1800s, the United States established a new federal government. Its founding documents have inspired millions.

Attempts at Greater British Control After the French and Indian War, colonists objected to increased British taxes and control. As punishments and rebellions grew harsher, the First Continental Congress met. Its members rejected the idea of independence. Still, that Congress turned out to be the start of the U.S. government.

The Fight for Independence On July 4, 1776, the Second Continental Congress declared that the United States was an independent nation. Thomas Jefferson and others wrote the Declaration of Independence. It states that "all men are created equal." Despite this, the Declaration's framers did not believe that it applied to women or to minorities. Slavery continued. At the Battle of Yorktown in 1781, the British surrendered.

A New Government Takes Shape The Articles of Confederation set out the rules of the first U.S. federal government. But under the Articles, the central, federal, government had little power and the states were bound together only loosely. In 1787, delegates created rules for a new federal government under the Constitution. It provided for a stronger central government that balanced power among three branches. The Bill of Rights was soon added to the Constitution, guaranteeing many individual freedoms. However, the Constitution failed to abolish slavery or protect Native Americans. Women and non-White people could not vote or hold office.

U.S. Political Parties Begin The country's first president, George Washington, opposed the formation of political parties. However, two parties soon developed. The Federalists wanted a stronger central government. The Democratic-Republicans wanted Congress and the rest of the federal government to have fewer powers.

Civic Literacy: Ideals of the Founders An important issue in this chapter is the impact of the revolutionary ideas of the founders of the United States. Ideas in the Declaration of Independence and the U.S. Constitution not only built the country, they sent shock waves around the world. However, living up to the promises in those documents has often been challenging.

New York Social Studies Framework

Key Idea 11.2: Constitutional Foundations

European colonization in North America prompted cultural contact and exchange among diverse peoples; cultural differences and misunderstandings at times led to conflict. A variety of factors contributed to the development of regional differences, including social and racial hierarchies, in colonial America.

Source: *New York State Grades 9–12 Social Studies Framework*

Civic Literacy Essay: Close Reading

Stated simply, the tasks involved in the Civic Literacy Document-Based Essay (see page 5) are:

1. Read the documents that relate to constitutional and civic issues.
2. Analyze the documents.
3. Describe the historical context of a constitutional or civic issue.
4. Explain the efforts of individuals, groups, and/or governments to address this issue.
5. Discuss how successful those efforts were
   OR
   Discuss the impact of the efforts on the United States and/or American society.

The foundation of the civic literacy document-based essay is established in the first task: close reading. Close reading is the careful interpretation of a text. It often requires reading for a second or third time to fully absorb the meaning of a text. When you read closely, you make an effort to understand the main idea, important details, and the tone or attitude of the writer, among other traits. The boxes in the margin of this book contain notes that help you closely read the primary sources, so you will get lots of practice.

Application: Samuel Adams was called a "firebrand" of the revolution because his words often inflamed sentiments and motivated people to act. Closely read the following excerpt from a speech he gave to the Continental Congress the day before the Declaration of Independence was signed. On the lines below it, write the main idea and two vivid details.

> "We cannot suppose that our opposition has made a corrupt and dissipated nation more friendly to America, or created in them a greater respect for the rights of mankind. We can therefore expect a restoration and establishment of our privileges, and a compensation for the injuries we have received, from their want of power, from their fears, and not from their virtues. The unanimity and valor, which will effect an honorable peace, can render a future contest for our liberties unnecessary."

_____

_____

_____

Key Terms by Theme

Governance
Boston Massacre (p. 39)
First Continental Congress
   (p. 40)
Thomas Jefferson (p. 44)
George Washington (p. 44)
Alexander Hamilton (p. 45)
Articles of Confederation (p. 51)
separation of powers (p. 55)

Bill of Rights (p. 55)
judicial review (p. 62)

Civics
Crispus Attucks (p. 39)
John Adams (p. 39)
Thomas Paine (p. 43)
Declaration of Independence
   (p. 44)

John Locke (p. 44)
Great Compromise (p. 52)
Federalists (p. 52)

Economy
boycott (p. 38)
Boston Tea Party (p. 40)
Coercive Acts (p. 40)
"Intolerable Acts" (p. 40)
tariff (p. 60)

Analyze a Primary Source

King George III of Britain, Proclamation of 1763

Read Closely: Cause
Thinking about causes and effects can help you better understand the history you read. What caused George III to write this proclamation? Circle the event he refers to in the first paragraph.

Read Closely: Power and Authority
The king describes his people as "loving Subjects" and expects them to obey every rule he creates. As this lesson shows, many of his subjects disagreed with him.

Read Closely: Effect
Notice cause-effect relationships that historical documents describe. What new rules did the king make after the event at Paris? Underline them in the second and third paragraphs.

Whereas We have taken into Our Royal Consideration the extensive and valuable Acquisitions in America, secured to Our Crown by the late Definitive Treaty of Peace, concluded at Paris . . . and being desirous that all Our loving Subjects . . . may avail themselves with all convenient Speed, of the great Benefits and Advantages which must accrue therefrom to their Commerce, Manufactures, and Navigation, We have thought fit . . . to issue this Our Royal Proclamation. . . .

And whereas it is just and reasonable and essential to Our Interest and the Security of Our Colonies, that the several Nations or Tribes of Indians with whom We are connected, and who live under Our Protection should not be molested or disturbed . . . no Governor . . . in any of Our other Colonies or Plantations in America, do presume for the present . . . [may] grant Warrants of Survey, or pass Patents for any Lands beyond the Heads or Sources of any of the Rivers which fall into the Atlantic Ocean. . . .

And whereas great Frauds and abuses have been committed in the purchasing Lands of the Indians, to the great Prejudice of Our Interests, and to the great Dissatisfaction of the said Indians; in order to prevent such Irregularities for the future, and to the End that the Indians may be convinced of Our Justice and determined Resolution to remove all reasonable cause of Discontent, We do . . . enjoy and require that no private Person do presume to make any Purchase from the said Indians of any Lands reserved to the said Indians.

Given at our Court at St. James's the 7th Day of October 1763 in the Third Year of our Reign.

Sources: http://www.digitalhistory.uh.edu/disp_textbook.cfm?smtID=3&psid=159 http://avalon.law.yale.edu/18th_century/proc1763.asp

British Efforts at Control

Before the French and Indian War, British citizens in the American colonies enjoyed many of the same basic rights as citizens in Great Britain. Britain allowed the colonies to govern themselves without much interference. Its colonial policy was one of salutary neglect. That meant leaving the colonies alone, but in a way that benefited them.

- The British did not enforce laws that required the colonies to trade only with Britain.

- The British did not collect taxes from the colonists.

- Colonists had the right to establish popular assemblies in the colonies. However, they were not allowed to vote for representatives in the British Parliament.

Britain won the French and Indian War. However, the conflict left the country in need of tax money. The victory also meant Britain had more land to control than ever. British efforts to gain political and economic control resulted in strict laws on the colonists. These efforts also resulted in enraged protests.

Proclamation of 1763 After the French and Indian War, Great Britain decided to enforce its trade laws and station a permanent military force in the colonies. Britain wanted to stabilize the western frontier and prevent Native American rebellion. The Proclamation of 1763 forbade the colonists from settling west of the Appalachian Mountains. The colonists were furious because that is exactly what they wanted to do. They also believed that faraway Britain was interfering too much in colonial affairs.

Stamp Act The British Parliament and king also decided to tax the American colonies without the consent of their assemblies. In 1765, Britain established a stamp tax on colonial newspapers and legal documents.

What difference did a few stamps make? The Stamp Act was actually a tax on every event that required the use of a printed paper. Buying a newspaper or playing cards now required paying a tax. So did getting married or writing a will. Even worse in the eyes of colonists was that the Stamp Act seemed to set a precedent, making new, more expensive taxes more likely. Facing strong opposition from the colonies, Britain repealed the Stamp Act in 1766.

> **Read Closely: Cause and Effect**
> One event can directly or indirectly affect future events. Identify two effects that resulted from Britain's military victory.

Arguments Over the Stamp Act	
For	**Against**
- By defeating the French, Britain protected the colonists from the French and their Native American allies.	- The British Parliament should not be able to raise taxes without the approval of colonial assemblies. Taxation without representation was unfair.
- The policy of salutary neglect was too costly.	- Colonists had fought in the French and Indian War but had no say about taxes.
- The colonists should share the costs of the war and of their own defense.	- Colonists wanted to settle west of the Appalachian Mountains.

> ***Civic Literacy:***
> ***Inequality*** The colonists contended that the king and Parliament treated them more poorly than they treated residents of Britain. Colonists' desire to rise above second-class citizenry dogged the British Empire over centuries—even up through the middle of the 20th century in Africa and South Asia.

Townshend Acts In 1767, Britain passed more laws that cracked down on the colonies:

- It stopped the New York Assembly from passing laws until it paid the expenses of British troops in the area.

- It taxed paper, paint, tea, lead, and glass.

- It added officers and ships to make sure that the colonists paid customs duties on imported products.

The Townshend Acts threatened the colonists' established ability to govern themselves. They caused such a storm of protest that Britain repealed most of them in 1770. Only the tax on tea remained.

Tea Act In 1773, Britain gave the British East India Company a monopoly on selling tea in the colonies. In other words, American colonists could not buy tea from the Dutch or any other sellers. In the early 1700s, only rich people drank tea. But by the mid-1700s, it was becoming more available. Like the British, many American colonists drank tea twice a day. In 1749, a Swedish visitor to Albany described the habits of the people there: "Their breakfast is tea." When the British made tea more expensive, the colonists were reminded of that insult daily.

Initial Colonial Reaction

It was one thing to resent the actions of the Crown, but what could be done in response? Colonist began to further organize their efforts to resist what they saw as tyranny from their far-off overlords.

Boycotts A **boycott** is a refusal to buy a product, use a service, or participate in something as a protest. American colonists peacefully used their economic power by refusing to buy taxed goods. In 1769, a Virginian named Martha Jaquelin wrote to a friend in Britain. "I have given up the Article of Tea," she wrote. "But some are not quite so tractable [agreeable]. However, if we can convince the good folks on your side [of] the Water of their Error, we may hope to see happier times."

Colonists also boycotted cloth. Weaving parties became popular as colonists made their own clothes. "Save your Money, and save your Country!" one group from the Boston Town Meeting urged.

Stamp Act Riots In contrast to peaceful boycotts, some protests were violent. Mobs in Boston destroyed the homes of tax collectors, including the lieutenant governor. Riots erupted in seaports from New Hampshire to Georgia.

A secret group called the Loyal Nine met in Boston to plan Stamp Act protests. Eventually, its members became part of a larger group called the Sons of Liberty. This group protested the Stamp Act throughout the 13 colonies. Samuel Adams, one of the founding fathers of the United States, was a member of both groups. The Sons of Liberty began considering whether they should respond to taxation attempts with weapons. "It does not require a majority to prevail," Adams wrote. Instead, it took "an irate, tireless minority, keen on setting brushfires of freedom in the minds of men."

Boston Massacre Because of vandalism, threats, and violence, colonial authorities asked Britain for protection. In response, Britain sent soldiers to Boston. They arrived in October 1768.

Tensions continued to run high in the Boston area. Boycotts continued. In 1770, the Sons of Liberty put "Importer" signs on some shops and harassed

Read Closely: Connections
How individuals choose to spend their money can affect economies and governments. How might the colonists' boycotts have affected Britain?

customers. A Loyalist who tried to take down one of the "Importer" signs fought with a group of boys who threw rocks at him. He shot and killed one of the boys, who was 11 years old.

On March 5, 1770, rumors swirled about what British soldiers might do. A crowd gathered and began pelting soldiers with snow and ice. Some colonists begged the soldiers not to fire. One of the soldiers, panicking, fired his weapon even though there had been no order to do so. Other soldiers also fired. Five people died, including a Black man named **Crispus Attucks**. This became known as the **Boston Massacre**.

Crispus Attucks A sailor and rope maker, Attucks was most likely a former slave. He was probably of African and Native American descent. At the time of his death, Boston did not allow White people and non-White people to be buried together. Boston officials ignored that law so that all those who died in the massacre could be buried in the same grave.

Decades after Attucks's death, abolitionists and civil rights activists praised his courage. Dr. Martin Luther King, Jr. wrote in 1964, "He is a reminder that the African-American heritage is not only African but American and it is a heritage that begins with the beginning of America." Today many people remember Attucks as the first casualty of the American Revolution.

Read Closely: Turning Point
Identify events that either cause a change in the direction of history or that symbolize a change that is happening. In what way was the Boston Massacre a turning point?

Source: Wikimedia Commons

Crispus Attucks

After the Massacre By the next morning, the soldiers and their captain were under arrest. Future president **John Adams** was part of the men's defense team in court. Adams showed that the situation was chaotic and the soldiers were under pressure. Of the eight men who were on trial for murder, six were found not guilty. The other two were found guilty, but of the lesser charge of manslaughter. Their thumbs were branded as punishment.

Why was the Boston Massacre important?

Civic Literacy:
Ideas and Beliefs
Today a fair trial is considered an essential human right. Many societies today believe that even those accused of shocking crimes deserve an impartial judge and a jury that weighs evidence fairly.

• It led to the royal governor removing all soldiers from Boston.

• Different accounts of the conflict circulated. Some blamed the colonists. Others blamed the soldiers. These accounts influenced people's views, making them more loyalist or rebellious in outlook.

• It showed that tension between colonists and soldiers could result in armed conflict.

The Boston Tea Party and Beyond

Many colonists were still angry that they were being taxed on tea without their consent. In 1773, the East India Company sent massive shipments of tea to the American colonies.

In New York and Philadelphia, colonists persuaded local officials to deny the tea ships permission to unload. Those ships sailed back to England with their tea. In Maryland and New Jersey, some colonists set fire to the tea. But the governor of Massachusetts decided that the tea must get through.

Blockade in Boston The governor asked the British navy to block Boston Harbor. No ships could leave until the tea was unloaded. The standoff lasted 20 days. Samuel Adams and others tried to negotiate with the governor during that time.

Then a group of colonists dressed as Native Americans boarded multiple ships in the harbor. They hacked open 342 tea crates and threw the tea into the harbor. A Boston newspaper reported that the colonists did this "without the least damage to the ships or any other property." Many who took part in what became known as the **Boston Tea Party** wanted to avoid looting. Their focus was the tea mainly because they believed the tax was levied in an unfair manner. In addition, colonists objected to the British East India Company's monopoly on tea.

In his diary, John Adams wrote about the Tea Party. "There was no other Alternative but to destroy it or let it be landed," he wrote. "To let it be landed would be giving up the Principle of Taxation by Parliamentary Authority, against which the Continent have struggled for 10 Years."

Coercive Acts The British Parliament struck back, passing the **Coercive Acts** in 1774. These acts closed Boston to shipping as punishment for the Boston Tea Party. They also weakened the Massachusetts legislature and nearly shut down Boston's economy. The colonists condemned these acts and others as **"Intolerable Acts."**

The new acts were not limited to punishing Boston. Royal governors in the colonies gained the right to house troops in empty buildings. Britain also declared that the territory between the Ohio and Mississippi Rivers would now shift to the jurisdiction of Quebec—another British colony, but a substantially French speaking and Catholic one.

Britain was trying to bring the American colonies under control as British subjects and taxpayers. However, the long period of salutary neglect made the crackdown seem severe. Britain had repealed harsh laws and taxes before, so many colonists thought that would happen again.

First Continental Congress As a result of the Coercive Acts, the colonists held the **First Continental Congress** in Philadelphia in 1774. Each American colony except Georgia sent delegates. These delegates disagreed about their purpose. Some believed that they should work out an agreement to ease tensions with Britain. Others wanted the Congress to be the start of a new, independent government.

At the First Continental Congress, the delegates rejected the idea of becoming an independent country. Instead, they supported a boycott on British goods. But the start of the American Revolution was not far away. The Continental Congress was the beginning of an independent government in the United States.

<aside>
Read Closely: Patterns
As you read, notice actions or events that seem to take a similar path. Can you identify a general pattern of how relations between Britain and the American colonies played out?
</aside>

<aside>
Read Closely: Central Effect
As you read, focus on why things happen the way they do. What central effect do you think the First Continental Congress had on the delegates?
</aside>

Application: Interpret a Primary Source

Read the excerpt and answer the questions that follow it.

Letter from Cadwallader Colden, Acting Governor of New York, 1765

No doubt you have heard of the Riot at Boston and of the Seditious Discourses and threats at New York. James McEvers had accepted the office of Distributor of Stamps. . . . Yesterday he sent me a Resignation of his office, being terrified by the suffering and ill usage the Stamp officer met with at Boston, and the threats he has received at New York.

Notwithstanding all of this I hope with the assistance I expect to defeat all their Measures & that the Stamps shall be delivered in proper time after their arrival. I shall not be intimidated.

The People of New York are surprisingly excited to sedition by a few Men, but I hope their wicked designs will be defeated and their machinations end in their obtaining the reward they deserve. You may believe that these things employ my thoughts and that great prudence is required in my Conduct at this time.

Source: The Colden Papers, Collections of the New York Historical Society, 1914.

1. What major conflict ended in the years preceding Colden's letter, and how did this affect the circumstances surrounding his writing?

_____

_____

_____

_____

_____

2. Why did the Stamp Act have the effect that Colden describes in the document?

_____

_____

_____

_____

_____

3. Based on what you have read in this lesson, what perspective did Stamp Act opponents have about Colden and other officials who were loyal to the king?

_____

_____

_____

_____

**Conceptual Understanding
11.2b** Failed attempts to mitigate the conflicts between the British government and the colonists led the colonists to declare independence, which they eventually won through the Revolutionary War, which affected individuals in different ways.

The United States sought its freedom through military victory over its home country. But it also sought freedom by presenting new ideas about human rights. Eventually, these ideas changed the balance of power on a global scale

Analyze a Primary Source

From the Declaration of Independence, 1776

Read Closely: Purpose
As you read a primary source, think about why its author or authors wrote it. Circle the phrase in the first paragraph that explains why the authors wrote the Declaration.

Read Closely: Ideas
The authors of the Declaration based their writing on the work of the philosopher John Locke (1632–1704). He wrote that men are "by nature all free, equal, and independent."

Read Closely: Bias
Active readers look for words and phrases that indicate a one-sided or slanted viewpoint. Underline words and phrases in the second paragraph that show the authors' bias against King George and the British government. If you need to, look up words in a dictionary.

When in the Course of human events, it becomes necessary for one people to dissolve the political bands which have connected them with another, and to assume among the powers of the earth, the separate and equal station to which the Laws of Nature and of Nature's God entitle them, a decent respect to the opinions of mankind requires that they should declare the causes which impel [cause] them to the separation.

We hold these truths to be self-evident [readily apparent], that all men are created equal, that they are endowed by their Creator with certain unalienable Rights, that among these are Life, Liberty and the pursuit of Happiness.—That to secure these rights, Governments are instituted among Men, deriving their just powers from the consent of the governed, —That whenever any Form of Government becomes destructive of these ends, it is the Right of the People to alter or to abolish it, and to institute new Government, laying its foundation on such principles and organizing its powers in such form, as to them shall seem most likely to effect their Safety and Happiness. Prudence, indeed, will dictate that Governments long established should not be changed for light and transient [temporary] causes; and accordingly all experience hath shewn, that mankind are more disposed to suffer, while evils are sufferable, than to right themselves by abolishing the forms to which they are accustomed. But when a long train of abuses and usurpations [instances of power being seized], pursuing invariably the same Object evinces [clearly shows] a design to reduce them under absolute Despotism, it is their right, it is their duty, to throw off such Government, and to provide new Guards for their future security. —Such has been the patient sufferance of these Colonies; and such is now the necessity which constrains them to alter their former Systems of Government. . . .

Source: https://www.archives.gov/founding-docs/declaration-transcript

Colonists Declare Independence

At first, most Americans thought of fighting the British only to defend their rights. They rejected the idea of fighting for independence. However, many changed their minds because of new ideas as well as outbreaks of violence.

Paine Argues for "Common Sense" Many American colonists read "Common Sense," a pamphlet by **Thomas Paine**. He referred to tyrants as "royal brutes." Paine boldly set forth the arguments for American independence. To him, it made no sense for a small island kingdom like Great Britain to rule over vast American lands at a great distance. Paine's small pamphlet had a huge impact. Within a few weeks of its publication, it sold more than 150,000 copies.

Colonists Monitor British Troop Movements On the night of April 18, 1775, three men—Paul Revere, William Dawes, and Samuel Prescott—warned the colonists that British troop movements threatened their weapons stockpiles. A British scouting party surprised the three and arrested Revere. Dawes and Prescott escaped. Prescott delivered a warning to the town of Concord, Massachusetts.

Gunfire at Lexington and Concord The first shots of the American Revolution rang out in the Massachusetts towns of Lexington and Concord. On April 19, 1775, British troops marched into Lexington and fired on a small band of armed Americans. The British then tried to march to Concord. Colonial farmers firing from behind trees and stone walls drove them back. In all, 273 British soldiers were killed or wounded, with 95 casualties on the colonial side.

Source: New York Public Library Digital Collections / Wikimedia Commons

The Battle of Lexington

The Continental Congresses Hammer Out Ideas Delegates from the colonies met in Philadelphia twice. Their goal was to plan united action to defend their rights.

- The First Continental Congress (1774) asked Britain to repeal its taxes and overturn other harsh measures. But the British did not.

- The Second Continental Congress (1776) met after the British and Americans clashed at Lexington and Concord and then at Bunker Hill outside Boston. On July 4, 1776, the congress announced its decision to declare the independence of a new nation: the United States.

> **Read Closely: Diplomacy**
> When you are reading about an independence movement, look for factors that caused a breakdown in communication between representatives of the two sides. What happened between the first and second Continental Congresses that affected the congress members' actions?

Purpose of the Declaration of Independence **Thomas Jefferson** was the main author of the **Declaration of Independence**. He eloquently stated the reasons for leaving Britain and becoming an independent nation. He created one of the founding documents of the United States.

The Declaration was also an announcement to the other European powers that a new country was open for alliances. By backing the United States, France and Spain could harm their hated rival, Britain.

Ideas in the Declaration of Independence The Declaration draws on theories of the philosopher **John Locke**. It argued that governments must represent the people, have limited power, and recognize basic human rights. When any government violates the people's natural rights, the people have the right to "alter or to abolish" that government. This viewpoint was revolutionary in an age where most of the countries of Europe were ruled by absolutist monarchies that would reject Locke's ideas at least in part or, more likely, altogether.

A second section of the Declaration lists specific grievances against the British king to show that Britain repeatedly violated the colonists' rights. The grievances included the following:

- dissolving colonial assemblies

- keeping British troops in the colonies

- "imposing taxes without [the colonists'] consent"

In the original draft, Jefferson criticized the British for taking part in the slave trade and maintaining a system "where men should be bought and sold." However, the Second Continental Congress, in debating and editing the Declaration, eliminated that wording. This was done, in large part, to keep Southern slaveholders on board with the document. Jefferson's criticism rang hollow anyway, as he was a prominent slaveholder.

John Hancock and other delegates meeting in Philadelphia were the first to sign the Declaration. Copies circulated throughout the colonies to explain the reasons for the war and the colonial leaders' vision for a future United States.

Long-Term Impacts of the Declaration of Independence The Declaration was the first formal document in which a people claimed to have the right to choose their government. Eventually, this startling idea affected people all over the world—first in France and then in many other countries.

The Declaration's revolutionary ideas have profoundly affected world history. Inspired by its principles, people in many nations—including countries as diverse as France, Liberia, and Vietnam—have used the Declaration to justify their own struggles for independence. In the United States, the Declaration served as a vital document in the later fight to end slavery, since it stated that all men were created equal.

The Revolutionary War

The first year of war was a desperate one for the largely untrained, disorganized revolutionary troops. Fighting a losing battle to defend New York City in July 1776, revolutionary commander General **George Washington** and his army barely managed to escape disaster. The troops retreated across the Hudson River to New Jersey.

Read Closely: Turning Point
As you read, look for factors that could have changed the course of history. How might U.S. history have been different if the congress members had kept the wording about slavery?

Read Closely: Cause and Effect
As you read, look for causes and effects, even if those effects are unintended. What unintended consequences did the Declaration have?

By the end of the first year, British troops and mercenaries, or hired troops, from Germany occupied Boston and New York. The American capital, Philadelphia, fell to the British in 1777.

No one city or region was the center of the war. According to Washington's aide **Alexander Hamilton**, "our hopes are not placed in any particular city, or spot of ground, but in preserving a good army furnished with proper necessaries, to take advantage of favorable opportunities, and waste and defeat the enemy by piece-meal."

Turning Points Washington desperately needed a victory to keep American hopes alive. He launched a surprise attack on Trenton, New Jersey, on December 25, 1776. His men routed the British.

A second turning point was a decisive American victory at Saratoga, New York, in October 1777. Americans showed enough strength in this battle to convince France to give them military and naval help. This news came as a relief to Washington and his men, who were suffering from inadequate food and clothing while camped at Valley Forge in Pennsylvania during the severe winter of 1777–1778.

General Washington Washington's troops suffered at Valley Forge from the freezing weather and lack of food. "No bread, no meat, no soldier!" the men shouted. But Washington and his wife Martha were there with them. Martha brought supplies from Mount Vernon, the Washingtons' home.

Source: New York Public Library Digital Collections / Wikimedia Commons

Washington at Valley Forge

Washington's command of the army was critical to the revolution's success. People called him the "soul and sword" of the American Revolution. Washington later became the first president of the United States. He served for two terms. Although he owned slaves, he wrote in his will that his slaves should be freed when his wife died.

Impacts of the War on Workers Wars always have unintended consequences. The American Revolution changed how everyday people worked.

- Many men became soldiers. That meant other people—often women and young people—had to take over their jobs on farms and in cities.

- The Continental Congress began printing its own money to pay for the war. It printed almost $250 million. People could not exchange the money for gold or silver. That meant few workers would accept it as payment. (The colonist Mercy Otis Warren called this money "immense heaps of paper trash.") Workers preferred payment in gold, silver, or barter.

> **Read Closely: Summary**
> Active readers are able to summarize the events they read. How would you summarize American military progress in 1776? What about in 1777?

Read Closely: Predictions
As you read, make predictions about what might happen next. How do you think the strength or weakness of U.S. currency during the Revolution affected the power of the U.S. government?

Read Closely: Motivations
As you read, think about why key figures in history acted the way they did. What do you think motivated Colonel Tye and his men to fight the patriots?

Read Closely: Patterns
One way to appreciate historical patterns is to see how they still exist in your lifetime. For example, wars and upheavals have often changed the status of women. How has the status of women changed since the time of the Revolutionary War?

• The idea that "all men are created equal" meant that society became closer to equal. For example, free White men began calling themselves "Mr." Before the war, that title was only for landowners. Although American society was not equal in a modern sense, it had more equality than many other countries of the time.

Impacts of the War on African Americans At the time of the Revolution, about 2.5 million people lived in the 13 colonies. About 460,000 of them were enslaved. Most of those enslaved people were of African descent. There were very few free Black people in the American colonies at this time.

African Americans generally fought for whichever side promised them freedom. African American soldiers fought alongside White soldiers at the battles of Lexington, Concord, and Bunker Hill. Some were free, others were earning their freedom through service, and still others would return to bondage. However, George Washington stopped the recruitment of African American soldiers in 1775. He did not allow their recruitment again until 1778, after the Continental Army had shrunk dramatically from disease and desertion.

The British used the rebels' stance against Black recruits to their advantage. The royal governor of Virginia offered freedom to any soldier who could escape enslavement and join their ranks. As a result, more African Americans fought for the British.

The escaped slave Colonel Tye was probably the most famous and feared guerrilla commander of the Revolutionary War. He raided the farms and homes of patriot families and captured patriot officers in New York and New Jersey. The British paid him and gave him the title of colonel. Tye and his men often raided the homes of the people who had enslaved them. Tye was a member of the Black Brigade, an elite force of 24 Black loyalists.

Impacts of the War on Women At the time of the Revolution, women did not vote, hold elected office, or officially fight in battle. However, their contributions were significant and long lasting:

• One young woman warned townspeople about British troop movements, just as Paul Revere had. In 1777, 16-year-old Sybil Ludington learned that the British planned to invade Danbury, Connecticut. She rode 40 miles through the night to warn the militia her father led. They intercepted the British and drove them back to their ships.

• Many women took over their husbands' responsibilities while they fought in the war. Abigail Adams, wife of future president John Adams, ran the couple's farm while John was away. She bought land and supervised construction, planting, and harvesting. In one of her letters to her husband, she called herself a "farmess."

• Women who supported American independence cut ties with friends and family members who were loyal to Britain. Lucy Knox, the wife of an army officer, left her entire loyalist family when she married. She never saw them again.

• Some women took up arms against British soldiers. Margaret Cochran Corbin fired a cannon on British troops in Manhattan after her soldier husband was killed in action. During the battle, she sustained severe injuries that affected her for the rest of her life. Corbin was the first woman to receive a U.S. military pension.

Impacts of the War on Native Americans

During the Revolution, Native Americans had three choices. They could fight for the patriots, fight for the loyalists, or try to stay neutral. The Declaration of Independence faults King George for sending "merciless Indian Savages" to harm the colonists. This description shows the way in which many colonists viewed Native Americans.

Not every member of every tribe chose the same side. Some tribes, such as the Creek, stayed neutral throughout the war. Others stayed neutral at first and then chose a side after an attack. And some tribes, such as the Abenaki, sent men to fight on both sides.

Native American Tribes in the Revolutionary War	
Tribes Supporting the Patriots	**Tribes Supporting the British and Loyalists**
• Oneida (New York) • Wabanaki Confederacy: Penobscot, Passamaquoddy, Pigwacket, Micmac, Maliseet (Maine, New Brunswick, Nova Scotia) • Stockbridge-Mohican (New York) • Potawatomi (Great Lakes) • Catawba (South Carolina)	• Cherokee (Carolinas, Georgia) • Mohawk, Onondaga, Seneca, Cayuga (New York) • Shawnee (Ohio, Kentucky) • Miami (Great Lakes) • Wyandot, or Huron (Michigan) • Chickasaw (Mississippi, Alabama, Tennessee) • Choctaw (Mississippi)

Native American women helped decide whether to ally with a side or stay neutral. Mary Brant was the daughter of a Mohawk leader called a sachem. She also had several children with a loyalist who supervised Indian affairs for the Northern colonies. Brant influenced other Mohawks to back Britain. She also spied for Britain and supplied the British with ammunition.

Victory at Yorktown During the last years of the war, the armies fought in the South. Fighting in Georgia and the Carolinas between 1778 and 1780 saw victories and defeats for both sides. By mid-1781, Britain's commanding general, Lord Cornwallis, had moved north into Virginia, setting up a base at Yorktown on Chesapeake Bay. Seeing an opportunity, Continental and French forces surrounded Yorktown by land, while French ships cut the British off by sea. Trapped, Cornwallis surrendered at Yorktown in October 1781. For all practical purposes, this ended the war's ground fighting and assured victory for the Americans.

American and British diplomats signed the Treaty of Paris in 1783. This finally ended the war. In the treaty, Great Britain recognized the existence of the United States as an independent country. The Mississippi River was the western border of the new American nation.

Read Closely: Differences
Recognizing distinctions is one way to better understand history. Native American tribes chose different sides on the issue of the American Revolution, and some stayed neutral. Why do you think that was?

Application: Interpret a Primary Source

Read the excerpt and answer the questions that follow it.

Letter from Abigail Adams to Her Husband John Adams, March 31, 1776

I long to hear that you have declared an independency—and by the way in the new Code of Laws which I suppose it will be necessary for you to make I desire you would Remember the Ladies, and be more generous and favourable to them than your ancestors. Do not put such unlimited power into the hands of the Husbands. Remember all Men would be tyrants if they could. If perticuliar care and attention is not paid to the Laidies we are determined to foment a Rebellion, and will not hold ourselves bound by any Laws in which we have no voice, or Representation.

That your Sex are Naturally Tyrannical is a Truth so thoroughly established as to admit of no dispute, but such of you as wish to be happy willingly give up the harsh title of Master for the more tender and endearing one of Friend. Why then, not put it out of the power of the vicious and the Lawless to use us with cruelty and indignity with impunity. Men of Sense in all Ages abhor those customs which treat us only as the vassals [subordinate or dependent] of your Sex. Regard us then as Beings placed by providence under your protection and in immitation of the Supreme Being make use of that power only for our happiness.

Response from John Adams, March 31, 1776

As to your extraordinary Code of Laws, I cannot but laugh. We have been told that our Struggle has loosened the bands of Government every where. That Children and Apprentices were disobedient—that schools and Colleges were grown turbulent—that Indians slighted their Guardians and Negroes grew insolent to their Masters.

But your Letter was the first Intimation that another Tribe more numerous and powerfull than all the rest were grown discontented.—This is rather too coarse a Compliment but you are so saucy, I wont blot it out.

Depend upon it, We know better than to repeal our Masculine systems.

Source: Massachusetts Historical Society, Adams Family Papers

1. Active readers think about the historical context of primary sources. According to Abigail Adams, what rights did women have at the time she wrote this letter? According to the chapter, what rights were women denied at the time?

   _____

   _____

   _____

   _____

   _____

2. Compare and contrast the tone of the two letters. What attitude does each letter writer express?

_____

_____

_____

_____

_____

3. As you read primary sources, evaluate them for reliability. What bias does Abigail show? What biases does John show?

_____

_____

_____

_____

_____

Abigail Adams

John Adams

Lesson 3 *Development of the Constitution*

The form of government created for the United States in 1787 by the framers of the Constitution has endured for more than 200 years. No other written constitution in the world has been in force for so long. What features of the Constitution have made U.S. government stable yet flexible enough to respond to changing needs?

Analyze a Primary Source

from the Constitution of the United States, 1787

Read Closely: Purpose
As you read a primary source, think about why it was written. According to the framers of the Constitution, what is it designed to do? Circle each purpose the framers list in the first paragraph.

Read Closely: Power and Authority
A constitution is the framework of a government. In many ways, the U.S. Constitution made the federal government stronger than the state governments. What powers did the Constitution forbid the states to have? Underline them.

Read Closely: Historical Context
Consider the context in which a primary source was produced. Under British rule, the colonists had to obey a king who was not elected and who ruled until death. Remembering this, the framers of the Constitution provided for a president but limited that person's power.

We the People of the United States, in Order to form a more perfect Union, establish Justice, insure domestic Tranquility, provide for the common defence, promote the general Welfare, and secure the Blessings of Liberty to ourselves and our Posterity [descendants], do ordain [decree] and establish this Constitution for the United States of America. . . .

All legislative Powers herein granted shall be vested [given legal power] in a Congress of the United States, which shall consist of a Senate and House of Representatives. . . .

The Congress shall have Power To lay and collect Taxes, Duties, Imposts and Excises, to pay the Debts and provide for the common Defence and general Welfare of the United States. . . .

No State shall enter into any Treaty, Alliance, or Confederation; . . . coin Money; emit Bills of Credit; make any Thing but gold and silver Coin a Tender in Payment of Debts; pass any Bill of Attainder, ex post facto Law, or Law impairing the Obligation of Contracts, or grant any Title of Nobility. . . .

The executive Power shall be vested in a President of the United States of America. He shall hold his Office during the Term of four Years.

The judicial Power of the United States, shall be vested in one supreme Court, and in such inferior Courts as the Congress may from time to time ordain and establish. The Judges, both of the supreme and inferior Courts, shall hold their Offices during good Behaviour, and shall, at stated Times, receive for their Services, a Compensation, which shall not be diminished during their Continuance in Office.

Source: National Archives, https://www.archives.gov/founding-docs/constitution-transcript

Articles of Confederation

What was the best way to govern the new country? The United States began with the **Articles of Confederation**. But its rules and structure kept the government weak in some ways.

Drafting the Articles During and after the American Revolution, delegates from the 13 original colonies, which later became states, met as a congress. Their job was to make laws for the United States.

In 1777, this congress drew up the Articles of Confederation. The states approved the articles in 1781. The Articles of Confederation was the first constitution for the United States.

Source: Smithsonian National Postal Museum / Wikimedia Commons
A stamp commemorating the Articles of Confederation

Successes of Government under the Articles of Confederation Congress under the Articles had two major achievements. First, it brought the Revolutionary War to a successful end. Second, it established a workable plan in 1787 for governing the western lands between the Appalachian Mountains and the Mississippi River. Called the Northwest Ordinance, the plan abolished slavery in the lands it covered.

Weaknesses of Government under the Articles of Confederation Congress had the power to declare war, make peace, and conduct foreign affairs under the Articles. However, due to its structure, the government lacked the power to act in many important avenues.

- The U.S. government under the Articles was a one-house lawmaking body, called the Congress (or Continental Congress). There was no executive branch to enforce the laws and no system of national courts to interpret them.

- Each state had equal representation in Congress by a delegation. Each delegation could cast just one vote on each issue.

- For a law to pass, two-thirds of the states had to approve it. To change the Articles of Confederation, the states had to agree unanimously to the change.

- Congress could not collect taxes directly. Instead, the states provided money for its expenses.

- Congress could not regulate commerce between the states. In other words, it had no control over any business deals, sales, or business-related traffic that crossed state lines.

- The paper money it printed was neither backed by gold or silver, nor was it exclusive. States were free to create their own currencies. So, the federal currency did not retain its value.

In the 1780s, economic troubles and political unrest caused many Americans to doubt whether their young country could survive under a weak central government.

> **Read Closely: Evaluation**
> As you read about government rules and policies, think about whether they did what their framers meant them to do. Did the Articles make the federal government economically strong or weak? Why might the framers have wanted an economically weak federal government?

The Constitution Emerges

Delegates from the states met in Philadelphia in 1787. The meeting's stated goal was to amend the Articles of Confederation. However, this plan soon changed. The delegates agreed to replace the existing plan of government with a new constitution. Then each group of delegates would bring the constitution to its home state for ratification, or approval.

Debated Issues The delegates disagreed sharply on three issues: representation, slavery, and trade. Larger states (those with larger populations) like Virginia insisted that the number of each state's representatives in the newly organized Congress should be proportional to the size of its population. In other words, states with more people should have more representatives. States with smaller populations like New Jersey wanted the number of representatives to be the same for each state.

Enslaved people made up a large part of the South's population. For this reason, Southern delegates suggested that slaves be counted in a state's population for representation purposes but not for tax purposes. Northern delegates proposed counting enslaved people for tax purposes but not for representation. Also, most northerners at the convention hoped to end the slave trade. Southerners feared that such action could lead to the end of slavery.

Southern delegates thought foreign commerce should not be taxed. The South imported many goods made in Britain. A tax on imports would make foreign goods more expensive. Northerners thought foreign commerce should be taxed. Their region was beginning to make goods that competed with imports. A tax on foreign goods might help these domestic "infant industries" grow. The Southern states, which shipped cotton and tobacco to Britain, also opposed taxing exports.

How Debates Were Resolved At the convention, the delegates resolved each controversy through compromise. The following solutions were part of what became known as the **Great Compromise**:

- A bicameral, or two-house, Congress: In the House of Representatives, states would be represented in proportion to their populations; in the Senate, all states would be represented equally.

- The "three-fifths compromise": Three-fifths of a state's enslaved population would be counted for purposes of taxation and representation.

- On the slave trade: Congress could pass no law ending the slave trade for 20 years, until 1808, and the tax on enslaved people entering the country could not exceed $10 per person.

- On international trade: Congress received the power to tax imports but not exports.

Federalists and Antifederalists

The debate over the ratification of the U.S. Constitution split the U.S. leadership. Supporters of ratification, such as Alexander Hamilton, became known as **Federalists**. They argued that the Constitution would provide stability that was absent under the Articles of Confederation. Opponents of ratification wanted a bill of rights to protect individual freedoms. This group, led by Thomas Jefferson, became known as the Antifederalists.

Civic Literacy: Slavery Even at the birth of the United States, people had strongly differing opinions on whether enslaving other people was moral. Conflicts over slavery eventually led to a bloody civil war. Although slavery is illegal almost everywhere today, it still exists in the form of human trafficking.

Read Closely: Stakeholders The stakeholders in a society always face benefits and risks when a country's form of government changes. How did the Great Compromise benefit people in higher-population states? How did it benefit people in lower-population states?

The Federalist Papers A series of essays by three Federalists (James Madison, Alexander Hamilton, and John Jay) explained the need for a new federal plan of government. Each essay explained why the new Constitution would strengthen the national government and protect personal liberties. When published as a book, the essays became a classic work. They defend the idea of a representative government that has powers divided among three branches.

The Antifederalist Papers Opponents of ratification included two leaders of the American Revolution: Patrick Henry and Samuel Adams. They feared that the central government under the Constitution might become too strong. They believed it could crush people's liberties. As originally written, the Constitution lacked a bill of rights. The Antifederalists believed this was proof that the government would not respect people's rights.

In 1788, the Antifederalist Mercy Otis Warren published an essay that criticized the proposed Constitution. "There is no security in the profered [proposed] system, either for the rights of conscience or the liberty of the Press," she warned. Further, she stated that "there is no provision for a rotation, nor anything to prevent the perpetuity of office in the same hands for life; which by a little well timed bribery, will probably be done, to the exclusion of men of the best abilities from their share in the offices of government."

Source: Kenneth C. Zirkel / Wikimedia Commons
Statue of Mercy Otis Warren in front of Barnstable County Courthouse, Massachusetts

The Proper Size for a Republic Some Antifederalists believed that the United States was too large for the suggested structure. Historically, successful republics (such as ancient Greek or Renaissance Italian city-states) had been geographically small enough for residents to quickly learn about important issues. They could even gather, in some cases, to work out important issues. But the distance from Massachusetts to Georgia was so great, and travel and communication were so slow, that some felt the new government could not be responsive to the people.

Future president James Madison disagreed. In *Federalist* essay number 10, he said that the size of the country was an advantage. It would be difficult, he argued, for one group to take over when there were so many groups that believed different things.

Protecting Individual Rights Each state called a special convention in which delegates voted for or against the proposed Constitution. The Federalists won the first three states by large majorities. But there was strong opposition in Massachusetts and Virginia.

The Federalists overcame this opposition by promising to add a bill of rights as the new government's first order of business. Even so, the vote to ratify the Constitution was far from unanimous. New York's convention, for example, voted to ratify by the slim majority of 30–27. Ratification by the required number of states (nine) happened in June 1788.

Read Closely: Turning Point
Pay attention to the order of major events to understand how each affected the others. The Federalists agreed to create a bill of rights immediately after ratification. In what way was this a turning point in U.S. history?

The New Federal Government

The framers of the Articles of Confederation described the agreement as "a firm league of friendship" among states. But the new Constitution was much more than that. It gave the federal government more power and described that power more clearly than the Articles had.

Federal/State Division of Power The Constitution includes a supremacy clause. In other words, if a federal law conflicts with a state law, the state law is invalid. The laws that Congress makes are the "supreme Law of the Land."

The supremacy clause gave the new federal government far more power and authority than it had under the Articles of Confederation. Since then, conflicts over federal power and states' rights have erupted at many times in the nation's history.

The president acts . . .

| **Another branch checks . . .** |

1. Makes a treaty with a foreign government — The Senate rejects the treaty (fails to ratify it by a two-thirds vote).

2. Commits certain "crimes and misdemeanors" — The House impeaches the president; the Senate votes to remove the president from office.

3. Vetoes an act of Congress — Congress overrides the veto by a two-thirds vote of each house.

4. Makes an appointment to a Cabinet post — The Senate rejects the president's nominee.

Congress acts . . .

Another branch checks . . .

1. Enacts a bill — The president vetoes Congress's act.

2. Enacts a bill that is signed by the president — The Supreme Court declares Congress's act to be unconstitutional.

The Supreme Court acts . . .

Another branch checks . . .

1. Declares an act of Congress unconstitutional — Congress proposes a constitutional amendment.

2. Declares an action of the president unconstitutional — The president appoints a new justice to the Supreme Court (if there is a vacancy).

Separation of Powers at the Federal Level The framers of the Constitution created a system for distributing the legislative, executive, and judicial powers of government among three separate branches. This is known as the **separation of powers**, since it gives each of the three branches of the federal government its own special area of responsibility.

- Congress, as the legislative branch, would make the nation's laws.

- The president, as the head of the executive branch, would enforce those laws.

- The federal courts, as the judicial branch, would interpret the laws. In other words, they would decide what the laws mean and how people should apply them in different situations.

By creating three branches, each with a different area of responsibility, the framers hoped to prevent one official or group from gaining all or most of the powers of government.

Creation of Checks and Balances A second great principle of the Constitution has to do with the way the three branches interact with one another.

The framers gave each branch some powers to participate in the decisions of the other branches. For this reason, each branch tries to gain the approval of the other branches for its policies and decisions. Without this approval, its policies may fail.

Americans call this system of partially shared responsibility checks and balances. Each branch can check, or block, the actions of the other branches. Powers are balanced, which stops any one branch from dominating the others.

Judicial Independence In a free society, judges need to be independent. Otherwise, political parties or individuals will be able to influence them or force them to decide cases in ways that unfairly favor one side over another. An independent judiciary can make fair decisions that uphold the rule of law. Alexander Hamilton wrote, "The complete independence of the courts of justice is peculiarly essential in a limited Constitution."

The Constitution protects judges in two ways. It allows lifetime appointments to any judge who continues to meet ethical and moral standards. It also does not allow Congress or the president to punish judges by lowering their pay.

The Bill of Rights

What was in the Bill of Rights? And what rights does the bill leave out?

Rights and Protections A bill of rights is a document that lists actions that government officials may not take. Its purpose is to prevent abuses of power and protect people's liberties.

Soon after the Constitution was adopted, one of the first acts of the new Congress was to propose a series of amendments to the Constitution. This document became known as the **Bill of Rights**. These ten amendments were proposed in 1789 and ratified as a group in 1791.

Included Rights Among the freedoms and rights the Bill of Rights guarantees are the following:
- freedom of religion
- freedom of speech and the press
- right to free assembly
- right to keep and bear arms

> **Read Closely: Comparison**
> As you read, compare ideas and events with others you have read about in the past. How was the new form of U.S. government similar to and different from what the 13 colonies had under British rule?

> **Read Closely: Cause and Effect**
> As you read, think about the effects of the ideas or laws you are learning about. What are some effects of an independent judiciary?

- right to a fair trial
- freedom from unreasonable searches by the police
- freedom from cruel and unusual punishments

Who decides what a fair trial is or what cruel and unusual punishment is? That is up to the courts to interpret.

Originally, the Bill of Rights protected citizens from the powers of the federal government only. That changed when the Fourteenth Amendment to the Constitution passed in 1868. After that, the rights these amendments guaranteed were gradually extended to state governments as well.

Sovereignty of the People Another way that the Constitution balances power is through the Tenth Amendment. This amendment says that the federal government has only the rights that the Constitution grants. Any other rights belong to the states or to the people.

The Constitution does not name these reserved powers. States traditionally have had authority over such matters as health and safety, marriage and divorce, regulation of businesses, and licensing of professions. The Constitution allows states to keep control in those and other areas.

Excluded Rights The U.S. Bill of Rights was inspired by earlier documents that guaranteed certain individual freedoms. These included the Magna Carta in England. Around the world, the Bill of Rights has influenced the creation of other charters of human rights. However, the bill did not protect everyone's rights.

Who was left out?

- The Constitution failed to abolish slavery, even after African Americans had fought in the Revolutionary War.

- The Constitution failed to guarantee that women receive equal treatment, including the right to vote. Women did not even have the right to hold property in their own name. They also lacked the right to be the legal guardians of their own children.

- The Constitution failed to guarantee the right to vote to all White males. Some states required voters to own land.

- The Constitution failed to protect Native Americans and their lands.

The Bill of Rights is the first 10 amendments to the Constitution. Since then, the United States has amended its Constitution 17 more times. It is in this ability to change and grow that one of the greatest strengths of the Constitution lies. No document, no matter how thoughtfully conceived, can possibly foresee changes brought about by forces such as technology or the evolution of social norms. The content of the amendments shows how the country has changed and continues to change.

Read Closely: Connections
Look for connections between what you are reading about and your everyday life. Examining how these concepts have affected you will help you understand them. How do these rights affect how you live?

Read Closely: Change
As you read, note that some level of change is a constant throughout history. Based on what you have read in this lesson, why do you think it has been necessary for Americans to make the changes they have to the Constitution?

Application: Interpret a Primary Source

Read the excerpt and answer the questions that follow it.

Constitution of the Cherokee Nation, July 12, 1839

Whereas our Fathers have existed, as a separate and distinct Nation, in the possession and exercise of the essential and appropriate attributes of sovereignty, from a period extending into antiquity, beyond the records and memory of man:

And whereas those attributes, with the rights and franchises which they involve, remain still in full force and virtue, as do also the national and social relations of the Cherokee people to each other and the body politic, excepting in those particulars which have grown out of the provisions of the treaties of 1817 and 1819 between the United States and the Cherokee Nation, under which a portion of our people removed to this country and became a separate community:

But the force of circumstances having recently compelled the body of the Eastern Cherokees to remove to this country, thus bringing together again the two branches of the ancient Cherokee family, it has become essential to the general welfare that a union should be formed, and a system of government matured, adapted to the present condition, and providing equally for the protection of each individual in the enjoyment of all his rights:

Therefore we, the people composing the Eastern and Western Cherokee Nation, in National Convention assembled, by virtue of our original and unalienable rights, do hereby solemnly and mutually agree to form ourselves into one body politic, under the style and title of the Cherokee Nation. . . .

And also that all rights and title to public Cherokee lands on the east or the west of the river Mississippi, with all other public interests which may have vested in either branch of the Cherokee family, whether inherited from our Fathers or derived from any other source, shall henceforward vest entire and unimpaired in the Cherokee Nation, as constituted by this union.

Source: Library of Congress https://www.loc.gov/law/help/american-indian-consts/PDF/28014182.pdf

1. Active readers think about the historical context of primary sources. According to the document, what happened to the Cherokee people in the past that this document will change?

   _____

   _____

2. Compare and contrast this constitution with the excerpt from the U.S. Constitution at the beginning of this lesson. What similarities and differences do you notice?

   _____

   _____

3. As you read primary sources, think about their purpose. What is the purpose of the Cherokee constitution?

   _____

   _____

Conceptual Understanding
11.2d Under the new Constitution, the young nation sought to achieve national security and political stability, as the three branches of government established their relationships with each other and the states.

Read Closely: Historical Context
George Washington served two terms as president. In his last speech before leaving office, he offered advice to Americans.

Read Closely: Audience
When reading a speech, remember that the speaker's audience affects the content of his or her presentation. In this speech, Washington speaks directly to an assemblage of people, but he's really speaking to the country as a whole. What quality does he tell them is most important in their government? Circle the word or phrase he uses.

Read Closely: Point of View
A primary source often reveals the point of view of its author. Based on this excerpt, what was Washington's opinion of factions? Underline words or phrases he uses to describe them.

Analyze a Primary Source

from George Washington's Farewell Address, 1796

The unity of Government which constitutes you one people, is also now dear to you. It is justly so; for it is a main pillar in the edifice [structure] of your real independence, the support of your tranquility at home, your peace abroad; of your safety; of your prosperity; of that very Liberty which you so highly prize. But as it is easy to foresee, that from different causes and from different quarters, much pains will be taken, many artifices [tricks] employed, to weaken in your minds the conviction of this truth. . . .

All obstructions to the execution of the Laws, all combinations and associations, under whatever plausible character, with the real design to direct, controul, counteract, or awe the regular deliberation and action of the constituted authorities, are destructive of this fundamental principle, and of fatal tendency. They serve to organize faction, to give it an artificial and extraordinary force—to put in the place of the delegated will of the nation, the will of a party, often a small but artful and enterprizing minority of the community; and, according to the alternate triumphs of different parties, to make the public administration the mirror of the ill concerted and incongruous projects of faction, rather than the organ of consistent and wholesome plans digested by common councils, and modified by mutual interests.

However combinations or associations of the above description may now and then answer popular ends, they are likely in the course of time and things, to become potent engines, by which cunning, ambitious and unprincipled men will be enabled to subvert the power of the people, and to usurp [overtake] for themselves the reigns of government; destroying afterwards the very engines which have lifted them to unjust dominion [rule].

Source: The National Archives, https://founders.archives.gov/documents/Washington/99-01-02-00963

George Washington and the Presidency

After the states ratified the Constitution, voters elected representatives and states elected senators to be part of the first Congress. The 13 states chose a group of electors (special voters for president and vice president). These electors unanimously chose George Washington as the first president. By April 1789, both the first president and the first Congress were in office. But because the system was new, no one could be certain how well it would work.

Washington's Cabinet George Washington served two terms as president (1789–1797). More than any later president, he made decisions and adopted policies that strongly influenced the nature of the U.S. government.

The Constitution says nothing about the president's advisers. But Washington met with a cabinet, which is a group of advisers. They were Secretary of State Thomas Jefferson, Secretary of the Treasury Alexander Hamilton, Secretary of War Henry Knox, and Attorney General Edmund Randolph.

Thanks to Washington, the cabinet is now a permanent part of the executive branch. Today, cabinet positions include the secretaries of agriculture, commerce, defense, education, energy, health and human services, homeland security, housing and urban development, interior, justice, labor, state, transportation, treasury, and veterans' affairs.

Washington expected to receive conflicting advice from his cabinet members. He wanted to show the young nation that the newly formed government was united and politically stable despite these differences. Political stability means that a country's government is not constantly changing. Flawed or contested elections, revolutions, and coups are very rare or do not happen.

Taxation and Rebellion To raise money, Congress put a tax on whiskey makers. News of the whiskey tax provoked an armed revolt among whiskey-producing farmers in western Pennsylvania. This was the Whiskey Rebellion.

Washington sent troops to put down the rebellion. This showed that the federal government had real power to act effectively in a crisis. But not everyone approved of Washington's use of a large army to deal with the rebellion. Thomas Jefferson said the government's action was like using "a meat axe to kill a spider."

Peaceful Transfer of Power Washington decided to serve only two terms (eight years). He worried that the American people might believe that a presidency should last the rest of the president's life. Power passed to John Adams, who was elected president for one term.

The successful transfer of power increased the political stability of the United States. It showed Americans and Europeans that a new president could be elected without bloodshed. The ideas in the Constitution were becoming real.

Farewell Address Washington gave a speech when he left office. In it, he offered advice to his successors and to the American people.

Washington strongly opposed the formation of political parties or factions. "The alternate domination of one faction over another, sharpened by the spirit of revenge . . . is itself a frightful despotism," he warned. If political infighting became strong enough, people would let a king or dictator take power.

In France, a revolution overthrew the French monarchy in 1789. Like the Americans, the French wanted to increase equality, and they believed in Enlightenment ideas. But in the United States, public opinion was divided on whether to help the new French Republic. Washington stayed neutral. In his Farewell Address, he urged the United States to "steer clear of permanent alliances with any portion of the foreign world."

Read Closely: Impact of Time
Noticing changes over time will help you understand how the U.S. government has changed. What do the more recent cabinet positions tell you about the government's changing priorities?

Read Closely: Importance of Place
To understand the importance of geography in history, think about where the different countries you read about are located on the globe. How might the relative locations of the United States and France have contributed to the U.S. ability to maintain its neutrality?

Hamilton and Economic Planning

Members of the government drew up plans to succeed economically as well as to survive politically. New York's Alexander Hamilton was in charge of the treasury. He proposed measures for strengthening the government's finances.

Hamilton's Economic Plan Hamilton's plan focused on three areas:

1. Repay the debts of the states and the national government, in order to increase the legitimacy of the federal government.

2. Establish a national bank to stabilize the currency situation and the overall national economy.

3. Create tariffs to protect new U.S. industries from foreign competition. A **tariff** is a tax on goods that come into or leave a country.

Debate Surrounding the Plan Jefferson and Madison opposed Hamilton's plan. His policies favored business interests and the North rather than farming interests and the South. Jefferson believed the plan would give the federal government too much power at the expense of the states. But it provided financial stability for the new nation and added to its economic growth. Congress eventually enacted Hamilton's economic plan after a bitter struggle. Conflict over Hamilton's financial plan caused the formation of two bitterly opposed political parties. Leading the parties were rival members of Washington's cabinet: Alexander Hamilton and Thomas Jefferson.

The Federalists and Loose Construction Hamilton's party was the Federalists. They favored government policies that would help Northern merchants. To a lesser extent, the policies would also help Southern planters. The merchants approved Hamilton's program. Why?

- They thought it would help make the national government strong and stable. (Stable government makes a healthy economy more likely. Stable government also helps with national security, which is the ability of a country to protect itself from attack.)

- They wanted a national bank to give loans to new businesses.

- They hoped tariffs would protect new industries in the United States from foreign competition.

On constitutional issues, the Federalists argued for loose construction. The Constitution states that Congress can "make all Laws which shall be necessary and proper for carrying into Execution the foregoing Powers, and all other Powers vested by this Constitution in the Government of the United States, or any Department or Officer thereof." Legal experts call this the elastic clause because it gives Congress so much flexibility.

Federalists believed courts should interpret the Constitution broadly. In other words, courts should rule that creating a national bank was legal even though the Constitution said nothing about creating a national bank.

The Democratic-Republicans and Strict Construction Thomas Jefferson led the Democratic-Republicans. They favored policies that would help farmers and ordinary people. The party opposed Hamilton's financial plan for several reasons.

Read Closely: Compare
Comparing similar events across time is an effective strategy as you read. It helps you connect what you are learning with what you already know. How were political parties at the time you are reading about similar to U.S. political parties today?

- Full payment of the national debt by buying back government bonds would benefit speculators. These are people who buy and sell bonds and other property in the hope of making profits. (Bonds are financial instruments that governments sell to investors.)

- A national bank would give loans to Northern merchants. However, it would be less likely to lend money to western and Southern farmers.

- Tariffs would drive up prices and hurt farmers. The Democratic-Republicans knew the government needed tariffs to pay off the nation's debts. But they disliked them and did little to support them.

Jefferson and the Democratic-Republicans argued for strict construction of the Constitution. They believed that the federal government should do only what specific clauses of the Constitution allowed.

Read Closely: Context
Keep in mind the era in which political events happened. Why were the opinions of farmers and planters so important at this time? Why didn't the party issues have more to do with the needs of women, Native Americans, and African Americans?

America's First Political Parties		
	Federalists	**Democratic-Republicans**
Leaders	Alexander Hamilton John Adams John Marshall	Thomas Jefferson James Madison James Monroe
Geographic strength	Strongest support among merchants of the Northeast	Strongest support among farmers of the South and West
Position on Hamilton's financial plan	Favored all parts of the plan (establishing central bank, funding the debt, protecting infant industries)	Opposed all parts of the plan
Position on constitutional issues	Favored loose construction of the Constitution to give the national government maximum power	Favored strict construction of the Constitution to limit the national government's powers and safeguard the independent powers of the states
Position on foreign policy	Though partial to the British, supported Washington's Proclamation of Neutrality	Though partial to the French, supported Jefferson's attempts to maintain U.S. neutrality during the Napoleonic Wars

Impact of the Supreme Court

The executive branch and the legislative branch exercised their powers. What about the judicial branch? In the country's early years, the Supreme Court issued three key decisions that still affect U.S. laws today.

Marbury v. Madison (1803) Just before leaving office, President John Adams appointed William Marbury as a federal court judge. But Thomas Jefferson, the next president, opposed this move. He told his secretary of state, James Madison, not to carry out the appointment.

Marbury argued that a 1789 law gave the Supreme Court the power to force Madison to give Marbury his appointment. But the Court disagreed. It said the Constitution did not authorize the 1789 law. Thus that law was null and void.

The Court's decision established the principle of **judicial review**. In such cases that the Court hears, its justices decide whether laws are consistent with the Constitution. Unconstitutional laws are invalid.

***McCulloch v. Maryland* (1819)** At issue in this case was whether a state government could collect a tax from a bank that the U.S. government had set up. The Chief Justice of the Supreme Court, John Marshall, argued that a state could not tax a federal agency. He said that the federal government was supreme under the Constitution. This case established the idea that a state law could be nullified (declared void) if it was found to conflict with a federal law.

***Gibbons v. Ogden* (1824)** At issue in this case was whether a state (New York) could give one steamship company the sole right to operate on an interstate waterway (the Hudson River). In his decision, Chief Justice Marshall stated that trade is commerce and Congress controls commerce between states. Therefore, New York's law was invalid.

The ruling helped define interstate commerce. It also gave the federal government more power to regulate businesses that operate in more than one state.

How the Court Strengthened the Powers of the Federal Government The cases that Marshall decided had lasting effects on the United States. The decisions increased the power of the national government. They also decreased the power of the states.

Marshall also expanded the power and influence of the Supreme Court. Using judicial review, the nation's highest court could strike down any laws that it considered to be unconstitutional.

Read Closely: Turning Point
While reading, think about how certain people might have changed the course of history. How might the United States be different if Marshall had ruled in favor of states' rights rather than federal rights?

Transfer of Power: 1800 vs. 2000

The United States experienced a peaceful transfer of power when Adams succeeded Washington. However, the nation had not yet experienced a close election. What would happen when two political parties each received about half the votes? Two extremely close elections—in 1800 and 2000—provided answers.

Presidential Election of 1800 During the first 13 years of U.S. government under the Constitution, three leaders dominated: George Washington, Alexander Hamilton, and John Adams. That Federalist era ended in 1800. Adams was defeated for reelection by two candidates of the Democratic-Republican Party—Thomas Jefferson and Aaron Burr.

Roles of the Electoral College and Congress in 1800 According to the Constitution during this era, states selected presidential electors in the same number as their representation in Congress. Each state's electors would vote for two people. The person who gained the most votes (and had more than 50 percent of the votes) won the presidency. The person in second place became vice president.

In the 1800 election, Jefferson and Burr had the same number of electoral votes. So the election was decided by a vote of the House of Representatives.

Jefferson finally won, but only after much confusion in Congress and suspense in the nation.

To avoid tie votes in the future, Congress proposed changing the electoral college system by means of the 12th Amendment. The change meant that each elector would cast one ballot for president and a second ballot for vice president. The states adopted this amendment in 1804. The amendment has worked well. Since its adoption, there have been no tie votes like that of 1800.

Presidential Election of 2000 The 2000 presidential election was one of the most dramatic and controversial in U.S. history. The two major candidates were Vice President Al Gore, the Democrat, and Texas Governor George W. Bush, the Republican. Both targeted centrist voters.

More than 100 million Americans cast ballots. For weeks afterward, the results remained in doubt. Gore received over 500,000 more popular votes nationwide than Bush did. Gore also carried the large coastal and Northern industrial states. Bush won popular majorities and electoral votes in the South, Southwest, and in parts of the Midwest. The election turned on the results in Florida.

Roles of the Electoral College and the Supreme Court in 2000 It appeared that Bush had won Florida's popular vote by a margin of a few hundred votes. Gore charged that votes had been miscounted in crucial counties. He also said that many votes went uncounted because of mechanical problems and poor ballot design. A process of court rulings and vote recounting lasted for weeks.

In *Bush v. Gore*, the Supreme Court ruled 5–4 that the Florida recount had to stop. The state's scheduled meeting of its electoral college imposed time limits that had passed. The hand recount of votes violated the 14th Amendment, which provides for equal protection of the laws. Bush thus won the electoral college vote. He had 271 votes to Gore's 266.

In 1800 and 2000, hotly contested elections caused rage and anguish. However, in neither case was there bloodshed or revolution. Each time, the government managed a peaceful transfer of power, while still pointing to serious flaws in the electoral system.

Source: State Library and Archives of Florida / Wikimedia Commons

An official examines a disputed ballot in Palm Beach County, Florida.

> **Read Closely: Compare**
> Look for similarities in historical events. How were the elections of 1800 and 2000 similar?

Application: Interpret a Primary Source

Read the excerpt and answer the questions that follow it.

Diary of Elizabeth De Hart Bleecker, New York City, 1799

Saturday, December 21
   The Bells of every Church were muffled and rung from twelve to one
O'clock—they are to continue ringing them the same every day till the 24th . . .
on account of the death of General Washington.

Friday, December 27
   Mr John Shaw was flogg'd [whipped or beaten] in Wall Street by Col.
Mansfield—the occasion of it was this—a few days after the news of General
Washington's death arriv'd, Mr. Shaw said, in the presence of a number
of gentlemen in the Coffee House, that "it was a pity, General Washington
had not died five and twenty years ago"—he repeated the expression in
the evening in the Insurance Room in the presence of Colonel Mansfield,
who, having serv'd under Washington, could scarce refrain from drubbing
[beating] him at the time, but considering himself as only a visitor in the
room, & unwilling to make any disturbance, he took no notice of it—Mr.
Shaw's speech was soon spread about, and he was universally censur'd
[criticized] for it—this evening in coming down Wall Street, he met Col. M.,
& stopping him, said he had understood he had been telling tales of him—
Col. M. reply'd he only mention'd what he heard him say—Mr S. said it was
a . . . lie, the words were scarcely utter'd, ere Col. M had his arm up, and the
great the mighty Mr John Shaw fell—some persons coming up, interpos'd
[came between], & Col. Mansfield left him, after having severely bruis'd
him, & given him a pretty black eye.

Source New York Public Library

1. Active readers think about the historical context of primary sources.
   According to the diary entries, what were Americans' opinions of George
   Washington at the time of his death? Support your answer with evidence from
   the diary entries.

   _____

   _____

   _____

   _____

2. Consider what you have learned about Washington in this chapter and in the diary entries. Based on this information, what effect did Washington's death have on Americans?

_____

_____

_____

_____

_____

3. Authors show bias or point of view in their writing. Bleecker calls Washington's critic "the great the mighty Mr John Shaw." Based on the diary entries, what do you think was Bleecker's opinion of Shaw? Support your answer with evidence from the diary entries.

_____

_____

_____

_____

_____

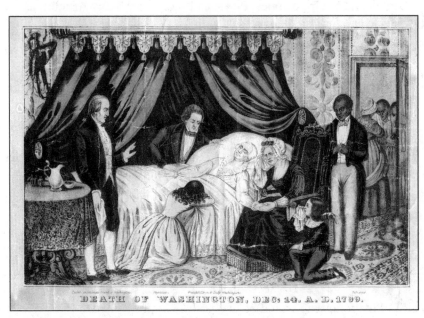

DEATH OF WASHINGTON, DEC: 14. A. D. 1799.

Source: Cornell University Library / Wikimedia Commons

Death of Washington

Multiple-Choice Questions

Questions 1 and 2 refer to the excerpt below.

A. New York Merchants Respond to the Stamp Act

AT a general Meeting of the Merchants of the City of New-York, trading to Great-Britain, . . . to consider what was necessary to be done in the present Situation of Affairs, with respect to the Stamp Act, and the melancholy [sad] State of the North-American Commerce, so greatly restricted by the Impositions and Duties established by the late Acts of Trade: They came to the following Resolutions, viz. [namely]

• **First,** That in all Orders they send out to Great-Britain, for Goods or Merchandize, of any Nature, Kind of Quality whatsoever, usually imported from Great-Britain, they will direct their Correspondents [business partners] not to ship them, unless the Stamp Act be repealed: It is nevertheless agreed, that all such Merchants as are Owners of, and have Vessels already gone, and now cleared out for Great-Britain, shall be at Liberty to bring back in them, on their own Accounts, Crates and Casks of Earthen Ware, Grindstones, Pipes, and such other bulky Articles, as Owners usually fill up their Vessels with.

• **Secondly,** It is further unanimously agreed, that all Orders already sent Home, shall be countermanded [cancelled] by the very first Conveyance [communication]; and the Goods and Merchandize thereby ordered, not to be sent, unless upon the Condition mentioned in the foregoing Resolution.

• **Thirdly,** It is further unanimously agreed, that no Merchant will vend [sell] any Goods or Merchandize sent upon Commission from Great-Britain, that shall be shipped from thence after the first Day of January next, unless upon the Condition mentioned in the first Resolution.

• **Fourthly,** It is further unanimously agreed, that the foregoing Resolutions shall be binding until the same are abrogated [repealed] at a general Meeting hereafter to be held for that Purpose.

Source: Resolutions of Merchants, New York, October 31, 1765

1. Which of the following would be the best use of this source?

   1. To provide a list of the provisions of the Stamp Act
   2. As evidence of the New York government's response the Stamp Act
   3. To show how a group of American businessmen planned to resist the Stamp Act
   4. To indicate how successful the Stamp Act was at raising revenue

2. Which of the following best summarizes the suggested course of action?

   1. The merchants were advised to order large quantities of supplies before the Stamp Act went into effect.
   2. The merchants intended to boycott British goods until the Stamp Act was repealed.
   3. Ships carrying British goods would not be allowed to dock in New York.
   4. Plans were prepared to participate in the Boston Tea Party.

Questions 3–5 refer to the excerpt below.

B. Thomas Paine's *The American Crisis*

THESE are the times that try men's souls: The summer soldier and the sunshine patriot will, in this crisis, shrink from the service of his country but he that stands it NOW, deserves the love and thanks of man and woman. Tyranny, like hell, is not easily conquered; yet we have this consolation with us, that the harder the conflict, the more glorious the triumph. What we obtain, too cheap, we esteem too lightly:—'Tis dearness only that gives every thing its value. Heaven knows how to set a

Source: Cornell University Library / Wikimedia Commons
Thomas Paine

proper price upon its goods; and it would be strange indeed, if so celestial an article as Freedom should not be highly rated. Britain, with an army to enforce her tyranny, has declared, that she has a right (not only to TAX) but "to BIND us in ALL CASES WHATSOEVER," and if being bound in that manner is not slavery, then is there not such a thing as slavery upon earth. Even the expression is impious, for so unlimited a power can belong only to God.

Whether the Independence of the Continent was declared too soon, or delayed too long, I will not now enter into as an argument; my own simple opinion is that had it been eight months earlier, it would have been much better. We did not make a proper use of last winter, neither could we while we were in a dependent state. However, the fault, if it were one, was all our own; we have none to blame but ourselves. But no great deal is lost yet; all that Howe has been doing for this month past is rather a ravage than a conquest which the spirit of the Jersies a year ago would have quickly repulsed, and which time and a little resolution with soon recover.

Source: Thomas Paine, *The American Crisis*, Number 1, December 1776

3. Which of the following best describes the author's intention in this excerpt?

   1. To boost the morale of the American people
   2. To urge British soldiers to desert and join the American cause
   3. To tell the Americans that they would probably lose the war
   4. To complain about the unjust tax on British goods

4. Which of the following claims does Paine make?

   1. That tyranny is easily conquered

   2. That freedom should not be highly rated

   3. That General Howe had already conquered the "Jersies" a year before

   4. That things would have gone better if Independence had been declared during the previous winter

5. Who are the stakeholders to whom Paine is appealing?

   1. The British government

   2. The American people

   3. Wives of soldiers and patriots

   4. General Howe's army

Questions 6–8 refer to the excerpt below.

C. Petition of the Philadelphia Synagogue to Council of Censors of Pennsylvania

By the tenth section of the frame of government of this commonwealth, it is ordered that each member of the general assembly of representatives of the freemen of Pennsylvania, before he takes his seat, shall make and subscribe a declaration, which ends in these words, "I do acknowledge the scriptures of the old and new testament to be given by divine inspiration," to which is added an assurance, that "no further or other religious test shall ever hereafter be required of any civil officer or magistrate in this state."

   Your memorialists beg leave to observe, that this clause seems to limit the civil rights of your citizens to one very special article of the creed; whereas by the second paragraph of the declaration of the rights of the inhabitants, it is asserted without any other limitation than the professing the existence of God, in plain words, "that no man who acknowledges the being of a God can be justly deprived or abridged of any civil rights as a citizen on account of his religious sentiments." But certainly this religious test deprives the Jews of the most eminent rights of freemen, solemnly ascertained to all men who are not professed atheists.

Source: *The Freeman's Journal or The North-American Intelligencer* (Philadelphia), January 21, 1784

6. What problem does this petition address?

   1. The fact that Jews do not have any rights under Pennsylvania law
   2. The fact that atheists do not have any rights under Pennsylvania law
   3. The fact that no religious test is required to be a magistrate in Pennsylvania
   4. The fact that only Christians are allowed to serve in Pennsylvania's general assembly

7. How do the petitioners support their claim that they should be allowed to serve in the Pennsylvania general assembly?

   1. By saying that they are freemen of Pennsylvania
   2. By arguing that Jews are not atheists
   3. By pointing out that Pennsylvania's civil rights apply only to Christians
   4. By quoting the declaration of rights of Pennsylvania's inhabitants

8. In what way does this petition reflect change and continuity in American history?

   1. It shows an attempt to deny a group certain rights because of their religion, in spite of laws originally intended to guarantee them full rights.
   2. It shows that discrimination on the basis of religion has been enshrined in laws throughout U.S. history, from the landing of the Pilgrims and the Puritans to the present.
   3. It shows that non-Christians have always been considered second-class citizens in what is now the United States.
   4. It shows that the United States was established as a Christian nation from the very beginning.

Short-Essay Questions

Study the two documents and answer the question that follows.

D. An Early Plan to Unite the Thirteen Colonies

It is proposed that humble application be made for an act of Parliament of Great Britain, by virtue of which one general government may be formed in America, including all the said colonies, within and under which government each colony may retain its present constitution, except in the particulars wherein a change may be directed by the said act, as hereafter follows.

1. That the said general government be administered by a President-General, to be appointed and supported by the crown; and a Grand Council, to be chosen by the representatives of the people of the several Colonies met in their respective assemblies. . . .

16. That for these purposes they have power to make laws, and lay and levy such general duties, imposts, or taxes, as to them shall appear most equal and just (considering the ability and other circumstances of the inhabitants in the several Colonies), and such as may be collected with the least inconvenience to the people; rather discouraging luxury, than loading industry with unnecessary burdens.

Source: Benjamin Franklin and Thomas Hutchinson, Albany Plan of Union, 1754

E. Observations of an English Clergyman on the American Colonies

America is formed for happiness, but not for empire. In a course of 1,200 miles I did not see a single object that solicited charity. But I saw insuperable causes of weakness, which will necessarily prevent its being a potent state. . . .

A voluntary association or coalition, at least a permanent one, is almost as difficult to be supposed: for fire and water are not more heterogeneous than the different colonies in North America. Nothing can exceed the jealousy and emulation which they possess in regard to each other. The inhabitants of Pennsylvania and New York have an inexhaustible source of animosity in their jealousy for the trade of the Jerseys. Massachusetts Bay and Rhode Island are not less interested in that of Connecticut. . . . Even the limits and boundaries of each colony are a constant source of litigation.

In short, such is the difference of character, of manners, of religion, of interest, of the different colonies, that I think, if I am not wholly ignorant of the human mind, were they left to themselves there would soon be a civil war from one end of the continent to the other, while the Indians and Negroes would, with better reason, impatiently watch the opportunity of exterminating them all together.

Source: Andrew Burnaby, *Travels through the Middle Settlements in North-America in the Years 1759 and 1760*, 1775

1. In a short essay, describe the historical context surrounding the two documents above. Then identify and explain the similarity and difference between the ideas described in these documents.

Study the two documents and answer the question that follows.

F. John Locke on Natural Rights

But though this be a state of liberty, yet it is not a state of licence: though man in that state have an uncontroulable liberty to dispose of his person or possessions, yet he has not liberty to destroy himself, or so much as any creature in his possession, but where some nobler use than its bare preservation calls for it. The state of nature has a law of nature to govern it, which obliges every one: and reason, which is that law, teaches all mankind, who will but consult it, that being all equal and independent, no one ought to harm another in his life, health, liberty, or possessions . . . [and] when his own preservation comes not in competition, ought he, as much as he can, to preserve the rest of mankind, and may not, unless it be to do justice on an offender, take away, or impair the life, or what tends to the preservation of the life, the liberty, health, limb, or goods of another.

And that all men may be restrained from invading others rights, and from doing hurt to one another, and the law of nature be observed, which willeth the peace and preservation of all mankind, the execution of the law of nature is, in that state, put into every man's hands, whereby every one has a right to punish the transgressors of that law to such a degree, as may hinder its violation: for the law of nature would, as all other laws that concern men in this world, be in vain, if there were no body that in the state of nature had a power to execute that law, and thereby preserve the innocent and restrain offenders.

Source: John Locke, *The Two Treatises on Government*, 1689

G. Samuel Adams on the Rights of the American Colonists

The natural liberty of man is to be free from any superior power on earth, and not to be under the will or legislative authority of man, but only to have the law of nature for his rule. . . .

Government was instituted for the purposes of common defence, and those who hold the reins of government have an equitable, natural right to an honorable support from the same principle that "the laborer is worthy of his hire." But then the same community which they serve ought to be the assessors of their pay. Governors have no right to seek and take what they please; by this, instead of being content with the station assigned them, that of honorable servants of the society, they would soon become absolute masters, despots, and tyrants. . . .

In short, it is the greatest absurdity to suppose it in the power of one, or any number of men, at the entering into society, to renounce their essential natural rights, or the means of preserving those rights; when the grand end of civil government, from the very nature of its institution, is for the support, protection, and defence of those very rights; the principal of which, as is before observed, are Life, Liberty, and Property. . . .

Source: Samuel Adams, *The Rights of the Colonists*, 1772

2. In a short essay, describe the historical context surrounding the two documents above. Then analyze and explain the author's purpose in the first document. How does his point of view affect the document's reliability as a source of evidence?

CHAPTER 3

Expansion, Nationalism, and Sectionalism (1800–1865)

Chapter Overview

In the 1800s, the United States expanded its territory and grew its economy. However, Northern and Southern states developed differently in terms of economics, transportation, and society.

The United States Becomes Stronger The Louisiana Purchase doubled the size of the country. It also led to conflicts with Native Americans and with Britain. These conflicts sparked the War of 1812. In this war, the British burned the U.S. Capitol and the White House. However, the United States won some military victories. It also gained favorable terms in the peace agreement.

A more powerful United States issued the Monroe Doctrine. It warned European powers not to colonize any more locations in the Western Hemisphere.

Political and Sectional Struggles Even as the United States became bigger and stronger, regional conflicts caused concern. Some Southern states wanted to nullify (declare void) U.S. laws that they considered to be unconstitutional.

New states joining the Union upset the delicate balance between free and slaveholding states. To address these issues, lawmakers created the Missouri Compromise (1820), the Compromise of 1850, and the Kansas-Nebraska Act (1854). In spite of these efforts, violent conflicts over slavery increased.

Civil War Severs the Country When the antislavery candidate Abraham Lincoln won the presidency, some Southern states that feared for the future of slavery left the Union. They called their new government the Confederate States of America. The North had more people and factories. The South had better generals. Also, for most of the war, the Confederacy fought a defensive war in its own territory—both advantages.

During the war, the North's reason for fighting changed. Instead of merely keeping the United States together, the goal became to eliminate slavery. African American soldiers helped to tip the balance and defeat the Confederacy.

Civic Literacy: Equality One major idea in this chapter touches on the principle that humans are created equal. African Americans, women, and Native Americans were far from equal during this era. However, the idea that people in these groups had rights gained traction, if slowly. The issue of equal rights continues to be a struggle throughout the United States and the world.

New York Social Studies Framework

Key Idea 11.3: Expansion, Nationalism, and Sectionalism

As the nation expanded, growing sectional tensions, especially over slavery, resulted in political and constitutional crises that culminated in the Civil War.

Source: *New York State Grades 9–12 Social Studies Framework*

Civic Literacy Essay: Analyze the Documents

As you have read, the first task in completing the civic literacy document-based essay is reading each document closely. (See page 35.) On the exam, each of the six documents is followed by a question that tests your understanding of what you read, requiring you to analyze the texts. The notes in the marginal boxes of this book can help you develop your skill of analyzing texts, since many include a question at the end and room for you to write your analysis or interpretation.

Ask questions such as the following to analyze the documents.

Questions for Analyzing Texts:

- Who is the author?
- What is the author's purpose?
- Who is the audience?
- What possible bias might the author have?
- In what historical circumstances was the text written?
- What is the author's argument?
- What evidence does the author use to support the argument?
- How do multiple documents relate to one another? Is there a clear cause-and-effect relationship between them? Do they show continuity or change?

Application: Read the document on the next page as you start the next lesson. The boxes in the margin answer three of the above questions—those related to purpose, cause and effect, and historical context. Answer the following question to analyze the text further.

What is one way in which the document shows continuity or change?

_____

_____

_____

Key Terms by Theme

Civics
nullification (p. 83)
Missouri Compromise (p. 85)
Dred Scott (p. 88)
Gettysburg Address (p. 90)

Economics
interchangeable parts (p. 78)

Geography
Louisiana Purchase (p. 75)

Governance
Andrew Jackson (p. 76)
Monroe Doctrine (p. 76)
Tecumseh (p. 76)
spoils system (p. 80)
secession (p. 91)
habeas corpus (p. 94)

Movement
Indian Removal Act (p. 80)

Trail of Tears (p. 80)
manifest destiny (p. 86)

Social Structures
Sojourner Truth (p. 79)
abolitionist (p. 84)
Frederick Douglass (p. 84)
Lucretia Mott (p. 85)
John Brown (p. 88)

Nationalism Strengthened and Challenged

In her autobiography from 1883, Harriet Robinson described what it was like to work as a young girl in the textile mills. She began working in mills in Lowell, Massachusetts, in 1835, when she was 10. She was a "mill girl" until she was 23.

Analyze a Primary Source

From the Autobiography of Harriet H. Robinson, 1883

Read Closely: Purpose
As you read a primary source, think about why the writer wrote it. Robinson published her memoir in 1883. One of her purposes for writing was to tell her readers about an earlier time—the 1830s.

Read Closely: Cause and Effect
Looking for descriptions of causes and effects can help readers better understand historical events. In what part of the third paragraph does Robinson describe a long-term effect of the mill girls' work? Circle the sentence.

Read Closely: Historical Context
It can be difficult to understand how much wages were worth nearly 200 years ago. How much were mill workers paid? How did that compare with other jobs that women could get at the time? In the second and fourth paragraphs, underline information on wages that women and girls earned.

In 1832, Lowell was little more than a factory village. . . . Stories were told all over the country of the new factory place, and the high wages that were offered to all classes of work-people; stories that reached the ears of mechanics' and farmers' sons and gave new life to lonely and dependent women in distant towns and farmhouses. . . . Troops of young girls came from different parts of New England, and from Canada. . . .

The very young girls were called "doffers." They "doffed," or took off, the full bobbins from the spinning-frames, and replaced them with empty ones. These mites worked about fifteen minutes every hour and the rest of the time was their own. . . . They were paid two dollars a week. The working hours of all the girls extended from five o'clock in the morning until seven in the evening, with one half-hour each, for breakfast and dinner. Even the doffers were forced to be on duty nearly fourteen hours a day. This was the greatest hardship in the lives of these children. . . .

The most prevailing incentive to labor was to secure the means of education for some male member of the family. To make a *gentleman* of a brother or a son, to give him a college education, was the dominant thought in the minds of a great many of the better class of mill-girls. . . . There are many men now living who were helped to an education by the wages of the early mill-girls.

We can hardly realize what a change the cotton factory made in the status of the working women. Hitherto . . . her labor could command but small return. If she worked out as servant, or "help," her wages were from 50 cents to $1 a week; or, if she went from house to house by the day to spin and weave, or do tailoress work, she could get but 75 cents a week and her meals. . . . A woman was not supposed to be capable of spending her own, or of using other people's money.

Source: Annenberg Learner, https://www.learner.org/workshops/primarysources/lowell/docs/factory2. html, https://www.learner.org/workshops/primarysources/lowell/before.html

Events Boost National Spirit

Nationalism is a belief that one's country is a unified whole. It shows itself when the importance of sectionalism becomes secondary and the recognition of national citizenship comes to the fore. In the early 1800s, political, military, technological, and social events all added to feelings of nationalism.

The Louisiana Purchase By 1800, pioneer families had moved beyond the Appalachian Mountains into Kentucky, Tennessee, and what would soon be the state of Ohio. These lands were already part of the United States. In 1803, the French emperor Napoleon Bonaparte made an extraordinary offer. He would sell New Orleans and the Louisiana Territory to the United States. Napoleon offered a bargain price—about $15 million.

This offer, however, presented a problem to U.S. President Thomas Jefferson. The Constitution says nothing about whether the national government may expand the country's borders. But to turn down the offer would be to miss out on probably the greatest land sale in history. Jefferson asked the Senate to ratify the treaty with France and buy Louisiana.

Read Closely: Values
Historians try to explain what information, reasons, or values led people to act as they did. What positive effects might a strong sense of nationalism cause? What about negative effects?

The Louisiana Purchase, 1803

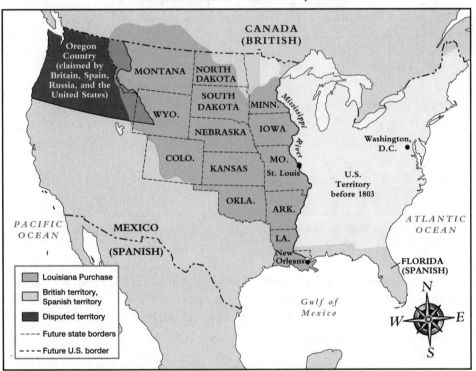

Map legend:
- Louisiana Purchase
- British territory, Spanish territory
- Disputed territory
- - - - Future state borders
- -·- Future U.S. border

The Louisiana Purchase and Nationalism The **Louisiana Purchase** cost the U.S. government three cents per acre of land. It doubled the size of the country. It opened a vast territory for expansion and settlement—territory that had no previous sectional identification. It was American territory. Gaining this territory added to a sense of nationalism and optimism about the future. James Monroe, the future president who helped broker the deal with France, enthusiastically supported the purchase. "Under prudent management it may be made to do much good as well as to prevent much evil," he wrote.

Tecumseh's Rebellion and Tensions with Britain Native Americans of the Great Lakes region reacted to the pressure of Americans settling on their lands. Tecumseh, the man who emerged as their leader, saw that the encroaching

Read Closely: Geography
A country's geography can greatly affect its politics and economics. What new political or economic advantages did the Louisiana Purchase give the United States?

Americans tried to divide the Native Americans, thereby weakening them. "You want by your distinctions of Indian tribes in allotting to each a particular track of land to make them to war with each other," **Tecumseh** wrote to the governor of the Indiana Territory. For many years, Tecumseh led raids against forts and towns while also making alliances with other Native Americans from places as far afield as Florida, Iowa, Missouri, and even Canada.

Westerners complained that Tecumseh's forces used weapons that Britain supplied. A group of young southerners and westerners in Congress were called "war hawks." These men resented British support of Native Americans and thought a war with Britain might allow the United States to capture British Canada. And Americans from all over the country resented British interference with U.S. shipping and trade. Congress declared war against Great Britain in 1812.

The War of 1812 At first, the war went badly for the United States. An attempted invasion of Canada failed. Later, British forces captured Washington, D.C. The British set fire to government buildings, including the Capitol and the White House.

But the United States won a naval victory on Lake Erie in 1813. U.S. forces also defeated Tecumseh that year. And General **Andrew Jackson** led a military victory at New Orleans in 1815. The treaty ending the war did not award any territory or money to either side.

The War of 1812 is also called the "second war for independence." After the war, Great Britain ended its policy of stopping American ships and seizing their cargoes. The United States emerged from the war as a respected member of the community of nations.

How the War of 1812 Strengthened Nationalism The war boosted the spirit of nationalism. For his victory at New Orleans in 1815, Andrew Jackson became a national hero. A witness to one of the war's battles, Francis Scott Key, expressed his national pride in a poem. A version of that poem later became the U.S. national anthem.

People recognized that the peace treaty gave nothing to either side. But many Americans felt proud to have fought the mighty British Empire to a draw. After the War of 1812, the United States was united as never before. A tide of nationalist feeling swept the country. The Federalist party stopped being a major force in American politics. The Democratic-Republican candidate for president, James Monroe, was almost unopposed in his two campaigns for president. People called the eight years of his presidency (1817–1825) the Era of Good Feelings.

The Monroe Doctrine Rebel groups in South America and Central America drew inspiration from the American and French revolutions. These groups led successful revolts against the colonial rule of Spain, Portugal, and France. President Monroe and Secretary of State John Quincy Adams feared that the monarchies of Europe might try to reconquer those lands.

In 1823, Monroe created a message called the **Monroe Doctrine**. He sent it to Congress, but it was really a warning to Spain and other European powers. It stated the following:

- The Western Hemisphere was closed to any further colonization by a European power.

- The United States would firmly oppose attempts by a European power to intervene in the affairs of the Western Hemisphere.

- The United States would not involve itself politically in the affairs of Europe.

Read Closely: Inference
When you make an inference, you form an opinion based on the facts and details that are available to you. The treaty that ended the war did not award land or money to Britain or the United States. What inference can you make based on this information?

Read Closely: Shifts
Paying attention to the name of an era can help you see how events are shifting. Why would the decline of one of two political parties help cause an "era of good feelings"?

Monroe's policy had the full support of the new nations of Latin America and Great Britain. In fact, Britain had initially suggested that the two countries issue a joint declaration ruling out any future European colonization in the Americas. However, Monroe decided the United States should issue the doctrine on its own. For more than 100 years, American leaders considered it the foundation for U.S. policy toward Europe and Latin America.

How the Monroe Doctrine Strengthened Nationalism In a letter to Thomas Jefferson, Monroe wrote that the United States should not "entangle ourselves" in European conflicts. The Monroe Doctrine was isolationist and favored neutrality. Instead of becoming involved in European politics, the United States would stick to its own hemisphere.

Economic Growth

Political change often happens because of economic forces. In the early 1800s, economic differences among the North, the South, and the West grew. These differences caused political strains and growing conflict.

The Market Revolution After the American Revolution, the U.S. economy changed. More settlers farmed more land and had more crops to sell. Local governments began forming companies that built roads and canals. The roads and canals meant that farmers could get more crops to more markets faster.

Not only were there more crops to buy, but there were more manufactured items as well. In the 1700s, people manufactured many items at home. During the market revolution, people with the means and vision to do so began to build mills. They hired people to work in the mills for wages. The workers used machines to create many items per hour. Manufactured goods became cheaper and easier to find.

Not every part of the country changed in the same way. In the South, most plantation owners invested in slaves rather than in mills, machines, or transit networks. And the U.S. government and settlers excluded Native Americans from the market revolution.

Technology and Transportation New technologies spurred on the market revolution. In the early 1800s, steamboats increased the speed of water transportation, allowing boats to travel against the current or wind. In the 1830s and 1840s, companies built railroads. Railroads made it much faster to send goods over land.

Geography was an important factor in Northern industrial growth. Many rivers in the North provided water power for running machinery. They also served as natural highways for transporting goods. Connecting the rivers was a network of roads and canals.

The construction of the Erie Canal, one of the most important of the era, ended in 1825. By connecting Lake Erie to the Hudson River, it connected the entire Great Lakes region to the Atlantic Ocean, and so, Europe and beyond. More locally, the canal allowed merchants and farmers to ship goods in one continuous voyage between New York City and ports on Lake Erie.

> **Read Closely: Synthesize**
> As you read, put together the information you are learning with what you already know. Why would farmers need to get their crops to market quickly? Think about the qualities that crops such as fruit, corn, and grains share.

Major Canals and Roads, 1820–1850

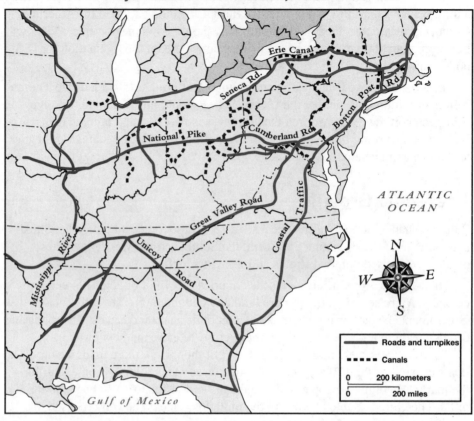

ATLANTIC OCEAN

Gulf of Mexico

Erie Canal
Seneca Rd.
Boston Post Rd.
National Pike
Cumberland Rd.
Great Valley Road
Coastal Traffic
Mississippi River
Unicoy Road

	Roads and turnpikes
	Canals

0 200 kilometers
0 200 miles

N
W E
S

Read Closely: Perspective
As you read, think about how different people at the time likely reacted to new developments. How might a musket buyer react to the invention of a musket that had interchangeable parts? How might a skilled artisan who hand-crafted muskets react to that same development?

Read Closely: Motivation
As you read, think about what reasons people may have had to react as they did. Why would some Southerners criticize Northern factory owners and say that their workers were like slaves?

Growth of Domestic Industries After the War of 1812, the United States became more self-sufficient. It already had many natural and human resources. It used these to develop a factory system. In a factory system, workers have specialized jobs. Instead of making an entire item, each worker might complete only one step in the process of making that item.

Factories grew even faster when they started using interchangeable parts in manufacturing. The inventor Eli Whitney helped develop this technique. For example, people used to make muskets one at a time, by hand. Each musket was one of a kind and hard to repair. But Whitney showed that muskets could be made with standardized, **interchangeable parts**, making them easy to assemble and repair. This idea could be applied to other products, as well.

The number of factories and textile mills increased throughout the North and especially in New England, where there was plenty of water power. Thousands of immigrants arriving yearly at the ports of Boston and New York provided a supply of cost-effective labor.

Mill Life The life of a machine operator in a New England textile mill was far different from the life of a skilled craftworker in a home workshop. Most wage earners in New England's textile mills were women and children. Many migrated from farms to factories to take advantage of the new textile jobs.

At first, working conditions were reasonable. Workers had their own homes. However, the mill owners began to require 12 to 14 hours of work a day, six days a week. Wages were low and working conditions were bad. Critics of the factory system—especially Southerners—said factory workers were "wage slaves."

In general, however, working conditions in U.S. factories were better than those in England. This was the case because in the United States, labor was more scarce. Some American mill owners provided their workers with housing and meals. But they deducted the cost of these benefits from workers' pay.

Increased Demand for Enslaved Labor To supply their textile mills, British manufacturers of the 1780s and 1790s needed more cotton. The Southern United States was a main supplier. However, removing the seeds from cotton plants was a slow, difficult job. Enslaved people did this work.

In 1793 Eli Whitney invented the cotton gin. It did the separating mechanically. Whitney thought his machine would reduce the demand for enslaved labor. But the machine made cotton more profitable for Southerners to grow. The institution of slavery actually grew instead.

As demand for cotton increased, Southern farmers began to move west into such territories as Alabama, Mississippi, Louisiana, Arkansas, and Texas. Plantation owners in the new regions supplied cotton to the Northern textile mills. Slavery became still more important in the South, and the regional differences of the growing country diverged further.

Changing Roles for Women In the North, new jobs opened up for many women as mill workers and factory workers. In Lowell, Massachusetts, most of the workers who made cloth were women. Lowell mill workers published their own magazine. Some of these workers went on to careers as writers, editors, and labor organizers.

In the South, wealthy White women on plantations supervised their homes. They also entertained relatives, friends, and business associates. Their style of living depended on the efforts of their slaves.

Enslaved women worked as hard as enslaved men in the fields. They also took care of their own homes and children. In the plantation houses, enslaved women cooked, sewed, and took care of the owners' children. Black women often gave birth to slave owners' children, either through relationships or through rape. These children had no legal rights.

In a famous speech, abolitionist and formerly enslaved person **Sojourner Truth** spoke forcefully about women. She demanded, "I could work as much and eat as much as a man—when I could get it—and bear the lash [whip] as well! And ain't I a woman?"

Status of Free Black People Although a majority of African Americans in the United States were enslaved, most in the pre–Civil War North were free. However, these free Black people did not have the full rights of citizenship. Most cities and towns denied them the right to vote. Only in the New England states did African American men have the right to vote.

Throughout most of the North, African Americans were segregated. Black children could not attend schools with White children. Churches often refused to accept Black members. As a result, many African Americans formed their own churches.

In some Northern states, African Americans were not allowed to serve on juries or testify in criminal cases. Black people often faced angry White mobs who did not want to compete with them for jobs.

Read Closely: Cause and Effect
Noticing causes and effects in what you read can help you better understand it. What was the expected effect of the invention of the cotton gin? What was the actual effect?

Read Closely: Economics
As you read about people from other eras, think about how economics affected their everyday lives. How were economic opportunities different for women in the North and in the South?

The Jacksonian Era

Andrew Jackson won election to the presidency in 1828. This presidential race marked a major change in the American political system.

The Rise of Political Democracy Back in 1824, John Quincy Adams had defeated Jackson in the presidential race. That was the last election to be decided by the House of Representatives. By 1828, all but two states had put the voters in charge of selecting presidential electors. Electoral voters would now follow the wishes of the people, who chose the electors with their votes.

By 1828, most states no longer required voters to own land. That meant there was a larger turnout than in the previous election. Jackson benefited from this change. Public opinion was becoming increasingly important in electing U.S. presidents.

Andrew Jackson was the candidate of the Democratic-Republicans. Voters considered him a "man of the people" instead a member of the rich elite. He was popular with the farmers and frontiersmen of the South and West and with workers in Eastern cities.

The Spoils System President Jackson adopted as his motto "Let the people rule." As the victor in the election of 1828, Jackson dismissed from federal employment some officials who were not Democrats and replaced them with his own Democratic supporters. The rewarding of political supporters with government jobs is known as the **spoils system**. Later presidents, whether Whig or Democrat, followed Jackson's example. Those who supported the spoils system considered it democratic at the time because it meant that government jobs would go to ordinary people ("the common man"), not to a specially educated and privileged group. However, Jackson's love of the common people did not extend to Native Americans in the Southeast.

Indian Removal Act For more than 200 years, Native Americans (the original settlers of North America) and pioneers had fought frequently. As Europeans emigrated to the United States in large numbers, they pushed Native Americans farther west. In 1829, a gold rush on Cherokee land in Georgia made Native American lands even more valuable.

Andrew Jackson was a champion of democracy for people of his own social class. He favored western farmers and pioneers. However, he had little sympathy for people who were not White. He reasoned that a policy of Indian removal would end conflict between Whites and Native Americans. He supported the **Indian Removal Act** (1830) and the forced removal of Native Americans from their lands east of the Mississippi River.

In the 1832 Supreme Court case *Worcester v. Georgia*, Chief Justice John Marshall ruled that the state of Georgia had no authority over the Cherokees' lands. Therefore, Georgia could not force the Cherokee to leave. President Jackson ignored the Court's ruling. He supposedly said, "Marshall made his decision, now let him enforce it."

Under the terms of the Indian Removal Act, the U.S. government signed more than 90 removal treaties with Native American groups. Some Native Americans left peacefully for the lands set aside for them in the Indian Territory west of the Mississippi River. (This land later became Oklahoma.) Others fought before the U.S. government forced them to submit.

The most tragic of the forced removals happened in 1838 and 1839. About 15,000 Cherokee men, women, and children from Georgia traveled 800 miles west through cold and rain. On this **Trail of Tears**, about 4,000 people died— many from starvation.

Read Closely: Sequence
While reading, look for words and phrases that signal the order of events. What happened in the presidential election that came before 1828?

_____

_____

_____

_____

Read Closely: Interpret
As you read a historical text, look for deeper or unspoken meaning in the actions of historical figures. What did Jackson mean when he supposedly said that Marshall could enforce the decision?

_____

_____

_____

_____

Application: Interpret a Primary Source

Read the excerpt and answer the questions that follow it.

Cherokee Chief John Ross Protests Treaty of New Echota, 1836

A delegation was appointed on the 23rd of October, 1835, by the General Council of the nation, clothed with full powers to enter into arrangements with the Government of the United States. . . . The delegation failing to effect an arrangement with the United States commissioner, then in the nation, proceeded, agreeably to their instructions in that case, to Washington City. . . .

After the departure of the Delegation, a . . . spurious [false] Delegation . . . proceeded to Washington City with [a] pretended treaty, and by false and fraudulent representations supplanted in the favor of the Government the legal and accredited Delegation of the Cherokee people. . . . And now it is presented to us as a treaty, ratified by the Senate, and approved by the President [Andrew Jackson]. . . .

By . . . this instrument, we are despoiled of our private possessions. . . . We are stripped of every attribute of freedom and eligibility for legal self-defence. Our property may be plundered before our eyes; violence may be committed on our persons; even our lives may be taken away, and there is none to regard our complaints. We are denationalized; we are disfranchised. We are deprived of membership in the human family! We have neither land nor home, nor resting place that can be called our own. And this is effected by the provisions of a compact which assumes the venerated, the sacred appellation [name] of treaty.

We are overwhelmed! Our hearts are sickened, our utterance is paralized. . . .

The instrument in question is not the act of our Nation; we are not parties to its covenants [agreements]; it has not received the sanction of our people. . . .

Source: PBS, https://www.pbs.org/wgbh/aia/part4/4h3083t.html

1. As you read, think about the historical context of the primary source. Based on what you have read in this lesson, what were relations like between the Cherokee Nation and the United States before Chief Ross wrote this letter?

_____

_____

2. Consider what you have learned about the Cherokee in this lesson and in the primary source. Based on this information, what effect did Ross's letter have?

_____

_____

3. Authors often show point of view in their writing. How would you describe the point of view of John Ross in this letter? Which words or phrases show his emotions? Support your answer with details from the letter.

_____

_____

**Conceptual Understanding
11.3b** Different perspectives concerning constitutional, political, economic, and social issues contributed to the growth of sectionalism.

Angelina Grimké (1805–1879) grew up on a slaveholding plantation in South Carolina. But along with her sister Sarah, she opposed the institution from an early age. The sisters also resented the limited educational opportunities afforded women at the time. Both left the South in their twenties, moving to the North and becoming members of the Society of Friends—the Quakers. The two were deeply involved in the abolition movement, writing and speaking from the point of view of Southerners who were well acquainted with the horrors of slavery.

Analyze a Primary Source

Angelina Grimké Speaks During a Riot, 1838

Read Closely: Historical Context
Grimké gave this speech at an antislavery convention. Many Northerners opposed the abolition of slavery. Many people were also horrified at the idea of a woman speaking in public, especially to an audience of women and men. The day after she gave this speech, a mob burned down the building where she gave it.

Read Closely: Purpose
As you read a speech, think about why it was written. According to Grimké, why did she give this speech? Circle the sentence in the second paragraph where she states her purpose.

Read Closely: Evidence
While reading speeches, think about what evidence the speaker presents. Which of Grimké's words and phrases provide evidence that slavery is unjust? Underline them.

[A yell from the mob without the building.] Do you ask, "what has the North to do with slavery?" Hear it—hear it. Those voices without tell us that the spirit of slavery is *here*, and has been roused to wrath by our abolition speeches and conventions. . . .

As a Southerner I feel that it is my duty to stand up here to-night and bear testimony against slavery. I have seen it—I have seen it. I know it has horrors that can never be described. I was brought up under its wing: I witnessed for many years its demoralizing influences, and its destructiveness to human happiness. It is admitted by some that the slave is not happy under the *worst* forms of slavery. But I have *never* seen a happy slave. . . . (Just then stones were thrown at the windows,—a great noise without [outside], and commotion within.) What is a mob? What would the breaking of every window be? What would the levelling of this Hall be? Any evidence that we are wrong, or that slavery is a good and wholesome institution? What if the mob should now burst in upon us, break up our meeting and commit violence upon our persons—would this be any thing compared with what the slaves endure? No, no. . . . I thank the Lord that there is yet life left enough to feel the truth, even though it rages at it—that conscience is not so completely seared as to be unmoved by the truth of the living God.

Source: *History of Pennsylvania Hall which was Destroyed by a Mob on the 17th of May,* 1838 Negro Universities Press, A Division of Greenwood Publishing Corp, New York, 1969

Perspectives on States' Rights

One of the great constitutional debates of the 1800s was the issue of **nullification**. That is the belief that states have the right to nullify (disregard) laws the federal government passed. Southerners felt a great attachment to their own region. They jealously guarded states' rights. They were convinced that the states had every right to secede from the Union if the national government tried to interfere too much with local matters.

The Virginia and Kentucky Resolutions One of the first examples of nullification happened in 1798. Congress had just passed the Alien and Sedition Acts. The main purpose of these acts was to intimidate supporters of the Democratic-Republican Party.

The Alien Act allowed the president to deport foreigners living in the United States who might be dangerous to the public safety. The Sedition Act allowed the government to fine and imprison anyone who wrote "scandalous and malicious writing or writings against the government" or encouraged people to rebel.

State legislatures in Virginia and Kentucky passed resolutions that protested these measures. Both states claimed the right to nullify the acts as unconstitutional. Thomas Jefferson wrote the Kentucky resolutions, and James Madison wrote the Virginia resolutions. Years later, Madison backed away from his support for nullification.

Tariffs Anger the South A tariff is a tax on imported goods, and in the 1800s, tariffs actually provided a significant amount of the federal government's revenue. Because of tariffs, goods produced outside the United States were more expensive than goods produced within the United States. Tariffs helped the North more than the South because most of the country's factories were in the North. Southerners had to pay higher prices for goods and received little or no benefit from the tariffs.

John C. Calhoun of South Carolina led the Southern resistance to high tariffs. While vice president under Andrew Jackson, Calhoun published an essay supporting the right of the states to nullify national law. Calhoun said states could nullify a tariff passed in 1828 because it benefited one section of the country at the expense of another.

To President Jackson, Calhoun's ideas seemed like treason. At a political dinner in 1830, the president offered a brief toast. "Our Federal Union," he said, "it must be preserved." In response Calhoun offered, "The Union—next to our liberty, the most dear."

The Nullification Crisis In 1832, Congress eliminated some parts of the tariff. But many Southerners were still dissatisfied. South Carolina called a special state convention, which declared the tariffs of 1828 and 1832 "null, void, and no law."

South Carolina threatened to withdraw from the Union if the federal government tried to collect tariffs in Southern ports. In other words, South Carolina talked of seceding. That means leaving the Union to become an independent republic.

A furious President Jackson threatened to send troops into South Carolina. But Senator Henry Clay saved the day by proposing a compromise. Clay persuaded Congress to pass a new tariff act in 1833. This new act gradually reduced tariff rates. South Carolina then repealed its Ordinance of Nullification. For the moment, both sides avoided violent conflict.

> **Read Closely: Cause and Effect**
> While reading, think about the effects of new laws and other innovations. What effects might the Alien and Sedition Acts have on a government and its people?

> **Read Closely: Point of View**
> Be aware that different groups can have diverging opinions about historical events. How did most factory owners probably view tariffs? How did most planters and farmers probably view them?

The Abolitionist Movement Some Americans were outraged at the conditions faced by enslaved people. Beatings were common. Children born into slavery were the property of the plantation owners. Owners could separate families and sell them to different owners.

The spirit of the American Revolution led to a significant **abolitionist** movement, which sought to end slavery. New Yorkers founded their first antislavery society in 1785. Between 1777 and 1804, all the U.S. states north of Maryland abolished slavery.

Most Southerners did not own slaves. However, slavery was the foundation of the Southern economy and society in many ways. The movement to defend and promote slavery tore apart the United States.

Nat Turner's Rebellion Some enslaved people fought back even though there was little hope of success and the penalty for revolt was death. Nat Turner led a slave revolt in Virginia in 1831. Fifty-nine White people died in the revolt, which authorities soon stopped. Nat Turner evaded capture for six weeks, but authorities finally captured, tried, and executed him. Fifty-five people convicted of helping Turner were executed, and White mobs killed as many as 200 more enslaved Black people in the rebellion's aftermath.

William Lloyd Garrison and *The Liberator* A White reformer named William Lloyd Garrison helped launch the abolitionist movement. He published an antislavery newspaper, *The Liberator*, beginning in 1831. He demanded an immediate end to slavery without compensating slave owners for their loss. The Constitution allowed slavery, so Garrison condemned it as "a covenant with death and an agreement with Hell."

Frederick Douglass At age 20 in 1838, **Frederick Douglass** escaped from slavery. After that, he dedicated himself to the cause of African American freedom and equal rights. Large crowds listened to him speak about the injustice of slavery. "Liberty for all, chains for none," he insisted.

Douglass founded a newspaper called the *North Star* in Rochester, New York. He also wrote the story of his life, *The Autobiography of Frederick Douglass*. Throughout his life, Douglass appreciated the importance of learning. He wrote, "Once you learn to read, you will be forever free."

Sojourner Truth Sojourner Truth (1797–1883) was a previously enslaved woman from New York. After 1843, she took on the name of Sojourner Truth, traveling widely and preaching. She spoke against slavery and for women's rights, mesmerizing crowds throughout the North with her speaking style. Truth fought slavery and segregation for the rest of her life.

Harriet Beecher Stowe and *Uncle Tom's Cabin* A White woman from Connecticut, Stowe was the author of one of the most influential novels ever written: *Uncle Tom's Cabin*. It tells the story of a kind, elderly slave, Uncle Tom. A vicious slave overseer, Simon Legree, savagely kills Tom.

Published in 1852, the book caused a sensation. Northerners felt moral outrage at its depiction of the evils of slavery. Southerners complained that it presented a false picture of Southern society.

Women Demand Expanded Rights

The fights for the abolition of slavery and for improvements in women's rights turned out to be closely related. Not all activists supported both causes. However, female abolitionists were improving their skills at organizing, speaking publicly, and writing. As a result, many of them began to advocate for their own rights as well. Remember that women still did not have the right to vote. In spite of this, many were extremely active in the reform movements of the 1830s and 1840s

The Grimké Sisters Angelina Grimké and Sarah Grimké were White and from South Carolina. They were abolitionists and early supporters of women's rights. Both sisters spoke before Northern groups. They described the experiences of enslaved people on their parents' plantation.

In "An Appeal to the Christian Women of the South," written in 1836, Angelina encouraged Southern White women to demand laws that would end slavery. "The women of the South can overthrow this horrible system of oppression and cruelty," she said.

Lucretia Mott As teacher in Poughkeepsie, New York, **Lucretia Mott** became interested in women's rights when she found out that she was earning half of what the male teachers earned. Mott founded an antislavery society, but the organizers of an antislavery convention would not let her be a delegate. Why? Because she was a woman. She spent much of her later life focused on expanding women's rights.

The Seneca Falls Convention "All men and women are created equal." That is one of the most famous passages from the Declaration of Sentiments. Activists presented the declaration at a women's rights convention at Seneca Falls, New York, in 1848. Mott and others helped organize the convention, which was the first of its kind. The declaration included demands for the following rights:

- to vote and hold elected office
- to hold property in their own names
- to manage their own incomes
- to be the legal guardians of their own children

The framers of the declaration modeled it after the Declaration of Independence. However, many people ridiculed the idea that women should be able to vote. That idea remained controversial for the rest of the century and beyond.

The Fight Over Slavery's Expansion

As the United States expanded, Northerners and Southerners argued bitterly over whether slavery should expand into new territories. Congress passed compromises, but these turned out to be temporary.

Missouri Compromise Southern slave owners who moved to the Missouri Territory brought their slaves with them. In 1819, the people of Missouri applied for admission to the Union as a new state—one that allowed slavery. But Missouri's admission would end the fragile balance of power between slave states and free states.

In 1820, Congress passed a measure known as the **Missouri Compromise**.

- Missouri would enter the Union as a slave state.
- Maine would enter the Union as a free state. (It had previously been part of Massachusetts.)
- All territory north of the 36°30′ line of latitude in the lands of the Louisiana Purchase would be closed to slavery. (That latitude was the southern border of Missouri.)

Read Closely: Obstacles
While reading, consider setbacks and hardships that people in history faced. Why would it have been difficult for Southern women to end slavery?

Read Closely: Spread of Ideas
While reading, notice which ideas capture people's imaginations at different times and places. How did the Declaration of Independence influence the Declaration of Sentiments?

Read Closely: Balance of Power
Maintaining a balance of power between different groups can prevent controversies and violence. How might Congress have changed once free states outnumbered slave states?

Manifest Destiny In the 1800s many Americans believed their country was destined to expand westward. They thought the United States should and would expand at least as far as the Pacific coast. They wanted the United States to be the dominant nation in North America.

However, Mexico already possessed large parts of the West. Americans' idea of **manifest destiny** threatened Mexico's control of its territory.

Texas In colonial times, Texas, California, and the lands in between had been part of the Spanish empire. When the Mexicans revolted against Spanish rule in 1821, Texas and California became the northern part of the new nation of Mexico.

By the mid-1830s, there were more American settlers in Texas than Mexicans. Those Americans often defied Mexico's laws, including its ban on slavery. They declared Texas an independent nation in 1836.

For nine years, Texas was independent. Then its leaders applied for admission to the Union as a state. Northerners opposed this because slavery was well established there. In 1845, Congress made Texas the 28th state. This annexation led to worsening relations with Mexico.

The Mexican-American War A Democratic president, James K. Polk, believed strongly in expansion. His desire to gain western lands was largely responsible for the outbreak of a war with Mexico. The immediate cause of the war was a disputed boundary between Texas and Mexico.

Two U.S. armies struck south into Mexican territory. One army occupied northern Mexico. A second army forced the Mexicans to surrender their capital, Mexico City, in 1848. A third American army marched to California. It quickly overcame Mexican defenders. In 1848, California became American territory.

In the treaty ending the Mexican War, the United States paid the token sum of $15 million to Mexico for the huge territory extending from Texas's western border all the way to the California coast. The Rio Grande became the Texas–Mexico border.

Read Closely: Diplomacy
Maintaining good relations between the governments of different countries is diplomacy. How would the idea of manifest destiny make diplomacy with neighboring countries more difficult?

Lands Added to the United States, 1783–1853

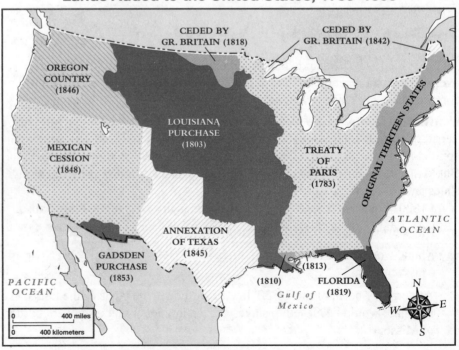

The Compromise of 1850 California was the first of the new territories to apply for admission as a state. The South was alarmed because California insisted on being admitted as a free state. This would upset the balance of free states and slave states. It would increase the representation in Congress of the nonslave states and give the North a majority in Congress. Congress passed another compromise:

- California would become a free state. In other parts of the Mexican Cession, settlers would decide by majority vote whether to allow slavery.

- Buying and selling enslaved people at public auction in Washington, D.C., would no longer be allowed.

- Government officials in the North would help capture escaped slaves and return them to their masters in the South. This Fugitive Slave Act had heavy fines for those who disobeyed.

Read Closely: Values
As you read, think about the beliefs that different groups of people hold. Why would an abolitionist object to the Fugitive Slave Act?

The Compromise of 1850

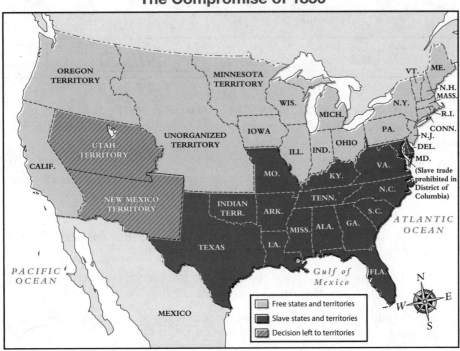

The Kansas-Nebraska Act Both Kansas and Nebraska were north of the 36°30' line. According to the Missouri Compromise of 1820, slavery would not be allowed there. But Southerners hoped to end this restriction. Congress decided that settlers in Kansas and Nebraska would decide for themselves whether to allow slavery.

In Kansas, fighting broke out between Southern, proslavery settlers and Northern, antislavery settlers. Armed clashes in "Bleeding Kansas" warned of the nationwide civil war that would soon follow.

The United States After the Kansas-Nebraska Act, 1854

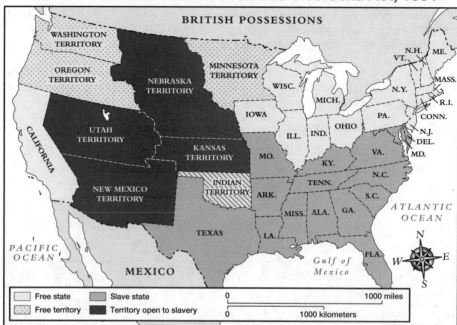

Speak and Listen: Understanding Visuals
In a small group, take turns describing one of the four regions identified by different colors or patterns on the map. Describe the status of slavery in the region in 1854, as well as what you know about the economics, politics, and culture of the region in 1854 and today.

The Dred Scott Decision The enslaved man **Dred Scott** was 61 years old, married, and had two daughters. He had lived in the slave state of Missouri. His owner took him to Illinois, a free state.

Returning to Missouri, Scott went to court to sue for his freedom. He argued that he had lived in free territory and therefore should be declared a free citizen.

In 1857, the Supreme Court ruled that Scott's petition was not valid. Chief Justice Roger Taney, a Southerner, wrote:

- "The people of the Negro race are not included, and were not intended to be included, under the word 'citizens' in the Constitution. . . ."

- Even free African Americans could not sue in a federal court, since they were not citizens of the United States.

- Slaves brought into free territory remained slaves because they were property.

- The Missouri Compromise, which had excluded slavery from free territory, was unconstitutional because it denied slave owners their property rights.

Southern slave owners were pleased with the Court's decision. In the North, many people were shocked to think that all western territories were now thrown open to slavery. Some had moral objections to slavery. Others hoped to keep the territory for White settlers only.

Read Closely: Balance of Power
As you read, notice threats to, or changes in, the balance of power among different groups. How did the Dred Scott decision change the balance of power in the United States?

John Brown's Raid White abolitionist **John Brown** believed in using violence to fight slavery. In Kansas in 1856, Brown and his sons murdered five supporters of slavery in retaliation for the deaths of antislavery settlers. In 1859, Brown led an attack on a federal arsenal in Harpers Ferry, Virginia (later West Virginia). The plot failed. Brown was captured, tried, and hanged. Northern abolitionists saw Brown as a martyr. To Southerners, he was a fanatic. It's easy to see that the territorial and philosophical divide in the United States meant that by the end of the 1850s, the Union was in peril.

Application: Interpret a Primary Source

Read the excerpt and answer the questions that follow it.

From "To My Old Master," by Frederick Douglass, 1848, Rochester, New York

Oh! sir, a slaveholder never appears to me so completely an agent of hell, as when I think of and look upon my dear children. It is then that my feelings rise above my control. . . . The grim horrors of slavery rise in all their ghastly terror before me; the wails of millions pierce my heart and chill my blood. I remember the chain, the gag, the bloody whip; the death-like gloom overshadowing the broken spirit of the fettered bondman [enslaved person in chains]; the appalling liability of his being torn away from wife and children, and sold like a beast in the market. Say not that this is a picture of fancy [an imagined story]. You well know that I wear stripes [scars from whipping] on my back, inflicted by your direction. . . . All this, and more, you remember, and know to be perfectly true, not only of yourself, but of nearly all of the slaveholders around you.

At this moment, you are probably the guilty holder of at least three of my own dear sisters, and my only brother, in bondage. These you regard as your property. They are recorded on your ledger, or perhaps have been sold to human flesh-mongers, with a view to filling your own ever-hungry purse. Sir, I desire to know how and where these dear sisters are. Have you sold them? or are they still in your possession? What has become of them? are they living or dead. . . . Write and let me know all about them. If my grandmother be still alive, she is of no service to you, for by this time she must be nearly eighty years old. . . . send her to me at Rochester, or bring her to Philadelphia, and it shall be the crowning happiness of my life to take care of her in her old age.

Source: Library of Congress, https://www.loc.gov/item/mfd.21024/

1. As you read, look for information about the historical context of the primary source. Douglass published this letter in his newspaper after hearing that his former owner, Thomas Auld, had been described as a kindly slave owner. Why do you think Douglass published the letter rather than just sending it to Auld?

   _____

   _____

2. Think about the excerpt from Angelina Grimké at the start of this lesson. Both Grimké and Douglass saw the effects of slavery firsthand. How does Douglass's perspective differ from that of Grimké?

   _____

   _____

3. Authors often write with their audience in mind. Douglass's audience was not only the slave owner but also the readers of his newspaper. How might this letter have affected newspaper readers? Support your answer with details from the letter.

   _____

   _____

Conceptual Understanding
11.3c Long-standing disputes over states' rights and slavery and the secession of Southern states from the Union, sparked by the election of Abraham Lincoln, led to the Civil War. After the issuance of the Emancipation Proclamation, freeing the slaves became a major Union goal. The Civil War resulted in tremendous human loss and physical destruction.

Read Closely: Historical Context
A *score* is another word for 20. "Four score and seven years ago" means 87 years ago. Lincoln is talking about 1776, the year of the Declaration of Independence. The Declaration says that "all men are created equal"—a concept Lincoln believed was essential to American values.

Read Closely: Purpose
While reading a speech, think about why the speaker wrote it. What is the purpose of Lincoln's speech? Look at the second paragraph and circle his reason for speaking.

Read Closely: Audience
Lincoln delivered this speech to Union supporters who had witnessed death and destruction as a result of the war. What phrases and sentences in the third paragraph could help convince audience members that those sacrifices were worthwhile? Underline them.

President Lincoln delivered this speech at the dedication of the National Cemetery at Gettysburg, Pennsylvania, on November 19, 1863. One of the most decisive battles of the Civil War had taken place at Gettysburg just over four months earlier.

Analyze a Primary Source

Abraham Lincoln Delivers the Gettysburg Address, 1863

Four score and seven years ago our fathers brought forth on this continent, a new nation, conceived in Liberty, and dedicated to the proposition that all men are created equal.

Now we are engaged in a great civil war, testing whether that nation, or any nation so conceived and so dedicated, can long endure. We are met on a great battle-field of that war. We have come to dedicate a portion of that field, as a final resting place for those who here gave their lives that that nation might live. It is altogether fitting and proper that we should do this.

But, in a larger sense, we can not dedicate—we can not consecrate [make holy]—we can not hallow—this ground. The brave men, living and dead, who struggled here, have consecrated it, far above our poor power to add or detract. The world will little note, nor long remember what we say here, but it can never forget what they did here. It is for us the living, rather, to be dedicated here to the unfinished work which they who fought here have thus far so nobly advanced. It is rather for us to be here dedicated to the great task remaining before us—that from these honored dead we take increased devotion to that cause for which they gave the last full measure of devotion—that we here highly resolve that these dead shall not have died in vain—that this nation, under God, shall have a new birth of freedom—and that government of the people, by the people, for the people, shall not perish from the earth.

Source: University of Virginia, https://millercenter.org/the-presidency/presidential-speeches/november-19-1863-gettysburg-address

Causes and Capabilities

Through compromise after compromise, lawmakers had managed to keep the United States together. What would happen if and when the compromises broke down? Would slave-holding states leave peacefully? Or would there be all-out war?

The Election of Lincoln Abraham Lincoln strongly opposed slavery. In his famous "house divided" speech, he said, "I believe this government cannot endure permanently half slave, and half free." And yet, he did not believe the federal government had the power to end slavery immediately. Angry feelings between Northerners and Southerners dominated politics in 1860. In a four-way presidential race, Lincoln won. However, he received only 40 percent of the popular vote.

A Confident South When an individual state decides to leave the United States, it is called **secession**. Many Southerners believed the North would not go to war over secession. Even if war came, Southerners believed they would get support from abroad. They thought Britain would back the South because Britain needed cotton for its factories.

Most Southern Whites owned no slaves. But a majority of them supported slavery as part of the Southern way of life. Slave owners and their supporters believed Lincoln and his Republican Party wanted to end slavery everywhere.

Southern States Secede One month after Lincoln's election, South Carolina left the Union. Other Southern states followed. The 11 Southern states that seceded had their own national constitution and central government. They called their nation the Confederate States of America.

Lincoln tried to convince the South not to secede. He reminded the South that the Fugitive Slave Act was still the law of the land. He said his administration would not interfere with slavery in the states where it existed. He supported an amendment that would guarantee slavery permanently in the states where it existed. But none of these arguments stopped Southern secession.

Fort Sumter A month after Lincoln's inauguration, a conflict triggered civil war. U.S. forces held Fort Sumter, an island fortress in the harbor of Charleston, South Carolina. South Carolina insisted that the troops surrender the fort to the South. Lincoln refused and sent food and supplies to the fort. Confederate troops opened fire on the fort, and the war began.

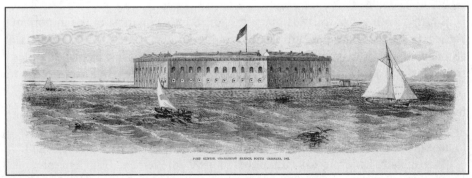

Source: Getty Images

An engraving of Fort Sumter in Charleston harbor, South Carolina, 1861

Strengths of the Union and the Confederacy In general, the South had a better army for fighting a short war, but the North's vast economic resources gave it the advantage in a longer war. The war turned out to be long. It lasted four years, from 1861 until 1865.

North and South in the Civil War	
Union Advantages	**Confederate Advantages**
• **Population:** In 1860, 22 million people lived in northern states. The South had 6 million free citizens and 3 million enslaved people. • **Industrial capacity and farming:** The Union's many factories and farms could produce massive amounts of war goods and food supplies. The South had little industry. Its farms produced mostly cotton rather than food. • **Transportation:** The North had more railroads and canals. • **Foreign relations:** Other countries recognized the United States as a legitimate nation. The South failed to achieve this recognition. • **Naval superiority:** The South had far fewer warships than the North. The North was able to blockade Southern ports and cut off vital supplies.	• **Strategic position:** In war, it is generally easier to defend a position than to attack it. Instead of launching risky offensives, the South needed to repulse Northern assaults. • **Preparation for war:** Southerners had a stronger military tradition than Northerners. Most Southern White men knew how to shoot and ride. They needed less training than Union soldiers did. • **Military leadership:** Southern generals, including Robert E. Lee and Thomas J. "Stonewall" Jackson, were far superior to most Northern generals. • **Morale:** Southern troops were defending their homeland. Therefore, their fighting spirit was usually greater than that of Northern troops. • **Foreign trade:** Britain relied on Southern cotton as raw material for its textile factories. Confederate leaders believed that Britain would pressure the North to accept secession.

Read Closely: Geography
As you read, think about how geography affects countries. What geographic advantages did each side have?

War Grips the Nation

As the country plunged into conflict, both sides expected a quick victory. Both were surprised that the war dragged on. Over the years, the North's motivation for fighting changed.

Read Closely: Costs of War
While reading, think about the effects of casualties on each side. Why would the North be able to bear more casualties than the South?

Southern Victories In 1861 and 1862, the South won most of the important battles. In the first Battle of Bull Run, a smaller Southern army led by Thomas "Stonewall" Jackson defeated a larger Union army. The battle was just 30 miles from Washington, D.C. In 1862, a second Union army lost at Bull Run.

Antietam In 1862, U.S. General George McClellan stopped an advance by General Robert E. Lee and the army of Virginia. The Battle of Antietam happened in Maryland. Lee had crossed the Potomac River from Virginia, hoping to take the war to the North. All previous battles had been fought in the South.

At Antietam, Union forces outnumbered the Confederates. But General McClellan refused to commit his whole army to the battle. In contrast, Lee used every soldier. The result was a draw. But people considered it a Union victory when Lee left the battlefield first. He and his army retreated back into Virginia.

The battle had cost more than 2,000 Union lives and 1,500 Confederate lives. There were more than 22,000 casualties.

Halting the Southern army had important consequences for both sides. Britain and France decided not to involve themselves in the conflict, although they appeared to sympathize with the South.

Gettysburg In 1863, the South's brilliant general, Robert E. Lee, decided on a bold invasion of the North. He made his way to the town of Gettysburg, Pennsylvania, with an army of about 71,000 men. But the Union Army was able to beat them to the area, taking control of a number of important, strategic positions near the town. After two days of fighting for specific positions, and heavy casualties, Lee decided on a frontal attack.

A 15,000-man Confederate assault was repulsed by dug-in Federal troops who inflicted heavy casualties. One Union soldier wrote home telling what happened: "We cut them down by thousand so much so that the ground was covered with dead and wounded."

That night General Lee retreated from Pennsylvania. Twice Lee had tried to take the war to the North, first at Antietam and then at Gettysburg. It was the last time Southern armies would threaten Northern territory.

The cost of the battle was terrible. More than 180,000 men were involved in the fighting. In three days, more than 10,000 men died. Another 56,000 were wounded. The loss of life at Gettysburg was so severe that officials created a national cemetery at the site.

Gettysburg Address At an official ceremony at the cemetery, Lincoln gave a two-minute speech, now called the **Gettysburg Address**. It is one of the most memorable and inspiring speeches in American history. Lincoln showed that the Union was fighting not only for a military victory but for universal values, such as those in the Declaration of Independence.

The Gettysburg Address had long-term effects on the country. Lincoln made it clear that the war was not only to preserve the Union but also to fight for human equality.

Vicksburg One day after the battle of Gettysburg, Union troops under General Ulysses S. Grant captured a fortress at Vicksburg, Mississippi. This victory gave the North control of the Mississippi River and split the South in two. It cut off Confederate states on the west side of the river (Texas, Arkansas, and western Louisiana) from the rest of the Confederacy.

The Expansion of Federal Power

During the war, President Lincoln presided over a notable expansion of the power of the federal government. For example, he signed into law the National Bank Act (1863), which created both a national banking system and a national currency. He also signed the Morrill Act, which created so-called land-grant colleges. But more controversially, certainly at the time, he suspended some of the rules and laws the United States had developed over time. As commander in chief of the armed forces, Lincoln also issued a proclamation that freed enslaved people in Confederate states. (This affected only those relatively few enslaved people living in Union-controlled parts of the Confederacy.)

Civil liberties are basic rights and freedoms that people can exercise without government interference. For example, Americans have the right to speak freely and the right to a fair trial. During the war, civil liberties suffered as Lincoln made the defeat of the South his priority.

> **Read Closely: Geography**
> As you read about battles, find out where each battle site is located. What psychological effects might have been the result of a Confederate victory that was far into Northern territory?

> **Read Closely: Turning Point**
> Pay attention to the order of major events to find out how each affected the others. In what way was the Battle of Vicksburg a turning point in the Civil War?

Suspension of Habeas Corpus Lincoln feared that people loyal to the Confederacy would take over Maryland. He contacted General Winfield Scott and ordered him to suspend **habeas corpus** if public safety was in danger.

Habeas corpus is Latin for "you have the body." It is a court order that requires law enforcement officials to bring a prisoner to court. Then a judge decides whether that person should stay in jail. Habeas corpus prevents a president, general, police chief, or other authority from putting people behind bars indefinitely and without due process of law. Note, however, that the Constitution allows for the suspension of habeas corpus when "in cases of rebellion or invasion the public safety may require it." (Article I, Section 9)

While habeas corpus was suspended, officers arrested hundreds of people but did not put them on trial. Army officers arrested the mayor and police chief of Baltimore and members of the state legislature. The charge was "giving aid and comfort in various ways to the insurrection."

By the end of the war, at least 15,000 people had suffered arrest and imprisonment without formal trials. Also, military courts tried and convicted some civilians. After the war, a Supreme Court decision held that military courts cannot place civilians on trial if state and federal courts are functioning.

Read Closely: Motivation
As you read, think about the reasons people in history had for acting as they did. Why might a wartime leader be more likely to suspend civil liberties?

Should Lincoln Have Suspended Habeas Corpus?	
Arguments For	**Arguments Against**
• Rebels were trying to destroy the country. • The Constitution allows habeas corpus to be suspended. • Lincoln was acting in the spirit of the Constitution.	• By suspending habeas corpus, Lincoln was taking an action as president that was specifically given to Congress. • Such power in the hands of a president could lead to one-person rule.

Emancipation Proclamation On January 1, 1863, Lincoln issued the Emancipation Proclamation. In this document, Lincoln declared that slaves in the Confederate states were now free. He wrote that "such persons of suitable condition will be received into the armed service of the United States."

Emancipation means freedom. But this proclamation did not immediately free many slaves. The border states of Delaware, Kentucky, Maryland, and Missouri had remained loyal to the Union. Slavery continued to exist in those states. The proclamation applied to the Confederate states, which did not recognize Lincoln's authority.

However, the proclamation was significant. Most people understood that slavery would probably be abolished throughout the nation if the North won. Enslaved people throughout the South made their way to Union lines, seeking freedom.

In addition, the emancipation provided a moral basis to the war. It made freeing the slaves a major Northern goal. Great Britain, which had abolished slavery in the 1830s, was reluctant to aid the South despite a need for cotton.

But not all Union supporters welcomed the proclamation. There were those who wanted to restore the Union without disturbing slavery—particularly in the border states. In New York City, laborers (often Irish immigrants) resented being drafted to fight a war that would emancipate people they feared would take their jobs. They took to the streets in mid-July 1863, attacking African-American people and businesses. Hundreds, maybe a thousand, people were killed—mostly Black men.

Read Closely: Cause and Effect
As you read, consider the effects of proclamations and other laws. What were some possible effects of welcoming formerly enslaved men into the U.S. military?

The Union Prevails

Although the South had done well in battle early in the war, the North's advantages made the difference in the war's later years. The Union's advantages in population and industry, coupled with its naval superiority, eventually took their toll. In the war's later years, the Union had another important advantage: African American soldiers.

African American Participation in the War When the war began, neither the North nor the South allowed African Americans to enlist in its armed forces. Thousands of free Black men in the North tried to enlist but were turned away. As the war continued, the U.S. government changed its policy. It allowed freed Southern slaves and free Northern Black men to serve in racially segregated army units.

At first, military officials assigned African American soldiers to tasks other than fighting. For example, they cooked meals and built defensive walls. But beginning in 1863, African American troops served in battle.

By war's end, more than 180,000 African Americans had joined the Union armed forces. About 38,000 had lost their lives.

Source: Getty Images

Abraham Lincoln and Senator Charles Sumner salute Union Troops.

Sherman's March to the Sea In 1864 and 1865, General William T. Sherman led a Northern army on a campaign of destruction. His army marched east from Tennessee to the Georgia coast and then north to the Carolinas. For the first time in the war, troops deliberately destroyed civilian lands and crops. "War is hell," said Sherman, and he made the Confederacy feel the truth of his statement.

Richmond and Appomattox As the capital of the Confederacy, Richmond, in central Virginia, was an important military objective. On April 2, 1865, Lee's battered army was forced to retreat, allowing Union forces to take the Confederate capital. Seven days later, Lee surrendered his army to Grant at Appomattox Court House. The war was over.

> **Read Closely: Inferences**
> Use the information you are learning to make inferences ("educated guesses" based on reasons and evidence) about groups of people. Consider the restrictions Northern White men put on African American soldiers. What inference can you draw about the Northerners' beliefs about African Americans?

> **Read Closely: Military Tactics**
> Consider how military policies and actions affect the course of a war. When a general or government allows soldiers to burn civilians' land and destroy their crops, that is often called "total war." From a military perspective, what are possible advantages and disadvantages of total war?

The North and the South in the Civil War

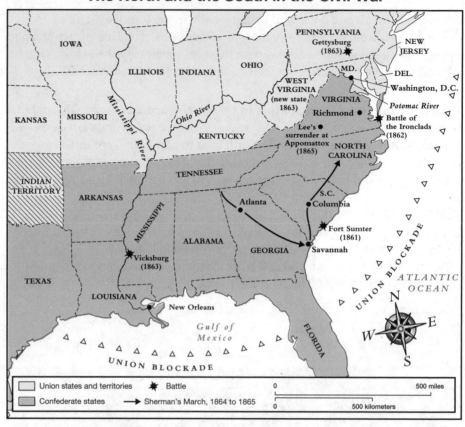

"With Malice Toward None" Lincoln won reelection in 1864. In his second inaugural address, he spoke about slavery. He said, "All knew that this interest was somehow the cause of the war." He noted that "neither party expected for the war the magnitude or the duration which it had already attained."

Lincoln tried to bring the nation together. He ended his speech with these words: "With Malice toward none, with charity for all, with firmness in the right, as God gives us to see the right, let us strive on to finish the work we are in, to bind up the nation's wound, to care for him who shall have borne the battle, and for his widow and orphans; to do all which may achieve and cherish a just and a lasting peace among ourselves and with all nations."

A month into Lincoln's second term, John Wilkes Booth, a Southern sympathizer, shot and killed the president as he watched a theater production.

Thirteenth Amendment The Thirteenth Amendment made slavery illegal in every state in the Union. It passed by two-thirds of Congress in 1864, and three-quarters of the states approved it in 1865. The Thirteenth Amendment freed people who had been enslaved all their lives.

Impacts of the War The Civil War led to tremendous human loss. About 1.5 million men served in the U.S. military, and about 800,000 fought for the Confederacy. The total death toll is unknown, but today, historians estimate that between 750,000 and 850,000 soldiers died. In total, about 2 percent of the country's population died in the war.

The war also led to physical destruction. Troops on both sides burned homes, farms, and factories, either to punish civilians or to prevent crops and other resources from falling into opponents' hands. Reconstructing the country would take decades.

Application: Interpret a Primary Source

Read the excerpt and answer the questions that follow it.

Letter from Samuel Cabble, Union Soldier

Dear Wife i have enlisted in the army i am now in the state of Massachusetts but before this letter reaches you i will be in North Carlinia and though great is the present national dificulties yet i look forward to a brighter day When i shall have the opertunity of seeing you in the full enjoyment of fredom i would like to no if you are still in slavery if you are it will not be long before we shall have crushed the system that now opreses you for in the course of three months you shall have your liberty. great is the outpouring of the [Black people] that is now rallying with the hearts of lions against that very curse that has seperated you an me yet we shall meet again and oh what a happy time that will be when this ungodly rebellion shall be put down and the curses of our land is trampled under our feet i am a soldier now and i shall use my utmost endeavor [effort] to strike at the rebellion and the heart of this system that so long has kept us in chains . . . remain your own afectionate husband until death—Samuel Cabble

Source: National Archives, https://www.archives.gov/education/lessons/blacks-civil-war/article.html

1. As you read, look for information about the historical context of the primary source. Cabble was a 21-year-old African American who had been enslaved. Based on this information, what can you conclude about the spelling, punctuation, and grammar in this letter?

   _____

   _____

   _____

   _____

2. While reading a primary source, look for examples of cause and effect to help you understand ideas. According to Cabble, what would be the effects of a Union victory?

   _____

   _____

   _____

   _____

3. Authors often write to express their point of view. Based on his letter, what was Cabble's view of the Civil War? Support your answer with details from the letter.

   _____

   _____

   _____

   _____

Multiple-Choice Questions

Questions 1–3 refer to the excerpt below.

A. Contemporary Account of Nat Turner's Rebellion

In consequence of the alarming increase of the Black population at the South, fears have been long entertained, that it might one day be the unhappy lot of the Whites, in that section, to witness scenes similar to those which but a few years since, nearly depopulated the once flourishing island of St. Domingo of its White inhabitants—but, these fears have never been realized even in a small degree, until the fatal morning of the 22d of August last, when it fell to the lot of the inhabitants of a thinly settled township of Southampton county (Virginia) to witness a scene horrid in the extreme!—when FIFTY FIVE innocent persons (mostly women and children) fell victim to the most inhuman barbarity.

The melancholy and bloody event was as sudden and unexpected, as unprecedented for cruelty—for many months previous an artful Black, known by the name of Nat Turner, (a slave of Mr. Edward Travis) who had been taught to read and write, and who hypocritically and the better to enable him to effect his nefarious designs, assumed the character of a Preacher, and as such was sometimes permitted to visit and associate himself with many of the Plantation Negroes, for the purpose (as was by him artfully represented) of christianizing and to teach them the propriety of their remaining faithful and obedient to their masters; but, in reality, to persuade and to prepare them in the most sly and artful manner to become the instruments of their slaughter!—in this he too well succeeded, by representing to the poor deluded wretches the Blessings of Liberty, and the inhumanity and injustice of their being forced like brutes from the land of their nativity, and doomed without fault or crime to perpetual bondage, and by those who were not more entitled to their liberty than themselves!—he too represented to them the happy effects which had been attended the united efforts of their brethren in St. Domingo, and elsewhere, and encouraged them with the assurance that a similar effort on their part, could not fail to produce a similar effect, and not only restore them to liberty but would produce them wealth and ease! . . . A plan was by him next devised when, where and how to commence the attack—it was to be before the break of day on the morning of the 22d, on the defenceless and thinly settled inhabitants in the neighborhood of the Cross Keys, Southampton county, twenty miles above Murfreesboro'.

Source: Samuel Warner, *Authentic and Impartial Narrative of the Tragical Scene*, 1831

1. On the basis of this excerpt, which of the following might be a good reason to question the reliability of Warner's account?

   1. It sensationalizes the attack.
   2. It was based on previous newspaper accounts.
   3. The author purports to know Nat Turner's intentions.
   4. Since the author was not present, his account is completely fictional.

2. Based on this excerpt, which of the following best seems to describe the author's bias?

   1. He probably sympathized with the slaves, but condemned their use of violence.
   2. He probably approved of the use of violence in the cause of freedom.
   3. He probably supported the continuation of slavery.
   4. He probably worried that slaves would rise up in rebellion and take over the government as they had in St. Domingo.

3. What parallels does the author draw between Nat Turner's rebellion and events in St. Domingo?

   1. Both were successful slave uprisings.
   2. Both were led by men who claimed to be preachers.
   3. Both showed why it was dangerous to teach slaves to read and write.
   4. Both resulted in the violent deaths of Whites.

B. An Early Description of Manifest Destiny

The far-reaching, the boundless future will be the era of American greatness. In its magnificent domain of space and time, the nation of many nations is destined to manifest to mankind the excellence of divine principles; to establish on earth the noblest temple ever dedicated to the worship of the Most High—the Sacred and the True. Its floor shall be a hemisphere—its roof the firmament [sky] of the star-studded heavens, and its congregation an Union of many Republics, comprising hundreds of happy millions, calling, owning no man master, but governed by God's natural and moral law of equality, the law of brotherhood—of "peace and good will amongst men." . . .

Yes, we are the nation of progress, of individual freedom, of universal enfranchisement. Equality of rights is the cynosure of our union of States, the grand exemplar of the correlative equality of individuals. . . . We must onward to the fulfilment of our mission—to the entire development of the principle of our organization—freedom of conscience, freedom of person, freedom of trade and business pursuits, universality of freedom and equality. This is our high destiny, and in nature's eternal, inevitable decree of cause and effect we must accomplish it. All this will be our future history, to establish on earth the moral dignity and salvation of man—the immutable [unchangeable] truth and beneficence [doing good] of God. For this blessed mission to the nations of the world, which are shut out from the life-giving light of truth, has America been chosen; and her high example shall smite unto death the tyranny of kings, hierarchs [people in authority], and oligarchs, and carry the glad tidings of peace and good will where myriads [great numbers] now endure an existence scarcely more enviable than that of beasts of the field. Who, then, can doubt that our country is destined to be *the great nation* of futurity?

Source: John O'Sullivan, "The Great Nation of Futurity," *The United States Democratic Review* 6 (1839)

4. In this article, John O'Sullivan describes manifest destiny several years before he actually used that term in another article on the annexation of Texas. How does this excerpt show the impact of time and place on the ideas expressed here?

   1. By comparing the United States to a church
   2. By exhibiting an ultrapatriotic view of the United States
   3. By referring to conflicts with other nations
   4. By suggesting that freedom is less important than expansion

5. On the basis of your reading of this excerpt, who are manifest destiny's stakeholders?

   1. All Americans
   2. American businesses
   3. Kings, hierarchs, and oligarchs
   4. Religious congregations

Questions 6–8 refer to the excerpt below.

C. The Citizenship Question

Source: Wikimedia Commons

Dred Scott, c. 1857

The question is simply this: Can a Negro, whose ancestors were imported into this country, and sold as slaves, become a member of the political community formed and brought into existence by the Constitution of the United States, and as such become entitled to all the rights, and privileges, and immunities, guarantied by that instrument to the citizen? One of which rights is the privilege of suing in a court of the United States in the cases specified in the Constitution. . . .

We think they [people of African ancestry] are not [citizens], and that they are not included, and were not intended to be included, under the words "citizens" in the Constitution, and can therefore claim none of the rights and privileges which that instrument provides for and secures to citizens of the United States. On the contrary, they were at that time considered as a subordinate and inferior class of beings, who has been subjugated by the dominant race, and, whether emancipated or not, yet remained subject to their authority, and had no rights or privileges but such as those who held the power and the Government might choose to grant them.

It is not the province of the court to decide upon the justice or injustice, the policy or impolicy [unsuitableness to the end in view], of these laws. The decision of that question belonged to the political or law-making power; to those who formed the sovereignty and framed the Constitution. The duty of the court is, to interpret the instrument they have framed, with the best lights we can obtain on the subject, and to administer it as we find it, according to its true intent and meaning when it was adopted.

Source: Chief Justice Roger B. Taney, Ruling in the case of *Dred Scott* v. *Sandford*, 1857

6. How does Taney justify his denial of citizenship to people of African ancestry?

    1. He says that they are not citizens because they cannot file lawsuits.
    2. He says only slaves born in the United States can be citizens.
    3. He says that the Constitution did not consider them citizens.
    4. He says only emancipated slaves can be citizens.

7. How does this ruling reflect change and continuity in American history?

    1. It is the first time a Supreme Court ruling recognized that free African Americans have all the rights, privileges, and immunities of citizens.
    2. It marks a change in the status of African Americans, from people imported as slaves to members of the political community.
    3. It says that emancipated slaves do not have the same rights as free-born African Americans.
    4. It is one of many rulings restricting the rights of African Americans based on a narrow interpretation of the Constitution's intent.

8. What was the result of the ruling in *Dred Scott* v. *Sandford*?

    1. Dred Scott was allowed to sue for his freedom.
    2. Scott won his freedom, but did not automatically become a citizen.
    3. No Black person, whether free or slave, could claim U.S. citizenship.
    4. Chief Justice Taney was removed from the Supreme Court.

Short-Essay Questions

Study the two documents and answer the question that follows.

D. Declaration of Sentiments

We hold these truths to be self-evident; that all men and women are created equal; that they are endowed by their Creator with certain inalienable rights; that among these are life, liberty, and the pursuit of happiness; that to secure these rights governments are instituted, deriving their just powers from the consent of the governed. Whenever any form of Government becomes destructive of these ends, it is the right of those who suffer from it to refuse allegiance to it, and to insist upon the institution of a new government, laying its foundation on such principles, and organizing its powers in such form as to them shall seem most likely to effect their safety and happiness. . . . But when a long train of abuses and usurpations, pursuing invariably the same object, evinces a design to reduce them under absolute despotism, it is their duty to throw off such government, and to provide new guards for their future security. Such has been the patient sufferance of the women under this government, and such is now the necessity which constrains them to demand the equal station to which they are entitled.

Source: Elizabeth Cady Stanton, Declaration of Sentiments, 1848

E. An Abolitionist's Creed

I am a believer in that portion of the Declaration of American Independence in which it is set forth, as among self-evident truths, "that all men are created equal; that they are endowed by their Creator with certain inalienable rights; that among these are life, liberty, and the pursuit of happiness." Hence, I am an Abolitionist. Hence, I cannot but regard oppression in every form— and most of all, that which turns a man into a thing—with indignation and abhorrence. Not to cherish these feelings would be recreancy [shameful cowardice] to principle. They who desire me to be dumb on the subject of slavery, unless I will open my mouth in its defense, ask me to give the lie to my professions, to degrade my manhood, and to stain my soul. I will not be a liar, a poltroon, or a hypocrite, to accommodate any party, to gratify any sect, to escape any odium or peril, to save any interest, to preserve any institution, or to promote any object. Convince me that one man may rightfully make another man his slave, and I will no longer subscribe to the Declaration of Independence. Convince me that liberty is not the inalienable birthright of every human being, of whatever complexion or clime [region or climate], and I will give that instrument to the consuming fire. I do not know how to espouse freedom and slavery together.

Source: William Lloyd Garrison, "No Compromise with the Evil of Slavery," 1854

1. In a short essay, describe the historical context surrounding the two documents above. Then identify and explain the similarities and differences between the ideas expressed in these documents.

Study the two documents and answer the question that follows.

F. Southern Reaction to Lincoln's Election

CHARLESTON, S. C., *November* 8, 1860.—Yesterday on the train, just before we reached Fernandina, a woman called out: "That settles the hash." Tanny touched me on the shoulder and said: "Lincoln's elected." "How do you know?" "The man over there has a telegram."

The excitement was very great. Everybody was talking at the same time. One, a little more moved than the others, stood up and said despondently: "The die is cast; no more vain regrets; sad forebodings are useless; the stake is life or death." "Did you ever!" was the prevailing exclamation, and some one cried out: "Now that the Black radical Republicans have the power I suppose they will [John] Brown us all. " No doubt of it. . . .

I now wish I had a chronicle of the two delightful and eventful years that have just passed. Those delights have fled and one's breath is taken away to think what events have since crowded in. Like the woman's record in her journal, we have had "earthquakes, as usual"—daily shocks.

At Fernandina I saw young men running up a Palmetto flag, and shouting a little prematurely, "South Carolina has seceded!" I was overjoyed to find Florida so sympathetic, but Tanny told me the young men were Gadsdens, Porchers, and Gourdins, names as inevitably South Carolinian as Moses and Lazarus are Jewish.

Source: Mary Boykin Chesnut, *A Diary from Dixie*, 1860–1865 (first published in 1905)

G. Lincoln on the Civil War in 1865

Neither party expected for the war the magnitude or the duration which it has already attained. Neither anticipated that the cause of the conflict might cease with or even before the conflict itself should cease. Each looked for an easier triumph, and a result less fundamental and astounding. . . . Fondly do we hope, fervently do we pray, that this mighty scourge of war may speedily pass away. Yet, if God wills that it continue until all the wealth piled by the bondsman's [slave's] two hundred and fifty years of unrequited toil shall be sunk, and until every drop of blood drawn with the lash shall be paid by another drawn with the sword, as was said three thousand years ago, so still it must be said "the judgments of the Lord are true and righteous altogether."

   With malice toward none, with charity for all, with firmness in the right as God gives us to see the right, let us strive on to finish the work we are in, to bind up the nation's wounds, to care for him who shall have borne the battle and for his widow and his orphan, to do all which may achieve and cherish a just and lasting peace among ourselves and with all nations.

Source: Abraham Lincoln, Second Inaugural Address, March 4, 1865

2. In a short essay, describe the historical context surrounding the two documents above. Then analyze and explain how the point of view of Chesnut's diary excerpt affects its reliability as a source of evidence.

Period 1

Document #1

From the Articles of Confederation 1781

Article II. Each state retains its sovereignty, freedom and independence, and every Power, Jurisdiction and right, which is not by this confederation expressly delegated to the United States, in Congress assembled.

Article III. The said states hereby severally enter into a firm league of friendship with each other, for their common defence, the security of their Liberties, and their mutual and general welfare, binding themselves to assist each other, against all force offered to, or attacks made upon them, or any of them, on account of religion, sovereignty, trade, or any other pretence whatever.

Source: founders.archives.gov

1. What were the circumstances under which the Articles of Confederation were first created?

_____

_____

_____

_____

Document #2

FEDERALIST No. 10

James Madison

To the People of the State of New York:

AMONG the numerous advantages promised by a well constructed Union, none deserves to be more accurately developed than its tendency to break and control the violence of faction. The friend of popular governments never finds himself so much alarmed for their character and fate, as when he contemplates their propensity to this dangerous vice. He will not fail, therefore, to set a due value on any plan which, without violating the principles to which he is attached, provides a proper cure for it. The instability, injustice, and confusion introduced into the public councils, have, in truth, been the mortal diseases under which popular governments have everywhere perished. . . .

Source: foundingfathers.info

2. In Federalist No. 10 Madison argues to end factions by creating a well constructed Union. Given the conditions in 1787 is this a strong argument for the new constitution? Explain.

_____

_____

_____

_____

Document #3

South Carolina Exposition and Protest (1828)

by John C. Calhoun [written during the Nullification Crisis]

If it be conceded, as it must be by every one who is the least conversant with our institutions, that the sovereign powers delegated are divided between the General and State Governments, and that the latter hold their portion by the same tenure as the former, it would seem impossible to deny to the States the right of deciding on the infractions of their powers, and the proper remedy to be applied for their correction. The right of judging, in such cases, is an essential attribute of sovereignty, of which the States cannot be divested without losing their sovereignty itself, and being reduced to a subordinate corporate condition. In fact, to divide power, and to give to one of the parties the exclusive right of judging of the portion allotted to each, is, in reality, not to divide it at all; and to reserve such exclusive right to the General Government (it matters not by what department) to be exercised, is to convert it, in fact, into a great consolidated government, with unlimited powers, and to divest the States, in reality, of all their rights, it is impossible to understand the force of terms, and to deny so plain a conclusion.

Source Johnson, Allen, ed., *Readings in American Constitutional History, 1776–1876, Part 1*

3. How does Calhoun see the division of powers between the Federal and State governments in danger?

_____

_____

_____

_____

Document #4

This excerpt was first published in the abolitionist newspaper *The North Star* on April 3, 1851. It discusses the Fugitive Slave Law passed by Congress on September 18, 1850.

The following resolutions were adopted at the recent Convention of the Western New York Anti-Slavery Society, held in Corinthian Hall: Resolved [Agreed], . . .That they who teach obedience to the Fugitive Slave Law, while they admit that the law is unjust, cruel and disgraceful, prove themselves destitute of moral principle, if not of moral sense, and they are to be ranked with the hardened and obdurate [heartless] creatures who, for a few paltry dollars, will perform the disgusting office of slave-catcher to the slaveholder. . . . Resolved, That we regard the Fugitive Slave Law of the last Congress as a conspiracy against the liberties of our country, which ought to be resisted at all hazards of property and life, by all who love God and revere [honor] the memories of our revolutionary fathers.

Source: *The North Star,* April 3, 1851

4. What action is likely to follow from the people who support this resolution?

_____

_____

_____

_____

Document #5

Declaration of the Immediate Causes Which Induce and Justify the Secession of South Carolina from the Federal Union. Adopted December 24, 1860

These ends it endeavored to accomplish by a Federal Government, in which each State was recognized as an equal, and had separate control over its own institutions. The right of property in slaves was recognized by giving to free persons distinct political rights, by giving them the right to represent, and burthening them with direct taxes for three-fifths of their slaves; by authorizing the importation of slaves for twenty years; and by stipulating for the rendition of fugitives from labor. We affirm that these ends for which this Government was instituted have been defeated, and the Government itself has been made destructive of them by the action of the non-slaveholding States. Those States have assume the right of deciding upon the propriety of our domestic institutions; and have denied the rights of property established in fifteen of the States and recognized by the Constitution; they have denounced as sinful the institution of slavery; they have permitted open establishment among them of societies, whose avowed object is to disturb the peace and to eloign the property of the citizens of other States. They have encouraged and assisted thousands of our slaves to leave their homes; and those who remain, have been incited by emissaries, books and pictures to servile insurrection.

Source: Gillman, Howard, and Graber, Mark A., *The Complete American Constitutionalism: Volume 5, Part 1*

5. How might the arguments of South Carolina in 1860 be seen as similar to those by the founding fathers in the Declaration of Independence in 1776?

_____

_____

_____

_____

Document #6

WILLIAM LLOYD GARRISON, "NO COMPROMISE WITH THE EVIL OF SLAVERY" (1854)

The abolitionism which I advocate is as absolute as the law of God, and as unyielding as his throne. It admits of no compromise. Every slave is a stolen man; every slaveholder is a man stealer. By no precedent, no example, no law, no compact, no purchase, no bequest, no inheritance, no combination of circumstances, is slaveholding right or justifiable. While a slave remains in his fetters, the land must have no rest. Whatever sanctions his doom must be pronounced accursed.

Source: Thompson, Bradley C., ed., *Antislavery Political Writings, 1833–1860*

6. How would proponents on each side of the slavery debate view Garrison's speech?

_____

_____

_____

_____

7. **Civic Literacy Document-Based Essay:** Select two examples of actions or opinions that affected the creation of a strong federal government before 1865 and for each (1) describe the historical circumstances, (2) discuss to what extent it led to a stronger or weaker federal system and (3) explain how this action or opinion influenced the government of the United States.

_____

_____

_____

_____

_____

_____

_____

_____

_____

_____

_____

_____

_____

_____

_____

_____

_____

_____

_____

_____

_____

_____

_____

_____

CHAPTER 4

The Post–Civil War Era (1865–1900)

Chapter Overview

From the middle to the end of the 19th century, the United States grappled with serious issues surrounding civil rights and opportunities for both U.S. citizens and those wishing to become so.

Reconstruction For 12 years after the war, Northern troops occupied parts of the South. These postwar years are known as Reconstruction. New amendments to the Constitution abolished slavery throughout the United States, gave citizenship to formerly enslaved people, and removed hurdles to voting based on race. But once Reconstruction was over, Southern states systematically deprived African Americans of their civil rights.

Women's Rights Many reformers who had worked tirelessly for the abolition of slavery now turned their attention to women's rights. Two of the most important rights were the right of married women to own and manage their own property and the right to vote.

Westward The building of the nation's first transcontinental railroad opened the interior of the country to White settlement. But first Native Americans, the original occupants of that land, had to be removed. After a series of wars, Native Americans were placed on reservations and deprived of their traditional livelihood. By 1890, increased population densities in the West revealed that a western "frontier" no longer existed.

New Populations Following the Mexican War, the United States annexed much of the land in the Southwest. Along with the land came most of the Mexicans who already lived there—some for centuries. The peace treaty with Mexico gave them citizenship and recognized their property rights. However, Anglo-American settlers who wanted their land did not recognize those rights.

Chinese immigrants were first attracted in large numbers by the California gold rush. More were recruited to build the western portion of the first transcontinental railroad. In spite of their contributions, they were denied the right to become citizens. In 1882, Congress passed a law prohibiting any more Chinese immigration.

Civic Literacy: Discrimination The issue of discrimination against Americans and recent immigrants runs throughout this chapter. African Americans, women, Native Americans, Mexican Americans, and Chinese immigrants all experienced discrimination on the basis of race, sex, or ethnicity.

New York Social Studies Framework

Key Idea 11. 4: The Post–Civil War Era

Reconstruction resulted in political reunion and expanded constitutional rights. However, those rights were undermined, and issues of inequality continued for African Americans, women, Native Americans, Mexican Americans, and Chinese immigrants.

Source: *New York State Grades 9–12 Social Studies Framework*

Civic Literacy Essay: Describe Historical Circumstances

The first requirement of the civic literacy essay itself is that it describe historical circumstances surrounding the constitutional or civic issue that is the focus of the prompt. Contextualization helps you make historical connections by placing historical documents within a larger context. This means connecting historical documents with what else was happening at the same time, looking at how the event fits in with events that came before and after it, and examining what larger processes were at play. Below are some of the historical thinking skills that will help you place the documents provided in context:

- Identify the impact of time and place.

- Identify relationships in time.

- Identify stakeholders and issues.

- Identify issues related to point of view or bias.

Think of the "five Ws" (Who, What, When, Where, Why) that you may have learned in elementary school. When you are analyzing a document or thinking about a historical event, ask yourself questions based on the five Ws to help you see the larger context.

Application: To help you contextualize, write a question you could ask about a document or issue for each of the five Ws:

Who: ——————————————————————————————

What: ——————————————————————————————

Where: ——————————————————————————————

When: ——————————————————————————————

Why: ——————————————————————————————

Key Terms by Theme

Governance
Andrew Johnson (p.115)
Reconstruction (p.115)
Black Codes (p. 117)
Jim Crow (p. 118)
Wounded Knee Creek (p. 131)
reservation (p. 132)
Chinese Exclusion Act (p. 138)

Civics
Freedmen's Bureau (p. 116)

Plessy v. Ferguson (p. 118)
separate but equal (p. 119)

Social Structures
carpetbaggers (p. 117)
scalawags (p. 117)
Ku Klux Klan (KKK) (p. 118)
Seneca Falls Convention (p. 123)
Elizabeth Cady Stanton (p. 123)
suffragist (p. 123)

Susan B. Anthony (p. 123)

Movement
Homestead Act (p. 129)
manifest destiny (p. 135)

Identity
Plains Indians (p. 130)
assimilation (p. 132)
nativist (p. 138)

Lesson 1 *Reconstruction and Repression*

Conceptual Understanding 11.4a Between 1865 and 1900, constitutional rights were extended to African Americans. However, their ability to exercise these rights was undermined by individuals, groups, and government institutions.

Booker T. Washington was nine years old when he was freed from slavery in 1865. In his autobiography, he describes attending evening classes after working all day. While working in a coal mine, he heard of a "great school for colored people"—the Hampton Institute. After graduating, Washington taught Native Americans in Hampton's night school for a year before a new opportunity presented itself. A new school was opening in Alabama to train African American teachers. When Alabama officials approached Hampton's Institute's founder to suggest a White man to take charge of the school, he instead suggested Washington. The Tuskegee Institute opened on July 4, 1881, and became Washington's life-work.

Analyze a Primary Source

Booker T. Washington, Former Slaves' Desire for Education

Read Closely: Specifics
When reading a primary source, recognizing specific details helps make general points more concrete, and therefore, easier to understand and recall. Circle the words or phrases in this excerpt that tell you the specific sort of education that African Americans wanted.

Read Closely: Evidence
Specific evidence in a primary source helps bolster the value of a primary source. Washington provides reasons for African Americans' misconceptions about education. What evidence does he provide for their desire for a classical education? Underline the phrase or sentence that explains this.

Read Closely: Comparing
Comparisons help readers to see a writer's point from a new perspective. Washington compares the federal government during Reconstruction to a mother and the freed slaves to her children. During Reconstruction, Freedmen's Bureaus cared for formerly enslaved people by providing clothing, food, and medical care.

The years from 1867 to 1878 I think may be called the period of Reconstruction. This included the time that I spent as a student at Hampton and as a teacher in West Virginia. During the whole of the Reconstruction period two ideas were constantly agitating the minds of the colored people, or, at least, the minds of a large part of the race. One of these was the craze for Greek and Latin learning, and the other was a desire to hold office.

It could not have been expected that a people who had spent generations in slavery, and before that generations in the darkest heathenism, could at first form any proper conception of what an education meant. In every part of the South, during the Reconstruction period, schools, both day and night, were filled to overflowing with people of all ages and conditions, some being as far along in age as sixty and seventy years. The ambition to secure an education was most praiseworthy and encouraging. . . .

During the whole of the Reconstruction period our people throughout the South looked to the Federal Government for everything, very much as a child looks to its mother. This was not unnatural. The central government gave them freedom, and the whole Nation had been enriched for more than two centuries by the labor of the Negro. Even as a youth, and later in manhood, I had the feeling that it was cruelly wrong in the central government, at the beginning of our freedom, to fail to make some provision for the general education of our people in addition to what the states might do, so that the people would be the better prepared for the duties of citizenship.

Source: Booker T. Washington, *Up from Slavery: An Autobiography* (Garden City, N.Y.: Doubleday & Co., 1901), pages 80–83.

Constitutional Reforms

After four years of fighting, mostly in the South, the former Confederacy was in ruins. In addition, Southern planters and farmers had lost their captive labor force when Lincoln's Emancipation Proclamation began the process of freeing 4 million enslaved African Americans. In the North, the Republican government in Washington had to solve two problems: how to readmit the Southern states to the Union, and how to protect the rights of formerly enslaved people.

Initial Plans

President Lincoln favored lenient treatment of the South. He did not want the Southern states treated as conquered territory, but to be readmitted with equal status to those of the North. He proposed two conditions for a seceded state's readmission:

1. ten percent of the state's voters would need to take an oath of allegiance to the United States

2. the new state government would be required to abolish slavery

But Lincoln was assassinated before he had a chance to guide his plan through Congress.

After Lincoln's assassination, his vice president, **Andrew Johnson**, became president. Many Northern Republicans distrusted Johnson, a Democrat from Tennessee—one of the states that had seceded. Johnson's plan for reconstruction was similar to Lincoln's. However, he added a third condition for readmission of a seceded state: it must deny the right to vote to certain Confederate leaders. Johnson did not trust Southern aristocrats and wanted to show his support for the small tradespeople and farmers of the South.

Congressional Reconstruction Radical Republicans in Congress wanted to punish the South for its role in the war by treating the seceded states as conquered territories. They also wanted to grant political rights to the newly freed slaves. Under their plan, the South would be occupied by federal troops and governed by army generals. The troops would be withdrawn from a state after it had adopted a new state constitution acceptable to Congress.

The Radical Republicans were able to pass their **Reconstruction** plan in spite of Johnson's repeated vetoes. By far the most important measures passed by the Radical Republicans were three Constitutional amendments guaranteeing the rights of newly free African Americans. These amendments are sometimes referred to as the Civil War Amendments or the Reconstruction Amendments.

Thirteenth Amendment (1865) This amendment made slavery illegal in every state of the Union, not just the Confederacy. The thirteenth is the only amendment in United States history to carry the signature of a president. In signing it, Lincoln demonstrated his commitment to ending slavery for good.

Fourteenth Amendment (1868) This amendment defined the rights of American citizenship as follows: "All persons born or naturalized in the United States, and subject to the jurisdiction thereof, are citizens of the United States and of the state wherein they reside." In addition, the Fourteenth Amendment prohibited the states from interfering with the "privileges and immunities" of citizens of the United States. Thus all African Americans (including freed slaves) were to be U.S. citizens with rights equal to those of other citizens.

The Fourteenth Amendment also prohibited the states from depriving a person of life, liberty, or property without due process of law. Nor could the states deny a citizen the equal protection of the laws. The rights protected by the Constitution now applied, in theory, to the state governments as well as the federal

Read Closely: Main Idea
Locate and understand the main idea of a primary source. This can often, but not always, be found in the source's concluding sentences. Throughout this excerpt, Washington provides examples of the former slaves' need and desire for an education. He concludes by saying that this will prepare them to be better citizens.

Read Closely: Motivation
When you read about disagreements between individuals or groups, think about the motivations behind their actions. President Johnson's plan for reconstruction was similar to Lincoln's, but Radical Republicans opposed it. What might have been their motivation for this?

Read Closely: Details
The Fourteenth Amendment defines citizenship, but does not refer to race. Why do we know that former slaves were now considered to be citizens?

Read Closely: Details
Writers often start a paragraph with a general idea and then provide details. How does the paragraph on the Freedmen's Bureau show this pattern?

government. In practice, state governments in the South waged a campaign to deny African Americans equal protection under the Constitution for nearly another hundred years.

Fifteenth Amendment (1870) The Fifteenth Amendment stated the following: "The right of citizens of the United States to vote shall not be denied or abridged by the United States or by any State on account of race, color, or previous condition of servitude." It did not, however, guarantee African Americans the ability to vote. State governments in the South used other means, described below, to deny the vote to their Black fellow citizens.

Reconstruction

For African Americans in the South, making the transition from slavery to freedom was an enormous challenge. At first, they had high hopes that the U.S. government would protect their rights and help them to take their place in Southern society as landowning farmers.

The Northern victory in the Civil War and the ending of slavery gave formerly enslaved people an opportunity to move to both the North and the West. In addition, Reconstruction policies gave African Americans in the South a chance to seek economic advancement, acquire an education, and gain some social equality. The federal government's protection of these rights during the Reconstruction period was absolutely revolutionary in nature.

Freedmen's Bureau A new U.S. government agency that emerged after the war was the **Freedmen's Bureau** (1865). Its task was to aid the nearly 4 million former slaves, or freedmen. In the South, the bureau built and operated schools for African Americans, who as slaves had deliberately been kept illiterate. Thousands of formerly enslaved people took advantage of the educational opportunities provided by the Freedmen's Bureau by attending schools and colleges for the first time. The bureau also provided emergency aid in the form of clothing, food, and medical supplies.

Source: Wikimedia Commons

The man representing the Freedmen's Bureau is shown here as the only barrier against racial violence.

African Americans in Government In the early years of Reconstruction (1868–1872), Black people in the South had the full support of Northern Republicans and U.S. troops. During this period, many African Americans won election to seats in Southern legislatures, and 14 served in the U.S. Congress. Half of the Black lawmakers were former slaves, and half had attended college. As a group, they supported causes such as the protection of civil rights and federal aid to education.

Republicans in the South During Reconstruction, thousands of Northerners moved to the South, seeing opportunities for both political power and economic gain. Northerners campaigned for seats in the legislatures created by the South's new state constitutions. They ran as Republicans and counted on African Americans' support at the polls.

In 1868, seven Southern states held elections. Aided by the nearly unanimous support of freedmen, Northern Republicans won four (of seven) governorships, ten (out of fourteen) seats in the U.S. Senate, and twenty (out of thirty-five) seats in the U.S. House of Representatives.

White Southerners accused these Northerners of profiting from the region's economic distress and political weakness. They scornfully referred to these Northern transplants as **carpetbaggers**. But they considered fellow White Southerners who cooperated with the Northerners to be even worse. Called **scalawags**, these people were believed to have only one motive: to share in the Northerners' corrupt schemes.

The chief interests of many White Southerners during Reconstruction were as follows:

- to revive their war-torn economy

- to regain control of their state governments

- to reduce the political power of Black Southerners, and

- to deny these freedmen advancement and equality in society

The End of Reconstruction As time passed, many Northerners grew tired of Reconstruction. They became less concerned about protecting the rights of African Americans and more interested in private pursuits. By 1875, the Civil War had been over for ten years. Many people wanted to put it behind them by withdrawing troops from the South. As public opinion shifted, Radical Republicans lost their grip on Congress. Toward the end of President Ulysses S. Grant's first term (1869–1872), there was a more moderate Congress. In 1872, Congress passed the Amnesty Act, which restored voting rights to about 160,000 former Confederates.

Segregation, Violence, and Restriction

The first year after the Civil War was a time of terrible confusion. Southerners held conventions to organize new postwar state governments. President Johnson accepted the conventions as legitimate if they complied with the terms of his Reconstruction plan.

Black Codes Each of these conventions drew up a list of measures for restricting the rights of former slaves. These measures were known as **Black Codes**. These restrictions included prohibiting African Americans from carrying firearms, starting businesses, appearing on the streets after sunset, renting or leasing farmland, and traveling without a permit.

> **Read Closely: Similarity and Difference**
> Recognizing similarities in different terms can help you understand their relationship. The nicknames *carpetbaggers* and *scalawags* refer to two different kinds of people. How were they similar and how did they differ?

Read Closely: Actions and Reactions

Historians look at events and try to explain what happened and why. Often an action causes a reaction, which in turn leads to another reaction. What led to the Black Codes, and what happened as a result of them?

White Southerners argued that the codes were necessary to maintain order. But to other Americans, it was obvious that they were meant to deprive African Americans of their civil rights. The Civil Rights Act of 1866 combated the Black Codes by giving the federal government the authority to protect the civil rights of Black Americans.

The Ku Klux Klan Former Confederate soldiers and other White Southerners wanted to regain political power. In every Southern state, they formed secret societies such as the Knights of the White Camellia and the **Ku Klux Klan (KKK)**. The KKK was formed in 1866 in Pulaski, Tennessee. Its first leader was former Confederate general Nathan Bedford Forrest. Members dressed in White sheets and other disguises to hide their identities. They used lynchings, the burning of African American homes and schools, and other attacks to terrorize the newly-freed African American population.

The Ku Klux Klan and other secret societies grew in number and strength. In response, Congress passed the Enforcement, or Force, Acts in 1870 and 1871. For a brief time, these allowed Federal troops to combat the Klan and other groups committing acts of terror against African Americans. Also in response, some Black Southerners took up arms in defense of their homes and families. In spite of any short-term successes by Federal forces, it became clear that the government either could not or would not enforce its own civil rights laws.

Election of 1876 and Compromise of 1877 By 1876, federal troops occupied only three Southern states: South Carolina, Florida, and Louisiana. After troops left the rest of the South, the Democrats returned to power. In those states, the Democratic candidate for president, Samuel Tilden of New York, won every electoral vote. The Republican candidate, Rutherford B. Hayes, could claim victory in only the three occupied states. Even in those states, however, there were contradictory sets of returns.

A special commission was called to decide who had won. Republicans on the commission outnumbered Democrats, and Hayes was declared the winner by one electoral vote. Southern Democrats were angered, but the political crisis was solved by compromise. Meeting in secret, Republican and Democratic leaders agreed that Hayes would be the next president. In exchange, Hayes would order the last federal troops to leave the South. The North's commitment to Reconstruction was over, and African Americans in the South were abandoned to White political rule.

Civil Rights Cases Many White Americans, in the North as well as in the South, regarded Black people as their social inferiors. In many cities in both regions, authorities enforced racial prejudice through practices that kept Black and White people from mixing in public places—railroad cars, streetcars, restaurants, hotels, and so on.

The Civil Rights Act of 1875 prohibited owners of railroads, restaurants, and other public places from discriminating against African American customers. For a few years, the law was generally obeyed. Beginning in 1881, however, Southern states adopted "**Jim Crow**" laws that enforced strict segregation of the races. By the 1890s, segregation was the rule everywhere in the South. African Americans were strictly prohibited from entering public places that had been reserved "for Whites only."

In 1896, when it upheld the ***Plessy v. Ferguson*** decision, the Supreme Court endorsed such racial segregation. Homer Plessy, a Black citizen of Louisiana, sued a railroad company for preventing him from entering a railroad car set aside for Whites. In this landmark decision, the Supreme Court ruled in favor of the property owner and against the African American petitioner. Because the railroad provided "**separate but equal**" facilities for Blacks, the Court decided that the equal protection clause of the Constitution had not been violated. (In reality, while facilities for African Americans were decidedly separate, they were by no means equal.) For many years the Court used the standard of "separate but equal" to justify segregation.

Restrictions on Voting Rights Southern Whites generally blamed Republicans for the hardships they suffered from war and Reconstruction. After Reconstruction, they made sure that Democrats in their region would be strong enough to win every Southern election. In a short time, the South became virtually a one-party region. From 1880 to 1924, Democratic candidates for president won all the electoral votes of the Southern states.

The Fourteenth Amendment had temporarily deprived Confederate officers of their vote. After Reconstruction, the Southern states found ways to prevent Black citizens from voting. In this way, they could ensure that the Democratic Party would return to power. Each Southern state passed a number of laws that made it either difficult or impossible for African Americans to vote. Between these laws and intimidation by groups such as the Ku Klux Klan, African Americans, who would have voted for Republican candidates, were kept from voting. The Southern states returned to the Democratic Party.

Read Closely: Unintended Consequences
Sometimes actions have unintended consequences. The Radical Republicans wanted to punish the South with a harsh Reconstruction plan. How did this end up backfiring on them?

Methods Used to Prevent African Americans from Voting		
Method	**Voting Law**	**How the Law Discriminated Against African Americans**
1. Literacy test	Voters must take a test to prove they can read and write.	Many freedmen had never been taught to read or write. Examiners would deliberately pass Whites and fail Blacks.
2. Poll tax	Citizens must pay a tax to the state before being allowed to vote.	Most black Southerners were denied the opportunities and resources available to their White counterparts and therefore, could not afford to pay the tax.
3. "Grandfather clause"	A person whose grandfather had voted before 1867 could vote without having to pass a literacy test.	Only White people had grandfathers who voted before 1867.

Civic Literacy: Power
Before the Civil War, slaveholders had power over African Americans in the South. During Reconstruction, Radical Republicans used their power to try to reshape the politics of the South and give civil rights to the freed slaves. After Reconstruction, Southern Whites reasserted their power over African Americans.

Freedmen Persevere

Before the Civil War, the enslaved African Americans of the South were denied citizenship. The Thirteenth Amendment ended slavery and the Fourteenth Amendment made citizens of all people "born or naturalized within the United States." For most African Americans, the road to citizenship had taken almost 250 years. Along that road, many African Americans had fought in both the Revolutionary War and the Civil War, seeking freedom. Citizenship, however, did not mean true equality. A series of court rulings following the Reconstruction period held that "separate but equal" did not violate the Fourteenth Amendment.

Read Closely: Contrasting Terms
The word *however* often signals a contrast with an idea expressed previously, such as distinguishing between two similar words. What point is the author trying to make by contrasting *citizenship* and *equality*?

African American Hopes For Black Southerners, making the transition from slavery to freedom was an enormous challenge. At first, they had high hopes that the U.S. government would protect their rights and help them take their place in Southern society as landowning farmers.

In the early years of Reconstruction, it was widely rumored that the government would give every formerly enslaved family in the South 40 acres of land and a mule. Radical Republicans, who favored the idea of distributing land to freed slaves, fed these hopes. The adoption of the Fifteenth Amendment gave African Americans reason to believe that the U.S. government would do everything in its power to protect their civil rights as voters. But the end of Reconstruction and the withdrawal of federal troops dashed those hopes.

Economic Realities The poorest Southerners, both Black and White, could not afford to pay rents or buy mules for plowing. They were forced to farm plots owned by big landowners. In return for farming a piece of land, they paid a certain share of the crop to the landlord. These sharecroppers, as they were called, were often unable to pay their debts for many reasons—worn out land, crop failures, low crop prices, high prices for farm supplies, and so on. Thus, many African Americans were still economically in bondage.

The Exodusters In 1862, Congress passed the Homestead Act, which granted 160 acres of public land in the American West to anyone who was all of the following:

- At least 21 years old or the head of a family

- Able to pay a small filing fee

- Willing to work and improve the land (including building a residence)

This act gave thousands of African Americans in the South a chance to own land. They moved to Kansas, Nebraska, the Indian Territory (now Oklahoma), the Dakota Territory, and elsewhere in the West. More than 25,000 African Americans left the South for Kansas alone during the 1870s and 1880s in a migration known as the Exoduster Movement. There, Black farmers found racial attitudes somewhat more hospitable than they had been in the South.

The Morrill Acts and Black Colleges The Land Grant College Act of 1862, or the Morrill Act, provided grants of land to finance colleges of agriculture. Because most Southern public educational institutions were racially segregated, Congress passed a Second Morrill Act in 1890. It required states with racially segregated public education systems to create a land-grant institution for Black students whenever one was created for White students. As a result, public land-grant institutions were established in each of the Southern states. Eventually, there were 16 such institutions for African Americans, offering courses in agriculture and in mechanical and industrial subjects.

Before this, most of the Black colleges and universities in the South had been established with the assistance of Northern religious organizations. One exception, the Tuskegee Institute, was created by the Alabama State Legislature, with a yearly appropriation of $2,000. Its first principal was Booker T. Washington, a formerly enslaved man who had worked his way through the Hampton Normal and Agricultural Institute in Virginia, which had been founded by the American Missionary Association.

Speak and Listen: Point of View With a partner, take turns describing why the point of view of some African Americans in 1880 was hopeful and the point of view of others was not. Take notes on what your partner says.

Application: Interpret a Primary Source

Read the excerpt and answer the questions that follow it.

Testimony of a Black Congressman

Think of it for a moment; here am I, a member of your honorable body, representing one of the largest and wealthiest districts in the State of Mississippi, and possibly in the South; a district composed of persons of different races, religions, and nationalities: and yet, when I leave my home to come to the capital of the nation, to take part in the deliberations of the House and to participate with you in making laws for the government of this great Republic, . . . I am treated, not as an American citizen, but as a brute. Forced to occupy a filthy smoking-car both night and day, with drunkards, gamblers, and criminals; and for what? Not that I am unable or unwilling to pay my way; not that I am obnoxious in my personal appearance or disrespectful in my conduct; but simply because I happen to be of a darker complexion. If this treatment was confined to persons of our own sex we could possibly afford to endure it. But such is not the case. Our wives and our daughters, our sisters and our mothers are subjected to the same insults and to the same uncivilized treatment. . . . The only moments of my life when I am necessarily compelled to question my loyalty to my Government or my devotion to the flag of my country is when I read of outrages having been committed upon innocent colored people and . . . when I leave my home to go traveling.

Source: John R. Lynch, member of the U.S. House of Representatives from Mississippi, 1872

1. Describe the context in which a member of Congress was treated in this fashion.

   _____

   _____

   _____

2. What effect do you think the situation Lynch describes had on Black Southerners during this era?

   _____

   _____

   _____

3. How reliable do you think Congressman Lynch's description is? Explain your reasoning.

   _____

   _____

   _____

Lesson 2 *Exclusion of Women Continues*

Conceptual Understanding
11.4b The 14th and 15th Amendments failed to address the rights of women.

Isabella Bomfree was born into enslavement in New York in 1797. In 1827, an abolitionist family bought her freedom. She moved to New York City a year later, and in 1843, changed her name to Sojourner Truth. After meeting Elizabeth Cady Stanton and Susan B. Anthony, she became a women's rights activist. Truth never learned to read or write, but she was a powerful and charismatic speaker. In 1867 she traveled to New York, where she addressed the first annual meeting of the American Equal Rights Association. Truth died in 1883.

Analyze a Primary Source

Sojourner Truth on Equal Rights for Women

Read Closely: Comparison
Speakers sometimes use comparisons to make their case more forcefully. Notice that this formerly enslaved woman compares men who have rights to slaveholders. Find the passage where Truth tells her listeners whom she is addressing when she says, "you think, like a slaveholder, that you own us" and underline it.

Read Closely: Main Idea
Speakers often repeat their main idea numerous times in a speech to really drive it home. Toward the end, Truth notes that Black men have been given the right to vote. There are references to "our rights," but only two to "equal rights." Circle the two references to equal rights.

Read Closely: Form of the Source
As you read this excerpt, keep in mind that it was not a written speech. Sojourner Truth never learned to read or write, but she was a powerful speaker. Try reading her words aloud to get a better feeling for the impact this speech would have made on her audience.

I have been forty years a slave and forty years free, and would be here forty years more to have equal rights for all. I suppose I am kept here because something remains for me to do; I suppose I am yet to help to break the chain. I have done a great deal of work; as much as a man, but did not get so much pay. I used to work in the field and bind grain, keeping up with the cradler [the person cutting the grain]; but men doing no more, got twice as much pay; so with the German women. They work in the field and do as much work, but do not get the pay. We do as much, we eat as much, we want as much. I suppose I am about the only colored woman that goes about to speak for the rights of the colored women. I want to keep the thing stirring, now that the ice is cracked. What we want is a little money. You men know that you get as much again as women when you write, or for what you do. When we get our rights we shall not have to come to you for money, for then we shall have money enough in our own pockets; and maybe you will ask us for money. But help us now until we get it. It is a good consolation to know that when we have got this battle once fought we shall not be coming to you any more. You have been having our rights so long, that you think, like a slaveholder, that you own us. I know that it is hard for one who has held the reins for so long to give up; it cuts like a knife. It will feel all the better when it closes up again. I have been in Washington about three years, seeing about these colored people. Now colored men have the right to vote. There ought to be equal rights now more than ever, since colored people have got their freedom.

Source: Sojourner Truth, Address to the First Annual Meeting of the American Equal Rights Association, May 9, 1867

Women's Changing Roles

In the 1800s, expectations of women began to evolve beyond merely serving their families as wives, mothers, and homemakers. But their second-class status in a male-dominated society remained the same. Women had no political power, but many found ways to expand their roles through moral influence. Women took an active role in the fight for the abolition of slavery. Many of the men in the movement, such as the Black abolitionist Frederick Douglass, were allies in the fight for women's rights, including the right to vote. One by one, women broke down barriers to education, employment, and full citizenship.

New Opportunities The Civil War opened up new opportunities for women. With so many men off fighting, women had to take on the roles of teachers, office workers, and shop assistants. In the South, women managed plantations that often included hundreds of enslaved individuals. Thousands of women from both the North and the South served in the war as nurses. More than a million men were killed or wounded in the Civil War. A generation of women—single, widowed, or with disabled husbands—had to support themselves and their families.

After the war, more women had an opportunity to attend colleges and enter professions formerly reserved for men. Women soon dominated the teaching profession—as many as a quarter of all women in New England spent at least some of their lives teaching school children. Nursing also was now open to women. Still others became social workers. But these professions were related to traditional women's roles—childcare and caring for the ill and less fortunate.

> **Read Closely: Turning Point**
> The word *after* suggests a shift from one phase to another. The Civil War was perhaps the biggest turning point in American history. How did it affect women's lives?

Demands for Voting and Property Rights

In 1848, the American women's movement formally commenced at the **Seneca Falls Convention** in New York state. **Elizabeth Cady Stanton** was the chief author of the convention's Declaration of Sentiments, based on the Declaration of Independence. The Declaration argued that the government and society oppressed women. It demands that women be considered full citizens, with the same rights and privileges as men. Among those rights was the right to vote. It was the only one of 12 resolutions that did not pass unanimously. Many thought it went too far, and would hurt the chances of equality in other areas, including property rights, divorce laws, education, and employment.

Upon its publication, the Declaration was ridiculed and criticized by social conservatives, both male and female, who disagreed with the idea of female equality. In time, many of the 68 women and 32 men who had signed it ended up renouncing it.

Suffrage Movement The United States Constitution did not originally guarantee suffrage (the right to vote). It was left up to the states, but it was limited to free men. Most states limited suffrage to men who owned land. Some required voters to pay a tax. By 1820, most states had eliminated the landowning requirement. The tax requirement disappeared more gradually. Still, none of the states permitted women to vote.

The woman suffrage movement proper was born at the Seneca Falls Convention. Participants in the movement (which included both men and women) were known as **suffragists**. Their leaders included **Susan B. Anthony**, Elizabeth Cady Stanton, and Lucy Stone.

Extending Suffrage After the Civil War, the Fourteenth Amendment extended citizenship to former slaves by making any person born or naturalized in the United States a citizen. It also prohibited the states from denying the right to vote to any male citizen who was at least 21 years old. The Fifteenth Amendment specifically said that the right to vote could not be denied to any citizen "on account of race, color, or previous condition of servitude."

Anthony and Stanton opposed passage of the Fourteenth and Fifteenth Amendments as they were worded. The Fourteenth Amendment was the first time the Constitution specifically limited suffrage to men. The Fifteenth Amendment failed to protect the right of women to vote. Anthony and Stanton wanted women included along with African American men. As Stanton wrote, "If that word 'male' be inserted, it will take us a century at least to get it out."

Source: Wikimedia Commons

The Judiciary Committee of the House of Representatives receiving a deputation of female suffragists.

Read Closely: Importance of Place

To understand the importance of geography in history, notice why events happen in one place rather than another. Most of the leaders of the woman suffrage movement lived in the East, but women first achieved the right to vote in the West. How did geography help them accomplish this?

Some suffragists concentrated on trying to persuade each state legislature to grant equal voting rights to women. It was in the western territory of Wyoming, in 1869, that women first achieved the right to vote. By 1896, seven states and territories in the West had granted women the right to vote. By 1910, women in most Western states voted in large numbers, while most women in the East were still denied voting rights. One possible reason for the West's leadership was men's realization that Western women had made many sacrifices and had played a crucial role in settling the frontier.

A Constitutional Amendment The suffrage movement continued into the Progressive Era (1890–1920). Susan B. Anthony worked to win support for an amendment to the U.S. Constitution guaranteeing voting rights for women in *all* the states. This amendment was first introduced in Congress in 1878, but male lawmakers rejected it. Recall that an amendment requires two-thirds of each house of Congress and three-fourths of the state legislatures or conventions. Suffragists persisted by reintroducing the amendment in every session of Congress for the next 40 years.

The suffragists kept up the pressure, asking how the United States could be a democracy if women could not vote. A new generation of suffragists led by Alice Paul and Carrie Chapman Catt replaced the older leadership. Though some men in the Progressive Movement supported suffrage, many thought women should not become involved in politics. Finally in 1919, Congress passed the amendment giving women the right to vote. To become the Nineteenth Amendment, however, at least 36 states had to ratify it.

The first states to ratify were Wisconsin and Michigan. The 36th and final state was Tennessee. Pro- and anti-suffrage activists descended upon Nashville, lobbying the members of the Tennessee House. On August 18, 1920, Harry Burn, a young legislator from East Tennessee, cast the deciding vote. Although Burn wore a red rose indicating that he was against ratification, he voted for the amendment. After his historic vote, Burn had to hide from an anti-ratification mob. The next day he explained that a letter from his mother changed his mind: "I know that a mother's advice is always safest for her boy to follow, and my mother wanted me to vote for ratification."

Property Rights Originally, American property laws followed English common law, under which a woman's property became her husband's upon marriage. This began to change in 1809 when Connecticut passed a law allowing married women to write wills. In 1839, Mississippi became the first state to pass a married women's property act. It guaranteed a married woman's right to the income from her property and protected it from being taken to pay her husband's' debts. However, husbands had the sole right to sell and manage the property.

In 1848—the same year as the Seneca Falls Convention—the state of New York passed the Married Women's Property Act. The basic provisions of that act were as follows:

- A woman retained ownership of any real and personal property she owned at the time of her marriage as well as the income from that property.

- A woman was not liable for her husband's debts.

- A husband was not allowed to dispose of his wife's property except to pay certain debts.

- Any property a married woman received as a gift to herself was her own property and could not be disposed of by her husband.

- Any contracts between two people planning to marry would remain in force after their marriage.

Other states used the New York law as a model for their own laws. By the mid-1870s, most other northern states had passed married women's property acts, and by the end of the century, each of the rest of the states had passed a version.

Susan B. Anthony

Susan Brownell Anthony was born in Adams, Massachusetts, in 1820. She was raised as a Quaker and was inspired throughout her life by the Quaker belief in equality for all. She taught from 1839 to 1849, first in a Quaker seminary and then a female academy. In 1849, Anthony returned to her parents' home near Rochester, New York, where she met many leading abolitionists, including her father's friends Frederick Douglass and William Lloyd Garrison. She became a passionate abolitionist.

In 1851 she met Elizabeth Cady Stanton, one of the organizers of the Seneca Falls Convention and author of the Declaration of Sentiments. (Anthony had not attended the convention, although her mother and a sister had.) The two women became close friends and for the rest of their lives, fought together for women's rights. Anthony campaigned for the reformation of married women's property rights in New York. She also served in the American Anti-Slavery Society. During the early years of the Civil War, she fought for the emancipation of enslaved people.

Read Closely: Contrast
A sentence that begins with *However* often describes a contrast with an idea expressed previously. What is the function of the word *however* at the beginning of the last sentence in the paragraph about property rights?

Read Closely: Motivation
When reading about a person's actions, consider how motivations shape those actions. What likely motivated Susan B. Anthony to become an abolitionist, and later to become a leader in the fight for women's rights?

Fight for Equal Rights Susan B. Anthony, Elizabeth Cady Stanton, and Frederick Douglass founded the American Equal Rights Association in 1866. Douglass had been the only African American at the Seneca Falls Convention, and was one of 32 men who signed the Declaration of Sentiments. He continued to work for women's rights until his death in 1895.

In 1868 Anthony became the publisher and Stanton the editor of *The Revolution*, a weekly women's rights newspaper. *The Revolution* dealt with subjects not normally discussed in mainstream publications such as sex education, domestic violence, and divorce. That year she also organized the Working Women's Association of New York. In May 1869 she and Stanton formed the National Woman Suffrage Association. Anthony became the organization's chief spokesperson.

Source: Library of Congress

Elizabeth Cady Stanton (left) and Susan B. Anthony, 1899

Fight for Woman Suffrage After leaving *The Revolution* in 1870, Anthony went on a series of lecture tours to help pay off the paper's debts. Often accompanied by Stanton, she traveled to California, Michigan, Colorado, and other states to rally support for woman suffrage. She was arrested for voting in the 1872 presidential election. She was found guilty and fined, but never paid the fine.

In 1878 Anthony and Stanton drafted a Constitutional amendment stating, "The right of citizens of the United States to vote shall not be denied or abridged by the United States or by any State on account of sex." It was introduced to Congress that year and every year until it was finally passed in 1918.

In 1890 the National Woman Suffrage Association merged with the more conservative American Woman Suffrage Association to form the National American Woman Suffrage Association. Anthony served as president of the organization from 1892 until 1900. By the time of her death in 1906, she had become a national heroine. A phrase from her last speech, "Failure is Impossible," became the motto of a new generation of suffragists.

Application: Interpret a Primary Source

Read the excerpt and answer the questions that follow it.

Woman Suffrage Must Be Non-Partisan

Every one must see that for a part of the suffrage women to thus ally themselves with the Republican party, another portion with the Democratic party, another with the Populist, another with the Prohibition, another with the Nationalist, and yet another with the Socialist Labor party, would be to divide and distract public thought from women as suffragists to women as Republicans, Populists, etc. To do this may be "good politics," for the different political parties, but it would surely be very "bad politics" for amendment No. XI. . . .

Of course each of the political parties, old and new, would be glad of the help of the women throughout this fall campaign, but who can fail to see that the women who should join one alliance would thereby lose their influence with the men of each of the other parties. They would at once be adjudged partisans, working for the interest of the party with which or to which they were allied. Women of California, you cannot keep the good will and win the good votes of all the good men of all the good parties of the State by allying yourselves with one or the other or all of them! . . .

It is very clear to every student of politics that what is "good politics" for political parties is "mighty poor politics" for a reform measure dependent upon the votes of the members of all parties. It will be time enough for the women of California to enroll themselves as Republicans, Democrats, Populists, etc., after they have the right to vote secured to them by the elimination of the word "male" from the suffrage clause of the constitution.

Source: Susan B. Anthony, article in the *San Francisco Call*, August 2, 1896

1. How does the voting status of women in California fit in with that of women in the West at this time?

   _____

   _____

2. Did the proponents of another reform movement, the anti-slavery movement take the same nonpartisan approach that Anthony urged on proponents of the suffrage movement? Explain.

   _____

   _____

3. To what degree do you think one should be wary of Susan B. Anthony as a source of unbiased information on this topic?

   _____

   _____

Lesson 3 *Destiny and Destruction in the West*

In 1879 Helen Hunt Jackson attended a lecture in Boston by Standing Bear, a leader of the Ponca tribe of Nebraska who had been moved to Indian Territory in Oklahoma in 1878. She was shocked to hear how Native Americans were treated and decided to research and expose the issue, which she did in her book *A Century of Dishonor.* .

Analyze a Primary Source

Helen Hunt Jackson on Government Mistreatment of Native Americans

Read Closely: Analysis
Closely analyze writings such as this to determine the object of the author's criticism. Jackson is critical of the treatment Native Americans received both from White settlers and from the government. Underline the phrase in which Jackson describes the U.S. government's treatment of Native Americans.

Read Closely: Metaphors
A metaphor is a word or phrase that is used to make a comparison, but not taken literally. In the second paragraph, circle the metaphor Jackson uses to describe the treatment Native Americans have suffered throughout their history.

Read Closely: Causes
Read primary sources closely to determine not just outcomes, but causes as well. In the third paragraph, Jackson describes the way in which attitudes about Native Americans turned to actual prejudice over the course of two or three generations.

There is not among these three hundred bands of Indians one which has not suffered cruelly at the hands either of the Government or of White settlers. The poorer, the more insignificant, the more helpless the band, the more certain the cruelty and outrage to which they have been subjected. This is especially true of the bands on the Pacific slope. These Indians found themselves of a sudden surrounded by and caught up in the great influx of gold-seeking settlers, as helpless creatures on a shore are caught up in a tidal wave. There was not time for the Government to make treaties; not even time for communities to make laws. The tale of the wrongs, the oppressions, the murders of the Pacific-slope Indians in the last thirty years would be a volume by itself, and is too monstrous to be believed.

It makes little difference, however, where one opens the record of the history of the Indians; every page and every year has its dark stain. The story of one tribe is the story of all, varied only by differences of time and place; but neither time nor place makes any difference in the main facts. Colorado is as greedy and unjust in 1880 as was Georgia in 1830, and Ohio in 1795; and the United States Government breaks promises now as deftly as then, and with an added ingenuity from long practice.

One of its strongest supports in so doing is the wide-spread sentiment among the people of dislike to the Indian, of impatience with his presence as a "barrier to civilization," and distrust of [them] as a possible danger. The old tales of the frontier life, with its horrors of Indian warfare, have gradually, by two or three generations' telling, produced in the average mind something like an hereditary instinct of unquestioning and unreasoning aversion which it is almost impossible to dislodge or soften.

There are hundreds of pages of unimpeachable testimony on the side of the Indian; but it goes for nothing, is set down as sentimentalism or partisanship, tossed aside and forgotten.

Source: Helen Hunt Jackson, *A Century of Dishonor* (Boston: Roberts Brothers, 1889), pages 337–338.

Policies Spur Expansion

When the Republican Party came to power in 1861, one of its main goals was to support agricultural progress by practically giving away public lands in the West. For this purpose, Congress gave land grants to western railroads. The lawmakers assumed, correctly, that the railroads would sell land to farmers at very low prices. Congress also enacted two laws for disposing of public lands.

Homestead Act (1862) Congress in 1862 passed the **Homestead Act**. It provided available public lands at no financial cost to those willing to settle on them. By the terms of this law, any citizen or immigrant intending to become a citizen could acquire 160 acres of federal land simply by farming it for five years. Labor, not money, was the price of a homestead.

Morrill Act (1862) This act gave huge tracts of federal land to the states. The only condition was that the states build colleges on the land for teaching "agricultural and mechanical arts." In addition, they taught military tactics as well as classical studies. These land-grant colleges were extremely important in providing a practical higher education to members of the working classes. The Hatch Act of 1887 provided funding for agricultural research at each land-grant college. Research at the land-grant colleges developed new technology that helped farmers increase their crop yields.

The importance of these schools, at the time of their founding and later even more so, can hardly be overstated. They immediately offered an avenue for higher education that went beyond traditional subjects, such as the ministry or law. These land-grant colleges grew over time to become some of the best known and most prestigious universities in the United States and beyond, including Cornell University (in New York), the University of Illinois (Urbana-Champaign), and the University of Wisconsin (Madison).

Pacific Railroad Act (1862) In 1845, New York entrepreneur Asa Whitney proposed a railroad that would link the East with the Pacific. In 1861 a young engineer named Theodore Judah convinced congressional leaders to pass the Pacific Railroad Act. President Lincoln signed it into law the following year. The route of the proposed railroad passed over almost totally unsettled territory. To encourage railroad companies to risk their money, the act granted to them sections of land along the route. Sections were arranged in a checkerboard pattern. Half the land squares would go to the railroad companies, and half would be kept by the government for sale to would-be settlers.

> **Read Closely: Motivations**
> When you are reading about the actions of governments, consider how motivations shape those actions. What motivations led to the passage of the Homestead Act, the Morrill Act, and the Pacific Railroad Act in 1862?

The Race to Lay Track The building of a transcontinental railroad across the western plains to the Pacific coast was to be one of the great achievements of Northern industry during and after the Civil War. Two private companies were formed to build the railroad. One, the Central Pacific Railroad, started in Sacramento, California, heading east. The Union Pacific Railroad headed west from Omaha, Nebraska. Both companies faced challenges. Central Pacific crews had to cut tunnels through the Sierra Nevada, the great Pacific coast mountain range. Union Pacific crews had to fight off Native Americans on the Great Plains. Then they had to blast tunnels through mountain passes in the towering Rockies.

After three years of work, the crews came together in 1869 in Promontory, Utah. Representatives of both railroads took turns pounding in the final spike (which was gold) uniting the east and west sections. This undertaking had massive consequences for the nation. The length of time it took to travel from the East to California was reduced from six months to just two weeks.

Source: Yale University Libraries / Wikimedia Commons

East and West shaking hands at the laying of the last rail of the Union Pacific Railroad

Read Closely: Turning Point
The word *after* is often used to suggest a shift from one phase to another. How did the completion of the first transcontinental railroad cause a shift?

The Closing of the Frontier After the completion of the first transcontinental railroad, other western railroads quickly followed. Between 1865 and 1900, the number of miles of railroad tracks in the United States grew from 35,000 to 260,000 miles. This was nearly eight times as much track in just 35 years. By the end of the century, the United States had many more miles of railroad than there were in all of Europe, including Russia. The railways spurred the growth of population, and along with it business and trade grew as well.

The railroad companies were even more eager than the U.S. government to encourage farmers to go West. After all, a railroad's chief business was hauling freight from one place to another. If there were no settlers on the empty plains, there would be no business for a western railroad. To recruit settlers, railroad companies sent agents to Europe as well as to U.S. cities. Railroads' land grants from the U.S. government were offered for sale to would-be settlers at bargain prices. As a result, by 1890, the frontier had ceased to exist.

Consequences for Native Americans

Before 1850, the land between Missouri and California was referred to as the Great American Desert because it seemed dry, barren, and impossible to farm. The region consisted of two main parts: the Great Plains and the Great Basin. The Great Plains were flat grasslands stretching about 400 miles from the banks of the Missouri River to the Rocky Mountains. The Great Basin was a desert lowland that stretched about 700 miles between the Rocky Mountains and the Sierra Nevada range.

People of the Plains The Native Americans had an entirely different view of the Great Plains. For them, the Plains were filled with plants and animals that provided support for their way of life. Millions of shaggy buffalo provided almost all that the **Plains Indians** needed. They were a source of meat for food, pelts for clothing, skins for shelter, bones for tools, and dried manure for fuel. The buffalo-hunting societies (including the Blackfeet, Cheyenne, Comanche, and Sioux) viewed the Plains with religious awe and respect. To them, the land and the life it supported were sacred.

The Arrival of White Settlers Starting in about 1850, Easterners began to view the so-called Great American Desert in a new light. The settling of this region occurred in three stages. First came people hoping to strike rich deposits of gold and silver in the western mountains. Then came people who hoped to make their fortune raising and selling cattle. Finally came the homesteaders, farm families who hoped for enough rain to raise wheat and corn for a profit.

During the gold rushes of 1849 and 1859, settlers pushed west in ever-greater numbers. As a result of the Homestead Act, the end of the Civil War, and the growth in railroads, millions of new settlers moved into the rolling Plains and the Great American Desert. This movement would have severe consequences for Native Americans. Unlike the White settlers from the East, they could not conceive of dividing the land into privately owned plots and using it for personal gain. The Native Americans believed that the land and its wealth belonged to all.

Treaties and Legal Status U.S. treaties guaranteed the Native Americans' right to this land for "as long as the rivers shall run and the grass shall grow." But in the 1850s, as settlers started building mining towns and cattle towns in the region, the people's way of life was again threatened. Despite treaty rights, Native Americans had their land taken from them as the settlers moved West in larger and larger numbers. Often the U.S. military supported the takeover of Native Americans' lands. Thus, the treaties offered little protection for Native Americans.

Native American Wars (1850–1900) Since the first Europeans set foot on the continent, White settlers had fought Native Americans for land. As the frontier moved west beyond the Mississippi River, these wars also shifted westward. The final chapter in the long conflict was fought on the last frontier—the Great Plains.

The Sioux, who hunted buffalo on the plains of Wyoming, were the first of many Plains people to attack U.S. military posts in the region. The high point of their war was a battle on the Little Bighorn River in Montana in 1876. Led by Chief Crazy Horse, the Sioux killed 210 U.S. soldiers, including Lieutenant Colonel George Custer. In 1890, the U.S. Army took its revenge, killing about 300 Sioux at **Wounded Knee Creek** in South Dakota. The fighting was less a battle than a massacre. The Sioux at Wounded Knee, including women and children, were cut down as they fled from the scene. This event ended Sioux resistance. They moved to a reservation in South Dakota.

Other Native Americans tribes resisted being forced onto reservations. In Oregon in 1877, a tribe of about 500 Nez Percé tried to escape over mountain trails to Canada. However, U.S. troops caught up with them and forced them to surrender. The Apache of Arizona were the last Native American tribe to fight U.S. troops. After they submitted in 1900, most Native Americans lived peaceably but unhappily on reservations.

Although Native Americans challenged White settlers and U.S. troops, they never won a war against them. They lost for three reasons:

1. They fought as separate tribes rather than a single, united nation.

2. Most tribes were small, often numbering fewer than a thousand people.

3. Although they had rifles as well as bows and arrows, Native Americans lacked their foes' advanced weapons, such as the cannon and machine gun.

> **Read Closely: Differences**
> Words such as *unlike* indicate that the text is describing a difference. In this case, it signals a difference in attitudes toward the land. How did the attitudes of Native Americans toward the land differ from those of White settlers?

The Reservation System The lands assigned to subjugated Native American societies by the U.S. government, called **reservations**, were not their native lands. Often members of feuding tribes were forced to live together on a reservation. Native Americans who had been nomadic hunters were forced to become farmers. They were not allowed to leave their reservation without permission. They were either encouraged or forced to dress like Whites. Christian missionaries tried to force them to give up their spiritual beliefs.

Reservation lands were often barren and poorly suited to supporting life. Unable to hunt for their food as in the past, Native Americans were reduced to lives of poverty and hopelessness. Many of the U.S. government agents who ran the reservations were corrupt. They often pocketed the funds intended for Native Americans' welfare.

The Dawes Act In the 1880s, some White Americans began to recognize that Native Americans were not being treated fairly. The reformer Helen Hunt Jackson published *A Century of Dishonor* in 1881. The book chronicles the nation's unjust treatment of Native Americans. It describes massacres of Native Americans by the U.S. Army and uses government documents to prove that the government never honored any of its treaties with Native Americans. Jackson sent a copy of her book to every member of Congress in the hope that they would pass reforms.

Reform-minded lawmakers in Congress hoped to improve conditions on the reservations by encouraging Native Americans to adopt the lifestyle of U.S. farmers. In 1887, Congress passed the Dawes Act, which offered 160-acre plots on the reservations to the heads of households. It was assumed that Native American farmers would become self-supporting and "Americanized." But people with a nomadic hunting culture did not become model farmers overnight. Rather than keeping homesteads for themselves, many rented or sold them to White settlers for cash.

Forced Assimilation Another attempt to replace American Indian culture with White culture came with the establishment of the Carlisle Boarding School in 1879. Native American children at Carlisle were given Americanized names and clothing and even mainstream haircuts. Students were also forced to attend Christian church services. Their Native American games were replaced by sports such as football and baseball.

In 1911, Carlisle defeated Harvard in a major football upset. In the following year, the Carlisle football team defeated Army. Jim Thorpe, who led Carlisle to victories in both games, also won two Olympic medals in 1912. Thorpe is regarded as one of the greatest athletes in U.S. history. The school survived until 1918. In its time, it served as a model for other boarding schools throughout the nation whose goal was **assimilation** of Native Americans into the dominant White culture.

Read Closely: Contrasts
The word *but* can often indicate a contrast in two competing points. How does this word indicate a contrast between Native Americans' old way of life and the new one the government tried to impose on them?

Application: Interpret a Primary Source

Read the excerpt and answer the questions that follow it.

The Testimony of Standing Bear, 1879

Half facing the audience again, [Standing Bear] let his gaze drift far out through a window. His tone grew tense.

"I seem to stand on the bank of a river. My wife and little girl are beside me. In front the river is wide and impassable, and behind are perpendicular cliffs. No man of my race ever stood there before. There is no tradition to guide me."

Then he described how a flood started to rise around them and how, looking despairingly at the great cliffs, he saw a steep, stony way leading upward. . . . Finally he saw a rift in the rocks and felt the prairie breeze strike his cheek.

"I turn to my wife and child with a shout that we are saved.

"We will return to the Swift Running Water that pours down between the green islands. There are the graves of my fathers. There again we will pitch our tepee and build our fires.

"But a man bars the passage. He is a thousand times more powerful than I. Behind him I see soldiers as numerous as the leaves of the trees. They will obey that man's orders. I too, must obey his orders. If he says that I cannot pass, I cannot. The long struggle will have been in vain. My wife and child and I must return and sink beneath the flood. We are weak and faint and sick. I cannot fight."

He paused with bowed head. Then, gazing up into Judge Dundy's face with an indescribable look of pathos and suffering, he said in a low, intense tone:

"You are that man." No one who merely reads the speech can possibly imagine its effect on those people who knew of the Poncas' sufferings when they heard it spoken by the sad old chief in his brilliant robes.

The U.S. judge ruled in favor of Standing Bear. He said the Poncas and their chief could return to their homeland in the Dakotas.

Source: Thomas H. Tibbles, *Buckskin and Blanket Days*

1. What was the broader political context for Standing Bear's 1879 testimony?

_____

_____

_____

2. Was this result for Standing Bear, short lived as it was, similar to or different from the outcomes that most Native American societies experienced? Explain.

_____

_____

_____

3. What do you think might be the ultimate purpose of a document of this kind?

_____

_____

_____

Lesson 4 *Immigrants in the West*

The Treaty of Guadalupe Hidalgo (1848) ended the war between the United States and Mexico. As a result of the treaty, Mexico gave up 55 percent of its territory to the United States. The treaty promised U.S. citizenship to Mexicans living in those territories. It also guaranteed that their property rights would be honored.

Analyze a Primary Source

The Treaty of Guadalupe Hidalgo

Close Reading: Form of the Source
The source of this excerpt is a treaty between the United States and Mexico, which accounts for its complicated language. The entire treaty contains 23 articles. This article deal with issues of citizenship and property rights of Mexicans who lived in or owned property in the region being annexed by the United States.

Read Closely: Details
In a primary source such as this, the details hold great significance for people's everyday lives—here concerning matters of citizenship. The treaty states that if Mexican citizens stay in the territory in question but do not make their decision about citizenship within a certain amount of time, they will automatically be considered U.S. citizens. Circle the phrase that indicates the time limit.

Close Reading: Key Point
The key point often appears in the first sentence of a paragraph. The first sentence of the third paragraph of Article VIII tells us that this paragraph deals with property that belonged to Mexican citizens who did not live in the territory at the time the treaty was ratified. This is the key point. The rest of the paragraph discusses the rights of those property owners.

ARTICLE VIII

Mexicans now established in territories previously belonging to Mexico, and which remain for the future within the limits of the United States, as defined by the present treaty, shall be free to continue where they now reside, or to remove at any time to the Mexican Republic, retaining the property which they possess in the said territories, or disposing thereof, and removing the proceeds wherever they please, without their being subjected, on this account, to any contribution, tax, or charge whatever.

Those who shall prefer to remain in the said territories may either retain the title and rights of Mexican citizens, or acquire those of citizens of the United States. But they shall be under the obligation to make their election within one year from the date of the exchange of ratifications of this treaty; and those who shall remain in the said territories after the expiration of that year, without having declared their intention to retain the character of Mexicans, shall be considered to have elected to become citizens of the United States.

In the said territories, property of every kind, now belonging to Mexicans not established there, shall be [absolutely] respected. The present owners, the heirs of these, and all Mexicans who may hereafter acquire said property by contract, shall enjoy with respect to it guarantees equally ample as if the same belonged to citizens of the United States.

Source: Treaty of Guadalupe-Hidalgo, February 2, 1848

The United States and Mexico Clash

In the 1800s, many Americans came to believe that their country was destined to expand westward. They spoke of the "**manifest destiny**" of the United States to expand at least as far as the Pacific coast and to be the dominant nation in North America. A large part of the West, however, was part of the Republic of Mexico. From the Mexicans' point of view, the U.S. idea of manifest destiny posed a challenge and a threat to their control of the northern territory of their country.

American Expansion Four western territories were added to the United States between 1845 and 1853, most of them from Mexico:

- Texas won its freedom from Mexico in 1836 and the U.S. government annexed it in 1845.

- Oregon Country became part of the United States in 1846 as the result of a treaty with Great Britain.

- California and much of the Southwest were ceded to the United States in 1848 by the Treaty of Guadalupe Hidalgo.

- The very southern parts of the present-day states of Arizona and New Mexico were purchased from Mexico in 1853.

Treaty of Guadalupe Hidalgo (1848) In the treaty ending the Mexican War, the United States paid $15 million to Mexico for the huge territory extending from Texas's western border to the Pacific coast. In addition, the United States agreed to relieve Mexico of responsibility for paying $3.2 million in debts to U.S. citizens. The Rio Grande became the U.S.–Mexico border. The treaty offered citizenship to the 75,000 Mexicans that were living in what is now the U.S. Southwest. It also promised that Mexicans would be allowed to keep their property or dispose of it as they saw fit.

As a result of the Mexican War, the United States gained a large Mexican American population. Mexico had lost over half of its land and natural resources to the United States. Mexico's resentment over the U.S. conquest of its northern provinces in the Mexican War lingered for many generations.

> **Read Closely: Results**
> Writers use key phrases, such as "as a result," to indicate a cause-and-effect relationship. In this paragraph, the Mexican War was the cause. There were many results, but only a few are mentioned here. Which of these results had the most significant long-term effect on the United States?

The Annexation of Texas, Mexican Cession, and Gadsden Purchase

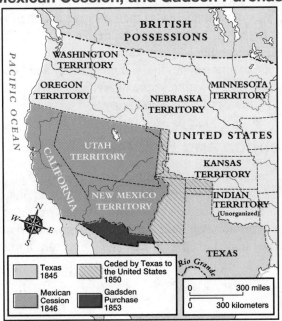

Legend:
- Texas 1845
- Mexican Cession 1846
- Ceded by Texas to the United States 1850
- Gadsden Purchase 1853

0   300 miles
0   300 kilometers

Mexican Americans Endure Discrimination

Compared with the rest of Mexico, these lands were sparsely populated. Most of the population—approximately 50,000 people—lived in New Mexico, *not* in Texas or California. After Mexico won its independence from Spain, the Mexican government granted large plots of land to men who were loyal to the new republic. The Mexicans who lived in these territories were proud of their heritage and of the large and successful *ranchos* they had developed.

Immediate Effects of the Treaty Approximately 90 percent of the Mexicans living in what became U.S. territory stayed to become citizens of the United States. They immediately became second-class citizens. Violence against Mexican Americans began almost immediately. During the California gold rush of 1849, Anglo miners denied the area's original Mexican settlers shares of the profits from mines. In some cases, vigilantes falsely accused Mexican Americans of crimes, held fake trials, and lynched them before jeering audiences.

Throughout the Southwest, Anglo-Americans swept in and simply took the lands they wanted from the Mexican Americans who owned them. In spite of the treaty's promises, corrupt governments favored Anglos in land disputes. When Mexican Americans tried to get their lands back in court, judges and lawyers often allowed the cases to drag on until the original landowners were left broke.

Mexican Americans Fight Back Occasionally, Mexican Americans fought back against the Anglo settlers who had stolen their lands. In 1889, several hundred formed *Las Gorras Blancas* ("the White Caps") in New Mexico. In addition to reclaiming stolen land, they wanted to intimidate Whites to prevent further land seizures. When violence failed to produce lasting changes, they tried running for offices in local elections. However, those attempts were suppressed because of fears that they would jeopardize the territory's chance for statehood.

Anti-Latino Discrimination Many former landowners found themselves with no choice but to take low-paying jobs as farm workers or as laborers in mines or on railroads. Anglo-Americans often looked down on the culture of the Mexicans, resulting in prejudice and discrimination. In spite of laws that banned businesses from importing laborers, employers seeking cheap labor actually sent recruiters into Mexico to convince more Mexicans to come to the United States. The Southern Pacific Railroad was one of those companies.

Anti-Latino discrimination grew along with immigration. States passed laws intended to deprive Mexican Americans of their heritage and their rights. Latinos were often barred from Anglo businesses. As time went on, Latinos found themselves increasingly segregated from Anglos in urban *barrios*. Those communities actually helped them maintain their ethnic identity and language. They developed their own economy, with restaurants, grocery stores, and other businesses that catered to members of their community.

Chinese Contribution and Exclusion

The first wave of Chinese immigrants to the United States came in the 1820s. By the end of 1849, there were barely 650 Chinese living in the United States. The discovery of gold in California resulted in a great gold rush that year as thousands of people sought fortunes. Chinese immigrants began to arrive in California in the 1850s. They hoped to strike it rich and then return home. By

Read Closely: Similarity
Recognizing similarities in historical events is one way to see how they fit into a broader context. How is the treatment of Mexican Americans similar to the treatment of Native Americans?

1852, over 25,000 Chinese immigrants had arrived. The Chinese were the first non-Europeans who arrived in large numbers of their own free will, unlike Africans who were enslaved and forcibly transported to the Americas.

Chinese and the Central Pacific Railroad Chinese labor soon became indispensable in developing the United States. In the 1860s, agents of the Central Pacific Railroad Company recruited thousands of men from China. They would have the difficult task of building the western half of the first transcontinental railroad. Eventually, 12,000 of the company's 13,500 workers were Chinese immigrants. They built some of the most hazardous parts of the railroad by dynamiting tunnels through the Sierra Nevada range. They were forced to work from dawn to dusk in very dangerous conditions. They had to sleep in tents in the middle of winter. Many Chinese laborers lost their lives in this dangerous work.

In June 1867, Chinese railroad workers went on strike—the largest labor strike of the era. They demanded shorter workdays, better working conditions, and to be paid the same as White workers. Chinese workers were paid between $26 and $35 a month, working 12 hours a day, six days a week. They had to provide their own food and tents. White workers earned $35 a month, plus their food and shelter. To break the strike, Central Pacific management cut off food and other supplies to the laborers. The railroad did not end up meeting any of the workers' demands.

Chinese Immigration Chinese workers on the transcontinental railroad had proven themselves to be more than a match for their difficult work. They were praised not only for their strength and endurance, but also for their brains and skill. The 1868 Burlingame-Seward Treaty with China eased immigration restrictions. At first, American businesses welcomed the steady flow of low-cost Chinese labor.

By 1880, over 300,000 Chinese lived in the United States. Most of them lived in California, and most of them were men. Even as late as 1890, fewer than 5 percent of the U.S. Chinese population was female. Few Chinese immigrants planned to stay permanently in the United States, intending to return to China after they made their fortunes. But many were forced to stay because they could not afford to return home. Those who remained were often stuck in low-paying, menial jobs—virtual slavery that was called "coolie" labor.

Discrimination Against Chinese From the very earliest days of the Republic, the Chinese were victims of discriminatory laws. The Naturalization Act of 1790 prohibited Chinese immigrants—as well as all other non-Whites—from becoming citizens through naturalization. The California constitution of 1879 specifically prohibited the state, counties, municipalities, and public works from hiring Chinese workers. According to the constitution, the fact that they were not eligible to become citizens made them "dangerous to the well-being of the State." The constitution encouraged cities and towns either to remove Chinese residents from within their limits or to keep them in "prescribed portions" of their limits. The state also required special licenses for Chinese-run businesses.

Chinese immigrants met with suspicion and hostility. They were barred from owning property, testifying in court, having their families join them, or marrying non-Chinese people. They were thus forced to band together and rely on family or benevolent associations. These were organizations designed not only to support the communities but also to defend them against discrimination. Chinatowns such as that in San Francisco became social and cultural centers. The Chinese created communities with their own social services, schools, places of worship, and health-care systems.

Read Closely: Differences
Words such as *unlike* indicate that the text is describing a difference between two things. In what significant way did the two largest groups of non-European immigrants to the United States differ?

Read Closely:
Causes Historical events usually have many causes. One way historians show them is through examples. What events led Congress to pass a law stopping Chinese immigration after earlier encouraging it?

Nativism A **nativist** is someone who believes that foreign-born people pose a threat to the majority culture and should be stopped from entering the country. At different times in the 19th century, nativists made organized attempts to exclude certain immigrant groups—not just Chinese and Japanese, but also Irish Catholics, East European Jews, and Italians.

A nationwide depression in the 1870s resulted in growing anti-Chinese feelings. Chinese laborers became scapegoats. During this period, there were labor troubles, and Chinese laborers were repeatedly used as replacement labor, which created further resentment. There was talk of Asian people coming to the United States by the millions and overwhelming White American culture. In Western states and territories, anti-Chinese riots broke out to protest the "yellow peril." In response to the nativist fears and prejudice, Congress passed a law halting Chinese immigration.

Chinese Exclusion Act (1882) Immigration by any Chinese people was halted by the **Chinese Exclusion Act**. As the first major restriction on immigration to the United States, it was a turning point in U.S. immigration policy. However, Chinese immigrants learned to use the U.S. court system to challenge exclusion and many other forms of discrimination. In 1897, the case of a Chinese man who had been born in the United States went to the U.S. Supreme Court. The Court's decision, based on the first clause of the Fourteenth Amendment, upheld the legal right of citizenship for any person born in the United States.

The Act remained in effect until 1943. The U.S. government repealed it in response to Japanese World War Two propaganda that consistently reminded China, a U.S. ally, of this discriminatory practice. U.S. President Franklin Roosevelt told legislators that repeal of the Act corrected a "historic mistake," but in reality, little changed in the short term. Only 105 immigration visas per year were initially allotted for Chinese immigrants.

"HOODLUMS" PELTING CHINESE EMIGRANTS ON THEIR ARRIVAL AT SAN FRANCISCO.

Source: Getty Images

"Hoodlums" in San Francisco attack Chinese immigrants.

Application: Interpret a Primary Source

Study the political cartoon and answer the questions that follow it.

THE ONLY ONE BARRED OUT.
Enlightened American Statesman.—" We must draw the line *somewhere*, you know."

Source: Library of Congress / Wikimedia Commons

1882 cartoon commenting on what type of immigrants are deemed
acceptable in the United States

1. Describe the U.S. economic and political context for this cartoon, drawn
   in 1882.

   _____

   _____

2. What does the caption refer to? Why does it say that the man representing
   Chinese Immigration is "the only one barred out"? [Note: The term *Fenian*
   refers to Irish Catholics who were devoted to the Irish nationalist cause.]

   _____

   _____

   _____

3. Name one way that the cartoonist's depiction of characters in his work betrays
   bias toward his subjects.

   _____

   _____

   _____

Multiple-Choice Questions

Questions 1–3 refer to the excerpt below.

A. Elizabeth Cady Stanton on Women's Rights

John Stuart Mill says the generality of the male sex cannot yet tolerate the idea of living with an equal at the fireside, and here is the secret of the opposition to woman's equality in the State and the Church; men are not ready to recognize it in the home. This is the real danger apprehended in giving woman the ballot, for as long as man makes, interprets and executes the laws for himself, he holds this whole matter pretty much in his own power under any system. Hence when he expresses the fear that liberty to woman would upset the family relation, he acknowledges that her present condition of subjection [enslavement] is not of her own choosing, and that if she had the power the whole relation would be essentially changed. And this is just what is coming to pass, the kernel of the struggle we witness to-day. This is woman's transition period, from slavery to freedom, and all the social upheavings, before which the wisest and bravest stand appalled, are but necessary incidents in her progress to equality.

Conservatism cries out we are going to destroy the family. Timid reformers answer, the political equality of woman will not change it. They are both wrong. It will entirely revolutionize it. When woman is man's equal the marriage relation cannot stand on the basis it is on today. But this change will not destroy it. As human statutes and state constitutions did not create conjugal [marital] and maternal love, they cannot annul them. We can trust the laws of the universe, even if the speeches and resolutions of a woman's rights convention seem to conflict with them. Is family life with the mass of mankind to-day so happy and satisfactory that it needs no improvement? Change is not death, neither is progress destruction.

Source: Elizabeth Cady Stanton, "On Marriage and Divorce," 1871

1. What was Stanton's chief purpose in writing this excerpt?

   1. To argue for a change in marriage laws
   2. To argue for the abolition of slavery
   3. To argue for women's right to vote
   4. To suggest that women in unhappy marriages should get divorced

2. Which of the following is one of the arguments Stanton uses to support her claim that giving women equal rights will not destroy the family?

   1. Men are not ready to recognize women's equality in the home.
   2. Men make, interpret, and execute laws.
   3. Under the present system, women are little more than slaves.
   4. Since laws and constitutions did not create marital and maternal love, changing them will not destroy it.

3. What recent event might have inspired Stanton to write this article?

   1. The Civil War had recently ended.
   2. Congress had passed the Civil War Amendments.
   3. Congress was debating an Equal Rights Amendment.
   4. The South was in the midst of Reconstruction.

Questions 4 and 5 refer to the excerpt below.

B. The Pacific Railway Act of 1863

Sec. 2. And be it further enacted, That the right of way through the public lands be . . . granted to said company for the construction of said railroad and telegraph line; and the right . . . is hereby given to said company to take from the public lands adjacent to the line of said road, earth, stone, timber, and other materials for the construction thereof; said right of way is granted to said railroad to the extent of two hundred feet in width on each side of said railroad where it may pass over the public lands. . . . The United States shall extinguish as rapidly as may be the Indian titles to all lands falling under the operation of this act . . .

Sec. 3. And be it further enacted, That there be . . . granted to the said company, for the purpose of aiding in the construction of said railroad and telegraph line, and to secure the safe and speedy transportation of mails, troops, munitions of war, and public stores thereon, every alternate section of public land, designated by odd numbers, to the amount of five alternate sections per mile on each side of said railroad, on the line thereof, and within the limits of ten miles on each side of said road . . . Provided, That all mineral lands shall be excepted from the operation of this act; but where the same shall contain timber, the timber thereon is hereby granted to said company . . .

Source: An Act to aid in the Construction of a Railroad and Telegraph Line from the Missouri River to the Pacific Ocean, and to secure to the Government the Use of the same for Postal, Military, and Other Purposes, 1862

4. How did Congress justify helping private railway companies build a transcontinental railway?

    1. It would be used to transport mail, troops, and munitions.

    2. It would be built on public land.

    3. The railway would clear the land to create a right-of-way.

    4. It would allow the U.S. government to take over Native American lands.

5. Which of the following stakeholders suffered as a direct result of the Pacific Railway Act?

    1. Miners

    2. Farmers

    3. Native Americans

    4. Union Pacific stockholders

Questions 6–8 refer to the excerpt below.

C. A Native American's Account of Signing a Treaty

Tul-lux Hol-li-quilla . . . further says that he was present ten years later, at the Warm Springs Agency, when Superintendent of Indian Affairs, Huntington, came to the Agency and called the Indians together, or at least those who were convenient, at that time, as Huntington's stay at the Agency was very short—less than twenty four hours; that during the time Huntington was there and about the time of the meeting, I arrived at the Agency with a load of wood; Huntington looking out of the window seeing me, called and said "Come in here and sign this paper, you are one of the good young Indians." I went into the room where Huntington was and he explained to me that he had a paper which he wanted me to sign; that the said paper had reference to the trouble then on between the Whites and the Piutes. He stated that the said paper would protect us when leaving the agency, when fishing, hunting or gathering berries; that if we would sign the paper passes would be issued whenever we left the reservation, which would show the White men that we were not Piutes and it was·with this understanding that I signed the paper presented, by Huntington. Absolutely nothing whatever was said by Huntington, or anyone else present at the said meeting, concerning our fishing rights or fishery. I am sure that we would have refused to sign any papers that would take from us such a precious right; that it was about a year later when we learned, through newspapers published in Portland, Oregon, that Huntington had deceived us and induced us to sign away our fishing rights.

Source: Affadavit of Tul-lux Hol-li-quilla regarding the treaties of 1855 and 1865, August 10, 1915

6. Which of the following would be the best use of this affadavit as a source?

    1. A biography of Tul-lux Hol-li-quilla
    2. A history of the Bureau of Indian Affairs
    3. A history of the Piutes
    4. A book documenting mistreatment of Native Americans by the U.S. government

7. Why did Tul-lux Hol-li-quilla sign the document?

    1. The Piutes had asked him to act in their behalf.
    2. Huntington had told him that it would protect his people when they left the reservation.
    3. Huntington had offered to reimburse the tribe in exchange for signing over their fishing rights.
    4. Superintendent Huntington had flattered him, calling him "one of the good young Indians."

8. What happened as a result of Tul-lux Hol-li-quilla's signing the document?

    1. Huntington was able to resolve the differences between the Whites and the Piutes.
    2. The Whites would know that Tul-lux Hol-li-quilla's people were not Piutes.
    3. He unwittingly gave up his people's fishing rights.
    4. Tul-lux Hol-li-quilla's people would be allowed to leave the reservation to fish, hunt, and gather berries.

Short-Essay Questions

Study the two documents and answer the question that follows.

D. A Radical Republican Congressman on Reconstruction

We have turned, or are about to turn, loose four million slaves without a hut to shelter them or a cent in their pockets. The infernal [hellish] laws of slavery have prevented them from acquiring an education, understanding the commonest laws of contract, or of managing the ordinary business of life. This Congress is bound to provide for them until they can take care of themselves. If we do not furnish them with homesteads, and hedge them around with protective laws; if we leave them to the legislation of their late masters, we had better have left them in bondage. Their condition would be worse than that of our prisoners at Andersonville. If we fail in this great duty now, when we have the power, we shall deserve and receive the execration [cursing] of history and of all future ages.

Source: Thaddeus Stevens, speech to the House of Representatives, December 18, 1865

E. An African American Abolitionist on Reconstruction

It is said by some: "We have done enough for the negro." Yes, you have done a great deal for the negro, and, for one, I am deeply sensible of it, and grateful for it. But after all, what have you done? We were slaves—and you have made us free—and given us the ballot. But the world has never seen any people turned loose to such destitution as were the four million slaves of the South. The old roof was pulled down over their heads before they could make for themselves a shelter. They were free! free to hunger; free to the winds and rains of heaven; free to the pitiless wrath of enraged masters, who since they could no longer control them, were willing to see them starve. They were free, without roofs to cover them, or bread to eat, or land to cultivate, and as a consequence died in such numbers as to awaken the hope of their enemies that they would soon disappear. We gave them freedom and famine at the same time. The marvel is that they still live. What the negro wants is, first, protection to the rights already conceded by law, and, secondly, education. Talk of having done enough for these people after two hundred years of enforced ignorance and stripes is absurd, cruel, and heartless.

Source: Frederick Douglass, speech to the Pennsylvania Society for Promoting the Abolition of Slavery, April 14, 1875

1. In a short essay, describe the historical context surrounding the two documents above. Then identify and explain the similarities and differences between the events described in these documents.

Study the two documents and answer the question that follows.

F. A Chinese Merchant Appeals to Congress

We are natives of the empire of China, each following some employment or profession—literary men, farmers, mechanics or merchants. When your honorable government threw open the territory of California, the people of other lands were welcomed here to search for gold and to engage in trade. The ship-masters of your respected nation came over to our country, lauded the equality of your laws, extolled the beauty of your manners and customs, and made it known that your officers and people were extremely cordial toward the Chinese. Knowing well the harmony which had existed between our respective governments, we trusted in your sincerity. Not deterred by the long voyage, we came here presuming that our arrival would be hailed with cordiality and favor. But, alas! what times are these! —when former kind relations are forgotten, when we Chinese are viewed like thieves and enemies, when in the administration of justice our testimony is not received, when in the legal collection of the licenses we are injured and plundered, and villains of other nations are encouraged to rob and do violence to us! Our numberless wrongs it is most painful even to recite.

Source: Pun Chi, Appeal to Congress to Protect the Rights of Chinese, ca. 1860

G. The Chinese Exclusion Act

SEC. 2. That the master of any vessel who shall knowingly bring within the United States on such vessel, and land or permit to be landed, any Chinese laborer, from any foreign port or place, shall be deemed guilty of a misdemeanor, and on conviction thereof shall be punished by a fine of not more than five hundred dollars for each and every such Chinese laborer so brought, and maybe also imprisoned for a term not exceeding one year.

SEC. 3. That the two foregoing sections shall not apply to Chinese laborers who were in the United States on the seventeenth day of November, eighteen hundred and eighty, or who shall have come into the same before the expiration of ninety days next after the passage of this act, and who shall produce to such master before going on board such vessel, and shall produce to the collector of the port in the United States at which such vessel shall arrive, the evidence hereinafter in this act required of his being one of the laborers in this section mentioned; nor shall the two foregoing sections apply to the case of any master whose vessel, being bound to a port not within the United States, shall come within the jurisdiction of the United States by reason of being in distress or in stress of weather, or touching at any port of the United States on its voyage to any foreign port or place: Provided, That all Chinese laborers brought on such vessel shall depart with the vessel on leaving port.

Source: An Act to execute certain treaty stipulations relating to Chinese, 1882

2. In a short essay, describe the historical context surrounding the two documents above. Then analyze and explain how the point of view of the first document affects its reliability as a source of evidence.

CHAPTER 5

Industrialization and Urbanization (1870–1920)

Chapter Overview

After the Civil War, the American economy grew rapidly, fueled by bountiful natural resources. The boom increased the nation's wealth, but it also led to some problems.

Industrialization New technologies gave rise to huge new industries. Extremely driven business people tried to dominate their industries until the government was forced to regulate unfair business practices. By 1900, the United States had displaced Great Britain as the world's largest economy.

Urbanization and Immigration U.S. cities grew as foreign immigrants and rural migrants sought jobs in urban factories. The waves of immigrants that came to the United States during this period were unlike previous settlers, in that most did not speak English and many were not Protestants. Many of them ended up living in crowded urban tenements and doing thankless or dangerous work for low wages.

Agricultural Movements In the West, farmers and railraods battled over shipping prices, with railroads offering lower prices to corporations and sticking farmers with the bill. As farm production increased, prices for farmers' produce dropped again and again. Mounting debt left farmers at the mercy of Eastern bankers. As a result, they organized to make changes.

The Labor Movement Big businesses took advantage of workers, requiring them to work long hours in unsafe conditions for low wages. Workers were powerless on their own but found strength in numbers, joining labor unions for a chance of better working conditions.

The Progressive Era A new wave of reformers pressed for changes. Muckrakers published exposés of big business, overcrowded tenements, unsanitary meatpacking plants, lynchings, and other evils. Some reformers worked to improve the lives of women, immigrants, and African Americans. The government stepped in with regulations on housing, the food and drug industries, and big business. And women finally won the right to vote.

Civic Literacy: Reform Throughout the history of the United States, elected officials and everyday citizens have take n it upon themselves to champion movements to help reform and improve government, industry, and a broad range of societal issues.

New York Social Studies Framework

Key Idea 11.5: Industrialization and Urbanization

The United States was transformed from an agrarian to an increasingly industrial and urbanized society. Although this transformation created new economic opportunities, it also created societal problems that were addressed by a variety of reform efforts.

Source: *New York State Grades 9–12 Social Studies Framework*

Civic Literacy Essay: Gather Evidence to Explain

After contextualizing (see page 113), you can move on to the task of explaining the efforts individuals, groups, and governments made to address the civic or constitutional issue at the heart of the prompt. The New York Regents say that explaining means "to make plain or understandable; to give reasons for or causes of; to show the logical development or relationship of." This part of the task has two main steps. First, think of all the efforts made to address the issue. Use the information in documents as well as information you learned in class. Consider efforts by

- **individual people** (leaders of a movements, for example)

- **groups of people** (labor unions, for example)

- **governments** (local, state, and federal)

These efforts can include protests, laws, court decisions, strikes, elections, boycotts, and many other endeavors. Gathering this evidence relies on a careful reading and analysis of the documents provided as well as accurate recollection of information from your reading and other studies. Write down every example you can think of—you don't have to use them all in your essay.

Application: Practice gathering evidence and explaining it as you read this lesson. Gather evidence about what efforts individuals, groups, and governments made to keep industry in check. Write down everything you learn about these efforts and make them understandable. Explain reasons, causes, and logical developments and relationships among the efforts.

Key Terms by Theme

Economics
Second Industrial Revolution (p. 151)
Bessemer process (p. 151)
trust (p. 152)
rebate (p. 153)
assembly line (p. 153)
American Federation of Labor (p. 162)
Industrial Workers of the World (p. 164)
socialism (p. 164)

Governance
Sherman Antitrust Act (p. 154)
platform (p. 160)
Theodore Roosevelt (p. 171)

Movement
push factors (p. 157)
pull factors (p. 157)

Civics
the Grange (p. 160)
Populist Party (160)
Nineteenth Amendment (p. 168)

Eighteenth Amendment (p. 169)
muckraker (p. 170)
Upton Sinclair (p. 170)
Ida B. Wells (p. 172)

Social Structures
Progressive Era (p. 167)
prohibition (p. 168)
Jane Addams (p. 170)
W.E.B. Du Bois (p. 172)

Lesson 1 Industrialization Transforms Economy

Conceptual Understanding 11.5a New technologies and economic models created rapid industrial growth and transformed the United States.

Andrew Carnegie believed that those who had wealth should use their wealth to make the world a better place for everyone. He made half a billion dollars from his Carnegie Steel Corporation, making him the richest man in the world. By the time he died, he had made charitable donations of 90 percent of his fortune.

Analyze a Primary Source

Andrew Carnegie on the "Gospel of Wealth"

Read Closely: Main Point
Authors often make their main point near the beginning of their writing. Carnegie believes that the wealthy have an obligation to the less fortunate. In the first paragraph, circle the term he uses for excess wealth—anything above what is necessary to live modestly and provide for dependents.

Read Closely: Contrasts
Carnegie uses the word *but* in the second paragraph to mark the contrast between two types of charity—providing assistance to the less fortunate so that they can help themselves, and providing outright handouts.

Read Closely: Point of View
Carnegie wants his readers to believe that wealthy people who do not follow his example will be judged by the public. Underline the phrase that best indicates his attitude toward those who don't use the bulk of their wealth to help others.

This, then, is held to be the duty of the man of wealth: first, to set an example of modest, unostentatious [not showy] living, shunning display or extravagance; to provide moderately for the legitimate wants of those dependent upon him; and after doing so to consider all surplus revenues which come to him simply as trust funds, which he is called upon to administer, and strictly bound as a matter of duty to administer in the manner which, in his judgment, is best calculated to produce the most beneficial results for the community— the man of wealth thus becoming the mere agent and trustee for his poorer brethren, bringing to their service his superior wisdom, experience, and ability to administer, doing for them better than they would or could do for themselves. . . .

In bestowing charity, the main consideration should be to help those who will help themselves; to provide part of the means by which those who desire to improve may do so; to give those who desire to rise the aids by which they may rise; to assist but rarely or never to do all. Neither the individual nor the race is improved by almsgiving [handouts]. Those worthy of assistance, except in rare cases, seldom require assistance. . . . Everyone has, of course, cases of individuals brought to his own knowledge where temporary assistance can do genuine good, and these he will not overlook. . . .

The man who dies leaving behind him millions of available wealth, which was his to administer during life, will pass away "unwept, unhonored, and unsung," no matter to what uses he leaves the dross [rubbish] which he cannot take with him. Of such as these the public verdict will then be: "The man who dies thus rich dies disgraced."

Such, in my opinion, is the true Gospel concerning Wealth, obedience to which is destined some day to solve the problem of the Rich and the Poor, and to bring "Peace on earth, among men good will."

Source: Andrew Carnegie, "Wealth," in the *North American Review*, 1889

Technology Drives Change

Historians call the period between the end of the Civil War and the beginning of World War I the **Second Industrial Revolution**. The United States was blessed with abundant natural resources such as iron, coal, and oil. Those resources, along with people willing to invest and a seemingly endless supply of labor, fueled the tremendous economic and industrial growth that marked this period.

The Industrial Revolution took off with the development of the **Bessemer process** for the mass production of steel. This was the first process developed to make steel inexpensively. Inexpensive steel fed other industrial systems that in turn, spurred growth. The railroad system benefited greatly from this situation, expanding quickly and widely. This allowed for rapid transport of raw materials and finished products throughout the nation.

Near the end of the period, improvements in workflow boosted industrial output and brought down prices. These innovations included the creation of the assembly line and new management techniques designed to increase efficiency. These advances in turn helped to create a consumer economy that demanded ever newer and more innovative products.

Transportation Following the Civil War, one of the most important factors in the industrialization of the United States was the growth of transportation. Before the Civil War, Most transportation in the United States took place on roads, rivers, and canals. Although the development of these networks pushed the country forward, it took the railroad to truly unite the growing nation. The development of the railroad is one of the great achievements of the United States.

On the eve of the Civil War, railroads ran through major cities of the United States, linking East and West. As noted earlier, the first transcontinental railroad was completed in 1869. After its completion, other western railroads followed in rapid succession. By the end of the century, a network of railroads crisscrossed the United States, creating a national market for agricultural and manufactured goods.

> **Read Closely: Contrast**
> The word *although* is used here to indicate a shift. What shift in transportation took place?

Transcontinental Railroads, 1900

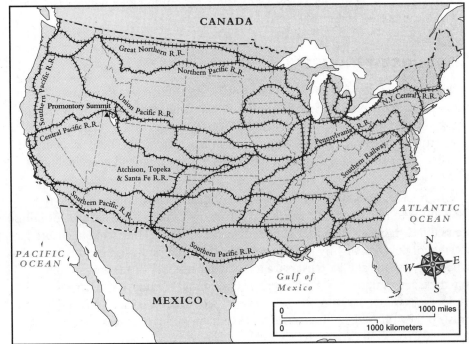

New Energy Sources In the early 1800s, coal became the main fuel powering railway locomotives. Mines along the Appalachian Mountains from Pittsburgh, Pennsylvania, to Birmingham, Alabama, produced coal by the ton. As railroads and factories grew, so did coal production, from approximately 30 million tons in 1870 to more than 200 million tons by 1900.

Before the Civil War, homes were lighted mainly by small lamps that burned either whale oil or vegetable oil. In 1859, Edwin Drake dug the first oil well in Titusville, Pennsylvania. Kerosene, a relatively clean fuel made from petroleum, began to be used for home lighting. Soon oil became a big business in the United States. Early refiners of kerosene considered gasoline and other petroleum products worthless and disposed of them. It wasn't until the invention of the automobile in 1892 that gasoline became recognized as a valuable fuel.

Since 1802, inventors had been trying to use electricity to produce light. But it wasn't until 1878 that U.S. inventor Thomas Edison developed the first successful electric light bulb. In the 1880s, he lit the homes of prominent New Yorkers like J. P. Morgan using small, individual generators. In 1882, with Morgan's financial backing, Edison started a business that would become General Electric. Later that year Edison opened the first central power plant in the United States, in lower Manhattan. With electricity readily available, inventors developed new electric-powered fans, irons, sewing machines, power tools, and household appliances.

Edison's "invention factory" employed a team of scientists and engineers who worked together on research projects. It is the direct forerunner of modern industrial laboratories. Among the hundreds of inventions developed there were the alkaline battery, the phonograph, and the motion picture camera.

Communications In the new industrial age, using electricity to send messages greatly speeded up communications. The electric telegraph system, developed by Samuel Morse in 1837, used Morse code to transmit messages through a wire. Thousands of miles of telegraph wires already connected American cities before the Civil War. In 1876, the invention of the telephone by Scottish immigrant Alexander Graham Bell gave people the ability to talk with each other over long distances. By 1900, some 1.3 million telephones were in use in American homes and businesses.

Captains of Industry

In the 50 years following the Civil War, the United States was transformed from a war-ravaged nation to the world's greatest industrial superpower. However, as of yet, it had not become a military or diplomatic superpower. A small group of pioneering businessmen played a large part in this transition. These "captains of industry" helped create the greatest industries of their time and ours, including oil, steel, automobiles, and finance.

Oil John D. Rockefeller invested his savings in an oil-refining company in 1865. Oil refining was then a fiercely competitive industry. The chances of failure seemed much greater than the chances of success. Rockefeller tried to ensure the survival of his company by taking control of the entire industry. He formed a new supercorporation called a **trust**, through which a number of firms are combined to reduce competition and control prices throughout an industry. After his competitors were near ruin, Rockefeller persuaded them to join his Standard Oil Trust. If they refused, he threatened to drive them out of business.

He nearly succeeded. In 1870, when Rockefeller organized the Standard Oil Company, he had about 200 competitors. Ten years later, only a few of them were still in business. Standard Oil accounted for 90 percent of the oil refined in the United States. Rockefeller defeated his competitors by using the following tactics:

- He persuaded railroads to give **rebates** to Standard Oil, which allowed him to charge lower prices for oil until his competitors were forced out of business. (A rebate is a return of a portion of the railroad's shipping charges.)

- Rockefeller moved swiftly to buy out struggling firms.

- Standard Oil built pipelines to transport its oil. In this way, the company avoided railroad freight charges and gained another competitive advantage.

Steel Scottish-born Andrew Carnegie came to the United States in the 1840s with no money. He educated himself by borrowing books from a private library whose owner lent a book a week to working boys. During the Civil War, Carnegie was superintendent of the Union's military railroads and telegraph lines in the East. After the war he formed a successful company that built steel bridges.

Then in 1870, he built his own steel works. In order to keep production costs low, he hired the brightest executives, managers, scientists, and engineers and invested in the latest technology. He was the first U.S. steelmaker to use the Bessemer process, which allowed him to make steel quickly at a lower cost. Carnegie made tough bargains with railroads to keep down shipping costs. And he did everything in his power to drive competitors out of business.

In 1901, Carnegie sold his steel company for nearly $500 million to a group of bankers led by J. P. Morgan. In spite of his competitive drive, Carnegie did not view wealth as the end goal. His motto was "to spend the first third of one's life getting all the education one can; to spend the next third making all the money one can; to spend the last third giving it all away for worthwhile causes."

Automobiles In 1908 Henry Ford declared, "I will build a motor car for the great multitude." Previously, automobiles had been luxuries for the wealthy. Ford and his engineers developed a new process of mass production. The manufacturing method was as innovative as the car itself. Instead of workers moving about to pick up various automobile parts, Ford had them stand in one spot as cars moved past them on a moving conveyor belt. Without moving from their places in the **assembly line**, workers repeated the same operations over and over. A chassis could be completed in just 93 minutes. Ford also raised the pay of his workers to reduce the company's high turnover rates, so that his efficient plant could run smoothly with contented, well-trained employees. He almost doubled salaries to $5 a day and reduced the workday from nine hours to eight hours.

Finance Financier John Pierpont Morgan was born to a wealthy and distinguished New England family. In the late 1850s he followed his father into the banking business. Then in 1871 he formed a partnership that would later be known as J. P. Morgan & Company. During the late 19th century, he reorganized and consolidated financially troubled railroads. Eventually, he controlled one-sixth of the nation's railways. He helped organize U.S. Steel and General Electric, as well as other major corporations.

During Morgan's time, the United States had no central bank. In 1895, he helped rescue the nation's gold standard by arranging a loan of more than $60 million to the federal government. During the financial panic of 1907, he convinced a group of leading financiers to stabilize the stock market by bailing out

Read Closely: Similarities
As you read, finding similarities between historical people and events can help you understand how certain people achieved what they did. What similar practice or practices helped make Rockefeller, Carnegie, and Morgan wealthy?

Read Closely: Motivation
While many industrialists were ruthless, paying their workers as little as possible, Henry Ford paid his workers almost double the going rate. Why would he do this if he didn't have to?

faltering financial institutions. In 1912, a congressional committee investigated Morgan and other Wall Street financiers for conspiring to control American banking and industry. As a result of that investigation, Congress created the Federal Reserve System in 1913 and passed the Clayton Antitrust Act in 1914.

Regulating the Giants

In the 1870s and 1880s the trend toward monopoly control was all too clear. In every industry it seemed that businesses were becoming less and less competitive as more and more of them merged. When companies have little or no competition, they are free to set prices for their goods and/or services. When a company has a monopoly in a particular field, workers, too, are left without choices. That company can set wages as they like, as well. The government faced public and political pressure to do something to restrain the actions of big business and to maintain some level of competition.

Early Attempts at Regulation Railroads competed with one another for business on long routes. They commonly made up for their losses by overcharging farmers for the less competitive shorter hauls. To fight high railroad rates, farmers took political action. They persuaded several state legislatures in the 1870s to pass laws regulating the freight rates of railroad companies. Companies facing regulation challenged the laws in court. In the case of *Wabash, St. Louis, and Pacific Railway v. Illinois* in 1886, the Supreme Court ruled that railroad rates set by state laws interfered with Congress's exclusive power to regulate interstate commerce.

Interstate Commerce Act To regulate certain practices of railroad companies, Congress passed the Interstate Commerce Act in 1887. The act created the Interstate Commerce Commission (ICC) to enforce the following regulations:

- Railroad rates had to be "reasonable and just."

- Pools—associations of competing railroads that agreed to charge customers the same amount—were illegal.

- Returning rebates to favored customers was illegal.

- Railroads could not charge more for a short haul than for a long haul.

At first the commission's powers were limited, but they expanded under later amendments to the law.

Sherman Antitrust Act The **Sherman Antitrust Act** of 1890 was the first major attempt to restrain the growth of monopolies. It stated that "every contract, combination in the form of a trust or otherwise, or conspiracy, in restraint of trade or commerce . . . is hereby declared to be illegal." However, the law was poorly and vaguely written. Terms such as *trust, conspiracy*, and *restraint of trade* were not defined. As a result, no trusts were successfully prosecuted in the 1890s. Weak as it was, however, the Sherman Antitrust Act established the principle that government had the right and the duty to break up trusts and other forms of monopoly.

"Trust-Busting" Court Cases Theodore Roosevelt was the first president to make a serious effort to enforce the Sherman Antitrust Act. He amazed people when he announced his decision to prosecute the Northern Securities Company, a powerful holding company that controlled several western railroads. In its 1904 decision in *Northern Securities Co. v. United States*, the Supreme Court ruled that the president's move to break up Northern Securities was proper and constitutional. After this victory, Roosevelt broke up other business combinations, including the John D. Rockefeller's Standard Oil Company.

Read Closely: Cause and Effect
Look for phrases such as "as a result," which signal the effect of an action or policy. What actions by J. P. Morgan led to new government regulations?

Read Closely: Distinguish Terms
Keep an eye out for sentences that begin with the word *However.* They often describe a contrast with an idea expressed previously. What difference is indicated here?

Application: Interpret a Primary Source

Read the excerpt and answer the questions that follow it.

The Value of Rebates

The reason for rebates was that such was the railroads' method of business. A public rate was made and collected by the railroad companies, but, so far as my knowledge extends, was seldom retained in full; a portion of it was repaid to the shippers as a rebate.

By this method the real rate of freight which any shipper paid was not known by his competitors nor by other railroad companies, the amount being a matter of bargain with the carrying company [railroad]. Each shipper made the best bargain that he could, but whether he was doing better than his competitor was only a matter of conjecture [opinion]. Much depended upon whether the shipper had the advantage of competition of carriers.

The Standard Oil Company of Ohio, being situated at Cleveland, had the advantage of different carrying lines, as well as of water transportation in the summer. Taking advantage of those facilities, it [Standard Oil] made the best bargains possible for its freights [shipping costs]. Other companies sought to do the same. . . .

The profits of the Standard Oil Company did not come from advantages given by railroads. The railroads, rather, were the ones who profited by the traffic of the Standard Oil Company, and whatever advantage it received in its constant efforts to reduce rates of freight was only one of the many elements of lessening cost to the consumer which enabled us to increase our volume of business the world over because we could reduce the selling price.

Source: John D. Rockefeller, *Random Reminiscences of Men and Events*, 1909

1. How would you describe the industrial situation in the United States during the era about which Rockefeller is reminiscing in this excerpt? Describe the era's positive and negative aspects.

   _____

   _____

2. What effect did the practice Rockefeller describes have on competition in his industry? Why?

   _____

   _____

3. Summarize Rockefeller's assessment of rebate schemes in the final paragraph above. Is his position credible? Why or why not?

   _____

   _____

   _____

Conceptual Understanding
11.5b Rapid industrialization and urbanization created significant challenges and societal problems that were addressed by a variety of reform efforts.

Samuel Gompers (1850–1924) came to the United States from England as a teenager. A cigar maker by trade, he organized the American Federation of Labor (A.F. of L.) in 1886. Gompers had little faith in political solutions to workers' problems, focusing instead on securing better pay and conditions for workers. Gompers served as the AFL's first president, a position he held until his death. The following excerpt is taken from a speech Gompers gave before a group of workers and union leaders in Louisville, Kentucky, on May 1, 1890.

Analyze a Primary Source

Samuel Gompers on the Goals of the American Federation of Labor

Read Closely: Evidence
In the final paragraph, Gompers says workers want higher wages. They had just received a raise in the last year, but still want more. Circle the amount of the previous year's pay increase.

Read Closely: Contrasts
Gompers uses the word *wealth* twice in this excerpt. In the first paragraph he is referring to wealth figuratively, referring to a person's improved mental state. In the last paragraph he uses the word in its literal sense, to refer to material riches.

Read Closely: Justification
Note that while Gompers admits that it is true that workers will always want more, he points out that this is not without reason. In the third paragraph, underline the phrase that Gompers uses to justify workers' demands for higher wages.

Why, when you reduce the hours of labor, say an hour a day, just think what it means. Suppose men who work ten hours a day had the time lessened to nine, or men who work nine hours a day have it reduced to eight hours; what does it mean? It means millions of golden hours and opportunities for thought. Some men might say you will go to sleep. Well, some men might sleep sixteen hours a day; the ordinary man might try that, but he would soon find he could not do it long. He would have to do something. He would probably go to the theater one night, to a concert another night, but he could not do that every night. He would probably become interested in some study and the hours that have been taken from manual labor are devoted to mental labor, and the mental labor of one hour will produce for him more wealth than the physical labor of a dozen hours. . . .

What we want to consider is, first, to make our employment more secure, and, secondly, to make wages more permanent, and, thirdly, to give these poor people a chance to work. The laborer has been regarded as a mere producing machine. . . .

We want eight hours and nothing less. We have been accused of being selfish, and it has been said that we will want more; that last year we got an advance of ten cents and now we want more. We do want more. You will find that a man generally wants more. . . . You ask a workingman, who is getting two dollars a day, and he will say that he wants ten cents more. . . . We live in the latter part of the Nineteenth century. In the age of electricity and steam that has produced wealth a hundred fold, we insist that it has been brought about by the intelligence and energy of the workingmen, and while we find that it is now easier to produce, it is harder to live. We do want more, and when it becomes more, we shall still want more.

Source: Samuel L. Gompers, "What Does the Working Man Want?" 1890

Urbanization and Immigration

The increasing industrialization of the United States after the Civil War encouraged millions of people to move to the cities of the East and Middle West. These urban newcomers included native-born Americans from rural areas, freed slaves from the South, and immigrants from Europe and Asia. People moved to cities for both economic reasons (jobs) and cultural reasons (schools, museums, theaters, and sports). African Americans also moved in hopes of escaping racial discrimination and repression in the South, with mixed results.

Jobs The primary reason people moved to the cities was for jobs. In the industrial age, cities grew larger mainly because of the factories that were built in them. To ship goods, industrialists located their factories near transportation centers, such as railroad terminals and steamship ports. Workers moved in to take advantage of the factory jobs. Near the factories, owners of real estate saw opportunities to rent housing to the workers. Merchants then opened shops catering to workers' needs. Thus, as cities grew in population, the variety of goods and services available also grew, fueling yet more growth.

Public Education City schools were better equipped and offered more complete courses of study than did rural ones. The movement for compulsory, or required, education was largely urban driven. Progressive reformers and labor activists both wanted children out of factories and in schools. Between 1865 and 1900, elementary school enrollments in the United States more than doubled. The number of U.S. high schools rose from about 400 in 1860 to more than 6,000 in 1900. Schools also improved in quality as more teachers received professional training. Earlier educators had mainly taught reading, writing, and arithmetic. After 1900, however, occupational training and citizenship education were considered equally important in many schools.

Read Closely: Change
As you read, note the significance of changes because you take something for granted. What do the changes mentioned in this paragraph tell you about public education by 1900?

Patterns of Immigration The greatest influx of immigrants to the United States occurred between the 1840s and the 1920s. Between the 1840s and the 1870s, German and Irish immigrants predominated. Beginning in 1896, immigrants from southern and eastern Europe—Italians, Jews, and Slavic people from the Austro-Hungarian Empire—were the most numerous. They were called "new immigrants" because their cultures were different from those of the earlier "old immigrant" groups from western and northern Europe.

Push-Pull Factors Reasons for immigration varied. In general, however, every person's or family's decision was based on two factors. Conditions in the home country that were bad and could no longer be tolerated were known as **push factors**. Conditions in the country they were immigrating to that promised to be better than those at home were known as **pull factors**.

In the Industrial Age, Europe's population experienced astonishing growth—from 140 million in 1750, to 260 million in 1850, and to 400 million in 1914. Farmland was scarce compared to the abundance of land on the western frontier of the United States. Harsh laws could be as bad as economic troubles. As a religious and ethnic minority, Jews in Russia and Poland lived in fear of pogroms—violent mob attacks on a religious or ethnic minority. In many countries of eastern Europe, people resented laws requiring boys of 15 and 16 to serve in a monarch's army. These are just some of the factors that pushed emigrants out of their native lands.

Many Europeans thought U.S. factory jobs might be easier to find and pay better wages than those near home. Also, railroad companies with Western lands to sell and steamship companies seeking passengers sent agents to Europe to promote the idea of emigration. Recruiters gave the impression that, after a few years of work, everyone could expect to become rich in the United States. Steamship lines offered tickets for the ocean voyage to New York City for as little as $25 per person. These were among the factors pulling immigrants to the United States.

European Immigrants: When They Came and Why		
Nationality	Period of Greatest Immigration	Main Push Factor
Irish	1840s–1850s	Failure of potato crop and resulting famine
Germans	1840s–1880s	Economic depression; oppression following failed revolutions
Scandinavians (Danes, Swedes, Norwegians, Finns)	1870s–1900s	Poverty; shortage of farmland
Italians	1880s–1920s	Poverty; shortage of farmland
Eastern Europeans (Poles, Russians, and others—including Jews)	1880s–1920s	Political oppression; religious persecution; poverty

Read Closely: Differences
Recognizing differences is one way to understand events in history. What differences might make native-born Americans feel concern about the "new immigrants"?

The Americanization Process The experience of leaving one's native country to live in an unknown place is usually a difficult and painful one. Certainly it was difficult for the Italians, Scandinavians, Greeks, and eastern Europeans. Their way of life in the "old country" was far different from life in the United States. By settling in ethnic neighborhoods, immigrants sought to preserve the customs and language that they had known in Europe. At the same time, most tried hard to learn English and adopt American ways. Usually, the immigrants' children became Americanized far more easily than their parents. The increase in the amount and quality of U.S. education went hand-in-hand with the rise in immigration. It reflected Americans' desire to have children of immigrants embrace the nation's language and culture.

Reactions to the "New" Immigration The immigrant population in the United States was a blend of two groups. One consisted of early immigrants and their descendants—native-born Americans who had more or less lost touch with their families' immigrant past. Most of them were Protestants of British descent. The other group was made up of foreign-born people from many lands. A large number of them were Catholic or Jewish.

The cultural values of native-born European Americans influenced their attitudes toward foreign-born newcomers. The native-born became concerned after 1890 when the number of people arriving from southern, central, and eastern Europe began to exceed all the rest. In 1910, for example, 725,000 persons came from these areas, while only 200,000 came from western and northern Europe. In the period from 1891 to 1915, "new immigrants" numbered over 11 million of the 15.5 million immigrants from Europe.

The antiforeign attitudes of many native-born Americans were reflected in the National Origins Act of 1924, which established quotas for immigrants from each country. However, the law prohibited altogether the immigration of Chinese, Japanese, and other Asian people.

Civic Literacy: Societal Conflict
The late 19th century was a time of many conflicts—between native-born Americans and immigrants, between farmers and railroads and Eastern bankers, and between labor and management. Some of these conflicts remain today.

Agrarian Issues and Movements

For farmers, the post–Civil War era was both the best of times and the worst of times. Because of advances in science and technology, American farmers were more productive than ever before. At the same time, farmers received discouragingly low prices for each pound of cotton and each bushel of wheat. In short, farmers succeeded as never before—and also failed as never before.

While land was cheap, everything else about a farmer's business was expensive: farm machinery, tools, buildings, seed, horses, and mules. Farmers also had to pay for grain storage and rail freight. They relied heavily on credit from merchants and loans from banks.

Naturally, farmers resented always being at the mercy of railroads, merchants, and banks. They were particularly upset when they succeeded in growing a large crop only to receive prices far below those of previous years. This condition—good crop, poor price—happened as often as not in the 1870s, 1880s, and 1890s. As prices sank, farm debts soared.

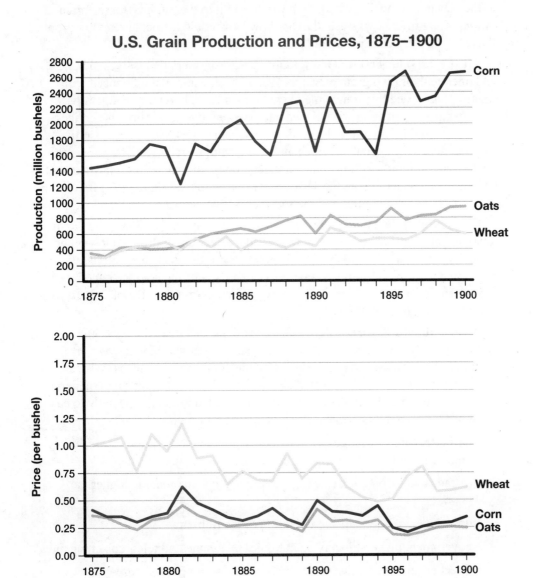

U.S. Grain Production and Prices, 1875–1900

Twice farmers turned to politics to solve their problems. Midwestern farmers battled the railroads in the Grange movement of the 1870s. Then farmers of the South and West campaigned against northeastern bankers in the Populist movement of the 1890s.

The Grange Movement The Patrons of Husbandry, otherwise known as **the Grange**, was founded in 1867 as a society for bringing farm families together for social purposes. Soon, however, Grange meetings focused on the economic issues troubling the farmers: how to cope with falling grain prices and rising railroad rates.

Read Closely: Shifts
The word *however* often indicates a contrast with an idea that has been expressed previously. How did the purpose of the Grange meetings change soon after they were founded?

Farmers complained about the common railroad practice of charging low rates for a long haul (for example, Chicago to New York) and a much higher rate for a short haul (for example, Springfield, Illinois, to Chicago). Railroads competed with one another for business on the long routes. They made up for their losses by overcharging farmers for the less competitive shorter hauls.

Farmers also complained about the high charge for the storage of their wheat and corn in grain elevators. Farmers could choose to sell their grain directly to the elevator company, which then would sell it to the public. But the price farmers were offered was usually very low. How could farmers break free from the crushing rates charged by others?

Grangers Take Action One solution was for farmers themselves to build and operate their own grain elevators. The new elevators were financed with money contributed by Grange members to businesses known as cooperatives. A cooperative is an enterprise owned and operated by those using its services. Besides operating the grain elevators at reasonable rates, Grange cooperatives lowered prices for needed supplies by buying from merchants in large quantities.

To fight high railroad rates, the Grangers took political action. They persuaded several state legislatures in the 1870s to pass laws regulating both the freight rates of railroad companies and the storage rates of elevator companies.

The Populist Party Farm prices rose briefly in the early 1880s, and Grange membership declined. But later in the decade, prices again dropped lower and lower. At one point farmers burned their corn for fuel rather than sell it at the prevailing low price. Embittered farmers in all parts of the country joined a movement that eventually became a new political party—the People's Party, also known as the **Populist Party**.

The Populist Platform of 1892 Populist delegates assembled in Omaha, Nebraska, in the summer of 1892 for their party's first national convention. Included in their new party's **platform** (statement of political ideas) were a number of reform ideas that caused a sensation when the nation's newspapers reported them. For the time, Populists' ideas sounded radical, especially to east-coast bankers and industrialists. They wanted the following:

Read Closely: Analysis
When you analyze text, it becomes possible to see why some things occurred while others did not. The Populist Party's platform included a number of demands for reforms. Some of them were eventually met. Which of the demands listed at right would be considered most radical, and why?

- unlimited silver coinage (thereby increasing the money supply, which they believed would increase crop prices and ease their debt burden)

- a graduated income tax (the higher the person's income, the higher the tax rate)

- government ownership and operation of the railroads

- government ownership and operation of telephone and telegraph companies

- direct election of U.S. senators (rather than by state legislatures)

- an eight-hour workday for all factory workers

The Populists drew many votes in 1892. The Populist candidate for president, James Weaver, received almost 9 percent of the popular vote and 22 electoral votes. Other Populists were elected to the U.S. Congress and to state legislatures in the South and West. For a brand-new party, it was an impressive showing. However, Democrat Grover Cleveland won the presidency (for a second, nonconsecutive time) by a wide margin.

The Election of 1896 At the Democratic convention of 1896, a member of Congress from Nebraska, William Jennings Bryan, declared that farmers would triumph over city bankers. Bryan, who supported unlimited silver coinage, defeated conservative Democrats to win the nomination. At the Populists' convention of 1896, a majority favored the idea of nominating the Democrats' candidate. After all, they reasoned, who could match Bryan's ability to rally the nation behind the Populists' favorite cause, silver? To satisfy those who opposed Bryan's nomination, the Populists chose their own vice presidential candidate.

Read Closely: Word Choice
Notice the use of the words *however* and *although* in this paragraph. Both words are used to indicate an outcome that might be seen as surprising. Why might Bryan's loss of the election have surprised people?

Source: U.S. National Archives / Wikimedia Commons

William Jennings Bryan speaking on stage during the 1896 presidential campaign

Even with the support of both the Democrats and the Populists, however, Bryan lost the election. The Republican candidate, William McKinley, who opposed the silver coinage idea, won the presidency. Although Bryan carried the South and much of the West, he failed to win the crucial electoral votes of the East. Many Eastern workers feared inflation. McKinley convinced them that silver coinage would cause high prices, which in turn would bring on a depression and the loss of jobs. This election marked a turning point for the country. Immigration, urbanization, and industrialization resulted in increased electoral power for big cities, almost all of which were in the East.

Bryan's defeat and improved farm prices after 1896 caused a rapid decline of the Populist Party. After 1900, Populists were no longer elected to Congress. Nevertheless, the two major parties eventually adopted many of the reforms in the Populist platform of 1892. In 1913 two reforms—the graduated income tax and direct election of senators—would form the basis of constitutional amendments. The Populist Party demonstrated that even if a third party failed to elect many candidates, it could still have a major influence on national policy.

The Nascent Labor Movement

The growth of industry and big business created problems for industrial workers. To minimize their labor costs, most manufacturers kept wages as low as possible. They often demanded from their workers a 60- to 70-hour workweek. Factories were often cold in winter and hot in summer. Ventilation was poor. Machines had few safeguards to prevent accidents. If an accident injured or killed a worker, it was considered the worker's fault, not the employer's. Factory workers were powerless as individuals to persuade large corporations to treat them better. To be more effective, they organized into large labor unions.

The Knights of Labor Organized in 1869, the Knights of Labor was the first union to become a major economic force. Unlike earlier unions, the Knights of Labor invited both skilled and unskilled workers of all kinds to join. The Knights excluded no one. African Americans and Whites, women and men, foreign-born and native-born all joined the union.

The Knights of Labor avoided strikes for many years, instead trying to settle labor disputes through arbitration. It established cooperatives that the workers owned and operated. More than anything, though, the Knights of Labor wanted to establish an eight-hour workday.

In 1885, the Knights of Labor surprised the nation by winning a major strike against a railroad company. Following the strike, membership in the union shot up to 700,000. But its triumph was short-lived. In 1886, during a labor rally in the Haymarket section of Chicago to protest earlier police brutality, an anarchist (someone who believes government is harmful and unnecessary) threw a bomb into a group of police officers. The police responded by firing into the crowd. In the end, seven police officers were killed along with at least four (and as many as eight) civilians. More than 90 police and civilians were wounded or injured as well. Since the Knights of Labor had organized the rally, it was blamed for the incident. In its aftermath, workers left the Knights of Labor in droves. By the 1890s, membership had dwindled to a small number.

The American Federation of Labor Samuel Gompers organized the **American Federation of Labor (AFL)** in 1886. In the wake of the Haymarket Riot, many departing members of the Knights of Labor joined the new organization. In altered form, the A.F. of L. still exists as the largest union in the United States.

As the leader of a union of cigar makers, Gompers had the idea of bringing other crafts unions together in a single organization. The federation, or loose association, of unions that he organized in 1886 permitted member unions to continue their separate existence. The A.F. of L. leadership set overall policy for achieving the objectives held in common by the various crafts unions.

Read Closely: Turning Point
As you read, look for events that significantly change the course of history. The Haymarket Riot was a major turning point in the history of the labor movement in the United States. How did it affect the Knights of Labor and the American Federation of Labor?

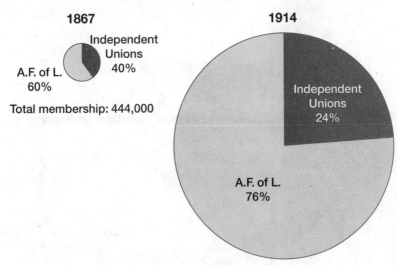

Labor Union Membership, in 1897 and 1914

1867

Independent Unions 40%

A.F. of L. 60%

Total membership: 444,000

1914

Independent Unions 24%

A.F. of L. 76%

Total membership: 2,647,000

Membership in the A.F. of L. grew steadily. By 1900, half a million workers belonged to crafts unions in the A.F. of L. It focused strictly on goals that directly benefited workers: higher wages, shorter working hours, and better working conditions. Unions in the A.F. of L. tended to discriminate against Black workers and women. As a result, employers often used African Americans to fill the jobs of striking union members. Their reputation as "strikebreakers" only increased the racial prejudice of the A.F. of L. membership.

The International Ladies' Garment Workers' Union In 1900, workers in the women's clothing industry organized the International Ladies' Garment Workers' Union (ILGWU) to protest low pay, long hours, and unsafe working conditions. Most of its members were Jewish immigrants employed in sweatshops. In 1909, the ILGWU organized the first garment strike of 20,000 shirtwaist (blouse) makers, mostly women and children. In the end, the workers won a pay raise and a shorter workweek. A second strike a year later led to the establishment of an arbitration board to settle disputes between labor and management.

The American Railway Union In 1893, locomotive fireman Eugene V. Debs formed the American Railway Union (ARU) to represent all railroad employees. In August 1893, the Great Northern Railroad began cutting wages. In response to further wage cuts, ARU members voted to strike in April 1894, shutting down the railroad for 18 days. Ultimately, the strike was successful and workers' wages were restored. This success attracted new members, and for a time, about 2,000 new members a day joined the ARU.

The workers who produced Pullman sleeping cars were among those new members. (Pullman sleeping cars were immensely popular and luxurious sleeper cars for trains.) In May 1894, they voted to strike, also over wage cuts. The ARU voted to support the Pullman workers by refusing to work on any trains that included Pullman cars. The Pullman strike became a nationwide struggle between the American Railway Union and the railroad managers association. In order to break the strike, railway officials ordered Pullman cars to be pulled on U.S. mail trains. When ARU members refused to work on mail trains, the government would step in. President Grover Cleveland did, in fact, send troops to end the strike. Debs was arrested and jailed for six months for conspiracy to interfere with the mail, and the ARU collapsed.

> **Read Closely: Contrasts**
> Take note of how similar events can sometimes have differing outcomes. Members of the American Railway Union voted to strike twice within the union's first year, but with very different results. How did the results of the two strikes differ?

THE CONDITION OF THE LABORING MAN AT PULLMAN.—

Source: U.S. National Archives. Wikimedia

A July 1894 labor newspaper cartoon shows a Pullman Company laborer squeezed between low wages and high rent.

Industrial Workers of the World Founded in 1905, the **Industrial Workers of the World (IWW)** was a radical labor organization that opposed capitalism and promoted **socialism**. In the socialist system, the means of production (factories, mines, and so on) would be owned by the workers, not just a few wealthy individuals. The IWW opposed the American Federation of Labor's refusal to include unskilled laborers in its unions. Among its founders were "Big Bill" Haywood of the Western Federation of Miners. One of the IWW's aims was for workers to control the means of production. The IWW scored its greatest victories in mining and lumber industries of the Pacific Northwest.

Reactions to Strikes Workers' strikes were extremely common in the late 19th and early 20th centuries. Many ended in violence, as strikers clashed with police and even state and federal troops. These strikes involved labor disputes with some of the nation's biggest corporations. Most Americans supported the government's use of troops to break strikes. They viewed strike leaders as revolutionaries who challenged the traditional values of society. But a growing minority sympathized with the unions and pointed to the unhappy plight of the workers—their low wages, long hours, and unhealthy working conditions. Government in the 1800s consistently sided with business against unions. But as will become apparent, it would change its policies to support both business and labor in the 20th century.

Application: Interpret a Primary Source

Read the excerpt and answer the questions that follow it.

Farmers Speak Out

In a country possessing so many facilities of cheap production this discouraging aspect of agriculture must be and is the result of other than natural causes. The annual additions of wealth [to the nation's economy] under the enlightened system of agriculture are enormous, but from the unequal divisions of the profits of labor and the unjust discriminations made against it, the enlistments of [economic records on] property show that the farmers of the United States are not prospering. While it [agriculture] is rapidly extinguishing all debts and restoring an equilibrium [stability] to the currency of the country, its votaries [those devoted to agriculture] are deprived of a just share of the rewards of their toil. . . . Transportation companies are allowed to make and unmake prices at will by their unjust and discriminating tariffs and freights [shipping costs]. Subsidies and tariffs are created to protect other industries to the prejudice [harm] of agriculture. Commerce is shackled [chained]. . . . Agricultural property is made to bear an unequal and undue proportion of taxation to afford [make possible] exemptions and privileges to other industries. Monopolies are permitted to assume power and control and exercise prerogatives [rights] and privileges justly belonging to sovereignty [national government]. Encouraged by legislation and stimulated by power, they have grown dictatorial and imperious [overbearing] in their demands, unrelenting in their exactions [excessive fees], and cruel and unmerciful in their impositions [levies]. Society has become extravagant and is now a heedless [uncaring] spendthrift of the painful earnings of labor. Government has become proud and autocratic [using absolute power], while her toiling laborers are humiliated in their poverty.

Source: Proceedings of the Thirteenth Session of the National Grange, 1879

1. Briefly describe the situation of farmers in the period spanning the end of the Civil War to the beginning of the 20th century.

_____

_____

2. What complaints does the speaker have about the railroad industry, and how did the Grangers translate their discontent into political solutions?

_____

_____

3. Describe what aspects of this speaker's perspective on the agricultural climate make him both a reliable and unreliable source of information.

_____

_____

Conceptual Understanding
11.5b Rapid industrialization and urbanization created significant challenges and societal problems that were addressed by a variety of reform efforts.

On a trip to Europe with her friend Ellen Starr, Jane Addams visited a settlement house in London's East End. She resolved to open a similar establishment in an underprivileged area of Chicago. In 1889 she and Starr leased Hull House, a large home in the Chicago slums. There they intended "to provide a center for a higher civic and social life; to institute and maintain educational and philanthropic enterprises and to investigate and improve the conditions in the industrial districts of Chicago." Addams received the Nobel Peace Prize in 1931. The following excerpt is from an 1892 address she gave to a conference of social workers.

Analyze a Primary Source

Jane Addams on the Need for Social Settlements

Read Closely: Geography
Geography is often an important aspect of historical writings. The location of Hull House was an important part of its mission. Underline the phrase that Addams uses to explain why she located Hull House where she did.

Read Closely: Details
According to Addams, while America stood for democratic ideals, the goal had only been partially achieved. Circle the word that indicates the area in which the democratic ideal *had* been extended.

Read Closely: Contrasts
In the fourth and fifth sentences of the second paragraph, Addams contrasts the rights that had been extended to African Americans and immigrants in the name of democracy with the reality of the rest of their existence.

Hull House, which was Chicago's first Settlement, was established in September, 1889 . . . in the belief that the mere foothold of a house, easily accessible, ample in space, hospitable and tolerant in spirit, situated in the midst of the large foreign colonies which so easily isolate themselves in American cities, would be in itself a serviceable thing for Chicago. Hull House endeavors to make social intercourse express the growing sense of the economic unity of society. It is an effort to add the social function to democracy. It was opened on the theory that the dependence of classes on each other is reciprocal; and that as "the social relation is essentially a reciprocal relation, it gave a form of expression that has peculiar value." . . .

It is not difficult to see that although America is pledged to the democratic ideal, the view of democracy has been partial, and that its best achievement thus far has been pushed along the line of the franchise [right to vote]. Democracy has made little attempt to assert itself in social affairs. We have refused to move beyond the position of its eighteenth-century leaders, who believed that political equality alone would secure all good to all men. We conscientiously followed the gift of the ballot hard upon the gift of freedom to the negro, but we are quite unmoved by the fact that he lives among us in a practical social ostracism [exclusion]. We hasten to give the franchise to the immigrant from a sense of justice, from a tradition that he ought to have it, while we dub him with epithets [abusive nicknames] deriding [ridiculing] his past life or present occupation, and feel no duty to invite him to our houses. We are forced to acknowledge that it is only in our local and national politics that we try very hard for the ideal so dear to those who were enthusiasts when the century was young. We have almost given it up as our ideal in social intercourse.

Source: Jane Addams, "The Subjective Necessity of Social Settlements," 1892

Governmental Reforms

One of the most remarkable periods of reform began shortly before 1900 and reached a climax in the presidential election of 1912. The reformers called themselves "progressives" and gave a name to the era they dominated—the **Progressive Era**. Some of the era's important changes occurred at the federal level of government.

Income Tax The Sixteenth Amendment (1913) gave Congress the power to collect a tax on incomes. The tax was considered democratic because originally it was collected only from people with extremely high incomes. It was also a progressive, or graduated, income tax. A progressive tax has a rate schedule that increases as a person's reported income increases. People with higher incomes pay a higher percentage in tax, while people with lower incomes pay a lower percentage in tax.

Direct Election of Senators The Seventeenth Amendment (1913) changed the method of voting for U.S. senators. Previously, they had been elected by state legislatures. Now they were elected directly by the voters in each state. This helped reduce the influence of special interests, particularly big business, in the selection of senators.

Federal Reserve System Before President Woodrow Wilson's administration (1913–1921), there had been no federal system for expanding or contracting the nation's money supply as the needs of business or the economy at large fluctuated. Wilson recognized that the growing industrial nation required an organized banking system.

In the past, private banks often had too little money in reserve, or kept in their vaults. If hundreds of customers tried to withdraw their money at the same time, a bank with a low reserve might collapse and fail, or go bankrupt. Many banks failing at once could cause the entire U.S. economy to sink into a depression. Wilson was determined to bring some order to the banking system to avoid such bankruptcies. Such "panics" had occurred as late as 1907.

The progressive solution to this problem, supported by Wilson, was to create a system of central banks called the Federal Reserve System. Under this system, private banks would keep their cash reserves in 12 Federal Reserve regional banks. A small group of U.S. officials—the Federal Reserve Board, or "Fed," made the general policy for these banks. The Fed could decide the actual percentage of reserves that banks must hold with their regional Federal Reserve Bank.

The regional banks could make loans to private banks around the country at interest rates set by the Fed. The loans consisted of paper money printed by the U.S. government as Federal Reserve notes. (This is the paper money Americans have used ever since Congress passed the Federal Reserve Act in 1913.) In addition, the Fed could determine the interest rate or "federal funds rate" charged by banks on "overnight loans" made to other banks.

Most important was the ability of the Fed to sell bonds to, or buy bonds from, the banks. In this way, the Fed could decrease or increase the amount of money banks had available to lend out to businesses. This affected the amount of money in circulation. Thus, the Federal Reserve System made it possible for the supply of currency to expand or contract according to the changing needs of business. This allowed the U.S. government to influence the entire national economy. This is essentially how the Federal Reserve System has operated throughout its history.

> **Read Closely: Previous Information**
> Try to apply information that you have already learned to your present reading. Recall that J. P. Morgan led a group of financiers to bail out ailing financial institutions during the 1907 panic. Why would it be preferable to have a government agency to help avoid such panics?

Women Demand the Vote

Women had worked for many years to gain the right to vote. The woman suffrage movement continued into the Progressive Era. The suffragists kept up the pressure for a constitutional amendment, asking how the United States could be a democracy if women could not vote. The older leadership was replaced by a new generation of suffragists led by Alice Paul and Carrie Chapman Catt. Some men in the Progressive Movement supported suffrage, but many thought women should not become involved in politics.

Read Closely: Contrast
The word *but* can often signify a contrast between two competing points. How does it contrast the attitudes of men in the Progressive Movement toward woman suffrage?

Source: Library of Congress / Wikimedia Commons

Suffrage parade, New York City, May 1912

Nineteenth Amendment   The suffragists' efforts got what they wanted with the passage in 1920 of the **Nineteenth Amendment**. It was nicknamed the "Susan B. Anthony Amendment" in honor of the leader who had first championed it. The amendment stated: "The right of citizens of the United States to vote shall not be denied or abridged by the United States or by any state on account of sex." Suddenly, the number of people eligible to vote in U.S. elections nearly doubled.

Temperance and Prohibition

Beginning in the 1830s, many women joined the temperance movement to fight against the production, sale, and abuse of alcohol. The movement sprung from an intense period of Protestant religious revivalism. Reformers argued that excessive consumption of alcohol increased the poverty of working-class families. Many factory owners supported prohibition as well, hoping to increase the productivity of their workers. But the push for temperance also had roots in anti-immigrant and anti-Catholic sentiments. For example, German immigrants' affection for beer helped bring anti-immigrant and anti-saloon forces together. Temperance advocates persuaded lawmakers in several states to prohibit the production and sale of alcoholic beverages. By the end of the 1850s, 13 states had passed **prohibition** laws.

Anti-Saloon League The Anti-Saloon League (ASL) was founded in 1893 as a state organization in Ohio. Within two years it had become a national organization with branches across the country. The League did not align itself with any political party. It worked with and promoted any politician who supported its only goal—the prohibition of the production and sale of alcohol in the United States. The League actively worked against politicians who did not support its goal.

Source: New York Times / Wikimedia
Carrie Nation with her hatchet

The ASL's activities, energetically advanced by its determined leader, Wayne Wheeler, expanded after 1913. That year, the states ratified the 16th Amendment to the Constitution, which created the national income tax. Prior to the passage of the 16th Amendment, up to 40 percent of federal funding came from liquor taxes. With funding no longer a stumbling block, ASL and other temperance activists were empowered to pressure lawmakers for national prohibition

Temperance Leaders Women played a strong role in the fight for prohibition. The most famous of the temperance crusaders were Frances Willard and Carry Nation. Willard supported both temperance and suffrage. She led the Woman's Christian Temperance Union (WCTU), which also supported progressive legislation that favored workers. Nation often used a more direct approach. She was known to march into the saloons of Kansas, wielding a hatchet, and destroying shelves of bottled liquor. Her unconventional approach and numerous arrests brought nationwide publicity to the temperance movement. But her ultimate impact on the success of the prohibition movement paled in comparison to that of mainstream groups such as the ASL and the WCTU.

Prohibition In 1919, the temperance movement achieved its goal with the ratification of the **Eighteenth Amendment**, which prohibited the manufacture and sale of alcoholic beverages in the United States. After the amendment was ratified, Congress passed the National Prohibition Act, commonly referred to as the Volstead Act, to enforce it.

Civic Literacy: Ideas and Beliefs Inspired by the idea of social progress, the progressive movement evolved into a political movement. Those involved in the movement believed that problems such as poverty, greed, racism, and violence could be addressed through reforms such as safe home and work environments.

The Impacts of Individual Reformers

Journalists were critically important to the Progressive Movement. Their books and articles prompted Americans to address the wrongs of society. Other progressives were concerned with the welfare of people living in urban slums. They were at the forefront of what was called the "social justice movement."

Muckrakers and Reform Monthly magazines like the *Ladies' Home Journal* and *McClure's* ran lengthy articles about corruption in government and shocking conditions in factories and slums. The writers of these articles drew attention to dirty politics, or "muck"—anything that seemed dishonest, immoral, and ugly. Theodore Roosevelt referred to these writers as "**muckrakers**." The muckrakers continued to influence later generations of journalists who, today, are known as investigative reporters.

The founder of *McClure's Magazine* hired Ida Tarbell as a reporter in 1894. Her book *History of the Standard Oil Company* (1904) was first published as a series of articles in the magazine. Tarbell's thorough account of John D. Rockefeller's monopolistic methods and unfair practices helped define the muckrakers' techniques.

In 1905, **Upton Sinclair** went undercover to investigate conditions in the Chicago stockyards for a socialist weekly. Originally appearing as a series of articles in *Appeal to Reason*, Sinclair's work *The Jungle* was published as a book in 1906. In his novel, Sinclair followed the lives of a family of Lithuanian immigrants who struggle to survive, living in slums and working dangerous, poorly paid jobs. He had hoped to create sympathy for workers—many of them immigrants—in the meatpacking industry. However, his book aroused widespread disgust in regard to food safety, causing Sinclair to remark, "I aimed at the public's heart and by accident I hit it in the stomach."

The public outcry following the book's publication led directly to the Meat Inspection Act (1906), which provided for federal inspection of meat. A related law, the Pure Food and Drug Act (1906), regulated the manufacture of foods and required commercially bottled and packaged medicines to be truthfully and fully labeled.

The Settlement House Movement A settlement house was a building located in a poor immigrant neighborhood where women and children could go for help in adjusting to American life. **Jane Addams**, a college graduate with an urge toward public service and reform, visited a settlement house called Toynbee Hall in London in 1888. Deeply impressed by the social services being provided there, Addams was determined to replicate the model in the United States. Addams and Helen Gates Starr established Hull House in Chicago in 1889. Following a similar model, Lillian Wald founded Henry Street Settlement in New York City in 1893.

Both settlement houses provided activities to keep poor children from the dangers of unsupervised play on city streets. They offered free classes for immigrants in English as well as classes in the arts, literature, and music. Addams, Wald, and other social workers became experts on the problems of urban poverty. They used their knowledge to persuade state legislatures to enact laws to protect children—especially laws to abolish child labor.

Early Fight for Birth Control Many working-class women risked their lives and suffered increased poverty because of frequent pregnancies and births.

> **Read Closely: Motivation**
> Looking for a person's motivations for their actions can be a helpful tool in understanding history. Upton Sinclair's book *The Jungle* led to the passage of the Meat Inspection Act of 1906. What was his intention when he wrote *The Jungle*?

Working as a nurse among immigrant families in New York City, Margaret Sanger witnessed their struggles. She believed that women who wanted it should be given information on ways to prevent pregnancy. In 1914, she started publishing a magazine on birth control and opened the first birth control clinic in Brooklyn. Her clinic and her book *What Every Girl Should Know* (1916) launched a movement for informed parenthood that gained strength in later decades.

Tenement Reform The Danish immigrant journalist and photographer Jacob Riis set out to describe the grim living conditions of typical immigrants in New York City. His 1890 book, *How the Other Half Lives*, shocked many middle-class readers with its detailed descriptions and photographs of overcrowded and unsanitary conditions in tenements—cheap, run-down, poorly maintained apartment buildings.

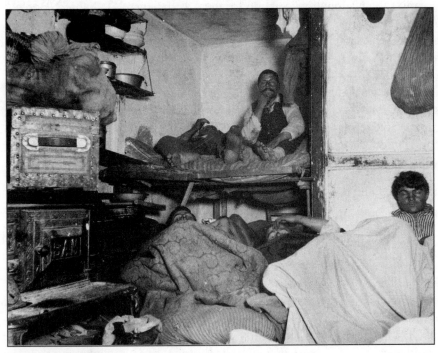

Source: Wikimedia Commons

Lodgers in a crowded New York tenement pay 5 cents a spot, 1889.

Riis's book provoked action. New York's state legislature and its reform-minded governor, **Theodore Roosevelt**, created the New York State Tenement Housing Commission in 1900. In turn, it established a commission for New York City, home to many of the tenements.

As concern grew about high death rates from infectious diseases, the state of New York passed a new tenement law in 1901. It called for new buildings to have windows that opened into courtyards rather than air shafts. The new law also required indoor rather than outdoor bathrooms. To make sure the law was followed, inspectors checked on new building construction. The improved sanitary conditions resulted in healthier living conditions and a decreased death rate.

> **Speak and Listen: Impact**
> With a partner, discuss two ways Jacob Riis made a lasting impact on American society. Give concrete examples. Also discuss any other writers you know were influential.

Movement for African American Rights Recall that Jim Crow laws had established racial segregation in the South in the 1880s and 1890s. During the Progressive Era, African American leaders challenged these laws and tried to win the support of White reformers. The best-known leader of African Americans in the Progressive Era was Booker T. Washington. (See Chapter 4.) Many White business leaders and politicians consulted Washington about the education and training of African Americans for skilled industrial jobs. Washington was frequently called to the White House to advise Theodore Roosevelt.

Another leader of the movement for African American rights was Harvard-educated scholar **W.E.B. Du Bois**. In 1905, he launched what became known as the Niagara Movement at a meeting of Black reformers in Niagara Falls, Canada. (They met there because hotels on the New York side of the border refused to give them rooms.) The movement focused on publicizing and protesting acts of injustice against African Americans.

In 1909, members of the Niagara Movement joined with White reformers to organize the National Association for the Advancement of Colored People (NAACP). The organization was dedicated to protecting the rights of African Americans. It also helped defend those accused of crimes merely because of their race. Du Bois edited the NAACP's magazine, *The Crisis*.

At the time, most White Americans didn't concern themselves with the issue of civil rights for African Americans. Even so, during the Progressive Era, NAACP lawyers managed to win a number of civil rights cases in the Supreme Court. Between 1915 and 1917, the Court declared the following to be unconstitutional:

- The grandfather clause

- A segregated housing law

- The practice of denying African Americans the right to serve on juries

- The practice of denying African Americans the right to run for office in party primaries

One of the NAACP's founders was **Ida B. Wells**. She was an African American muckraking journalist from Tennessee who dedicated her career to the cause of racial justice. Wells lost several friends to lynchings, or hangings, by mobs of Whites. This inspired her to launch a crusade against lynching. In 1895 she published *A Red Record*, in which she thoroughly documented the evil. Her work helped bring this violence to the attention of the public.

Read Closely: Details
Details in a reading can often point to broader facts about history and society. How does the paragraph about the Niagara Movement illustrate injustice against African Americans?

Application: Interpret a Primary Source

Read the excerpt and answer the questions that follow it.

How the Other Half Lives

Long ago it was said that "one half of the world does not know how the other half lives." That was true then. It did not know because it did not care. The half that was on top cared little for the struggles, and less for the fate of those who were underneath, so long as it was able to hold them there and keep its own seat. There came a time when the discomfort and crowding below were so great, and the consequent upheavals so violent, that it was no longer an easy thing to do, and then the upper half fell to inquiring what was the matter. Information on the subject has been accumulating rapidly since, and the whole world has had its hands full answering for its old ignorance.

In New York . . . the boundary line of the Other Half lies through the tenements. . . . Today three-fourths of its people live in the tenements, and the nineteenth century drift of the population to the cities is sending ever-increasing multitudes to crowd them. The fifteen thousand tenant houses that were the despair of the sanitarian in the past generation have swelled into thirty-seven thousand, and more than twelve hundred thousand persons call them home. The one way out he saw—rapid transit to the suburbs—has brought no relief. We know now that there is no way out; that the "system" that was the evil offspring of public neglect and private greed has come to stay, a storm-centre forever of our civilization. Nothing is left but to make the best of a bad bargain.

Source: Jacob Riis, Introduction to *How the Other Half Lives*, 1890

1. Based on this excerpt, what can we assume was Riis's intention, his broader mission, in writing *How the Other Half Lives*?

_____

_____

2. Riis talks about the population of the tenements in the second paragraph. Describe in your own words the situation he lays out. Why did the situation develop as it did?

_____

_____

3. Describe who you think Riis's audience is in this excerpt. What about Riis might make his audience more likely to accept his viewpoint and findings?

_____

_____

Multiple-Choice Questions

Questions 1–3 refer to the excerpt below.

A. Frances Willard to the 20th Annual Conference of the WCTU in Chicago

The Prohibition agitation in America has not been as great in the past year as formerly, and the reasons are not far to seek. A presidential campaign always lowers the moral atmosphere for a year before it begins and a year after it is over. Legislators become timid, politicians proceed to "hedge," journalists, with an eye to the loaves and fishes, furl their sails concerning issues that have at best only a fighting chance; the world, the flesh, and the devil get their innings, and the time is not yet. In the past year the attention of the nation has been focused

Source: Library of Congress / Wikimedia Commons

Frances Willard

on the World's Fair and the endless difficulties to which that has given birth. There has been an incalculable amount of ill-will set in motion as the result of personal financial interest and ignoble ambition. All this savours [tastes] not the things of God or of humanity. The re-adjustment of political parties is still inchoate [only partly in existence]; men's hearts are failing them for fear; leaders in the traditional party of moral ideas have thrown off all disguises and grounded any weapons of rebellion they may once have lifted against the liquor traffic. The financial panic has rivetted the attention of the public on their own dangers and disasters, and the spirit of money-making has lamentably invaded the ranks of the temperance army itself; but prohibition is as lively an issue to-day as emancipation was in 1856; an issue that stirs such deadly hatred is by no means dead. It is still quick with fighting blood, and its enemies know this even better than its friends. . . .

Source: Frances Willard, Annual Address to the Women's Christian Temperance Union, 1893

1. Which of the following is one of the reasons Willard gives for less "Prohibition" agitation in the previous year?

    1. Presidential campaigns lower the moral atmosphere.
    2. The Progressive Party had promised to ban the sale of alcohol.
    3. Law enforcement had cracked down on demonstrations by agitators.
    4. Congress had passed a constitutional amendment banning the sale and distribution of alcoholic beverages.

2. How does this excerpt illustrate both change and continuity in the temperance movement?

    1. It shows how the movement for the emancipation of slaves had evolved into a temperance movement after the Civil War.
    2. The temperance movement had begun years before but suffered setbacks in 1893 from which it would recover, eventually achieving its goal of prohibition.
    3. Political parties that had been in existence since before the Civil War were going through re-adjustments but would continue into the next century.
    4. Greed had led to a financial panic, which focused the attention of the public temporarily on money-making and self-interest.

3. To what other historical event or cause does Willard compare prohibition?

    1. A presidential election
    2. The World's Fair
    3. Emancipation
    4. The financial panic

Questions 4 and 5 refer to the excerpt below.

B. Eugene Debs on Becoming a Socialist

In 1894 the American Railway Union was organized and a braver body of men never fought the battle of the working class.

Up to this time I had heard but little of Socialism, knew practically nothing about the movement, and what little I did know was not calculated to impress me in its favor. I was bent on thorough and complete organization of the railroad men and ultimately the whole working class, and all my time and energy were given to that end. My supreme conviction was that if they were only organized in every branch of the service and all acted together in concert they could redress their wrongs and regulate the conditions of their employment. The stockholders of the corporation acted as one, why not the men? It was such a plain proposition—simply to follow the example set before their eyes by their masters—surely they could not fail to see it, act as one, and solve the problem.

It is useless to say that I had yet to learn the workings of the capitalist system, the resources of its masters and the weakness of its slaves. Indeed, no shadow of a "system" fell athwart my pathway; no thought of ending wage-misery marred my plans. I was too deeply absorbed in perfecting wage-servitude and making it a "thing of beauty and a joy forever."

It all seems very strange to me now, taking a backward look, that my vision was so focalized [focused] on a single objective point that I utterly failed to see what now appears as clear as the noonday sun—so clear that I marvel that any workingman, however dull, uncomprehending, can resist it.

But perhaps it was better so. I was to be baptized in Socialism in the roar of conflict and I thank the gods for reserving to this fitful occasion the fiat, "Let there be light!"—the light that streams in steady radiance upon the broadway to the Socialist republic.

Source: Eugene V. Debs, "How I Became a Socialist" in *The Comrade*, April 1902

4. How could the excerpt above best be used?

   1. As a source for an article explaining the workings of capitalism
   2. As a source for an article explaining what socialism is
   3. As a source for a history of American labor unions
   4. As a source for a book explaining how to organize a labor union

5. What problem did Debs hope to solve by turning to socialism?

   1. The way in which stockholders were reimbursed
   2. The growing power of labor unions
   3. The government's ability to stop strikes
   4. The poor conditions of the working class

Questions 6–8 refer to the excerpt below.

C. Ford on the First Assembly Line

A Ford car contains about five thousand parts—that is counting screws, nuts, and all. Some of the parts are fairly bulky and others are almost the size of watch parts. In our first assembling we simply started to put a car together at a spot on the floor and workmen brought to it the parts as they were needed in exactly the same way that one builds a house. When we started to make parts it was natural to create a single department of the factory to make that part, but usually one workman performed all of the operations necessary on a small part. The rapid press [pressure] of production made it necessary to devise plans of production that would avoid having the workers falling over one another. . . .

The first step forward in assembly came when we began taking the work to the men instead of the men to the work. We now have two general principles in all operations—that a man shall never have to take more than one step, if possibly it can be avoided, and that no man need ever stoop over.

. . . In short, the result is this: by the aid of scientific study one man is now able to do somewhat more than four did only a comparatively few years ago. That line established the efficiency of the method and we now use it everywhere. The assembling of the motor, formerly done by one man, is now divided into eighty-four operations—those men do the work that three times their number formerly did.

Source: Henry Ford, "The First Assembly Line," 1913

6. Which of the following best describes Ford's probable purpose in writing this essay?

1. To explain how to avoid workplace accidents
2. To provide an excuse for cutting jobs at his factory
3. To make sure that he got credit for inventing the assembly line
4. To explain the reasons for the development of the assembly line

7. How does this excerpt illustrate a turning point in history?

1. It describes the creation of the first automobile factory.
2. It describes a revolutionary change in manufacturing.
3. It describes the scientific revolution.
4. It describes a new way to build houses.

8. What was the main reason for the development of the assembly line?

1. To improve efficiency
2. To introduce scientific study into the workplace
3. To make it easier for one person to build a motor
4. To reduce the amount of factory space needed to build each vehicle

Short-Essay Questions

Study the two documents and answer the question that follows.

D. Conditions in a Sausage Factory

There was never the least attention paid to what was cut up for sausage; there would come all the way back from Europe old sausage that had been rejected, and that was moldy and White—it would be dosed with borax and glycerine, and dumped into the hoppers, and made over again for home consumption.

There would be meat that had tumbled out on the floor, in the dirt and sawdust, where the workers had tramped and spit uncounted billions of consumption germs. There would be meat stored in great piles in rooms, and the water from leaky roofs would drip over it, and thousands of rats would race about on it. It was too dark in these storage places to see well, but a man could run his hand over these piles of meat and sweep off handfuls of the dried dung of rats. These rats were nuisances, and the packers would put poisoned bread out for them; they would die, and then rats, bread, and meat would go into the hoppers together. This is no fairy story and no joke; the meat would be shoveled into carts, and the man who did the shoveling would not trouble to lift out a rat even when he saw one—there were things that went into the sausage in comparison with which a poisoned rat was a tidbit.

Source: Upton Sinclair, *The Jungle*, 1906

Source: U.S. National Archives and Records Administration / Wikimedia Commons

A meatpacking plant in Omaha, Nebraska, 1910

E. From the Meat Inspection Act of 1906

For the purposes hereinbefore set forth the Secretary shall cause to be made, by inspectors appointed for that purpose, an examination and inspection of all meat food products prepared for commerce in any slaughtering, meat-canning, salting, packing, rendering, or similar establishment, and for the purposes of any examination and inspection and inspectors shall have access at all times, by day or night, whether the establishment be operated or not, to every part of said establishment; and said inspectors shall mark, stamp, tag, or label as "Inspected and passed" all such products found to be not adulterated; and said inspectors shall label, mark, stamp, or tag as "Inspected and condemned" all such products found adulterated, and all such condemned meat food products shall be destroyed for food purposes, as hereinbefore provided, and the Secretary may remove inspectors from any establishment which fails to so destroy such condemned meat food products: *Provided*, That subject to the rules and regulations of the Secretary the provisions of this section in regard to preservatives shall not apply to meat food products for export to any foreign country and which are prepared or packed according to the specifications or directions of the foreign purchaser, when no substance is used in the preparation or packing thereof in conflict with the laws of the foreign country to which said article is to be exported; but if said article shall be in fact sold or offered for sale for domestic use or consumption then this proviso shall not exempt said article from the operation of all the other provisions of this chapter.

Source: Federal Meat Inspection Act of 1906

1. In a short essay, describe the historical context surrounding the two documents above. Then identify and explain the cause-and-effect relationship between the events described in these documents.

Study the two documents and answer the question that follows.

F. Lynch Law in America

Our country's national crime is *lynching*. It is not the creature of an hour, the sudden outburst of uncontrolled fury, or the unspeakable brutality of an insane mob. It represents the cool, calculating deliberation of intelligent people who openly avow that there is an "unwritten law" that justifies them in putting human beings to death without complaint under oath, without trial by jury, without opportunity to make defense, and without right of appeal. . . .

During the last ten years a new statute has been added to the "unwritten law." This statute proclaims that for certain crimes or alleged crimes no negro shall be allowed a trial; that no White woman shall be compelled to charge an assault under oath or to submit any such charge to the investigation of a court of law. The result is that many men have been put to death whose innocence was afterward established; and to-day, under this reign of the "unwritten law," no colored man, no matter what his reputation, is safe from lynching if a White woman, no matter what her standing or motive, cares to charge him with insult or assault.

It is considered a sufficient excuse and reasonable justification to put a prisoner to death under this "unwritten law" for the frequently repeated charge that these lynching horrors are necessary to prevent crimes against women. . . .

But the negro resents and utterly repudiates the effort to blacken his good name by asserting that assaults upon women are peculiar to his race. The negro has suffered far more from the commission of this crime against the women of his race by White men than the White race has ever suffered through his crimes. Very scant notice is taken of the matter when this is the condition of affairs. What becomes a crime deserving capital punishment when the tables are turned is a matter of small moment when the negro woman is the accusing party.

Source: Ida B. Wells-Barnett, "Lynch Law in America," *The Arena,* January 1900

JOHN HARTFIELD WILL BE LYNCHED BY ELLISVILLE MOB AT 5 O'CLOCK THIS AFTERNOON

Governor Bilbo Says He is Powerless to Prevent it—Thousands of People are Flocking Into Ellisville to Attend the Event—Sheriff and Authorities are Powerless to Prevent it.

Source: Headlines from the *Jackson Daily News*. Story was reported from Hattiesburg, Mississippi, June 26, 1919

2. In a short essay, describe the historical context surrounding the two documents above. Then analyze and explain how the purpose of the first document affects its reliability as a source of evidence.

CHAPTER 6

The Rise of U.S. Power
(1890–1920)

Chapter Overview

In the late 19th and early 20th centuries, the United States began to play a more prominent role on the world stage. As a result, the country took actions and assumed roles that were controversial to many Americans and contrary to traditional policies and ideals.

Imperialism After expanding from the Atlantic to the Pacific, Americans began to debate further expansion. By 1900, the United States had annexed Samoa and Hawaii, and a war with Spain brought Puerto Rico, Guam, and the Philippines under direct U.S. control. Then in 1903, the United States helped engineer the secession of Panama from Colombia. As a result, the United States was able to build the Panama Canal, connecting the Atlantic and Pacific Oceans.

Intervention In the early 20th century, U.S. presidents re-interpreted the Monroe Doctrine. This rethink allowed them to justify sending troops into other countries in the Western Hemisphere, such as Haiti, the Dominican Republic, and Nicaragua. U.S. intervention in Mexico during that country's revolution affected relations between the two countries for many years.

World War I During the late 19th century, the nations of Europe had formed two major alliances—the Allied Powers (Britain, France, Russia, and Italy) and the Central Powers (Germany, Austria-Hungary, Bulgaria, and the Ottoman Empire). In August 1914, events led to a "world war" pitting the alliances against one another. The United States tried to remain neutral, but the United States eventually declared war on Germany. The arrival of large numbers of U.S. troops in Europe helped the Allies defeat the Central Powers.

Effects of the War The war changed the U.S. economy. As men went off to fight in Europe, women replaced them in the workplace. In what became known as the Great Migration, African Americans left the South to find work in factories in the North. After the war, the United States experienced an economic recession.

Civic Literacy: The Press During this era, newspapers had enormous influence over popular opinion. Owners of large newspapers ran sensational headlines to shock the public and sell more newspapers. These tactics ended up influencing public policy as well, and media outlets have similar power today.

New York Social Studies Framework

Key Idea 11.6: The Rise of American Power
Numerous factors contributed to the rise of the United States as a world power. Debates over the United States' role in world affairs increased in response to overseas expansion and involvement in World War I. United States participation in the war had important effects on American society.

Civic Literacy Essay: Organize Your Evidence

After writing everything you have learned and remembered, organize your evidence. Review your notes, looking for patterns related to the task.

The organizational pattern you choose will depend on the task, the evidence you have collected, and your argument (see page 223). The chart below shows some of the different organizational patterns you might use.

Type of Order	Description
Chronological (Time) Order	Arranges evidence in the order in which efforts and events happened
Spatial Order	Arranges evidence according to location (Southern United States, New England, the West for example)
Order of Importance	Arranges evidence according to its importance or impact (from least to most important or most to least important)
Developmental Order	Arranges evidence according to a logical pattern in which one development leads to the next—a chain of causes and effects, for example
Comparison and Contrast	Arranges evidence according to similarities and/or differences

Application: Make a list of highlights of your experiences in school. Then try organizing them in two different organizational patterns. Which do you think would make the most interesting arrangement? Give reasons for your answer.

Key Terms by Theme

Geography
Panama Canal (p. 188)
Roosevelt Corollary (p. 189)
Woodrow Wilson (p. 190)

Governance
imperialism (p. 185)
Queen Liliuokalani (p. 185)
William McKinley (p. 185)
protectorate (p. 187)

Allied Powers (p. 193)
Central Powers (p. 193)
Fourteen Points (p. 197)
Treaty of Versailles (p. 198)
reparations (p. 198)

Identity
self-determination (p. 197)
nativist (p. 206)

Movement
Great Migration (p. 204)

Social Structures
social Darwinism (p. 185)
Red Scare (p. 206)
Ku Klux Klan (KKK) (p. 206)

Conceptual Understanding
11.6a In the late 1800s, various strategic and economic factors led to a greater focus on foreign affairs and debates over the United States' role in the world.

The Anti-Imperialist League formed in 1898 to fight U.S. annexation of the Philippines under the Treaty of Paris. Its members included many prominent Americans—former president Benjamin Harrison, industrialist Andrew Carnegie, and author Mark Twain, among others. The League nearly succeeded in its goal: the Treaty of Paris was ratified by a single vote on February 6, 1899.

Analyze a Primary Source

Platform of the American Anti-Imperialist League

Read Closely: Purpose
When you analyze a primary source, keep in mind its purpose—the reason it was written. This is the platform, or set of goals, of the Anti-Imperialist League, which was formed to oppose the annexation of the Philippines. Circle the word that indicates the organization's *main* goal for the Philippines.

Read Closely: Contrasts
In historical documents, look for contrasts that point to key ideas. In both the first and the fifth paragraphs, the author uses the phrase "criminal aggression" to contrast U.S. actions in the Philippines with the effect of those actions on the United States. Underline the phrases that describe the effects this aggression had on the United States.

Read Closely: Allusion
In the first paragraph, the author uses two familiar phrases: "life, liberty and the pursuit of happiness" and "governments derive their just powers from the consent of the governed." His audience likely would have recognized the allusions to the Declaration of Independence.

We hold that the policy known as imperialism is hostile to liberty and tends toward militarism, an evil from which it has been our glory to be free. We regret that it has become necessary in the land of Washington and Lincoln to reaffirm that all men, of whatever race or color, are entitled to life, liberty and the pursuit of happiness. We maintain that governments derive their just powers from the consent of the governed. We insist that the subjugation of any people is "criminal aggression" and open disloyalty to the distinctive principles of our Government.

We earnestly condemn the policy of the present National Administration in the Philippines. It seeks to extinguish the spirit of 1776 in those islands. We deplore the sacrifice of our soldiers and sailors, whose bravery deserves admiration even in an unjust war. We denounce the slaughter of the Filipinos as a needless horror. We protest against the extension of American sovereignty by Spanish methods.

We demand the immediate cessation of the war against liberty, begun by Spain and continued by us. We urge that Congress be promptly convened to announce to the Filipinos our purpose to concede to them the independence for which they have so long fought and which of right is theirs.

The United States have always protested against the doctrine of international law which permits the subjugation of the weak by the strong. A self-governing state cannot accept sovereignty over an unwilling people. The United States cannot act upon the ancient heresy [controversial opinion] that might makes right.

Imperialists assume that with the destruction of self-government in the Philippines by American hands, all opposition here will cease. This is a grievous error. Much as we abhor the war of "criminal aggression" in the Philippines, greatly as we regret that the blood of the Filipinos is on American hands, we more deeply resent the betrayal of American institutions at home. . . .

Whether the ruthless slaughter of the Filipinos shall end next month or next year is but an incident in a contest that must go on until the Declaration of Independence and the Constitution of the United States are rescued from the hands of their betrayers. . . .

Source: "Platform of the American Anti-Imperialist League," 1899

Strategic and Economic Interests

Americans disagreed about whether the United States should adopt a policy of **imperialism**. It was obvious that the United States, like the nations of Europe, was rapidly industrializing. It was also obvious that U.S. trade was growing. Should the United States now enter the race for overseas colonies?

Arguments for Expansion After Americans had settled the western land frontier, some business leaders looked for new economic frontiers—new markets and new investment opportunities. Many Americans believed that Manifest Destiny now justified increasing the U.S. role in world affairs. This new vision of Manifest Destiny led the United States to acquire coaling stations for its growing fleet of steamships. These stations, located in the Pacific and the Caribbean, supplied coal to help ships run. They also served as naval bases for the U.S. military.

Some people argued that less-developed regions of the world would benefit from being governed by the civilizations of the West. They wanted to spread Christianity and Western civilization. This belief was based on **social Darwinism**, which promoted the idea of biological or genetic superiority of some peoples and, therefore, nations. Perceived "cultural superiority," and often racial superiority, was used to justify expansion.

Arguments Against Expansion Some Americans opposed expansion on both moral and practical grounds. They thought the United States should focus on trade without political involvement. Some feared it was inevitable that foreign involvement would lead to foreign wars. Even some businesspeople questioned the need for territorial gains. They argued that wars would harm rather than help overseas trade.

Some Americans argued that democracy would suffer if the United States took over foreign places. In doing so, it would deny the people who lived there their political rights and independence. Opponents believed that Manifest Destiny had ended with the expansion to the Pacific. There was no justification for cultural or military expansion to Asia and Latin America. Others had less lofty justifications for their beliefs. They opposed expansion on the grounds that it would allow large numbers of non-White people to become Americans.

Annexation of Samoa A group of islands called Samoa lies in the South Pacific Ocean. In 1878, the United States negotiated the right to build a coaling station there. In 1889, war nearly broke out as Germany and Great Britain also expressed interest in establishing bases in the islands. Then in 1899, Germany and the United States agreed to divide Samoa. Each would took control of different islands—without consulting the Samoan people.

Acquisition of Hawaii In 1887, the independent kingdom of Hawaii allowed the United States to build a coaling station in Pearl Harbor. Six years later, with the help of U.S. Marines, a group of American sugar growers overthrew Hawaii's **Queen Liliuokalani**. They hoped the United States would annex the islands. When President Grover Cleveland refused, Hawaii became an independent republic. But the next president, **William McKinley**, pushed to make Hawaii a U.S. territory. In 1900, the Senate approved the annexation of Hawaii.

> **Read Closely: Bias**
> Understanding a person's bias for their actions is crucial to understanding history. How did the idea of cultural superiority provide a "moral" justification for European and American imperialism?

The Spanish-American War

In 1895, a revolt against Spanish rule broke out in Cuba, one of Spain's few remaining colonial holdings. Three years later, the United States declared war against Spain over the Cuba question. More than any other event, this war represented a turning point in U.S. foreign policy. The United Stated gained a swift and decisive victory. This showed that the United States was now becoming a major military power as well as a leading economic power.

Causes of War The American people's sympathy for the Cuban people rebelling against an oppressive regime played a large role in bringing about the war with Spain. Americans' sympathies were fanned by sensational headlines in the newspapers, especially the New York City newspapers owned by William Randolph Hearst and Joseph Pulitzer. Both publishers were guilty of "yellow journalism," squeezing all the sensation they could out of the violent conflict in Cuba. They greatly exaggerated reports of Spanish atrocities against the Cuban people.

In February 1898, the USS *Maine*, a battleship anchored in the harbor of Havana, Cuba, exploded and sank. About 250 of its crew died. The cause of the explosion was never discovered. U.S. newspapers, however, blamed Spain for blowing up the ship. Editorials in the yellow press called for war to liberate Cuba from Spanish rule. "Remember the *Maine*" became a battle cry.

There were other reasons for war. Cuba's location made it an ideal naval base for U.S. ships. Many thought that an island only 90 miles from Florida should not belong to a European power. Many felt that an independent (or U.S.-dominated) Cuban government would better protect the $50 million U.S. investment in Cuba's sugar and tobacco plantations.

Decision for War Not everyone favored the idea of a war with Spain. Some business leaders feared that such a war might lead to the destruction of American-owned properties. There was also a good diplomatic reason for avoiding war. After the sinking of the *Maine*, Spain agreed to virtually all of the U.S. demands concerning Cuba. This included granting Cuba independence. Nevertheless, in April 1899, President McKinley asked Congress for a declaration of war against Spain. Congress readily complied.

REMEMBER THE MAINE! AND DON'T FORGET THE STARVING CUBANS!

Source: Historical Society of Pennsylvania / Wikimedia Commons

This cartoonist used graphic images in hope of spurring support for U.S. action.

The Spanish-American War lasted only about four months. It was fought in two areas—the islands of Cuba and Puerto Rico in the Caribbean and the Philippine Islands in the Pacific. The United States won every major battle.

In Cuba, a troop of U.S. volunteers known as the Rough Riders won fame for their charge up San Juan Hill under future U.S. president Theodore Roosevelt. However, they didn't arrive until *after* two segregated regiments of African American "buffalo soldiers." Later, these fighters saved the Rough Riders from near certain defeat and death. Shortly afterward, the Cuban port of Santiago surrendered. At the same time, the neighboring island of Puerto Rico fell to U.S. forces.

In the Philippines, the U.S. Navy distinguished itself in a devastating attack against the Spanish fleet in Manila Bay. Commander George Dewey's overwhelming victory in this naval battle made him an American hero. The Filipinos, like the Cubans, had been fighting for their independence from Spain when the war began. They celebrated the U.S. victory at Manila Bay. But they were soon disappointed when independence did not follow.

Read Closely: Contrast
A sentence that begins *However* often describes a contrast with an idea expressed previously. In reference to the Rough Riders and the "buffalo soldiers," what is being contrasted, and why is this important?

Results of the Spanish-American War

In and around this time, a number of European countries, chiefly Great Britain, France, and Germany, were fully engaged in imperialism. They had already carved up vast areas of Africa and Asia. U.S. politicians and the American public were divided on whether becoming an imperial power was the right thing to do.

Treaty of Paris The terms of the Treaty of Paris, signed in December 1898, were as follows:

- Spain gave two islands to the United States: Puerto Rico in the Caribbean and Guam in the Pacific.

- Spain granted Cuba its independence, but Cuba became a U.S. **protectorate**—a nominally independent country that is controlled by a foreign power.

- Spain "sold" the Philippines to the United States for $20 million.

American public opinion was sharply divided. Some wanted the Philippines to be a U.S. territory. Others thought Filipinos should have their independence.

Imperialist Argument Imperialists argued that colonial expansion was necessary. It had the potential to build the reputation of the United States as a world power. They argued that the Philippines were bound to fall under the influence of one Western power or another. If that was so, they were better off under U.S. rule than under a nondemocratic government, such as Germany.

Anti-Imperialist Argument The anti-imperialists were led by William Jennings Bryan, the Democratic candidate for president in 1900. They warned that the United States would be abandoning its own commitment to democracy if it ruled territory on the other side of the Pacific. They also feared that the possession of islands near Asia would draw the United States into Asian politics and wars.

Constitutional Issues In a series of cases known as the Insular Cases, the Supreme Court in 1901 ruled that the Constitution did not fully cover colonial possessions. The extent to which the Constitution applied to colonies would be determined by Congress. This decision confirmed what the anti-imperialists had feared. The democratic ideals enshrined in the Declaration of Independece and the Constitution would not apply to U.S. colonies.

Revolt in the Philippines The Filipinos resented being traded from one colonial power to another. In 1899, rebel troops that had fought against Spain turned their weapons against U.S. forces. To put down the uprising, President McKinley sent 70,000 additional troops to the Philippines. By the time the rebellion ended in 1902, over 20,000 Filipino combatants and 4,200 U.S. soldiers had perished. More than 200,000 Filipino civilians, too, had died, due to combat, disease, and famine.

U. S. Imperialism in the Western Hemisphere

U.S. imperialism was just as active in what the country considered its own sphere of influence—the Americas. The United States justified its interference in Latin America and the Caribbean through an extension of the Monroe Doctrine.

Panama Canal As early as the 1850s, there had been plans to dig a canal through a narrow strip of land in Central America—the region known as Panama. The benefits of such a canal were clear:

- It would cut in half the sailing time from New York to San Francisco.

- It would greatly help the trade of all nations of the world.

- It would also eliminate the dangerous voyage over stormy seas at the tip of South America.

When Theodore Roosevelt became president in 1901, Panama belonged to the South American republic of Colombia. Roosevelt offered to pay Colombia $10 million for the right to lease the land through which the canal would pass. He was furious when Colombia refused his offer. Roosevelt's response was to support a 1903 uprising in Panama against Colombian rule.

The uprising lasted only a few hours. U.S. Navy forces prevented Colombian troops from stopping the so-called revolution. Roosevelt quickly recognized the government of the new Republic of Panama. In return, Panama quickly agreed to U.S. terms for leasing a canal zone through the country. Work on the canal began soon afterward.

The building of the **Panama Canal** was one of the engineering marvels of the 20th century. Enormous locks and dams had to be built to control the canal's water level. These structures allowed ships to move section-by-section through the canal. Entire towns had to be erected to house all the workers. As many as 40,000 or more workers toiled on the canal at some points, mostly laborers from poor Caribbean Islands. Just over 5,600 workers died from accidents or disease during construction. After seven years, the "big ditch" was completed in 1914. Theodore Roosevelt lived to see ocean-going ships move through the canal that was begun under his administration.

Read Closely: Effect
To fully appreciate the significance of a historical decision, be alert to any contradictory effects it has. For example, one argument imperialists used to justify the U.S. takeover of the Philippines was to keep them from being taken over by a nondemocratic government. What was the actual result of U.S. rule in the Philippines?

Roosevelt Corollary Recall that the Monroe Doctrine of 1823 had warned European nations not to interfere in the internal politics of Latin American nations. Implied in this warning was the idea that the United States would protect the countries of Latin America from outside interference. Also implied was the assumed right of the United States to send troops into any threatened country to the south. The policy of intervention would be applied several times in the early years of the 20th century.

Roosevelt used the Monroe Doctrine to justify his interventionist policy in Latin America. Several Latin American nations had failed to pay their debts to Great Britain, Germany, and other European nations. Roosevelt recognized that Europeans might use debt as an excuse for intervention in indebted countries. To avoid this possibility, he said that the United States might intervene in a Latin American country if its debts were far overdue. This extension to the Monroe Doctrine is known as the **Roosevelt Corollary**.

From Latin Americans' viewpoint, however, the Roosevelt Corollary was an unfair expansion of U.S. military power into the affairs of independent nations. The corollary, they reasoned, was not for their protection but to help maintain the dominant position of the United States.

Applying his corollary in 1904, President Roosevelt sent U.S. troops to occupy the capital of the Dominican Republic, an island country in the Caribbean Sea. The troops remained long enough to make sure that the Dominican Republic paid its debts. In addition to the Dominican Republic, other areas in the West Indies were also treated as American protectorates. These nations included Haiti and Cuba.

> **Read Closely: Similarities**
> Look for similarities in ideas and policies to help identify historical trends. What similarities exist between the ideas of those who supported control of the Philippines and the ideas behind the Roosevelt Corollary?

THE BIG STICK IN THE CARIBBEAN SEA

Source: Wikimedia Commons
Roosevelt applied the proverb, "Speak softly, and carry a big stick," to regional politics. It meant that negotiations with Latin American countries were always backed by the threat of military consequences.

Dollar Diplomacy President William Howard Taft believed that the United States should protect U.S. businesses that invested in Latin America. He also believed that the United States had the right to force a Latin American country to repay loans it owed to U.S. banks. These monetary reasons for intervention resulted in what was called dollar diplomacy. For example, Taft sent U.S. Marines to Nicaragua in 1912, when a civil war there threatened to prevent repayment of a large U.S. bank loan.

Wilson and Intervention President **Woodrow Wilson** said that he did not believe in dollar diplomacy. But he did believe in keeping order, especially in troubled areas close to the United States. U.S. military forces occupied Haiti from 1916 to 1934 and the Dominican Republic from 1917 to 1925 to put down civil wars. Latin Americans throughout the region deeply resented the U.S. policy of intervention.

Wilson's most serious problem in Latin America was the result of a 1910 revolution in Mexico. Wilson disliked what he considered to be the ruthless methods of a Mexican dictator named Victoriano Huerta. In 1914, U.S. troops occupied the Mexican port of Veracruz after several U.S. sailors were jailed there. Wilson withdrew the troops after Huerta agreed to resign. The new Mexican government of Venustiano Carranza was immediately challenged by rebel forces under Pancho Villa.

On March 9, 1916, Villa raided the town of Columbus, New Mexico, about three miles north of the border with Mexico. Although Villa's troops were repulsed by U.S. Cavalry soldiers stationed there, 19 Americans lost their lives and the town was severely damaged.

Wilson retaliated by sending 10,000 U.S. troops into northern Mexico where they pursued Villa for nearly a year. Wilson avoided formally going to war, however. Early in 1917, he ordered the removal of U.S. troops and formally recognized the Carranza government as legitimate. But Mexicans' bitter memories of U.S. intervention had a negative effect on U.S.-Mexican relations for many years.

Source: Wikimedia Commons
U.S. Navy troops turn over control of Veracruz to troops from the U.S. Army.

Application: Interpret a Primary Source

Read the excerpt below and answer the questions that follow it.

A Plea from the Queen of Hawaii to the President of the United States

MY GREAT AND GOOD FRIEND: It is with deep regret that I address you on this occasion. Some of my subjects, aided by aliens, have renounced their loyalty and revolted against the constitutional government of my Kingdom. They have attempted to depose me and to establish a provisional government, in direct conflict with the organic [traditional] law of this Kingdom. Upon receiving incontestable proof that his excellency the minister plenipotentiary [official representative] of the United States, aided and abetted their unlawful movements and caused United States troops to be landed for that purpose, I submitted to force, believing that he would not have acted in that manner unless by the authority of the Government which he represents.

This action on my part was prompted by three reasons: The futility of a conflict with the United States; the desire to avoid violence, bloodshed, and the destruction of life and property, and the certainty which I feel that you and your Government will right whatever wrongs may have been inflicted upon us in the premises. In due time a statement of the true facts relating this matter will be laid before you, and I live in the hope that you will judge uprightly and justly between myself and my enemies.

This appeal is not made for myself personally, but for my people who have hitherto always enjoyed the friendship and protection of the United States. . . .

I now ask you that in justice to myself and to my people that no steps be taken by the Government of the United States until my cause can be heard by you.

Source: Letter from Queen Liliuokalani of Hawaii to U.S. President Benjamin Harrison, January 18, 1893

1. Describe the historical context surrounding this letter.

_____

_____

2. What effect did Queen Liliuokalani's letter hope to have?

_____

_____

3. How did Liliuokalani hope to sway the president of the United States to right the wrongs that have been inflicted on Hawaii?

_____

_____

Lesson 2 *World War I*

President Woodrow Wilson tried to keep the United States from involvement in World War I. In early 1917, however, events and circumstances drove the country into the conflict. Shortly after Congress declared war on Germany, Wilson issued an appeal to the American people, asking them to do everything possible for the war effort.

Analyze a Primary Source

"Do Your Bit for America"

Read Closely: Intended Audience
When you analyze a primary source, think about the people the writer intended to read it. This piece is an appeal to the American people in general. Circle the name of the specific group that Wilson views as the most important.

Read Closely: Claim and Evidence
One way to engage with a primary source is to think about whether the writer is making a claim and, if so, what evidence he or she provides to support that claim. Wilson claims that there is a need to make sure of large harvests. Underline the evidence he provides for this need.

Read Closely: Purpose
Wilson's purpose is to inspire all citizens to do their "bit" to help win the war. Wilson assures his readers that the work of civilians on the home front—factory workers, miners, and especially farmers—is just as necessary and important as the work of soldiers under fire.

> The industrial forces of the country, men and women alike, will be a great national, a great international, service army—a notable and honored host engaged in the service of the nation and the world, the efficient friends and saviors of free men everywhere.
>
> Thousands—nay, hundreds of thousands—of men otherwise liable to military service will of right and of necessity be excused from that service and assigned to the fundamental, sustaining work of the fields and factories and mines, and they will be as much part of the great patriotic forces of the nation as the men under fire.
>
> I take the liberty, therefore, of addressing this word to the farmers of the country and to all who work on the farms: The supreme need of our own nation and of the nations with which we are cooperating is an abundance of supplies, and especially of foodstuffs.
>
> The importance of an adequate food supply, especially for the present years is superlative. Without abundant food, alike for the armies and the peoples now at war, the whole great enterprise upon which we have embarked will break down and fail.
>
> The world's food reserves are low. Not only during the present emergency, but for some time after peace shall have come, both our own people and a large proportion of the people of Europe must rely upon the harvests in America.
>
> Upon the farmers of this country, therefore, in large measure rests the fate of the war and the fate of the nations. May the nation not count upon them to omit no step that will increase the production of their land or that will bring about the most effectual cooperation in the sale and distribution of their products?
>
> The time is short. It is of the most imperative importance that everything possible be done, and done immediately, to make sure of large harvests.
>
> I call upon young men and old alike and upon the able-bodied boys of the land to accept and act upon this duty—to turn in hosts [large numbers] to the farms and make certain that no pains and no labor is lacking in this great matter.
>
> **Source:** Woodrow Wilson, Proclamation to the American People, April 15, 1917

The War's Beginning and Progress

Before the outbreak of World War I, U.S. troops had fought abroad in Latin America and in Asia. However, they had never fought in Europe. How and why did the United States become involved in a terribly destructive European war? What were the consequences of U.S. involvement?

"The Great War," as it was called at the time, began in August 1914 and ended in November 1918. The United States participated in the war on the side of Great Britain and France but did not enter the war until April 1917. Before that came nearly three years of brutal warfare on multiple fronts that devastated Europe. This tragic conflict had multiple short- and long-term causes.

Long-Term Causes of World War I The major long-term causes of World War I were nationalism, militarism, and imperialism. In an attempt to maintain a balance of power, European nations had formed two major alliances. Great Britain, France, Russia, and Italy formed an alliance known as the **Allied Powers**. Germany, Austria-Hungary, the Ottoman Empire, and Bulgaria formed the **Central Powers**. These alliances made it likely that a war between any two nations of Europe would automatically involve both nations' allies—quickly exploding into a continent-wide conflict.

European Alliances in World War I

European military alliances at the start of World War 1, 1914

The core of these divides, in part, can be traced to the Franco-German War of 1870–1871. The quick defeat of France by a coalition of German states, headed by Prussia, had a number of important effects:

- It cemented the unification of individual German states and confederations into a powerful German state.

- It ended the predominance of France in continental Europe.

- In the treaty that ended the war, France was forced to pay huge war reparations (5 billion francs). In addition, Germany annexed all of the eastern French province of Alsace and half of Lorraine.

- France was left humiliated and hungry for revenge.

Read Closely: Motivations
When you read about the actions of individuals or countries, consider how motivations shape these actions. What motivated the nations of Europe to form rival alliances?

In the 20 years before 1914, tensions between rival powers had been steadily building in Europe. Great Britain was concerned about Germany's ambitions for colonies and its strengthening navy. It also worried about Germany's growing industrial economy. Austria-Hungary worried about the rebellious attitude of Serbs and other Slavic peoples in its empire. The aging Austrian monarch also worried about support for Serbia by the world's largest Slavic nation, Russia. Russia, in turn, worried about Germany's support for Austria-Hungary.

Short-Term Causes of World War I The spark that ignited World War I was the assassination of the heir to the throne of Austria-Hungary, the Archduke Franz Ferdinand, and his wife. They were shot on the streets of Sarajevo, a city in Austria-Hungary. (Sarajevo is now the capital of Bosnia and Herzegovina.) The assassin Gavrilo Princip was a citizen of neighboring Serbia. He was also a member of a band of Serbian nationalists called the Black Hand. The group hoped to bring about the collapse of Austria-Hungary so that Serbs within the empire could join independent Serbia.

Austria-Hungary blamed Serbia for the attack. It presented Serbia with an ultimatum. Serbia agreed to most of the demands. Even so, Austria-Hungary declared war on Serbia and began bombarding Belgrade, the Serbian capital, on July 29, 1914.

The allies of the Austrians and the Serbs quickly called their armies into a state of readiness for war. A huge Russian army moved to defend Serbia. At the same time, Germany came to the aid of Austria-Hungary. Recognizing that Germany and Russia would likely be at war, France and Great Britain prepared to defend their Russian ally and themselves. Germany declared war on Russia on August 1 and on France on August 3. German troops marched into neutral Belgium on the same day. The next day Great Britain declared war on Germany.

Years of Neutrality In 1914, most Americans, including the president, believed that the war in Europe did not concern the United States. They viewed the Atlantic Ocean as a barrier separating their country from the problems of Europe. Also, many recalled Thomas Jefferson's advice to avoid "entangling alliances."

As a neutral country, the United States continued to trade with the countries of Europe. But Germany's chances for victory in the war depended in large part on keeping supplies from reaching its enemies. It could achieve this goal by using a weapon new to warfare—the submarine.

Germany had by far the greatest number of submarines. It used them with deadly effect against British ships. Beginning in early 1915, Germany also used its submarines to sink any ships that crossed into waters close to Great Britain. Many of those ships carried American cargo and American passengers.

In May 1915, a British passenger liner, the *Lusitania,* steamed into the "war zone" near Ireland. A German submarine torpedoed and sank it. Unknown to the passengers, the ship carried weapons as part of its cargo. More than 1,000 people lost their lives, including 128 Americans. News of the tragedy led many Americans to fear that their country might be drawn into the war after all. In several strongly worded protests, however, President Wilson persuaded Germany to abandon its policy of sinking unarmed ships without warning.

Build-Up to U.S. Involvement As citizens of an English-speaking country, most Americans felt strong ties to Great Britain. They also sympathized with the French, remembering that France had helped win U.S. independence. Americans also realized that both France and Great Britain had democratic governments. France and Great Britain's enemies, on the other hand, were ruled by monarchs.

The British navy blockaded German ports. As a result, most U.S. trade during the war was with the British and the French. In fact, the U.S. banks loaned money to Britain and France so they could purchase war materials from U.S. manufacturers.

Policymakers in the U.S. government feared German victory in the war for two reasons. First, the German economy before the war showed great strength. Its products competed strongly with U.S. goods in international markets. Second, and more importantly, U.S. military leaders worried about threats to U.S. security if Germany won the war and gained the upper hand in the Atlantic Ocean. German naval ascendancy in the Atlantic might hurt U.S. trade. It would also increase Germany's ability to intervene in Latin America.

At the beginning of the war, Germany invaded the neutral country of Belgium in order to strike next at France. Americans viewed this invasion as cruel and unfair. It was the action of a bully. Skillful propagandists in Great Britain and France made the most of Germany's reputation as a military aggressor. They invented stories of German cruelty that were widely printed in U.S. newspapers. Pictures of the German emperor (or *kaiser*), Wilhelm, made him appear especially villainous.

As the war dragged on, people in all the fighting nations suffered greatly. The death tolls on both the Eastern Front (Russia) and the Western Front (France) were staggering. Especially along the Western Front, troops dug into trenches became locked in a tragic stalemate. By the end of 1916, millions had died from artillery fire, poison gas, tank attacks, and machine-gun bullets. But all was in vain. There were no significant gains by either side.

Read Closely: Details
To understand how the United States managed to remain neutral during the early years of the war, pay attention to the specific reasons. What details help explain U.S. neutrality?

Read Closely: Geography
Many readers understand history best when they can visualize where events occurred. Look at a map showing the Allied Powers and Central Powers. What geographical challenges did each alliance face?

Source: Imperial War Museums / Wikimedia Commons
British troops ready ladders for an assault on German trenches near Arras, France, in April 1917.

Civilians suffered along with the soldiers. Suffering was especially great in Germany, where the British blockade cut off shipments of food supplies. The German people were hungry, nearly starved. Conditions in Russia were even worse. There, the people decided, led by opportunistic Communist revolutionaries, that the only hope for relief from desperate poverty and suffering lay in revolution.

From Neutrality to War

President Wilson worked hard for neutrality. However, he began to accept the need for preparedness. He asked Congress for more funds to build up the army and the navy. In addition, Wilson established a Council of National Defense to increase cooperation between the U.S. military and private industry.

Opposition to U.S. Involvement Most Americans had voted for Wilson a second time in 1916 because he "kept us out of war." Opponents of the war pointed out that the causes of the war had little to do with the United States. Socialists and some unions opposed the war because it pitted workers from one country against workers from another. Some argued that the war was little more than a capitalist scheme for making money. Pacifists opposed fighting in any war, believing that disputes should be settled peacefully.

Short-Term Causes of U.S. Involvement In January 1917, Germany announced that its submarines would sink without warning any ships entering British waters. German leaders recognized they risked drawing the United States into the war on the British side. But they hoped that submarine damage to British shipping would end the war before U.S. troops could be trained for combat.

Early in 1917, the British intercepted and decoded a telegram from the German foreign secretary, Arthur Zimmermann, to the German minister in Mexico. In it, Germany promised to help Mexico win back former Mexican territories in the United States if Mexico would ally itself with Germany upon a U.S. declaration of war on Germany. The British sent the Zimmermann telegram to the U.S. government. Its publication in U.S. newspapers caused a sensation.

In March 1917, news came of the overthrow of the Russian monarch, known as the *tsar,* Nicholas II. Americans were excited by the news. They expected the new government in Russia to be democratic. President Wilson was especially pleased. As a leading champion of democracy, Wilson was willing to fight for democracies in Europe such as France and Great Britain. Now that their ally, Russia, was more democratic, Wilson believed he could lead the United States to war on the side of democracies.

Source: Wikimedia Commons

A figure representing Germany (and the devil) tempts Mexico with the prospect of retrieving territory lost to the United States in 1848.

Decision for War On April 2, 1917, the president went to Congress to deliver one of the most eloquent and memorable speeches in U.S. history. He called Germany's submarine policy "warfare against mankind." He went on to say that "we desire no conquest," but that "the world must be made safe for democracy." Members of Congress stood up and cheered. Four days later, they voted almost unanimously for a U.S. declaration of war against Germany.

Mobilizing for War Never before had the United States fought in a war on European soil. To help win the war, Wilson and his advisers recognized that all the resources of the nation—farms, factories, businesses, labor unions, men, women, even children—had to participate in a determined national effort. A number of U.S. business leaders were called to Washington to set up a War Industries Board. The board helped factories change both their products and their methods to meet wartime needs. As a result, U.S. factories turned out vast quantities of supplies for the war.

The federal government asked everybody to make daily sacrifices. Americans soon grew accustomed to "meatless" and "wheatless" days. The conservation effort made a huge difference in the amount of food shipped overseas in 1917 and 1918. For an entire year, the main U.S. contribution to the Allied forces in France was to keep them supplied with food, guns, ships, airplanes, and other goods. This economic contribution was vital.

U.S. Sends Troops to Europe U.S. troops didn't arrive on the front in large numbers until the summer of 1918. Unlike the war-weary troops of Europe, the members of the American Expeditionary Forces (AEF) were fresh and ready for action. Under the command of General John J. Pershing, they at first fought in British and French units. By the end of the war, Pershing commanded over 1 million U.S. and French soldiers. The United States had developed a modern fighting force. It was equipped with machine guns and tanks, as well as an efficient support organization that could move supplies thousands of miles quickly.

Last Big Push Russia had left the war. It signed an armistice with the Central Powers in December 1917. Now Germany could concentrate on the Western Front. An all-out German offensive in March 1918 almost succeeded in reaching Paris. The drive was finally turned back. U.S. troops arrived in time for a massive counterattack that eventually won the war.

The first great thrust by U.S. troops occurred between September 12 and 16, 1918, along a section of the frontline trenches called the St. Mihiel Salient. Another assault, beginning September 26, drove the exhausted and demoralized Germans through the Argonne, a forest in northwestern France. By early November, the retreating Germans had been pushed back almost to the border of their own country.

Allied Victory, Wilson's Defeat

The war ended on November 11, 1918. Germany signed an armistice and conceded defeat. In the United States, crowds went wild with excitement and joy.

Wilson's Fourteen Points Woodrow Wilson sought a lasting peace settlement. In January 1918, Wilson had proposed his **Fourteen Points**, a program for world peace. Some of the key points addressed peoples' and countries' desire for **self-determination**, or freedom to decide their own political status.

> **Read Closely: Turning Points**
> As you read, identify turning points—events that change the course of history. What were two significant turning points that helped bring World War I to its conclusion?

- creation of an independent Polish state
- restoration of territories seized and occupied during the war
- adjustment of the borders of Austria-Hungary and the Turkish portion of the Ottoman Empire according to the principle of self-determination
- a degree of self-determination for people living in lands colonized by European powers

Other points addressed the need for a new set of international arrangements.

- an end to secret treaties
- recognition of every nation's right to freedom of the seas in peace and war
- a reduction of weapons
- establishment of a general association of nations to keep the peace by resolving disputes between nations

Negotiating Peace The German government recognized Wilson's Fourteen Points as a basis for a just peace. It asked Wilson to arrange the armistice. Wilson traveled to France to meet with other leaders to negotiate the terms of the peace treaty. Only the victors were present at these discussions, which took place in the palace at Versailles, near Paris. The people of Europe greeted Wilson as a hero. As the conference continued through the early months of 1919, however, the hard realities of European politics overwhelmed Wilson's plan for peace.

Unlike Wilson, the leaders of France, Great Britain, and Italy wanted a peace treaty that would punish their wartime enemies. The victorious European powers had suffered huge losses of life and property. France had lost more than 1.5 million soldiers and Britain approximately 1 million. The United States had suffered approximately 115,000 military deaths.

The European Allies wanted to make sure that Germany would never rise again as a major military power. They also wanted a treaty that would force Germany to pay for war damages. Because the United States entered the war late and suffered far fewer casualties, the other Allied leaders discounted U.S. opinions. Therefore, Wilson found it difficult to achieve the goals he set out in the Fourteen Points.

Treaty of Versailles The treaty that finally emerged from the conference, known as the **Treaty of Versailles**, included the following provisions:

- Alsace and Lorraine (seized by Germany in 1871) would be returned to France.
- Poland, whose independence had been lost for more than a hundred years, would again be an independent country.
- Germany would lose all of its colonial holdings, which were extensive.
- Germany would be required to pay **reparations**, punitive payments imposed by the winning side in a war, amounting to a staggering $33 billion).
- Germany would be made to disband its armed forces and agree never to have an army of more than 100,000 men.
- Germany would accept full responsibility for causing the war. (This provision was known as the war guilt clause.)
- An association of nations, the League of Nations, would be created to reduce the chance of future wars.

Read Closely: Contrast
Recognizing distinctions is one way to understand the different options available in history. President Wilson went to Europe with a plan for peace, the Fourteen Points. The other Allies had very different ideas. In what ways did the Treaty of Versailles differ from Wilson's Fourteen Points?

New Nations of Eastern Europe, 1919

A separate treaty with Austria broke up the Austro-Hungarian Empire. It reduced Austria to less than a third of its former size. Four new republics were carved from its territory: Austria, Hungary, Czechoslovakia, and Yugoslavia.

The Treaty of Versailles was very harsh on Germany, but it was less severe than France and Great Britain had originally wanted. Wilson succeeded in softening the terms slightly. Still, the treaty was considered vengeful by many, and Wilson feared it might cause Germany to rebel against its terms.

The treaty included a few of Wilson's Fourteen Points in modified form. He was happy about one diplomatic victory. He had succeeded in persuading others at the conference to include the League of Nations as part of the treaty. All signers of the treaty were committed to joining the League. Wilson hoped the League would eventually correct the treaty's faults.

League of Nations and the United States Senate Politics in the United States proved just as difficult as politics in Europe. Members of President Wilson's own Democratic Party generally supported the treaty that he brought home with him from Paris. But Republicans in Congress were much less enthusiastic. Some were firmly opposed. To win approval of the Versailles treaty, Wilson had to win the votes of senators from both parties.

The Constitution requires that two-thirds of the Senate must ratify all treaties. Wilson could count on a majority of senators supporting the treaty, but a two-thirds vote was uncertain. Republicans opposing the treaty included two groups, isolationists and reservationists. Isolationists rejected the treaty outright because it would involve too many commitments abroad. Reservationists would accept the treaty only if certain clauses, called reservations, were added to it. Henry Cabot Lodge of Massachusetts, a bitter enemy of the president, led the reservationist faction in the Senate.

The chief issue of Lodge and the reservationists to the Versailles Treaty was Article 10 of the Covenant of the League of Nations. In the opinion of the treaty's opponents, this article could be used to force the United States into a war that Congress did not approve.

In September 1919, Wilson began a national tour to defend the League of Nations and the treaty. After a speech in Colorado, however, the president fell seriously ill and had to return to the White House. Then in October, he suffered a stroke that paralyzed one side of his body. For several months he was unable to provide leadership for the ratification of the treaty.

The vote in the Senate to ratify the treaty was set for early November. A majority would have voted in favor of the treaty if it included Senator Lodge's reservations. However, Wilson indicated that the reservations were not acceptable. He instructed Democratic senators to vote no. Ratification failed. A later vote for the treaty without reservations also failed to win two-thirds approval.

Had Wilson been willing to accept Lodge's reservations, the treaty likely would have passed. Instead, the United States, which had proposed the League of Nations, was the only major power not to ratify it. President Warren Harding, a Republican, signed a separate U.S. peace treaty with Germany in 1921. It contained nothing about the League of Nations and passed the Senate easily.

> **Read Closely: Stakeholders**
> Stakeholders are people, or groups of people, who are involved in or affected by important decisions in a place or event. Explain how stakeholders ruined the chances for Senate ratification of the Treaty of Versailles.

Source: Wikimedia Commons
A 1920 cartoon, "Getting Together on the Peace Treaty," mocks both sides for their bitter struggle over the Treaty of Versailles.

Application: Interpret a Primary Source

Read the excerpt below and answer the questions that follow it.

Democratic Party Platform
Article V. Preparedness

Along with the proof of our character as a Nation must go the proof of our power to play the part that legitimately belongs to us. The people of the United States love peace. They respect the rights and covet the friendship of all other nations. They desire neither any additional territory nor any advantage which cannot be peacefully gained by their skill, their industry, or their enterprise; but they insist upon having absolute freedom of National life and policy, and feel that they owe it to themselves and to the role of spirited independence which it is their sole ambition to play that they should render themselves secure against the hazard of interference from any quarter, and should be able to protect their rights upon the seas or in any part of the world. We therefore favor the maintenance of an army fully adequate to the requirements of order, of safety, and of the protection of the nation's rights, the fullest development of modern methods of seacoast defense and the maintenance of an adequate reserve of citizens trained to arms and prepared to safeguard the people and territory of the United States against any danger of hostile action which may unexpectedly arise; and a fixed policy for the continuous development of a navy, worthy to support the great naval traditions of the United States and fully equal to the international tasks which this Nation hopes and expects to take a part in performing. The plans and enactments of the present Congress afford substantial proof of our purpose in this exigent [urgent] matter.

Source: Democratic Party Platform, June 14, 1916

1. This excerpt is one section of the Democratic Party platform in 1916, when Woodrow Wilson was running for re-election. What was the historical context at the time the playform was announced?

   _____

   _____

2. What events had taken place that would have prompted the Democrats to think war might be inevitable?

   _____

   _____

3. `What is the purpose of this section? How do you know?

   _____

   _____

Lesson 3 *The Home Front*

Conceptual Understanding 11.6c World War I had important social, political, and economic effects on American society.

A red flag has long been used as a symbol of the people's rights against oppressive governments. During the 19th century, it became associated with Socialist movements and protests in Europe. Even before the Soviet Union adopted the red flag, American socialists carried it in protests. In July 1917, 8,000 socialists held a peace parade in Boston. A mob of soldiers and sailors attacked them on Boston Common, beating many up and taking away their red flags. Soon after the war was over, socialists carried the red flag in a parade on Fifth Avenue in New York City. A week after the end of World War I, the mayor of New York banned the display of the red flag.

"Down with the Red Flag"

Read Closely: Symbolism
As you read, note that throughout history, symbols can be extremely powerful. Flags serve as symbols. The Stars and Stripes flag represents the United States and all the things the United States stands for. Underline the phrase that indicates what the editorial believes the red flag stands for.

Read Closely: Audience
The purpose of an editorial is to influence public opinion. This editorial in the *Washington Post* was written in response to a socialist demonstration in New York City. Circle the word or words that indicate the audience that the writer hopes will take responsibility for putting an end to bolshevism and anarchy.

Read Closely: Impact
While this editorial sets out to spur a government crackdown on bolshevism and anarchy, the author's word choices have another effect. By references to European bolshevism and aliens preaching against the U.S. government, writings such as this fanned the flames of intolerance and xenophobia, the fear and hatred of foreigners.

The red flag of bolshevism [Soviet communism] and anarchy [rejection of all forms of government], though displayed in a parade of socialists, no longer has any place in the United States. It signifies defiance of law, order, and constitutional government. It is an insult to the Stars and Stripes.

The liberty of the world has just been won at an awful sacrifice of blood and treasure. Shall that liberty be tainted and polluted by the anarchy of bolshevism? Is the autocracy [absolute rule] of kings and emperors to be succeeded by the autocracy of the mob? Is America to be the scene of activity for soviets and soldiers and workmen's councils, with license for the mob to rob and pillage and with no protection to life and liberty?

Let the red flag be squelched [crushed] at the very beginning! The activities of crack-brained [crazy] radicals and unreconstructed aliens who fail to appreciate the blessings of a free government must be suppressed. Following recent socialist demonstrations which have ended in riots, the board of aldermen of New York has adopted an ordinance prohibiting the display of red flags in parades or public meetings in that city and fixing a maximum penalty of $100 fine and ten days' imprisonment for violation of it. And the New York police are ready with valiant nightsticks to enforce it, backed by 3,000,000 loyal citizens willing to assist. . . .

Not alone should states and municipalities prohibit the display of the flag of anarchy, but the federal government should take any steps within its power to crush anarchy in whatever form it may take. With bolshevism rampant in Europe, we may expect a flock of radical agitators in the United States in the near future, come here to preach the gospel which has worked such havoc in Russia and which is threatening the safety of the governments set free by the war. Every alien who comes to these shores and begins preaching against the United States government should be imprisoned at once. Deportation is not sufficient; it would merely leave him free to afflict some other land.

Source: "Down with the Red Flag" editorial, *The Washington Post*, November 28, 1918

Mobilization Affects Economy

When World War I began, the U.S. economy was in recession. The United States had long been a debtor nation. Its financial institutions and businesses owed debts to other nations. Great Britain and other European countries had played a dominant role in banking, industry, and trade for a long time. After the United States entered the war, domestic industrial production shifted from civilian to war goods. The U.S. government took action to guide economic activity through agencies such as the War Industries Board. Between 1914 and 1918, about 3 million people were added to the military and half a million to the government.

The War's Effect on the Economy

The war changed the nation's economic condition permanently. Before the war, London was the financial capital of the world. After the war, financial leadership shifted to New York. The United States increasingly began investing internationally. As such, it took on the global economic role that Great Britain had traditionally played.

To carry out the war, the European Allies had borrowed more than $10 billion to finance their war efforts. After the war, U.S. policymakers believed that other nations should promptly repay their debts to the United States. Because of its loans to Great Britain and France during the war, the United States became the world's greatest creditor nation—one to whom debts are owed. U.S. presidents of the 1920s insisted that the Allies pay back at least a sizable portion of their war debts.

New Jobs for Women and Minorities World War I changed the nature of the American workforce. The war created new employment opportunities for women. With millions of men in the armed forces, women began filling jobs once thought suitable only for men. They became factory workers, railroad conductors, and farmers. They made shells in munitions plants and enlisted in the Nurse Corps of the army and navy. The war increased the need for telephone operators, secretaries, and sales personnel. Women soon made up a majority in these occupations. They also maintained their dominance in more traditional female occupations for the era—teaching and nursing.

Farmers in the Southwest needed workers to plant and harvest crops. Between 1917 and 1920, about 100,000 migrants from Mexico came to settle permanently in Texas, New Mexico, Arizona, and California.

African Americans also filled factory jobs vacated by departing troops. A migration of African Americans to Northern cities had begun before the war. It increased significantly as a result of the new job opportunities.

Postwar Recession During World War I, prices of many American-made goods increased. Because most were exported or used by the military, fewer goods were available to U.S. consumers. During this period, wages did not keep pace with rising prices. By 1921, unemployment had increased from 2 percent during the war to nearly 12 percent. At the same time, exports and the production of armaments dropped.

As the demand for goods decreased, businesses went bankrupt. People who were unemployed or whose wages did not keep pace with prices could no longer afford to purchase goods and services. Added to this was the drop in farm income. European farmers once again began to grow products that had been imported from the United States during the war. These conditions caused the United States to fall into a recession, which lasted from 1920 to 1922.

Read Closely: Turning Point
The words *before* and *after* often indicate turning points in history. World War I was a major turning point in history. How does the text use these words to signify a turning point related to World War I?

The Great Migration

In what is called the **Great Migration**, Southern African Americans moved to Northern cities in great numbers. Between 1910 and 1930, the Black population of Northern cities grew from 1 million to 2.5 million. As with most migrations, push-pull factors—causes that drive migrants from their origin and draw them to their destination—were at work.

African Americans Postwar Some 300,000 African American men joined the military fight to make the world "safe for democracy." When they returned home from the war, they were no longer willing to go back to being treated as second-class citizens. Thus, the 1920s saw increased confrontations between Black and White Americans. The era also saw the formation and strengthening of organizations that challenged African Americans' second-class citizenship.

Many of the confrontations between Black and White Americans occurred in cities in the South. One of the most deadly took place in Tulsa, Oklahoma, in June 1921. Like other U.S. cities, Tulsa was segregated. However, the city's African American Greenwood District was nationally recognized. The affluent community's thriving business district was referred to as the "Black Wall Street."

The Tulsa riot was sparked by rumors that a young Black male had assaulted a White woman. After an inflammatory report in the *Tulsa Tribune*, an army of White people looted and burned Greenwood. When the rioting was over, 35 city blocks had been reduced to charred ruins. More than 1,400 Black-owned homes and businesses had been burned to the ground. As many as 300 people were killed, and nearly 10,000 Black Tulsans were left homeless. Many Black residents of the South felt they could no longer tolerate the second-class status that led to such violence.

Push Factors Poor economic conditions in the South and the virtual slavery of sharecropping were factors in the exodus of African Americans to Northern cities. Factories in the urban North typically paid three times what Black workers could earn in the rural South. But the main push factor was the brutal realities of Jim Crow laws. These only increased after World War I. African Americans risked being jailed or even lynched if they defied White rule. In 1927 alone, 24 lynchings took place throughout the South. Many were sparked by suspected or rumored sexual encounters between Black males and White females.

The Great Migration, 1900–1929

Pull Factors The main pull factor was the promise of steady jobs in Northern factories. During World War I, the enlistment of Northern factory workers coupled with the slowing of immigration from Europe created a labor shortage in the North. Companies began to recruit Black Southerners to work in factories, in steel mills, and on the railroads. The *Chicago Defender* and other African American newspapers carried reports of good wages and better living conditions in large industrial cities such as Chicago, Detroit, and New York.

Reception of African Americans in the North Many White Northerners felt threatened by the arrival of African Americans in large numbers. In Chicago in 1919, riots broke out between Black and White people on a segregated beach. A total of 38 people died in the fighting that resulted. Race riots broke out in other Northern cities as well. In Northern communities, as in the South, African Americans found segregation not only on beaches but also in housing, schools, and clubs. Even the Northern African American establishment tended to look down on these rural newcomers. All sections of the country were failing to achieve racial fairness.

By their mere presence, however, these African Americans were able to convince some Northerners to pay attention to the greater injustices endured by Black Americans who remained in the South. The migrants changed their own lives and the lives of their children. African American troops returning from Europe helped create a "New Negro movement" that fostered racial pride and self-expression. It, in turn, gave rise to the cultural movement known as the Harlem Renaissance.

Challenges to Freedoms and Tolerance

Congress passed the Espionage Act in 1917 and the much harsher Sedition Act in 1918. These laws imposed heavy fines and prison sentences for the following antiwar actions:

- spying and aiding the wartime enemy
- interfering with the recruitment of soldiers
- speaking against the government's campaign to sell bonds to finance the war
- urging resistance to U.S. laws
- using "disloyal, profane, scurrilous, or abusive language" about the American form of government, flag, or military uniform

In addition, the federal government empowered the U.S. Post Office to remove any antiwar materials from the mails.

About 1,500 people who spoke out against the war were arrested under the Espionage and Sedition Acts. In 1918, Eugene Debs, who had been the Socialist Party's candidate for president in 1908 and 1912, was sentenced to ten years in prison for making an antiwar speech. (He was again the candidate in 1920 and received his highest vote total while behind bars.) Emma Goldman, an anarchist, received a two-year prison term for her antiwar activities. After serving her sentence, she was deported to the Soviet Union.

Schenck v. United States Another dissenter who went to jail was Charles Schenck, the general secretary of the Socialist Party. Schenck had mailed about 15,000 leaflets urging men to oppose the military draft. After being tried and convicted under the Espionage Act, Schenck appealed to the U.S. Supreme Court. He argued that his First Amendment rights to freedom of speech and the press had been violated.

Read Closely: Causes
While reading, pay attention to all causes for an event, not just the obvious ones. Every event has numerous causes, some more obvious than others. What are two causes for the labor shortage during World War I?

Civic Literacy: Movement of Citizens
The Great Migration of African Americans from the rural South to the urban North began around 1916. It profoundly affected African Americans and the broader U.S. society. In 1900, 90 percent of all African Americans lived in the South, and 75 percent lived on farms. By 1970, fewer than half of the nation's African Americans lived in the South, and only 25 percent of them lived in rural areas.

In the case of *Schenck v. United States* (1919), the Supreme Court ruled unanimously against Schenck. It upheld the constitutionality of the Espionage Act. Justice Oliver Wendell Holmes wrote the decision, in which the court ruled that the right to free speech was not absolute. In ordinary times, wrote Holmes, the mailing of Schenck's leaflets would have been protected under the First Amendment. However, Holmes went on, every act of speech must be judged according to the circumstances in which it is committed. For example, "the most stringent protection of free speech would not protect a man in falsely shouting fire in a theatre and causing a panic." Furthermore, speech that would be harmless in a time of peace might threaten the public safety in a time of war.

The question to be asked, according to Holmes, was whether or not an act of speech posed a "clear and present danger" to the public. If it did, then Congress had the power to restrain such speech. The "clear and present danger" test, first stated in the Schenck case, was often applied in later free-speech cases.

Red Scare The Communist revolution in Russia fueled **nativist** fears about the loyalties of foreign-born residents of the United States. Nativists thought foreign-born radicals might attempt to overthrow the U.S. government. Their fears turned to action in the **Red Scare** of 1919 and 1920. Attorney General A. Mitchell Palmer organized a series of raids—the so-called Palmer raids—to arrest and deport immigrants suspected of disloyalty. Federal agents were told to search for damaging evidence in homes and businesses and in the offices of political groups. Often they did so without search warrants. Before the raids ended, nearly 600 people were forced to leave the United States as unwanted "Reds," or Communists. Fear of perceived radical thinkers persisted throughout the 20th century.

Xenophobia Life in the 1920s was generally prosperous for people of the middle class, who were largely native-born, White Americans. It was less so for ethnic minorities and the foreign born. Especially in rural communities, there was distrust of big cities where large numbers of Italian and Jewish immigrants had settled. Most immigrants were hard working and law abiding. However, many people accused them of being responsible for city slums and crime or of being Communists.

Recall that the **Ku Klux Klan (KKK)** was a secret society that terrorized freed slaves in the South after the Civil War. The Klan made a comeback following the film *The Birth of a Nation* (1915), which glorified the organization. During the 1920s, millions of people in all parts of the country openly wore the KKK's white-hooded costume in parades. The main goal of the Klan was to maintain the supremacy of the White Protestant majority. In addition to African Americans, the Klan now viewed Roman Catholics, Jews, and immigrants as threats and regularly targeted them. Its growing membership made the Klan an important force in the politics of many states. The governors of Oregon and Indiana actually owed their elections to the Klan's support.

Read Closely: Contrast
A sentence that begins with the word *However* often describes a contrast with an idea expressed previously. In this case, what contrast is being made?

Read Closely: Differences
Recognizing distinctions is one way to understand differences between two places, trends, or events. How did the Ku Klux Klan of the 1920s differ from the KKK of the Reconstruction era?

Application: Interpret a Primary Source

Read the excerpt below and answer the questions that follow it.

Letter to the Editor of the *Chicago Defender*

Dear Sir: Although I am a stranger to you but I am a man of the so called colored race and can give you the very best or reference as to my character and ability by prominent citizens of my community by both White and colored people that knows me although am native of Ohio whiles I am a northern desent were reared in this state of Mississippi. Now I am a reader of your paper the Chicago Defender. After reading your writing ever wek I am compell & persuade to say that I know you are a real man of my color you have I know heard of the south land & I need not tell you any thing about it. I am going to ask you a favor and at the same time beg you for your kind and best advice. I wants to come to Chicago to live. I am a man of a family wife and 1 child I can do just any kind of work in the line of common labor & I have for the present sufficient means to support us till I can obtain a position. Now should I come to your town, would you please to assist me in getting a position I am willing to pay whatever you charge I dont want you to loan me not 1 cent but *help* me to find an occupation there in your town now I has a present position that will keep me employed till the first of Dec. 1917. now please give me your best advice on this subject. I enclose stamp for reply.

Source: Letter from Marcel, Mississippi, October 4, 1917, in *The Journal of Negro History*, October 1919

1. Why would this letter have been written at this time?

_____

_____

_____

_____

2. How is this letter related to other events covered in this lesson?

_____

_____

_____

_____

3. What was the writer's purpose in this letter?

_____

_____

_____

_____

Multiple-Choice Questions

Questions 1–3 refer to the excerpt below.

A. Theodore Roosevelt's Corollary to the Monroe Doctrine

It is not true that the United States feels any land hunger or entertains any projects as regards the other nations of the Western Hemisphere save such as are for their welfare. All that this country desires is to see the neighboring countries stable, orderly, and prosperous. Any country whose people conduct themselves well can count upon our hearty friendship. If a nation shows that it knows how to act with reasonable efficiency and decency in social and political matters, if it keeps order and pays its obligations, it need fear no interference from the United States. Chronic wrongdoing, or an impotence which results in a general loosening of the ties of civilized society, may in America, as elsewhere, ultimately require intervention by some civilized nation, and in the Western Hemisphere the adherence of the United States to the Monroe Doctrine may force the United States, however reluctantly, in flagrant cases of such wrongdoing or impotence, to the exercise of an international police power. . . . Our interests and those of our southern neighbors are in reality identical. They have great natural riches, and if within their borders the reign of law and justice obtains, prosperity is sure to come to them. While they thus obey the primary laws of civilized society they may rest assured that they will be treated by us in a spirit of cordial and helpful sympathy. We would interfere with them only in the last resort, and then only if it became evident that their inability or unwillingness to do justice at home and abroad had violated the rights of the United States or had invited foreign aggression to the detriment of the entire body of American nations. . . .

Source: Theodore Roosevelt, annual message to Congress, December 6, 1904

1. Which of the following best summarizes Roosevelt's intention in making this speech?

    1. To assure the world that the United States was no longer interested in imperialism

    2. To warn European powers not to attempt to interfere in the affairs of the nations of the Western Hemisphere

    3. To assert the United States' right to intervene in other nations of the Western Hemisphere

    4. To urge Congress to authorize the annexation of neighboring countries to the south

2. Under what circumstances does Roosevelt say the United States should act as a police power?

    1. When another nation in the Western Hemisphere elects a president of whom the United States do not approve

   2. When another country is guilty of chronic wrongdoing or violates the rights of the United States

   3. When another country attempts to form an alliance with a nation outside the Western Hemisphere

   4. When the people of another nation rise up in rebellion against a ruler who is friendly to the United States

3. How does this excerpt illustrate change and continuity in American history?

   1. It shows that the United States has abandoned the idea of Manifest Destiny.

   2. It repeals the Monroe Doctrine and replaces it with the Roosevelt Corollary.

   3. It extends the Monroe Doctrine, promising that the United States will come to the aid of nations throughout the world that are threatened by foreign interference.

   4. It invokes the Monroe Doctrine against European intervention in the affairs of other nations of the Western Hemisphere while asserting the U.S. right to intervene in those nations.

Questions 4–6 refer to the excerpt below.

B. The Supreme Court on Restricting First Amendment Rights

Of course, the document would not have been sent unless it had been intended to have some effect, and we do not see what effect it could be expected to have upon persons subject to the draft except to influence them to obstruct the carrying of it out. The defendants do not deny that the jury might find against them on this point.

But it is said, suppose that that was the tendency of this circular, it is protected by the First Amendment to the Constitution. Two of the strongest expressions are said to be quoted respectively from well known public men. It well may be that the prohibition of laws abridging the freedom of speech is not confined to previous restraints, although to prevent them may have been the main purpose . . . . We admit that, in many places and in ordinary times, the defendants, in saying all that was said in the circular, would have been within their constitutional rights. But the character of every act depends upon the circumstances in which it is done. The most stringent protection of free speech would not protect a man in falsely shouting fire in a theatre and causing a panic. It does not even protect a man from an injunction against uttering words that may have all the effect of force. The question in every case is whether the words used are used in such circumstances and are of such a nature as to create a clear and present danger that they will bring about the substantive evils that Congress has a right to prevent. It is a question of proximity and degree. When a nation is at war, many things that might be said in time of peace are such a hindrance to its effort that their utterance will not be endured so long as men fight, and that no Court could regard them as protected by any constitutional right.

Source: Chief Justice Oliver Wendell Holmes, Majority Opinion, *Schenck v. United States*, March 3, 1919

4. What was the impact of time or place on this Supreme Court ruling?

   1. It upholds a law that curtailed First Amendment rights during the First World War.

   2. It prohibits the use of quotations from public persons in subversive documents.

   3. It limits the freedom of expression of foreign-born anarchists.

   4. The ruling had nothing to do with either time or place.

5. How did Holmes's justify his ruling against Schenck?

   1. He had determined that Schenck was an anarchist plotting to overthrow the government of the United States.

   2. He wanted to keep Socialists and Communists out of the United States.

   3. He determined that Schenck's attempt to obstruct the draft in time of war posed a clear and present danger.

   4. He wanted to keep Schenck from encouraging workers in defense industries to go on strike for better working conditions.

6. How does Holmes support his claim that Schenck's constitutional rights had not been violated?

   1. He says that Schenck was a Socialist and therefore not protected by the Constitution.

   2. He says that Schenck should be imprisoned as a German sympathizer.

   3. He says that Schenck attempted to make it appear that the dangerous quotations in his flyer were made by well-known public men.

   4. He says that some things that might be said in time of peace are detrimental to the war effort and therefore are not protected by the Constitution.

Questions 7 and 8 refer to the excerpt below.

C. An Anarchist Describes Her Deportation During the "Red Scare"

Hardly had the last wire been sent when the corridor filled with State and Federal detectives, officers of the Immigration Bureau and Coast Guards. I recognized Caminetti, Commissioner General of Immigration, at their head. The uniformed men stationed themselves along the walls, and then came the command, "Line up!" A sudden hush fell upon the room. "March!" It echoed through the corridor.

Deep snow lay on the ground; the air was cut by a biting wind. A row of armed civilians and soldiers stood along the road to the bank. Dimly the outlines of a barge were visible through the morning mist. One by one the deportees marched, flanked on each side by the uniformed men, curses and threats accompanying the thud of their feet on the frozen ground. When the last man had crossed the gangplank, the girls and I were ordered to follow, officers in front and in back of us.

We were led to a cabin. A large fire roared in the iron stove filling the air with heat and fumes. We felt suffocating. There was no air nor water. Then came a violent lurch; we were on our way.

I looked at my watch. It was 4:20 A.M. on the day of our Lord, December 21, 1919. On the deck above us I could hear the men tramping up and down in the wintry blast. I felt dizzy, visioning a transport of politicals doomed to Siberia, the étape [a place to confine prisoners in transit] of former Russian days. Russia of the past rose before me and I saw the revolutionary martyrs being driven into exile. But no, it was New York, it was America, the land of liberty! Through the port-hole I could see the great city receding into the distance, its sky-line of buildings traceable by their rearing heads. It was my beloved city, the metropolis of the New World. It was America, indeed, America repeating the terrible scenes of tsarist Russia! I glanced up—the Statue of Liberty!

Source: Emma Goldman, *Living My Life*, 1931

7. Which of the following is a similarity that Goldman notes in this excerpt?

    1. She likens the uniformed men to the Gestapo in Nazi Germany.
    2. She says her experience of being herded was similar to the experiences of Jews being shipped to concentration camps.
    3. She compares her experience to the exile of political prisoners in Russia.
    4. She compares her experience to a long trek through the snows of a Russian winter.

8. Which of the following best describes how Goldman's experience differed from the experience of the revolutionaries in tsarist Russia?

    1. She was not allowed to take any of her belongings with her.
    2. She was being deported from a land where people are supposedly free.
    3. She chose to leave the United States voluntarily.
    4. The place where she and the others were held was not at all like the place where Russian prisoners were confined when they were sent into exile.

Short-Essay Questions

Study the two documents and answer the question that follows.

D. The 1898 Treaty of Paris Ending the Spanish–American War

Article I.
Spain relinquishes all claim of sovereignty over and title to Cuba. And as the island is, upon its evacuation by Spain, to be occupied by the United States, the United States will, so long as such occupation shall last, assume and discharge the obligations that may under international law result from the fact of its occupation, for the protection of life and property.

Article II.
Spain cedes to the United States the island of Porto Rico and other islands now under Spanish sovereignty in the West Indies, and the island of Guam in the Marianas or Ladrones.

Article III.
Spain cedes to the United States the archipelago known as the Philippine Islands . . . . The United States will pay to Spain the sum of twenty million dollars ($20,000,000) within three months after the exchange of the ratifications of the present treaty.

Article IV.
The United States will, for the term of ten years from the date of the exchange of the ratifications of the present treaty, admit Spanish ships and merchandise to the ports of the Philippine Islands on the same terms as ships and merchandise of the United States.

Source: Treaty of Peace Between the United States and Spain, December 10, 1898

E. Mark Twain on Imperialism

I left these shores, at Vancouver, a red-hot imperialist. I wanted the American eagle to go screaming into the Pacific. It seemed tiresome and tame for it to content itself with the Rockies. Why not spread its wings over the Philippines, I asked myself? And I thought it would be a real good thing to do.

I said to myself, here are a people who have suffered for three centuries. We can make them as free as ourselves, give them a government and country of their own, put a miniature of the American constitution afloat in the Pacific, start a brand new republic to take its place among the free nations of the world. It seemed to me a great task to which had addressed ourselves.

But I have thought some more, since then, and I have read carefully the treaty of Paris, and I have seen that we do not intend to free, but to subjugate the people of the Philippines. We have gone there to conquer, not to redeem. . . .

It should, it seems to me, be our pleasure and duty to make those people free, and let them deal with their own domestic questions in their own way. And so I am an anti-imperialist. I am opposed to having the eagle put its talons on any other land.

Source: Mark Twain, New York *Herald* (October 15, 1900)

1. In a short essay, describe the historical context surrounding the two documents above. Then identify and explain the cause-and-effect relationship between the ideas described in these documents.

Study the two documents and answer the question that follows.

F. Over There

Verse
Johnnie, get your gun, get your gun, get your gun,
Take it on the run, on the run, on the run,
Hear them calling you and me,
Ev'ry son of liberty.
Hurry right away, no delay, go today,
Make your daddy glad to have had such a lad,
Tell your sweetheart not to pine,
To be proud her boy's in line.

Chorus
Over there, over there
Send the word, send the word over there
That the Yanks are coming, the Yanks are coming,
The drums rum-tumming ev'rywhere
So prepare, say a pray'r
Send the word, send the word to beware
We'll be over, we're coming over,
And we won't come back till it's over over there!

Verse
Johnnie, get your gun, get your gun, get your gun,
Johnnie, show the Hun you're a son of a gun,
Hoist the flag and let her fly,
Yankee Doodle do or die.
Pack your little kit, show your grit, do your bit,
Yankees to the ranks from the towns and the tanks,
Make your mother proud of you
And the old Red, White, and Blue.

Source: George M. Cohan (composer/lyricist), 1917

G. World War I U.S. Army Air Service Recruiting Poster

Source: *United States Air Force*

2. In a short essay, describe the historical context surrounding the two documents above. Then analyze and explain how the purpose of the lyrics to "Over There" affects the use of the song as a reliable source of evidence.

Period 2

Document #1

14th Amendment

All persons born or naturalized in the United States and subject to the jurisdiction thereof, are citizens of the United States and of the State wherein they reside. No State shall make or enforce any law which shall abridge the privileges or immunities of citizens of the United States; nor shall any State deprive any person of life, liberty, or property, without due process of law; nor deny to any person within its jurisdiction the equal protection of the laws.

---

1. How did this section of the 14th amendment reflect the drastic changes made in US society in the 1860s?

    _____

    _____

    _____

    _____

Document #2 A

Kensington, Ill.,

August 17, 1894.

To His Excellency, the Governor of the State of Illinois:

We, the people of Pullman, who, by the greed and oppression of George M. Pullman, have been brought to a condition where starvation stares us in the face, do hereby appeal to you for aid in this our hour of need. We have been refused employment and have no means of leaving this vicinity, and our families are starving. Our places have been filled with workmen from all over the United States, brought here by the Pullman Company, and the surplus were turned away to walk the streets and starve also. There are over 1600 families here in destitution and want, and their condition is pitiful. We have exhausted all the means at our command to feed them, and we now make this appeal to you as a last resource. Trusting that God will influence you in our behalf and that you will give this your prompt attention, we remain,

Yours in distress,

THE STARVING CITIZENS OF PULLMAN

Source: historymatters.gmu.edu

Document #2 B

A story published in the *New York Times* on July 5, 1894, was headlined "Debs Wildly Talks Civil War." Quotes from Eugene V. Debs appeared at the beginning of the article:

"The first shot fired by the regular soldiers at the mobs here will be the signal for civil war. I believe this as firmly as I believe in the ultimate success of our course.

"Bloodshed will follow, and 90 percent of the people of the United States will be arrayed against the other 10 percent. And I would not care to be arrayed against the laboring people in the contest, or find myself out of the ranks of labor when the struggle ended. I do not say this as an alarmist, but calmly and thoughtfully."

Source: *New York Times*, "Debs Wildly Talks Civil War," July 5, 1894

2. How do documents A and B show differing ways that working people reacted to labor difficulties?

_____

_____

_____

_____

Document #3

Excerpt from William Jennings Bryan's Cross of Gold speech 1896.

"You come to us and tell us that the great cities are in favor of the gold standard. I tell you that the great cities rest upon these broad and fertile prairies. Burn down your cities and leave our farms, and your cities will spring up again as if by magic. But destroy our farms and the grass will grow in the streets of every city in the country."

Source: historymatters.gmu.edu

3. How does this excerpt help to explain one of the major ideas of the Populist Movement of the late 1880s?

_____

_____

_____

_____

Document #4

The following is an excerpt from the decision in the Supreme Court Case United States v. Cruikshank, 92 U.S. 542 (1875);

The Fourteenth Amendment prohibits a State from depriving any person of life, liberty, or property without due process of law, and from denying to any person within its jurisdiction the equal protection of the laws, but it adds nothing to the rights of one citizen as against another. It simply furnishes an additional guaranty against any encroachment by the States upon the fundamental rights which belong to every citizen as a member of society. The duty of protecting all its citizens in the enjoyment of an equality of rights was originally assumed by the States, and it still remains there. The only obligation resting upon the United States is to see that the States do not deny the right. This the Amendment guarantees, but no more. The power of the National Government is limited to the enforcement of this guaranty.

Source: supreme.justia.com

4. How does this decision reflect the larger issues found in the dissatisfaction with the Federal government's role in Reconstruction and states' rights in general?

_____

_____

_____

_____

Document #5 A

From a pamphlet distributed by the National Association Opposed to Woman Suffrage.

VOTE NO ON WOMAN SUFFRAGE

BECAUSE 90% of women either do not want it, or *do not care*.

BECAUSE it means *competition* with men instead of *co-operation*.

BECAUSE 80% of the women eligible to vote are married and can only double or annul their husbands' votes.

BECAUSE it can be of no benefit commensurate with the additional expense involved.

BECAUSE in some States more voting women than voting men will place the Government under petticoat rule.

BECAUSE it is unwise to risk the good we already have for the evil which may occur.

Source: *The Atlantic*, "Vote No on Women Suffrage: Bizarre Reasons for Not Letting Women Vote," November 6, 2012

Document #5 B

Thomas Wentworth Higginson, minister and activist, wrote this pro-suffrage pamphlet.

"It would never do for women to vote, it would lead to such divisions in families." But political divisions do not, after all, make men quarrel half so much as religious divisions; and if you allow women to do their own thinking in religion, why not in politics? Besides, nothing makes a man so coaxing and persuasive as when he tries to induce his neighbor to vote "our ticket." Husbands who are boors all the rest of the year would become patterns of politeness for a month before election day,—if the wives only had a vote!

"The polls are not decent places for women, at present." Then she is certainly needed there to make them decent. Literature was not decent, nor was the dinner table, till she was admitted to them, on equal terms. But already, throughout most parts of the country, the ballot-box is as quiet a place to go as the Post-office; and where it is not so, the presence of one woman would be worth a dozen policemen.

"Politics are necessarily corrupting." Then why not advise good men, as well as good women, to quit voting?"

Source: docsteach.org

5. What is the relationship between document 5 A and document 5 B?

_____

_____

_____

_____

Document #6

Chinese Exclusion Act; May 6, 1882

An Act to Execute Certain Treaty Stipulations Relating to Chinese

Whereas, in the opinion of the Government of the United States the coming of Chinese laborers to this country endangers the good order of certain localities within the territory thereof: Therefore,

Be it enacted by the Senate and House of Representatives of the United States of America in Congress assembled, That from and after the expiration of ninety days next after the passage of this act, and until the expiration of ten years next after the passage of this act, the coming of Chinese laborers to the United States be, and the same is hereby, suspended; and during such suspension it shall not be lawful for any Chinese laborer to come, or having so come after the expiration of said ninety days, to remain within the United States.

Source: avalon.law.yale.edu

6. What is the historical importance of this act?

_____

_____

_____

_____

7. **Civic Literacy Document-Based Essay:** Select two examples of actions by the government of the United States, individuals or groups that had an impact on the rights of individuals or groups and for each example (1) describe the action taken, (2) discuss the historical circumstances describing the action and (3) discuss to what extent the action either furthered or limited the rights of individuals or groups.

_____

_____

_____

_____

_____

_____

_____

_____

_____

_____

_____

_____

_____

_____

_____

_____

_____

_____

_____

_____

_____

_____

CHAPTER 7

Prosperity and Depression (1920–1939)

Chapter Overview

Between 1920 and 1939, the American economy experienced a great boom followed by a historic collapse. The period was also characterized by important governmental and social changes on numerous fronts.

Social Changes Women in American began to challenge their traditional roles. More and more women began working full time (though for lesser wages), young women became more independent and self-sufficient, and the image of the free-spirited flapper became a reflection of the liberalization of 1920s society. The Prohibition reform movement successfully criminalized the sale of alcohol in 1919, but it effectively made criminals of everyday citizens and fueled the rise of organized crime in big cities.

African American Culture African Americans continued to struggle for social and economic equality during the 1920s. The growing economy did provide opportunity for African Americans, especially in and around urban centers. Culturally, literary and artistic success in African American communities—especially in Harlem, New York—crossed racial lines into mainstream America. Racial pride spurred the creation of African American political and social organizations such as the NAACP.

The Bottom Falls Out The Depression that began in 1929 would last for nearly a decade. Unemployment soared, banks closed, customers lost their life savings, and millions of Americans went bankrupt, losing their homes. Unemployment and poverty were rampant. President Hoover's approach to relief counted on helping businesses that, if successful, would then employ people. But Americans wanted more and more-direct help. New President Roosevelt took a more active approach, using the abilities—and funds—of the federal government to try to kick-start the economy (with mixed results). By 1939, the economy had made great strides, but times were still tough for most Americans.

Civic Literacy: Economics Political parties and their representatives in government have contrasting ideas about the role of the government in the economy. Presidents Coolidge and Hoover (Republicans) believed in a business-friendly role for government that would allow success to "trickle down" to average citizens. When that failed, Roosevelt implemented very activist federal programs to more directly help citizens affected by the collapse of the economy.

New York Social Studies Framework

Key Idea 11.7: Prosperity and Depression The 1920s and 1930s were a time of cultural and economic changes in the nation. During this period, the nation faced significant domestic challenges, including the Great Depression.

Source: *New York State Grades 9–12 Social Studies Framework*

Civic Literacy Essay: Develop a Thesis

The final task in the civic literacy essay prompt is in some ways the most challenging because it requires you to make an evaluation. This task asks you to discuss either the extent to which the efforts of individuals, groups, and governments were effective or the impact the efforts had on the United States or American society. The New York Board of Regents defines *discuss* as making "observations about something using facts, reasoning, and argument; to present in some detail." (See page 289 for more on discussing.)

Develop a Claim A thesis, or claim, is a nonfactual statement asserted to be true. It is a statement about which people can disagree because it requires an explanation or evaluation. A historically defensible claim is one that can be supported with sound historical evidence. For example, the Declaration of Independence claims that "all men are created equal; that they are endowed by their Creator with certain unalienable rights; that among these are life, liberty, and the pursuit of happiness." This claim was not based on any historical facts but rather on the Enlightenment ideals of European philosophers such as Locke and Rousseau. It became a goal for the Founding Fathers who wrote the U.S. Constitution.

The claim for the civic literacy essay will focus on either how effective the efforts you described were in accomplishing their goals or the extent of their impact on the United States or American society. Within those general frameworks there is much room for variation—your evidence will guide you in crafting the most succinct thesis statement.

Application: Read the following document-based essay question and a thesis statement developed to address it. Evaluate the thesis statement on how clearly it asserts a meaningful claim.

Civic Literacy Document-Based Question: Choose *two* federal government actions that have expanded or limited the rights of individuals and for *each* (1) describe the historical circumstances that led to the government action and (2) discuss the impact of the action on the United States and/or American society.

Thesis Statement: The Alien and Sedition Acts and the ratification of the Fourteenth Amendment were two actions by the government that affected the rights of individuals in the United States.

Key Terms by Theme

Civics
Scopes Monkey Trial (p. 228)

Economics
Great Depression (p. 238)
Dow Jones Industrial Average (p. 238)
Hooverville (p. 240)

Geography
Dust Bowl (p. 243)

Governance
Herbert Hoover (p. 239)

Franklin D. Roosevelt (p. 240)
New Deal (p. 240)
Social Security Act (p. 242)

Social Structures
flapper (p. 225)
evolution (p. 227)
Harlem Renaissance (p. 231)
Langston Hughes (p. 231)
Zora Neale Hurston (p. 231)
Paul Robeson (p. 232)
jazz (p. 233)

Duke Ellington (p. 233)
Louis Armstrong (p. 233)
W.E.B. Du Bois (p. 233)
National Association for the Advancement of Colored People (NAACP) (p. 233)

Technology
Henry Ford (p. 237)

The 1920s: Social Change and Continuity

Conceptual Understanding 11.7a The 1920s was a time of cultural change in the country, characterized by clashes between modern and traditional values.

The 1920s was characterized by clashes between modern and traditional values. In the years after World War I, the White supremacist group the Ku Klux Klan experienced a resurgence. African Americans, Roman Catholics, Jews, and immigrants were viewed as threats and were regular targets for intimidation—and sometimes murder—by the Klan. The African American academic, author, and civil rights advocate W.E.B. Du Bois considered the reasons for the rise of the KKK beyond simple racism.

Analyze a Primary Source

W.E.B. Du Bois, "The Shape of Fear," *The North American Review*, June 1926

Read Closely: Claim
When reading a primary source such as this, identifying the specific claim the author makes helps readers understand how to interpret the evidence that follows. Underline what Du Bois claims caused the resurgence of the KKK.

Read Closely: Cause and Effect
To back up their claims, authors often identify a cause-and-effect relationship between ideas, factors, or groups. Du Bois suggests a cause and effect has created "The Shape of Fear." Notice how he clearly describes the feared and fearful.

Read Closely: Conclusion
An effective conclusion binds a writer's claims and evidence into a clear summation. Du Bois has made a case for why he thinks the KKK has resurfaced so strongly after World War I. Circle his conclusion to this analysis.

What is the cause of all this? There can be little doubt but that the Klan in its present form is a legacy of the World War. Whatever there was of it before that great catastrophe was negligible and of little moment. The wages of War is Hate; and the End, and indeed the Beginning, of Hate is Fear. The civilized world today and the world half-civilized and uncivilized are desperately afraid. The Shape of Fear looms over them. Germany fears the Jew, England fears the Indian; America fears the Negro, the Christian fears the Moslem, Europe fears Asia, Protestant fears Catholic, Religion fears Science. Above all, Wealth fears Democracy. These fears and others are ancient or at least longstanding fears. But they are renewed and revivified today because the world has at present a severe case of nerves; it feels it necessary to be nervous because the Unexpected has happened.

Source: W.E.B. Du Bois, "The Shape of Fear," *The North American Review*, June 1926

Challenges to Social Norms

After the turmoil of World War I and the relatively progressive policies of President Wilson, Americans elected Warren G. Harding, who promised a "return to normalcy" during the 1920 election campaign. Harding was a conservative and his administration adopted laissez-faire policies that relaxed the regulation of business. However, this hands-off approach was coupled with the enactment of protectionist tariffs on imported goods. His administration was beset by scandals, as numerous men he trusted and placed in important roles used their positions for personal enrichment. Harding died in office in 1923 and was succeeded by his Vice President Calvin Coolidge, who went on to win the 1924 election.

Coolidge said, "The chief business of the American people is business"—a sentiment that echoed the pro-industry attitude of Harding. At times, however, this meant that federal regulatory bodies that were conceived as checks on corporate excess acted instead as facilitators of business expansion. During the Coolidge administration, big business and the wealthy gained greatly and increased their share of the country's wealth. Although all may have seemed well, society and the economy were changing rapidly in the 1920s. The Harding and Coolidge's governments, however, did not recognize or adapt to the economic changes.

Flappers and Freud During the 1920s, increasingly liberal, urban cultural values began to replace traditional, rural cultural values in the United States. Fads like the dance craze called the "Charleston" became cultural touchstones. The swinging sounds of jazz dominated. Young women called "**flappers**" raised the hemlines of their skirts above the knee, cut their hair short, danced to jazz in clubs, and lived independently of parents and husbands. They shocked the older generations, who worried that greater freedom and full-time employment for women would lead to a breakdown of the traditional family.

Sigmund Freud pioneered the field of psychoanalysis and his ideas became very popular in the United States. Freud held that individuals could resolve their emotional problems through talking about them, probing unconscious memories, and interpreting the past events and dreams of the patient. His theories and practices provided a new way to view and interpret human behavior that was not grounded in religion or conventional modes of rationality.

Women on the Rise As evidenced by the emergence of flappers, women in the 1920s began to challenge old assumptions about their role in society. Several developments made this possible:

- World War I had created new employment opportunities for millions of women, and many continued working after the war ended.

- Time-saving devices like refrigerators, washing machines, vacuum cleaners, and other household appliances became commonplace and made it possible for middle-class women to enter the workforce in record numbers.

- There was a great expansion in white-collar occupations such as telephone operator, clerk, stenographer, and teacher.

As early as 1920, women made up approximately 21 percent of the total workforce. Though women received lower wages than men for the same work, their economic freedom fueled social independence, and many young women moved away from home to live on their own.

Read Closely: Causation
As you read, think about how certain facts apply to other people or concepts. How do you think the federal policy that favored big business impacted most Americans' lives?

Read Closely: Inference
Try to make inferences to see how one idea or fact might have broad social or cultural effects. Radio—the world's first electronic mass media—exploded in home use during the 1920s. How might radio have contributed to the faddism and growing popularity of new music like jazz?

The adoption of the Nineteenth Amendment in 1920 gave women throughout the United States the right to vote. During the struggle for its adoption, women organized demonstrations, picket lines, and hunger strikes, which helped them realize their ability to influence public policy.

Prohibition and the Volstead Act In 1919, the states ratified the Eighteenth, or Prohibition, Amendment. For decades, Carrie Nation and other temperance reformers had pushed to end the manufacture and sale of alcoholic beverages in the United States. A strong coalition of anti-alcohol forces emerged on the road to Prohibition. Protestant clergy and worshipers who equated the abuse of alcohol with sinfulness found common cause with Progressive reformers who believed alcohol abuse contributed many of the social ills they hoped to amend.

The Anti-Saloon League (ASL) lobbied lawmakers relentlessly and formed alliances with any group that it felt would further its cause—from Democrats and Republicans to the KKK and the NAACP. After the amendment's ratification, Congress passed the National Prohibition Act—more popularly known as the Volstead Act (after Minnesota Representative Andrew J. Volstead)—which provided enforcement of Prohibition. Supporters of the amendment argued that banning alcohol would improve the country's morals, lower crime rates, reduce alcohol consumption (especially among the young), and improve the health of Americans.

Ironically, Prohibition caused a huge increase in certain types of crime. Prohibition caused millions of otherwise law-abiding citizens to obtain alcohol illegally. Alcohol was either manufactured illegally in the United States or smuggled in from Canada and other foreign sources. Liquor smugglers known as bootleggers made huge profits, and in cities like New York and Chicago, they organized criminal gangs that survived by bribing the police and violently eliminating criminal rivals. Federal officials fought a losing battle to enforce Prohibition until 1933, when the 18th Amendment was repealed by another amendment, the 21st Amendment.

Forces Fight Change

Life in the 1920s was generally good for members of the middle class, who were largely native-born, White Americans. It was not so good for ethnic minorities and the foreign born. Especially in rural communities, people distrusted big cities where large numbers of Italian and Jewish immigrants had settled. Although most immigrants were hardworking and law abiding, many people accused the foreign born of being responsible for city slums and crime.

The Ku Klux Klan Returns The Ku Klux Klan (KKK) was originally a secret society of southern Whites who terrorized freed slaves after the Civil War. The Klan made a comeback following the release of the 1915 film *The Birth of a Nation*, which glorified the Klan. During the 1920s, millions of people in small towns in the North, South, and Midwest openly wore the KKK's white-hooded costume in town parades.

The Klan's national membership peaked at 4 million in the 1920s. Its main goal was to maintain what its members believed was the supremacy and purity of the White, Protestant majority. African Americans, Roman Catholics, Jews, and immigrants were viewed as threats and were regular targets for Klan intimidation and violence—including cross burning, flogging, and lynching (primarily of African American men). Its growing membership made the organization an important force in the politics of many states. The governors of Oregon and Indiana, for example, owed their elections to the Klan's support.

Quota Acts of the 1920s The United States instituted a series of laws in the 1920s to limit the number of immigrants allowed to legally enter the country. The federal government passed three such acts during the decade. Each set of limits was based upon immigrants' country of birth and the number of people from that country who had been in the United States at the time of a previous census:

- In 1921, the Emergency Quota Act went into effect. The annual quota for each country was calculated at 3 percent of the total number of foreign-born persons from that country recorded in the 1910 U.S. census. The quota did not apply to immigrants from countries of the Western Hemisphere.

- The Immigration Act of 1924 lowered the quota further, changed the census date (from 1910 to 1890), and based the quota on all people present in the census, not just foreign-born people. It allowed only 2 percent of the total number of persons from any country recorded in the 1890 census. It also eliminated immigration from Asian countries altogether.

The changes brought about by the 1924 act clearly targeted immigration by people from certain parts of the world. By changing the census date (from 1910 to 1890) and criteria, the government chose a time when people from western and northern Europe dominated the total pool of U.S. residents. Lawmakers intended to drastically reduce the number of immigrants to be accepted from southern and eastern Europe, many of whom were Roman Catholic or Jewish and poor. These traits, among others, made them undesirable in the eyes of Americans with nativist beliefs.

The quota acts of the 1920s delivered the results that lawmakers intended. During the peak period of immigration from 1901–1910, more than 8 million immigrants—mostly from Italy, Russia, and the Austro-Hungarian Empire—arrived in the United States. After 1924, an overall total of only 165,000 immigrants were allowed per year, with that number further reduced to 150,000 from 1929 forward. People from these regions were limited to a small percentage of these reduced totals.

The Scopes Monkey Trial Beginning in the late 19th century, an ongoing debate developed between liberal Christians who sought to make Christianity more relevant to contemporary life, and conservative Christians, who wanted to preserve what they considered the fundamental ideas of Christianity. The fundamentalists, as they were called, believed that every word of the Bible was literally true. Fundamentalist ideas held sway throughout rural America in the 1920s, especially in the South. On the contrary, a more liberal, modernist approach to Christianity was more common in urban areas. This and other factors contributed to a deep cultural and geographic divide in the United States. Fundamentalists waged war against modernist ideas—they rejected Charles Darwin's theory of **evolution** and attempted to stop the teaching of evolution in the public schools.

Read Closely: Reasoning
Popular culture sources such as movies, novels, and even advertisements reflect broader trends in societies, and, therefore, history. The massively popular *The Birth of a Nation* clearly posed the Ku Klux Klan as heroes who could save America. Why do you think the Klan had such a resurgence during the 1920s?

Read Closely: Connections
As you read, look for parallels between different movements and ideas in a text. Fundamentalism grew during the late teens and 1920s. Temperance crusaders were able to get Prohibition enacted in 1919. What do these two movements suggest about the Americans who promoted them?

The clash between urban and rural cultures reached a boiling point in a highly publicized trial in Tennessee in 1925. The defendant was a biology teacher in Dayton, Tennessee, named John Scopes. He had purposely defied a Tennessee law against teaching Darwin's theory of evolution in public schools. The law had been passed because Darwin's ideas ran counter to fundamentalist doctrine, which taught that believers should interpret the Bible literally. Famous Chicago lawyer Clarence Darrow defended Scopes. The prosecutor was William Jennings Bryan, a believer in fundamentalism and a politician from an earlier era who unsuccessfully ran for president in 1896, 1900, and 1908.

The so-called **Scopes Monkey Trial** received international attention because it served as a proxy battle between science and religion. Reading about the trial in their newspapers, city people tended to side with Scopes and Darrow. Rural, church-going Americans tended to side with the prosecution. Scopes and Darrow lost the case, but the court fined him only $100—and a higher court in Tennessee later reversed the trial court's verdict.

In spite of Scopes' conviction, Darrow was widely considered to have bested Bryan in court, and some states rejected anti-evolution laws similar to Tennessee's in the years that followed. However, such anti-evolution laws remained in place in Tennessee and other states until they were ruled unconstitutional by the U.S. Supreme Court—more than 40 years later in 1968.

Civic Literacy: Separation of Church and State The Scopes trial is one of many legal and cultural clashes between segments of the population that disagree over the extent to which, if any, religion should play a role in education. Some, for example, want to be able to apply public education funds to help pay tuition at religious schools. Does using public money for religious schooling violate the Constitution's separation?

Source: Wikimedia Commons

Anti-evolution books on sale in Dayton, Tennessee

Application: Interpret a Primary Source

Read the excerpt and answer the questions that follow it.

Charlotte Perkins Gilman, "Is America Too Hospitable?"
October 1923

There is a question, sneeringly asked by the stranger within our gates: "What is an American?" The American, who knows he is one but has never thought of defining himself, is rather perplexed by the question. A simple answer is here suggested: "Americans are the kind of people who make a nation which every other nationality wants to get into." The sneering stranger then replies: "By no means. It is not your nation we admire—far from it! It is your great rich country we want to get into."

The amazing thing is the cheerful willingness with which the American people are giving up their country to other people, so rapidly that they are already reduced to a scant half of the population. No one is to blame but ourselves. The noble spirit of our founders, and their complete ignorance of sociology began the trouble. They honestly imagined that one kind of man was as good as another if he had the same opportunity—unless his color was different. Consequently they announced, with more than royal magnificence, that this country was "an asylum for the poor and oppressed of all nations." [Quotation is from General George Washington, General Orders, April 18, 1783.]

What is an American? The only kind of person on earth who invites all creation to crowd him out of house and home. And even he is beginning dimly to wonder if it is not time to withdraw the invitation.

Source: Charlotte Perkins Gilman, "Is America Too Hospitable?" *The Forum*, October 1923

1. Does Gilman's opinion reflect the broader mood in the United States at the time of her writing? Explain.

_____

_____

2. How was the reaction to immigration in the 1920s similar to or different from the reaction of Americans in the past?

_____

_____

3. Closely examine Gilman's language in the excerpt. What bias does she betray in her writing?

_____

_____

_____

Lesson 2 *African American Culture Blossoms*

Conceptual Understanding
11.7b African Americans continued to struggle for social and economic equality while expanding their own thriving and unique culture. African American cultural achievements were increasingly integrated into national culture.

African Americans continued to struggle for social and economic equality while expanding their own thriving and unique culture. Black cultural achievements were increasingly integrated into national culture. Following World War I, the United States witnessed a flowering of African American arts. Artistic and intellectual activity flourished in Black communities in the bigger U.S. cities. In the early 1920s, Harlem—a Black neighborhood north of Central Park in New York City—became the epicenter of what became known as the Harlem Renaissance

Analyze a Primary Source

Langston Hughes, "The Negro Artist and the Racial Mountain," 1926

Read Closely: Point of View
Identifying and pondering a writer's point of view help a reader better understand a source. Hughes is writing from an artist's perspective. His belief in the need for artists to express what's in their hearts informs his opinions throughout this article. Underline evidence of Hughes's conviction that artists must stay true themselves in their art.

Read Closely: Parallels
Writers often use parallel structure to help make a point. Notice Hughes's attitude toward White and African American audiences to his work. He equates both audiences by describing his attitude in very similar ways.

Read Closely: Purpose
Hughes is addressing African American culture and society here. His extolling the works of African American artists is purposeful—he's making a point to his culture. Circle a phrase that identifies Hughes's intended audience for this essay.

Let the blare of Negro jazz bands and the bellowing voice of Bessie Smith singing Blues penetrate the closed ears of the colored near-intellectuals until they listen and perhaps understand. Let Paul Robeson singing Water Boy, and Rudolph Fisher writing about the streets of Harlem, and Jean Toomer holding the heart of Georgia in his hands, and Aaron Douglas drawing strange Black fantasies cause the smug Negro middle class to turn from their White, respectable, ordinary books and papers to catch a glimmer of their own beauty. We younger Negro artists who create now intend to express our individual dark-skinned selves without fear or shame. If White people are pleased we are glad. If they are not, it doesn't matter. We know we are beautiful. And ugly too. The tom-tom [drum] cries and the tom-tom laughs. If colored people are pleased we are glad. If they are not, their displeasure doesn't matter either. We build our temples for tomorrow, strong as we know how, and we stand on top of the mountain, free within ourselves.

Source: Langston Hughes, "The Negro Artist and the Racial Mountain," *The Nation*, June 23, 1926

The Harlem Renaissance

As part of the Great Migration, African Americans from the South moved to northern cities to escape brutal Jim Crow laws and attitudes. As a result, Black populations in cities like Chicago, Detroit, and New York increased markedly—nearly doubling over a 20-year span. New York City's Harlem neighborhood became a hotbed of intellectual and arts culture for African Americans, peaking during the 1920s. The **Harlem Renaissance** was the result of a number of factors: the Great Migration, the rising economic and civil rights expectations of African Americans returning from World War I, and a newfound interest and pride in African traditions of music and folk art. Many talented writers, performers, and musicians, and intellectuals settled in Harlem and rose to fame.

Read Closely: Infer Causation
As you make your way through a text, making inferences can help further your overall grasp of what you are reading. How might a growing African American community help spur interest in the arts and traditions of its people?

Population of Central Harlem

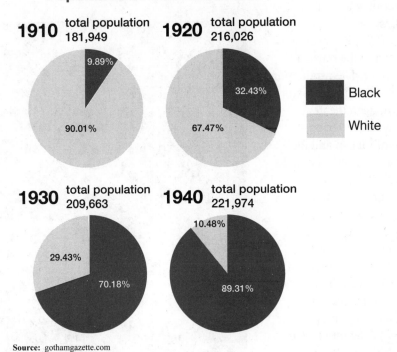

Source: gothamgazette.com

Writers The best known of the Harlem poets were James Weldon Johnson, Countee Cullen, and **Langston Hughes**. Hughes used Black vernacular—everyday, spoken language—and his love of jazz in expressing THE frustrations and difficulties faced by African Americans living in an age of discrimination and segregation. In his poem "Harlem (Dream Deferred)," Hughes asks:

"What happens to a dream deferred?

Does it dry up

like a raisin in the sun? . . .

Maybe it just sags

like a heavy load

Or does it explode?"

African American novelists of the era explored modern life, cultural history, and folklore in their work:

- **Zora Neale Hurston** was an anthropologist, and she wrote fiction and nonfiction as well as satires about African American life. Her novel *Their Eyes Were Watching God* (1937) draws on her academic studies to incorporate black folk traditions from the South.

Read Closely: Interpretation
Take the time to look more deeply into works of art you encounter in your reading. Langston Hughes' poem "Harlem (Dream Deferred)" is one of the best known from the Harlem Renaissance. Based on the excerpt you read, what does Hughes suggests happens by the final line?

- Jean Toomer explored experimental avenues of expression. His modernist novel *Cane* (1933) was composed of character sketches, poetry, and variations in narrative style.

- Claude McKay, author of *Home to Harlem* (1927), was born in Jamaica and immigrated to the United States in 1912. The racism encountered in his adopted nation led him to become one of the more radical voices of the Harlem Renaissance.

Performers was. A former All-American football player and valedictorian at Rutgers College in New Jersey, **Paul Robeson**, became one of the most celebrated actors living in Harlem. He first gained fame for his 1924 performance in Eugene O'Neill's play *Emperor Jones*. Robeson would later play the title role in Shakespeare's *Othello*, which ran on Broadway for 296 performances—longer than any other Shakespeare play.

In 1927, Robeson was the lead in the musical *Showboat*. The production was the first in the history of American theater to deal with the serious issue of racism and the problems faced by Black Americans. *Showboat* also broke ground artistically as a coherent drama with music and lyrics completely integrated into the plot. (Previously, musicals were light, often-trivial comedies interspersed with popular songs.) It featured Black and White performers on the same stage, too, another rare event during the period. Robeson's performance of "Ol' Man River" was one of the most memorable songs of the musical.

Source: Library of Congress

Paul Robeson appearing as Othello during his record-breaking run on Broadway

Read Closely: Turning Point
As you read, look for events and people that drive and signal major changes in history and culture. Both Paul Robeson and Josephine Baker became famous well beyond African American audiences alone. How might performers like them have influenced the wider White culture in America?

Josephine Baker was another notable African American stage artist of the period. Born Freda Josephine McDonald in St. Louis, Missouri, Baker was doing street-corner dancing in her hometown when a vaudeville show recruited her. From there, she headed to New York City, where she gained fame as a comic dancer during the Harlem Renaissance. As her fame grew, she became more vocal in her objection to racial segregation, refusing to perform for segregated audiences. She immigrated to France in 1925, where she performed freely for all audiences and became a sensation and cultural icon. Fluent in both English and French, Baker became the first Black woman to star in a major motion picture—the French film *Zouzou* (1934). She received the Croix de Guerre, a French military honor, for assisting the French resistance during the Nazi occupation of France in World War II.

Jazz African American musicians were the principal creators of the most popular music of the 1920s—**jazz**. The music developed in New Orleans around 1900. Musical historians consider jazz one of the unique, original American art forms, combining elements of European and African musical traditions. By the 1920s, jazz had traveled north to Chicago and New York City. Its vibrant, fast-moving tempo expressed the spirit of the times. Several standout performers from the era went on to become legends of American music:

- Pianist, bandleader, and composer **Duke Ellington** created thousands of pieces of music over his career. He excelled at creating innovative arrangements and getting the most from the talented players who flocked to play with the master.

- Trumpet player and singer **Louis Armstrong** grew up in New Orleans, right alongside the music he became known for. Armstrong's technical ability, inventiveness, and spontaneity were matched only by the joy he displayed while playing.

- Blues singer Bessie Smith sang the hard knocks of life with a fire and emotional intensity that made her one of the top recording artists of the 1920s, popular with both Black and White listeners.

Black Nationalism and Pride

In the majority of cases, talent and ability did not lead to acceptance for African American and other minority artists. In Harlem at the famous Cotton Club, African Americans worked as entertainers, but they were seldom seen as customers. Movie producers and directors rarely cast African Americans in anything but stereotyped roles (servants, maids, and so on). Popular Black entertainers were often not allowed to stay in the hotels or to eat in the restaurants in which they provided the entertainment. Jim Crow laws in the South and less overt though still segregationist laws in the North continued to pose social and economic challenges for African Americans.

W.E.B. Du Bois and the NAACP Beginning in the early 1900s, the Harvard-educated scholar and writer **W.E.B. Du Bois** became one of the most important leaders of the movement for African American rights. He was instrumental in forming the **National Association for the Advancement of Colored People (NAACP)** in 1909, which joined White and Black reformers together under one banner. The organization strove to protect the rights of African Americans and help defend those accused of crimes merely because of their race. NAACP lawyers managed to win a number of civil rights cases in the Supreme Court. Between 1915 and 1917, the Court declared the following to be unconstitutional: segregated housing laws, denying African Americans the right to serve on juries, and preventing African Americans the right to run for office.

In 1910, Du Bois also helped found the NAACP publication *The Crisis*. This magazine, which Du Bois edited for its first 24 years, was an influential outlet for intellectual discussion and debate. It had a circulation of over 100,000 readers by 1920. *The Crisis* published many of the Harlem Renaissance writers, including Langston Hughes, Countee Cullen, and Jean Toomer.

The NAACP grew in size and public stature throughout the 1920s. Writer James Weldon Johnson was the organization's first Black executive secretary.

Read Closely:
Indirect Results
In historical texts, look for less obvious outcomes of historical trends or events. The 1920s is called "The Jazz Age," partly because of the dominance of the new American style of music. In what ways might jazz have unified the African American community across the United States?

Read Closely:
Increased Impact
As you read, be on the lookout for ways that individuals and groups collaborate to increase their impact. The NAACP gained traction as an organization after combining the efforts of Black and White racial justice groups. How might the racial make-up of the NAACP have been important to its growth and success in the 1920s?

The NAACP Legal Defense Fund raised money for the many court battles the national organization fought. Walter F. White, a Georgia-born journalist and activist with African American heritage, became one of the organization's most prominent investigators. He would later lead the NAACP when Johnson retired as executive secretary.

White's tenure was extremely productive for the association. The NAACP played a key role in keeping an avowed segregationist off the Supreme Court and reversing the *Plessy v. Ferguson* "separate but equal" doctrine. During the Depression, the NAACP focused on economic justice issues that disproportionately affect African American workers. Walter White served as an advisor to First Lady Eleanor Roosevelt, who was an NAACP board member, and lobbied her to try to influence the president's anti-discrimination policies.

Marcus Garvey While the NAACP worked for integration, a Jamaican immigrant named Marcus Garvey, whose parents had been enslaved, worked for the exact opposite. Coming to the United States in 1916, Garvey was deeply offended by the second-class status of African Americans. He thought African Americans needed to take pride in their African heritage. In Jamaica, he had organized the Universal Negro Improvement Association (UNIA), which sponsored a "Back to Africa" movement.

Garvey urged African Americans not to seek acceptance by the White majority. Instead, he believed that they should build their own institutions and leave the United States for Africa, their ancestors' homeland. In the United States, UNIA attracted about half a million members—no small number for such a radical organization among an overall Black population of about 10.4 million in 1920. Garvey's political leadership ended in 1925 when he was convicted of using the mail to defraud investors. In 1927, the U.S. government deported him to Jamaica.

Source: Wikimedia Commons

A stock certificate for the Black Star Line, begun by Marcus Garvey as a way to promote trade by Black organizations and as a way to transport African Americans who wanted to return to Africa.

Application: Interpret a Primary Source

Read the excerpt and answer the questions that follow it.

James Weldon Johnson, "Race Prejudice and the Negro Artist," 1928

[T]here is a common, widespread, and persistent stereotyped idea regarding the Negro, and it is that he is here only to receive; to be shaped into something new and unquestionably better. The common idea is that the Negro reached America intellectually, culturally, and morally empty, and that he is here to be filled—filled with education, filled with religion, filled with morality, filled with culture. In a word, the stereotype is that the Negro is nothing more than a beggar at the gate of the nation, waiting to be thrown the crumbs of civilization.

Through his artistic efforts the Negro is smashing this immemorial stereotype faster than he has ever done through any other method he has been able to use. He is making it realized that he is the possessor of a wealth of natural endowments and that he has long been a generous giver to America. He is impressing upon the national mind the conviction that he is an active and important force in American life; that he is a creator as well as a creature; that he has given as well as received; that he is the potential giver of larger and richer contributions.

In this way the Negro is bringing about an entirely new national conception of himself; he has placed himself in an entirely new light before the American people. I do not think it too much to say that through artistic achievement the Negro has found a means of getting at the very core of the prejudice against him by challenging the Nordic [related to the countries of Scandinavia] superiority complex. A great deal has been accomplished in this decade of "renaissance."

Source: James Weldon Johnson, "Race Prejudice and the Negro Artist," *Harper's*, November 1928.

Speak and Listen:
Impact With a partner, take turns reading the second paragraph sentence by sentence. Then discuss ways in which African Americans have been "generous givers" to America. Identify specific gifts and discuss their relative importance. Which are most significant in shaping American society and culture?

1. Describe some of the artistic achievements of the Harlem Renaissance era that Johnson is referring to.

_____

_____

2. Where do you think African Americans were finally able, in the 1920s, to bring about "an entirely new national conception" of themselves?

_____

_____

3. Who is the author, James Weldon Johnson, and from what point of view does he approach this topic?

_____

_____

Lesson 3 *Prosperity Then Depression*

For many Americans, the 1920s was a time of prosperity. However, underlying economic problems, reflected in the stock market crash of 1929, led to the Great Depression. President Franklin D. Roosevelt's responses to the Great Depression increased the role of the federal government.

Analyze a Primary Source

Franklin Delano Roosevelt, Acceptance Speech at the Democratic Convention, July 2, 1932

Read Closely: Defining the Opponent
Roosevelt uses a familiar rhetorical device by defining his opponents in a negative light. Underline the phrases or sentences Roosevelt employs to define the Republican Party in power as the Depression began.

Read Closely: Counter Claim
Roosevelt is building a case against the policies of the Hoover administration and Republican Party. Notice how he presents the Republican belief that economic laws can't be altered because they are "made by nature," and then refutes that claim by pointing out that these laws were human made. Thus, they can be changed.

Read Closely: Call to Action
This is a persuasive speech, and Roosevelt is speaking to more than simply the nominating delegates at the Democratic National Convention. Circle the sentence where Roosevelt makes an appeal to the nation as a whole.

Our Republican leaders tell us economic laws—sacred, inviolable, unchangeable—cause panics which no one could prevent. But while they prate [speak idly] of economic laws, men and women are starving. We must lay hold of the fact that economic laws are not made by nature. They are made by human beings. Yes, when—not if—when we get the chance, the Federal Government will assume bold leadership in distress relief. For years Washington has alternated between putting its head in the sand and saying there is no large number of destitute people in our midst who need food and clothing, and then saying the States should take care of them, if there are. Instead of planning two and a half years ago to do what they are now trying to do, they kept putting it off from day to day, week to week, and month to month, until the conscience of America demanded action. . . .

I pledge you, I pledge myself, to a new deal for the American people. Let us all here assembled constitute ourselves prophets of a new order of competence and of courage. This is more than a political campaign; it is a call to arms. Give me your help, not to win votes alone, but to win in this crusade to restore America to its own people.

Source: excerpt from Franklin Delano Roosevelt, Acceptance Speech at the Democratic Convention, July 2, 1932

The Roaring Economy

Big businesses flourished and grew bigger and more powerful throughout the 1920s under the policies of the Calvin Coolidge and Herbert Hoover administration. By 1929, the 200 largest U.S. businesses controlled 49 percent of all corporate wealth in the country.

Workers Thrive in the Roaring Twenties For the majority of the 1920s, unemployment was very low—hovering around the 5 percent mark. Worker productivity rose as a result of new manufacturing methods that helped bring down manufacturing costs. Workers' wages increased, though the growth did not match the increases in productivity and company profits. An average factory worker earned $1,100 a year in 1919; by 1929, that annual income was $1,350. The fact that prices for consumer goods also fell during the period increased peoples' buying power.

Read Closely: Effects
Consider what effects arise from information you learn in a history text. What effect do you think did increasing household incomes and purchasing power have on the overall U.S. economy?

Gains in Productivity and Wages, 1909–1929

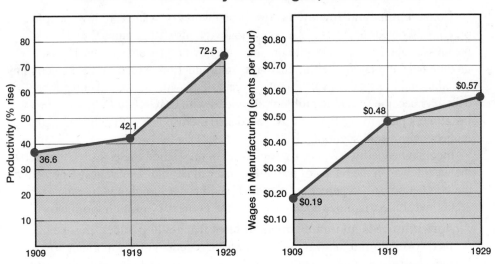

The Automobile Revolution The automaker **Henry Ford** applied the ideas of mass-production to his business. Making his Model T cars on assembly lines saved time, cut production costs, and enabled Model Ts to be sold in 1916 for only $400. Ford's efficient production methods were copied in other industries.

The automobile did for the 20th century what the railroad had done for the 19th century. It boosted the American economy and transformed American society. Between 1919 and 1928, the number of cars manufactured by U.S. companies exploded from 1.5 million to 4.7 million. By the end of the decade of prosperity, Americans owned more than 25 million cars—a startling number for a country with about 30 million households and a population of 123 million.

The millions of automobiles sold in the 1920s stimulated the growth of other industries:

- The rubber industry expanded to produce tires.
- The oil and gasoline industry provided fuel.
- The steel industry produced millions of tons of metal for auto bodies.
- Roadside hotels and restaurants were built all over the country to take advantage of the motorists' fondness for travel and tourism.

Read Closely: Symbolism
As you read, try to see that some information means more than simply the literal facts. The affordability of automobiles certainly allowed more Americans to buy cars. What might be some of the symbolic reasons why owning a car was so appealing to the average American worker?

Read Closely:
Potential Problem
Some information in a historical text will point toward future negative consequences. With new innovative products for the home, such as washing machines, radios, kitchen appliances, and more within reach, more and more people engaged in installment buying. What potential problems do you see with so much of the U.S. economy based on borrowing money?

Read Closely:
Different Impacts
As you read, seek out the different ways that events impact different groups. The impact of the Depression depended on where you lived. What are some ways people living in urban areas might have endured the Depression differently than those in rural or farming areas?

The Credit Boom Before the 1920s, ownership of automobiles, telephones, phonographs, radios, and other new technologies was limited to the rich. But as the economy grew and incomes increased, these technologies became available to millions of American consumers. To encourage people to buy new toasters, refrigerators, cars, and other products, businesses extended credit through installment buying. Rather than paying the entire price of the product upon purchase, consumers had the opportunity to spread out their payments in installments, even as they used the product. Millions of people went into debt to finance purchases.

Weaknesses Lead to a Crash

Although the 1920s seemed like a wondrous time of prosperity, some saw signs that problems were on the horizon. There were, in fact, a number of basic weaknesses in the economy that contributed to the economic collapse that became known as the **Great Depression**.

Consumption and Income Issues When workers' wages are low, people's purchasing power declines. As a result, many goods will go unsold and businesses begin to fail. Despite the increase in worker wages in the 1920s, income began to lag far behind increases in production, which made the economy unstable and too weak to sustain many years of growth. Increased consumer debt also became a serious problem. Provided with easy credit to buy on the installment plan, many families overburdened themselves with debt and had to reduce their overall spending.

Income inequality, too, became an issue. In the United States in 1929, much of the wealth was in the hands of a small number of people. The richest 5 percent of the population had 25 percent of the total income. The combined income of the 36,000 wealthiest families equaled that of the poorest 12 million families.

Agriculture Stagnation Farmers suffered from falling prices. European farms recovered from the war and there was less demand for American crops. Farmers borrowed money to purchase land and the newest equipment—tractors, tillers, and so on. They hoped to increase their income by ramping up production. Unfortunately, increased production tended to decrease prices. This period of overproduction, low prices, and crushing debt meant that the 1920s were less than "roaring" for U.S. farmers.

The Stock Market Crash During the 1920s, the risky practice of borrowing money to purchase stocks became more common. This was called buying stocks on margin. An investor could put down as little as 10 percent when purchasing stock, and the bank would put up the rest. For example, a person could purchase $100 of stock with $10 of cash and $90 borrowed money. If the stock went up in value by 20 percent, the person could sell it for $120, repay the loan, and profit handsomely on his or her cash investment of $10. The idea became widespread that it was perfectly safe to buy stock, wait for its price to rise, and sell it at a big profit.

Between 1922 and 1927, the value of the **Dow Jones Industrial Average** doubled. (The Dow Jones Average is a tool to help investors gauge the overall value and health of the stock market.) It then nearly doubled again in just the next two years. During that same period, however, the value of stocks owned on margin had nearly doubled as well—reaching a staggering $6.5 billion. Overconfidence in the stock market prevailed, but a reckoning loomed.

In 1928, **Herbert Hoover** became president in a landslide victory. Hoover had succeeded as an engineer, a business leader, and a Cabinet member under Presidents Harding and Coolidge. For the first six months of 1929, prosperity continued under Hoover. The bull (or rising) market on Wall Street reached its highest point in September 1929. Then the prices of stocks started to go down— sometimes slowly, sometimes in frightening drops. On Tuesday, October 29, thousands of people panicked and ordered their brokers on Wall Street to sell at any price. On that single day, known as Black Tuesday, the Dow Jones Average plummeted 25 percent, and the stock market lost an estimated $30 billion in value.

The Great Crash on Wall Street had four immediate and devastating economic consequences:

1. The billions of dollars in savings that people had used to buy stocks were largely wiped out.

2. Many individuals and businesses that owned stock on margin could not repay the loans and went bankrupt.

3. Banks failed when large numbers of depositors wanted to withdraw their funds all at once—an event known as a panic or a "run on the bank."

4. People lost confidence in the economy.

For years after the crash, people preferred to save what they could rather than to risk investing in new business ventures.

International Consequences In the 1920s, many other nations owed vast sums of money to the United States. Much of this debt stemmed from U.S. loans to European countries during and after World War I. This economic imbalance contributed to the economic collapse of 1929. International debts were largely repaid with loans from the United States. For example, the United States lent money to Germany so that Germany could pay reparations to England and France. England and France, in turn, could then repay loans to the United States made during World War I. When the stock market crashed, the cycle of debt payments both in the United States and Europe came to a halt.

> **Read Closely: Policy Results**
> Presidents Harding, Coolidge, and Hoover all supported and advanced economic policies that favored big business, the banking industry, and investors. How might some of those policies directly contributed to bringing about the Great Crash and the Depression?

The Hoover Administration Responds

An economic crisis of this magnitude would challenge any government. President Hoover had very defined ideas about the limits of government involvement in the economy and society, and these were reflected in his response.

Hoover Bets on Business and Banks Hoover drew on his economic experience and past successes to try to halt the Depression. He enacted the following policies.

• Taxes were cut to enable consumers to buy more products.

• The amount of government money spent on public projects—the building of dams, highways, harbors, and so on—increased modestly.

• Federal funds were provided to struggling banks, railroads, and insurance companies to keep them from going bankrupt.

• The Federal Farm Board was established to help farmers and keep prices from falling.

• European nations were told that they could temporarily stop making payments on their war debts.

Despite these efforts, economic conditions did not improve. Many Americans felt Hoover's policies helped businesses rather the common people. Hoover disagreed with the idea of giving aid directly to individuals. He held a strong belief in "rugged individualism." Hoover believed in limited government and felt the actions of private businesses and individuals would be more successful. If businesses succeeded, everyone would benefit indirectly, as profits, in theory, would eventually make their way down to wage earners.

Read Closely: Federal Solutions
In many ways, Hoover's efforts to halt the Depression were similar to his and Coolidge's pro-business policies. What might be problematic about pursuing a similar course when the economy had crashed?

Rising Unemployment and Falling Prices, 1929–1932

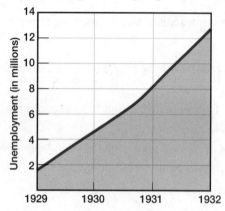
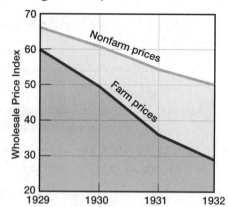

Unemployment and Hoovervilles In 1932, about 12 million workers—25 percent of the labor force—were unemployed. Those who had jobs worked fewer hours and for lower wages. Prices paid to farmers were desperately low. Factories produced only half of their 1929 output. By 1932, about 5,000 banks had closed their doors. Millions of Americans, both rich and poor, had lost their savings forever.

Unemployed people who could not pay even the lowest rents were forced into the streets. For food, they had to beg or line up for free meals served by private charities and churches. Homeless families slept in tents and shacks clustered in areas they mockingly called **Hoovervilles**. The sense of despair across the country was overwhelming.

FDR and The New Deal

In 1932 Americans expressed their dissatisfaction with Hoover and the Republican party by voting overwhelmingly for Democratic challenger **Franklin D. Roosevelt** and giving Democrats control of both houses of Congress. Roosevelt promised a **"New Deal"** for the American people. He believed that government should help people directly by giving them jobs with, or subsidized by, the government. The federally funded paychecks, in Roosevelt's view, would give people hope and revive the economy by giving people money to spend on goods and services.

Roosevelt also believed in trying out many ideas for solving the economic crisis. Roosevelt and his advisers (a group called the "Brain Trust") had three main goals:

- provide relief to the poor and unemployed

- bring about the recovery of businesses

- reform the economic system to correct the mistakes that had caused the Depression

In Roosevelt's first three months in office, known as the "Hundred Days," important laws were enacted that had a dramatic and long-lasting effect on the country.

Read Closely: Comparison
Comparing two different approaches to a historical event or crisis can help show why one was successful while the other faltered. Hoover and Roosevelt had two very different philosophies about the role government should play in fixing the American economy. How would you describe the two Presidents' approaches?

Banking and Stock Market Reforms After Roosevelt took office in 1933, he declared a nationwide bank holiday, closing all banks for four days. Congress passed the Emergency Banking Act, which allowed for the reopening of sound banks. The run on the banks stopped, and public confidence in them returned. Soon, most of the nation's banks were in business again. The Glass-Steagall Act of 1933 created the Federal Deposit Insurance Corporation (FDIC) and changed some banking practices. The FDIC gave government backing and insurance for bank deposits up to a certain amount so that depositors would not risk loss of their money.

The Securities and Exchange Commission (SEC) was created in 1934 to regulate pricing practices and require that basic data on stocks and bonds offered for sale be made public. A major goal was to curb margin buying and speculation.

Direct Federal Assistance Programs The 1933 Federal Emergency Relief Administration (FERA) provided federal money to the states to be used to create jobs for the unemployed. The Public Works Administration (PWA) provided relief by using federal money to pay for major construction projects. Private businesses hired by the PWA built roads, bridges, libraries, hospitals, schools, courthouses, and other public projects. The Civilian Conservation Corps (CCC), provided relief for unemployed young men, many from urban areas, between ages 18 and 25. They worked on conservation projects: flood control, soil conservation, forest replanting, and park construction. The Works Progress Administration (WPA) gave jobs, salaries, and skills to more than 8.5 million Americans who worked to construct 18,000 playgrounds, 124,000 bridges, 651,000 miles of highway, and much more.

One of the most ambitious New Deal programs was the Tennessee Valley Authority (TVA). The southern region watered by the Tennessee River was often flooded. The farmers living near the river had no electric power and were extremely poor. In 1933, Congress created the TVA to accomplish several goals:

- build dams to control floods

- build reservoirs to hold needed water

- build hydroelectric power plants to provide inexpensive electricity for the region

The Agricultural Adjustment Act (AAA) of 1933 paid farmers to take land out of production as a means of limiting production and raising farm prices. The money for these payments was to come from a "processing tax" on the industries that made the raw products into finished goods, such as mills that processed wheat into flour and cotton into cloth. The AAA also asked farmers to destroy a portion of their crops and livestock to raise the real income of farmers to "parity," that is, the higher price level that farmers had enjoyed before World War I.

> **Read Closely:**
> **Underlying Purpose**
> As you read, try to delve beneath the policies you learn about to understand why they were instituted. How would you describe the underlying purpose of the Roosevelt administration reforms on banking and the stock market?

> **Read Closely:**
> **Changing Attitudes**
> History is about people, so always consider how policies affect their beliefs and outlook, whether on a short- or long-term basis. How might the direct assistance programs of the New Deal have helped change the national attitude about the Depression?

New Deal Programs/Agencies	
Federal Emergency Relief Administration (FERA)	Established as a temporary measure to get monetary relief to citizens in need. Did this by granting money to state and local agencies.
Civilian Conservation Corps (CCC)	Provided jobs, mostly for young, single men, in the areas of natural resource conservation.
Public Works Administration (PWA)	Instituted to help reduce unemployment by funding large, public construction projects, such as roads, dams, bridges, and public buildings.
Agricultural Adjustment Administration (AAA)	Designed to return agriculture to profitability by paying subsidies to farmers who agreed to reduce production.
National Recovery Administration (NRA)	Designed to help the industries recover by allowing similar businesses to cooperate, through setting prices, wages, hours, and the like. Labor received assurances of collective bargaining rights.
Federal Deposit Insurance Corporation (FDIC)	Created to protect depositors' bank accounts up to a certain amount.
Tennessee Valley Authority (TVA)	Established to control flooding and provided electricity to the impoverished areas in and around the Tennessee River.
Works Progress Administration (WPA)	Gave paying work and job skills to millions of unemployed people while greatly improving U.S. infrastructure and services.

Read Closely: Perceptions
As you read, look for ways that legislation or other governmental acts affect the ways citizens see their lives and world. How might New Deal labor laws have changed the way the American worker perceived his or her role in the economy?

Business and Labor The National Recovery Administration (NRA), set up in 1933, encouraged business and labor leaders in every industry to draw up codes of fair practices. These included maximum hours of work, minimum wages, and goals for how many goods should be produced and at what price. The codes were designed to help businesses control production and raise prices and to help labor by putting people back to work and raising wages. To win the support of labor, a provision in the NRA act gave workers the right to organize into unions. The Wagner Act of 1935 guaranteed to all workers the right to join the union of their choice and thus to "bargain collectively" with their employer on such issues as wages, hours, and factory conditions.

To enforce the act, a National Labor Relations Board (NLRB) was empowered to supervise union elections, prevent unfair labor practices by employers, and compel employers to deal with whatever union the majority of workers chose to join. A few years later, the Fair Labor Standards Act of 1938 set minimum wages and maximum hours for workers in industries engaged in interstate commerce. The law also prohibited children under 16 from working in interstate commerce.

Social Security One of the most significant reforms of the New Deal came with the passage of the **Social Security Act** (1935). It established old-age insurance paid for by a joint tax on employers and employees. This ensured workers a monthly income when they reached age 65. The act also established unemployment compensation to give laid-off workers some income for a number of weeks while they sought new employment. Finally, the Social Security Act provided for federal grants to the states to assist in caring for the disabled, the blind, and dependent children.

Resistance and Court Challenges The New Deal legislation was very popular with most Americans as they saw a direct impact and improvement in their lives. However, some citizens and many Republican politicians rejected aspects of the New Deal, claiming the program gave the federal government too much power. The federal government had to defend some of its legislative programs in court. At that time, previous Republican presidents had appointed most of the Supreme Court. They struck down a number of the New Deal programs as unconstitutional, including the National Recovery Administration (NRA) and the Agricultural Adjustment Act (AAA).

Angered by the Supreme Court's decisions, Roosevelt proposed a scheme for increasing the number of justices on the court from 9 to 15—allowing him to appoint justices who would support his agenda. Legislators from both parties denounced this idea as an attempt to pack the Court. In 1937, the Democratic-controlled Congress defeated Roosevelt's plan because it attempted to undo the federal government's system of checks and balances.

The Dust Bowl As if the social and economic crisis of the Great Depression were not enough, some areas of the United States experienced a serious environmental crisis known as the **Dust Bowl**. In the early 1930s, farmers from Oklahoma, Arkansas, Kansas, and other areas of the Great Plains found that their land had turned to dust. Poor farming practices, a long-lasting drought, and high winds combined to cause widespread crop failures and dust storms. Thousands of poor farmers lost their income and land. In response, the New Deal's Soil Conservation Act (SCA) created the Soil Conservation Service (SCS) to reverse the effects of land mismanagement. Labor from the CCC and the WPA helped support the work of the SCS.

Read Closely: Responsibility
What does it say about the Democratically controlled Congress that it voted down Roosevelt's attempt to pack the Supreme Court?

Source: National Archives and Records Administration / Wikimedia Commons

A dust storm prepares to engulf the town of Rolla, Kansas, on April 14, 1935.

Application: Interpret a Primary Source

Read the excerpt and answer the questions that follow it.

Letter to First Lady Eleanor Roosevelt, from C.B.S., Rural Supervisor of Schools, Anderson County, Tennessee, January 26, 1936

My dear Mrs. Roosevelt,

You may think I am a very insignificant person to be writing to a person of your standing and ability but by reading your article and hearing your talks I know you are real and have an interest in people even my dear little needy boys and girls of the mountain schools.

I am Rural Supervisor of schools in my county. I have forty schools to supervise. Due to insufficient clothing and food many are unable to attend schools. I wish it were possible for you to see some of the conditions. It is not uncommon for a child to have but one dress or shirt. They have to stay at home the day the mother laundries [launders] them.

I am just wishing that in some of your groups that it would be possible to interest them in our needs. The Save the Children Fund, with headquarters in New York, has helped me some. Many children of my schools would be unable to attend school had it not been for this organization.

I hope you will not consider me rude for writing. I have my heart in the work. I realize a hungry or a cold child cannot learn too much.

Source: Margaret C. Moran, *U.S. History and Government: Readings and Documents,* Amsco School Publications, 2003

---

1. Describe the geographic and economic context of this letter.

_____

_____

2. How does the author's letter reflect the lives of many rural Americans during the Depression?

_____

_____

3. Do you think the author is describing the situation in his or her county truthfully? Why or why not?

_____

_____

Chapter 7 *Review*

Multiple-Choice Questions

Questions 1–3 refer to the excerpt below.

A Flapper Explains "Flapperhood"

I wonder if it ever occurred to any of you that it required brains to become and remain a successful flapper? Indeed it does! It requires an enormous amount of cleverness and energy to keep going at the proper pace. It requires self-knowledge and self-analysis. We must know our capabilities and limitations. We must be constantly on the alert. Attainment of flapperhood is a big and serious undertaking!

"Brains?" you repeat, skeptically. "Then why aren't they used to better advantage?" That is exactly it! And do you know who is largely responsible for all this energy's being spent in the wrong directions? You! You parents, and grandparents, and friends, and teachers, and preachers—all of you! "The war!" you cry. "It is the effect of the war!" And then you blame prohibition. Yes! Yet it is you who set the example there! But this is my point: Instead of helping us work out our problems with constructive, sympathetic thinking and acting, you have muddled them for us more hopelessly with destructive public condemnation and denunciation. . . .

We are the Younger Generation. The war tore away our spiritual foundations and challenged our faith. We are struggling to regain our equilibrium. The times have made us older and more experienced than you were at our age. It must be so with each succeeding generation if it is to keep pace with the rapidly advancing and mighty tide of civilization. Help us to put our knowledge to the best advantage. Work with us! That is the way! Outlets for this surplus knowledge and energy must be opened. Give us a helping hand.

Youth has many disillusionments. Spiritual forces begin to be felt. The emotions are frequently in a state of upheaval, struggling with one another for supremacy. And Youth does not understand. There is no one to turn to—no one but the rest of Youth, which is as perplexed and troubled with its problems as ourselves. Everywhere we read and hear the criticism and distrust of older people toward us. It forms an insurmountable barrier between us. How can we turn to them?

Source: Ellen Welles Page, "A Flapper's Appeal to Parents," *Outlook*, December 6, 1922

1. Which of the following claims made by Page is most plausible?

    1. It takes brains to be a successful flapper.

    2. The older generation is responsible for the existence of flappers.

    3. The younger generation is struggling to regain its equilibrium in the wake of the war.

    4. Parents have only made things worse by trying to help.

2. According to this excerpt, what impact did time and place have on the flapper?

1. American teenagers became flappers because of Prohibition.
2. The war and advancing of civilization contributed to create the flapper.
3. Without jazz, there would have been no flappers.
4. Flappers rejected the morality of the older generation.

3. According to Page, which of the following best describes the underlying problem facing the flapper generation?

1. They need outlets for their surplus knowledge and energy.
2. Prohibition has cut down on their opportunities to socialize.
3. The looming threat of war makes it impossible for them to think of the future.
4. Old people criticize and distrust them.

Questions 4 and 5 refer to the excerpt below.

B. A Texas Minister Defends the Ku Klux Klan

What do you really KNOW about the Ku Klux Klan? Have you heard both sides and carefully considered the facts with impartial fairness and without prejudice? Have you made an HONEST effort to learn the truth? Have you given the Klan a just, fair, and impartial trial? Are you "PLAYING THE GAME FAIR?," or have you condemned the Klan on the testimony of its enemies without hearing the other side? . . .

Enemies have tried every conceivable method to suppress the activities and growth of the Klan. They have tried mob violence, brickbats, clubs, and guns; they have tried frame-ups, courts, and investigations; they have tried lawsuits, injunctions, and false witnesses; they have tried crooks, liars, and traitors; they have tried wine, women, and graft; they have tried lawyers, judges, and governors;—in fact, they have tried all the hellish means, diabolical methods, and devilish schemes that the spirits of demons and fiendish minds of men, aided by his Satanic Majesty, could conceive and invent to wreck and destroy the Klan; but they have all miserably failed. In spite of the fiendish desire and hell born efforts to check its growth, disrupt its membership, and destroy its influence, the Klan marches steadily onward and upward toward the successful defeat of wrong, and a triumphant victory for the right.

Surely the hand of God is leading and the Spirit of God is hovering over this great movement. Nothing short of Divine Providence could ever have saved the Klan from wreck and ruin as it has passed through such trying ordeals and dangerous experiences. If this work be of men it will come to naught; but if it be of God you cannot stop it. The right will always prevail, and the wrong will fail.

Source: Rev. W. C. Wright, "The Ku Klux Klan Unmasked," ca. 1924

4. How does Wright support his claim that the enemies of the Ku Klux Klan have tried to suppress its activities?

1. He says that only Divine Providence has saved the Klan from destruction.

2. He says that movies have given people the wrong idea about the Klan and its goals.

3. He accuses them of trying to outlaw the wearing of white robes and hoods.

4. He provides a paragraph of ways in which they have supposedly tried to stop the Klan.

5. How does this excerpt illustrate change and continuity in history?

1. It shows that the public does not always see that there are good people on both sides of every issue.

2. It deals with a resurgence of the White supremacy in the 1920s that is similar to the one taking place today.

3. It shows that religion could be used to justify evil.

4. It shows that the public has always been at the mercy of "fake news."

Questions 6–8 refer to the excerpt below.

C. A Congressman on the Failure of Prohibition

What is the effect of Prohibition on general crime increase? Today, Leavenworth and Atlanta prisons, both federal penitentiaries, are so overcrowded that they are caring for several hundred convicts above the institutions' facilities. There are about 3,200 now in Leavenworth and 3,023 in Atlanta. Temporary dormitories for the two prisons probably will have to be provided in the industrial shops. Apparently the experiment in national regulation of local beverages and habits has been a failure and has brought with it increase rather than decrease in general crime. What is the remedy? . . .

I should like to see the Eighteenth Amendment repealed, power being retained by the Congress to protect the states from outside interference with their local laws, but while the Eighteenth Amendment is part of the Constitution I feel that there might be a substitute for the Volstead Act which would greatly improve the existing situation.

Repeal the Volstead Act and enact the following:

Section 1.—Each State shall for itself define the meaning of the words "intoxicating liquors" as used in Section 1 of Article XVIII of the Amendments to the Constitution of the United States, and each State shall itself enforce within its own limits its own laws on this subject.

Section 2.—Any person who transports or causes to be transported into any State any beverage prohibited by such State as being an "intoxicating liquor" should be punished by the United States by imprisonment for not more than 10 years or by a fine of not less than $10,000 nor more than $100,000, or by both such fine and imprisonment. . . .

The Volstead Act is certain to be modified. The Eighteenth Amendment, in the minds of the majority of the American people, was never intended to apply to wine, beer and cider, and by the adoption of such a law as I have proposed, those states which wish such beverages may obtain them legally even while the Eighteenth Amendment remains part of the Constitution.

Source: John Philip Hill, "A State's Rights Remedy for Volsteadism," *The North American Review,* Summer and Fall 1925

6. Which of the following best describes Hill's purpose in this excerpt?

   1. He wanted to repeal Prohibition.

   2. He hoped to end prison overcrowding.

   3. He wanted to make laws defining intoxicating liquors uniform throughout the U.S.

   4. He was proposing a modification in the way Prohibition was enforced.

7. What does Hill seem to believe is the underlying cause of the failure of Prohibition?

   1. Organized crime

   2. Regional attitudes toward what should be covered

   3. Overcrowded prisons

   4. Inadequate enforcement of the Eighteenth Amendment

8. The author proposes a solution to the problems caused by the Volstead Act. How did Congress eventually deal with them?

   1. By passing the Twenty-first Amendment

   2. By repealing the Volstead Act and replacing it with his suggested modifications

   3. By loosening penalties for possession and distribution of alcoholic beverages

   4. By stiffening penalties for possession and distribution of alcoholic beverages

Source: Wikimedia Commons

Pouring whisky into a sewer, July 1921

Short-Essay Questions

Study the two documents and answer the question that follows.

D. An Art Critic's Review of WPA Art

As this exhibition clearly shows, the Federal Art Project's work falls under two headings. First of all is the provision of relief for artists who need it. This is the temporary, incidental, and, from one point of view, the less important heading, although it is the first cause of the Project's being. The second division of the work constitutes a kind of artistic resettlement administration—the provision of works of art where such were never known before. This, from the long-range, cultural point of view, is the thing that counts most. The concentration of artists and the market for art in the large, glutted metropolitan centers is being broken down in many different ways. These new directions and new points of departure established by the Project account for the title given the exhibition as a whole—"Frontiers of American Art." . . .

The most permanent and obvious of the Project's "frontiers" is that of the adornment of public buildings with mural paintings, mosaics, sculpture, and so on. Some 1300 such works have been installed in tax-supported structures. This is the most risky of the several directions in which the project is going. A bad picture can be taken down, but once a mural or sculpture is set up in a public building, it is going to stay there a long time, and unless the work is of very high quality its effects will be bad. . . .

Source: Alfred Frankenstein, "The WPA Artists Lean On Their Brushes, *San Francisco Chronicle* (April 23, 1939)

E. WPA Mural in Coit Tower, San Francisco

Source: Wikimedia Commons

Uncredited workers in employ of the Works Progress Administration, including Ralph Stackpole, Bernard Zakheim, and faculty and students of the California School of Fine Arts, 1930s

1. In a short essay, describe the historical context surrounding the two documents above. Then identify and explain the cause-and-effect relationship between the events and ideas described in these documents.

Study the two documents and answer the question that follows.

F. Review of Zora Neale Hurston's First Novel from *The Crisis*

Now Miss Hurston has written a book, and despite the enthusiastic praise on the jacket by such eminent literary connoisseurs as Carl Van Vechten, Fannie Hurst, and Blanche Colton Williams, all sponsors for the New Negro, this reviewer is compelled to report that *Jonah's Gourd Vine* is quite disappointing and a failure as a novel . . .

The defects of Miss Hurston's novel become the more glaring when her work is placed bedside that of contemporary White authors of similar books about their own people—such as the first half of Fielding Burke's novel of North Carolina hillbillies, "Call Home the Heart," or two novels of Arkansas mountaineers, "Mountain Born" by Emmet Gowen and "Woods Colt" by T. R. Williamson. The first two names are, like Miss Hurston's, first novels, and we feel that it is not asking too much of her to expect that in writing novels about her own people she give us work of equal merit to these.

Lest this criticism of *Jonah's Gourd Vine* seem too severe, let us add that there is much about the book that is fine and distinctive, and enjoyable. Zora Hurston has assembled between the pages of the book a rich store of folklore. She has captured the lusciousness and beauty of the Negro dialect as have few others. . . These factors give the book an earthiness, a distinctly racial flavor, a somewhat primitive beauty which makes its defects the more regrettable. We can but hope that with time and further experience in the craft of writing, Zora Hurston will develop the ability to fuse her abundant material into a fine literary work.

Source: Andrew Burris, "The Browsing Reader," *The Crisis,* June 1934

G. Hurston Describes the Critical Reception of Her First Novel

Zora Neale Hurston won critical acclaim for two new things in Negro fiction. The first was an objective point of view. The subjective view was so universal that it had come to be taken for granted. When her first book, "Jonah's Gourd Vine," a novel, appeared in 1934, the critics announced across the nation, "Here at last is a Negro story without bias. The characters live and move. The story is about Negroes but it could be anybody. It is the first time that a Negro story has been offered without special pleading. The characters in the story are seen in relation to themselves and not in relation to the Whites as has been the rule. To watch these people one would conclude that there were no White people in the world. The author is an artist that will go far."

The second element that attracted attention was the telling of the story in the idiom—not the dialect—of the Negro. The Negro's poetical flow of language, his thinking in images and figures was called to the attention of the outside world. It gave verisimilitude to the narrative by stewing the subject in its own juice.

Source: Zora Neale Hurston, "Art and Such," 1938 (unpublished during Hurston's lifetime)

2. In a short essay, describe the historical context surrounding the two documents above. Then analyze and explain how the point of view of the second document affects its reliability as a source of evidence.

CHAPTER 8

World War II (1935–1945)

Chapter Overview

As the country slowly pulled out of the Great Depression through the 1930s, Americans had very little appetite for getting involved in world affairs. However, political and military developments in Europe and Asia eventually thrust the United States into a worldwide conflict.

The Rise of Fascism Spurs World War In the 1930s, Adolph Hitler and his Nazi Party consolidated power in Germany. Mussolini had done the same in Italy in the 1920s. Germany took aggressive action toward some of its neighbors, violating previous agreements. In 1939, Germany invaded Poland and World War II began. Tensions between the United States and Japan grew, and Japan's preemptive attack on Pearl Harbor in December 1941 abruptly ended the U.S. isolationist position.

The United States at War The United States prioritized the fight against Germany and Italy in Europe. The D-Day invasion of France in June 1944 was the turning point in the war in Europe. U.S. forces fought their way across the Pacific, island by island, to try to defeat the Japanese. When the war in Europe ended, U.S. military focus shifted to Japan. President Truman made the decision to use nuclear weapons against Japan in an attempt to put an end to the war. Japan quickly surrendered, ending World War II.

A National Effort When the war began, American industry shifted rapidly from consumer to war production. As more and more men left for the war, more and more women joined the workforce. The federal government forced Japanese Americans living on the West Coast, citizens or not, into internment camps.

The Holocaust At the end of the war, Germany's mass slaughter of the Jewish people and others was laid bare. Hundreds of German military personnel and civilian leaders were captured and brought to trial publicly at Nuremberg. Some were executed by hanging; others were sentenced to prison terms.

Civic Literacy: Citizens' Rights The internment of U.S. citizens of Japanese ancestry during World War II shows clearly that the rights of U.S. citizens can come under threat. The United States prides itself on being a nation where basic rights and freedoms are enshrined in law. However, this example shows that constant vigilance is required to ensure that the Constitution is able to withstand attacks from those who would resort to unlawful discrimination in times of peril.

New York Social Studies Framework

Key Idea 11.8: World War II The participation of the United States in World War II was a transformative event for the nation and its role in the world.

Source: *New York State Grades 9–12 Social Studies Framework*

Civic Literacy Essay: Write the Introduction

After you closely read and analyzed the documents, gathered and organized evidence, and developed an effective thesis statement, much of the hard work in writing your civic literacy document-based essay is complete. The most challenging task still remaining is to write an introduction that (1) serves as a blueprint for the rest of the essay and (2) casts the topic in a broader historical perspective.

The Introduction as Blueprint In generic terms, a good introduction conveys the framework or limits of the topic as well as a clear debatable and defensible claim. The introduction also suggests the organizational pattern and reasoning process that will unfold in the rest of the essay. In other words, it conveys (without saying), "Here's what I'm going to argue. Here's the reasoning process I am going to use to convince you. Here's the order I will use to present my ideas." The reasoning process may be causation, continuity and change, or comparison. Each reasoning process suggests a unique organization.

Historical Perspective A good introduction also relates the topic of the prompt to broader historical events, developments, or processes that occur before, during, or continue after the time frame of the question. In other words, it conveys (without saying), "Here's how this topic relates to what came before it/what came after it/what else was going on at the time or other aspects of society, and any number of broader historical patterns and trends."

Application: Find both the blueprint and historical perspective in the following introduction. How does the introduction answer these questions: What is the author's argument? What reasoning process will the author use? What order will the author likely use? How does the topic relate to broader historical events, developments, or processes?

The 13th, 14th, and 15th Amendments to the Constitution freed the enslaved people of the United States, made them citizens with equal protection under the laws, and granted adult males the right to vote. But states soon found ways to restrict those rights. Through a series of Civil Rights Acts, Congress attempted to guarantee the rights of all Americans, but African Americans still lack rights that White Americans take for granted. Martin Luther King's civil disobedience, Stokely Carmichael's Black Power movement, and the present-day Black Lives Matter movement are all parts of this ongoing struggle.

Key Terms by Theme

Civics
Executive Order 9066 (p. 269)
Eleanor Roosevelt (p. 278)

Identity
fascism (p. 255)
genocide (p. 275)
Holocaust (p. 275)

Governance
Adolf Hitler (p. 255)

Nazi Party (p. 255)
appeasement (p. 256)
D-Day (p. 261)
Operation Overlord (p. 261)
Winston Churchill (p. 264)
Joseph Stalin (p. 264)
Yalta Conference (p. 264)
Harry S. Truman (p. 266)
ration (p. 271)

Nuremberg Trials (p. 276)
United Nations (UN) (p. 276)
Hiroshima (p. 266)
Nagasaki (p. 266)

Technology
Manhattan Project (p. 266)

Conceptual Understanding
11.8a As situations overseas deteriorated, President Roosevelt's leadership helped to move the nation from a policy of neutrality to a pro-Allied position and, ultimately, direct involvement in the war.

While suffering through the Great Depression, many in the United States felt reluctant to get involved in the affairs of other countries. They looked on with increasing apprehension as Germany, Japan, and Italy grew more powerful and aggressive. As situations overseas deteriorated, President Roosevelt's leadership helped to move the nation from a policy of neutrality to a pro-Allied position. But when Japan attacked Pearl Harbor, the United States could no longer sit on the sideline.

Analyze a Primary Source

Representative Carl Curtis of Nebraska, U.S. House of Representatives, March 2, 1939

Read Closely: Details
Curtis makes it clear who he believes is stoking the fears of Americans in an attempt to gain support for war. Underline the subjects Curtis identifies.

Read Closely: Rationale
Curtis is opposed to the idea of going to war again so soon after World War I. Circle his rationale for his opposition to going to war.

Read Closely: Closing
Writers try to end an argument with something memorable. Curtis closes his comments by saying that the United States must "make the world safe for democracy," a phrase used to justify U.S. entry into World War I. He uses this quotation as a warning to not make the same mistake in 1939.

I would like to ask the question, What has happened in the last few months that imperils the safety of the United States? Who is it that is about to invade or attack us? What foreign nation has issued threatening statements concerning the United States?

When we trace down this war hysteria we find that it originates with high officials in the administration. It is the New Deal's spokesmen who have sounded the alarm. It is they who have flagrantly preached the doctrines of hate in an attempt to turn the American people against certain nations and in sympathy with others.

Individually, I may be in sympathy with certain things that go on in the world, and I may be very much out of sympathy with other things that happen. But as a congressman of the United States, that is none of my business, because it is the desire and wish of the American people that we do not police the world. . . . The American people are intelligent, they can detect the identity of such statements as "the democracies of the world must stand together," with the catch words that were used in 1917, such as "we are fighting a war to make the world safe for democracy."

Source: Representative Carl Curtis of Nebraska, U.S. House of Representatives, March 2, 1939

Fascist Aggression

Fascism is a type of government that controls all aspects of society and is led by an all-powerful dictator with the support of one political party. Although different types of fascism developed in different countries, they all shared some important characteristics:

- *Extreme nationalism:* total embrace of national culture as the foundation of personal identity coupled with rejection of foreign cultural and ideological influences

- *Opposition to democratic values:* belief in the power of elites and rejection of the ability of the masses to lead and govern through the vote

- *Totalitarianism:* ideological and physical domination of all aspects of society—legal, religious, educational, social, and even familial

- *Embrace of military values:* glorification of discipline, courage, strength, and obedience above all other traits

- *Scapegoating:* use of conspiracy theories and racial hatred to steer blame for social and economic problems onto minorities or political opponents

- *Anti-Communism/Anti-Socialism:* view of all types of leftist ideologies as foreign (often Jewish) conspiracies designed to sabotage the nation's natural strength and order

In Italy, the Fascist Party, led by Benito Mussolini, seized power in 1922. Anyone who criticized Mussolini's regime risked severe punishment.

Germany, after its defeat in World War I, suffered economic ruin, marked particularly by runaway inflation and severe unemployment. The penalties imposed by the Treaty of Versailles, which ended World War I, made the country's economic plight even worse. This treaty forced Germany to pay a crushing sum of money in reparations. It also had to surrender to France the Saar Valley, an important coal-mining region. The treaty also wounded German national pride by forcing the country to accept complete responsibility for causing World War I.

Many embittered Germans found an answer for their anger and disillusionment in the nationalistic speeches of **Adolf Hitler**. He led a fascist faction called the **Nazi Party**. Hitler turned the rage and frustration of the German masses against a minority group—Jewish people. In 1933, Hitler became chancellor (or prime minister) of Germany's government. He then seized absolute power as the Nazi leader and dictator of Germany.

In 1936, fascist leader Francisco Franco attempted to overthrow Spain's republican government. The Soviet Union sent aid to the Spanish government. Germany's Hitler and Italy's Mussolini aided Franco's fascist forces. Germany sent tanks and airplanes—state-of-the-art weapons of war—to the fascists. Limited Soviet assistance and volunteer fighters—including some sympathetic Americans—were no match for the help provided by Germany. In 1939, Spain fell to fascism.

Hitler's Rising Aggression: World War II Begins The rise of dictatorships in Nazi Germany and Fascist Italy were met with timid policies and inaction by the world's democracies. This led to the triumph of aggression and the failure of peace efforts.

Hitler violated the terms of the Treaty of Versailles first through a massive campaign of rearmament. Then in 1936 he ordered German troops into the Rhineland, a neutral, demilitarized territory along the frontier with France and Belgium. Two years later, he sent troops into Austria, effectively absorbing that

> **Read Closely: Cause and Effect**
> Notice how a text presents causation. For example, the third and fourth paragraphs describe the feelings of the German people after World War I. How did the German people's response to their post–World War I economy help someone like Hitler to rise to power?

country into Germany. Soon after, he announced his intention of seizing the Sudetenland. This region of Czechoslovakia bordered Germany and had a large German-speaking population.

Mussolini also began expanding militarily. His Italian army conquered territory in Africa. The African kingdom of Ethiopia, long an independent nation, mounted a valiant resistance. However, it fell to the Italian invaders in 1936.

While Germany and Italy engaged in aggressive military actions, Great Britain and France followed a policy of **appeasement**—the use of diplomacy and accommodation in an attempt to decrease tensions. British and French leaders applied this policy at the Munich Conference in 1938 by giving in to Hitler's demand to annex the Sudetenland. The British and French hoped they could trust his assurance that he wanted only the Sudetenland and nothing more. But only a few months after Munich, German troops occupied all of Czechoslovakia and then threatened Poland. In August 1939, Soviet leader Joseph Stalin entered the Molotov-Ribbentrop Pact with Hitler. In it, the two dictators publicly agreed not to attack one another for 10 years. Privately, they agreed to divide much of Eastern Europe between them, with each getting half of Poland.

On September 1, 1939, Germany invaded Poland and quickly took the western half. (The Soviet Union followed suit, taking the eastern half.) Appeasement had failed. The only way to stop Hitler would be through the use of armed force. Great Britain and France both declared war against Germany. World War II had begun.

During the first two years of World War II (1939–1941), the Allies (Great Britain, France, and allied democracies) suffered a series of crushing defeats. Wave after wave of German tanks, planes, and fast-moving troops overwhelmed

Speak and Listen: Previous Knowledge

World War II has been the subject of countless books, movies, and television shows. Discuss with a partner what you remember from them that can help provide context for the information you are reading.

World War II German Conquests in Europe

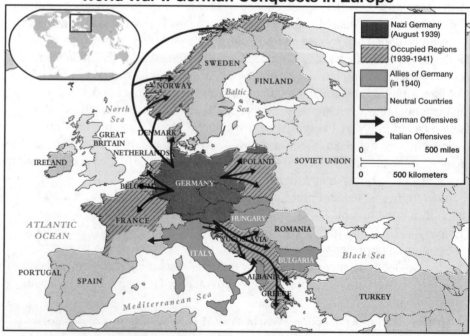

Nazi Germany quickly conquered most of Europe in the early years of the war.

Allied defenses. The Germans called this rapid and overwhelming method of attack *blitzkrieg*. Next, German armies swept into Belgium, the Netherlands, Denmark, and Norway. France managed only brief resistance. In June 1940, France fell to Nazi invaders.

The U.S. Position

Through the 1930s, the majority of the American people wanted their country to remain neutral. They wanted no part of another world war. Over time, however, President Roosevelt grew more and more concerned about the aggressive acts of Germany, Italy, Spain, and Japan. Japan committed similar acts of aggression against China throughout the 1930s. A group of Japanese military leaders dominated the government—they wanted Japan to be the supreme power in East Asia. Their strong-arm methods were similar to those of the European fascists. In 1931, Japanese troops marched into Manchuria and then invaded China's heartland in 1937.

Responding to the Japanese invasion of China, Roosevelt gave what was called the Quarantine Speech, proposing that democratic nations join together to quarantine, or isolate, aggressor nations. The purpose, he explained, would be "to protect the health of the [international] community against the spread of the disease." Isolationists were quick to criticize Roosevelt's speech. They feared the president's proposed policy might lead to American involvement in war. Public opinion polls showed that most Americans agreed with the isolationists, not with the president. Members of Congress were well aware of isolationist feelings. Between 1935 and 1937, Congress enacted the Neutrality Acts—laws designed to ensure U.S. neutrality in the event of war:

- No sale or shipment of arms nor loans or credit to belligerent, or warring, nations

- No traveling by U.S. citizens on the ships of belligerent nations

- Nonmilitary goods purchased by belligerent nations must be paid for in cash and transported on their own ships (known as the cash-and-carry principle)

United States Inches Toward War The outbreak of war in Europe in 1939–1940 and the success of the German army caused a sharp change in U.S. public opinion. People were more willing to help democratic Great Britain battle Hitler's forces. Most Americans understood that German victories in Europe could threaten U.S. security. In order to assist Great Britain once the war began, President Roosevelt moved quickly to change the earlier Neutrality Acts. Roosevelt persuaded Congress to pass a new Neutrality Act in 1939, which expanded the earlier cash-and-carry principle to include sales of arms and ammunition. To help the British defend themselves against crippling submarine attacks, President Roosevelt in 1940 transferred to Britain 50 U.S. destroyers (small warships used to escort and protect larger ships). In exchange, the United States was given eight British naval and air bases, extending from Newfoundland to South America. Called the Destroyers for Bases Agreement, this was another significant break from the principles of the Neutrality Acts.

Withering under the daily German attacks, the British needed more war supplies than the cash-and-carry program could deliver. Roosevelt persuaded Congress to pass the Lend-Lease Act in 1941. This authorized the lending, or leasing, of war supplies to Great Britain, Free France, and, later, the Soviet Union. Roosevelt felt the United States should act as the arsenal of democracy.

> **Read Closely: Context**
> Note how the text describes the general feeling of American citizens to what looked like impending war in Europe. Think, too, about the U.S. economic situation at this time as well. What might be some of the reasons the American public held isolationist attitudes toward U.S. foreign policy?

> **Read Closely: Turning Point**
> When reading historical texts, look for decisive events that change the course of a country or its people. Why do you think public opinion in the U.S. changed as the war progressed in Great Britain?

These policies enacted in less than two years meant that U.S. neutrality was over. The United States was not yet at war. However, it was committing much of its economic resources to help fight off the German assault.

U.S.-Japanese Tensions

Throughout the 1930s, U.S. foreign policy makers had been alarmed by Japan's acts of aggression in China. They viewed such acts as violations of the U.S. Open Door policy to which Japan had agreed. Established in 1899 and 1900 under President William McKinley, the Open Door Policy, among other things, sought to ensure Chinese territorial integrity.

In 1940, the United States put an embargo on a list of U.S. exports that Japan needed to maintain its war machine. Under the embargo, Japan could no longer purchase U.S. oil, aviation gasoline, scrap iron, and steel. President Roosevelt also froze all Japanese assets in U.S. banks. Japan could no longer use these bank deposits to purchase U.S. goods. Though these actions affected the Japanese government and military, they made no changes in Japanese policies toward China. By 1941, Japan controlled much of northern China. Japanese naval and air assaults gained them the islands of the Netherlands East Indies (now Indonesia), and after France fell to Germany, the French colony of Indochina (present-day Vietnam, Laos, and Cambodia) fell to Japan.

Negotiations between the United States and Japan continued into 1941. The United States remained firm in its demand that Japan leave mainland China. However, Japanese leaders were not willing to give up the Chinese territory they controlled. In fact, Japanese leaders were planning to attack other Pacific territories in order to secure some of the materials embargoed by the United States. Although formal negotiations between the two countries continued, Japanese leaders had already decided to risk war with the United States.

Pearl Harbor

In 1941, Japan believed that the United States might soon enter the war to oppose Japan's planned invasion of Indonesia. Japanese military leaders made the fateful decision to launch a surprise attack on the U.S. naval fleet in the Pacific. If the attack succeeded in destroying the fleet, Japan's generals hoped that the U.S. Navy would take a long time to recover. Japan hoped to achieve all of its war aims before that happened.

Early Sunday morning, December 7, 1941, hundreds of Japanese planes bombed a fleet of ships docked at the U.S. naval base at Pearl Harbor, Hawaii. In all, 8 battleships and 11 other ships were either sunk or disabled, 150 U.S. planes were destroyed, and 2,335 soldiers and sailors were killed. (Japan also bombed U.S. bases in the Philippines and the island of Guam that day.)

The next day, President Roosevelt asked Congress for a declaration of war against Japan. December 7, he said, was "a date which will live in infamy." Congress voted overwhelmingly for war. Japan's allies in Europe—Germany and Italy—responded by declaring war on the United States. Now that U.S. territory had been attacked, the American people put aside their isolationist feelings and enthusiastically took up the war effort.

Read Closely: Trends
Historians often present similar developments to show trends during a period. Look for the similarities between actions that make them a trend. How might the fascist German, Italian, and Spanish governments' actions in Europe have influenced Japan's actions in China?

Read Closely: Point of View
As you read, look for events and trends that might have helped people more readily alter their point of view. After Japan bombed Pearl Harbor, the American point of view toward war clearly changed. What preceding events might have made it easier for the nation to embrace going to war so completely?

Application: Interpret a Primary Source

Read the excerpt and answer the questions that follow it.

President Franklin Roosevelt, Fireside Chat (Radio), December 9, 1941

The course that Japan has followed for the past ten years in Asia has paralleled the course of Hitler and Mussolini in Europe and in Africa. Today, it has become far more than a parallel. It is actual collaboration so well calculated that all the continents of the world, and all the oceans, are now considered by the Axis strategists as one gigantic battlefield. . . .

On the road ahead there lies hard work—grueling work—day and night, every hour and every minute. I was about to add that ahead there lies sacrifice for all of us. But it is not correct to use that word. The United States does not consider it a sacrifice to do all one can, to give one's best to our nation when the nation is fighting for its existence and its future life . . .

In these past few years—and, most violently, in the past three days—we have learned a terrible lesson. It is our obligation to our dead—it is our sacred obligation to their children and our children—that we must never forget what we have learned.

And what we all have learned is this: There is no such thing as security for any nation—or any individual—in a world ruled by the principles of gangsterism. There is no such thing as impregnable defense against powerful aggressors who sneak up in the dark and strike without warning. We have learned that our ocean-girt [surrounded by an ocean] hemisphere is not immune from severe attack—that we cannot measure our safety in terms of miles on any map.

Source: President Franklin Roosevelt, Fireside Chat (Radio), December 9, 1941

1. Describe the context for Roosevelt's "chat." What was the situation in Europe?

_____

_____

2. Roosevelt was one year into his third term as president when Japan attacked Pearl Harbor. How do you think citizens viewed Roosevelt when he delivered this Fireside Chat?

_____

_____

3. Roosevelt uses specific language to describe Japan and Germany's actions. What effect do you think this language had on the listener?

_____

_____

Lesson 2 *The United States at War*

Conceptual Understanding 11.8a As situations overseas deteriorated, President Roosevelt's leadership helped to move the nation from a policy of neutrality to a pro-Allied position and, ultimately, direct involvement in the war.

U.S. entry into World War II had a significant impact on American society. The major goal of the Allied strategy was to defeat Nazi Germany first and then focus on Japan and Asia. American forces were split between the fighting on the European and Pacific fronts.

Analyze a Primary Source

First Lieutenant Joseph Hallock, 21-year-old Bombardier Aboard a B-17 Flying Fortress in Europe

Read Closely: Details
In telling a story, writers and speakers often provide specific details about what they saw, experienced, and felt in order to bring the scene alive to the reader. As you read, notice how Hallock describes what he went through in very concrete, specific language.

Read Closely: Realities of War
Firsthand descriptions of historical events are able to convey emotion and immediacy in a way that secondhand descriptions cannot. Hallock doesn't shy away from describing the realities of war he experienced as a bombardier. Underline two places where Hallock depicts the violence of war.

Read Closely: Personal Reflection
Hallock provides some insight into how he was feeling and experiencing the events—which is a characteristic of a first-person narrative like this interview. Circle instances where the reader learns how Hallock felt rather than simply how he reacted.

We had a feeling, though, that this Augsburg [Germany] show was bound to be tough, and it was. We made our runs and got off our bombs in the midst of one hell of a dogfight [midair battle]. Our group leader was shot down and about a hundred and fifty or two hundred German fighters swarmed over us as we headed for home. Then, screaming in from someplace, a 20-millimeter cannon shell exploded in the nose of our Fort. It shattered the plexiglas, broke my interphone and oxygen connections, and a fragment of it cut through my heated suit and flak suit. I could feel it burning into my right shoulder and arm.

I crawled back in the plane, wondering if anyone else needed first aid. I found that two shells had hit in the waist of the plane, exploding the cartridge belts stored there, and that one waist gunner had been hit in the forehead and the other in the jugular vein. I thought, "I'm wounded, but I'm the only man on the ship who can do this job right." I placed my finger against the gunner's jugular vein, applied pressure bandages, and injected morphine into him. Then I sprinkled the other man's wound with sulfa powder. We had no plasma aboard, so there wasn't much of anything else I could do . . . Then I crawled back to the nose of the ship to handle my gun, fussing with my wounds when I could and making use of an emergency bottle of oxygen.

The German fighters chased us for about forty-five minutes. They came so close that I could see the pilots' faces, and I fired so fast that my gun jammed. I went back to the left nose gun and fired that gun till it jammed. By that time we'd fallen behind the rest of the group, but the Germans were beginning to slack off. It was turning into a question of whether we could sneak home without having to bailout.

Source: *New Yorker Magazine*, August 12, 1944

The War in Europe

When the United States entered the war, Germany had for two years been able to invade countries across Europe and in North Africa with relative ease. Hitler's move into the Soviet Union proved more of a challenge. Several months before Pearl Harbor, Hitler broke his nonaggression pact with Stalin by launching a massive assault against the Soviet Union.

As 1942 began, Hitler faced three formidable foes: the United States, the Soviet Union, and Great Britain. His days of easy victory were over. Almost immediately after Hitler attacked the Soviet Union, the United States provided military aid to the Soviet Union. Additional assistance under the Lend-Lease Program followed. As a result, a wave of U.S. military equipment made its way to the Soviet Union. This was crucial in that country's defense of its homeland and its later offensive against Germany.

Although Japan attacked Pearl Harbor, Allied strategy required that Nazi Germany be defeated first. It took the Allies more than three years (1942–1945) to win back the territories conquered by German and Italian armies in the first two years of the war. The single most important turning point was Hitler's decision to invade the massive and populous Soviet Union. The decision proved to be a fatal blunder. German invaders in the Soviet Union suffered a crushing defeat at the Battle of Stalingrad (1942–1943).

Meanwhile, in the North African desert, a British force under General Bernard Montgomery defeated the Germans in a tank battle at El Alamein. Soon after in 1943, combined assaults by British and American armies forced the surrender of the German army in North Africa. From their African bases, the Allies were able to invade the Mediterranean island of Sicily. They then began a long and bloody campaign to liberate Italy from Mussolini's control.

D-Day On June 6, 1944 (code name: **D-Day**), Allied forces left England to begin **Operation Overlord**—a massive drive to liberate France. The invading force included 11,000 planes, 600 warships, and 176,000 men. It was the largest amphibious (sea-to-land) assault in history. Crossing the English Channel, the assault force achieved its objective of securing beachheads on the coast of Normandy (northern France). From there, Allied forces under U.S. General Dwight Eisenhower, the Supreme Allied Commander in Western Europe, fought for control of Normandy and then all of France. Allied forces liberated Paris nearly three months later, on August 25, and continued their push eastward toward Germany.

From the other direction, Soviet troops also moved rapidly toward Berlin. In April 1945, American and Soviet troops met for the first time on German territory near the Elbe River. Seeing that the end was near, Hitler committed suicide. Germany surrendered unconditionally on May 7, 1945 (V-E Day), ending the war in Europe.

> **Read Closely: Causation**
> As you read, look for the causation in historical events. The text makes the point that the Soviet Union presented Hitler and the German army its toughest resistance to invasion. What were some of the contributing factors that caused Germany's failure in the Soviet Union?

World War II in Europe, 1943–1945

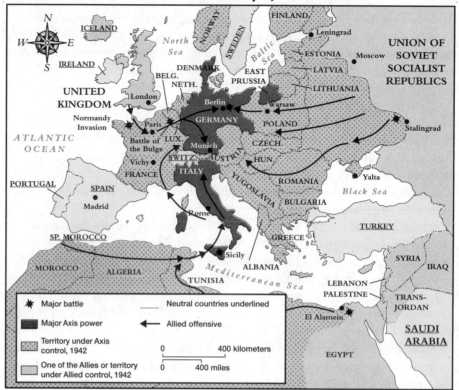

Legend:
- ★ Major battle
- ■ Major Axis power
- ▨ Territory under Axis control, 1942
- ▢ One of the Allies or territory under Allied control, 1942
- ___ Neutral countries underlined
- ← Allied offensive

0 — 400 kilometers
0 — 400 miles

Advances in Military Technology

In the 20 years between World War I and World War II, military technologies advanced rapidly. Weapons became more precise and more powerful, while also increasing their range and speed. Machine guns used in World War II were more portable (lighter weight) and were able to fire more rounds more quickly and more accurately. Tanks, which were introduced and saw limited use during World War I, advanced greatly by the time they were employed during World War II. They could maneuver better, travel faster, withstand attacks better, and deliver deadlier fire. They became major weapons of devastation on the battlefield.

The War at Sea Submarines were used to great success by Germany's naval forces during the First World War. Their advanced U-boats could carry up to a dozen torpedoes. They could stay underwater for up to two hours. During World War II, the submarines used by both Allied and Axis powers could carry more torpedoes and stay under water much longer. Another technology—sonar—was improved as well. It helped more effectively detect submarines as well as incoming torpedoes.

World War II aircraft carriers also changed the war at sea. These massive vessels could transport attack aircraft anywhere in the world by sea. The Japanese attack on Pearl Harbor provided clear evidence of aircraft carriers' importance. The Japanese attack in Hawaii was entirely carrier based. As the war went on, it became clear that carrier strength in the Pacific would go a long way toward deciding who would eventually gain the upper hand.

The Air War Air power had advanced far beyond the limitations of the previous war. During World War I, the plane was still a new technology. But by the late 1930s, flight technology was much more sophisticated. Warplanes could fly much faster and farther. They could carry more and bigger bombs. Air combat was a key element of the war. Bombers on both sides delivered devastating bomb payloads on towns, factories, and energy facilities. They were also used to take out strategic elements like bridges, railways, and dams. Faster fighter planes attacked enemy bombers, protected their own bombers, and strafed (machine-gunned) enemy troop columns and positions.

Radar helped detect distant objects via radio waves. Britain had developed an advanced system that helped the Royal Air Force defend the country against German air attacks during the 1940 Battle of Britain. American research during the war led to a more effective microwave radar.

Advances in rocketry also contributed greatly to the air war. Germany developed the V-2 rocket, which used liquid, rather than solid, fuel. This allowed for more efficient and greater thrust. Its range was 200 miles and it was equipped with more than 1,500 pounds of explosives. Germany launched more than 1,000 V-2 rockets at London alone in the final nine months of the war.

Read Closely: Technology
As you read about the impacts of technology in a historical text, think about the technologies developed in the future. What are some of the innovations developed during World War II that we now live with every day in even more advanced states?

FDR's Leadership

President Roosevelt and his administration were more concerned with the developments in Europe in the late 1930s than was most of the American public. The rise of fascist governments and Hitler's military buildup in Germany posed a threat to democracies in Europe and perhaps around the world. Roosevelt appeared to know that this unchecked aggression could eventually draw the United States into the war. As Germany began to invade its European neighbors, Roosevelt seemed more prepared to act than the isolationist sentiments of Congress and the country would allow.

Changing the Neutrality Acts in 1939, exchanging American destroyers with Britain for naval air bases in 1940, and the Lend-Lease Act of 1941 to help Britain, France, and the Soviet Union battle German forces were all indications that Roosevelt was preparing the country for a war footing. In August 1941, President Roosevelt and British Prime Minister Winston Churchill met on a battleship anchored off the coast of Newfoundland, Canada. At this meeting, they formulated a statement of common war aims known as the Atlantic Charter:

- recognition of the right of all nations to self-determination

- U.S.-British understanding that neither power would seek to gain territory from the war

- the disarmament of aggressor nations

- a "permanent system of general security" in the future

Read Closely: Patterns
In analyzing events or human actions, historians look for patterns—repeated behavior that suggests a reason or meaning for the results. Consider Roosevelt's attitude and actions before the bombing of Pearl Harbor. What do Roosevelt's policies before the country was pulled into the war suggest about his leadership abilities?

In November 1941, American code breakers had learned that Japan planned an attack against the United States. But when it would happen was unclear. After the December 7 bombing of Pearl Harbor, Roosevelt asked the Congress to declare war on Japan the following day. On December 9, Roosevelt sought to calm and assure the nation in a fireside chat about the declaration of war. "We will make very certain that this form of treachery shall never endanger us again," he told the country. "We must begin the great task that is before us by abandoning once and for all the illusion that we can ever again isolate ourselves from the rest of humanity."

Allied Leader Roosevelt quickly established himself as a leader of the Allied war against Hitler and Germany. He met many times with British Prime Minister **Winston Churchill**. Together, they settled strategy differences and coordinated their country's efforts. Relations with the Soviet Union and its leader **Joseph Stalin** were more complicated. The Soviets did not coordinate their attacks on German forces with the Western powers. Roosevelt felt it was necessary that the Soviet Union, Britain, and the United States be on good terms when the war ended and peacetime efforts began. Roosevelt, Churchill, and Stalin met at the **Yalta Conference** in February 1945 as the war neared its end. Stalin agreed to join the U.S. fight against Japan after Germany surrendered. Stalin also agreed to establish democracies in the eastern European countries the Soviets had occupied. However, he went back on his agreement in the years after the war.

Source: National Archives and Records Administration / Wikimedia Commons

Churchill, Roosevelt, and Stalin at the Yalta Conference

Read Closely: Context
The conditions or environment surrounding an event often provides important context for how or why something happened. Upon the U.S. entry to the war, Roosevelt asserted himself as a leader of the Allied efforts against Hitler and Germany. What conditions allowed Roosevelt to assume such a role?

During the last year of World War II, Roosevelt had another political battle to fight at home: the 1944 presidential election. His deteriorating health made campaigning and running a war extremely taxing. But Roosevelt and running mate Harry Truman won by an electoral landslide. It was the fourth consecutive term for Roosevelt.

The War in the Pacific

While American forces focused on the war in Europe, Japan continued to make strides in Asia and the Pacific islands. The United States couldn't wait for the war in Europe to end. It had to fight on two fronts.

Early in 1942, the British colony of Malaya fell to the Japanese. In early May, U.S. forces in the Philippines surrendered to the Japanese. Japan now controlled much of Asia and the islands of the South Pacific. U.S. naval and military leaders developed a strategy known as island hopping. In order to get within striking distance of Japan, American forces would concentrate on winning only the most strategically located islands. Others would be left under Japanese control. Bloody, fierce fighting raged on each targeted island. Fearsome casualties mounted on both sides.

Aircraft carrier warfare played a key role in the Pacific for both countries. Japan continued to have success against U.S. naval forces. Both countries combined air, naval, and ground attacks on the islands over which they fought. In early June 1942, the Battle of Midway proved an important early turning point in the Pacific war. American ships and planes defeated Japanese forces in several major battles. It is believed that this victory probably saved Hawaii from Japanese occupation.

It would be another two years until a more decisive battle would turn the tide to the U.S. forces. In October 1944, the Battle of Leyte Gulf spanned four days. Leyte was a Philippine island. U.S. air and naval forces destroyed Japanese carriers and ultimately regained control of the Philippine Islands.

World War II in the Pacific, 1941–1945

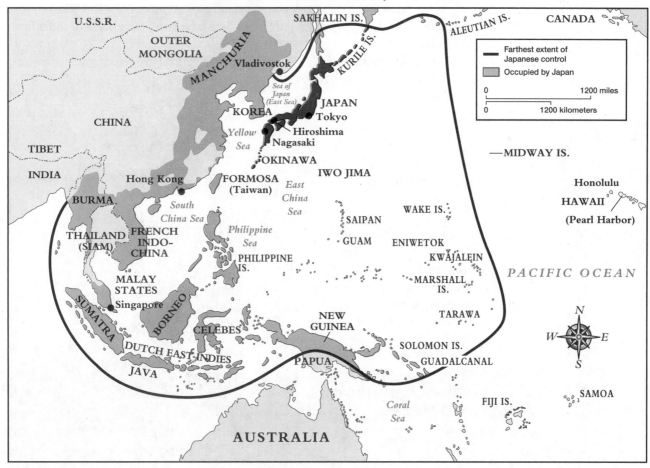

The Atomic Bomb In 1932, the great physicist Albert Einstein had left Germany for the United States, never to return. Einstein feared that Germany would develop an atomic bomb. He feared that an atomic bomb in the hands of Germany would lead to the defeat of the Allies. So, he wrote a letter to President Roosevelt in 1939 recommending that the United States develop such a bomb first. Roosevelt heeded the advice of Einstein and others, committing U.S. funds to the **Manhattan Project**. Based in Los Alamos, New Mexico, the project employed scientists who had fled Europe alongside U.S scientists in the race to become the first nuclear power.

In April 1945, less than three months after being sworn in for his fourth term, President Roosevelt died. His successor, Vice President **Harry S. Truman**, had to decide what to do with newly developed, immensely destructive atomic bomb. At the time, Truman and his military advisers were planning to invade the Japanese homeland in order to achieve final victory. But casualty estimates for such an invasion were chilling: between 400,000 and 1 million U.S. fatalities, with twice as many wounded. If Truman decided to use the new bomb, American lives might be saved. But if nuclear weapons were used, hundreds of thousands of Japanese civilians would be condemned to death.

Truman decided to use the bomb. He reasoned that the bomb's destructiveness might force Japan to surrender. Then the planned U.S. invasion could tbe canceled. On August 6, 1945, a single U.S. plane dropped an atomic bomb on the city of **Hiroshima**. Three days later, a second atomic bomb was dropped on the city of **Nagasaki**. The two explosions instantly killed more than 100,000 Japanese civilians. Many thousands more died later from the effects of radiation poisoning.

Truman was right. The use of the atomic bomb convinced Japan to surrender. General Douglas MacArthur presided over the formal Japanese surrender aboard the U.S. battleship *Missouri* on September 2, 1945. Thus ended the most destructive war in history. The total death toll for all nations: 17 million military deaths and probably more than twice that number in civilian deaths. The U.S. death toll was about 400,000. No nation since has ever used a nuclear weapon against another nation.

Source: Wikimedia Commons

The Atomic Bomb Dome, now a peace memorial, was one of the few buildings not destroyed by the atomic blast in Hiroshima.

Read Closely: Comparison
Comparing military campaigns and strategies can help one understand the nature and details of battles more clearly. The war in Europe was fought primarily on the ground and in the air. The war in the Pacific was primarily an air and sea battle. What are some of the important differences between these two types of campaigns?

Read Closely: Rationale
Understanding why events occurred or why people did what they did is one of the hallmarks of historical inquiry. President Truman was faced with an overwhelming decision about whether or not to use the atomic bomb. What else might have contributed to Truman's decision to drop the bombs on Japan?

Application: Interpret a Primary Source

Read the excerpt and answer the questions that follow it.

President Harry S. Truman, Press Release Alerting the Nation About the Atomic Bomb, August 6, 1945

Sixteen hours ago, an American airplane dropped one bomb on Hiroshima and destroyed its usefulness to the enemy.

It is an atomic bomb. It is a harnessing of the basic power of the universe. The force from which the sun draws its power has been loosed against those who brought war to the Far East.

We are now prepared to obliterate more rapidly and completely every productive enterprise the Japanese have above ground in any city. We shall destroy their docks, their factories, and their communications. Let there be no mistake; we shall completely destroy Japan's power to make war.

It was to spare the Japanese people from utter destruction that the ultimatum of July 26 was issued at Potsdam. [The Potsdam Declaration demanded Japan unconditionally surrender or face "prompt and utter destruction."] Their leaders promptly rejected that ultimatum. If they do not now accept our terms they may expect a rain of ruin from the air, the like of which has never been seen on this earth. . . .

The fact that we can release atomic energy ushers in a new era in man's understanding of nature's forces. Atomic energy may in the future supplement the power that now comes from coal, oil, and falling water, but at present it cannot be produced on a basis to compete with them commercially. . . .

I shall recommend that the Congress of the United States consider promptly the establishment of an appropriate commission to control the production and use of atomic power within the United States. I shall give further consideration and make further recommendations to the Congress as to how atomic power can become a powerful and forceful influence towards the maintenance of world peace.

Source: President Harry S. Truman, Press Release Alerting the Nation About the Atomic Bomb, August 6, 1945

1. What was the state of World War II at the time Truman decided to drop the first atomic bomb on Japan?

_____

_____

2. What effect do you think Truman's message had on U.S. citizens?

_____

_____

3. What may have been Truman's purpose for informing the public about this action many hours after it had happened?

_____

_____

Lesson 3 *The Domestic Impacts of World War II*

U.S. victory in World War II depended almost as much on the work of civilians as on the fighting of the armed forces. During nearly four years of U.S. participation in the war, all Americans had to adjust to the unusual demands of wartime.

**Conceptual Understanding
11.8b** United States entry into World War II had a significant impact on American society.

Analyze a Primary Source

War Manpower Commission, United States Employment Service, Mobile, Alabama, 1942

Read Closely: Government Programs
As you read, notice the language this government pamphlet uses to encourage women to take wartime jobs. The traditional roles of both women and men had to change during the war, and some men and women had difficulty adopting a new attitude about their roles.

Read Closely: Argument
This is a persuasive document the War Manpower Commission distributed in Mobile, Alabama, to convince women to join the war effort. Underline some of the reasons given for why women should work during the war.

Read Closely: Urgency
Take note of how special historical circumstances force governments into almost-desperate pleas to their citizens. The U.S. military needed to ramp up all weapon and supply production quickly and in massive numbers. Circle instances where the writer makes the case for acting on this plea as soon as possible.

To the Women of Mobile:

You are needed in the war jobs and in other essential civilian jobs directly aiding the war effort in Mobile NOW. Manpower has been practically exhausted. Housing available at this time will not permit the bringing into Mobile of the thousands of additional workers required for the shipyards and other war and essential industries. We must depend upon you—upon womanpower. There are idle machines in war plants which you can operate. There are idle jobs in the shipyard that you can fill. There are jobs in stores, offices, transportation, restaurants, hospitals in which you can render essential war service.

Hitler will not come to our shores if we build the ships which can transport our soldiers and our war materials overseas. We are training the armies, we are building the airplanes, tanks, guns and trucks, to do the job that must be done. But they will be of little use if we do not build the ships that can transport them to the battle zones.

Many of you are already in war jobs and are rendering essential service to our common country in the hour of need. We do not ask that you give up one essential job to take another. We do appeal to you, however, to take a job in which you can aid in the war program. Those of you who are not engaged in war work or essential civilian employment, we do urge you to take the training which will equip you for such a job, or if they have the training, to take the job NOW without delay.

Women have responded nobly to the call to war service throughout the Nation. Many are employed in the shipyards in Mobile now. Many are at Brookley Field. [Brookley Field in Mobile, Alabama, was the primary Air Force supply base in the southeast during World War II.] Still others are in plants which are producing the war supplies essential to victory. Women who have never worked before are employed in stores and other necessary business establishments. Women have proved their efficiency in war work. Throughout our country they are doing the work which many believed could be done only by men.

Source: War Manpower Commission, United States Employment Service

The Effects of Mobilization

Even before the United States entered World War II, Congress enacted a selective service law, or draft, in September 1940. (This law passed by only one vote in the House of Representatives.) Every man between the ages of 21 and 35 was required to register for possible mandatory admission into the armed forces. By 1945, a total of 12.5 million men and women were in uniform—approximately one out of three of the eligible group. Unemployment declined from approximately 25 percent in 1933 to less than 10 percent in 1941 and to a little more than 1percent in 1944. This represented a record low for unemployment in modern American history.

New services and volunteer organizations came into being during World War II. The Civil Air Patrol (CAP), established in 1941, organized and deployed volunteers in key missions, including aerial anti-submarine patrols. German U-boats were a constant threat on the East Coast of the United States. These enemy submarines sank more than 200 Allied ships in 1942 alone. Volunteers offered to fly reconnaissance missions to spot German submarines. Eventually, CAP planes were given depth charges, bombs set to explode underwater at a preset depth, and authorized to attack enemy submarines. In Florida, the Coast Guard organized a flotilla of private boats known as the Mosquito Fleet to watch for U-boats and other threats. Nationwide, thousands of civil defense volunteers were trained to spot enemy planes and other threats.

When the United States entered the war, Allied hopes for victory depended largely on the speed with which U.S. factories could turn out war goods. Government officials encouraged companies in every industry to stop producing consumer goods. Instead, they needed to produce ships, planes, bombs, bullets, and other military supplies. As the chief supplier of war materials for the Allied cause, the United States acted as "the arsenal of democracy." The cost of the war was staggering. The United States spent billions of dollars on the war effort. Citizens were encouraged to buy war bonds to support the war effort.

> **Read Closely: National Effort**
> The federal government was preparing for war before the country was ready to engage in it. Once war was declared, the nation mobilized quickly. Why might the country have reacted so quickly to the call to war against Germany and Japan?

Japanese Internment

After Japan's attack on Pearl Harbor, many Americans treated citizens of Japanese descent with great suspicion and hostility. However when the U.S. government had a well-connected, Japanese-speaking naval officer conduct a thorough investigation of the Japanese American community, he reported in 1941 that the vast majority of Japanese immigrants were completely loyal to the United States. This was true to an even greater extent among their U.S.-born children. He found further that Japanese officials in the United States distrusted Japanese Americans. They regarded Japanese Americas as "cultural traitors" who could not be trusted to aid Imperial Japan's cause.

In spite of their widespread loyalty, Japanese Americans suffered throughout the war from prejudice and discrimination. President Roosevelt yielded to the general prejudice by authorizing **Executive Order 9066**. The order, in effect, authorized the removal of all Japanese Americans from their homes in California and other western states. In 1942, the U.S. army seized 117,000 Japanese Americans (70,000 of whom were U.S. citizens) and transported them to barracks within barbed-wire compounds called "relocation centers." Most were released before the war's end. However, those suspected of disloyalty (about 18,000) were kept in a relocation center in California until Japan surrendered in 1945.

Source: National Archives and Records Administration / Wikimedia Commons

Members of the Mochida family awaiting transportation to an internment camp

Civic Literacy: Addressing Historical Wrongs
In 1982, a presidential commission concluded that the imprisonment of Japanese Americans was "not justified by military necessity," as the Supreme Court had found. Rather, it was the result of "race prejudice, war hysteria, and a failure of political leadership."

According to historian Arthur Link, the treatment of Japanese Americans in World War II was "the greatest single violation of civil rights in American history." But the Supreme Court did not see it that way. In a case decided in 1944, *Korematsu v. United States*, the Court determined that the removal of Japanese Americans was justified as a matter of military necessity. Robert H. Jackson was one of three Justices who dissented from the majority decision. He wrote that Mr. Korematsu "has been convicted of an act not commonly a crime. It consists merely of being present in the state whereof he is a citizen, near the place where he was born, and where all his life he has lived." In recent years, many Japanese Americans who suffered loss and humiliation during World War II have received official apologies from the U.S. government as well as small sums of money to partly compensate them for damages.

A True Group Effort

World War II was by no means a strictly military campaign. President Roosevelt, state governors, city mayors, and citizen and religious organizations called for all Americans to contribute to the war effort—at home or in battle.

Womanpower As the government drafted young men into military service, women took their place in the workforce. The number of women in the U.S. labor force went from about 15 million in 1941 to about 19 million in 1945. A popular song of the period celebrated a character known as Rosie the Riveter, who represented women working on assembly lines in support of the war effort:

All the day long, whether rain or shine

She's a part of the assembly line

She's making history, working for victory

Rosie, brrrrrrrrrrr, the riveter.

Source: National Museum of American History / Wikimedia Commons

World War II poster encouraging women to join the industrial workforce

American women also made contributions in the military by enlisting in support units (but not in combat units) in all branches of the military. For example, women who joined the Women's Army Corps (WACs) served in the United States and overseas as drivers, radio operators, office staff, and even supply pilots. Military nurses were almost always women.

Rationing With American industry shifting from peacetime to wartime production, many goods were in short supply. Crucial products such as clothing, sugar, meat, rubber for tires, and gasoline were all **rationed**. Americans received coupon books. These allowed the purchase of rationed items in accordance with the number of coupons they had received for that product. A special government agency, the Office of Price Administration, monitored retail prices to ensure that the prices of products in short supply did not rise too high and cause inflation.

Entertainers Hollywood and popular musical stars also contributed to the war effort. The composer Irving Berlin wrote patriotic songs to inspire Americans. His "God Bless America" was performed by singer Kate Smith in 1942. In concerts around the country, Smith's singing of this patriotic song helped to sell millions of dollars of war bonds. Film stars like Bob Hope organized shows for the USO (United Service Organizations) that took movie and recording stars around the globe to entertain U.S. soldiers. One of the most popular songs among the soldiers of World War II was Irving Berlin's "White Christmas" sung by Bing Crosby.

African Americans at War More than a million African Americans served in the U.S. armed forces during World War II. But here as elsewhere, their hopes for equal treatment were unmet; they were placed in segregated units. Some questioned the sacrifice they were asked to make in fighting racism abroad when they suffered racism at home. James G. Thompson, of Wichita, Kansas, came up with a Double V Campaign. He explained in a letter to a Pittsburgh newspaper that as the V was being used as a sign of victory over the tyranny of the Axis forces, "[L]et colored Americans adopt the double VV for a double victory: The first V for victory over our enemies from without, the second V for victory over our enemies within. For surely those who perpetrate these ugly prejudices here are [seeking] to destroy our democratic form of government just as surely as the Axis forces."

> **Read Closely: Cause and Effect**
> Keep an eye out for cause-and-effect relationships in historical texts. The text describes the variety of ways different Americans contributed to the U.S. effort in World War II. What effect do you think the war effort at home had on the American public?

Application: Interpret a Primary Source

Read the excerpt and answer the questions that follow it.

President Franklin D. Roosevelt, Fourth Inaugural Address, January 20, 1945

We Americans of today, together with our allies, are passing through a period of supreme test. It is a test of our courage—of our resolve—of our wisdom—our essential democracy.

If we meet that test—successfully and honorably—we shall perform a service of historic importance which men and women and children will honor throughout all time.

As I stand here today, having taken the solemn oath of office in the presence of my fellow countrymen—in the presence of our God—I know that it is America's purpose that we shall not fail.

In the days and in the years that are to come we shall work for a just and honorable peace, a durable peace, as today we work and fight for total victory in war.

We can and we will achieve such a peace.

We shall strive for perfection. We shall not achieve it immediately—but we still shall strive. We may make mistakes—but they must never be mistakes which result from faintness of heart or abandonment of moral principle.

I remember that my old schoolmaster, Dr. Peabody, said, in days that seemed to us then to be secure and untroubled: "Things in life will not always run smoothly. Sometimes we will be rising toward the heights—then all will seem to reverse itself and start downward. The great fact to remember is that the trend of civilization itself is forever upward; that a line drawn through the middle of the peaks and the valleys of the centuries always has an upward trend."

Our Constitution of 1787 was not a perfect instrument; it is not perfect yet. But it provided a firm base upon which all manner of men, of all races and colors and creeds, could build our solid structure of democracy.

And so today, in this year of war, 1945, we have learned lessons—at a fearful cost—and we shall profit by them.

We have learned that we cannot live alone, at peace; that our own well-being is dependent on the well-being of other nations far away. We have learned that we must live as men, not as ostriches, nor as dogs in the manger.

We have learned to be citizens of the world, members of the human community.

We have learned the simple truth, as Emerson said, that "The only way to have a friend is to be one." We can gain no lasting peace if we approach it with suspicion and mistrust or with fear.

We can gain it only if we proceed with the understanding, the confidence, and the courage which flow from conviction.

Source: President Franklin D. Roosevelt, Fourth Inaugural Address, January 20, 1945

1. World War II was still happening when Roosevelt delivered this speech. What does the speech reveal about his thoughts on the outcome of the war?

_____

_____

_____

_____

_____

_____

2. What point do you think Roosevelt is making when he describes "what we have learned"?

_____

_____

_____

_____

_____

3. Who do you think Roosevelt's intended audience (or audiences) is for this speech?

_____

_____

_____

_____

_____

Lesson 4 *The Holocaust*

As Allied troops retook formerly German-held lands, they began to discover the Nazis' grim system of slave labor and death camps. One of the first encountered was Maidanek, on the outskirts of Lublin, Poland. Correspondent Alexander Werth of the British Broadcasting Corporation (BBC) was with Soviet troops when they liberated the camp. However, Werth's report on the camp was so horrifying that the BBC refused to air it, thinking it must be Soviet propaganda.

Analyze a Primary Source

Inside a Nazi Death Camp: Alexander Werth, BBC and *London Sunday Times* correspondent, Maidanek Camp, Poland, July 1944

Read Closely: Eyewitness Accounts
Eyewitness accounts provide direct information about what one person experienced and observed. Historians will check eyewitness accounts against other factual accounts to determine how reliable the writer or speaker is.

Read Closely: Question
Writers will sometimes insert a question into a narrative to highlight a certain event or add emphasis to a particular thought. Underline a sentence where Werth employs this rhetorical device.

Read Closely: Setting
Notice the details the writer provides in order to evoke a visual image for the reader. Circle two sentences in which Werth describes the setting for these atrocities.

We stopped outside a large barrack marked *Bad und Desinfektion II* (Bath and Disinfection 2). "This," somebody said, "is where large numbers of those arriving at the camp were brought in."

The inside of this barrack was made of concrete, and water taps came out of the wall, and around the room there were benches where the clothes were put down and *afterwards* collected. So this was the place into which [prisoners] were driven. Or perhaps they were politely invited to "Step this way, please?" Did any of them suspect, while washing themselves after a long journey, what would happen a few minutes later? Anyway, after the washing was over, they were asked to go into the next room; at this point even the most unsuspecting must have begun to wonder. For the "next room" was a series of large square concrete structures, each about one-quarter of the size the bathhouse, and, unlike it, had no windows. The . . . people . . . were driven or forced from the bathhouse into these dark concrete boxes— about five yards square—and then, with 200 or 250 people packed into each box—and it was completely dark there, except for a small light in the ceiling and the spy hole in the door—the process of gassing began. First some hot air was pumped in from the ceiling and then the pretty pale-blue crystals of Cyclon [Zyclon B—Werth mistakenly called it "Cyclon."] were showered down on the people, and in the hot wet air they rapidly evaporated. In anything from two to ten minutes everybody was dead.

Source: Alexander Werth, BBC and *London Sunday Times* correspondent, Maidanek Camp, Poland, July 1944

An Adequate U.S. Reaction?

Almost two decades before World War II started, Adolf Hitler was a proponent of removing the Jewish people from Germany. He wrote that Jews were an evil race of people (not a religion), and he and the Nazi Party referred to Jews as "subhuman." When Hitler took over the government in 1933, he began discriminatory policies against the Jewish people. First came a boycott of Jewish-owned stores and then a wholesale dismissal of Jews from civil service jobs. Government legal actions followed. By 1938, physical violence against Jews and their businesses and synagogues erupted.

Once the war began, Germany held more and more Jewish people in camps. German special forces began mass shootings of Jewish people during the offensive against the Soviet Union. These shootings alone resulted in the deaths of more than 1.4 million people. In 1942, Germany began to systematically exterminate the Jews of Europe in concentration camps. The Nazis and many German citizens considered this "the final solution to the Jewish question."

As early as December 1942, the U.S., Britain, and the Soviet Union governments were aware of the mass slaughter in German-occupied territories. The three countries, however, took no demonstrable action to address the crisis. A couple of years later, as U.S. troops moved across Germany, they came upon the concentration camps recently abandoned by the Nazis. In these camps, they found a few survivors of the Nazi **genocide**. The survivors told horrifying stories of being shipped in trains to the camps to where their friends and loved ones suffered death in a gas chamber or were worked to death. About 6 million Jews were killed in the **Holocaust**. Other peoples considered unworthy by the Nazis suffered as well:

- ethnic Poles (more than 1.8 million killed)

- Serbs (over 300,000)

- Roma, formerly called "Gypsies" (more than 100,000)

- people with disabilities (about 270,000)

- gay and lesbian people (more than 5,000)

- Jehovah's Witnesses (more than 2,500)

Source: United States Holocaust Memorial Museum / Wikimedia Commons

Survivors of the Dachau concentration camp in southern Germany cheer U.S. troops arriving to liberate them.

Thousands who died in the Holocaust might have survived if the United States had changed its immigration policy. Hitler had come to power in the 1930s and began to persecute the Jewish minority. In response, many refugees from Nazi Germany hoped to gain admission to the United States. About 175,000 immigrants from German-controlled territory were accepted. But hundreds of thousands more were denied entry, even though the immigrant quota for Germany was not filled.

The Nuremburg Trials

For nearly an entire year after the war with Germany ended (November 1945–October 1946), a unique series of trials took place in Nuremberg, Germany. The defendants were former military and political leaders of the defeated Nazi government that the Allies were able to arrest. (Some, like Hitler, killed themselves before they could be captured.) These leaders were accused of war crimes, especially the mass murder of Jews in Nazi concentration camps. Judges at the **Nuremberg trials** represented the victorious nations of World War II, including the United States.

The chief prosecutor for the Nuremberg trials was United States Supreme Court Justice Robert Jackson, a strong defender of individual rights. Jackson was one of the Supreme Court Justices who dissented from the majority opinion in *Korematsu v. United States*, which allowed Federal internment camps for Japanese Americans during the war. As chief prosecutor at Nuremberg, he challenged the actions and accounts of high-ranking Nazi officials, such as Hermann Goering. At the start of the trials, Jackson stated of the accused, "They are living symbols of racial hatreds, of terrorism and violence, and of the arrogance and cruelty of power." He made clear that this was not an indictment of the German people as a whole. Rather the prosecution was aimed at those who conspired to commit "abnormal and inhumane conduct."

Of 24 defendants, 19 were convicted, 10 of whom were executed. In addition, other military trials in Germany led to lesser punishments for some 500,000 former Nazis. Some Nazis who escaped capture were later found and brought to trial. For example, the Nazi SS man in charge of deportations, Adolph Eichmann, was captured in Argentina in 1960. He was executed in Israel in 1962. (The SS was an elite Nazi police and military unit.) Klaus Barbie, the ruthless head of the Gestapo in Lyon, France, was extradited from Bolivia in 1983 and imprisoned for life in France. (The Gestapo was the Nazi political police unit.) The Nuremberg trials established the precedent that national leaders could be held responsible for "crimes against humanity." The last known Nuremberg-convicted Nazi officer, Martin Sandberger, passed away in 2010.

The United Nations is Born

Having fought in two horribly destructive world wars, the United States and its allies wanted to ensure that future world peace would be built on a firm foundation. The **United Nations (UN)** was an international attempt to create a forum for countries across the globe to diminish conflicts and seek peaceful resolutions.

The United States and its allies sent representatives to a conference in San Francisco in April 1945. Their purpose was to replace the post–World War I League of Nations with a new peacekeeping organization. The United Nations' purpose would mirror that of the League. Representatives from the member nations would meet to settle disputes and stop acts of aggression like those that had led to World War II.

When the UN was formed, its members tried to learn from where the League of Nations had failed.

League of Nations	United Nations
Its Covenant was drawn up by only the victors of World War I.	Its Charter was drawn up at a conference of 50 countries.
Decisions could only be made by unanimous vote of all members. (Each member effectively had a veto.)	Decisions would be made by some form of majority vote. (China, France, Russia, the United Kingdom, and the United States have veto power, but only in the Security Council.)
Its Covenant did not negate a country's right to start a war (as long as it had gone through a mandated process).	Its Charter recognized no legitimate circumstances under which a country can legally start a war.
It had no mechanism by which to enforce its mandates.	It has the power to institute mandatory enforcement measures, such as economic sanctions or military measures.
Its Covenant had no provisions for the promotion of human welfare.	Its Charter has specific sections mandating the promotion of economic and social development, particularly among less-developed countries.

According to the UN Charter (the constitution of the United Nations), all member nations were entitled to vote in the UN General Assembly on almost any international issue. A smaller group of nations, the UN Security Council, could call on member nations to take military action in a crisis. But such a decision had to be approved by all five permanent members on the Security Council. The permanent members were the Soviet Union (now Russia), Great Britain, France, China, and the United States. Six non-permanent members of the Security Council—a number later increased to ten—would rotate among other nations, each of which would serve two-year terms.

The UN established special agencies for various purposes. An Economic and Social Council would attempt to reduce hunger and improve health care in the poorer countries of the world. A Trusteeship Council would make decisions concerning the colonies given up by Germany and Japan. An International Court of Justice would decide legal questions referred to it by disputing nations.

In 1945, by a vote of 82 to 2, the U.S. Senate approved U.S. membership in the United Nations. In doing so, the United States signaled to the world that it would not again return to a policy of isolationism. As the world's most powerful nation—and also the only nation with atomic weapons at that time—the United States was now prepared to play a leading role in world affairs.

United Nations Universal Declaration of Human Rights In 1948, the United Nations General Assembly approved a document called the Universal Declaration of Human Rights. The list of rights included in this document was based largely on earlier documents that were important to the development of Western democracies (for example, the British Magna Carta of 1215 and the

Read Closely: Stakeholders Stakeholders are people or entities with an interest in the outcome of an event or development. Although all UN members were stakeholders, why do you think the five permanent members of the UN Security Council held more sway than other countries in security matters?

U.S. Declaration of Independence of 1776). The Declaration of Human Rights, however, went beyond the earlier documents. It included not only civil and political rights but also economic and social rights:

- freedom of speech and religion
- freedom of movement and asylum
- equality before the law
- the right to a fair trial
- the right to participate in government
- the right not to be subjected to torture

The wide-ranging document also included economic, social, and cultural rights:

- the right to have food, clothing, housing, medical care, and to receive an education
- the right to benefit from social security and a decent standard of living
- the right to work, to receive equal pay for equal work, and to form labor unions
- the right to marry and raise a family
- the right to maintain one's culture

Source: Wikimedia.

Eleanor Roosevelt displays the Universal Declaration of Human Rights in Spanish.

Read Closely: Personality
Note that historical figures' individual personalities play a role in their achievements. Eleanor Roosevelt was one of the most well-known women in the world after World War II. Why might Roosevelt have been such a successful advocate for passing the Universal Declaration of Human Rights?

Former First Lady **Eleanor Roosevelt** played an important role in getting the UN to adopt the Universal Declaration of Human Rights. In 1945, Eleanor Roosevelt became the U.S. representative to the newly formed United Nations. She served there until 1951. In 1946, she was elected chair of the United Nations Human Rights Commission. Roosevelt had a public history as an advocate for child welfare and equal rights for women and racial minorities. She was also known for her overall concern for humanity. This made her a formidable proponent of the declaration. Her leadership on the commission won the respect of her male colleagues at the UN. This helped lead to the passage of the Universal Declaration of Human Rights in 1948.

Application: Interpret a Primary Source

Read the excerpt and answer the questions that follow it.

Eleanor Roosevelt, Speech to the United Nations, Paris, France, December 9, 1948

In giving our approval to the Declaration today it is of primary importance that we keep clearly in mind the basic character of the document. It is not a treaty; it is not an international agreement. It is not and does not purport to be a statement of law or of legal obligation. It is a Declaration of basic principles of human rights and freedoms, to be stamped with the approval of the General Assembly by formal vote of its members, and to serve as a common standard of achievement for all peoples of all nations.

We stand today at the threshold of a great event both in the life of the United Nations and in the life of mankind. This Universal Declaration of Human Rights may well become the international Magna Carta of all men everywhere. We hope its proclamation by the General Assembly will be an event comparable to the proclamation of the Declaration of the Rights of Man by the French people in 1789, the adoption of the Bill of Rights by the people of the United States, and the adoption of comparable declarations at different times in other countries.

At a time when there are so many issues on which we find it difficult to reach a common basis of agreement, it is a significant fact that 58 states have found such a large measure of agreement in the complex field of human rights. This must be taken as testimony of our common aspiration first voiced in the Charter of the United Nations to lift men everywhere to a higher standard of life and to a greater enjoyment of freedom. Man's desire for peace lies behind this Declaration. The realization that the flagrant violation of human rights by Nazi and Fascist countries sowed the seeds of the last world war has supplied the impetus [motivation] for the work which brings us to the moment of achievement here today.

Source: Eleanor Roosevelt, Speech to the United Nations, Paris, France, December 9, 1948.

1. Why do you think Roosevelt dedicated part of her speech to defining what the Universal Declaration of Human Rights is not?

_____

_____

2. Why might Roosevelt have chosen to compare the Universal Declaration to other foundational documents from other countries?

_____

_____

3. How might Roosevelt's biases inform her speech to the UN?

_____

_____

Multiple-Choice Questions

Questions 1–3 refer to the excerpt below.

A. Japanese Relocation Begins Following Executive Order 9066

The greatest forced migration in American history was getting under way today.

Along the entire Pacific Coast, and from the southern half of Arizona, some 120,000 enemy aliens and American-born Japanese were moving, or preparing to move, to areas in which the threat of possible espionage, sabotage or fifth column activities would be minimized.

None of the Japanese had actual orders to get out of the coastal military area designated yesterday by Lieut. Gen. John L. DeWitt, Western defense and Fourth Army commander, but all had his warning that eventually they must go.

Before deadlines are set for clearing of the area—twice as large as Japan itself—there is much to be done by the Army and by governmental agencies co-operating with it in working out a program that will call for the least possible economic confusion.

Thomas C. Clark, alien control co-ordinator, said in Los Angeles he hoped Japanese might be removed from coast prohibited areas within 60 days, but that "we are not going to push them around."

"We are going to give these people a fair chance to dispose of their properties at proper prices," Mr. Clark said. "It has come to our attention that many Japanese farmers have been stampeded into selling their properties for little or nothing."

Sixty-five chapters of the Japanese-American Citizens League, which claims a membership of 20,000 American-born Japanese, will hold meetings soon in 300 communities "to discuss methods by which they can correlate their energies and co-operate extensively in the evacuation process."

Source: "Japanese on West Coast Face Wholesale Uprooting," *The San Francisco News*, March 4, 1942

1. What is one of the problems the Japanese faced as they were forcibly removed from their homes?

    1. They had not been given time to pack their personal belongings.
    2. Parents were being separated from their children.
    3. Some farmers had been pressured to sell their land for next to nothing.
    4. The Japanese-American Citizens League was holding meetings to correlate efforts to resist the evacuation.

2. Which of the following best explains the way in which the events described in this article reflect the impact of time and place?

    1. They followed a "Gentlemen's Agreement" between the United States and Japan that restricted Japanese immigration.
    2. They were the result of the Japanese attack on Pearl Harbor and the subsequent executive order that allowed for the removal of any persons deemed a threat by the military.

3. They came after cities with large Japanese populations had become frustrated by their attempts to force people to live in designated areas.

4. They reflected the efforts of the state of California to take over land that had belonged to Japanese farmers.

3. Which of the following most accurately describes the reliability of this article as a source?

1. It is unreliable. The piece is clearly government propaganda intended to make the Japanese removal seem more humane than it was.

2. It is somewhat unreliable. The reporter is clearly sensationalizing the events described.

3. It is somewhat reliable. It exhibits a clear pro-government bias.

4. It is reliable. It appears to present the facts in a straightforward manner.

Questions 4–6 refer to the excerpt below.

B. Recommended Enlistment of Navaho Indians as "Code Talkers"

1. Mr. Philip Johnston of Los Angeles recently offered his services to this force to demonstrate the use of Indians for the transmission of messages by telephone and voice-radio. His offer was accepted and the demonstration was held for the Commanding General and his staff.

2. The demonstration was interesting and successful. Messages were transmitted and received almost verbatim. In conducting the demonstration messages were written by a member of the staff and handed to the Indian; he would transmit the messages in his tribal dialect and the Indian on the other end would write them down in English. The text of messages as written and received are enclosed. The Indians do not have many military terms in their dialect so it was necessary to give them a few minutes, before the demonstration, to improvise words for dive-bombing, anti-tank gun, etc.

3. Mr. Johnston stated that the Navaho is the only tribe in the United States that has not been infested with German students during the past twenty years. These Germans, studying the various tribal dialects under the guise of art students, anthropologists, etc., have undoubtedly attained a good working knowledge of all tribal dialects except Navaho. For this reason the Navaho is the only tribe available offering complete security for the type of work under consideration. It is noted in Mr. Johnston's article (enclosed) that the Navaho is the largest tribe but the lowest in literacy. He stated, however, that 1,000 — if that many were needed — could be found with the necessary qualifications. It should also be noted that the Navaho tribal dialect is completely unintelligible to all other tribes and all other people, with the possible exception of as many as 28 Americans who have made a study of the dialect. This dialect is thus equivalent to a secret code to the enemy, and admirably suited for rapid, secure communication.

4. It is therefore recommended that an effort be made to enlist 200 Navaho Indians for this force. In addition to linguistic qualifications in English and their tribal dialect they should have the physical qualifications necessary for messengers.

Source: Maj. Gen. Clayton B. Vogel, Memorandum to the Commandant, U.S. Marine Corps, March 6, 1942

4. What evidence does Vogel provide in support of his claim that the demonstration of "code talking" was successful?

   1. He said that the Navaho did not have many military terms in their dialect.

   2. He said that the Navaho had not been "infested" by German students.

   3. He said he was enclosing the text of messages as they were written and received.

   4. He said that the Navaho were the largest tribe but had the lowest literacy rates.

5. Why did Vogel think that using the Navaho language would be a good way to transmit messages?

   1. Germans had been studying various tribal dialects and had a good working knowledge of them.

   2. The Navaho were the largest tribe but had the lowest literacy rates.

   3. The Navaho dialect used hieroglyphics as its written language, and only other Navaho could read them.

   4. The Navaho dialect was equivalent to a secret code.

6. What happened as a result of the demonstration Vogel describes?

   1. He recommended that the Navaho teach their dialect to other tribes to improve intertribal communications.

   2. He recommended that the U.S. military enlist 200 Navajo to serve as code talkers.

   3. He recommended that the Bureau of Indian Affairs open schools to improve Navaho literacy rates.

   4. He recommended that the Navaho update their vocabulary so that it would include military terms and other vocabulary associated with modern life.

Questions 7 and 8 refer to the excerpt below.

C. Women in War Industry

Source: Office for Emergency Management, Office of War Information, Domestic Operations Branch, Bureau of Special Services, ca. 1943

7. How are the women portrayed in this poster similar to each other?

   1. They are all doing work that would normally have been done by men.
   2. They are all war widows.
   3. They are all married women.
   4. They are all women who previously worked in peacetime industries.

8. Why was this poster created?

   1. As a tribute to women
   2. As a photo montage honoring working women
   3. To inspire women to work in war industries
   4. As propaganda to intimidate the Axis powers by making them think that women in the United States were stronger than their women

World War II (1935–1945)   283

Short-Essay Questions

Study the two documents and answer the question that follows.

D. FDR's "The Four Freedoms"

In the future days, which we seek to make secure, we look forward to a world founded upon four essential human freedoms.

The first is freedom of speech and expression—everywhere in the world.

The second is freedom of every person to worship God in his own way—everywhere in the world.

The third is freedom from want—which, translated into world terms, means economic understandings which will secure to every nation a healthy peacetime life for its inhabitants—everywhere in the world.

The fourth is freedom from fear—which, translated into world terms, means a world-wide reduction of armaments to such a point and in such a thorough fashion that no nation will be in a position to commit an act of physical aggression against any neighbor—anywhere in the world.

That is no vision of a distant millennium. It is a definite basis for a kind of world attainable in our own time and generation. That kind of world is the very antithesis of the so-called new order of tyranny which the dictators seek to create with the crash of a bomb.

To that new order we oppose the greater conception—the moral order. A good society is able to face schemes of world domination and foreign revolutions alike without fear.

Since the beginning of our American history, we have been engaged in change—in a perpetual peaceful revolution—a revolution which goes on steadily, quietly adjusting itself to changing conditions—without the concentration camp or the quick-lime in the ditch. The world order which we seek is the cooperation of free countries, working together in a friendly, civilized society.

This nation has placed its destiny in the hands and heads and hearts of its millions of free men and women; and its faith in freedom under the guidance of God. Freedom means the supremacy of human rights everywhere. Our support goes to those who struggle to gain those rights and keep them. Our strength is our unity of purpose.

To that high concept there can be no end save victory.

Source: Franklin D. Roosevelt, State of the Union Address, January 6, 1941

E. The Struggle for the Rights of Man

I have come this evening to talk with you on one of the greatest issues of our time—that is the preservation of human freedom. I have chosen to discuss it here in France, at the Sorbonne, because here in this soil the roots of human freedom have long ago struck deep and here they have been richly nourished. It was here the Declaration of the Rights of Man was proclaimed, and the great slogans of the French Revolution—liberty, equality, fraternity—fired the imagination of men. I have chosen to discuss this issue in Europe because this has been the scene of the greatest historic battles between freedom and tyranny. I have chosen to discuss it in the early days of the General Assembly because the issue of human liberty is decisive for the settlement of outstanding political differences and for the future of the United Nations.

The decisive importance of this issue was fully recognized by the founders of the United Nations at San Francisco. Concern for the preservation and promotion of human rights and fundamental freedoms stands at the heart of the United Nations. Its Charter is distinguished by its preoccupation with the rights and welfare of individual men and women. The United Nations has made it clear that it intends to uphold human rights and to protect the dignity of the human personality. In the preamble to the Charter the keynote is set when it declares: "We the people of the United Nations determined . . . to reaffirm faith in fundamental human rights, in the dignity and worth of the human person, in the equal rights of men and women and of nations large and small, and . . . to promote social progress and better standards of life in larger freedom." This reflects the basic premise of the Charter that the peace and security of mankind are dependent on mutual respect for the rights and freedoms of all.

Source: Eleanor Roosevelt, Speech on Human Rights, Sorbonne, Paris, September 28, 1948

1. In a short essay, describe the historical context surrounding the two documents above. Then identify and explain how the ideas in these documents mark a turning point.

Study the two documents and answer the question that follows.

F. The Scene at Dachau Concentration Camp after Liberation

Marc Coyle reached the camp two days before I did and was a guard so as soon as I got there I looked him up and he took me to the crematory. Dead SS troopers were scattered around the grounds, but when we reached the furnace house we came upon a huge stack of corpses piled up like kindling, all nude so that their clothes wouldn't be wasted by the burning. There were furnaces for burning six bodies at once, and on each side of them was a room twenty feet square crammed to the ceiling with more bodies - one big stinking rotten mess. Their faces purple, their eyes popping, and with a hideous grin on each one. They were nothing but bones & skins. Coyle had assisted at ten autopsies the day before (wearing a gas mask) on ten bodies selected at random. Eight of them had advanced T.B. [tuberculosis], all had typhus and extreme malnutrition symptoms. There were both women and children in the stack in addition to the men.

While we were inspecting the place, freed prisoners drove up with wagon loads of corpses removed from the compound proper. Watching the unloading was horrible. The bodies squooshed and gurgled as they hit the pile and the odor could almost be seen.

Behind the furnaces was the execution chamber, a windowless cell twenty feet square with gas nozzles every few feet across the ceiling. Outside, in addition to a huge mound of charred bone fragments, were the carefully sorted and stacked clothes of the victims—which obviously numbered in the thousands. Although I stood there looking at it, I couldn't believe it. The realness of the whole mess is just gradually dawning on me, and I doubt if it ever will on you.

Source: Pfc. Harold Porter, letter to his mother and father, Dachau, May 7, 1945

G. Opening Statement at the Nuremberg War Crimes Trials

The privilege of opening the first trial in history for crimes against the peace of the world imposes a grave responsibility. The wrongs which we seek to condemn and punish have been so calculated, so malignant, and so devastating, that civilization cannot tolerate their being ignored, because it cannot survive their being repeated. That four great nations, flushed with victory and stung with injury stay the hand of vengeance and voluntarily submit their captive enemies to the judgment of the law is one of the most significant tributes that Power has ever paid to Reason. . . .

In the prisoners' dock sit twenty-odd broken men. Reproached by the humiliation of those they have led almost as bitterly as by the desolation of those they have attacked, their personal capacity for evil is forever past. It is hard now to perceive in these men as captives the power by which as Nazi leaders they once dominated much of the world and terrified most of it. Merely as individuals their fate is of little consequence to the world.

What makes this inquest significant is that these prisoners represent sinister influences that will lurk in the world long after their bodies have returned to dust. We will show them to be living symbols of racial hatreds, of terrorism and violence, and of the arrogance and cruelty of power. They are symbols of fierce nationalisms and of militarism, of intrigue and war-making which have embroiled Europe generation after generation, crushing its manhood, destroying its homes, and impoverishing its life. They have so identified themselves with the philosophies they conceived and with the forces they directed that any tenderness to them is a victory and an encouragement to all the evils which are attached to their names. Civilization can afford no compromise with the social forces which would gain renewed strength if we deal ambiguously or indecisively with the men in whom those forces now precariously survive.

Source: Robert H. Jackson, Opening Statement, Trial of the Major War Criminals before the International Military Tribunal, Nuremberg, November 21, 1947

2. In a short essay, describe the historical context surrounding the two documents above. Then analyze and explain how the point of view of the letter affects its reliability as a source of evidence.

CHAPTER 9

The Cold War (1945–1990)

Chapter Overview

After World War II, ideological differences led to political tensions between the United States and the Soviet Union. For more than 40 years, the world's superpowers—the United States and the Soviet Union—engaged in a Cold War that had implications across the globe.

Eastern Europe, Korea, and Vietnam After World War II, the Soviet Union wanted to maintain control of Eastern European countries that they helped free from Nazi control and then occupied. In the end, Eastern Europe, including part of Germany, fell under Soviet domination. The ideological battle between democracy and communism flared up in actual wars in the 1950s in Korea, and in the 1960s, in Vietnam.

The Nuclear Arms and Space Races The Cold War was also fought in space and in the realm of nuclear technology. A four-decade nuclear competition between the superpowers ensued, with occasional boiling points and defensive-minded treaties to try to limit any potential damage. The Soviet Union took the lead in the space race in the 1950s, but it was the United States, fulfilling the vision of President John F. Kennedy, that first landed men on the moon.

Influence in the Middle East After the establishment of the state of Israel after World War II, the Middle East became a hotbed of conflict between Arabs and Jews and the United States and the Soviet Union. U.S. dependence on Middle Eastern oil afforded the region's countries some leverage in its dealings with the United States. Diplomatic efforts of multiple U.S. presidents had mixed results in tamping down the ongoing conflicts between Israel and its Arab neighbors.

The Cold War Ends The Reagan administration's military build-up, its willingness to engage in diplomacy, and the failing Soviet economy helped bring about a peaceful end to the Cold War. Diplomatic efforts between the two countries and a new spirit of openness and tolerance in Soviet society acted as a catalyst for the emergence of democratic governments in Eastern Europe, the breakup of the Soviet Union, and, ultimately, the fall of the Berlin Wall that symbolized Cold War's beginning 40 years earlier.

Civic Literacy: Declaring War According to the Constitution, the power to declare war belongs to Congress alone. Once war is declared, the president, as commander-in-chief, directs the armed forces. However, in the Cold War period, two conflicts that are generally referred to as wars, in Korea and Vietnam, took place under orders of the president but without a formal declaration of war by Congress. Did the executive branch overstep its authority in these cases?

New York Social Studies Framework

Key Idea 11. 9: The Cold War In the period following World War II, the United States entered into an extended era of international conflict called the Cold War that influenced foreign and domestic policy for more than 40 years.

Source: *New York State Grades 9–12 Social Studies Framework*

Civic Literacy Essay: Write the Supporting Paragraphs

The supporting paragraphs in your essay will demonstrate your skill in using evidence. They will also demonstrate your ability to follow an organizational pattern that makes the best presentation of your evidence.

Evidence and Organization Suppose your thesis asserts that the struggle by African Americans to abolish slavery and win citizenship rights had a significant positive impact on American society. You have already gathered as many facts, examples, and details as possible as evidence relevant to your thesis—that is, directly connected to your topic (see page 149). You have also likely determined the best organizational pattern for your evidence (see page 183).

Discussing: The Heart of the Argument Your main task in writing the supporting paragraphs is to discuss— "to make observations about something using facts, reasoning, and argument; to present in some detail," as the New York Board of Regents explains it. You want to prove that your thesis is reasonable. You can use several types of support:

- Facts: In *Plessy v. Ferguson* (1896), the Supreme Court established the "separate but equal" standard. However, in 1954, the Supreme Court overturned that decision in the case *Brown v. Board of Education.* Arguing the case against *Plessy* was a future justice, Thurgood Marshall.

- Reasoning: The efforts to stop the protesters in Birmingham, Alabama in 1963, including the use of high-powered hoses and police dogs, marked a turning point in the civil rights movement. Those images were broadcast across the nation, strengthening the impact of the efforts of the determined protesters.

- Argument: Dr. King's charismatic leadership, his nonviolent approach to protest, and his spiritual foundation combined to make the civil rights movement an indelible part of American culture. It uplifted Blacks and Whites together. These efforts led to legislation that made significant progress in protecting the rights of all minorities.

Application: As you read the sources in this lesson, identify facts, reasoning, and argument.

Key Terms by Theme

Governance
Cold War (p. 291)
iron curtain (p. 292)
containment (p. 292)
Marshall Plan (p. 293)
North American Treaty
    Organization (NATO) (p. 293)
Tonkin Gulf Resolution (p. 295)
John F. Kennedy (p. 299)
Berlin Wall (p. 299)
Fidel Castro (p. 301)
Henry Kissinger (p. 301)
realpolitik (p. 302)

détente (p. 302)
Palestine (p. 305)
Israel (p. 305)
Jimmy Carter (p. 307)
Ayatollah Khomeini (p. 308)
Mikhail Gorbachev (p. 311)
glasnost (p. 311)
perestroika (p. 311)

Civics
War Powers Act (p. 296)
McCarthyism (p. 293)
Watergate (p. 296)

Technology
National Aeronautics and Space
    Administration (NASA) (p. 300)

Economics
Organization of Petroleum
    Exporting Countries (OPEC)
    (p. 306)

Lesson 1 *The Struggle for Influence*

Though the United States and the Soviet Union were allies during World War II, it was a temporary agreement in what was a generally poor relationship between the two countries. After World War II, the two countries reached some agreements in the formation of the United Nations, but the United States quickly came to see its former ally as a threat to freedom and democracy.

Analyze a Primary Source

President Harry Truman, Address of the President of the United States, March 12, 1947

Read Closely: Building a Case

Notice how Truman builds his case by describing specific examples of aggressive actions by totalitarian regimes against free people. Underline the specific instances Truman describes in building his case.

Read Closely: Alternatives

In a speech such as this, the speaker will often present the situation as black and white. The listeners are presented with two starkly different alternatives. Circle the contrasting language Truman uses to show the differences between the two choices.

Read Closely: Doctrine

Truman closes this section of his speech outlining what he feels the U.S. policy toward the other nations of the world should be. It is a far more interventionist U.S. foreign policy than the country has adopted previously. Notice, however, that the language he uses to pledge U.S. support for oppressed people and countries is purposely not militaristic.

To ensure the peaceful development of nations, free from coercion, the United States has taken a leading part in establishing the United Nations. The United Nations is designed to make possible lasting freedom and independence for all its members. We shall not realize our objectives, however, unless we are willing to help free peoples to maintain their free institutions and their national integrity against aggressive movements that seek to impose upon them totalitarian regimes. This is no more than a frank recognition that totalitarian regimes imposed on free peoples, by direct or indirect aggression, undermine the foundations of international peace and hence the security of the United States.

The peoples of a number of countries of the world have recently had totalitarian regimes forced upon them against their will. The Government of the United States has made frequent protests against coercion and intimidation, in violation of the Yalta agreement, in Poland, Rumania, and Bulgaria. I must also state that in a number of other countries there have been similar developments.

At the present moment in world history nearly every nation must choose between alternative ways of life. The choice is too often not a free one. One way of life is based upon the will of the majority, and is distinguished by free institutions, representative government, free elections, guarantees of individual liberty, freedom of speech and religion, and freedom from political oppression.

The second way of life is based upon the will of a minority forcibly imposed upon the majority. It relies upon terror and oppression, a controlled press and radio; fixed elections, and the suppression of personal freedoms.

I believe that it must be the policy of the United States to support free peoples who are resisting attempted subjugation by armed minorities or by outside pressures.

I believe that we must assist free peoples to work out their own destinies in their own way.

Source: President Harry Truman, Address of the President of the United States, March 12, 1947

Impacts of Wartime Conferences

Beginning in 1943, Great Britain, the United States, and the Soviet Union met in a series of conferences. These took place to discuss strategy for winning the war and for shaping the world after the war ended. The first meeting took place in Tehran, Iran's capital.

Conference	Result
Tehran (November 1943)	- The Allies agreed that the Soviet Union would focus on freeing Eastern Europe from German control while Britain and the U.S. would concentrate on Western Europe. - Britain and the United States agreed to a Soviet demand to shift some Polish territory to the Soviet Union, to be made up by Poland gaining territory elsewhere, mostly from Germany.
Yalta (February 1945)	- Stalin wanted more control over Eastern European countries, citing the Soviet Union's disproportionately large sacrifice due to the war. - Roosevelt wanted those countries to be free and democratic. - Stalin accepted Roosevelt's position and agreed to help the United States fight against Japan.
Potsdam (July 1945)	- Germany would be disarmed and divided into four occupation zones (British, U.S., French, and Soviet). - The former German capital Berlin would also be divided into zones of occupation. - War criminals in both Japan and Germany would be put on trial. - Japan would be occupied chiefly by U.S. troops. - Polish territory would be granted to the Soviet Union.

The agreement concerning Poland was met with criticism. Some felt the United States and Britain conceded too much to the Soviets. The agreement, they argued, practically invited the Soviets to occupy Poland and dominate the countries of Eastern Europe. At the time of the Yalta Conference, Soviet troops were already well established in Eastern Europe.

The Cold War Begins During the postwar years, the U.S. worried about the Soviet Union expanding its power by supporting Communist revolutions and gaining control over other nations. The Soviets feared U.S. power. Only the United States had nuclear weapons, and it had dropped two of them on Japan.

Postwar hostility between the Soviet Union and the United States was also based on two opposing political ideologies. The United States was a democracy with a capitalist economy. The U.S.S.R was a communist country and economy. The two nations' rivalry after World War II was called the **Cold War** because the conflict didn't involve armies fighting against each other.

As soon as World War II ended, the Soviet Union used occupation troops in Eastern Europe to achieve political control of the region. In 1945 and 1946, elections took place in Poland, Romania, Bulgaria, and Hungary. However, they were far from free or fair elections. The occupying Soviet military supported the Communist parties in each of these countries. In each country, Communists took control of the police, the newspapers, and the radio stations. Unsurprisingly, the Communist candidates won these rigged elections. Czechoslovakia did have a free

> **Read Closely: Patterns**
> When reading historical texts, recognizing patterns helps provide a broader understanding of events. What patterns can you identify in the meetings of the Big Three?

election, but in 1948 the Soviet-backed Communists forced the Czech leaders to leave office. Seven Eastern European states were now Soviet satellite countries.

In Germany, the postwar plan was for a brief occupation followed by unification under a democratically elected government. But because of the conflict between the Soviet Union and the other occupying powers, Germany remained divided into two parts. There was a freely elected western part (West Germany) and a Communist controlled Soviet satellite (East Germany).

Soviet domination of the Eastern European countries meant that they were cut off from contact with the West. East Europeans could not travel and were forbidden to read Western publications or listen to broadcasts from the West. In 1946, the great British wartime leader Winston Churchill gave a speech in Fulton, Missouri. In it, he famously said that an "**iron curtain**" had fallen across Europe, dividing it into Soviet controlled Eastern Europe and the democracies of Western Europe.

U.S. Containment Policy

The Cold War between the United States and the Soviet Union went beyond the issues of controlling countries or territories. The two countries battled in many ways:

- engaging in an arms race to build more powerful nuclear weapons
- giving military aid to rebel or government forces that leaned toward communism or democracy
- increasing espionage efforts against one another
- creating and distributing propaganda that condemned the opposing nation and its way of life
- engaging in a space race to be the first to make gains in space exploration
- using the United Nations General Assembly and Security Council to condemn actions of the rival power

These Cold War tactics dominated world politics from about 1945 to 1989. As a result, the world was often in a state of high tension.

The United States feared that the Soviet Union would continue its Eastern European aggression into Western Europe and elsewhere. In 1947, American scholar and diplomat George Kennan proposed an answer to this problem. He suggested that "the main element of any United States policy toward the Soviet Union must be that of a long-term, patient but firm and vigilant containment of Russian expansive tendencies. . . ." **Containment** became the guiding U.S. policy during the 40 years of the Cold War.

The Truman Doctrine and The Marshall Plan In 1947, the government of Greece was in danger of being overthrown by Greek Communists. If Greece fell, then Turkey was also vulnerable to being swept into the Soviet orbit. Truman decided to contain the Communist threat with millions in U.S. military aid for both countries. In his statement to Congress, which became known as the Truman Doctrine, the president said: "The free peoples of the world look to us for support in maintaining their freedoms. If we falter in our leadership, we may endanger the peace of the world—and we shall surely endanger the welfare of our own Nation." U.S. aid to Greece and Turkey helped these countries maintain democratic institutions and societies.

At the same time, the Western European economies were still in poor shape from the destructive effects of war. Communist parties in France and Italy fed on people's frustrations. In both countries, they won large numbers of supporters. To contain the rising tide of communism and Soviet influence, Truman's Secretary of State George Marshall proposed an ambitious program of foreign aid. From 1948 to 1951, Congress approved $12 billion of economic assistance to Europe, a huge sum for that time. The **Marshall Plan**, as it was called, helped to bring about European recovery. By 1951, Communist control of France and Italy was no longer a serious possibility.

The Berlin Airlift and NATO In 1948, the Soviet Union announced that the British, French, and Americans could no longer transport supplies over land to Berlin through the Soviet zone of occupation. Contrary to Soviet hopes, Truman pledged that the United States would not abandon West Berlin. Truman ordered the U.S. Air Force to bring supplies to West Berlin by air. This Berlin Airlift flew in supplies day after day for almost a year. By 1949, the Soviets ended their land blockade to West Berlin.

In 1949, the United States did something it had never done before. It committed itself to a permanent military alliance in peacetime. It became part of the **North Atlantic Treaty Organization (NATO)**. Other members included 11 other countries: Great Britain, France, Italy, Belgium, the Netherlands, Denmark, Norway, Iceland, Portugal, Luxembourg, and Canada. The treaty countries agreed that "an armed attack against one or more of them in Europe or North America shall be considered an attack against all." NATO's primary purpose was to deter the Soviet Union from aggression and thus to avoid war.

Fear of Communism and McCarthyism In 1950, the U.S. Congress passed anti-Communist legislation known as the McCarran Act. The aim was to make organizations accused of either receiving support from Communists or including Communist members to reveal their members and financial statements. It also prohibited Communists (or members of Communist-front organizations) to work for national defense industries or be allowed entry into the United States. Fear of Communist influences and subversion was especially intense in the early 1950s.

The person most responsible for arousing public fears was Wisconsin Senator Joseph McCarthy. He conducted Senate committee hearings in which he accused many government officials of being "Communist sympathizers." McCarthy's committee also investigated famous actors and writers, as well as educators and others. Their constitutional rights were disregarded and many lost their jobs. They had trouble finding new employment because businesses would blacklist, or refuse to hire, those under investigation.

In mid-1954, McCarthy chaired televised hearings that turned the tide of public opinion against him. Many were seeing McCarthy in action for the first time, and they did not like what they saw. He interrupted and bullied witnesses and made reckless use of unsubstantiated charges. As a result, McCarthy quickly lost both his supporters and his power. In December 1954, the Senate voted to censure McCarthy for improper conduct that damaged the reputation of the Senate. The term **McCarthyism** has come to mean "the use of reckless and unfair accusations in the name of suppressing political disloyalty."

Truman's War in Korea

In 1950, the United States became involved in a war in Korea. One of the war's underlying causes was U.S. opposition to communism. The immediate cause was a sudden attack by North Korean armed forces against the territory of South Korea.

> **Read Closely: Defining Terms**
> Earlier the text defined the political and economic differences between the United States and the Soviet Union. How did these different political and economic ideas contribute to the Cold War between the countries in the years after World War II?

> **Read Closely: Mass Media**
> Look for connections between historical and political events and media figures and methods. Why do you think McCarthy went after actors and writers in his crusade? How did the media contribute to his downfall?

At the end of World War II, the Japanese occupation forces were driven out of Korea by Soviet armies arriving from the north and American armies arriving from the south. Soviets and Americans agreed that the 38th parallel of latitude should be the temporary dividing line between their zones of occupation. North Korea was backed by Communist Soviet Union and South Korea had U.S. support.

Read Closely: Connections
As you read, make connections between what historical figures say and what they do. How do the events leading to the Korean War illustrate the Truman Doctrine in action?

Hoping that the UN could manage Korea's problems, U.S. troops left the country in 1949. But in June 1950, a North Korean army marched across the 38th parallel into South Korea. In response, President Truman ordered U.S. troops into South Korea and called on the United Nations to aid in South Korea's defense. At the time, the Soviet Union had withdrawn its representative from the UN. As such, it had lost its veto power in the Security Council.

China Complicates the War At first, the U.S. military forces and their international allies suffered a series of defeats. The commander of the UN forces was U.S. General Douglas MacArthur. But a surprise attack behind enemy lines pushed the North Koreans back toward the Chinese border. MacArthur's attack caused China to come to the aid of North Korea. Thousands of Chinese soldiers drove the UN forces south in retreat to the 38th parallel. MacArthur urged President Truman to permit him to bomb Chinese bases in Manchuria, a part of China, in order to stop the Chinese attack. Truman refused. He wanted to pursue a limited war in Korea. He feared that bombing China would result in a larger and more dangerous war.

The war in Korea dragged on through 1952. Despite much loss of life, neither side could win decisive victories. The war became stalemated near the 38th parallel. Truce talks started in July 1951. The 1952 Republican candidate for president, General Dwight D. Eisenhower, promised to "go to Korea" to end the fighting. As president-elect, he carried out his promise. An armistice was finally signed in June 1953, re-establishing the 38th parallel as the line between the opposing forces.

Read Closely: Central Cause
Much of U.S. military and political intervention in other countries between 1950 and the late 1980s was caused by the Cold War goal of containing the spread of communism. Why do you think two different presidents—Eisenhower and Kennedy, both military veterans—took such modest steps in their containment efforts over the course of a decade?

Korean War: Military Casualties				
	South Korea	**United States**	**China**	**North Korea**
Dead	217,000	36,600	600,000	406,000
Wounded	430,000	103,300	716,000	1,500,000

The Vietnam War

Similarly to the situation in Korea, in the 1950s, Vietnam became divided. There was a Communist north, supported by the Soviet Union, and a non-Communist south, supported by the United States. To help support U.S. interests in the region, President Eisenhower sent a few hundred military advisers to help train South Vietnamese troops.

When John Kennedy became president in 1961, he continued supporting South Vietnam's government. He increased the number of U.S. military personnel from 2,000 advisors in 1961 to 16,000 troops in 1963. But by the mid-1960s, the Communist opposition within South Vietnam appeared to be gaining strength. This alarmed U.S. policymakers wary of a "domino effect" in Southeast Asia. If Vietnam fell to communism, would its neighbors quickly follow?

Johnson Escalates the War Lyndon Johnson, who became president after Kennedy's assassination in 1963, promised "no wider war" in Vietnam. But he soon changed this policy to counter the strong support given to South Vietnamese Communist fighters, the Viet Cong, by the North Vietnamese government, China, and the Soviet Union. Johnson felt that the widespread use of U.S. troops was now necessary.

In August 1964, reports claimed that North Vietnamese gunboats had attacked two U.S. ships in the Gulf of Tonkin off the coast of North Vietnam. (These reports later proved inaccurate.) In response, Congress overwhelmingly approved the **Tonkin Gulf Resolution**. The resolution effectively turned over to the president the power to use the armed forces in Vietnam in any way he saw fit.

Early in 1965, U.S. planes began bombing enemy targets in the North. At the same time, U.S. combat troops arrived in South Vietnam by the thousands. In little more than three years, the number of U.S. troops in Vietnam rose from 184,000 in 1965 to 536,100 in 1968.

In January 1968, Communist forces launched an all-out attack against targeted cities in South Vietnam. The capital city, Saigon, was in danger of being taken. Though the Communist forces were pushed back, their so-called Tet Offensive had dramatically demonstrated their strength. It also forced Americans to recognize the possibility that the war could go on for much longer.

Student Protests As the war continued, more and more young Americans were drafted into military service and sent to Vietnam. A rising number of these young Americans were wounded or killed in action. People began to question whether the United States was fighting for a worthwhile cause. Many college students protested the war. They publicly set fire to their draft cards and occupied buildings on college campuses.

The president and his military advisers stated many times that U.S. and South Vietnamese forces would eventually win the war. Many Americans, however, no longer accepted official reports about the war. The many public protests against the war were one reason that Lyndon Johnson surprised the world in 1968 by announcing that he would not seek re-election.

Nixon and Vietnam The next president, Richard Nixon, struggled to deal with the war in Vietnam and with the antiwar movement at home. In March 1969, Nixon announced a military strategy called Vietnamization. U.S. troops were to gradually withdraw while at the same time intensively training South Vietnamese troops to carry on the war. Nixon also carried out another part of his strategy

Read Closely: Trends
Historians often show developments at different times to show larger trends over an extended period. The Constitution requires Congress to declare war. But the U.S. Congress did not do so in the cases of Korea or Vietnam. Why do you think this was the case for these two conflicts?

U.S. Troop Buildup in Vietnam, 1964–1968

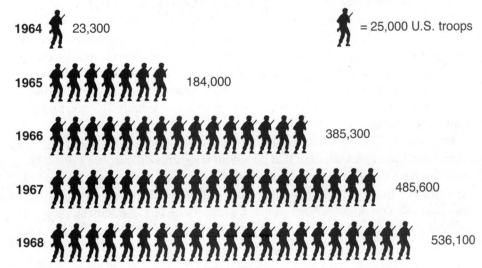

1964 — 23,300

= 25,000 U.S. troops

1965 — 184,000

1966 — 385,300

1967 — 485,600

1968 — 536,100

in secret. He ordered a series of bombing raids over Cambodia to cut off North Vietnamese supply routes into South Vietnam. Even Congress was unaware of the bombing at first.

Americans continued to protest the Vietnam War in growing numbers. On November 15, 1969, more than 250,000 protesters gathered in Washington, D.C., and marched from the Washington Monument to the White House. In 1972, as more U.S. troops left Vietnam, Nixon ordered the continuous bombing of North Vietnam. These raids hit its capital, Hanoi, for the first time in the war. At the same time, South Vietnamese forces continued to lose ground to the Communists.

In early 1973, after long and difficult negotiations, President Nixon agreed to peace terms that had the approval of South and North Vietnam. U.S. troops would leave Vietnam, and elections would be held to determine South Vietnam's future. The civil war in Vietnam continued for almost two more years. Ultimately, South Vietnam fell to the Communist North in 1975.

The War Powers Act Many members of Congress regretted the Tonkin Gulf Resolution, which had given total war-making power to President Johnson. They wanted to limit the president's power in the future. Congress passed the **War Powers Act** in 1973. These were the act's major provisions:

- Within 48 hours of sending troops into combat, the president must inform Congress of the reasons for the action.

- If U.S. troops are involved in fighting abroad for more than 90 days, the president must obtain Congress's approval to continuing the use of troops or bring them home.

Watergate President Nixon had won re-election in 1972 by a huge margin. But soon after his second term began, the **Watergate** crisis broke. During the campaign period, five men had been arrested attempting a late-night break-in at Democratic National Committee offices in the Watergate office building in Washington, D.C. In time, news reports suggested that the crime might have been planned by members of the White House staff and perhaps by the president himself.

The Federal Bureau of Investigation (FBI) investigated the Watergate affair. Two investigative reporters for the *Washington Post* revealed that suspicions about certain officials close to the president might be well founded. The most dramatic investigation was conducted by a Senate committee and was televised to the nation. Throughout 1973, Nixon repeatedly claimed that he had no previous knowledge of the break-in and that he had not attempted to cover it up.

The Senate committee learned that the president had taped every conversation that took place in his White House office. It requested that the president turn over the tapes as evidence. Nixon released some tapes but not others, citing "executive privilege." The case went to the Supreme Court, and the Court ruled against Nixon. The tapes revealed that he had participated in an effort to protect those responsible for the Watergate break-in. His actions—attempting to cover up a crime—were criminal.

On August 8, 1974, rather than face impeachment and removal from office, Nixon announced on television that he would resign his office. Vice President Gerald Ford was swiftly sworn in as the new president. It was the first time in U.S. history that a living president had left office before the end of his term. Watergate resulted in 48 convictions. Most of these were among Nixon administration officials and people who worked for his re-election.

Read Closely: Turning Point
Analyze how events develop to understand key moments in history. The American public became more engaged and enraged about the Vietnam War as it progressed. What might be a turning point in the public's attitude from supporting the war effort to demanding it end?

Read Closely: Impact
Historians like to evaluate the impact of events on cultures and societies. Examining developments over time can lead one to make reasonable assessments on such impacts. In light of the Vietnam War and the Watergate Affair, how might you describe the attitude of the American public toward its leaders?

Application: Interpret a Primary Source

Read the excerpt and answer the questions that follow it.

President Lyndon Johnson, State of the Union, January 12, 1966

We will stay [in Vietnam] because a just nation cannot leave to the cruelties of enemies a people who have staked their lives and independence on America's solemn pledge—a pledge that had grown through the commitment of three American Presidents.

We will stay because in Asia and around the world are countries whose independence rests, in large measure, on confidence in America's word and in America's protection. To yield to force in Vietnam would weaken that confidence, would undermine the independence of many lands, and would whet the appetite of aggression. We would have to fight in one land, and then we would have to fight in another—or abandon much of Asia to the domination of Communists.

I wish tonight that I could give you a blueprint for the course of this conflict over the coming months, but we just cannot know what the future may require. We may have to face long, hard combat or a long, hard conference, or even both at once.

Until peace comes, or if it does not come, our course is clear. We will act as we must to help protect the independence of the valiant people of South Vietnam. We will strive to limit the conflict, for we wish neither increased destruction nor do we want to invite increased danger.

The war in Vietnam is not like these other wars. Yet, finally, war is always the same. It is young men dying in the fullness of their promise. It is trying to kill a man that you do not even know well enough to hate.

Therefore, to know war is to know that there is still madness in this world.

Yet we do what we must.

Source: President Lyndon Johnson, State of the Union, January 12, 1966

1. Johnson had greatly escalated the commitment of U.S. troops into Vietnam in the year before this speech. What do you think Johnson's intention was in describing the Vietnam War as he did?

_____

_____

2. What details does Johnson offer for the effects the war will have?

_____

_____

3. President Johnson served in the Navy during World War II. What do his closing remarks about soldiers reveal about Johnson's point of view on war?

_____

_____

Lesson 2 *The World on the Edge*

Conceptual Understanding
11.9b The United States and the Soviet Union engaged in a nuclear arms race that eventually led to agreements that limited the arms buildup and improved United States-Soviet relations.

During the Cold War, the United States and the Soviet Union battled on the world stage in various ways. One of the primary battles was a nuclear arms race that not only threatened both countries, but threatened countries all over the globe. President Eisenhower, a former five-star general, was uniquely placed to see the sources of this race and who might be in part responsible for it.

Analyze a Primary Source

President Dwight D. Eisenhower, Farewell Address to the Nation, January 17, 1961

Read Closely: Context
Notice how President Eisenhower describes the way the country's national defense has changed in such a short period of time. He presided over the evolution of the U.S. military from a traditional ground, air, and sea force to a more high-tech and deadly nuclear force.

Read Closely: Evidence
Pay close attention to the evidence a speaker gives to back up his or her claims. Eisenhower provides details to describe the efforts and resources the country has dedicated to this military overhaul. Underline some of the specific information Eisenhower offers as evidence.

Read Closely: Cautionary Claim
A veteran of war before becoming president, Eisenhower had a clear-eyed vision of what the United States' current military posture could mean. Circle the cautionary details Eisenhower offers for the nation going forward in the Cold War.

Until the latest of our world conflicts, the United States had no armaments industry. American makers of plowshares could, with time and as required, make swords as well. But now we can no longer risk emergency improvisation of national defense; we have been compelled to create a permanent armaments industry of vast proportions. Added to this, three and a half million men and women are directly engaged in the defense establishment. We annually spend on military security more than the net income of all United States corporations.

This conjunction of an immense military establishment and a large arms industry is new in the American experience. The total influence—economic, political, even spiritual—is felt in every city, every state house, every office of the Federal government. We recognize the imperative need for this development. Yet we must not fail to comprehend its grave implications. Our toil, resources and livelihood are all involved; so is the very structure of our society.

In the councils of government, we must guard against the acquisition of unwarranted influence, whether sought or unsought, by the military-industrial complex. The potential for the disastrous rise of misplaced power exists and will persist.

Disarmament, with mutual honor and confidence, is a continuing imperative. Together we must learn how to compose difference, not with arms, but with intellect and decent purpose. Because this need is so sharp and apparent I confess that I lay down my official responsibilities in this field with a definite sense of disappointment. As one who has witnessed the horror and the lingering sadness of war—as one who knows that another war could utterly destroy this civilization which has been so slowly and painfully built over thousands of years—I wish I could say tonight that a lasting peace is in sight.

Source: President Dwight D. Eisenhower, Farewell Address to the Nation, January 17, 1961

The Nuclear Arms Race

After World War II and the use of atomic weapons at Hiroshima and Nagasaki, the United States stood out as the world's most powerful military nation. But in 1949, the Soviet Union exploded its first atomic bomb. The United States was no longer the only nation in possession of the most destructive weapon ever made.

In 1952, the United States announced that it had developed a hydrogen bomb. This weapon was thousands of times more destructive than the atomic bomb. But only one year later, the Soviet Union announced that it, too, had developed and tested an H-bomb. The arms race was on. The two most powerful nations in the world competed with each other to produce more and more nuclear weapons. People recognized that much of the world might be destroyed if the Cold War ever turned into a hot, nuclear war.

Therefore in 1953, President Eisenhower proposed an atoms-for-peace plan to the United Nations. Under this plan, nations would pool their atomic resources for peaceful purposes. However, the Soviet Union refused to participate. The United States launched a limited version of the plan with Canada and its European allies. Western nations would now pursue peaceful uses for atomic power, such as the production of electricity.

The U-2 Incident and The Berlin Wall As the Cold War continued, tensions between the United States and the Soviet heightened in other areas. In 1960, the Soviet Union shot down a U.S. spy plane over its territory. The Soviets captured the American pilot Gary Powers. During the U-2 incident, as it was called, Soviet leader Nikita Khrushchev angrily charged the U.S. with spying using U-2 planes. Eisenhower denied it at first. But he later admitted that these planes were often used for spying. The pilot Powers was later exchanged for a Soviet spy. As a result of the incident, Khrushchev canceled a planned summit conference with President Eisenhower.

In January 1961, President **John F. Kennedy** took office. Soon afterward, he was tested by Soviet leader Khrushchev. After World War II, the Allies had divided both Germany as a whole, as well as the city of Berlin. In both cases, the eastern section came under Soviet control and France, Britain, and the United States controlled the western section. In 1955, West Germany joined the NATO alliance and East Germany joined the Soviet-sponsored Warsaw Pact. Berlin itself was situated nearly in the center of Soviet-controlled East Germany. By 1961, West Germany had become far more prosperous than Soviet-controlled East Germany. East Germans were flocking to the greater freedom and prosperity of West Berlin. This embarrassed the Soviet Union. Khrushchev threatened to sign a treaty with East Germany to allow the East German Communists to cut off all the food that came to West Berlin by land.

In June 1961, President Kennedy met Khrushchev at a summit conference in Vienna, Austria. Little was accomplished because Kennedy stood firmly in support of West Berlin. Two months later, the Soviets and their East German allies startled the world. They erected a concrete and barbed wire wall along the border between East Berlin and West Berlin. The purpose of the **Berlin Wall** was to prevent East Berliners from moving into the western section of the city. Many East Berliners tried to climb over the wall, tunnel under it, or even swim around it. Some succeeded, while others were caught or even shot by East German guards. Kennedy's response to the Berlin Wall was to travel to West Berlin. He assured the people there that the United States would never give in to Soviet pressures. In a public speech, Kennedy told the crowd "Ich bin ein Berliner" ("I am a Berliner."). By this he meant that any threat against West Berlin would be viewed as a threat against the United States.

> **Read Closely: Patterns**
> As you read, look for recurring patterns in a text. What patterns can you identify in the actions and reactions of the Soviet Union and the United States?

Sputnik and the Space Race In 1957, the Cold War literally reached into outer space. In that year, the Soviet Union launched *Sputnik*, the first artificial satellite to orbit Earth. The American public was shocked that the Soviet Union had beaten them into space. Eisenhower and Congress responded immediately by passing the Space Act of 1958. It created a new agency—the **National Aeronautics and Space Administration (NASA)**. Congress also enacted the National Defense Education Act (1958). It provided low-interest loans to college students majoring in math and science. Only four months after Sputnik, the United States responded by launching its first satellite—*Explorer I*. The space race was on.

Despite the massive U.S. effort to get out in front in the space race, the Soviet Union scored another first in 1961. It sent Yuri Gagarin into orbit. He became the first human to circle Earth in outer space. President Kennedy announced in 1961 that the United States intended to be the first nation to land a human being on the moon. Less than a month after Gagarin's journey through space, a NASA rocket lifted American astronaut Alan Shepard into space. Although he did not orbit Earth, Shepard returned safely in his space capsule. The U.S. space program had its first triumph.

Other breakthroughs soon followed. In February 1962, astronaut John Glenn spent five hours in space orbiting the Earth. But not every mission was a success. In 1967, astronauts Virgil Grissom, Edward White, and Roger Chaffee were killed when a fire broke out in their *Apollo I* space capsule during a pre-launch test.

In July 1969, the *Apollo 11* mission carried three astronauts from Earth to the moon and back. While Michael Collins remained in the spacecraft, Neil Armstrong and Edwin "Buzz" Aldrin landed on the surface of the moon in a lunar module. Millions of television viewers around the world watched in amazement as Armstrong set foot on the gray lunar surface. Few people who viewed the event will forget Neil Armstrong's words as he stepped out of the spacecraft onto the moon: "That's one small step for [a] man, one giant leap for mankind." The plaque Armstrong and Aldrin left on the moon read simply, "We came in peace."

Read Closely: Inference
Try to make inferences to see how one idea or action might have broader effects on society. The space race was another battlefield in the Cold War. How might President Kennedy's challenge to put a man on the moon have inspired American society in the 1960s?

Source: Wikimedia Commons

Buzz Aldrin on the surface of the moon, photographed by Neil Armstrong

Soviet Missiles in Cuba

One Cold War conflict between the United States and the Soviet Union took place close to the U.S. mainland. In 1959, a young Cuban revolutionary named **Fidel Castro** overthrew the government of military dictator Fulgencio Batista. At first, the United States thought the change in government might be beneficial. For years, Batista had ruthlessly suppressed Cubans' civil liberties. But Castro promptly seized U.S.-owned properties in Cuba and established a Communist regime similar to the one in the Soviet Union. U.S. policymakers realized that Cuba—a nation only 90 miles from U.S. shores—had fallen under Soviet influence.

In October 1962, photographs of Cuba taken from U.S. spy planes showed the presence of Soviet nuclear weapons. The missiles, so close to the shores of the United States, posed a direct threat to U.S. security. President Kennedy considered many options, including an air strike against Cuba. He decided to send U.S. Navy ships into Cuban waters to intercept Soviet ships that might be carrying missiles. Kennedy sent a message to Soviet leader Nikita Khrushchev. He demanded that Soviet ships carrying missiles to Cuba turn around and that the missiles already in Cuba be removed. Kennedy announced his actions in a televised speech to the U.S. public. People feared what would happen if Soviet ships tried to break through the U.S. naval blockade. Could this trigger an exchange of nuclear weapons between the superpowers?

Fortunately, Khrushchev backed down. He agreed to order the Soviet ships to turn around and later to remove the missiles from Cuba. In return, Kennedy agreed that the United States would not invade Cuba. He also secretly agreed to remove U.S. nuclear missiles that were already in Turkey, near the Soviet Union.

Kennedy's handling of the Cuban missile crisis was considered to be the greatest foreign policy success of his presidency. After the crisis, the threat of a nuclear confrontation subsided some. Both the Soviet Union and the United States became more cautious in their dealings with each other. Neither wanted to provoke another crisis like the one that had nearly caused a worldwide disaster.

Nuclear Test Ban Treaties and the Hot Line Interactions between the Soviet Union and the United States were not always so intense and alarming. One sign of improved U.S.-Soviet relations was the signing of a nuclear test ban treaty in 1963. The two superpowers agreed to end the testing of nuclear weapons in the atmosphere, in outer space, and underwater. Underground tests were still permitted. In 1967, another treaty banned putting nuclear weapons in orbit around the Earth or on the moon or other planets.

In another positive step, the two sides set up a direct telephone line, or "hot line," between the office of the U.S. president and that of the Soviet premier. This enabled the two leaders to communicate quickly in a time of crisis.

Détente and SALT

In 1969, Richard M. Nixon became president of the United States. During the 1950s, as Eisenhower's vice president, Nixon expressed hostility toward the Soviet Union, China, and other Communist nations. But after becoming president, Nixon adopted policies designed to lessen Cold War tensions. He even sought to scale back U.S. military commitments around the world. Nixon depended greatly on the advice of **Henry Kissinger**, his assistant for national security affairs and later his secretary of state.

> **Read Closely: Turning Point**
> Look for actions and reactions that make an important difference in the course of history. The Cuban missile crisis seemed to mark a shift in the Cold War. Why do you think the two sides began steps to de-escalate tensions?

Nixon and Kissinger believed that U.S. foreign policies should have a single goal. They should support the national self-interest of the United States. Kissinger argued that all countries pursued their own self-interest. Therefore, he thought, the United States should do the same in order to devise realistic and successful policies. This approach to foreign policy—focusing on realities rather than ideals—is known as **realpolitik**.

Nixon's attempt to reduce Cold War anxiety and to improve U.S.-Soviet relations was known as the policy of **détente**. This French word means "the relaxation of tensions." A principal goal of détente was to set limits on the production of nuclear weapons. During Nixon's first term as president, diplomats from the United States and the Soviet Union held a series of talks called the Strategic Arms Limitation Talks (SALT). They negotiated an important breakthrough in the arms race, limiting several weapons:

Read Closely: Continuity
To understand the significance of a historical development, consider how it developed on the basis of what came before it. How did Nixon's policy of détente build on the de-escalation steps of the Kennedy administration?

- long-range nuclear missiles

- intercontinental ballistic missiles (ICBMs)

- defensive (or antiballistic) missiles (ABMs)

In 1972, Nixon traveled to the Soviet Union where he met with Soviet Premier Leonid Brezhnev. The two signed the SALT agreement. The world breathed a little more easily when they saw the leaders of the two superpowers agree to reduce the growth and spread of nuclear weapons.

Nixon also agreed to end a U.S. trade ban from 1949. It had prohibited the shipment of U.S. goods to the Soviet Union. To help the Russian people through a bad food shortage, Nixon offered (and Congress later approved) the sale of $750 million worth of U.S. wheat to the Soviets. The U.S.-Soviet "grain deal," as it was called, pleased the Soviet Union—and U.S. farmers. Also in 1972, the United Nations proposed another disarmament accord. The Seabed Agreement pledged never to place nuclear weapons on the ocean floor. The Soviet Union and the United States were among the 100 nations that signed the agreement.

Source: Wikimedia Commons

Leonid Brezhnev (left) meets Richard Nixon (right) in June 1973 during the Soviet Leader's U.S. visit.

Application: Interpret a Primary Source

Read the excerpt and answer the questions that follow it.

President Richard Nixon, Televised Address to the Soviet People from the Kremlin Palace, May 29, 1972

With great power goes great responsibility. When a man walks with a giant tread, he must be careful where he sets his feet.

Speaking for the United States, I can say this: We covet no one else's territory, we seek no dominion over any other people. We seek the right to live in peace, not only for ourselves but for all the peoples of this earth.

Soviet citizens have often asked me, "Does America truly want peace?" [I] believe that our actions answer that question far better than any words could do. If we did not want peace, we would not have reduced the size of our armed forces by a million men, by almost one-third, during the past three years.

If we did not want peace, we would not have worked so hard at reaching an agreement on the limitation of nuclear arms; at achieving a settlement of Berlin; at maintaining peace in the Middle East; at establishing better relations with the Soviet Union, with the People's Republic of China, with other nations of the world.

In many ways, the people of our two countries are very much alike. Like the Soviet Union, ours is a large and diverse nation. Our people, like yours, are hardworking. Like you, we Americans have a strong spirit of competition.

Through all the pages of history, through all the centuries, the world's people have struggled to be free from fear. . . .

And yet time and again people have vanquished the source of one fear only to fall prey to another. Let our goal now be a world free of fear.

A world in which nation will no longer prey upon nation. In which human energies will be turned away from production for war, and toward more production for peace. . . . A world in which, together, we can establish that peace which is more than the absence of war. Which enables man to pursue those higher goals that the spirit yearns for.

Source: President Richard Nixon, Televised Address to the Soviet People from the Kremlin Palace, May 29, 1972

1. Why was Nixon's address to the Soviet people from the Kremlin an important marker for U.S.-Soviet relations during the Cold War?

   _____

   _____

2. How might the Soviet people have reacted to Nixon's speech from the Kremlin?

   _____

   _____

3. Throughout the speech, President Nixon focuses on the concerns of people as well as national issues. Why do you think he so often discusses the lives of American and Soviet citizens?

   _____

   _____

Lesson 3 *The Troubled Middle East*

American strategic interests in the Middle East grew with the Cold War, the creation of the State of Israel, and the increased United States dependence on Middle Eastern oil. The continuing nature of the Arab-Israeli dispute has helped to define the contours of American policy in the Middle East.

Analyze a Primary Source

President Dwight D. Eisenhower, Special Message to Congress, January 5, 1957

> The reason for Russia's interest in the Middle East is solely that of power politics. Considering her announced purpose of Communizing the world, it is easy to understand her hope of dominating the Middle East. This region has always been the crossroads of the continents of the Eastern Hemisphere. The Suez Canal enables the nations of Asia and Europe to carry on the commerce that is essential if these countries are to maintain well-rounded and prosperous economies. The Middle East provides a gateway between Eurasia and Africa.
>
> Then there are other factors which transcend the material. The Middle East is the birthplace of three great religions—Moslem, Christian and Hebrew. Mecca and Jerusalem are more than places on the map. They symbolize religions which teach that the spirit has supremacy over matter and that the individual has a dignity and rights of which no despotic government can rightfully deprive him. It would be intolerable if the holy places of the Middle East should be subjected to a rule that glorifies atheistic materialism. International Communism, of course, seeks to mask its purposes of domination by expressions of good will and by superficially attractive offers of political, economic and military aid.
>
> Under all the circumstances I have laid before you, a greater responsibility now devolves upon the United States . . . The action which I propose would . . . authorize the United States to cooperate with and assist any nation or group of nations in the general area of the Middle East in the development of economic strength dedicated to the maintenance of national independence. It would [also] authorize such assistance and cooperation to include the employment of the armed forces of the United States to secure and protect the territorial integrity and political independence of such nations.
>
> This program will not solve all the problems of the Middle East. The United Nations is actively concerning itself with all these matters, and . . . we are willing to do much to assist the United Nations in solving the basic problems of Palestine.
>
> **Source:** President Dwight D. Eisenhower, Special Message to Congress, January 5, 1957

Conceptual Understanding 11.9c American strategic interests in the Middle East grew with the Cold War, the creation of the State of Israel, and the increased United States dependence on Middle Eastern oil. The continuing nature of the Arab-Israeli dispute has helped to define the contours of American policy in the Middle East.

Read Closely: Point of View President Eisenhower begins his speech with a brief summary of recent history in the Middle East. Notice how he changes focus from the larger question of the Middle East to a more specific concern of the Cold War conflict between the United States and the Soviet Union.

Read Closely: Purpose Pay attention to the motives that a speaker attributes to the subjects of his or her speech. Underline the reasons Eisenhower suggests for the Soviet Union's interest in the region.

Read Closely: Symbolism The Middle East, according to Eisenhower, has a unique place in human history. Circle some of the symbolic meanings he ascribes to the Middle East.

The Region's Strategic Importance

The Middle East became a flashpoint for U.S. foreign policy after World War II ended, specifically with the creation of the State of Israel. In 1947, the United Nations voted to divide the British-controlled **Palestine** into two states—one Arab and one Jewish. The U.N. action resulted in violence between Jews and Arabs. In May 1948, **Israel** declared itself an independent state. Both the United States and the Soviet Union supported this development.

Most Arab nations objected to U.S. support of Israel even though they too received U.S. economic aid. Arab resentment against both Israel and the United States grew in the postwar years. This allowed the Soviet Union to gain influence in the Middle East, especially in Syria. In 1957, President Eisenhower moved to address this spreading Soviet influence. He established the U.S. policy of sending troops to any Middle Eastern nation that requested help against communism. The Eisenhower Doctrine was first tested in Lebanon in 1958. The presence of U.S. troops in Lebanon helped that country's government deal successfully with a Communist challenge.

The history of the Middle East in modern times has been marked by civil wars, revolutions, assassinations, invasions, and border wars. In dealing with each conflict, U.S. policymakers tried to balance three main interests:

1. support to the democratic State of Israel

2. support for Arab states to ensure a steady flow of Middle Eastern oil to the United States and its allies

3. prevention of increased Soviet Union influence in the region

A Volatile, Important Region From 1948 to 1973, Israel fought four wars with its Arab neighbors.

Wars	Outcome
1948–1949	Arab states attacked Israel in a failed attempt to crush the newly independent Jewish state.
Suez Crisis, 1956	Israel joined France and Great Britain in attacking Egypt. (After the United States condemned the attack, Israel withdrew.)
Six-Day War, 1967	Israel defeated Jordan, Syria, and Egypt in six days, occupied the bordering territories of the Golan Heights (Syria), the Sinai Peninsula and Gaza Strip (Egypt), and the West Bank (Jordan).
Yom Kippur War, 1973	Arab nations led by Egypt and Syria attacked Israel on the Jewish holy day of Yom Kippur. After fierce fighting and initial Arab victories, Israel mounted a successful counter-attack.

Civic Literacy:
Altered Worldview
After World War II, the United States began taking a more active and interventionist role in political and military conflicts across the globe. This was a marked break from the country's mainly isolationist approach to world affairs in its first 150 years. The Middle East has been the most consistent region for U.S. intervention over the past 70 years.

Territories Gained by Israel During the Six Day War, 1967

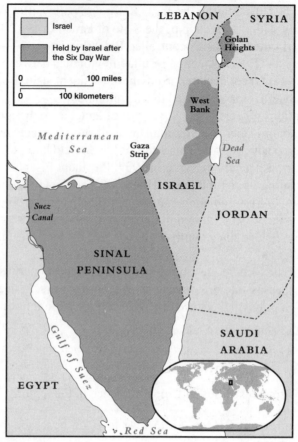

Map legend:
- Israel
- Held by Israel after the Six Day War

Scale: 0 – 100 miles; 0 – 100 kilometers

Map labels: LEBANON, SYRIA, Golan Heights, Mediterranean Sea, West Bank, Gaza Strip, Dead Sea, ISRAEL, Suez Canal, JORDAN, SINAI PENINSULA, Gulf of Suez, SAUDI ARABIA, EGYPT, Red Sea

During the Yom Kippur War, the United States conducted what became known as shuttle diplomacy. President Nixon's Secretary of State Henry Kissinger traveled back and forth between the warring nations to arrange a cease-fire. At stake was not only the security of Israel but also U.S.-Soviet relations. The United States supported Israel in the conflict while the Soviets supported Syria. A cease-fire was finally arranged after Israeli troops had successfully crossed into Egyptian territory. The end of the military crisis led immediately to the beginning of an economic crisis. Angered by U.S. support of Israel, several Arab nations announced an embargo on the shipment of oil to the United States and its Western allies.

The Oil Crises The Arab-Israeli war made Americans aware of their dependence on foreign oil. Arab countries used their control of Middle East oil fields to punish the United States for its support of Israel. Saudi Arabia, Iraq, Iran, and other nations were members of the **Organization of Petroleum Exporting Countries (OPEC)**. The 1973 Arab oil embargo on the sale of their oil to the United States made worldwide oil prices soar. This only added to the woes of the American economy. Between 1973 and 1974, the price of a barrel of oil jumped from $3 to $11.

The effects of increased oil prices went well beyond a rise in the price of gasoline. Manufacturing, services, construction—everything costs more when oil prices increase. The U.S. automobile industry was badly hurt. American consumers bought fewer American cars and more of the smaller, fuel-efficient imports from Japan and Europe. The oil shortage also led to long lines at gas stations. Presidents Nixon and Ford both urged Americans to conserve energy in their homes and on the road. OPEC eventually lifted its embargo in 1974. But it continued to limit production to keep oil prices high. When the crisis passed, however, the United States became even more dependent on foreign oil.

President **Jimmy Carter** had to deal with a second oil crisis in 1979. A political revolution in Iran caused a major cutback in that country's oil production. Oil prices climbed from about $11 a barrel to $40 a barrel. The shock to the world economy was severe. At U.S. gas stations, motorists waited in long lines to refill their tanks. They also had to pay more than a dollar a gallon for gas. (It cost about 80 cents a gallon before the oil shortage.) This second oil crisis reminded Americans that they were at the mercy of OPEC and upheavals in the Middle East. President Carter had already persuaded Congress to set up a new cabinet department—the Department of Energy. He urged the department to expand its search for practical forms of energy other than oil. In 1980, Congress approved $20 billion in research funds to develop synthetic fuels.

Read Closely: Unintended Consequences
Identify instances where one course of action leads to an unforeseen result. U.S. intervention in the Middle East in the 1970s was based on Eisenhower Doctrine policies. The oil embargo's effect on the U.S. economy was felt almost immediately. Why might the OPEC nations have chosen an embargo as a response to U.S. intervention in the Middle East?

U.S. Middle East Policy

President Jimmy Carter, elected in 1976, attempted to reduce tensions between Israel and its Arab neighbors. In 1978, he persuaded Egypt's president Anwar Sadat and Israel's prime minister Menachem Begin to meet informally to discuss peace at Camp David, the presidential compound in Maryland. For thirteen days, Carter worked with the two sides to find a way to resolve their differences. To the surprise of many, the three leaders announced that they had reached an agreement. In 1979, Egypt and Israel signed a peace treaty based on the Camp David Accords:

- Israel was to return the Sinai Peninsula to Egypt.

- Egypt formally recognized Israel as an independent nation.

- Israel and Egypt pledged to respect the border between them.

Many Egyptians and other Arabs bitterly condemned Sadat for making peace with Israel. Begin also faced severe criticism within his country for returning the Sinai Peninsula to Egypt. For their courage in agreeing to make peace with a former enemy, Anwar Sadat and Menachem Begin received the Nobel Peace Prize in 1978. Sadat's brave move for peace, unfortunately, cost him his life. Muslim extremists assassinated the Egyptian leader in 1981.

Carter faced Cold War complications in the Middle East during his presidency, as well. The United States and Soviet Union had coexisted under the Nixon administration policy of détente through much of the 1970s. But this policy changed after the Soviet invasion of Afghanistan, a Muslim nation located on the Soviet Union's southern border.

In 1978, a rebellion broke out in Afghanistan against the Soviet-backed Communist government. The Soviets invaded Afghanistan in December 1979 in an attempt to crush the rebellion. The movement of Soviet troops alarmed the Carter administration. U.S. officials feared that the Soviets might use Afghanistan as a base to seize oil fields in the Persian Gulf.

To punish the Soviets for their aggression, Carter instituted a grain embargo that reduced U.S. grain shipments to the Soviet Union. He also announced that U.S. athletes would not participate in the 1980 Moscow Summer Olympics. Additionally, Carter established the U.S. policy to use any means necessary to protect its interests in the Persian Gulf region. This included military force. Because of the Soviet invasion of Afghanistan, the era of détente between the superpowers effectively ended.

Read Closely: Turning Point
Look for actions and reactions that make an important difference in the course of history. The Camp David Accords were an important milestone in 20th-century Middle East politics. Why do you think Begin and Sadat both took the risk in agreeing to the Camp David Accords?

The Iran Hostage Crisis In 1979, Iranian revolutionaries broke into the U.S. Embassy in Iran's capital, Tehran. They captured 62 Americans and held 52 as hostages for more than a year. Many Iranians were angered by past U.S. policies toward their country. In 1953, the United States had helped overthrow the elected Iranian government, replacing it with a monarchy under Shah Mohammad Reza Pahlavi. In return, the Shah let the United States use Iran as a base for spying on the Soviet Union. Some Iranians condemned the Shah for brutally suppressing dissent. To do this, he used his secret police service, which was organized and trained with help from U.S. intelligence services.

Source: Wikimedia Commons

Iranian captors parade blindfolded U.S. hostages for the cameras.

Fundamentalist Muslims, whose leader was the exiled **Ayatollah Khomeini**, opposed the Shah, in part for modernizing Iran rather than following their interpretation of Islam. In 1979, Khomeini led a successful revolution against the Shah, who escaped the country and ultimately entered the United States for medical treatment. The continuing support of the Shah by the United States greatly angered the Iranian revolutionaries. In response, they stormed the U.S. Embassy in Tehran and seized and held American diplomats and citizens. The revolutionaries demanded that the Shah be returned to Iran for trial in exchange for the release of the hostages. Carter refused, saying that "the United States will not yield to blackmail."

In April 1980, Carter attempted a military rescue of the hostages. But the rescue effort failed when the helicopters carrying U.S. troops broke down in the Iranian desert. The Shah died in July 1980. However, months passed without any change in the hostage situation. The standoff with Iran over American hostages cast doubt on Carter's ability to successfully lead the country. This ultimately contributed to Carter's lost bid for reelection in 1980. On the day Carter left office, January 20, 1981—inauguration day for the new president Ronald Reagan—Iran announced the release of the hostages, 444 days after their capture.

Tragedy in Lebanon Early in his first term, President Reagan faced crisis in the Middle East as well. In the mid-1970s, Christian and Muslim factions in Lebanon, just north of Israel, erupted in what became an ongoing civil war. Syria, neighboring Lebanon to the east, intervened by supporting the radical Palestine Liberation Organization (PLO). Israel sent troops into southern Lebanon to retaliate for PLO terrorist attacks on Israel. In 1982, Israel bombarded the Lebanese capital Beirut and demanded and won a Palestinian withdrawal from the city.

President Reagan sought to keep the peace in Beirut and assist in the United Nations' supervised withdrawal. He ordered U.S. Marines to the embattled city as peacekeepers. The effort ended in tragedy on October 23, 1983, when terrorists exploded a massive truck bomb at the Marine barracks near Beirut, killing 241 Americans. (Fifty-eight French paratroopers were killed in a similar attack that day.) Four months later, President Reagan removed the troops.

Application: Interpret a Primary Source

Read the excerpt and answer the questions that follow it.

Elie Wiesel, Nobel Prize Acceptance Speech, December 10, 1986

Human rights are being violated on every continent. More people are oppressed than free. How can one not be sensitive to their plight? Human suffering anywhere concerns men and women everywhere. That applies also to Palestinians to whose plight I am sensitive but whose methods I deplore when they lead to violence. Violence is not the answer. Terrorism is the most dangerous of answers. They are frustrated, that is understandable, something must be done. The refugees and their misery. The children and their fear. The uprooted and their hopelessness. Something must be done about their situation. Both the Jewish people and the Palestinian people have lost too many sons and daughters and have shed too much blood. This must stop, and all attempts to stop it must be encouraged. Israel will cooperate, I am sure of that. I trust Israel for I have faith in the Jewish people. Let Israel be given a chance, let hatred and danger be removed from their horizons, and there will be peace in and around the Holy Land. Please understand my deep and total commitment to Israel: if you could remember what I remember, you would understand. Israel is the only nation in the world whose existence is threatened. Should Israel lose but one war, it would mean her end and ours as well. But I have faith. Faith in the God of Abraham, Isaac, and Jacob, and even in His creation. Without it no action would be possible. And action is the only remedy to indifference, the most insidious danger of all. Isn't that the meaning of Alfred Nobel's [the inventor of dynamite who founded the Nobel Prizes] legacy? Wasn't his fear of war a shield against war?

Source: Elie Wiesel, Nobel Prize Acceptance Speech, December 10, 1986

1. Author Wiesel survived the Nazi concentration camps during World War II and became an advocate for human rights throughout his life. How might his Nobel speech have been informed by his experience in World War II?

_____

_____

2. Why does Wiesel identify indifference as "the most insidious danger of all"?

_____

_____

3. What do you think Wiesel's primary purpose was in his speech accepting the Nobel Peace prize?

_____

_____

**Conceptual Understanding
11.9d** A combination of factors contributed to the end of the Cold War, including American policies and Soviet economic and political problems that led to the loss of Soviet control over Eastern Europe.

President Reagan's election in 1980 increased hostilities between the United States and the Soviet Union. The Reagan Administration's policies put constant pressure on the Soviet Union at a time when the unsustainable nature of the Soviet system in the modern world was becoming more and more clear. By 1985, with the rise to power of leader Mikhail Gorbachev, the Soviet Union began opening its society and economy to western influences.

Analyze a Primary Source

President Ronald Reagan, Remarks at the Brandenburg Gate, June 12, 1987

Read Closely: Metaphor
Metaphors can be powerful symbols—a writer can use metaphors to imprint a visual meaning on the reader. Notice how Reagan follows his description of the wall that divides Germans by calling it a "scar" on the land and people.

Behind me stands a wall that encircles the free sectors of this city, part of a vast system of barriers that divides the entire continent of Europe. From the Baltic, south, those barriers cut across Germany in a gash of barbed wire, concrete, dog runs, and guard towers. Farther south, there may be no visible, no obvious wall. But there remain armed guards and checkpoints all the same—still a restriction on the right to travel, still an instrument to impose upon ordinary men and women the will of a totalitarian state. Yet it is here in Berlin where the wall emerges most clearly; here, cutting across your city, where the news photo and the television screen have imprinted this brutal division of a continent upon the mind of the world. Standing before the Brandenburg Gate, every man is a German, separated from his fellow men. Every man is a Berliner, forced to look upon a scar.

Read Closely: Contrast
Writers will sometimes contrast opposing ideas to draw a clear distinction between them. Circle examples where Reagan contrasts the small steps the Soviet Union is taking with U.S. ideals.

And now the Soviets themselves may, in a limited way, be coming to understand the importance of freedom. We hear much from Moscow about a new policy of reform and openness. Some political prisoners have been released. Certain foreign news broadcasts are no longer being jammed. Some economic enterprises have been permitted to operate with greater freedom from state control.

Are these the beginnings of profound changes in the Soviet state? Or are they token gestures, intended to raise false hopes in the West, or to strengthen the Soviet system without changing it? We welcome change and openness; for we believe that freedom and security go together, that the advance of human liberty can only strengthen the cause of world peace. There is one sign the Soviets can make that would be unmistakable, that would advance dramatically the cause of freedom and peace.

Read Closely: Call to Action
Reagan makes a bold call to action for Gorbachev and the Soviet Union to prove they are serious about making reforms. Notice how Reagan combines the wall metaphor with the contrasting language of freedom.

General Secretary Gorbachev, if you seek peace, if you seek prosperity for the Soviet Union and Eastern Europe, if you seek liberalization: Come here to this gate! Mr. Gorbachev, open this gate! Mr. Gorbachev, tear down this wall!

Source: President Ronald Reagan, Remarks at the Brandenburg Gate, June 12, 1987

Contributing Factors

In 1972, President Nixon and Soviet leader Leonid Brezhnev signed the first Strategic Arms Limitation Treaty (SALT I). It applied only to the future production of defensive nuclear missiles. The two superpowers agreed to set an upper limit on the number of anti-ballistic missiles (ABMs) that each would produce. They hoped that having fewer missiles to defend against a nuclear attack would make each country less likely to launch an attack.

In 1979, President Carter and Soviet Premier Brezhnev signed a second strategic arms treaty, SALT II. It established a ceiling on the number of long-range offensive missiles that each superpower could produce and limited the number of cruise missiles, which could be launched from airplanes and submarines. Many members of the U.S. Senate feared that the SALT II treaty left the Soviet Union with a military advantage. But the Senate never had a chance to vote either for or against SALT II. Early in 1980, President Carter withdrew the treaty from consideration after he received reports that Soviet troops had invaded Afghanistan. Carter had worked hard through diplomatic means, but his labors were undercut.

President Ronald Reagan, on the other hand, had never believed that the Soviet Union could be trusted. In his 1980 campaign for the presidency, Reagan promised to increase military spending so that the United States could once again take the lead in the arms race. He kept his promise. In his first year in office, 1981, he asked Congress to approve huge increases in the defense budget for building new weapons systems. He wanted $1.5 trillion spent over a five-year period on new bombers, submarines, and missiles. Congress approved most of his requests.

The most ambitious and controversial of Reagan's proposals was to develop a "space shield"—the Strategic Defense Initiative (SDI). Critics of the idea thought it sounded like the popular movie *Star Wars*. The weapons would orbit Earth and, from outer space, shoot down Soviet missiles before they could reach U.S. targets. Though skeptical about SDI's cost and practicality, Congress voted for funds to explore the idea.

New Soviet Leadership Soviet leader Leonid Brezhnev died in 1982. He had presided over the slow decline of his country's economy. His first successor died after only 15 months in office, the second after 13 months. In March 1985, the Soviet Communist Party selected **Mikhail Gorbachev** to serve as general secretary of the Communist Party. Relatively young and energetic, he recognized national problems and proposed sweeping reforms to revitalize the Soviet system. For example, he instituted *glasnost*, or "openness," in which citizens were free to express their opinions openly about public issues without fear of reprisals. Glasnost marked a dramatic break with the previous system in which critics of government policy were often arrested and imprisoned.

To modernize the financial system, Gorbachev enacted a set of economic reforms called *perestroika*, "restructuring," which had far-reaching results:

- It loosened central government control of the economy.

- It allowed local bureaucrats and factory managers to make independent decisions.

- It allowed the mixing of private businesses and government welfare.

- It accepted that privately owned businesses had an incentive (the profit motive) to produce goods more efficiently than in the old centralized system.

> **Speak and Listen: Conflict**
> With a partner, discuss ways that nations can respond to conflicts. Discuss specific tools from the diplomatic, economic, and military spheres.

Gorbachev realized that the Soviet economy could not improve if a large percentage of the nation's resources went to its armed forces. Gorbachev was therefore eager to meet with U.S. leaders and reduce the costly and dangerous arms race.

Gorbachev and Reagan met three times to discuss arms control and other issues. At their third meeting in Washington, D.C. (December 1987), the two leaders made a significant breakthrough by signing a treaty to reduce missiles in Europe. These were intermediate range missiles that could travel hundreds of miles (compared with longer-range intercontinental ballistic missiles [ICBMs]). The Intermediate-range Nuclear Forces Treaty (INF Treaty) went far beyond the SALT treaties. Instead of just limiting future production of weapons, the INF Treaty dictated that all intermediate-range missiles in Europe be removed and dismantled. Gorbachev and Reagan established 1990 as the year when Europe would be completely free of intermediate-range nuclear weapons.

Source: Wikimedia Commons

Gorbachev and Reagan signing the INF Treaty at the White House, 1987

Read Closely: Turning Point
As you read, look for important developments that alter relationships or change the path of history. Why was the 1987 INF Treaty between the United States and the Soviet Union a pivotal event in the Cold War?

Historians offer a variety of causes for what led to the end of the Cold War and the subsequent collapse of the Soviet Union. Some cite the collapse of the Soviet economy after 75 years of Communist central planning. Others cite the U.S. military buildup under Reagan. He believed that peace through strength was the most effective means of dealing with the Soviet Union. As a result, defense spending grew 35 percent, creating the largest peacetime army in U.S. history. But Reagan also saw that circumstances had provided him the opportunity to engage Russia and enter negotiations. Indeed, Gorbachev felt that it was Reagan's willingness to limit arms, not build them, that most influenced the Russians. This allowed Gorbachev to defeat his conservative critics and begin the reforms that led to the end of the Cold War.

The Berlin Wall Falls

The collapse of Europe's Communist governments occurred with dramatic suddenness. In 1989, Poland held free elections, and the Communists lost. Because Gorbachev favored reform and openness, the Soviet Union accepted the results of the Polish elections. Soon, one country after another in Eastern Europe followed Poland's example. The voters of Hungary, Czechoslovakia, and Romania replaced single-party Communist regimes with multiparty political systems. For the first time in half a century, Eastern Europe was free from outside control. The "iron curtain" dividing Europe into two hostile camps was beginning to open.

At a summit in Malta, an island in the Mediterranean Sea in 1989, President George H.W. Bush and Soviet leader Gorbachev signed an agreement to substantially reduce their stockpiles of weapons. The United States also agreed to provide food and economic aid to the Soviet Union. Bush noted that the end of the Cold War had freed the United Nations to do its intended job: keep the peace. For his part, Chairman Gorbachev stated, "The arms race, mistrust, psychological and ideological struggle, all those should be things of the past."

East Germany was the last country to shed its Communist government. In November 1989, Germans on both sides of the Berlin Wall stormed the wall and tore it down. The wall had been a hated symbol of German division and the Cold War. East Germans accepted the West German government as their own. Germany was reunited in October 1990. The government of the new Germany pledged never again to take military action against its European neighbors.

Source: Wikimedia Commons

The Berlin Wall in 1988

Read Closely:
Cause and Effect
Recognize how causation in a text is sometimes not overtly stated but inferred by the way facts are presented. East and West Germans tore down the Berlin Wall in 1989. How might that political act have effected ensuing developments in the Soviet Union?

Because of large military expenditures and inefficient central planning, the Soviet economy could no longer deliver goods and services to its people. Critics called for an end of the Soviet system. In June 1991, Russian official Boris Yeltsin was elected head of the Russian Republic. Yeltsin was a reformer who had resigned from the Communist Party and who called for greater political openness.

In December 1991, after months of turmoil, the Soviet Union ceased to exist as a single nation. In its place were 12 independent republics, joined in what was known as the Commonwealth of Independent States (CIS). Estonia, Latvia, and Lithuania became independent countries that were promptly recognized as such by the UN.

Application: Interpret a Primary Source

Read the excerpt and answer the questions that follow it.

"Reagan and the Russians," *The Atlantic Monthly,* February 1994

The Soviet Union's defense spending did not rise or fall in response to American military expenditures. Revised estimates by the Central Intelligence Agency indicate that Soviet expenditures on defense remained more or less constant throughout the 1980s. . . .

A . . . more persuasive reason for the Soviet economic decline is the rigid "command economy" imposed by Stalin in the early 1930s. It did not reward individual or collective effort; it absolved Soviet producers from the discipline of the market; and it gave power to officials who could not be held accountable by consumers. . . . The command economy . . . was not a response to American military spending. The Soviet Union lost the Cold War, but it was not defeated by American defense spending. . . .

By the time Gorbachev became General Secretary, in March of 1985, he was deeply committed to domestic reform and fundamental changes in Soviet foreign policy. . . .

Gorbachev was not intimidated by the military programs of the Reagan Administration. "These were unnecessary and wasteful expenditures that we were not going to match," he told us. . . .

The Carter-Reagan military buildup did not defeat the Soviet Union. On the contrary, it prolonged the Cold War. Gorbachev's determination to reform an economy crippled in part by defense spending urged by special interests, but far more by structural rigidities, fueled his persistent search for an accommodation with the West. That persistence, not SDI, ended the Cold War.

Source: "Reagan and the Russians," Richard Ned Lebow and Janice Gross Stein, *The Atlantic Monthly,* February 1994

1. How does the article reflect upon the actions the United States and the Soviet Union took during the Reagan administration?

_____

_____

_____

_____

_____

2. How did Gorbachev's diplomatic agreements with Reagan about nuclear weapons affect his ability to tackle the USSR's worsening economic issues?

_____

_____

_____

_____

_____

3. How would you describe the purpose of this article? What kinds of evidence do the authors provide to support that purpose?

_____

_____

_____

_____

_____

Multiple-Choice Questions

Questions 1–3 refer to the excerpt below.

A. Nuclear Scientists on the Dangers of a Nuclear Arms Race

Secrecy will inevitably lead to an atomic armaments race: Under any conditions a large part of the scientific and industrialization of any great power will be directed toward the utilization of nuclear energy. A policy of secrecy is bound to lead to one of suspicion. Scientists of other countries will be spurred on to develop atomic bombs of their own in self-defense. This in turn, will lead to further emphasis on the military applications on our own part. The result will be an armaments race, with all its disastrous possibility.

The second large problem raised by the atomic bomb is that of its *tremendous destructive possibilities*. During the war years, all of our effort on the application of nuclear energy has been directed toward its destructive possibilities. Although much has been written about the wonderful new age on which we are about to enter, there is very little scientific information available on the subject of the constructive possibilities of the utilization of nuclear energy. However, we have been made strongly aware of the dangers inherent in the mishandling of this tremendous force by the peoples of the world. We have seen in the case of Hiroshima and Nagasaki that one crude, pioneering atomic bomb is sufficient to destroy a city of medium size. It is certain that further development will result in bombs of vastly greater destructive potential. The Pearl Harbor attack which destroyed most of Pacific Fleet may be dwarfed in a future war by a disaster in which as much as a quarter of our population and the major part of our industry will suddenly disappear. This may even be a conservative estimate of the damage that will occur before we are in a position to retaliate, if retaliation be any longer possible. It will be a small consolation to have the largest supply of the world's best bombs; it may be too late to use them. It is possible that we may not even know who our attackers are.

Source: Preliminary statement of the Association of Manhattan District Scientists, New York City Area, ca. August 1945

1. What evidence do the scientists give in support of their claims of the destructive possibilities of nuclear energy?

   1. They cite the devastation of Hiroshima and Nagasaki.
   2. They mention the destruction of the Pacific Fleet in the Pearl Harbor attack.
   3. They say that we have the largest supply of the world's best bombs.
   4. They say that there is little scientific information available on the constructive possibilities of nuclear energy.

2. Based on the content of this excerpt, which of the following represents the most plausible claim?

   1. Nuclear energy will have many constructive uses.

   2. The world is about to enter a wonderful new age.

   3. In the event of a nuclear war, much of our population and industrial capability would be destroyed.

   4. The bombing of Hiroshima and Nagasaki could have been avoided.

3. Why do the scientists think that secrecy is a problem?

   1. It can turn our allies into potential enemies.

   2. The destructive possibilities of atomic energy can only be known by bombing cities.

   3. If a nuclear war breaks out, we may not even know who our attackers are.

   4. It leads to suspicion, which will lead other countries to develop their own nuclear arsenals.

Questions 4 and 5 refer to the excerpt below.

B. The War Powers Act

SECTION 1. This joint resolution may be cited as the "War Powers Resolution".

   SEC. 2. (a) It is the purpose of this joint resolution to fulfill the intent of the framers of the Constitution of the United States and insure that the collective judgement of both the Congress and the President will apply to the introduction of United States Armed Forces into hostilities, or into situations where imminent involvement in hostilities is clearly indicated by the circumstances, and to the continued use of such forces in hostilities or in such situations.

   (b) Under article I, section 8, of the Constitution, it is specifically provided that the Congress shall have the power to make all laws necessary and proper for carrying into execution, not only its own powers but also all other powers vested by the Constitution in the Government of the United States, or in any department or officer thereof.

   (c) The constitutional powers of the President as Commander-in-Chief to introduce United States Armed Forces into hostilities, or into situations where imminent involvement in hostilities is clearly indicated by the circumstances, are exercised only pursuant to (1) a declaration of war, (2) specific statutory authorization, or (3) a national emergency created by attack upon the United States, its territories or possessions, or its armed forces.

   SEC. 3. The President in every possible instance shall consult with Congress before introducing United States Armed Forces into hostilities or into situations where imminent involvement in hostilities is clearly indicated by the circumstances, and after every such introduction shall consult regularly with the Congress until United States Armed Forces are no longer engaged in hostilities or have been removed from such situations.

Source: Joint Resolution Concerning the War Powers of Congress and the President, November 7, 1973

4. How does this document illustrate the impact of time and place?

   1. It was produced immediately after World War II, when the United States hoped to avoid future wars.

   2. It was produced in response to the war in Vietnam to keep the United States out of future wars of that nature.

   3. It was produced during the Iran hostage situation to prevent the United States from invading Iran.

   4. It was produced during Operation Desert Storm to limit the president's power to declare war.

5. How does this document represent a response to a problem?

   1. It is an attempt by Congress to revoke the president's role as Commander-in-Chief.

   2. It is an attempt by Congress to end future wars and remove troops immediately from areas of conflict.

   3. It is an attempt by Congress to limit the president's power in the future.

   4. It is an attempt by Congress to make the president solely responsible for any future wars.

Questions 6–8 refer to the excerpt below.

C. Preamble to the Camp David Accords

The search for peace in the Middle East must be guided by the following:

The agreed basis for a peaceful settlement of the conflict between Israel and its neighbors is United Nations Security Council Resolution 242, in all its parts.

After four wars during 30 years, despite intensive human efforts, the Middle East, which is the cradle of civilization and the birthplace of three great religions, does not enjoy the blessings of peace. The people of the Middle East yearn for peace so that the vast human and natural resources of the region can be turned to the pursuits of peace and so that this area can become a model for coexistence and cooperation among nations.

The historic initiative of President Sadat in visiting Jerusalem and the reception accorded to him by the parliament, government and people of Israel, and the reciprocal visit of Prime Minister Begin to Ismailia, the peace proposals made by both leaders, as well as the warm reception of these missions by the peoples of both countries, have created an unprecedented opportunity for peace which must not be lost if this generation and future generations are to be spared the tragedies of war. . . .

Peace requires respect for the sovereignty, territorial integrity and political independence of every state in the area and their right to live in peace within secure and recognized boundaries free from threats or acts of force. Progress toward that goal can accelerate movement toward a new era of reconciliation in the Middle East marked by cooperation in promoting economic development, in maintaining stability and in assuring security.

Security is enhanced by a relationship of peace and by cooperation between nations which enjoy normal relations. In addition, under the terms of peace treaties, the parties can, on the basis of reciprocity, agree to special security arrangements such as demilitarized zones, limited armaments areas, early warning stations, the presence of international forces, liaison, agreed measures for monitoring and other arrangements that they agree are useful.

Source: Accords between Egypt and Israel at Camp David, September 17, 1978

6. Which of the following best describes the stakeholders affected by the Camp David Accords?

   1. The United States and Israel
   2. Egypt and the Palestinians
   3. Israel and the Palestinians
   4. The people of the Middle East

7. Why were the Camp David Accords necessary?

   1. There had been four wars in 30 years in the Middle East.
   2. Israel and Egypt had both developed nuclear weapons.
   3. The United States no longer wanted to defend Israel in case of attack.
   4. The Suez Crisis had brought the world to the brink of a third world war.

8. How do the Camp David Accords illustrate continuity and change in history?

   1. They finally brought to an end the hard feelings that Jews had felt since being held in captivity in Egypt during biblical times.
   2. They ended hostilities between Egypt and Israel, although tensions in the Middle East continue to this day.
   3. Israel and Egypt finally recognized the need for a separate Palestinian state.
   4. They made it possible for Israel to return the seat of government to its historic capital, Jerusalem.

Short-Essay Questions

Study the two documents and answer the question that follows.

D. Senator McCarthy on "Enemies from Within"

As one of our outstanding historical figures once said, "When a great democracy is destroyed, it will not be from enemies from without, but rather because of enemies from within." . . .

The reason why we find ourselves in a position of impotency is not because our only powerful potential enemy has sent men to invade our shores . . . but rather because of the traitorous actions of those who have been treated so well by this Nation. It has not been the less fortunate, or members of minority groups who have been traitorous to this Nation, but rather those who have had all the benefits that the wealthiest Nation on earth has had to offer . . . the finest homes, the finest college education and the finest jobs in government we can give.

This is glaringly true in the State Department. There the bright young men who are born with silver spoons in their mouths are the ones who have been most traitorous. . . .

I have here in my hand a list of 205 . . . a list of names that were made known to the Secretary of State as being members of the Communist Party and who nevertheless are still working and shaping policy in the State Department. . . .

As you know, very recently the Secretary of State proclaimed his loyalty to a man guilty of what has always been considered as the most abominable of all crimes—being a traitor to the people who gave him a position of great trust—high treason. . . .

He has lighted the spark which is resulting in a moral uprising and will end only when the whole sorry mess of twisted, warped thinkers are swept from the national scene so that we may have a new birth of honesty and decency in government.

Source: Senator Joseph R. McCarthy, Lincoln Day Speech in Wheeling, West Virginia, February 9, 1950

E. "McCarthy Cries Again"

A couple of years ago Senator Joe McCarthy buckled on his armor and, like a twentieth-century Don Quixote, set out to slay the dragon of American Communism singlehanded. His intentions seemed noble as those of the good knight. But also like the good knight, who attacked a procession of monks and a flock of sheep under the impression that they were brigands and ogres, he got a little confused about the targets of his sallies.

Thus it has come to pass, as his crusade continues, that anyone who takes issue with him assumes the look of the Red dragon itself. Disagreement becomes lies or crookedness. An adverse editorial comment is automatically a "left-wing smear." And the senator charges treason against a countryman as recklessly as Don Quixote charged the windmill.

Mr. McCarthy has had a busy time of it, because there are a great many people who approve the purpose of his crusade, but object strongly to his methods. There are many publications which feel the same way. One of them is *Collier's*. Another is *Time*. And we at *Collier's* feel just a little discriminated against because, so far, the senator has ignored us while singling out *Time* and accusing it of "twisting and distorting the facts about my (McCarthy's) fight to expose and remove Communists from government."

This charge apparently grew out of a *Time* cover story on Senator McCarthy. The senator had earlier attacked it as a "vicious and malicious lie." But recently he employed a new tactic which was definitely not cricket.

Backed by the prestige of his office, he sent a letter to "practically all *Time* advertisers," according to his own statement, which, while it did not come right out and ask them to take their business elsewhere, suggested that they were doing their country a disservice by their continued support of the magazine. . . .

Senator McCarthy has set himself up as the final authority on loyalty and Americanism. He insists that his accusations are not to be doubted, and his judgment is not to be questioned. Yet, a few weeks after he wrote his letter to *Time*'s advertisers, he testified in Syracuse, New York that the *Washington Post* and the *New York* (Communist) *Daily Worker* "parallel each other quite closely in editorials." And when he was asked whether he would consider the *Christian Science Monitor* a "left-wing smear paper," he replied, "I can't answer yes or no."

Those are the statements of a man who is either woefully unperceptive or wholly irresponsible. And when such a man asks that his wild-swinging attacks be accepted without question, he is, to borrow his own words, not only ridiculous but dangerous.

Source: "McCarthy Cries Again," Editorial in *Collier's*, August 2, 1952

1. In a short essay, describe the historical context surrounding the two documents above. Then identify and explain the cause-and-effect relationship between the ideas described in these documents.

Study the two documents and answer the question that follows.

F. A Vietnam Veteran Speaks Out Against the War

In our opinion and from our experience, there is nothing in South Vietnam which could happen that realistically threatens the United States of America. And to attempt to justify the loss of one American life in Vietnam, Cambodia or Laos by linking such loss to the preservation of freedom, which those misfits supposedly abuse, is to us the height of criminal hypocrisy, and it is that kind of hypocrisy which we feel has torn this country apart.

We found that not only was it a civil war, an effort by a people who had for years been seeking their liberation from any colonial influence whatsoever, but also we found that the Vietnamese whom we had enthusiastically molded after our own image were hard put to take up the fight against the threat we were supposedly saving them from.

We found most people didn't even know the difference between communism and democracy. They only wanted to work in rice paddies without helicopters strafing them and bombs with napalm burning their villages and tearing their country apart. They wanted everything to do with the war, particularly with this foreign presence of the United States of America, to leave them alone in peace, and they practiced the art of survival by siding with whichever military force was present at a particular time, be it Viet Cong, North Vietnamese or American.

We found also that all too often American men were dying in those rice paddies for want of support from their allies. We saw first hand how monies from American taxes were used for a corrupt dictatorial regime. We saw that many people in this country had a one-sided idea of who was kept free by the flag, and Blacks provided the highest percentage of casualties. We saw Vietnam ravaged equally by American bombs and search and destroy missions, as well as by Viet Cong terrorism – and yet we listened while this country tried to blame all of the havoc on the Viet Cong.

Source: John Kerry, Speech on behalf of Vietnam Veterans Against the War before the Senate Foreign Relations Committee, April 23, 1971

G. "It Was Vital Not to Lose Vietnam by Force to Communism"

As of this point in my own research, I advance three propositions to explain why, how, and with what expectations the United States became involved in the Vietnam war.

First, U.S. involvement in Vietnam is not mainly or mostly a story of step by step, inadvertent descent into unforeseen quicksand. It is primarily a story of why U.S. leaders considered that it was vital not to lose Vietnam by force to Communism. Our leaders believed Vietnam to be vital not for itself, but for what they thought its "loss" would mean internationally and domestically. Previous involvement made further involvement more unavoidable, and, to this extent, commitments were inherited. But judgments of Vietnam's "vitalness"—beginning with the Korean War—were sufficient in themselves to set the course for escalation.

Second, our Presidents were never actually seeking a military victory in Vietnam. They were doing only what they thought was minimally necessary at each stage to keep Indochina, and later South Vietnam, out of Communist hands. This forced our Presidents to be brakemen, to do less than those who were urging military victory and to reject proposals for disengagement. It also meant that our Presidents wanted a negotiated settlement without fully realizing (though realizing more than their critics) that a civil war cannot be ended by political compromise.

Third, our Presidents and most of their lieutenants were not deluded by optimistic reports of progress and did not proceed on the basis of wishful thinking about winning a military victory in South Vietnam. They recognized that the steps they were taking were not adequate to win the war and that unless Hanoi relented, they would have to do more and more. Their strategy was to persevere in hope that their will to continue—if not the practical effects of their actions—would cause the Communists to relent.

Source: State Department official Leslie H. Gelb, Statement to Senate Committee on Foreign Relations, May 1972

2. In a short essay, describe the historical context surrounding the two documents above. Then analyze and explain how the point of view of Kerry's testimony affects its reliability as a source of evidence.

Civic Literacy Document-Based Essay

Period 3

Document #1

Evalyn Walsh McLean was the wife of the owner of the *Washington Post* and a pillar of Washington Society. She describes the scene as the Bonus Army first entered Washington and marched past her elegant mansion:

"On a day in June, 1932, I saw a dusty automobile truck roll slowly past my house. I saw the unshaven, tired faces of the men who were riding in it standing up. A few were seated at the rear with their legs dangling over the lowered tailboard. On the side of the truck was an expanse of white cloth on which, crudely lettered in black, was a legend, BONUS ARMY.

Other trucks followed in a straggling succession, and. on the sidewalks of Massachusetts Avenue where stroll most of the diplomats and the other fashionables of Washington were some ragged hikers, wearing scraps of old uniforms. The sticks with which they strode along seemed less canes than cudgels. They were not a friendly-looking lot, and I learned they were hiking and riding into the capital along each of its radial avenues; that they had come from every part of the continent. It was not lost on me that those men, passing anyone of my big houses, would see in such rich shelters a kind of challenge.

I was burning, because I felt that crowd of men, women, and children never should have been permitted to swarm across the continent. But I could remember when those same men, with others, had been cheered as they marched down Pennsylvania Avenue. While I recalled those wartime parades, I was reading in the newspapers that the bonus army men were going hungry in Washington."

Source: eyewitnesstohistory.com

1. What conflicting views does Mrs. McLean have of the people in the Bonus Army?

_____

_____

_____

_____

Document #2

March 12, 1933: Fireside Chat 1: On the Banking Crisis

By the afternoon of March 3 scarcely a bank in the country was open to do business. Proclamations temporarily closing them in whole or in part had been issued by the Governors in almost all the states.
It was then that I issued the proclamation providing for the nation-wide bank holiday, and this was the first step in the Government's reconstruction of our financial and economic fabric. The second step was the legislation promptly and patriotically passed by the Congress confirming my proclamation and broadening my powers so that it became possible in view of the requirement of time to entend (sic) the holiday and lift the ban of that holiday gradually. This law also gave authority to develop a program of rehabilitation of our banking facilities. I want to tell our citizens in every part of the Nation that the national Congress -- Republicans and Democrats alike -- showed by this action a devotion to public welfare and a realization of the emergency and the necessity for speed that it is difficult to match in our history.

Source: Millercenter.org

2. How does the new policy of a Bank Holiday change the government's role in the economy?

_____

_____

_____

_____

Document #3

Decision in the Supreme Court case, *Engle v. Vitale* (1962)

Justice Hugo Black wrote: "We think that by using its public school system to encourage recitation of the Regents' prayer, the State of New York has adopted a practice wholly inconsistent with the Establishment Clause…
It is no part of the business of government to compose official prayers for any group of the American people to recite as a part of a religious program carried on by government."

Source: supreme.justia.com

3. What specific right is being protected in the court's decision?

_____

_____

_____

_____

Document #4

Source: Wikimedia Commons

4. How did public expressions of opinion on Vietnam differ from earlier wars?

_____

_____

_____

_____

Document #5

Brown v. Board of Education of Topeka, 1954

   Segregation of White and Negro children in the public schools of a State
solely on the basis of race, pursuant to state laws permitting or requiring
such segregation, denies to Negro children the equal protection of the laws
guaranteed by the Fourteenth Amendment -- even though the physical facilities
and other "tangible" factors of White and Negro schools may be equal.

Source: ourdocuments.gov

5. In what vital way did this case change public policy?

_____

_____

_____

_____

Document #6

Senator Gaylord Nelson address to the first Earth Day crowd in 1970

I congratulate you, who by your presence here today demonstrate your concern and commitment to an issue that is more than just a matter of survival. How we survive is the critical question. Earth Day is dramatic evidence of a broad new national concern that cuts across generations and ideologies. It may be symbolic of a new communication between young and old about our values and priorities. Take advantage of this broad new agreement. Don't drop out of it. Pull together a new national coalition whose objective is to put Gross National Quality on a par with Gross National Product.

Source: Chomsky, Noam, Requiem for the American Dream: The 10 Principles of Concentration of Wealth and Power, 2017

6. What action(s) is being called for by Senator Nelson?

_____

_____

_____

_____

7. **Civic Literacy Document-Based Essay:** Select two documents that illustrate the changing role of the government in the period from 1920–1990 and for each (1) discuss the nature of the change, (2) describe the historical circumstances for the change and (3) discuss to what extent the role of the government was expanded or limited.

CHAPTER 10

U.S. Social and Economic Change (1945–Present)

Chapter Overview

When Eisenhower moved into the White House in 1953, he was the first Republican president in 20 years. Like his predecessors and the presidents who followed him, he was forced to face the difficult issues embedded in U.S. society.

African Americans A new generation of African American leaders emerged to lead the fight for civil rights. They created new organizations to further their cause. Some used sit-ins, boycotts, and marches to protest segregation, while others favored a more militant "Black Power" approach. Repeatedly, the Supreme Court found segregation laws to be unconstitutional. In the 1960s, Congress passed laws to try to guarantee civil rights and voting rights for all Americans.

Equal Rights for Others Other groups also began to demand more rights. Women were tired of being treated as second-class citizens. Native Americans fought assimilation and demanded the U.S. government honor the treaties it had signed. Mexican Americans demanded respect and better wages.

People with disabilities fought to remove barriers that prevented them from fully participating in the life of their communities. Members of the Lesbian, Gay, Bisexual, and Transgender (LGBT) community fought laws that discriminated against people because of their sexual identity.

The Environment A book about the dangers of pesticides sparked a movement to protect the environment. Congress enacted legislation to clean up the air and waterways and to protect endangered species. However, some conservatives opposed much of the program to protect the environment, viewing it as an impediment to free enterprise.

Government's Role Disagreements about what role the federal government should take go all the way back to the battles between the Federalists and Antifederalists in the late 1780s. President Johnson believed that it was up to the government to try to create a just society. President Reagan believed that social programs were a waste of money and that government should play a smaller role.

Civic Literacy: Equity One aspect of human rights is equality of access for all people to basic needs of life. Issues around access to health care and a job that pays a living wage played an important part in many of the movements and policies discussed in this chapter.

New York Social Studies Framework

Key Idea 11.10: U.S. Social and Economic Changes Racial, gender, and socioeconomic inequalities were addressed by individuals, groups, and organizations. Varying political philosophies prompted debates over the role of the federal government in regulating the economy and providing a social safety net.

Source: *New York State Grades 9–12 Social Studies Framework*

Civic Literacy Essay: Write the Conclusion

A strong conclusion helps create unity by circling back to the ideas in your introduction and thesis statement. The conclusion is also a good opportunity to extend and refine the ideas you have developed and woven throughout your essay.

Providing Unity While wrapping up your essay with a return to the ideas in your introduction helps provide unity, simply restating your thesis is not a strong way to end the essay. The conclusion, for example, would be a good place to mention the current state of inequality, such as the Black Lives Matter movement, the higher rates of poverty and hopelessness experienced by African Americans, and the attempts by several states to again restrict minorities' voting rights. This change extends the thesis statement rather than simply repeating it.

Demonstrating Depth An extension of your thesis statement such as the one above also helps demonstrate a deep understanding of the topic by referring to multiple factors, which ideally you will have introduced earlier in your essay. In order to demonstrate a deep understanding, your essay should be more analytical than descriptive. You should try to analyze, evaluate, and/ or create information. For example, you might connect the 14th Amendment's "equal protection" clause and the Jim Crow laws that maintained White supremacy to the Supreme Court decision in *Plessy v. Ferguson* that established the "separate but equal" doctrine for railway cars.

Other ways you can demonstrate a deep and complex understanding are to consider the significance of a source's credibility and limitations and explain why a historical argument is or is not effective. While most of the development of your complex understanding needs to be done within the body of your essay, you can use the conclusion to summarize or extend that understanding.

Application: In your own words, explain how you can use the conclusion of an essay to provide unity and to demonstrate depth of understanding.

_____

_____

_____

_____

Key Terms by Theme

Civics

Brown v. Board of Education of Topeka (p. 333)
Thurgood Marshall (p. 333)
Rosa Parks (p. 333)
Dr. Martin Luther King, Jr. (p. 333)
civil disobedience (p. 333)
Roe v. Wade (p. 342)
Russell Means (p. 342)

Economics

César Chávez (p. 343)
United Farm Workers (UFW) (p. 343)

Reaganomics (p. 350)
Great Recession (p. 351)
Americans with Disabilities Act (p. 344)

Governance

Defense of Marriage Act (DOMA) (p. 345)
Great Society (p. 349)
Barack Obama (p. 352)
Affordable Care Act (ACA) (p. 354)

Identity

National Organization for Women (p. 341)

American Indian Movement (AIM) (p. 342)
Lesbian, Gay, Bisexual, and Transgender (LGBT) (p. 345)

Movement

March on Washington (p. 335)

Social Structures

Betty Friedan (p. 341)
Gloria Steinem (p. 341)
Stonewall Inn riots (p. 345)

Lesson 1 *The Civil Rights Movement*

On August 28, 1963, Martin Luther King, Jr., stood on a speaker's platform near the Lincoln Memorial in Washington, D.C., and spoke to a crowd of more than 200,000 people as well as a huge television audience. In the most famous part of his speech, the civil rights leader spoke of his dream for a democratic nation.

Analyze a Primary Source

"I Have a Dream . . ."

Read Closely: Connections
Speakers will oftentimes make connections between their beliefs or main ideas and those of respected individuals or texts from the past. Dr. King quotes from the Declaration of Independence. Underline the part of that quotation that summarizes what the rest of this selection is about.

Read Closely: Rhetorical Device
A rhetorical device is a tactic that a writer or speaker uses to help add emphasis to a certain point or to make it more memorable. Notice Dr. King's skillful use of repetition in this speech, which helps him emphasize important points. Circle the repeated word in the final paragraph that helps us understand Dr. King's point of view.

Read Closely: Details
In the first paragraph, Dr. King refers to the "difficulties of today" that African Americans faced. Notice how he provides details about those difficulties in the second and third paragraphs—and how he contrasts them with a hoped-for future.

I say to you today, my friends, though, even though we face the difficulties of today and tomorrow, I still have a dream. . . . I have a dream that one day this nation will rise up and live out the true meaning of its creed: "We hold these truths to be self-evident; that all men are created equal." . . .

I have a dream that my four little children will one day live in a nation where they will not be judged by the color of their skin but by the content of their character. . . . I have a dream that one day in Alabama, . . . little Black boys and Black girls will be able to join hands with little White boys and White girls as sisters and brothers. . . .

This is the faith with which I return to the South. . . . With this faith we will be able to transform the jangling discords of our nation into a beautiful symphony of brotherhood. With this faith we will be able to work together, . . . knowing that we will be free one day.

Source: Martin Luther King, Jr., "I Have a Dream . . ."
For the full text of Dr. King's famous and moving speech, look online.

Early Events and Gains of the Movement

Brown v. Board of Education of Topeka Founded in 1909, the National Association for the Advancement of Colored People (NAACP) took a leading role in the fight for African Americans' civil rights during the 1950s and 1960s. One of its biggest victories was in the case of ***Brown v. Board of Education of Topeka***. That 1954 Supreme Court decision marked a turning point in the movement for civil rights for African Americans.

Previously, in the case of *Plessy* v. *Ferguson* (1896), the Supreme Court had ruled that segregation did not violate the Constitution, as long as there were "separate but equal" facilities for both Black and White Americans.

In the early 1950s, the school system of Topeka, Kansas, was segregated by law. Oliver Brown's African American family lived closer to an all-White elementary school than to an all-Black one. When he tried to enroll his daughter Linda in the White school, school officials turned him down. The NAACP filed a lawsuit on Brown's behalf against the Topeka Board of Education. When a federal court rejected the suit on the grounds that Topeka's schools were "separate but equal," Brown and the NAACP appealed to the U.S. Supreme Court.

The case was argued by **Thurgood Marshall**, an African American attorney who worked for the NAACP. In addition to legal arguments, he used research data that showed that African American children suffered damage as a direct result of living in a segregated society. The Supreme Court concluded that Topeka's school system and others like it violated the Fourteenth Amendment's guarantee of equal protection of the laws. The Court ordered an end to racial segregation of public schools with "all deliberate speed."

Montgomery Bus Boycott Many southern cities made African Americans sit at the back of city buses. In 1955 in Montgomery, Alabama, an NAACP official named **Rosa Parks** refused to give up her seat in the front of the bus to a White person. She was arrested and charged with violating the segregation laws. Protesting her arrest, a young Baptist minister, **Dr. Martin Luther King, Jr.,** urged African Americans in Montgomery to refuse to ride the city's buses. The bus boycott lasted for more than a year and was extremely effective. It hurt both the bus system and business in general. To end the boycott, the city of Montgomery agreed to desegregate its transportation system.

As a result of his involvement in the bus boycott, Martin Luther King, Jr., emerged as a prominent leader of the civil rights movement. A supremely gifted leader and speaker, King advocated nonviolence and **civil disobedience**, the refusal to obey a law due to a moral objection, to protest the segregation laws of the South. In 1957, he founded the Southern Christian Leadership Conference (SCLC) to coordinate the efforts of African American leaders to end racial segregation. Its methods included boycotts, sit-ins, and marches.

Not all African Americans agreed with King's approach. One of his earliest critics was Malcom X. Born Malcolm Little, he replaced his "slave name" with an *X* when he became a member of the Nation of Islam, an African American movement that combined elements of Islam with Black nationalism. Like King, he was a powerful speaker, and gave voice to the frustration and bitterness of many African Americans. Rather than aiming for integration, he thought that African Americans should focus on their own needs, and he urged his followers to fight back against those who violently abused them.

Civic Literacy: Inequality
Since the abolition of slavery, African Americans have been fighting for equality with White Americans. With the recognition in the 1950s that "separate but equal" was not real equality, they finally began to make real progress. Several landmark court cases and new laws protecting civil rights and voting rights made things better, but inequality persists.

Read Closely: Comparisons
Comparisons are useful to highlight similarities and differences. Martin Luther King and Malcolm X were both major figures in the civil rights movement. How were they similar and how were they different?

Little Rock School Desegregation Many White southerners opposed the Supreme Court's ruling to desegregate their school systems. The first major challenge to the Court's decision occurred in Little Rock, Arkansas, in 1957. The city's board of education had drawn up a desegregation plan and ordered a formerly all-White high school to admit a few African American students.

Source: U.S. Army / Wikimedia Commons

U.S. Army soldiers escort African American students into Central High School, Little Rock, Arkansas.

Arkansas's governor, Orval Faubus, posted units of the Arkansas National Guard around the school to stop African American students from entering. He said the troops were there to maintain order. When a federal court forbade Faubus to interfere, he removed the troops—but only after a mob of Whites had stopped the students from entering the building.

President Eisenhower was reluctant to become involved in the crisis. He recognized, however, that Faubus's actions challenged the authority of the federal government and the U.S. Supreme Court. He called the Arkansas National Guard into federal service and ordered it back to the high school, this time to protect the right of the African American students to enter the building. In addition, he sent hundreds of U.S. soldiers to Little Rock to keep order and to prevent any further trouble. Governor Faubus referred to these measures as an "occupation," but most Americans supported Eisenhower's actions.

The Turbulent Sixties

During the 1960s, several new organizations formed to work for civil rights. Some followed King's approach. They were committed to nonviolent methods and had a goal of integration. Others followed the lead of Malcolm X. They were willing to use violence in self-defense and focused more on building Black institutions. Ella Baker, a former NAACP official who had helped Martin Luther King organize the SCLC, founded the Student Nonviolent Coordinating Committee (SNCC) in 1960. The students who joined this organization participated in sit-ins and other peaceful demonstrations against Jim Crow laws in the South. In 1961, they began efforts to register southern African Americans to vote.

Speak and Listen:
Point of View
Both Faubus and Eisenhower called out the Arkansas National Guard. With a partner, discuss each official's point of view—their reason for calling on the National Guard. Which point of view most closely aligns with the founding principles of the United States, and why?

Birmingham Protest In the early 1960s several cities in the South did away with their segregation laws, but Birmingham, Alabama, was not one of them. In April 1963, protesters led by Martin Luther King, Jr., went to Birmingham to participate in a peaceful march through the center of the city. The Birmingham police attacked the marchers with dogs and electric cattle prods and sprayed them with powerful fire hoses. King was among the marchers arrested and jailed in Birmingham. In a famous letter from the Birmingham jail, King defended his reasons for breaking laws that he considered unjust.

March on Washington In the summer of 1963, civil rights leaders organized a massive demonstration in the nation's capital. The **March on Washington** for Jobs and Freedom (to give it its full name) was meant to alert Congress and the American people to the need for stronger civil rights laws. More than 200,000 African Americans and White supporters packed the Mall in front of the Lincoln Memorial on August 28. Both White and Black entertainers performed and leaders of the civil right movement spoke. Finally, Dr. King delivered a historic speech, referred to as his "I Have a Dream" speech, that moved the nation and the world. It was now apparent that the civil rights movement had grown into a powerful force for change.

Read Closely: Motivation
When you are reading about the actions of individuals, consider how motivations shape those actions. What motivations shaped civil rights workers' civil disobedience?

Source: U.S. National Archives and Records Administration / Wikimedia Commons

Prominent civil rights and labor union leaders take part in the March on Washington for Jobs and Freedom.

Read Closely: Effects
To fully appreciate the significance of a historical event, be alert to any contradictory effects it has. For example, the Freedom Summer organizers' goal was to help African Americans register to vote. What were the most visible results of their efforts?

Freedom Summer In 1964, Fannie Lou Hamer co-founded the Mississippi Freedom Democratic Party (MFDP) and challenged an incumbent Democratic congressman in the primary. As a member of SNCC, she helped recruit hundreds of college student volunteers from the North, most of them White, to help African American residents in Mississippi register to vote. During 1964's "Freedom Summer," more than a thousand volunteers were arrested and three were murdered. Thirty Black homes or businesses and thirty-seven Black churches were burned. Some of the violence was captured on national television, forcing the nation to focus on civil rights issues.

Selma To rally support for registering African American voters in Dallas County and throughout Alabama, Martin Luther King, Jr., and other SCLC activists organized a 54-mile march from Selma to the state capital of Montgomery in March 1965. The marchers were beaten by state troopers and harassed by hostile crowds. They finally reached Montgomery only after President Johnson sent federal troops to protect them

In 1963, only about 1 to 2 percent of African American voters in Dallas County, Alabama, were registered to vote. The city of Selma was the administrative center of Dallas County. Local officials kept Black voter registration low by limiting times during which people could register, using overly complicated paperwork, and employing arbitrary literacy tests. Activists from the Student Nonviolent Coordinating Committee campaigned to register Black voters, but their efforts were met by increasing violence from local law enforcement officials.

Source: Wikimedia Commons

Peaceful marchers make their way from Selma to Montgomery, Alabama, 1965.

Racial Unrest The South was not the only part of the country in which racial tensions flared. In northern cities, most African Americans lived in crowded, segregated neighborhoods where poverty and unemployment were common. Hearing news of churches being bombed and civil rights marchers being attacked and killed, many young African Americans became increasingly angry and distrustful of White people. The result was a violent outburst of discontent.

The first riots took place in the Watts neighborhood of Los Angeles in 1965. They began as a response to what local residents felt was a case of police brutality against an African American man. But the situaion quickly became a large-scale protest against a range of problems—from poverty and a lack of opportunity to the tense and often violent relationship that existed between the police and the people of Watts and other predominantly Black communities.

Violent confrontations between residents and police lasted six days and resulted in the deaths of 34 people. Just over 1,000 people were injured and about 4,000 were arrested. Rampant lawlessness led to looting and arson on a grand scale. Some estimates placed damage to property as high as $200 million.

Riots erupted again in the summer of 1966 and the summer of 1967. These outbreaks affected more than 167 cities. Among the worst hit were Detroit, Michigan, and Newark, New Jersey.

Tensions and unrest continued into the 21st century. Racial disparities in the justice system and law enforcement's use of force against Black Americans led to the Black Lives Matter movement in 2013. The 2020 killing of George Floyd by Minneapolis police sparked intense protests across the nation, the largest in U.S. history, and calls for reforms to police training and protocols.

Read Closely: Comparison
Protests of the 1960s started with a nonviolent approach but took a more aggressive stance, as with the Black Power movement near the end of the decade. Based on what you read about civil unrest of the 21st century and your own observations, how do the methods of the eras compare?

Black Power As a student at Howard University, Stokely Carmichael joined the SNCC. He was the youngest protestor arrested challenging segregation laws in Mississippi. He became increasingly frustrated as he saw civil rights volunteers beaten and murdered. In 1966, Carmichael became the SNCC's chairman. During a march in Mississippi that year he urged demonstrators to form a "Black Power" movement that rejected nonviolence and advocated self-defense. Carmichael believed that African Americans had to achieve political and economic power before they could be part of a multiracial society.

Assassinations Racial tensions in the 1960s led to the violent deaths of three African American leaders. Medgar Evers was a leader of the NAACP in Mississippi during the 1950s and into the 1960s. He built a reputation as an effective leader, helping organize protests and voter-registration drives throughout the state. In June 1963, someone shot and killed Medgar Evers in front of his home. A known White supremecist, Byron De La Beckwith, was arrested and charged with the murder. In spite of overwhelming evidence of his guilt, all-White juries in Mississippi failed to reach a verdict in his case, and he walked free. The case was reopened in the 1990s, however, and De La Beckwith was finally brought to justice, receiving a life sentence for murder.

Tensions between Malcolm X and the leader of the Nation of Islam, Elijah Muhammad, had been brewing for some time. In March 1964, he left Muhammad's organization. He began a more internationalist approach to African American issues by creating connections with African political and social organizations.But Malcolm could not escape the enmity casued when he left the Nation of Islam. Malcolm X was shot and killed in February 1965, and three members of the Nation of Islam were convicted for the slaying.

In April 1968, a sniper shot and killed Martin Luther King, Jr., as he stood on a motel balcony in Memphis, Tennessee. News of King's death touched off riots in many cities. Throughout the nation, Americans paid tribute to the man who had so courageously led the struggle for racial justice and democratic reform. In 1983, King became the only nonpresident to be honored with a federal holiday for his birthday.

Important Court Cases and Laws

During the 1960s, the efforts of local and national civil rights organizations began to bear fruit. A number of court decisions and laws began the long, and still unfinished, journey to turn the tide of inequality in the United States. Over time, however, some of these advances were challenged.

Civil Rights Act of 1964 This act authorized the U.S. attorney general to bring suit if an individual's civil rights were violated. It prohibited discriminatory practices on the basis of race, ethnicity, gender, or religion in many situations:

- in the services provided by such businesses as restaurants, hotels, motels, and gas stations

- in the use of government-operated facilities, such as public parks and pools

- in federally supported programs, such as urban renewal and antipoverty programs

- in workplaces of 100 or more workers or in labor unions of 100 or more members (a number later reduced to 25)

In effect, this act outlawed all Jim Crow laws and practices. No one could be denied equal rights or opportunities based on race.

The constitutionality of the Civil Rights Act of 1964 was upheld by the Supreme Court in the *Heart of Atlanta Motel, Inc. v. United States* (1964). In this case, a motel owner challenged the right of Congress to pass legislation outlawing discrimination in motels. The Court ruled that the Constitution's interstate commerce clause gave Congress the right to enact such legislation.

Voting Rights In 1964, Congress and the states ratified the Twenty-Fourth Amendment to the U.S. Constitution. It banned the use of the poll tax in federal elections. Soon afterward, many states abolished the **poll tax** as a requirement for voting in state and local elections as well.

The **Voting Rights Act of 1965** prohibited the use of literacy tests to keep African Americans, or anyone else, from voting. It also authorized the U.S. government to identify places where only a small percentage of African Americans had registered to vote. Federal registrars would then go to these places to help them register. Within a year, the number of Black southerners registered to vote had increased about 50 percent.

In *Shelby County v. Holder* (2013), however, the Supreme Court struck down a section of the Voting Rights Act. That act required nine entire states (and local government units in a further six states) with a history of discrimination to get clearance from Congress before changing voting rules in order to make sure racial minorities were not negatively affected. In the 5–4 opinion, the Court ruled that the formula Congress used had become outdated. Several states that had been required to seek clearance before changing their laws immediately passed laws requiring photo IDs to vote. The U.S. Justice Department indicated it would intervene as necessary to protect the voting rights of minorities.

Voting Rights and the 2020 Presidential Election

In 2022, 35 states requested or required photo IDs to vote. Many people claim this unfairly deprived African Americans and other groups of the right to vote. The American Civil Liberties Union (ACLU) estimated in 2022 that as many as 25 percent of Black people of voting age lack a government-issued photo ID.

Election of 2020 In the presidential election of 2020, nearly 67 percent of all eligible voters cast ballots—one of the largest turnouts of the last century. Almost 71 percent of White voters and 58 percent of non-White voters participated in the 2020 election. Voter participation numbers fueled the argument that voter supression is still taking place in the United States.

Joe Biden defeated incumbent Donald Trump by 7 million votes in 2020. Yet, without evidence, Trump claimed voter fraud and made efforts to reverse the election results, which showed weaknesses in the electoral system. These issues were remedied with the passage of the Electoral Count Reform Act of 2022.

Based on the 2020 election outcome, some Republicans and Trump supporters wanted changes to voting laws. Since the election, state legislatures have passed more than 30 laws, ranging from ID requirements to limits on mail-in voting. Some people claim that these efforts to make elections increasingly secure have only disenfranchised more minority voters.

January 6 Trump's claims of a fraudulent election and demands that his supporters "Stop the Steal" led to a rally at the White House on January 6, 2021—the day the Senate was to accept the election results. The rally moved the U.S. Capitol building and turned violent, leaving five people dead and many more injured. Trump was impeached by the House of Representatives for incitement of an insurrection, but the Senate fell short of the two-thirds vote needed to convict (his first impeachment in 2019 resulted in acquittal for abuse of power and obstruction of Congress).

Application: Interpret a Primary Source

Read the excerpt below and answer the questions that follow it.

Segregation and Education

Today, education is perhaps the most important function of state and local governments. Compulsory school attendance laws and the great expenditures for education both demonstrate our recognition of the importance of education to our democratic society. It is required in the performance of our most basic public responsibilities, even service in the armed forces. It is the very foundation of good citizenship. Today it is a principal instrument in awakening the child to cultural values, in preparing him for later professional training, and in helping him to adjust normally to his environment. In these days, it is doubtful that any child may reasonably be expected to succeed in life if he is denied the opportunity of an education. Such an opportunity, where the state has undertaken to provide it, is a right which must be made available to all on equal terms.

We come then to the question presented: Does segregation of children in public schools solely on the basis of race, even though the physical facilities and other "tangible" factors may be equal, deprive the children of the minority group of equal educational opportunities? We believe that it does.

Source: Chief Justice Earl Warren, *Brown v. Board of Education of Topeka*, 1954

1. Describe the events that led to this Supreme Court ruling.

_____

_____

_____

_____

2. In what way does this document mark a turning point in the fight for civil rights?

_____

_____

_____

_____

3. What purpose did this document serve?

_____

_____

_____

_____

Lesson 2 *Diverse Groups Fight for Rights*

Conceptual Understanding
11.10b Individuals, diverse groups, and organizations have sought to bring about change in American society through a variety of methods.

The question of the role and image of women was addressed in *The Feminine Mystique*, a 1963 book by Betty Friedan. Friedan criticized the common assumption that women are happiest at home rather than in the workplace. She argued that women were as capable as men in all respects and should have equal opportunity to pursue high-level jobs in business and the professions. Widely read and discussed, Friedan's book challenged women to redefine their role in society and to break away from a limited view of themselves.

Analyze a Primary Source

The Problem That Has No Name

Read Closely: Intended Audience
When you analyze a primary source, think about the person or people the writer intended to read it. In this case, the intended audience is implied. Circle the word or phrase that indicates the audience Friedan had in mind.

Read Closely: Claim
Writers often begin with a claim that is later reinforced by evidence. Underline the problem that Friedan claims women have buried in their minds?

Read Closely: Contrasts
After making her claim, Friedan amasses details describing the life of the suburban housewife. In the second paragraph, she describes a life that might have been the envy of earlier generations of women. But she goes on in the third paragraph to say that women who weren't satisfied with that life were ashamed to admit it.

The problem lay buried, unspoken, for many years in the minds of American women. It was a strange stirring, a sense of dissatisfaction, a yearning that women suffered in the middle of the twentieth century in the United States. Each suburban wife struggled with it alone. As she made the beds, shopped for groceries, matched slipcover material, ate peanut butter sandwiches with her children, chauffeured Cub Scouts and Brownies, lay beside her husband at night—she was afraid to ask even of herself the silent question—"Is this all?" . . .

The suburban housewife—she was the dream image of the young American women and the envy, it was said, of women all over the world. The American housewife—freed by science and labor-saving appliances from the drudgery, the dangers of childbirth and the illnesses of her grandmother. She was healthy, beautiful, educated, concerned only about her husband, her children, her home. She had found true feminine fulfillment. As a housewife and mother, she was respected as a full and equal partner to man in his world. She was free to choose automobiles, clothes, appliances, supermarkets; she had everything that women ever dreamed of. . . .

If a woman had a problem in the 1950's and 1960's, she knew that something must be wrong with her marriage, or with herself. Other women were satisfied with their lives, she thought. What kind of a woman was she if she did not feel this mysterious fulfillment waxing the kitchen floor? She was so ashamed to admit her dissatisfaction that she never knew how many other women shared it. If she tried to tell her husband, he didn't understand what she was talking about. She did not really understand it herself. . . .

Gradually I came to realize that the problem that has no name was shared by countless women in America.

Just what was this problem that has no name? What were the words women used when they tried to express it? Sometimes a woman would say "I feel empty somehow . . . incomplete." Or she would say, "I feel as if I don't exist."

Source: Betty Friedan, *The Feminine Mystique*, Chapter 1 (1963)

Women, Native Americans, and Chicanos Demand Social Change

African Americans were not the only group demanding social change. The 1960s were a hotbed of social change as women, Native Americans, Chicanos (Mexican Americans). Many of these movements were given catchy names by the media, such as "women's liberation," "red power," and "brown power."

The Modern Women's Movement During the 1950s, most middle-class women believed that their place was at home. Husbands were expected to provide the family's income while wives looked after the house and children. This traditional view of a woman's role was challenged in the 1960s by women known as feminists. **Betty Friedan's** book *The Feminine Mystique* hit a nerve and helped spawn a movement.

Friedan helped form the **National Organization for Women (NOW)** in 1966. The organization's goals included equal pay for equal work, daycare centers for the children of working mothers, and the passage of antidiscrimination laws. Another goal was to increase the awareness of women and men about the various ways that men unfairly dominated women's lives.

Many members of NOW had been active in the struggle to win civil rights for African Americans. They drew on this experience to organize marches and demonstrations and thereby attracted national attention. NOW also supported female candidates for office and lobbied for changes in laws. Able spokespersons for women's rights, such as **Gloria Steinem** and Bella Abzug, became nationally known. In the 1970s, Abzug won election to Congress as a representative from a district in New York City. Gloria Steinem founded the magazine *Ms.* that focused on feminist issues.

NOW still functions as a pressure group to help expand the political and economic rights of women. Despite progress, it is still concerned with the goal of equal pay for equal work and issues such as a woman's right to have an abortion. In order to achieve its goals, it maintains strong political involvement on both state and national levels.

The Equal Pay Act (1963) was one of the first laws to address gender discrimination. It prohibited unequal pay or benefits to men and women who work in equivalent jobs. It also provided guidelines for when unequal pay is permitted by factors other than gender. The Civil Rights Act of 1964 prohibited employers from discriminating on the basis of race, color, religion, sex, or national origin.

Source: Wikimedia Commons

Gloria Steinem on the cover of Ms. Magazine's 30th anniversary issue

> **Read Closely: Related Changes**
> One way to understand the significance of a development is to note how it is connected to changes elsewhere. Describe the similarities between feminists' goals with the Equal Rights Amendment and suffragists' goals in seeking the vote for women.

In 1972 Congress proposed an amendment to the Constitution. Called the Equal Rights Amendment (ERA), it stated: "Equality of rights under the law shall not be denied or abridged by the United States or any state on account of sex." For ten years, NOW and other feminist organizations campaigned for ERA to be ratified by the necessary number of states. The amendment gained ratification by 35 states, 3 states fewer than needed to become part of the Constitution. After ratification by Nevada in 2017 and Illinois in 2018, the number of states reached 37—still one vote short.

In 1972, Congress passed an education act that included a provision known as Title IX. It made gender discrimination illegal in determining participation in educational programs at institutions that received federal funding. As a result of Title IX, athletic activities for women expanded greatly. In addition, specialized, formerly all-male schools had to open their doors to both sexes.

The case of *Roe v. Wade* was another key event in women's movement. In 1970, a pregnant woman living in Texas wanted to have an abortion but could not do so because of Texas's law prohibiting abortions. The Supreme Court ruled the Texas law unconstitutional because it violated a woman's constitutional right to privacy. The Court said women had the right to have an abortion during the first six months of pregnancy. During the last three months of pregnancy, however, a state may ban abortions.

The decision in *Roe v. Wade* sparked controversy still that has not been resolved. Supporters argued that the right to privacy applies to a woman's body. Opponents argued that even during the first six months of pregnancy, the fetus is a person who has rights equal to those of any person after birth.

Nearly 50 years after *Roe*, the Supreme Court ruled again on abortion in *Dobbs v. Jackson Women's Health Organization* (2022). The Court reversed the *Roe* decision, stating that the Constitution does not protect the right to an abortion. Ultimately, this ruling allowed each state to determine abortion policy.

Native Americans Rights Founded in 1944, the National Congress of American Indians (NCAI) was the first political organization to represent all Native American tribes. It formed to oppose the federal government's policies of terminating tribal status and assimilating Native Americans. Under these policies, the government sought to end all treaty obligations to Native American tribes, eliminate reservations, and force American Indians to become part of the mainstream U.S. culture. While advocates of this policy saw it as ending a form of segregation, Native American activists saw it quite differently. Members of the NCAI advocated to get the federal government to honor treaties, preserve their native laws and culture, and improve the quality of life for Native Americans.

The U.S. Bureau of Indian Affairs (BIA) had failed for decades to raise living standards. A 1960 study found that Native Americans had a life expectancy of only 46 years, compared with 70 years for the U.S. population as a whole. Native Americans suffered from higher rates of malnutrition and unemployment than any other ethnic minority.

In 1972 the **American Indian Movement (AIM)**, a radical group, occupied the offices of the BIA in Washington, D.C., demanding that the U.S. government honor treaties signed a century or more earlier. The next year, more than 200 armed members of AIM, led by **Russell Means**, took control of the village of Wounded Knee on a South Dakota Sioux reservation. Wounded Knee had been the site of a massacre of Native Americans by U.S. troops in 1890. AIM remained in the village for two months. Their demands that treaty rights be reinstated were unsuccessful.

Read Closely: Differences
Recognizing distinctions is one way to understand the different options available in history. Two major organizations formed to represent Native Americans from all tribes. How did their methods differ?

President Nixon tried to provide greater self-determination for Native Americans. Traditional lands were returned to the Taos people in New Mexico, and Nixon increased the number of Native Americans employed in the Bureau of Indian Affairs. In 1975, soon after Nixon left office, Congress passed the Indian Self-Determination and Education Assistance Act. This law increased the role of Native Americans in directing their own education and government.

Chicano Movement Just as African Americans began to speak of Black Power, Mexican Americans, or Chicanos, organized a movement for "Brown Power." The leader of the movement was a gifted and determined labor organizer named **César Chávez**. Chávez had worked as a migrant farm laborer. Employers often took advantage of migrant workers desperate for work no matter how low the wage. Since migrant workers had no permanent address, it was hard to organize them into a labor union for group action. Despite the difficulties, Chávez and his cofounder Dolores Huerta succeeded in organizing a strong union of migrant workers called the **United Farm Workers (UFW)**.

For five years, from 1965 to 1970, Chávez and Huerta's union struggled to win better pay and greater respect for migrant farm laborers from the California landowners who employed them to harvest grapes. The union conducted a strike against the grape growers and also urged the American people to boycott California grapes. Like Martin Luther King, Jr., Chávez insisted that his movement be completely nonviolent. Eventually, the strike and the boycott succeeded in winning major concessions for the union and workers. In 1970, the largest grape growers in the state agreed to sign a contract with the UFW.

The Movement for Rights Broadens

The groundswell of desire for improved treatment under the law extended beyond gender and ethnic identities during this period. Through grassroots action and through legislative and judicial avenues, long ignored or oppressed groups gained access, justice, and dignity.

Source: Wikimedia Commons

César Chávez speaks at a farm workers' rally in 1974.

Rights of the Disabled People with physical disabilities protested in the 1960s that federal and state laws treated them unfairly. The disabled also suffered from discrimination in the job market. Congress responded by passing legislation designed to protect the rights of disabled persons.

Passed in 1975, the Education for All Handicapped Children Act provided strong support for children with learning disabilities. The law provided for testing to identify disabilities, a list of rights for disabled children and their parents, and funds to assist states and local school districts in providing programs in special education. It guaranteed children with disabilities between the ages of 3 and 21 a free and appropriate public education in the least restrictive environment.

The **Americans with Disabilities Act**, passed in 1990, gave 43 million mentally and physically challenged Americans protection against discrimination. Under this law, businesses were required to make employment available to disabled persons by providing "reasonable accommodations." These included restructuring jobs, changing workstation layouts, or altering equipment. All new public accommodations, such as hotels, restaurants, retail stores, and transit systems (both public and private), were required to be accessible to individuals with disabilities. Barriers to services in existing facilities were to be removed if such changes were readily achievable.

Rights of the Accused Under Chief Justice Earl Warren, who held the position from 1953 to 1969, the Supreme Court issued several rulings in landmark cases that guaranteed the rights of the accused in criminal cases:

Read Closely: Potential Problems
In all three of these cases, the Supreme Court ruled that people who have been accused of crimes still have rights guaranteed by the Constitution. What kinds of problems might these rulings create?

- *Mapp v. Ohio* (1961) This case involved the Fourth Amendment's protection against "unreasonable searches and seizures" of a suspected person's property. The Supreme Court ruled that evidence wrongly obtained by the police could not be admitted as evidence in the suspect's trial.

- *Gideon v. Wainwright* (1963) This case involved the Sixth Amendment's guarantee that a citizen accused of a crime shall "have the assistance of counsel for his defense." The Court ruled that a state must provide lawyers to indigent (poor) defendants in all **felony**, or serious, criminal cases.

- *Miranda v. Arizona* (1966) The Court ruled that the police cannot question someone about a crime before informing that person of his or her constitutional rights. The Supreme Court's decision stated: "Prior to any questioning, the person must be warned that he has a right to remain silent, that any statement he does make may be used as evidence against him, and that he has a right to the presence of an attorney." The police were required to read suspects their "Miranda rights" before questioning them.

Immigration Between 1921 and 1965, U.S. immigration laws had favored nationalities from Western Europe and discriminated against people from other parts of the world. The old quota system was replaced by the Immigration Act of 1965 that set new, less restrictive criteria to determine who would be allowed to immigrate each year. Preference would be given to skilled workers and professionals and to those with family ties to U.S. citizens.

The Immigration Reform and Control Act of 1986 placed heavy fines on employers who knowingly hired illegal aliens. At the same time, the law permitted illegal aliens who had entered the United States before 1982 to remain here as legal residents. The act did not, however, succeed in stopping the flow of illegal immigrants across the Mexican–U.S. border.

In 2015, then-presidential candidate Donald Trump promised a border wall, paid for by Mexico, to prevent illegal immigrants from entering the country. By the time President Trump left office in 2021, more than 400 miles of wall had been constructed at a cost of about $15 billion; however, it was financed with money from numerous federal projects—not by Mexico. One of Joe Biden's first acts as president was to halt construction of the border wall. Additionally, the Biden administration lifted various Trump-era restrictions on the number of visas issued to people entering the country.

In April 2022, Republican governors began busing thousands of asylum-seeking migrants, mainly from Central America, to Democratic-led locations, including New York City, Washington D.C., and Chicago. They wanted to make the point that if Democrats do not address immigration problems, they should bear the cost of immigrants' presence.

Gay Rights and the LGBT Movement In the 1950s and 1960s, it was illegal to be Gay. Police harassment of Gay and Transgender people was common in cities throughout the United States. In June 1969, New York City police raided a popular Gay bar, the Stonewall Inn. As they herded patrons into paddy wagons, the crowd began to fight back. Riots continued outside the bar for the next five days.

The **Stonewall Inn riots** marked the first time that members of this community fought back collectively and in large numbers to assert their rights. Beginning in 1970, Gay and Lesbian people began to hold annual Gay Pride parades in cities around the country to commemorate the riots. More importantly, the riots inspired a new generation of activists to fight for **Lesbian, Gay, Bisexual, and Transgender (LGBT)** rights. Within a few years, many states had decriminalized homosexuality, and many cities had passed ordinances prohibiting discrimination on the basis of sexual identity.

One of the first nationwide Gay rights policies came about when President Clinton removed the long-standing ban against Gay individuals serving in the armed forces in 1994. To make the military more comfortable with the change, Clinton said that Gay people could serve but only if they remained silent about their sexual preference. The policy became known as "Don't Ask, Don't Tell." The policy stirred up controversy in the military and civilian sectors.

In 1996, Congress passed the **Defense of Marriage Act (DOMA)**, which defined marriage as a union between one man and one woman. Because of this law, federal benefits were denied to same-sex couples. However in *United States v. Windsor* (2013) the Court ruled that the Defense of Marriage Act (DOMA) was unconstitutional. The majority ruled that it violated the rights of LGBT individuals and interfered with states' rights to define marriage. Then in 2015, the Court went even further. In the case of *Obergefell v. Hodges*, the Court ruled that the U.S. Constitution's guarantees of due process and equal protection under the law give same-sex couples the right to marry, thus making same-sex marriage legal nationwide.

Source: Wikimedia Commons

Citizens celebrate the Supreme Court decision that ruled the Defense of Marriage Act (DOMA) unconstitutional.

In 2022, the federal government passed the Respect for Marriage Act which offered more protections for same-sex couples. This legislation repealed the Defense of Marriage Act (DOMA). It guaranteed the rights and benefits of marriages for same-sex couples in federal law. The law affirmed that public acts, records, and proceedings will be recognized by all states. Additionally, it guaranteed marriage rights for interracial couples.

However, some states attempted to limit the gains made at the federal level by the LGBT community. According to the Human Rights Campaign (HRC), in 2022, states proposed 315 bills that were considered discriminatory toward LGBT people in education, health care, housing, employment, and other areas. Only 29 of those bills became law.

Students' Rights The Supreme Court decided several cases involving the rights of students:

- *Engel v. Vitale* (1962) The Court found that New York State's establishment of a prayer to be recited in public schools unconstitutional, arguing that this officially sanctioned prayer violated the principle of the separation of church and state.

- *Tinker v. Des Moines School District* (1969) The Court ruled that students could not be penalized for wearing black armbands to school to protest the Vietnam War. The Court argued that students do not "shed their constitutional rights to freedom of speech or expression at the schoolhouse gate."

- *New Jersey v. TLO* (1985) The Court ruled that school officials do not need a warrant if they have "probable cause," (a viable, legal reason) for searches in order to maintain order and discipline.

Environmental Issues

In 1962, Rachel Carson published *Silent Spring*, an alarming book that opened many Americans' eyes to dangers to the environment. Carson described how the pesticide DDT, a chemical spray widely used by farmers to kill insects, caused the deaths of enormous numbers of birds and fish. She also explained the damaging effects to the entire environment if wildlife vanished as a result of chemical pollution.

In the 1970s, Congress took a number of actions that it hoped would help improve the country's natural environment:

- In 1970, it established the Environmental Protection Agency (EPA). This agency had the power to enforce 15 previously enacted federal programs to protect the environment.

- Also in 1970, it passed the Clean Air Act. This allowed the EPA to set federal standards for monitoring the quality of the air.

- The Clean Water Act of 1972 empowered the agency to provide funding to help states and local governments clean up polluted rivers and lakes.

- In 1973, the Endangered Species Act prohibited any trade in endangered species or their products. It also required that federal agencies assess the impact on wildlife habitat of any proposed projects.

President Reagan wanted to deregulate the EPA, and questioned the agency's legitimacy. He and many other conservatives saw the regulations as inefficient and an unnecessary burden on many individuals, organizations, and businesses. He also questioned scientific evidence behind EPA regulations and considered many of the EPA's proposals as wasteful. He was opposed to additional environmental restrictions on industry.

Application: Interpret a Primary Source

Read the excerpt below and answer the questions that follow it.

President Obama's Speech After Same-Sex Marriage Ruling

Our nation was founded on a bedrock principle that we are all created equal. The project of each generation is to bridge the meaning of those founding words with the realities of changing times—a never-ending quest to ensure those words ring true for every single American.

Progress on this journey often comes in small increments. Sometimes two steps forward, one step back, compelled by the persistent effort of dedicated citizens. And then sometimes there are days like this, when that slow, steady effort is rewarded with justice that arrives like a thunderbolt.

This morning, the Supreme Court recognized that the Constitution guarantees marriage equality. In doing so, they have reaffirmed that all Americans are entitled to the equal protection of the law; that all people should be treated equally, regardless of who they are or who they love.

This decision will end the patchwork system we currently have. It will end the uncertainty hundreds of thousands of same-sex couples face from not knowing whether they're marriage, legitimate in the eyes of one state, will remain if they decide to move or even visit another. . . .

And this ruling is a victory for America. This decision affirms what millions of Americans already believe in their hearts. When all Americans are treated as equal, we are all more free. . . .

From extending full marital benefits to federal employees and their spouses to expanding hospital visitation rights for LGBT patients and their loved ones, we've made real progress in advancing equality for LGBT Americans in ways that were unimaginable not too long ago.

I know a change for many of our LGBT brothers and sisters must have seemed so slow for so long. But compared to so many other issues, America's shift has been so quick. . . .

And slowly made an entire country realize that love is love.

Source: President Barack Obama, speech after *Obergefell v. Hodges* Supreme Court ruling, 2015

1. Describe the historical context in which this Supreme Court case and subsequent speech occurred.

_____

_____

2. How did the *Obergefell* case mark a turning point for the LGBT community?

_____

_____

3. What was the main point of President Obama's speech? Identify a sentence from the speech that supports your answer.

_____

_____

Lesson 3 The Federal Government's Role Debated

In May of 1964, President Johnson announced his plans for a "Great Society" in this speech. The Great Society was the largest social reform movement in modern U.S. history. Its goals were eliminating poverty, ending inequality, reducing crime, and protecting the environment.

Analyze a Primary Source

President Johnson on "The Great Society"

Read Closely: Stakeholders
Notice that speakers often attempt to motivate people by giving them a stake in what they are trying to accomplish. In his speech, Johnson talks about people who will have a stake in helping to create the Great Society. Circle the word that indicates who these stakeholders are.

Read Closely: Problem
The Great Society was Johnson's solution for what he saw as the two biggest social problems plaguing the United States. In the third paragraph, he mentions them: poverty and racial injustice. Eliminating both of these evils was the primary goal of the Great Society.

Read Closely: Details
For the most part, this passage uses generalizations to discuss the goals of the Great Society. Johnson knew that his goals for the Great Society would not be met overnight. Underline the phrase that indicates how long he thinks it may take to achieve those goals.

The challenge of the next half century is whether we have the wisdom to use that wealth to enrich and elevate our national life, and to advance the quality of our American civilization.

Your imagination, your initiative, and your indignation will determine whether we build a society where progress is the servant of our needs, or a society where old values and new visions are buried under unbridled growth. For in your time we have the opportunity to move not only toward the rich society and the powerful society, but upward to the Great Society.

The Great Society rests on abundance and liberty for all. It demands an end to poverty and racial injustice, to which we are totally committed in our time. But that is just the beginning.

The Great Society is a place where every child can find knowledge to enrich his mind and to enlarge his talents. It is a place where leisure is a welcome chance to build and reflect, not a feared cause of boredom and restlessness. It is a place where the city of man serves not only the needs of the body and the demands of commerce but the desire for beauty and the hunger for community.

It is a place where man can renew contact with nature. It is a place which honors creation for its own sake and for what it adds to the understanding of the race. It is a place where men are more concerned with the quality of their goals than the quantity of their goods.

But most of all, the Great Society is not a safe harbor, a resting place, a final objective, a finished work. It is a challenge constantly renewed, beckoning us toward a destiny where the meaning of our lives matches the marvelous products of our labor.

So I want to talk to you today about three places where we begin to build the Great Society — in our cities, in our countryside, and in our classrooms.

Source: Lyndon B. Johnson, Commencement Speech at the University of Michigan, May 22, 1964

Johnson vs. Reagan

These two presidents' terms were separated by 12 years and three other presidents: Nixon, Ford, and Carter. U.S. culture changed notably between the terms of Johnson and Reagan. The differences in the eras are represented by the fact that these two presidents represented markedly different views of the role of government.

Lyndon Johnson and the Great Society President Johnson's far-reaching **Great Society** program affected all areas of American life, including health, education, housing, employment, immigration, and civil rights. Johnson's ideas for social legislation were not new. Democratic presidents Truman and Kennedy had offered similar proposals. But Congress had rejected many of the aspects of Truman's Fair Deal and Kennedy's New Frontier. Now, however, Johnson managed to persuade a Democratic Congress to enact much of his program.

He announced an "unconditional" War on Poverty. Johnson said that a country as prosperous as the United States should be able to eliminate poverty. As the first step toward this goal, he persuaded Congress to pass the Economic Opportunity Act of 1964, which authorized one billion dollars of federal money for antipoverty programs.

Another aspect of the War on Poverty was the VISTA program (Volunteers in Service to America). Modeled on the concept of President Kennedy's Peace Corps, VISTA sent volunteers to poor areas in the United States as well as to Native American reservations to provide training and technical support.

Beyond the War on Poverty, Johnson's Great Society created a number of other programs designed to improve Americans' lives. As of 2019, all of these initiatives still existed.

Great Society Programs	
Medicare	Guaranteed health insurance for most individuals 65 and older
Medicaid	Provided health insurance primarily for lower-income people under age 65
The National Endowment for the Arts	Supported the creation and performance of the arts, including theater, film, literature, music, and fine arts
The National Endowment for the Humanities	Supported education, research, and public programs in the humanities, including archaeology, history, literature, philosophy, and similar disciplines
The Corporation for Public Broadcasting	Helped distribute federal funds to educational program producers and stations nationwide
Job Corps	Helped young people find meaningful employment
Head Start	Helped low-income parents with the care and education of their young children

> **Read Closely: Motivation**
> Looking for motivations for a person's actions can be a helpful tool in understanding history. Johnson's Great Society was a very ambitious group of social programs. Why was he willing to spend a billion dollars to try to wipe out poverty?

Johnson's increased government spending added $42 billion, or 13 percent, to the national debt. Much of that was a result of the war in Vietnam, yet it was less than a third of the debt added by President Nixon. Every other president since Johnson has increased the debt by at least 30 percent. Too much debt can be a bad sign, for an individual or a country. However, most economists would reject the idea that the presence of a national debt is necessarily a problem.

Johnson signed the Revenue Act of 1964, which lowered the top tax rate from 91 percent to 70 percent and the corporate tax rate from 52 percent to 48 percent. These cuts spurred the economy enough that revenue increased from $94 billion in 1961 to $153 billion in 1968. Johnson's programs also boosted the gross domestic product, the total value of the goods and services a country produces in a given period, and the unemployment rate fell while he was in office.

Reagan and Supply-Side Economics President Ronald Reagan entered office in 1981, a time when the U.S. economy was in trouble. The Federal Reserve did its part to help end inflation by limiting the supply of money in the economy and allowing interest rates to rise. While these policies had the intended effect, reducing inflation and keeping it low, they helped bring about a serious recession in 1982. President Reagan's response to this economic crisis was based on a theory called supply-side economics.

This plan called for a reduction of federal income taxes. Reagan believed that tax relief for the wealthy would enable them to earn and spend more, thus stimulating the economy and adding new jobs. This in turn would result in more revenue for the federal government. At the same time, the government would make major cuts in welfare programs, which Reagan and other conservatives considered wasteful.

The inflation rate dropped to 6 percent in 1982 and less than 4 percent in 1983. But one of the causes of the lower inflation rate was a severe business recession. By late 1982, unemployment rose to about 11 percent. Prosperity returned in 1984 and continued for the remainder of the decade. Inflation ceased to be a serious problem. But another problem took its place: that of staggering budget deficits.

Reagan urged Congress to pass the Tax Reform Act in 1986. Previous tax laws had divided taxpayers into several brackets, according to their earned income. The higher the taxable income, the higher the percentage of income paid in taxes. The new law created only two tax brackets, putting millionaires in the same bracket as people earning $30,000 a year.

Critics of President Reagan's economic policy warned that "**Reaganomics**" would result in huge deficits. They were right. Reagan's tax cuts meant lower government revenues. At the same time, Reagan increased spending for defense by 35 percent, resulting in higher government expenditures overall. As a result, there were deficits eight years in a row and the national debt increased by 186 percent by the end of the 1980s.

Partly because of the debt burden, the government was less able to spend adequate sums for urgent needs such as highway repair and health care. Reagan's cuts in programs such as food stamps and Aid for Dependent Children forced many poor families deeper into poverty.

Financial Issues and Regulation

The Great Recession After George W. Bush's re-election in 2004, major economic problems began to surface. Housing prices had been increasing sharply. Many people bought houses they could not afford, expecting prices to continue to increase. Some banks approved loans for borrowers who might not be able to make the mortgage payments.

Some banks bundled mortgages together into bonds and resold them to investors and financial institutions. This added instability to financial markets while also fueling the already overheated housing market. Homebuilding corporations raced to create new subdivisions to take advantage of the inflated prices. The growing supply of housing created a "housing bubble."

In 2007, defaults on mortgages began to increase significantly. Many borrowers were unable to pay back their loans, forcing banks to **foreclose** on many more homeowners than in the past. (When a bank forecloses on a property, it seizes the property for nonpayment of a loan.) As foreclosed homes came back on the market, the supply of homes was greater than the demand. House prices started to fall, and more homeowners defaulted. Banks that had focused on home mortgages were threatened with bankruptcy as loans went unpaid.

Source: Getty Images

Risky real estate lending led to a wave of home foreclosures during the Great Recession.

The housing bubble led to a worldwide banking crisis that affected even the largest banks. This led banks to greatly restrict lending to both consumers and businesses. With credit unavailable, consumers cut back on their purchases. Businesses stopped hiring, shelved plans for expansion, and began laying off employees. The stock market fell dramatically because of the banking crisis and reduced corporate profits. By 2008, the unemployment rate had increased to eight percent and threatened to climb higher. The economy fell into a deep decline known as the **Great Recession**.

The Government Responds In 2008, Congress passed the Economic Stimulus Act to provide $152 billion in tax incentives for businesses, tax rebates for low- and middle-wage earners, and higher limits on mortgages guaranteed by the government.

Government economists deemed several large financial companies "too big to fail." That is, if one such company failed, trust in the U.S. financial system would suffer, creating a downward spiral leading to complete collapse. To keep these larger banks from going bankrupt, Congress passed the Emergency Economic Stabilization Act. One of the act's provisions was to provide $700 billion to help

Read Closely: Causes
Historical events usually have many causes. The Great Recession is no exception—one catastrophe led to another. What event triggered the beginning of the financial crisis?

offset the reduced value of assets held by these banks. This provided a financial cushion for banks until they could sell some of their troubled assets or see them increase in value.

To avoid a depression, the Federal Reserve, which supervises the banking system, took the following steps:

- dropped the interest rate it charges to zero

- purchased mortgages and government bonds from banks

- set up a temporary loan facility from which financial institutions could borrow additional funds

The administration of President **Barack Obama** (2009–2017) began in the midst of the Great Recession. President Obama and his economic team immediately took actions to improve the economy. The first step was a second stimulus act, the American Recovery and Reinvestment Act (2009). It provided $787 billion for tax cuts to individuals, funds for public works projects, incentives to hire workers, funds to states to avoid layoffs, and extended unemployment benefits.

In September 2009, the government provided $82 billion to General Motors and Chrysler to save them from collapse. This bail-out allowed them to modernize their production and distribution facilities and reduce their debt levels. The automakers took this opportunity to decrease the number of models they produced. In return for the infusion of cash, the government received shares of stock in the two companies.

With the economy still in recession, the president and Congress passed a $15 billion jobs bill in March 2010. The bill was supposed to encourage private industry to hire workers who had been laid off for more than 60 days. In addition, taking a cue from New Deal programs of the 1930s, Congress shifted $20 billion in unused stimulus funds to road building in the hope of increasing employment. Unemployment, however, remained at high levels.

In July 2010, Congress passed the Dodd-Frank Wall Street Reform and Consumer Protection Act. The law came about in response to the unsound practices of the "too big to fail" banks and other financial institutions. The act aimed to head off the need for future bailouts by taxpayers and to protect consumers from unfair practices by financial institutions. To help do this, it established two new agencies:

- the Financial Services Oversight Council, to identify risks to the economy posed by new financial practices and activities of large corporations

- the Consumer Financial Protection Bureau, to provide consumer protection in the financial sector

Economic Ups and Downs Over time, the United States recovered from the Great Recession and experienced significant economic growth. In 2017, the Tax Cuts and Jobs Act was signed by President Trump, lowering taxes for large businesses while still benefitting the average taxpayer. By 2019, the country had its lowest unemployment rate (3.5 percent) in decades, steady business growth, a booming stock market, overall family income growth, and record low poverty rates for many ethnic groups.

However, this economic success quickly disappeared at the beginning of the COVID-19 pandemic in 2020. Some of the most damaging effects of COVID were disrupted production, forced business closures, a weakened labor force, and slowed trade between nations. The country also had to deal with supply chain delays and rising gas and oil prices resulting from the war between Russia and Ukraine.

Social Welfare Programs

The U.S. government did not invest heavily in social welfare programs prior to the Great Depression. However, that national, and world, crisis overwhelmed the communal and private support systems that had previously existed. Destitute Americans clamored for federal assistance, and the administration of Franklin Roosevelt provided it. But many conservatives opposed aspects of the president's New Deal, seeing them as federal government overreach.

Social Security During his presidency (1953–1961), the Republican President Eisenhower disagreed with his fellow Republicans who wished to cut back social programs begun by the Democrats. In fact, he increased Social Security benefits for retired persons and brought many more workers under the protection of the Social Security system.

Senior citizens won a major legislative victory in 1975 when Congress passed a law linking Social Security benefits to the cost of living. If inflation caused the cost of living to increase, Social Security benefits would also rise automatically. The new provision was known as a cost-of-living adjustment (COLA). Increasing Social Security benefits was expensive, especially during the inflationary years of the late 1970s. To prevent the Social Security system from going bankrupt, Congress raised the Social Security tax in 1977.

In 1983, Congress passed the Social Security Reform Act. This act saved the system from financial collapse by speeding up planned increases in Social Security taxes and by delaying for six months a scheduled increase in benefits. The reform of 1983 was able to keep the system solvent. However, it is believed the system will be unable to meet its payment obligations by 2037. The retirement of baby boomers, people born between 1946 and 1964, will see a sharp rise in the number of people drawing benefits. The system will still be able to pay out an estimated 75 percent of promised benefits, so adjustments will have to be made, either in the amount of money going in or the expectations for benefits.

Medicare Senior citizens often encounter high costs of hospital care, doctor care, and other medical needs. To help them, Congress established a public health insurance program known as Medicare, which became part of the Social Security system in 1964. Under the program, persons over 65 were insured for a large part of the costs of health care.

In 2003, President George W. Bush and Congress agreed on the first major addition to Medicare benefits since its passage. It created a program to provide prescription drugs at lower-than-retail prices for Medicare recipients. As part of this new addition, Medicare paid most of the initial cost of drugs. The need for this program stems from the fact that medical prescriptions account for a much greater portion of health care costs than they did in 1964. Innovations in medicines treat more issues and, in turn, cost more.

Health Care Reform A top priority for President Obama was passage of a health care bill, which Congress debated for many months. In major speeches, President Obama noted the lack of insurance for more than 43 million Americans and the rising cost of health care coverage. Republicans strongly opposed the bill, claiming that it was too expensive and would lead to a government takeover of the health care industry. Democrats countered that there were too many uninsured people and that health care was a right.

Civic Literacy: Social Security
Security means feeling safe and free from worry. Since the Great Depression, our federal government has created a number of "safety nets" to provide security in one way or another. One of the most popular government programs is even called *Social Security*. Government programs that protect people's savings provide another type of security.

Read Closely: Course of Action
One way to engage with history is to consider the best course of action available. Do you think that provisions should be made for more money to fund full Social Security benefits beyond 2037? Or should people be asked to take less than full benefits beyond that date? Explain your choice.

Finally, in March 2010, President Obama signed the **Affordable Care Act (ACA)**, popularly known as "Obamacare," into law. The ACA had a number of vital elements:

- A requirement that all Americans have health insurance beginning in 2014

- Medicaid coverage for families with incomes up to 133% of the federal poverty level

- No denial of insurance for people with preexisting conditions

- No cancellation of policies for those who are ill

- An allowance for children under the age of 26 to remain on a parent's policy

To help pay for this expanded coverage, individuals who earn above $200,000 or families that earn over $250,000 would pay a special Medicare tax.

Percentage of Americans Without Health Insurance (2013 and 2014)			
Age Group	End of 2013 (%)	End of 2014 (%)	Net Change (%)
All Adults	17.1	12.9	-4.2
18 to 25	23.5	17.4	-6.1
26 to 34	28.2	22.6	-5.6
35 to 64	18.0	12.8	-5.2
65+	2.0	2.0	0.0

Source: Gallop-Healthways Well-Being Index

In campaign speeches, Donald Trump promised to "repeal and replace" Obamacare "very, very quickly" if he were elected. Two years after his inauguration, most of the Affordable Care Act was still in place. During the 2018 midterm elections, many Republicans who initially opposed Obamacare were promising to keep key elements of it. And many Democrats were calling for expansion into a form of "Medicare for all."

Federal Responses to COVID The effects worldwide of the COVID-19 pandemic were devastating. The effects in the United States were equally damaging and even heightened, in part, by the reluctance of many people to follow safety guidelines, inconsistent actions among the 50 states, and a slow response by the federal government. People accused President Trump of downplaying the virus's severity and a lack of urgency in organizing federal resources to fight COVID. However, the Trump administration did have success with Operation Warp Speed—a $10 billion program that aided pharmaceutical companies in the rapid development and production of a COVID vaccine—with the first shots being administered in the United States in December 2020.

The subsequent Delta and more-contagious Omicrom variants of the COVID virus provided a new series of challenges for the federal government. The Biden administration's efforts to combat the changing virus included increasing testing options, a more extensive vaccination program, a federal mask mandate, and financial support for those impacted by COVID. Despite the efforts and resources dedicated to limiting the effects of the virus, the Centers for Disease Control and Prevention (CDC) reported that the country suffered more than 80 million cases and more than 1 million COVID-related deaths by mid-2022.

Application: Interpret a Primary Source

Read the excerpt below and answer the questions that follow it.

"Too Big to Fail"

Although "too big to fail" (TBTF) has been a long-standing policy issue, it was highlighted by the financial crisis, when the government intervened to prevent the near-collapse of several large financial firms in 2008. Financial firms are said to be TBTF when policymakers judge that their failure would cause unacceptable disruptions to the overall financial system. They can be TBTF because of their size or interconnectedness. In addition to fairness issues, economic theory suggests that expectations that a firm will not be allowed to fail create moral hazard—if the creditors and counterparties of a TBTF firm believe that the government will protect them from losses, they have less incentive to monitor the firm's riskiness because they are shielded from the negative consequences of those risks. If so, TBTF firms could have a funding advantage compared with other banks, which some call an implicit subsidy.

There are a number of policy approaches—some complementary, some conflicting—to coping with the TBTF problem, including providing government assistance to prevent TBTF firms from failing or systemic risk from spreading; enforcing "market discipline" to ensure that investors, creditors, and counterparties curb excessive risk-taking at TBTF firms; enhancing regulation to hold TBTF firms to stricter prudential standards than other financial firms; curbing firms' size and scope, by preventing mergers or compelling firms to divest assets, for example; minimizing spillover effects by limiting counterparty exposure; and instituting a special resolution regime for failing systemically important firms. A comprehensive policy is likely to incorporate more than one approach, as some approaches are aimed at preventing failures and some at containing fallout when a failure occurs.

Source: "Summary," in *Systemically Important or "Too Big to Fail" Financial Institutions*, Congressional Research Service, September 24, 2018

1. What was the historical context that led to the creation of this document?

_____

_____

2. How does this document mark a turning point?

_____

_____

3. Who was the intended audience for this document?

_____

_____

Multiple-Choice Questions

Questions 1 and 2 refer to the excerpt below.

A. President Johnson's Remarks on the Signing of the Medicare Bill in the Presence of Former President Truman

I am so proud that this has come to pass in the Johnson administration. But it was really Harry Truman of Missouri who planted the seeds of compassion and duty, which have today flowered into care for the sick, and serenity for the fearful. Many men can make many proposals.

Many men can draft many laws. But few have the piercing and humane eye, which can see beyond the words to the people that they touch. Few can see past the speeches and the political battles to the doctor over there that is tending the infirm, and to the hospital that is receiving those in anguish, or feel in their heart painful wrath at the injustice which denies the miracle of healing to the old and to the poor. And fewer still have the courage to stake reputation, and position, and the effort of a lifetime upon such a cause when there are so few that share it.

But it is just such men who illuminate the life and the history of a nation. And so, President Harry Truman, it is in tribute not to you, but to the America that you represent, that we have come here to pay our love and our respects to you today. For a country can be known by the quality of the men it honors. By praising you, and by carrying forward your dreams, we really reaffirm the greatness of America.

It was a generation ago that Harry Truman said, and I quote him: "Millions of our citizens do not now have a full measure of opportunity to achieve and to enjoy good health. Millions do not now have protection or security against the economic effects of sickness. And the time has now arrived for action to help them attain that opportunity and to help them get that protection."

Well, today, Mr. President, and my fellow Americans, we are taking such action—20 years later.

Source: President Lyndon B. Johnson, Remarks on the Signing of the Medicare Bill, July 30, 1965

1. How does this excerpt best illustrate continuity and change?

    1. It is a tribute from one president to one of his predecessors.

    2. It shows that all Democratic presidents have the same goals.

    3. It acknowledges the fact that a recently passed program had first been championed by a president two decades before.

    4. It proves that the "repeal and replace" attitude of Republicans to universal health care is not new.

2. What support does Johnson give for his claim that President Truman "planted the seeds of compassion and duty" that led ultimately to the passage of the Medicare bill?

   1. He says that Truman drafted the law that eventually became the Medicare bill.
   2. He quotes a statement Truman made a generation before.
   3. He describes the political battles that ultimately led to the passage of the Medicare bill.
   4. He mentions the doctors and hospitals that care for the old and the poor.

Questions 3–5 refer to the excerpt below.

B. The Supreme Court Affirms Students' Free Speech Rights

Under our Constitution, free speech is not a right that is given only to be so circumscribed [restricted] that it exists in principle, but not in fact. Freedom of expression would not truly exist if the right could be exercised only in an area that a benevolent government has provided as a safe haven for crackpots. The Constitution says that Congress (and the States) may not abridge the right to free speech. This provision means what it says. We properly read it to permit reasonable regulation of speech-connected activities in carefully restricted circumstances. But we do not confine the permissible exercise of First Amendment rights to a telephone booth or the four corners of a pamphlet, or to supervised and ordained discussion in a school classroom.

If a regulation were adopted by school officials forbidding discussion of the Vietnam conflict, or the expression by any student of opposition to it anywhere on school property except as part of a prescribed classroom exercise, it would be obvious that the regulation would violate the constitutional rights of students, at least if it could not be justified by a showing that the students' activities would materially and substantially disrupt the work and discipline of the school. . . . In the circumstances of the present case, the prohibition of the silent, passive "witness of the armbands," as one of the children called it, is no less offensive to the Constitution's guarantees.

As we have discussed, the record does not demonstrate any facts which might reasonably have led school authorities to forecast substantial disruption of or material interference with school activities, and no disturbances or disorders on the school premises in fact occurred. These petitioners merely went about their ordained rounds in school. Their deviation consisted only in wearing on their sleeve a band of black cloth, not more than two inches wide. They wore it to exhibit their disapproval of the Vietnam hostilities and their advocacy of a truce, to make their views known, and, by their example, to influence others to adopt them. They neither interrupted school activities nor sought to intrude in the school affairs or the lives of others. They caused discussion outside of the classrooms, but no interference with work and no disorder. In the circumstances, our Constitution does not permit officials of the State to deny their form of expression.

Source: Justice Abe Fortas, Majority Opinion, *Tinker v. Des Moines Independent Community School Board*, February 24, 1969

3. What actions led to this court case?

    1. A school's attempt to forbid an antiwar protest

    2. A school's attempt to prohibit school prayers

    3. A school's attempt to force students to say the Pledge of Allegiance

    4. A school's attempt to prohibit discussion of the war in Vietnam

4. What was the effect of this Supreme Court decision?

    1. It affirmed the right of students to free speech as long as it took place outside of school hours.

    2. It affirmed students' freedom of speech, even if it interrupted school activities.

    3. It affirmed the right of students to force their views on other students.

    4. It affirmed students' freedom of speech as long as it did not disrupt regular school activities.

5. How does this case illustrate the impact of time and place?

    1. It shows that the Midwest in the 1960s was much more conservative than the rest of the nation.

    2. It came about as a result of the antiwar and free-speech movements of the 1960s.

    3. It shows how organized antiwar activity could lead to a truce in Vietnam.

    4. It paved the way for nationwide campus antiwar demonstration like the one at Kent State University in 1970.

Questions 6–8 refer to the excerpt below.

C. Reaganomics and the President's Men

No economist lays the entire blame for the current recession at the doorstep of Reaganomics. But judged on its own terms, Mr. Reagan's allegedly painless means to economic recovery has failed to deliver on its promise of simultaneous low inflation, robust growth and a balanced budget.

How could the nation have gone from hope to gloom in less than two years? It is a critical question as the 1982 election approaches. Yet there is another, possibly more significant question to be asked: How could Mr. Reagan's economic plan have been enacted in the first place? For it was a program that lacked any sort of traditional constituency in Congress or in the Government, a program whose premises were challenged by conservative and liberal economists alike and that was widely characterized as a risky gamble with the nation's future.

This question hovers over much of the current debate about Reaganomics, just as it hovered, unasked, over a somber meeting in the White House just two months ago. There, as the sun streamed in through the French doors of the Cabinet room, a combative President was pressing 25 Republican Congressmen to support a measure he himself would have ridiculed earlier, a $98 billion tax increase. Many in the room opposed the measure, including Representative Jack F. Kemp of suburban Buffalo, an early advocate of the so-called "supply-side" theory that deep tax cuts by themselves would spur economic recovery.

The room fell silent as Paul Laxalt, the rangy, silver-haired Senator from Nevada, spoke up. Mr. Reagan's closest friend on Capitol Hill, Mr. Laxalt not surprisingly supported the President in seeking the tax increase. But it was a poignant moment. The three-year tax cut, which had been at the heart of Mr. Reagan's economic program, and which had been enacted amid such promise the previous summer, had been a mistake, Mr. Laxalt said, and now it was time to take corrective action. After all, he reminded listeners, it wasn't as if they had all been true believers in supply-side economics. "If there had been a secret ballot in the Senate last year," he said, "there wouldn't have been more than 12 votes for the tax cut."

Source: Steven R. Weisman, "Reagonomics and the President's Men," *New York Times*, October 24, 1982

6. Which of the following is a plausible claim made by the author of this article?

   1. Reagan's economic policies would lower inflation, grow the economy, and balance the budget
   2. "Supply-side" economics would spur economic recovery
   3. Reagan's plan for economic recovery had failed
   4. Reagan's economic plan was supported by both conservative and liberal economists

7. According to the author, what was a major problem with Reaganomics?

   1. Congress had failed to pass the legislation necessary to make it work.
   2. The tax cut had been a mistake.
   3. The tax cut only benefited the wealthy.
   4. Only 12 senators supported supply-side economics.

8. How did Reagan propose to solve to the this problem?

   1. He hoped to gain more support from both conservatives and liberals.
   2. He wanted Congress to enact deeper tax cuts to spur economic recovery.
   3. He wanted Congress to extend the current tax cuts another three years.
   4. He wanted to raise taxes.

Short-Essay Questions

Study the two documents and answer the question that follows.

D. The Original Statement of Purpose of the National Organization for Women

We, men and women who hereby constitute ourselves as the National Organization for Women, believe that the time has come for a new movement toward true equality for all women in America, and toward a fully equal partnership of the sexes, as part of the world-wide revolution of human rights now taking place within and beyond our national borders.

The purpose of NOW is to take action to bring women into full participation in the mainstream of American society now, exercising all the privileges and responsibilities thereof in truly equal partnership with men.

We believe the time has come to move beyond the abstract argument, discussion and symposia over the status and special nature of women which has raged in America in recent years; the time has come to confront, with concrete action, the conditions that now prevent women from enjoying the equality of opportunity and freedom of choice which is their right, as individual Americans, and as human beings.

NOW is dedicated to the proposition that women, first and foremost, are human beings, who, like all other people in our society, must have the chance to develop their fullest human potential. We believe that women can achieve such equality only by accepting to the full the challenges and responsibilities they share with all other people in our society, as part of the decision-making mainstream of American political, economic and social life.

Source: National Organization for Women, Statement of Purpose, Adopted October 29, 1966

E. What's Wrong with "Equal Rights" for Women?

Of all the classes of people who ever lived, the American woman is the most privileged. We have the most rights and rewards, and the fewest duties. Our unique status is the result of a fortunate combination of circumstances.

1) We have the immense good fortune to live in a civilization which respects the family as the basic unit of society. This respect is part and parcel of our laws and our customs. It is based on the fact of life—which no legislation or agitation can erase—that women have babies and men don't.

If you don't like this fundamental difference, you will have to take up your complaint with God because He created us this way. The fact that women, not men, have babies is not the fault of selfish and domineering men, or of the establishment, or of any clique of conspirators who want to oppress women. It's simply the way God made us.

Our Judeo-Christian civilization has developed the law and custom that, since women must bear the physical consequences of the sex act, men must be required to bear the other consequences and pay in other ways. These laws and customs decree that a man must carry his share by physical protection and financial support of his children and of the woman who bears his children, and also by a code of behavior which benefits and protects both the woman and the children. . . .

In the last couple of years, a noisy movement has sprung up agitating for "women's rights." Suddenly, everywhere we are afflicted with aggressive females on television talk shows yapping about how mistreated American women are, suggesting that marriage has put us in some kind of "slavery," that housework is menial and degrading, and—perish the thought—that women are discriminated against. New "women's liberation" organizations are popping up, agitating and demonstrating, serving demands on public officials, getting wide press coverage always, and purporting to speak for some 100,000,000 American women. It's time to set the record straight. The claim that American women are downtrodden and unfairly treated is the fraud of the century. The truth is that American women never had it so good. Why should we lower ourselves to "equal rights" when we already have the status of special privilege?

Source: Phyllis Schlafly, Speech on behalf of STOP ERA, 1972

1. In a short essay, describe the historical context surrounding the two documents above. Then identify and explain the similarities and differences between the ideas expressed in these documents.

F. "Letter from a Birmingham Jail"

I am cognizant of the interrelatedness of all communities and states. I cannot sit idly by in Atlanta and not be concerned about what happens in Birmingham. Injustice anywhere is a threat to justice everywhere. We are caught in an inescapable network of mutuality, tied in a single garment of destiny. Whatever affects one directly, affects all indirectly. Never again can we afford to live with the narrow, provincial "outside agitator" idea. Anyone who lives inside the United States can never be considered an outsider anywhere within its bounds.

You deplore the demonstrations taking place in Birmingham. But your statement, I am sorry to say, fails to express a similar concern for the conditions that brought about the demonstrations. I am sure that none of you would want to rest content with the superficial kind of social analysis that deals merely with effects and does not grapple with underlying causes. It is unfortunate that demonstrations are taking place in Birmingham, but it is even more unfortunate that the city's White power structure left the Negro community with no alternative.

In any nonviolent campaign there are four basic steps: collection of the facts to determine whether injustices exist; negotiation; self purification; and direct action. We have gone through all these steps in Birmingham. There can be no gainsaying the fact that racial injustice engulfs this community. Birmingham is probably the most thoroughly segregated city in the United States. Its ugly record of brutality is widely known. Negroes have experienced grossly unjust treatment in the courts. There have been more unsolved bombings of Negro homes and churches in Birmingham than in any other city in the nation. These are the hard, brutal facts of the case. On the basis of these conditions, Negro leaders sought to negotiate with the city fathers. But the latter consistently refused to engage in good faith negotiation.

Source: Dr. Martin Luther King, Jr., Open Letter to "My Fellow Clergymen," April 16, 1963

G. "What We Want"

One of the tragedies of the struggle against racism is that up to now there has been no national organization which could speak to the growing militancy of young Black people in the urban ghetto. There has been only a civil rights movement, whose tone of voice was adapted to an audience of liberal Whites. It served as a sort of buffer zone between them and angry young Blacks. None of its so-called leaders could go into a rioting community and be listened to. In a sense, I blame ourselves, together with the mass media, for what has happened in Watts, Harlem, Chicago, Cleveland, Omaha. Each time the people in those cities saw Martin Luther King get slapped, they became angry; when they saw four little Black girls bombed to death, they were angrier; and when nothing happened, they were steaming. We had nothing to offer that they could see, except to go out and be beaten again. We helped to build their frustration. . . .

An organization which claims to speak for the needs of a community, as does the Student Nonviolent Coordinating Committee, must speak in the tone of that community, not as somebody else's buffer zone. This is the significance of Black Power as a slogan. For once, Black people are going to use the words they want to use, not just the words Whites want to hear. And they will do this no matter how often the press tries to stop the use of the slogan by equating it with racism or separatism.

An organization which claims to be working for the needs of a community, as SNCC does, must work to provide that community with a position of strength from which to make its voice heard. This is the significance of Black Power beyond the slogan.

Black Power can be clearly defined for those who do not attach the fears of White America to their questions about it. We should begin with the basic fact that Black Americans have two problems: they are poor and they are Black. All other problems arise from this two-sided reality: lack of education, the so-called apathy of Black men. Any program to end racism must address itself to that double reality.

Source: Stokely Carmichael, "What We Want," *The New York Review of Books*, September 22, 1966

2. In a short essay, describe the historical context surrounding the two documents above. Then analyze and explain how the point of view of Dr. King's letter affects its reliability as a source of evidence.

CHAPTER 11

The United States in a Changing World (1990–Present)

Chapter Overview

After the breakup of the Soviet Union, the world had one superpower: the United States. But this did not make the United States immune to attacks and other international problems.

Military Action and Inaction in the 1990s Iraq invaded Kuwait in 1990, endangering worldwide oil supplies. In 1991, the United States led a coalition of countries that liberated Kuwait through military means. Throughout the 1990s, U.S. presidents worried about "Vietnam syndrome." Lawmakers and the public did not want the United States to be in long wars in faraway places.

The War on Terror The September 11 attacks had their roots in decades of Islamic extremism. In response, the United States invaded Afghanistan. U.S. forces found and killed 9/11 mastermind Osama bin Laden in 2011. Near the same time, the United States invaded and occupied Iraq, believing that its leader, Saddam Hussein, was stockpiling dangerous weapons. This belief, however, proved unfounded.

Technology and Globalization As transportation and communication technologies improved, companies began spreading their business operations across many countries. Multinational corporations gained power and influence. Most governments supported free trade to boost their economies. However, some countries attracted multinationals by having weak laws protecting both worker rights and the environment.

In the late 1900s and early 2000s, China's government was Communist and autocratic. But China encouraged and supported free enterprise, and as a result, it became an economic powerhouse. The United States developed a complicated economic and geopolitical relationship with China.

Civic Engagement: Balancing Rights and Protections One issue in this chapter is the struggle to balance individuals' desire for freedom with their need for safety. After 9/11, Congress passed laws that made it easier for the government to monitor private communications. Did the laws really protect against attacks? Was the invasion of privacy worth the alleged benefit?

New York Social Studies Framework

Key Idea 11.11: The United States in a Changing World (1990–present)

The United States' political and economic status in the world has faced external and internal challenges related to international conflicts, economic competition, and globalization. Throughout this time period, the nation has continued to debate and define its role in the world.

Source: *New York State Grades 9–12 Social Studies Framework*

Civic Literacy Essay: Reread and Evaluate

Be sure to allow plenty of time to understand the task and gather your evidence before you start writing. That effort will likely make your writing easier and stronger. Also allow time to reread and evaluate your essay.

As you evaluate your essay, start at the most basic level: Did you fulfill the tasks the prompt requires? Check the key terms of the question and the key terms you use in your response, and be sure they align.

For an easy reminder of what else to look for as you evaluate your essay, remember this sentence: **The Clearest Essays Require Care.** The first letter of each word—*T, C, E, R,* and *C*—stands for a key element your essay must contain:

1. **Thesis/claim**: The thesis must make a reasonable claim that responds to the prompt and lays out an organizational pattern. It should consist of one or more sentences located in one place, either in the introduction or the conclusion.

2. **Contextualization**: *Describe* the historical context, relating the topic of the prompt to broader historical events, developments, or processes that occur before, during, or continue after the time frame of the question.

3. **Evidence**: *Explain* your thesis by providing a number of specific and relevant pieces of evidence, and clearly show how they support your thesis. Use evidence from the documents as well as your knowledge of history.

4. **Reasoning**: *Discuss* the topic using effective reasoning processes, such as comparison, continuity and change, or causation, to frame your argument. Use an organizational strategy appropriate to the reasoning process.

5. **Complexity**: Check that you have woven a complex understanding throughout your essay (or fully developed it in one place). For example, look for both causes and effects, similarities and differences, and continuities and changes; connections across and within periods; the significance of a source's credibility and limitations; and the effectiveness of a historical claim.

Key Terms by Theme

Civics
civil liberties (p. 375)
lobbyist (p. 382)

Economics
globalization (p. 380)
multinational corporations (p. 380)

Exchange
free trade (p. 380)
North American Free Trade
   Agreement (NAFTA) (p. 380)

trade war (p. 380)
trade deficit (p. 384)

Governance
coalition (p. 367)
sanctions (p. 368)
Operation Desert Storm (p. 369)
Persian Gulf War (p. 369)
Vietnam Syndrome (p. 369)
Patriot Act (p. 374)
Taliban (p. 374)

weapons of mass destruction
   (WMDs) (p. 376)
Operation Iraqi Freedom (p. 376)
Donald J. Trump (p. 380)
Mao Zedong (p. 383)
Tiananmen Square (p. 383)

Identity
ethnic cleansing (p. 370)
Osama bin Laden (p. 373)
al-Qaeda (p. 373)

Conceptual Understanding
11.11a The United States created a coalition to defeat Iraq in the Persian Gulf War (1991) but was reluctant to commit American military power through the rest of the decade.

In June 1991, the European country of Yugoslavia began to disintegrate along ethnic and religious lines. Initially, two of its regions, Croatia and Slovenia, declared independence. A war for territory quickly developed, mostly including Catholic Croatia, Orthodox Christian Serbia and partly Muslim Bosnia-Herzegovina. In Bosnia, Serbian-allied forces committed numerous atrocities against the region's Muslim residents. The interviewee below was only 14 years old at the time of the events he describes.

Analyze a Primary Source

Elvedin Pasic Testifies About War in the Former Yugoslavia, 2012

Read Closely: Human Geography
Human geography, the study of the interaction of people and geography, is often important to historical study. What parts of Pasic's testimony describe the ethnic groups that lived in his area? Underline them.

Q. Could you tell us the size and ethnicity of your village?

A. . . . My village, Hrvacani, was 100 percent Muslim ethnicity and approximately a hundred houses.

Q. And could you tell us where you went to school?

A. . . . My school in Vrbanjci was full of my friends, Serbs, Croats, and Muslims all together during that time. . . . Before the war, we shared the same classroom, playing basketball, soccer, and all activities. . . .

Q. And drawing your attention to May 1992, did you see any unusual activity around these villages, the Serb villages, that is?

Read Closely: Purpose
While reading court testimony, think about why the person being questioned is testifying. Circle the part of Pasic's testimony that shows he witnessed an act of war.

A. Yes. To our left where the Savici, the village, Serb village, was located we've noticed people digging trenches. Our neighbors, they were digging trenches. . . . They were digging trenches and getting ready for something. . . people in our village. . . decided to go and talk to our neighbors . . . they [said they] were just preparing for the military exercises . . . and not to worry about it. We are neighbors. That nothing should ever happen to us. . . .

Q. And was there a religious occasion celebrated in your village in May or June of 1992?

A. Yes, our holiday Bajram . . . we would go to our house and go from house to house, eat sweets, and celebrate the holiday with the family.

Read Closely: Audience
Prosecutors asked for Pasic to testify to remind people of a war that had happened 20 years earlier. Many reporters around the world described Pasic's testimony sympathetically.

Q. Was the – was Bajram interrupted in 1992?

A. Yes. On our second day we were attacked by our neighbors. . . . bombs and the shells started landing in our village. . . . It was horrible. . . . the shells were hitting houses and the ground was shaking.

Source: United Nations International Criminal Tribunal for the Former Yugoslavia

The Persian Gulf War

In the 1980s, the four major producers of oil in Southwest Asia were Saudi Arabia, Kuwait, Iran, and Iraq. All four countries are on the shores of the Persian Gulf. When conflicts broke out among them, many other countries around the world became involved.

The Iran-Iraq War In 1980, Iraq instigated a war with its neighbor to the east, Iran. Iraq, and its military dictator Saddam Hussein, wanted to take control of the mostly Arab oil-producing region of Iran that bordered Iraq. (Iraqis are Arab; Iranians are Persian.) Hussein also accused Iran of stirring rebellion among Iraq's Shi'ite Muslim majority. (Iran had an overwhelming Shi'ite majority, but Iraq was about 30 percent Sunni Muslim—including Saddam Hussein.) The war lasted eight years. It ended in a virtual stalemate. But while no land was gained, many lives were forever changed or lost. Estimates of total casualties run from 1 to 2 million, with as many as 500,000 killed on both sides.

Iraq Invades Kuwait With his land- and oil-grab in Iran thwarted, Hussein looked to another neighbor—Kuwait. Iraq had multiple reasons for wanting to invade the tiny country to its south:

- Hussein accused Kuwait of drilling into Iraqi territory, thereby stealing Iraqi oil.

- Hussein also accused Kuwait of helping drive down the global price of oil. This, he said, was an attack on the Iraqi economy and people.

- Kuwait refused to forgive Iraq's $14 billion debt—money lent to support Hussein's war against Iran.

- Kuwait was rich in oil and had occupied a strategic position on the Persian Gulf.

- Since Kuwait's beginning in 1962, Iraq had claimed Kuwait was part of Iraq.

On August 2, 1990, Iraq invaded and, within hours, occupied Kuwait. Iraq was now in control of 20 percent of the world's oil supply. To pressure Iraqi forces to withdraw, the United States and the United Nations put an embargo on Iraqi oil. In other words, most countries stopped buying oil from Iraq. The resulting drop in oil supplies quickly led to higher fuel prices.

President Bush Opposes Invasion The Iraqi invasion alarmed President George H. W. Bush and other world leaders for three reasons:

- It was an act of aggression by a strong nation against a weak one. (In 1990, Iraq had the world's fourth-largest military.)

- Iraq might next try to conquer the world's largest oil producer, Saudi Arabia.

- Iraq's military power could allow it to dominate other countries in the region.

President Bush ordered U.S. troops to Saudi Arabia. He announced a defensive effort called Operation Desert Shield. A 28-member United Nations **coalition** joined U.S. forces. The group included Great Britain, Saudi Arabia, Syria, Turkey, and Egypt.

A UN resolution gave its members permission to use force if Iraq did not leave Kuwait. The U.S. Congress voted in favor of the war resolution.

> **Read Closely: Cause and Effect**
> Recognize how a text presents causation. In this case, how did a political cause lead to an economic effect?

The United Nations Uses Economic Sanctions After Iraq invaded Kuwait, the United Nations levied economic **sanctions**, penalties for not complying with international law, on Iraq. It did so to try to influence the country's behavior. The United Nations wanted Iraq to stop invading other countries and to reduce its military forces.

Should One Country Impose Economic Sanctions on Another?	
In Favor	**Against**
• Allows one country (or several countries) to influence another country's behavior • No need for troops, weapons, or military force • Can be removed gradually in response to positive behavior from that country	• Possible increase in smuggling • Possible catastrophic damage to sanctioned country's economy • Unintended consequences possible: starvation, political chaos, violence, and so on

Operation Desert Storm In January 1991, thousands of planes from allied bases in Saudi Arabia attacked military targets in Iraq and Kuwait. The Iraqi army did little to fight back. After a month of bombing attacks, allied forces launched a massive ground attack against Iraqi positions in Kuwait and southern Iraq. Allied tanks swept across the desert into southern Iraq and Kuwait, followed by ground troops. Again, there was little resistance. But coalition troops stopped short of driving all the way to the Iraqi capital Baghdad and deposing Saddam Hussein. President George H.W. Bush decided against overthrowing Hussein for fear it might destabilize not just Iraq but the entire region.

Persian Gulf War, 1990–1991

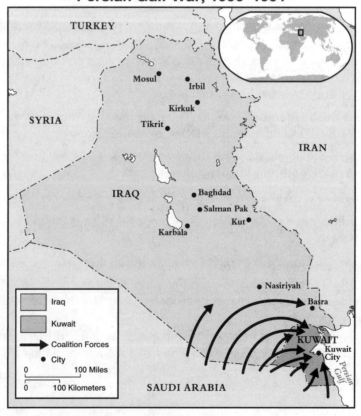

This combat phase was known as **Operation Desert Storm**. Bush announced in late February that the United States and its allies had won. In a cease-fire agreement, Iraq agreed to eliminate all poison gas and germ weapons. It also agreed to let UN observers inspect weapons-storage sites. To enforce the agreement, the United Nations kept economic sanctions in place until Iraq met all terms.

Positive Consequences of the Persian Gulf War As a result of the **Persian Gulf War**, Kuwait was again free. The war also ended Saddam Hussein's ambitions to control Middle East oil supplies and prices. The war led to military cooperation between Western Europe and the United States. Russia supported U.S. resolutions in the United Nations. To lessen the negative effects of sanctions, the United Nations established an Oil-for-Food program in 1997.

Negative Consequences of the Persian Gulf War Saddam Hussein stayed in power in Iraq. Critics said Bush should have sent troops into the Iraqi capital of Baghdad to oust the dictator. The president and his supporters argued that the coalition's aim was to remove Hussein from Kuwait, not from Iraq.

Even after the Oil-for-Food program began, the Iraqi economy remained shattered. According to the United Nations, malnutrition rates among children rose sharply, and hundreds of thousands of ordinary Iraqis starved to death.

Debates on Humanitarian Intervention

Democrat Bill Clinton won the presidency in 1992. His two terms in office marked a shift away from the policies of Republican Presidents Reagan and George H. W. Bush. Some of the most pressing decisions Clinton had to make related to whether to get involved in overseas conflicts.

Vietnam Syndrome The Vietnam War had a profound effect on U.S. foreign policy in the 1960s and 1970s. About 58,000 Americans died in the conflict. Still, the United States failed to defeat North Vietnam. This loss caused millions of Americans to question whether the United States should involve itself in distant conflicts. For many years, the American people did not want to become involved in foreign conflicts. Congress shared that reluctance. Experts called this behavior the **Vietnam syndrome**.

After the liberation of Kuwait, President George H. W. Bush said, "We've kicked the Vietnam syndrome once and for all." However, other conflicts under Bush's successor showed that it remained an issue for the United States.

Defending Human Rights The collapse of many Communist governments and the breakup of the Soviet Union shifted the balance of global power. New conflicts erupted in Bosnia, Rwanda, Kosovo, and elsewhere.

Some human rights activists argued that the United States had a duty to intervene in these conflicts. They said a wealthy and powerful country should not stand by while leaders murdered people based on their ethnicity or religion.

Yugoslavia Disintegrates A major problem facing the Bush and Clinton administrations was the breakup of Yugoslavia, a country in southeastern Europe. Yugoslavia was made up of six republics, including Slovenia, Croatia, Bosnia-Herzegovina, and Serbia. Of the six, Serbia had the most power.

In 1991, Bosnia declared itself independent, following the lead of Slovenia and Croatia. Serbia and the Bosnian Serbs that they supported began a brutal civil war against Muslim and ethnic Croatian Bosnians.

Read Closely: Motivation
Looking for a group's reasons for its actions can be a helpful tool in understanding history. What motivation did the United Nations probably have for insisting on inspections of weapons-storage sites?

Read Closely: Quotations
Notice which direct quotations the author or authors of a history text choose to include. What does the quotation from President Bush reveal about the Vietnam syndrome?

"Ethnic Cleansing" in Bosnia Forces under Serbian control killed thousands of Bosnian Muslims. They also expelled Muslims and non-Serbs from areas under their control. This practice came to be known as "**ethnic cleansing**." Millions of Bosnian Muslims and others fled.

The United States was reluctant to intervene in the Bosnian war. This was an aftereffect of the Vietnam syndrome. Also, the United States wanted Europe to take more responsibility for its own security.

NATO Intervenes In August 1995, President Clinton decided to work with the North Atlantic Treaty Organization (NATO) to take action. NATO is a military alliance of the United States, Canada, and many European nations. In Operation Deliberate Force, NATO began air attacks on Serbian forces.

In November 1995, the leaders of Bosnia, Croatia, and Serbia signed a treaty in Dayton, Ohio. Bosnia's civil war was over. The peace agreement divided Bosnia into two self-governing regions. A Muslim-Croat federation controlled 51 percent of the country, and a Serb republic held 49 percent. To keep the peace, NATO stationed troops in Bosnia. U.S. soldiers stayed in Bosnia until 2004.

Genocide in Rwanda Deliberately killing people who are part of a certain racial, political, religious, or cultural group is genocide. In 1994, a brutal civil war broke out in Rwanda, in central Africa, between rival ethnic groups—the Hutu and the Tutsi. The majority Hutu killed more than 800,000 Tutsi and moderate Hutu. About two million people fled the country. Many died from disease.

The Clinton administration knew a genocide might happen. However, Clinton decided not to send troops into the region, fearing that an intervention would lead to "another Vietnam." This was another clear example of the Vietnam syndrome.

The genocide lasted about 100 days. The United Nations intervened but had trouble finding countries that would send troops. Tutsi-led forces eventually captured the capital. Political and economic recovery took many years.

War in Kosovo Ethnic and religious conflict also led to war in Kosovo, a province in southern Yugoslavia. (By this time, Yugoslavia was composed of only Serbia and Montenegro.) Ninety percent of the people there were ethnic Albanians, most of whom were Muslim. The other 10 percent were Serbs, most of whom were Orthodox Christian. Albanian Muslims formed the Kosovo Liberation Army in 1996 to fight for independence from Yugoslavia.

Until 1999, Kosovo was a self-governing province within Yugoslavia. It had its own elected officials and Albanian-language schools. In that year, President Slobodan Milosevic of Yugoslavia took away Kosovo's self-rule. He forced its elected officials to resign. People rioted, and Serbian officials cracked down.

Milosevic authorized the murder of dozens of Albanian separatists in Kosovo. Serbian police burned the homes of thousands of Kosovo residents. People fled to Albania. Full-scale war erupted.

Another NATO Intervention The United Nations feared another "ethnic cleansing" operation. It called on both sides to agree to an immediate cease-fire or face NATO air strikes. Milosevic refused. In spring 1999, NATO began a massive air war against Yugoslav and Serbian forces. Milosevic accepted a peace plan a few months later. A 50,000-member multinational force entered Kosovo. Later that year, refugees returned. NATO troops remain in Kosovo. This peacekeeping mission is the longest in NATO history.

Russia's Invasion of Ukraine Russian President Vladimir Putin used the claim that NATO's eastward expansion over time has threatened Russia's security as justification for a February 2022 invasion of its western neighbor, Ukraine. NATO members responded with billions of dollars in humanitarian and military aid to Ukraine's defense of its homeland.

Read Closely: Euphemisms
A euphemism is a mild word or phrase that people use instead of a frightening or offensive word or phrase. As you read history, think about the true meanings of euphemisms. What word or phrase would it be accurate to use instead of *ethnic cleansing*?

Read Closely: Main Concept
After you read a section, you should be able to summarize the individual points into one overall message. Uniting smaller ideas into one underlying concept will help you make sure you understand what you have read. What is the concept in this section?

Application: Interpret a Primary Source

Read the excerpt and answer the questions that follow it.

Speech by UN Secretary-General Kofi Annan, 2004

The genocide in Rwanda should never, ever have happened. But it did. The international community failed Rwanda, and that must leave us always with a sense of bitter regret and abiding sorrow. . . .

I myself, as head of the UN's peacekeeping department at the time, pressed dozens of countries for troops. I believed at that time that I was doing my best. But I realized after the genocide that there was more that I could and should have done to sound the alarm and rally support. This painful memory, along with that of Bosnia and Herzegovina, has influenced much of my thinking, and many of my actions, as Secretary-General.

None of us must ever forget, or be allowed to forget, that genocide did take place in Rwanda, or that it was highly organized, or that it was carried out in broad daylight. No one who followed world affairs or watched the news on television, day after sickening day, could deny that they knew a genocide was happening, and that it was happening on an appalling scale. . . .

In Tanzania, a United Nations criminal tribunal continues to pursue the main perpetrators of the genocide. The tribunal has handed down pioneering verdicts: the first conviction for genocide by an international court; the first to hold a former head of government responsible for genocide; the first to determine that rape was used as an act of genocide; and the first to find journalists guilty of genocide. . . .

With these and other steps, the United Nations is doing what it can to help Rwanda find a path to lasting security and peace. . . .

Source: United Nations, https://www.un.org/press/en/2004/sgsm9223.doc.htm

1. As you read, look for information about the historical context of the primary source. Based on the information in the speech, what can you conclude about his perspective on the Rwandan genocide?

   _____

   _____

2. While reading a primary source, look for examples of similarities and differences to help you understand the events being described. What other part of the world does Annan say had a crisis similar to the one in Rwanda?

   _____

   _____

3. What purpose did Annan have in making this speech? Support your answer with details from the letter.

   _____

   _____

Conceptual Understanding 11.11b In response to the terrorist attacks of September 11, 2001, the United States launched the War on Terror, which involved controversial foreign and domestic policies.

"Freedom was attacked this morning by a faceless coward," President George W. Bush said on September 11, 2001. "And freedom will be defended." Extremists carried out a series of assaults on the United States. These terrorist actions had their roots in anti-Western ideas that had developed over decades. In the resulting War on Terror, the United States pursued terrorists, invaded Afghanistan, and eventually occupied Iraq. Congress also granted significant new powers to government agencies.

Analyze a Primary Source

Two Survivors from the World Trade Center Remember September 11, 2001

Read Closely: Historical Context
Praimnath, originally from Guyana, and Clark, a Canadian, both worked at the World Trade Center in New York City. They were among only four people who were at or above the tower's impact zone who survived.

Read Closely: Point of View
While reading history, consider the value of firsthand accounts. In what way do these firsthand accounts make the attacks vivid in a way that a third-person account might not? Circle details that make the accounts memorable.

Read Closely: Audience
People who have survived historic events often retell their experiences to help those who were not there, or who had not even been born yet, understand what happened. Which parts of these accounts gave you new information about the September 11 attacks? Underline them.

Stanley Praimnath, loan officer: It was the darkest day in my life. Loneliest day in my life. Most horrifying day in my life. When I looked out that window, towards the Statue of Liberty, and I saw that plane coming towards me, I was numb. This monstrous plane looking at me, like, "I'm taking you." Part of the 82nd floor collapsed. All of the walls were knocked flat. I was screaming! Crying! And praying out loud, "Lord! Help me! Please! Send somebody!" ... I felt like this strange force came over me. This power that I've never felt before. And I looked at this wall and I started to hit and punch and kick. And I busted a little hole. And Brian said, "I see your hand!"

Brian Clark, banker: And I heard this, Bang! Bang! Bang! Bang! Bang! Bang! Bang! . . . "Help! Help!" And I was able to grab onto something, whether it was his collar or we locked arms, I'm not sure, and then I lifted him out. And we fell on a heap on the floor, and we introduced ourselves. And he said, "Oh! Hallelujah! I'm Stanley!" And I said, "My name is Brian. We might be friends for life!" You know that sort of emotion overcame us. And then I said, "Come on, let's go. Let's get out of here."

Stanley Praimnath: So here I am, running, screaming, like everybody else. My Lord upheld this building. Then we were in perfect safety. The building collapsed. And here I am, got delivered, and I'm angry. Angry because all of these good people who were there, the firefighters, the cops, the EMS [emergency medical service] workers, all of these good people who were left in this building, which I am sure they were, that couldn't come down from the 81st or 82nd floor because of all of this debris. They perished. So, I'm angry.

Source: PBS Frontline, Voices of September 11, Faith and Doubt at Ground Zero

The September 11 Attacks

On September 11, 2001, a massive terrorist attack took place on U.S. soil. It horrified the nation and much of the world. The causes of the attack were complex, and the repercussions continue to this day.

The Attacks Islamic extremists hijacked four large planes. They flew two into the World Trade Center towers in New York City. Police officers and firefighters rescued as many people as they could before the towers collapsed. Nearly 3,000 people died.

Source: Getty Images

The World Trade Center towers' iconic status made them a target for anti-U.S. terrorists.

Terrorists flew a third plane into the Pentagon, the nation's military headquarters in Washington, D.C. Nearly 200 people died there. The building was badly damaged.

The hijackers planned to fly a fourth plane to Washington, D.C. However, passengers rushed the terrorists in the cockpit. That plane crashed in a field in Pennsylvania. All on board died, including 40 passengers and crew members and four hijackers.

The Attackers The 19 hijackers were Islamic extremists. All were followers of a wealthy Saudi fundamentalist, **Osama bin Laden**. He led a terrorist network called **al-Qaeda** ("the Base").

Roots of Islamic Extremism Tensions between the United States and Islamic fundamentalists go back to the 1920s. In 1928, a group called the Muslim Brotherhood emerged in Egypt. This Arab, Sunni Muslim movement preached a return to a form of Islam with no Western influences. As it spread throughout the Islamic world, anti-Western ideas spread with it.

Anti-Western, and specifically anti-American, beliefs fueled the Shi'ite Muslim–led 1979 Iranian revolution. That conflict toppled Iran's pro-American government and established an Islamic republic. Revolutionaries held 52 Americans hostage for more than a year.

> **Read Closely: Importance of Place**
> To understand the importance of geography in history, notice why events happen in one place rather than another. Why would terrorists focus on New York City and Washington, D.C., rather than less populous U.S. locations that might not be as well defended?

Read Closely: Differences
A political or social movement can experience changes over time. How did Islamic terror attacks change in the 1900s and in 2001?

Read Closely: Cause and Effect
Noticing causes and effects as you read will make it easier for you to understand the flow of historical events. What were some effects of the 9/11 attacks?

Read Closely: Turning Point
Pay attention to short-term and long-term consequences of an action in history. In what way were the 9/11 attacks a turning point in U.S. history?

Islamic Extremism in the 1980s and 1990s In 1993, Islamic terrorists bombed the basement of the World Trade Center. The bombers failed to topple the twin towers. However, the blast killed six people and injured more than 1,000.

Muslim militants bombed two U.S. embassies in Kenya and Tanzania in 1998. These attacks killed 224 people and wounded more than 5,000. Muslim militants also attacked the USS *Cole* in Yemen in 2000, killing 17 sailors.

Americans React to 9/11 The 9/11 attacks struck at major U.S. cities. Hundreds of thousands of Americans saw the destruction in person. Tens of millions more watched on television. The United States closed its airspace for two days, leaving thousands of airline travelers stranded. After 9/11, more Americans enlisted in the armed forces. Americans also donated $2.8 billion to 9/11-related charities.

President George W. Bush wanted an aggressive foreign policy. "I will not wait on events while dangers gather," he said. "I will not stand by as peril draws closer and closer." He described Iraq, Iran, and North Korea as an "axis of evil."

The War on Terror President Bush announced that the nation would fight terrorism across the globe. He said the United States would punish terrorists and any nations that protected them. He asked Congress for anti-terrorist legislation and funds to help rebuild parts of New York City.

The Patriot Act In October 2001, Congress passed the **Patriot Act**. The Act aimed to help the government fight terrorism at home:

- It made it easier for the federal government to get warrants to monitor phone calls and electronic communications among suspected terrorists.

- It allowed government agencies to share more information with one another.

- It gave the government more power to track money that might go to terrorists.

- It let the government detain foreigners who might be terrorists or terrorist supporters.

Invasion of Afghanistan The United States believed that the Afghan government was sheltering bin Laden and his al-Qaeda followers. Islamic fundamentalists called the **Taliban** ("students") controlled most of the country. President Bush demanded that the Taliban turn over bin Laden. They refused.

In October, the United States began air strikes. Joining an alliance of Afghans who opposed the Taliban, the U.S. Air Force struck military bases and troop sites. By early December, the Afghan alliance controlled most of the country. The Taliban's rule ended, but bin Laden was still at large. U.S. forces tracked down and killed bin Laden in Pakistan in 2011.

Afghanistan After Taliban Rule The United States (and about 30 NATO nations) kept troops in Afghanistan to try to stabilize the country. In 2004, Afghanistan had its first democratic presidential election. Regional warlords, fundamentalists, and the Taliban all continued to oppose democracy and the foreign military presence in the country. Military clashes continued and the Taliban even regained control of some areas. As of 2019, a small number of U.S. troops were still in Afghanistan.

The United States Withdraws Troops The Trump administration first made the agreement to remove the remaining U.S. troops from Afghanistan by May of 2021. President Biden also supported the evacuation of U.S. soldiers. Soon after the last troops had left, the Afghan government quickly collapsed, allowing the Taliban to reestablish control. The United States still considered the Taliban a terrorist organization and froze Afghan assest in U.S. banks. Eventually, much of the money was directed to humanitarian crises caused by the Taliban takeover.

The Constitution in Times of Crisis

How far will Americans go to feel safe? Congress, the president, and ordinary citizens struggled with this question after 9/11. Many people wanted government agencies to have more power to stop terrorists. However, giving the government powers that were too broad and sweeping would violate Americans' constitutional rights. The Fourth Amendment of the Constitution protects against unreasonable searches and seizures.

Impact of the Patriot Act Before 9/11, Congress focused on international terrorism. The Patriot Act focused on terrorism within the United States as well as abroad. It provided new penalties for bioterrorism and for attacks on mass transit systems. It also updated the law to reflect new technologies.

How helpful was the Patriot Act? A 2015 Justice Department report said the FBI could not name any specific instances in which its new mass surveillance powers helped agents crack terrorism cases. However, FBI Director Robert Mueller defended the Patriot Act. He said that trying to fight terrorism without it would be like having "one hand behind our backs."

The Act's Effects on Civil Liberties Patriot Act critics opposed suspending **civil liberties** for terrorism suspects. The government could now search personal records for links to terrorism. It could also detain foreign suspects while denying them lawyers and open hearings. The Act let the government spy on ordinary Americans as well as possible terrorists.

Electronic Surveillance Programs The Patriot Act let government officials collect phone and Internet metadata from U.S. citizens without their notice or consent. Metadata is information about information. Government officials could monitor who called whom and when. However, they could not monitor the actual conversations without getting a warrant from a judge.

Police used listening devices called wiretaps in their investigations. Under the Patriot Act, government intelligence agencies could too. In both cases, the investigators needed a warrant from a judge.

Changes to Surveillance Laws Many requirements of the Patriot Act expired in 2005. President Bush reauthorized the Act. In 2015, President Barack Obama signed a new law related to terrorism. It reauthorized many Patriot Act provisions. However, it ended bulk collection of Americans' phone and Internet metadata.

Read Closely: Course of Action
When reading, put yourself in the place of historical figures. It will help you understand how and why they made decisions. If you had been a member of Congress in 2001, would you have voted for the Patriot Act? Why or why not?

Civic Literacy: Freedom vs. Security Throughout history, governments have struggled with how to pass laws that strike the right balance, providing both freedom and security. Laws that are too lax allow people to conspire to attack the state or to harm other citizens. Laws that are too strict or too sweeping often end with innocent citizens being treated like criminals.

Regime Change in Iraq

President Bush continued to be concerned about Iraq, Iran, and North Korea. Many people in the U.S. government believed these countries either had nuclear weapons or were developing them. The president turned first to Iraq. His father (President George H.W. Bush) had helped defeat Iraq after its invasion of Kuwait but had not overthrown Iraq's dictator, Saddam Hussein.

Competing Groups in Iraq The country had three rival groups within it:

- Sunnis, one of the two major branches of Islam, made up about 32–37 percent of Iraq's population. For years, Sunnis had dominated the national government in Iraq.

- The Shiites, the other major branch of Islam, made up about 60–65 percent of the population. Shiite Muslims were a majority in Iraq and Iran.

- The Kurds, an ethnic rather than a religious group, were strong in northern Iraq. The overwhelming majority of Kurds were Sunni Muslims but identified most strongly as Kurds.

Iraqis by ethnicity

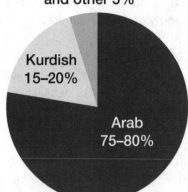

Turkmen, Assyrian and other 5%

Kurdish 15–20%

Arab 75–80%

Iraqis by religion

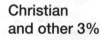
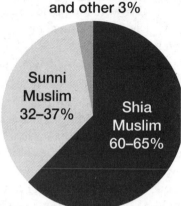

Christian and other 3%

Sunni Muslim 32–37%

Shia Muslim 60–65%

Source: CIA World Factbook

Read Closely: Comparisons
Noting how groups are distinctive even as they share some traits can help you understand how they act. How were the three competing groups within Iraq similar? How were they different?

Iraqi ruler Saddam Hussein ran a brutal dictatorship. He suppressed all dissent, denied basic human rights, and jailed or killed opponents. Saddam used poison gas to kill Kurds in 1988 and Shiites in 1991.

A Possible Preemptive Strike After 9/11, U.S. government officials began to consider an attack on Iraq. They contended that Iraq had developed **weapons of mass destruction (WMDs)** it might use against its neighbors. A WMD is a chemical, nuclear, biological, or other device designed to harm many people. In an attempt to head off an attack by the United States, Saddam Hussein allowed United Nations inspectors into Iraq in late 2002. The Iraqis appeared to comply with the UN resolutions regarding compliance with previous resolutions and inspections. However, the United States and Great Britain claimed Iraq was still hiding WMDs. U.S. President George W. Bush and British Prime Minister Tony Blair began seeking support for military action against Iraq.

Opposition to such an attack grew in Europe. Leaders of France, Germany, and Russia said UN weapons inspections should continue. They threatened to veto a U.S. resolution in the United Nations authorizing a coalition of military forces to invade Iraq.

The United States had the support of a smaller coalition. This group included Great Britain, Australia, and Spain. However, many Islamic nations feared warring against another Islamic country. Saudi Arabia asked the United States to withdraw its troops that had been stationed there since the Persian Gulf War.

Read Closely: Motivations
As you read, think about why people and countries act as they do. Why do you think Saudi Arabia asked the United States to withdraw troops?

Operation Iraqi Freedom In March 2003, the U.S.-led coalition launched an attack called "**Operation Iraqi Freedom**." By May, Iraqi military forces were defeated. U.S. soldiers captured Saddam Hussein, who was hiding in a hole in the ground. In 2006, an Iraqi court convicted him of crimes against humanity and hanged him.

Postwar Problems The United States occupied Iraq. Occupation forces needed to rebuild cities and restore electricity and water services. They also had to stop people from looting and provide jobs. But guerrilla and terrorist attacks posed an even greater challenge. These were often in the form of suicide bombings, and they targeted U.S. troops, coalition forces, and civilians. Many more U.S. soldiers died in these attacks than in the initial war. By April 2008, more than 4,000 Americans, and several hundred coalition soldiers, had died in the fighting.

The Iraqi people suffered in strikingly greater numbers than did U.S. and coalition soldiers in the war's aftermath. Military groups came together around different religious beliefs, ethnicities, and ideologies. Some fought each other and most fought the U.S. and coalition forces. The resulting casualties, added to those who perished in the war itself, were devastating. By one estimate, as many as 275,000 Iraqis died as a direct result of violence between 2003 and mid-2011.

The United States searched Iraq for weapons of mass destruction. They did not find any. U.S. officials changed their rationale for the war, saying that "regime change," removing Saddam Hussein, was enough reason to fight. Many Americans, both private citizens and people within the government, felt that without proof of WMDs, war had been sought under false pretenses. Many people wanted the United States to concentrate on fighting al-Qaeda.

Toward a New Iraqi Government In July 2003, the United States set up a 25-member Governing Council in Iraq. The council included Shiites, Sunnis, and Kurds. In March 2004, the Governing Council signed an interim constitution. It provided for the following:

- a federal system of government

- equal rights for all Iraqis, regardless of religion, ethnicity, or gender

- freedom of expression and worship

It also recognized the special role of Islamic law as a basis for Iraqi law. Experts considered this constitution one of the most democratic in the Middle East.

An interim Iraqi government took power in June 2004. However, ongoing conflicts between rival religious, ethnic, and political factions prevented peace or stability. U.S. troops, too, continued to be involved in armed confrontations. Most Iraqis still experienced shortages of electricity and clean water. Roads, bridges, schools, and hospitals were still in disrepair. Conditions slowly improved over time, with violence decreasing somewhat after 2007. The United States agreed to a timetable for withdrawing its troops, turning security operations over to Iraqi forces. The final U.S. withdrawal was complete by the end of 2011. Iraq's troubles, however, were far from over, as instability and factional fighting continued.

> **Read Closely: Connections**
> Consider how the different historical events you are reading about may be connected. Why would the occupation forces want to restore power and water, stop looters, and create jobs?

> **Read Closely: Context**
> Pay attention to the place and time in which an event happens. Why would the new constitution include a recognition of the special role of Islamic law?

Application: Interpret a Primary Source

Read the excerpt and answer the questions that follow it.

Muslims Denounce September 11 Attacks

The undersigned, leaders of Islamic movements, are horrified (ra`ahum) by the events of Tuesday, 11 Sept. 2001 in the United States which resulted in massive killing (qatl), destruction (tadmeer) and attack (i`tida) on innocent lives.

We express our deepest sympathies and sorrow. We condemn, in the strongest terms, the incidents (hawadith; word shared with Hebrew in "hadasah") which are against all human and Islamic norms. This is grounded in the Noble Laws of Islam which forbid all forms of attacks on innocents. God Almighty says in the Holy Qur'an: "No bearer of burdens can bear the burden [wizr] of another." (Surah al-Isra 17:15)

We also decry the targeting of the faith of Islam and its followers before the investigation determines the culprits. The condemnation (idanah) should be limited to them—who ever did it—and not extended to others.

With the obscurities (ghumuz, word shared with Hebrew) surrounding this incident and the multitude of parties with interest in such horrendous acts, the undersigned hope the investigators and the media will exercise caution. Do not hurry to pronounce a guilty party until you are sure of the forces (quwa, word shared with Hebrew) behind this horrific, painful (aleem) act (haadith, word shared with Hebrew).

We wish to convey our sincerest condolences to the families of the innocent victims and the American people.

Source: "Muslim Scholars and Intellectuals Condemn Attacks in New York and Washington," *Al-Quds Al-Arabi* newspaper, London,

1. Forty-six prominent Muslims signed this letter. They included politicians, scholars, and leaders from throughout the Muslim world. Based on this information, what can you conclude about the timing of this letter?

_____

_____

2. Based on this letter and on what you have read in this lesson, what effects were the letter writers concerned about?

_____

_____

3. Authors often write to accomplish multiple purposes. According to this letter, what three purposes did the letter writers have? Describe them in your own words.

_____

_____

Lesson 3 Technology and Globalization

Over the course of his life, Juan Trippe was consistently ahead of his time. He was an early aviator, flying missions during World War 1. He cofounded Pan American Airlines in 1927, becoming its first president. Pan American consistently led the way in early days of commercial aviation under Trippe's leadership. His position as an industry leader and commercial visionary placed him perfectly to predict the direction of the future economy.

Conceptual Understanding
11.11c Globalization and advances in technology have affected the United States economy and society.

Analyze a Primary Source

Juan Trippe Predicts Globalization, 1943

Read Closely: Historical Context
Trippe gave this speech during World War II. During that war, there were about 350,000 women who served in the armed forces and about 16 million men. Women did not serve in combat then. Alaska and Hawaii did not become U.S. states until 1959.

Tonight, as we are gathered here at the World Trade Dinner, two thoughts are uppermost in the minds of all of us. First, to win the war as speedily as possible. Second, to expand our system of free enterprise—our American way of life—in order to provide jobs at decent wages for the millions of fighting men who are now employed in strictly war industries. . . .

A century ago, we were one of the world's great trading nations. . . . When we . . . started moving west the interest and energies of our people turned inland. We lost interest in foreign trade. We concentrated on domestic development. That job was big enough to keep us occupied for a hundred years. With an energetic people, great natural resources, and freedom for the individual to rise as fast as his abilities would carry him, we built a great nation, and provided for our citizens a standard of living higher than anyone ever before dreamed of. . . .

Read Closely: Purpose
Trippe wanted to persuade his audience of three key ideas. What were they? Underline them in the first and last paragraphs.

Thanks to domestic transportation and communications, our forty-eight states are a neighborhood. New York and San Francisco are closer in time than were New York and Philadelphia a hundred years ago. And today, having accomplished all this in our own country, we can play our part in accomplishing the same thing throughout the world.

Man now stands on the threshold of the Age of Flight, the Air Age, when not just single nations or single continents, but the entire globe, will become one neighborhood. . . .

Read Closely: Point of View
As a business leader, Trippe saw globalization largely as a financial issue. In the last paragraph of this excerpt, what two things did he suggest that American businesses do? Circle his advice.

We in the United States should get our fair share of this vast future commerce. We must maintain our political and economic position in the world. Only by becoming once again a great world trading nation can we do this. Only in this way shall we be able to provide the millions of new jobs which must be found if our democracy, our system of free enterprise, our American way of life, is to endure. . . .

Source: from Juan Trippe, "Foreign Trade in the Air Age," address delivered October 26, 1943, New York City

The United States in a Global Age

Advances in technology make it easier than ever to communicate with people across the globe. A system of free trade makes it possible to buy and sell goods and services over long distances. But this interconnected world has had unexpected consequences.

What Is Globalization? The term **globalization** refers to the spreading of commerce and culture on a worldwide scale. Globalization began more than 2,000 years ago on the Silk Roads. These trading routes connected Eurasia. For the most part, traders on the Silk Roads moved luxury items—silk, spices, gems, and so on—from Asia to Europe. But today's globalization affects far more people. For most, using products and services that come from foreign countries is an everyday activity.

Globalization and Free Trade After World War II, many U.S. companies kept their headquarters in U.S. cities but opened factories in other nations. These were often in poorer countries that had lower labor costs, plentiful raw materials, or both. By the 1980s, the largest U.S. companies had turned themselves into **multinational corporations**. In other words, they did business in many countries.

Read Closely: Cause and Effect
Notice when one process or event influences or directly causes future outcomes. What was the effect of lower tariffs?

Tariffs made globalization more difficult. A tariff is a tax on goods that go out of or come into a country. From the 1990s forward, the governments of most countries kept tariffs low. This made international trade more profitable. **Free trade** means that people can buy from and sell to people in other countries with few or no tariffs.

NAFTA Many governments began to focus on free trade. President George H.W. Bush began negotiations for the **North American Free Trade Agreement (NAFTA)** with Mexico and Canada. His successor, President Clinton, completed them. NAFTA began in 1994. It ended tariffs on some goods and gradually removed them on others.

People who favored NAFTA said it would create jobs. They also said better economic conditions in Mexico would reduce illegal immigration to the United States. NAFTA critics said that companies would send jobs from the United States and Canada to Mexico. People in Mexico would work for less money.

Read Closely: Motivations
As you read about trade agreements, note the combination of ideas and goals that motivate people. Why do you think nations in Central and South America wanted to join NAFTA even though its results had been mixed?

After NAFTA The results of NAFTA were mixed. Mexico's imports and exports increased. This meant Mexican consumers got better, less expensive products. While some U.S. and Canadian companies moved jobs to take advantage of lower wage costs in Mexico, the job losses were not significant. For its part, Mexico did not see a closing of the wage gap between its workers and those of its NAFTA partners. In the end, the agreement did make the economies of the signatories more interdependent, which has been viewed both positively and negatively, depending on who one asks.

In 2004, NAFTA expanded to five Central American countries. In 2006 and 2007, some South American countries joined the agreement.

President **Donald J. Trump** opposed NAFTA. In 2018, he renegotiated a trade deal with Mexico and Canada. Trump also put new tariffs on Canadian steel and aluminum. Critics said Trump's actions could lead to a **trade war**, wherein other countries could levy tariffs against U.S. goods.

Globalization and Advances in Technology During the 1990s, the Internet began connecting many people around the globe. This communication system simplified aspects of doing business globally. A company could research and develop a product in one country. Then it could make it in a second country and sell it in still other countries.

Email and online shopping made ordering products faster. Shipping became more efficient. Trade grew. Imports and exports are now more than half of the total value of the goods and services produced in the world. The World Bank says that in the United States, trade as a percentage of the GDP in the U.S. grew from 9 percent in 1960 to 27 percent in 2017.

Source: Getty Images

Large container ships transport goods quickly and efficiently, fueling the global economy.

What happened because of these changes? Businesses and investments began to move beyond domestic and national borders. Globalization opened up opportunities for foreign investment and new manufacturing capacities worldwide.

Globalization's Positive Consequences Globalization has vastly increased world trade. It has opened up world markets for U.S. goods and services. People who favor globalization argue that it allows workers in poor countries to have higher living standards.

Living and working conditions have improved greatly in much of the world. In 2018, experts calculated that about half the world's population was middle class or rich. That is about 3.8 billion people. Never in human civilization had such a large percentage of people escaped poverty. However, globalization is only one of many factors that have changed the world economy.

Globalization's Negative Consequences Critics contend that globalization helps rich people and harms poor ones. Rich people get less expensive products to buy. Poorer people may earn less for their work or may lose their jobs. Globalization can allow economies to develop rapidly, but industrial production in the developing world often has negative consequences for the environment.

> **Read Closely: Synthesize**
> As you read this lesson, connect what you are learning to what you have learned in earlier lessons and from other sources. Based on that information, what other factors may have led to a reduction of the percentage of humans who live in poverty?

Multinational Corporate Influence

Some critics say that globalization makes multinational corporations more powerful than governments. Most governments have elections and other ways that average people can make their voices heard. But a multinational corporation may have only a small group of people in charge of it.

The Rise of Multinationals Multinational corporations have been a part of the American economy since the Dutch West India Company ran a trade-centered colony in what later became New York. But industrialization, globalization, and technology have made multinationals increasingly important in American life.

From the start of the industrial era, U.S. companies built factories overseas to sell products in those foreign markets. Over time, communication improved and shipping became more affordable. U.S. firms hired foreign companies to make products and then shipped them back to the United States to sell in the U.S. market. The overall cost was less because wage rates were lower in less-developed countries. In a word, U.S. corporations began to outsource manufacturing jobs.

Today, about half of Americans who work in the private sector work for large companies that have more than 500 employees. These large firms often pay higher wages than smaller businesses do. However, critics worry that some multinational corporations—only the very largest and most successful—have too much influence on the U.S. government and economy.

Corporate Influence on the United States Corporations argue that outsourcing improves profits. They insist it is necessary for companies to remain competitive. They suggest that outsourced workers can find other jobs. They also point out that lower labor costs drive down the cost of products for all Americans.

Issues of corporate influence and corporate responsibility continue to concern many Americans.

- Large corporations often pay little or no income tax.

- Some communities offer tens of millions of dollars in tax breaks for corporations to move there.

- Some critics believe that corporations such as Amazon, Google, and Apple will develop monopoly power in their industries. A company that has a monopoly controls all of a market. With no competition, it can set its prices as high as it wants to.

Corporate Influence on Other Countries Multinational corporations are often rich, powerful, and able to relocate their offices and factories to different countries. These qualities can make it challenging for governments to negotiate with them.

Corporations often hire lobbyists to influence politicians. A **lobbyist** is someone who works to influence lawmakers about a certain issue or industry. In a free society, lobbyists and the groups who pay them have a right to express themselves. Corporations are not the only groups to hire lobbyists. So do environmental groups, unions, religious organizations and many others. However, critics worry that the amount of money a huge multinational can spend on lobbying might have a disproportionate effect on lawmaking. Canada, Australia, and many other countries have restricted corporate lobbying.

Read Closely: Comparisons
While reading history, compare what you are learning about different people and groups. Why would wage rates be lower in less-developed countries than in developed ones?

Read Closely: Analysis
One way to grasp complicated events is to break them into smaller or more specific parts that are easier to understand. Why would a government try to control a company's monopoly power?

China's Economic and Strategic Rise

As the world's most populous nation, China offers the greatest opportunities in the world for U.S. commerce. However, China has repeatedly violated human rights. The United States and other countries have urged China to improve its human rights record. This pressure has been a barrier to full-scale trade with the United States.

China's Gradual Evolution China was a U.S. ally during World War II. U.S. policymakers hoped it would become a democracy. But Communists under **Mao Zedong**'s leadership took over the government of mainland China. In a Communist society, the government controls all, or nearly all, of the economy. During the Cold War, capitalist and Communist governments directly opposed one another.

From 1950 until 1970, the United States and China did not trade with each other. China's economy was based on farming, and it had little contact with other countries.

In 1972, President Richard Nixon visited China. He did this, in part, to put pressure on the Soviet Union. China and the Soviet Union had broken ties in 1960. Gradually, the United States and China began trading with each other.

Between 1978 and 1989, China's leaders made social and economic reforms. They let students criticize government policies and suggest ideas for making government more democratic. They opened their country to Western tourists. But most importantly, they significantly changed the Chinese economy. Led by Deng Xiaoping, China adopted the "Four Modernizations," introducing sweeping changes in key areas:

- Agriculture
- Industry
- Science and technology
- National defense

Investment and improvement in these areas was combined with a much greater engagement with the international economy. After 1984, a number of cities designated as "special economic zones" began to drive China's steady rise in manufacturing and international trade.

Crackdown in Tiananmen Square The spring of 1989 saw a brutal end to reform and openness in China. One hundred thousand students and other citizens had gathered in **Tiananmen Square** in the capital of Beijing. They demonstrated peacefully and urged the government to make democratic reforms. The government ordered troops to fire on the demonstrators. In a few hours, soldiers killed several thousand protesters.

The United States and other nations protested the massacre. For the most part, however, President George H.W. Bush followed much the same policy toward China as before. Congress passed economic sanctions on China, but he did not carry them out. Bush argued that the United States could best help the Chinese people by staying on good terms with China's government. President Clinton continued this policy, even while China was arresting its citizens who favored democratic reforms.

China's Economy Grows and Matures Over decades, the Chinese government allowed the economy to grow and develop even as government control over the Chinese people stayed strict. Between 1990 and 2015, China had the fastest-growing economy in the world.

> **Read Closely: Trends**
> Notice the gradual changes that take place in societies over time. How would you describe economic and political trends in China between World War II and 1989?

In 2011, China became the second-largest economy in the world, after the United States. It has reached the following milestones:

- the world's largest trading nation (as measured by the sum of exports and imports of goods)
- the largest exporter of goods
- the second-largest importer of goods
- the country with the most self-made female billionaires

Experts say that China's economy is now about the same size as the U.S. economy. But China has four times the population of the United States. That means China's economic power is likely to grow quickly.

A Trade Deficit China and the United States are major trade partners. The United States has a **trade deficit** with China. A trade deficit happens when one country buys more from another country than it sells to that country.

In 2018, the trade gap between the countries was $419 billion. In other words, the United States bought $419 billion more in goods from China than it sold to China. In 2018, President Trump expressed a desire to reduce the trade deficit. He imposed tariffs on $250 billion in Chinese goods, but demand for Chinese products remained high.

China and the United States: The Strategic Rivalry China's growing economic power changed its strategic relationship with the United States. Both countries sought markets for their products and inexpensive yet high-quality goods for their citizens. Their governments remained very different, though.

The Chinese government had far more control over individuals and businesses than did the U.S. government. China continued to be an authoritarian society ruled by the Communist Party, even as capitalism flourished there.

China undertook a program to modernize its military. It also took a more prominent role in regional and global issues. However, the Chinese government recognized the military and economic power of the United States. The relationship between the two countries will remain complicated.

Read Closely: Make Predictions
Look for patterns in events that can help you predict what will happen next. Based on what you know about China's population and economy, what is China's economic future likely to be?

Source: Wikimedia Commons

President Xi Jinping with President Donald Trump

Application: Interpret a Primary Source

Read the excerpt and answer the questions that follow it.

Teenager Speaks at United Nations Climate Conference, 2018

My name is Greta Thunberg. I am 15 years old. I am from Sweden. . . . Many people say that Sweden is just a small country and it doesn't matter what we do. **But I've learned you are never too small to make a difference. . . .**

You only speak of green eternal economic growth because you are too scared of being unpopular. You only talk about moving forward with the same bad ideas that got us into this mess, even when the only sensible thing to do is pull the emergency brake. You are not mature enough to tell it like it is. Even that burden you leave to us children. But I don't care about being popular. I care about climate justice and the living planet. Our civilization is being sacrificed for the opportunity of a very small number of people to continue making enormous amounts of money. **Our biosphere is being sacrificed so that rich people in countries like mine can live in luxury**. It is the sufferings of the many which pay for the luxuries of the few. . . .

You say you love your children above all else, and yet **you are stealing their future in front of their very eyes**.

Until you start focusing on what needs to be done rather than what is politically possible, there is no hope. **We can't solve a crisis without treating it as a crisis.** We need to keep the fossil fuels in the ground, and we need to focus on equity. And if solutions within the system are so impossible to find, maybe we should change the system itself. We have not come here to beg world leaders to care. You have ignored us in the past and you will ignore us again. We have run out of excuses and we are running out of time. We have come here to let you know that change is coming, whether you like it or not. The real power belongs to the people. Thank you.

Source: from Greta Thunberg, speech for the United Nations Climate Change Conference, December 15, 2018, Katowice, Poland,

> ***Speak and Listen:***
> ***Worldview*** With a partner or in a small group, talk about Greta Thunberg's worldview, or philosophy. Is it typical of young people's worldviews, or is hers unique? How does her worldview compare to your own? Be as specific as you can.

1. When reading a primary source, look for information about the historical context of the primary source. In 2018, Thunberg began a one-person climate strike outside the Swedish parliament each Friday. Her movement grew to more than 1,700 events in more than a dozen countries, as students skipped school on Fridays to demand that governments and corporations do more to solve climate change. Why might people object to these types of student protests?

_____

_____

_____

_____

2. Think about whether any of the events you are reading about could have a significant effect on future events. According to Thunberg, in what way is climate change a turning point in world history? Support your answer with details from the speech.

_____

_____

_____

_____

_____

3. Thunberg states, "We have not come here to beg world leaders to care." What is her purpose in giving this speech?

_____

_____

_____

_____

Source: Wikimedia Commons

Greta Thunberg at the front banner of a Fridays For Future demonstration in Berlin

Multiple-Choice Questions

Questions 1 and 2 refer to the excerpt below.

A. Resolved: That Humanitarian Intervention Does More Harm Than Good

The international community currently faces a global refugee crisis and mass atrocities in Iraq, Myanmar, Syria, Yemen, and beyond. How should the West respond?

Proponents of humanitarian intervention – the use of force to halt human rights abuses – argue that the world's most powerful militaries have a responsibility to protect innocent civilians around the world. Beyond saving lives, they argue, intervention deters would-be abusers and ensures global stability, thereby strengthening the liberal world order. But opponents argue that military intervention is thinly veiled Western imperialism, and subsequently, an assault on state sovereignty. And, it's ineffective: the West, with its military might, increases the death toll and worsens the conflicts it sets out to solve. Further, given recent waves of populism in the U.S., France, and U.K., they suggest that Western nations should spend their time looking inward rather than policing activity around the world.

For the Motion [arguments against intervention]:

- Despite good intentions, humanitarian intervention invariably leads to instability, occupation, and the death of innocent civilians.

- State sovereignty must be respected on the world stage. Unless acting in self-defense or facing an imminent threat, nations have no right to use military force against another state.

Against the Motion [arguments for intervention]:

- All U.N. member states have endorsed the Responsibility to Protect doctrine, a global political commitment to halt or prevent genocide and war crimes. These states have an obligation to uphold this promise.

- Violent civil wars often have spillover effects, leading to regional instability that could threaten global security.

Source: Debate Sponsored by the German Marshall Fund's Brussels Forum, Brussels, Belgium, March 9, 2018

1. According to this excerpt, which of the following is a problem for which humanitarian intervention might be considered an appropriate response?

   1. Western imperialism

   2. Waves of populism in the U.S., France, and the U.K.

   3. The liberal world order

   4. Mass atrocities in several countries

2. According to this excerpt, what is a frequent result of humanitarian intervention?

   1. The overthrow of ruthless dictators
   2. An increased death toll
   3. The establishment of stable democracies
   4. The global refugee crisis

Questions 3–5 refer to the excerpt below.

B. The Positive Side of Globalization

> Globalization, the increasing integration of world markets, has already done a lot of great things for Americans.
>
> It has helped America win the war on communism. It has freed Americans from government regulations and militant unions. It has assigned America the role of the world's best innovator. It has helped America sustain its lead as the world's largest economy.
>
> And it has helped Americans get wealthy and enjoy one of the world's highest standards of living.
>
> For the record, globalization is not new. The most recent opening of national and local markets to international trade and competition is a resumption of an old trend that began in the last quarter of the 19th century, which was interrupted in the first half of the 20th century by the rise of nationalism, communism and trade/military wars.
>
> Today's globalization is an American invention. It began with America's initiative to create GATT [General Agreement on Tariffs and Trade] (now WTO [World Trade Organization])/IMF [International Monetary Fund]/ World Bank – a regime to save its economy and the world from the threat of communism by creating a world market, which would help each country excel in what it does best.
>
> There's a well-tested economic theory behind the basic premise behind globalization: it is called comparative advantage. And it produced the hoped-for results. By the mid-1980s, the war against communism was won. The Soviet Union collapsed, and its satellite countries rushed to join America's world market regime.
>
> **Source:** Panos Mourdoukoutas, "Globalization Has Done a Lot of Great Things for Americans," *Forbes*, January 3, 2017

3. Which of the following best describes continuity and change in history as identified by the author in this excerpt?

   1. The author says out that globalization has done many great things for the United States.
   2. The author says that Americans have achieved one of the world's highest standards of living as a result of globalization.
   3. The author says that globalization began in the late 19th century, but today's globalization came about as a result of American-led international economic initiatives.
   4. The author says that globalization led to the collapse of the Soviet Union.

4. What evidence does the author offer in support of his claim that globalization has done a lot of great things for Americans?

   1. He says that today's globalization is an American invention.
   2. He says that the United States initiated the creation of several organizations to save our economy.
   3. He says that it opened up international markets for American products.
   4. He says that it has helped the United States remain the world's largest economy.

5. Which of the following best describes the author's probable purpose in writing this article?

   1. He wanted to show how globalization helped win the war on communism.
   2. He wanted to defend globalization from its detractors.
   3. He wanted to explain how globalization works.
   4. He wanted to provide a rationale for international economic organizations.

Questions 6–8 refer to the excerpt below.

C. A Brief Look at Relations Between the United States and China

The U.S.–China relationship is confronting its most daunting challenge in the forty years since the two countries established diplomatic ties. Current trends portend [warn of something bad] steadily worsening relations over the long term, with increasingly adverse consequences for all actors involved. Specifically, Beijing and Washington are transitioning from a sometimes contentious [likely to cause an argument] yet mutually beneficial relationship to an increasingly antagonistic, mutually destructive set of interactions. The often positive and optimistic forces, interests, and beliefs that sustained bilateral ties for decades are giving way to undue pessimism, hostility, and a zero-sum mindset in almost every area of engagement.

Both sides bear responsibility for this pervasive deterioration, but at present the United States under President Donald Trump is unquestionably contributing most publicly to it, primarily through its ill-considered rhetorical and other overreactions to perceived Chinese misbehavior. While nothing about this degenerating relationship is inevitable (despite the uninformed alarmist predictions of doomsayers on both sides), the threat of an even more precipitous and dangerous decline in the relationship is very real and demands serious corrective measures to avert a potential catastrophe.

To understand how we have reached this point and how to put the Sino-American relationship on a more positive path, analysts first need to dispel the simplistic and largely negative misconceptions about the past that predominate today, especially in the United States. Next, observers need to grasp the highly adverse structural and attitudinal trends driving the current negative dynamic, the serious dangers these trends pose for both countries and the world (including the possibility of a new Cold War), and the high stakes involved in correcting or mitigating [making less harmful] them. From that vantage point, policymakers may better discern which actions each side must take to stabilize and strengthen the relationship for their mutual benefit.

Source: Michael D. Swaine, "A Relationship Under Extreme Duress: U.S.-China Relations at a Crossroads", Carnegie Endowment for International Peace, January 16, 2019

6. How does this excerpt demonstrate the impact of time and place?

    1. It places the relationship of China and the United States in the context of a new Cold War.

    2. It describes current trends in the context of 40 years of renewed diplomatic ties.

    3. It describes President Trump's attempts to correct the trade imbalance by imposing tariffs.

    4. It describes Chinese retaliation against tariffs imposed by the United States.

7. According to Swaine, what is the chief reason for the deterioration of relations between the United States and China?

    1. President Trump's rhetoric and overreactions

    2. China's failure to renounce communism

    3. Chinese misbehavior (such as the theft of U.S. intellectual property and patents)

    4. A new Cold War

8. According to this excerpt, what is the first step in dealing with the problem of deteriorating relations between the United States and China?

    1. The United States needs to reestablish diplomatic relations with China.

    2. The Chinese need to stop stealing U.S. intellectual property and patents.

    3. Analysts need to get rid of their negative misconceptions about the past.

    4. The United States needs to prepare for a new Cold War.

Short-Essay Questions

Study the two documents and answer the question that follows.

D. Who Is the Enemy?

Who is this enemy that created an organization capable of inflicting such horrific damage on the United States? We now know that these attacks were carried out by various groups of Islamist extremists. The 9/11 attack was driven by Usama Bin Ladin.

In the 1980s, young Muslims from around the world went to Afghanistan to join as volunteers in a jihad (or holy struggle) against the Soviet Union. A wealthy Saudi, Usama Bin Ladin, was one of them. Following the defeat of the Soviets in the late 1980s, Bin Ladin and others formed al Qaeda to mobilize jihads elsewhere.

The history, culture, and body of beliefs from which Bin Ladin shapes and spreads his message are largely unknown to many Americans. Seizing on symbols of Islam's past greatness, he promises to restore pride to people who consider themselves the victims of successive foreign masters. He uses cultural and religious allusions to the holy Qur'an and some of its interpreters. He appeals to people disoriented by cyclonic change as they confront modernity and globalization. His rhetoric selectively draws from multiple sources—Islam, history, and the region's political and economic malaise.

Bin Ladin also stresses grievances against the United States widely shared in the Muslim world. He inveighed against the presence of U.S. troops in Saudi Arabia, which is the home of Islam's holiest sites, and against other U.S. policies in the Middle East.

Source: *The 9/11 Commission Report*: Executive Summary, 2004

E. A Former White House Chief of Staff Speaks Out on the Patriot Act

Recent tragic events have brought about a rapid reconsideration of the legal restrictions placed on law enforcement and the intelligence communities. On October 26, President Bush signed into law the USA Patriot Act (Patriot Act), which makes significant changes in the legal structure within which the law enforcement and intelligence communities operate. This article focuses on the key provisions of the Patriot Act that pertain to electronic surveillance and intelligence gathering. . . .

Many of the electronic surveillance provisions in the Patriot Act faced serious opposition prior to September 11 from a coalition of privacy advocates, computer users, and elements of high-tech industry. The events of September 11 convinced many in that coalition and overwhelming majorities in Congress that law enforcement and national security officials need new legal tools to fight terrorism. But we should not forget what gave rise to the original opposition—many aspects of the bill increase the opportunity for law enforcement and the intelligence community to return to an era where they monitored and sometimes harassed individuals who were merely exercising their First Amendment rights. Nothing that occurred on September 11 mandates that we return to such an era. If anything, the events of September 11 should redouble our resolve to protect the rights we as Americans cherish. Therefore, as the new powers granted under the Patriot Act begin to be exercised, we should not only feel more confident that our country has the tools to be safe but we should be ever vigilant that these new tools are not abused.

Source: John Podesta, "USA Patriot Act: The Good, the Bad, and the Sunset," *Human Rights Magazine*, Winter 2002

1. In a short essay, describe the historical context surrounding the two documents above. Then identify and explain the cause-and-effect relationship between the events described in these documents.

Study the two documents and answer the question that follows.

F. Who Really Triggered the Gulf War?

July 25, 1990 – Presidential Palace – Baghdad

U.S. Ambassador Glaspie – I have direct instructions from President Bush to improve our relations with Iraq. We have considerable sympathy for your quest for higher oil prices, the immediate cause of your confrontation with Kuwait. (pause) As you know, I lived here for years and admire your extraordinary efforts to rebuild your country. We know you need funds. We understand that, and our opinion is that you should have the opportunity to rebuild your country. (pause) We can see that you have deployed massive numbers of troops in the south. Normally that would be none of our business, but when this happens in the context of your threat s against Kuwait, then it would be reasonable for us to be concerned. For this reason, I have received an instruction to ask you, in the spirit of friendship – not confrontation – regarding your intentions: Why are your troops massed so very close to Kuwait's borders?

Saddam Hussein – As you know, for years now I have made every effort to reach a settlement on our dispute with Kuwait. There is to be a meeting in two days; I am prepared to give negotiations only this one more brief chance. (pause) When we (the Iraqis) meet (with the Kuwaitis) and we see there is hope, then nothing will happen. But if we are unable to find a solution, then it will be natural that Iraq will not accept death.

U.S. Ambassador Glaspie – What solutions would be acceptable?

Saddam Hussein – If we could keep the whole of the Shatt al Arab – our strategic goal in our war with Iran – we will make concessions (to the Kuwaitis). But, if we are forced to choose between keeping half of the Shatt and the whole of Iraq (i.e., in Saddam's view, including Kuwait) then we will give up all of the Shatt to defend our claims on Kuwait to keep the whole of Iraq in the shape we wish it to be. (pause) What is the United States' opinion on this?

U.S. Ambassador Glaspie – We have no opinion on your Arab – Arab conflicts, such as your dispute with Kuwait. Secretary (of State James) Baker has directed me to emphasize the instruction, first given to Iraq in the 1960's, that the Kuwait issue is not associated with America. (Saddam smiles)

Source: Transcript of a Meeting Between Iraqi President Saddam Hussein and U.S. Ambassador to Iraq April Glaspie, July 25, 1990

G. The U.S. Policy of Regime Change

As President Bush says frequently, the policy of the United States in Iraq is 'regime change.' That's a phrase widely interpreted to mean the overthrow of the government in Baghdad by any means necessary. The term itself isn't new. In the Iraqi context, it dates at least as far back as 1998, and the United States has a long history of changing regimes in other countries. But the administration's embrace of this expression is meant to represent a philosophical departure from previous policies. Its supporters see an opportunity to bring the benefits of freedom, democracy and free markets to closed societies everywhere from Iraq to China. A new kind of liberation theology, if you will. They point to the historical lessons of Germany and Japan after the Second World War and to the democracies that emerged following the collapse of the Soviet Union.

Critics see imperialism and a cynical disregard for what happened in the aftermath of other US-sponsored regime changes. They cite bloody repression in Guatemala, in Chile under Pinochet, Iran under the shah and in the former Zaire, now the Democratic Republic of Congo.

Is regime change a legitimate goal of foreign policy? Is it ever just or right? Does it make a difference if it means deposing an elected president in Chile or reinstating an elected president in Haiti? Where do you draw the line?

Source: Neal Conan, "U.S. Policy of Regime Change," Talk of the Nation, National Public Radio, September 25, 2002

2. In a short essay, describe the historical context surrounding the two documents above. Then analyze and explain how the purpose of the transcript of the meeting between Ambassador Glaspie and Saddam Hussein affects its reliability as a source of evidence.

Period 4

Document #1

Source: Wikimedia Commons

1. What First Amendment rights are being practiced in the actions of the people in this document?

_____

_____

_____

_____

Document #2

Ben Wizner from the ACLU said in regards to the arrest of Wikileaks founder Julian Assange:

"Criminally prosecuting a publisher for the publication of truthful information would be a first in American history, and unconstitutional. The government did not cross that Rubicon with today's indictment, but the worst case scenario cannot yet be ruled out. We have no assurance that these are the only charges the government plans to bring against Mr. Assange. Further, while there is no First Amendment right to crack a government password, this indictment characterizes as 'part of' a criminal conspiracy the routine and protected activities journalists often engage in as part of their daily jobs, such as encouraging a source to provide more information. Given President Trump's and his administration's well-documented attacks on the freedom of the press, such characterizations are especially worrisome."

Source: aclu.org

2. How would you summarize Mr. Wizner's point of view?

_____

_____

_____

_____

Document #3

Bill McKibben, author and founder of 350.org

We do, though; we face a crisis as great as any president has ever encountered. Here's how his paragraph looks so far: Since he took office, summer sea ice in the Arctic has mostly disappeared, and at the South Pole, scientists in May made clear that the process of massive melt is now fully under way, with 10 feet of sea-level rise in the offing. Scientists have discovered the depth of changes in ocean chemistry: that seawater is 30 percent more acidic than just four decades ago, and it's already causing trouble for creatures at the bottom of the marine food chain. America has weathered the hottest year in its history, 2012, which saw a drought so deep that the corn harvest largely failed. At the moment, one of the biggest states in Obama's union, California, is caught in a drought deeper than any time since Europeans arrived. Hell, a few blocks south of the U.N. buildings, Hurricane Sandy turned the Lower East Side of New York into a branch of the East River. And that's just the United States. The world's scientists earlier this spring issued a 32-volume report explaining exactly how much worse it's going to get, which is, to summarize, a lot worse even than they'd thought before. It's not that the scientists are alarmists – it's that the science is alarming. Here's how one Princeton scientist summarized the situation for reporters: "We're all sitting ducks."

Source: McKibben, Bill, Rolling Stone, "A Call to Arms: An Invitation to Demand Action on Climate Change," June 5, 2014

3. What actions would Mr. McKibben likely ask people to take to deal with this crisis?

_____

_____

_____

_____

Document #4

Jack Phillips, owner of Masterpiece Cakeshop in Denver, had argued that his cakes are works of art and that requiring him to bake them for same-sex weddings would force him to express a view that violated his religious beliefs.

Phillips, however, maintained during an interview with "Today," that he would "serve everybody."

"It's just that I don't create cakes for every occasion they ask me to create," he said.

"I don't discriminate against anybody — I serve everybody that comes in my shop," Phillips said. "I don't create cakes for every message that people ask me to create.

"This cake is a specific cake, a wedding cake is an inherently religious event and the cake is definitely a specific message," Phillips said, explaining his objection to making the wedding cake for the same-sex wedding.

Source: nbcnews.com

4. Identify the conflicting rights that are identified by Mr. Phillips' actions.

_____

_____

_____

Document #5

Memo from Secretary of Homeland Security Janet Napolitano, July 15, 2012, establishing the Deferred Action for Childhood Arrival policy

By this memorandum, I am setting forth how, in the exercise of our prosecutorial discretion, the Department of Homeland Security (DHS) should enforce the Nation's immigration laws against certain young people who were brought to this country as children and know only this country as home. As a general matter, these individuals lacked the intent to violate the law and our ongoing review of pending removal cases is already offering administrative closure to many of them. However, additional measures are necessary to ensure that our enforcement resources are not expended on these low priority cases but are instead appropriately focused on people who meet our enforcement priorities.

Source: dhs.gov

5. How does Secretary Napolitano's memo change how some immigrants in this country will be treated?

_____

_____

_____

_____

Document #6

From "How the Leader of Black Lives Matter Defines 'Power'"

"When George Zimmerman was acquitted… I wrote a post on Facebook that we later called 'A Love Letter to Black People,'" said Garza, the co-founder of Black Lives Matter, while speaking at the Lesbians Who Tech Summit in New York on Sept. 13.

Garza, a Black queer woman, is an Oakland-based organizer, writer, and public speaker who is currently the special projects director for the National Domestic Workers Alliance, the nation's leading voice for dignity and fairness for the millions of domestic workers in the United States.

"I wrote a post saying that we deserve to live," she continued. "That we deserve to live with dignity, no matter who we are, or where we come from. I ended that post by saying that our lives matter. And my sister, Patrisse [Cullors], put a hashtag in front of it."

Garza said she was confused by the mark: "I was like, 'What is this, why are you putting the pound sign?' I'm not quite a millennial."

Source: qz.com

6. What event(s) sparked the Black Lives Matter movement started by Ms. Garza?

_____

_____

_____

_____

7. **Civic Literacy Document-Based Essay:** Select two examples of individuals or groups taking civic action from 1990–2019 to make changes and for each example (1) identify the groups or individuals and their goals, (2) describe the historical circumstances of the action and (3) compare the actions taken to other historical actions by groups or individuals.

_____

_____

_____

_____

_____

_____

_____

_____

_____

_____

_____

_____

_____

_____

_____

_____

_____

_____

_____

_____

_____

_____

_____

_____

_____

_____

_____

_____

_____

_____

_____

Practice Regents Examination

Part 1—Stimulus-Based Multiple-Choice Questions

MCQ Set #1

Base your answers to questions 1 through 3 on the excerpt below and on your knowledge of social studies.

> The Burgesses of Assembly are elected, and return'd from all parts of the Country, viz. from each County two, and from James City one; which make up in all fifty one Burgesses, besides one Burgess to be sent by the Colledge, as the Charter directs. . . . The Freeholders [landowners] are the only Electors, and where-ever they have a Free-hold, (if they be not Women, or under Age) they have a Vote in the Election. . . . The Election is concluded by plurality of Voices; and if either Party be dissatisfied, or thinks he has not fair Treatment, he may demand a Copy of the Poll, and upon Application to the House of Burgesses shall have his Complaint inquired into. But to prevent undue Elections, many Acts have been there made agreeable to some lately enacted in England.
>
> The first business of a Convention, is to make choice of a Speaker, and to present him in full House to the Governor. Upon this occasion the Speaker in the name of the House, petitions the Governor to confirm the usual Liberties, and Priviledges of Assembly, namely, Access to his Person, whenever they shall have occasion; a freedom of Speech, and Debate in the House, without being further accountable; and a Protection of their Persons and their Servants from Arrest, &c. And these being granted by the Governor, they proceed to do Business, choosing Committees, and in other things, imitating as near as they can, the Method of the Honourable House of Commons in England.
>
> The Laws having duly past the House of Burgesses, the Council and the Governors Assent; they are transmitted to the Queen by the next Shipping, for her Approbation, her Majesty having another Negative Voice, on this Condition, that they immediately become Laws, and be in force upon the Governors first passing them, and so remain, if her Majesty don't actually repeal them, although she be not pleased to declare her Royal Assent.
>
> —Robert Beverley, *The History and Present State of Virginia, In Four Parts* (1705)

1. The best use of this excerpt would be to

    1. provide a description of Virginia's state government.
    2. indicate how laws are passed in Virginia.
    3. provide a description of Virginia's colonial government.
    4. to provide a model for the Constitution of the United States.

2. How did the legislative process of the House of Burgesses differ from that of a state legislature today?

   1. The House of Burgesses formed committees.

   2. Once legislation was passed by the House of Burgesses it went to the governor.

   3. Members of the House of Burgesses were guaranteed freedom of speech.

   4. Legislation had to be approved by the queen of England before it became law.

3. How does this passage illustrate the impact of time and place?

   1. The House of Burgesses was modeled after the English House of Commons, and adult male landowners had the right to vote.

   2. The Virginia colonists rebelled against rule by the queen of England.

   3. It describes the appointment of the governor by the House of Burgesses.

   4. Legislative sessions of the House of Burgesses were formally opened by the queen of England.

MCQ Set #2

Base your answers to questions 4 through 6 on the excerpt below and on your knowledge of social studies.

Parliament was influenced to adopt the pernicious Project, and assuming a new Power over them, have in the Course of eleven Years given such decisive Specimens of the Spirit and Consequences attending this Power, as to leave no Doubt concerning the Effects of Acquiescence under it. They have undertaken to give and grant our Money without our Consent, though we have ever exercised an exclusive Right to dispose of our own Property; Statutes have been passed for extending the Jurisdiction of Courts of Admiralty and Vice-Admiralty beyond their ancient Limits; for depriving us of the accustomed and inestimable Privilege of Trial by Jury in Cases affecting both Life and Property; *for suspending the Legislature of one of the Colonies;* for interdicting all Commerce to the Capital of another; and for altering fundamentally the Form of Government established by Charter, and secured by Acts of its own Legislature solemnly confirmed by the Crown; *for exempting the "Murderers" of Colonists from legal Trial, and in Effect, from Punishment;* for erecting in a neighbouring Province, acquired by the joint Arms of Great-Britain and America, a Despotism dangerous to our very Existence; *and for quartering Soldiers upon the Colonists in Time of profound Peace. It has also been resolved in Parliament, that* Colonists charged with committing certain Offences, shall be transported to England to be tried.

—Thomas Jefferson, A Declaration by the Representatives of the United Colonies of North-America, now met in Congress at Philadelphia, setting forth the Causes and Necessity of their taking up Arms, 6 July 1775

---

4. What major event had occurred 11 years earlier to cause the British to assume the new powers to which Jefferson refers?

   1. England passed a Bill of Rights.

   2. The American Revolution had begun.

   3. The French and Indian War ended.

   4. The Second Continental Congress adopted the Declaration of Independence.

5. Which of the following events occurred just before Jefferson issued this declaration?

   1. Crispus Attucks was killed in the Boston Massacre.
   2. Colonists dressed as Native Americans threw tea into the harbor in what came to be known as the Boston Tea Party.
   3. The Second Continental Congress adopted the Declaration of Independence.
   4. The first shots of the American Revolution were fired at Lexington and Concord.

6. How might this declaration be considered a turning point in American history?

   1. In it Jefferson articulates the grievances that led the colonists to declare independence.
   2. Jefferson is appealing to the American colonists to negotiate in an effort to avoid war.
   3. Jefferson is urging the colonists to engage in civil disobedience.
   4. Jefferson is arguing for the passage of the United States Constitution.

MCQ Set #3

Base your answers to questions 7 through 9 on the excerpt below and on your knowledge of social studies.

> At the proposal of the Russian Imperial Government, made through the minister of the Emperor residing here, a full power and instructions have been transmitted to the minister of the United States at St. Petersburg to arrange by amicable negotiation the respective rights and interests of the two nations on the northwest coast of this continent. A similar proposal has been made by His Imperial Majesty to the Government of Great Britain, which has likewise been acceded to. The Government of the United States has been desirous by this friendly proceeding of manifesting the great value which they have invariably attached to the friendship of the Emperor and their solicitude to cultivate the best understanding with his Government. In the discussions to which this interest has given rise and in the arrangements by which they may terminate the occasion has been judged proper for asserting, as a principle in which the rights and interests of the United States are involved, that the American continents, by the free and independent condition which they have assumed and maintain, are henceforth not to be considered as subjects for future colonization by any European powers. . . .
>
> —President James Monroe, Annual Message to Congress, December 2, 1823

7. What prompted President Monroe to issue this message to Congress?

   1. Russia and Great Britain were plotting to take over the northwest coast of North America.
   2. He wanted to let the nations of Europe know that the Americas were no longer open for colonization.
   3. He wanted to avoid a war between Russia and Great Britain from spreading to North America.
   4. He wanted Russia and Great Britain to help drive the Spanish out of their remaining colonies in the Americas.

8. What was the immediate result of Monroe's message?

   1. The United States guaranteed the independence of the new republics to our south.

   2. Russia and Great Britain both abandoned their colonies in North America.

   3. The United States annexed large portions of Mexico and Canada.

   4. There was a rush by European powers to establish colonies in the Americas before the Monroe Doctrine went into effect.

9. In what way could this be considered a turning point in history?

   1. The United States forced Russia to give up its colony on northwest coast of North American, which is now Alaska.

   2. The United States forced Great Britain to grant freedom to its North American colonies in what is now Canada.

   3. The United States claimed a position of leadership in defending the freedom of neighbors in the Americas.

   4. It forced Russia and Great Britain to form an alliance that would eventually help lead to World War I.

MCQ Set #4

Base your answers to questions 10 and 11 on the excerpt below and on your knowledge of social studies.

Slavery, like all other great systems of wrong, founded in the depths of human selfishness, and existing for ages, has not neglected its own conservation. It has steadily exerted an influence upon all around it favorable to its own continuance. And to-day it is so strong that it could exist, not only without law, but even against law. Custom, manners, morals, religion, are all on its side everywhere in the South; and when you add the ignorance and servility of the ex-slave to the intelligence and accustomed authority of the master, you have the conditions, not out of which slavery will again grow, but under which it is impossible for the Federal government to wholly destroy it, unless the Federal government be armed with despotic power, to blot out State authority, and to station a Federal officer at every cross-road. This, of course, cannot be done, and ought not even if it could. The true way and the easiest way is to make our government entirely consistent with itself, and give to every loyal citizen the elective franchise, —a right and power which will be ever present, and will form a wall of fire for his protection.

—Frederick Douglass, "Reconstruction," *Atlantic Monthly*, December 1866

---

10. What problem does Frederick Douglass address in this excerpt?

    1. the continuation of slavery in the north after the Civil War

    2. the continuation of racial discrimination in the South after the Civil War

    3. the despotic power of the federal government under Reconstruction

    4. the inability of the federal government to abolish slavery

11. How does Douglass suggest that the problem can be solved?

    1. by completely eliminating states' rights
    2. by arming the federal government with despotic power
    3. by stationing federal officers at every crossroad
    4. by extending the vote to all citizens

MCQ Set #5

Base your answers to questions 12 through 14 on the excerpt below and on your knowledge of social studies.

> Many people who believe in Birth Control as the means of voluntary motherhood say that the propaganda of the movement is directed too much to women and too little to men. They contend that the appeal should be to men quite as much as to women and that a strong effort should be made to arouse the masculine half of humanity to its responsibilities in relation to the evils growing out of the enslavement of the reproductive function.
>
> It is true that the propaganda of the Birth Control movement in America has been addressed almost entirely to women. It has been couched in the terms of woman's experience. Its prime importance to her has been continuously and consistently stressed. The reason for this course is at once fundamental and practical.
>
> The basic freedom of the world is woman's freedom. A free race cannot be born of slave mothers. A woman enchained cannot choose but give a measure of bondage to her sons and daughters. No woman can call herself free who does not own and control her body. No woman can call herself free until she can choose consciously whether she will or will not be a mother.
>
> —**Margaret Sanger, "A Parents' Problem or Woman's?"** in *Birth Control Review* **(March 1919)**

12. Which of the following claims does Sanger make in this excerpt?

    1. Men should take equal responsibility with women for birth control.
    2. Birth control is one more way for men to exercise control over women.
    3. Women should be able to control their own bodies and decide whether to be mothers.
    4. Abortion should remain legal so that women can safely terminate unwanted pregnancies.

13. Along with this excerpt, which of the following best illustrates change and continuity in 20th-century American history?

    1. the ratification of the 19th Amendment
    2. the ongoing fight over *Roe* v. *Wade*
    3. the enactment of Title IX
    4. the failure of the Equal Rights Amendment

MCQ Set #6

Base your answers to questions 14 through 16 on the excerpt below and on your knowledge of social studies.

> We intend to begin on the first of February unrestricted submarine warfare. We shall endeavor in spite of this to keep the United States of America neutral. In the event of this not succeeding, we make Mexico a proposal or alliance on the following basis: make war together, make peace together, generous financial support and an understanding on our part that Mexico is to reconquer the lost territory in Texas, New Mexico, and Arizona. The settlement in detail is left to you. You will inform the President of the above most secretly as soon as the outbreak of war with the United States of America is certain and add the suggestion that he should, on his own initiative, invite Japan to immediate adherence and at the same time mediate between Japan and ourselves. Please call the President's attention to the fact that the ruthless employment of our submarines now offers the prospect of compelling England in a few months to make peace.
>
> —Telegram from German Foreign Secretary Arthur Zimmermann to the German ambassador to Mexico, January 16, 1917

14. What was Zimmermann's main purpose in writing this telegram?

    1. to keep the United States neutral throughout the war
    2. to force the United States to enter the war
    3. to get England to sign a peace treaty with Germany
    4. to convince Mexico to ally itself with Germany if the United States entered the war

15. What actually happened as a result of this telegram?

    1. Both Mexico and Japan entered the war as German allies.
    2. The British intercepted the telegram and defeated Germany in the Battle of Britain.
    3. President Wilson asked Congress to declare war on Germany.
    4. Mexico and Japan both declared war on Germany.

16. In what way does this telegram mark a turning point in U.S. history?

    1. It was the first time the United States became involved in a European war.
    2. It was the first time submarines were used in war.
    3. It was the first time a telegram was sent across the Atlantic Ocean from Europe to the Americas.
    4. It marked the end of the policy known as the Monroe Doctrine.

MCQ Set #7

Base your answers to questions 17 through 19 on the excerpt below and on your knowledge of social studies.

Until last year I was of those mildly amused at the K.K.K. It seemed to me incredible that in 1925 such a movement could attract any number of people or become really serious. And then at first hand and at second I saw the Klan and its workings in widely different places.

I was lecturing in Akron, Ohio. Now Ohio is one of those States upon whose essential Americanism and devotion to the finer ideals of democracy I have long banked. There in the Middle West that finer flower of democracy, born in New England, and later choked by the industrialism of the East, had, to my mind, gone for replanting and renewal. I looked for sanity in the United States to come from a democratic appeal to the Middle West. And yet, there in Akron . . . I found the Klan calmly and openly in the saddle. The leader of the local Klan was president of the Board of Education and had just been tremendously busied in driving a Jew out of the public schools. The Mayor, the secretary of the Y.M.C.A., prominent men in many walks of life, were either open Klansmen or secret sympathizers. I was too astonished to talk. Throughout parts of Ohio, Illinois and Indiana I found a similar state of affairs.

What is the cause of all this? There can be little doubt but that the Klan in its present form is a legacy of the World War. Whatever there was of it before that great catastrophe was negligible and of little moment. The wages of War is Hate; and the End, and indeed the Beginning, of Hate is Fear. The civilized world today and the world half-civilized and uncivilized are desperately afraid. The Shape of Fear looms over them. Germany fears the Jew, England fears the Indian; America fears the Negro, the Christian fears the Moslem, Europe fears Asia, Protestant fears Catholic, Religion fears Science. Above all, Wealth fears Democracy. These fears and others are ancient or at least longstanding fears. But they are renewed and revivified today because the world has at present a severe case of nerves; it feels it necessary to be nervous because the Unexpected has happened.

—W. E. B. Du Bois, "The Shape of Fear," *The North American Review* (June 1926)

17. What support does Du Bois offer for his claim that the Ku Klux Klan was alive and well in 1925?

    1. He cites a rise in lynchings in the South.

    2. He mentions the existence of Jim Crow laws in the Midwest.

    3. He describes school segregation in places such as Kansas.

    4. He lists many community leaders in Akron, Ohio, who are members of the Ku Klux Klan.

18. What does Du Bois see as the cause for the revival of the Ku Klux Klan?

    1. He thinks it is a result of the World War.

    2. He thinks most people view it as a service club like the Rotary or Kiwanis.

    3. He thinks it is a response to the threat of socialism.

    4. He thinks that the Klan spread to the Midwest when African Americans moved north to work in factories during the World War.

19. What similarities does Du Bois see between what was going on in the United States and what was going on elsewhere in the postwar world?

   1. He says the influence of the Ku Klux Klan had spread to Europe, where it caused race riots.
   2. He equates the rise of the Ku Klux Klan with the rise of authoritarian governments in Europe.
   3. He blames fear of "the other," citing instances of this around the world.
   4. He relates the rise of the Ku Klux Klan to a postwar worldwide religious revival.

MCQ Set #8

Base your answers to questions 20 through 22 on the excerpt below and on your knowledge of social studies.

It is easy for you and for me to shrug our shoulders and to say that conflicts taking place thousands of miles from the continental United States, and, indeed, thousands of miles from the whole American Hemisphere, do not seriously affect the Americas—and that all the United States has to do is to ignore them and go about its own business. Passionately though we may desire detachment, we are forced to realize that every word that comes through the air, every ship that sails the sea, every battle that is fought does affect the American future.

Let no man or woman thoughtlessly or falsely talk of America sending its armies to European fields. At this moment there is being prepared a proclamation of American neutrality. This would have been done even if there had been no neutrality statute on the books, for this proclamation is in accordance with international law and in accordance with American policy.

This will be followed by a Proclamation required by the existing Neutrality Act. And I trust that in the days to come our neutrality can be made a true neutrality.

It is of the utmost importance that the people of this country, with the best information in the world, think things through. The most dangerous enemies of American peace are those who, without well-rounded Information on the whole broad subject of the past, the present and the future, undertake to speak with assumed authority, to talk in terms of glittering generalities, to give to the nation assurances or prophecies which are of little present or future value.

I myself cannot and do not prophesy the course of events abroad—and the reason is that because I have of necessity such a complete picture of what is going on in every part of the world, that I do not dare to do so. And the other reason is that I think it is honest for me to be honest with the people of the United States.

I cannot prophesy the immediate economic effect of this new war on our nation but I do say that no American has the moral right to profiteer at the expense either of his fellow citizens or of the men, the women and the children who are living and dying in the midst of war in Europe.

—Franklin D. Roosevelt, Fireside Chat, September 3, 1939

20. What event had just occurred to prompt President Roosevelt to broadcast this Fireside Chat?

    1. The Germans had sunk the *Lusitania*.

    2. France and Britain had declared war on Germany.

    3. The United States had withdrawn from the League of Nations.

    4. Japanese forces had bombed the U.S. naval base at Pearl Harbor.

21. What was Roosevelt's intention in broadcasting this Fireside Chat?

    1. He wanted to warn the American people against communist propaganda.

    2. He wanted to reassure the American people that the United States was ready to fight.

    3. He wanted to reassure the American people that the United States would try to stay out of the war.

    4. He wanted to warn the American people that anyone attempting to profit from the war would be imprisoned under the War Powers Act.

22. What course of action does Roosevelt say that the United States will take?

    1. It will sell weapons to both sides in the conflict.

    2. It will sell weapons to the Allies.

    3. It will break off diplomatic relations with Germany.

    4. It will remain neutral.

MCQ Set #9

Base your answers to questions 23 and 24 on the excerpt below and on your knowledge of social studies.

> As for McCarthy. Only a short-sighted or completely inexperienced individual would urge the use of the office of the Presidency to give an opponent the publicity he so avidly desires. Time and time again, without apology or evasion, I—and many members of this Administration—have stood for the right of the individual, for free expression of convictions, even though those convictions might be unpopular, and for uncensored use of our libraries, except as dictated by common decency.
>
> We have urged that America must be true to the principles of freedom and justice as applied to the individual if America herself is to remain free. Permit me to say that I think there would be far more progress made against so-called "McCarthy-ism" if individuals of an opposing purpose would take it upon themselves to help sustain and promote their own ideals, rather than to wait and wail for a blasting of their pet enemies by someone else. Frankly, in a day when we see journalism far more concerned in so-called human interest, dramatic incidents, and bitter quarrels than it is in promoting constructive understanding of the day's problems, I have no intention whatsoever of helping promote the publicity value of anyone who disagrees with me—demagogue or not!
>
> —President Dwight D. Eisenhower, Letter to his brother Milton Eisenhower, October 9, 1953

23. According to Eisenhower, what issues are at stake, and who will be affected by them?

    1. The right of individuals to believe as they want without fear of the government.

    2. The right of journalists to write human interest stories.

    3. Senator McCarthy's right to continue the hearings on communist infiltration without interference from the president.

    4. The right of those accused of being communist sympathizers to invoke the 5th Amendment to avoid incriminating themselves.

24. How does Eisenhower propose to respond to McCarthyism?

    1. He wants to have his attorney general stop McCarthy's hearings.

    2. He will campaign for McCarthy's opponent in the next election.

    3. He will continue to stand up for the rights of individuals without giving McCarthy the publicity he craves.

    4. He plans to tell journalists to promote constructive understanding of the day's problems.

MCQ Set #10

Base your answers to questions 25 and 26 on the excerpt below and on your knowledge of social studies.

Female-to-Male Earnings Ratio and Median Earnings of Full-Time, Year-Round Workers 15 Years and Older by Sex: 1960–2017

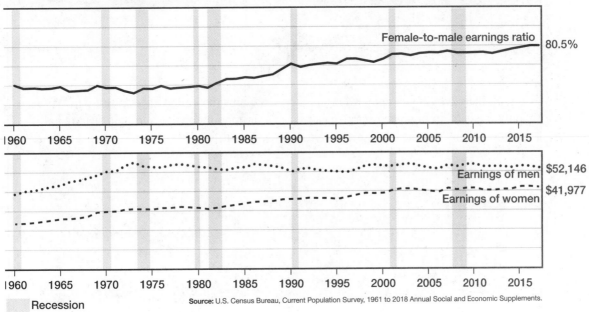

Source: U.S. Census Bureau, Current Population Survey, 1961 to 2018 Annual Social and Economic Supplements.

25. Which of the following best summarizes the main idea of these two charts?

    1. Average incomes have not increased much since 1961.

    2. Women's incomes have increased by nearly 20 percent in relation to men's incomes.

    3. Women's incomes are still substantially lower than men's incomes.

    4. Men continue to make substantially more than women for doing the same work.

26. Based on these two charts, which of the following is a plausible claim about the results of the Equal Pay Act?

    1. The act caused women's incomes to peak in the mid-1970s.

    2. The act was a complete failure since women still earn only about 80 percent of what men earn.

    3. The act was a failure because it only raised women's incomes from about 60 percent to about 80 percent of men's incomes.

    4. The act was probably responsible for shrinking the income gap between men and women.

MCQ Set #11

Base your answers to questions 27 and 28 on the excerpt below and on your knowledge of social studies.

U.S. Marines and Iraqis topple the statue of Saddam Hussein in Baghdad, Iraq, April 9, 2003

27. What historic event does this photograph commemorate?

    1. The killing of Osama bin Laden by U.S. Navy Seals.
    2. The fall of Baghdad during Operation Iraqi Freedom.
    3. The occupation of Baghdad during Operation Desert Storm.
    4. The trial and execution of Saddam Hussein.

28. Through the years, the United States has been responsible for many regime changes other than that in Iraq. Which of the following was an early instance of a U.S.-sponsored regime change?

    1. the forced abdication of Queen Liliuokalani of Hawaii
    2. Fidel Castro's communist revolution in Cuba
    3. the fall of the Berlin Wall
    4. the breakup of Yugoslavia

Part 2—Short-Essay Questions

Short Essay Question—Set #1

This Short Essay Question is based on the accompanying documents and is designed to test your ability to work with historical documents. Each Short Essay Question set will consist of two documents. Some of these documents have been edited for the purposes of this question. Keep in mind that the language and images used in a document may reflect the historical context of the time in which it was created.

Task: Read and analyze the following documents, applying your social studies knowledge and skills to write a short essay of two or three paragraphs in which you:

- Describe the historical context surrounding these documents.
- Identify and explain the ***relationship*** between the events and/or ideas found in these documents (Cause and Effect, *or* Similarity/Difference, *or* Turning Point).

In developing your short essay answer of two or three paragraphs, be sure to keep these explanations in mind:

Describe means "to illustrate something in words or tell about it"

Historical Context refers to "the relevant historical circumstances surrounding or connecting the events, ideas, or developments in these documents"

Identify means "to put a name to or to name"

Explain means "to make plain or understandable; to give reasons for or causes of; to show the logical development or relationship of"

Types of Relationships:

Cause refers to "something that contributes to the occurrence of an event, the rise of an idea, or the bringing about of a development"

Effect refers to "what happens as a consequence (result, impact, outcome) of an event, an idea, or a development"

Similarity tells how "something is alike or the same as something else"

Difference tells how "something is not alike or not the same as something else"

Turning Point is "a major event, idea, or historical development that brings about significant change. It can be local, regional, national, or global"

Document 1

[The Germans] have played their part in serving to convince us at last that that Government entertains no real friendship for us and means to act against our peace and security at its convenience. That it means to stir up enemies against us at our very doors the intercepted note to the German Minister at Mexico City is eloquent evidence.

We are accepting this challenge of hostile purpose because we know that in such a Government, following such methods, we can never have a friend; and that in the presence of its organized power, always lying in wait to accomplish we know not what purpose, there can be no assured security for the democratic Governments of the world. . . . We are glad, now that we see the facts with no veil of false pretense about them to fight thus for the ultimate peace of the world and for the liberation of its peoples, the German peoples included: for the rights of nations great and small and the privilege of men everywhere to choose their way of life and of obedience. The world must be made safe for democracy. Its peace must be planted upon the tested foundations of political liberty. We have no selfish ends to serve.

We desire no conquest, no dominion. We seek no indemnities for ourselves, no material compensation for the sacrifices we shall freely make. We are but one of the champions of the rights of mankind. We shall be satisfied when those rights have been made as secure as the faith and the freedom of nations can make them. . . .

Source: Woodrow Wilson, Joint Address to Congress, April 2, 1917

Document 2

Yesterday, December 7, 1941—a date which will live in infamy—the United States of America was suddenly and deliberately attacked by naval and air forces of the Empire of Japan.

The United States was at peace with that nation, and, at the solicitation of Japan, was still in conversation with its government and its emperor looking toward the maintenance of peace in the Pacific. Indeed, one hour after Japanese air squadrons had commenced bombing in the American island of Oahu, the Japanese ambassador to the United States and his colleague delivered to our secretary of state a formal reply to a recent American message. While this reply stated that it seemed useless to continue the existing diplomatic negotiations, it contained no threat or hint of war or armed attack.

It will be recorded that the distance of Hawaii from Japan makes it obvious that the attack was deliberately planned many days or even weeks ago. During the intervening time the Japanese government has deliberately sought to deceive the United States by false statements and expressions of hope for continued peace.

The attack yesterday on the Hawaiian Islands has caused severe damage to American naval and military forces. I regret to tell you that very many American lives have been lost. In addition, American ships have been reported torpedoed on the high seas between San Francisco and Honolulu. . .

The people of the United States have already formed their opinions and well understand the implications to the very life and safety of our nation.

As commander in chief of the Army and Navy I have directed that all measures be taken for our defense. But always will our whole nation remember the character of the onslaught against us.

No matter how long it may take us to overcome this premeditated invasion, the American people in their righteous might will win through to absolute victory. I believe that I interpret the will of the Congress and of the people when I assert that we will not only defend ourselves to the uttermost but will make it very certain that this form of treachery shall never again endanger us. . . .

I ask that the Congress declare that since the unprovoked and dastardly attack by Japan on Sunday, December 7, 1941, a state of war has existed between the United States and the Japanese Empire.

Source: Franklin D. Roosevelt, Request for a Declaration of War, December 7, 1941

Short-Essay Question—Set #2

This Short Essay Question is based on the accompanying documents and is designed to test your ability to work with historical documents. Each Short Essay Question set will consist of two documents. Some of these documents have been edited for the purposes of this question. Keep in mind that the language and images used in a document may reflect the historical context of the time in which it was created.

Task: Read and analyze the following documents, applying your social studies knowledge and skills to write a short essay of two or three paragraphs in which you:

- Describe the historical context surrounding Documents 1 and 2.
- Analyze Document 2 and explain how audience, or purpose, or bias, or point of view affects this document's use as a reliable source of evidence.

In developing your short essay answer of two or three paragraphs, be sure to keep these explanations in mind:

Describe means "to illustrate something in words or tell about it"

Historical Context refers to "the relevant historical circumstances surrounding or connecting the events, ideas, or developments in these documents"

Identify means "to put a name to or to name"

Explain means "to make plain or understandable; to give reasons for or causes of; to show the logical development or relationship of"

Types of Relationships:

Cause refers to "something that contributes to the occurrence of an event, the rise of an idea, or the bringing about of a development"

Effect refers to "what happens as a consequence (result, impact, outcome) of an event, an idea, or a development"

Similarity tells how "something is alike or the same as something else"

Difference tells how "something is not alike or not the same as something else"

Turning Point is "a major event, idea, or historical development that brings about significant change. It can be local, regional, national, or global"

Document 1

Merry Christmas

Merry Christmas, China

From the gun-boats in the river,

Ten-inch shells for Christmas gifts,

And peace on earth forever.

Merry Christmas, India,

To Gandhi in his cell,

From righteous Christian England,

Ring out, bright Christmas bell!

Ring Merry Christmas, Africa,

From Cairo to the Cape!

Ring Hallehuiah! Praise the Lord!

(For murder and rape.)

Ring Merry Christmas, Haiti!

(And drown the voodoo drums—

We'll rob you to the Christian hymns

Until the next Christ comes.)

Ring Merry Christmas, Cuba!

(While Yankee domination

Keeps a nice fat president

In a little half-starved nation.)

And to you down-and-outers,

("Due to economic laws")

Oh, eat, drink, and be merry

With a bread-line Santa Claus—

While all the world hails Christmas,

While all the church bells sway!

While, better still, the Christian guns

Proclaim this joyous day!

While holy steel that makes us strong

Spits forth a mighty Yuletide song:

SHOOT Merry Christmas everywhere!

Let Merry Christmas GAS the air!

Source: Langston Hughes, "Merry Christmas" (1930)

Document 2

Note: In the following excerpt, the ellipses (. . .) are part of the writer's style and do not indicate that something has been left out.

he wondered why he couldn't find work . . . a job . . . when he had first come to New York he had . . . and he had only been fourteen then . . . was it because he was nineteen now that he felt so idle . . . and contented . . . or because he was an artist . . . but was he an artist . . . was one an artist until one became known . . . of course he was an artist . . . and strangely enough so were all his friends . . . he should be ashamed that he didn't work . . . but . . . was it five years in New York . . . or the fact that he was an artist . . . when his mother said she couldn't understand him . . . why did he vaguely pity her instead of being ashamed . . . he should be . . . his mother and all his relatives said so . . . his brother was three years younger than he and yet he had already been away from home a year . . . on the stage . . . making thirty-five dollars a week . . . had three suits and many clothes and was going to help mother . . . while he . . . Alex . . . was content to lay and smoke and meet friends at night . . . to argue and read Wilde . . . Freud . . . Boccacio and Schnitzler . . . to attend Gurdjieff meetings and know things . . . Why did they scoff at him for knowing such people as Carl . . . Mencken . . . Toomer . . . Hughes . . . Cullen . . . Wood . . . Cabell . . . oh the whole lot of them . . . was it because it seemed incongruous that he . . . who was so little known . . . should call by first names people they would like to know . . . were they jealous . . . no mothers aren't jealous of their sons . . . they are proud of them . . . why then . . . when these friends accepted and liked him . . . no matter how he dressed . . . why did mother ask . . . and you went looking like that . . . Langston was a fine fellow . . . he knew there was something in Alex . . . and so did Rene and Borgia . . . and Zora and Clement and Miguel . . . and . . . and . . . and all of them . . .

Source: Richard Bruce Nugent, "Smoke, Lilies and Jade," *Fire!!* (November 1926)

Voting Rights

Document #1

Abigail Adams in a letter to her husband John Adams, March 31, 1776

"I long to hear that you have declared an independency. And, by the way, in the new code of laws which I suppose it will be necessary for you to make, I desire you would remember the ladies and be more generous and favorable to them than your ancestors. Do not put such unlimited power into the hands of the husbands. Remember, all men would be tyrants if they could. If particular care and attention is not paid to the ladies, we are determined to foment a rebellion, and will not hold ourselves bound by any laws in which we have no voice or representation."

Source: Adams Family Papers, Massachusetts Historical Society

1. What movement might be said to begin with this letter from Mrs. Adams?

_____

_____

_____

Document #2

Horace Greeley, editor of the New York Tribune, 1848

"When a sincere republican is asked to say in sober earnest what adequate reason he can give, for refusing the demand of women to an equal participation with men in political rights, he must answer, None at all. However unwise and mistaken the demand, it is but the assertion of a natural right, and such must be conceded."

Source: ap.gilderlehrman.org

2. What is the historical context for Mr. Greeley's statement?

_____

_____

_____

Document #3

Source: New York Heritage Digital Collections

JUST LIKE THE MEN! Votes for WHITE women.

3. How does this cartoon show a division that occurred in the women's suffrage movement?

_____

_____

_____

_____

Document #4

Voting Rights Act (1965)

    SEC. 4. (a) To assure that the right of citizens of the United States to vote is not denied or abridged on account of race or color, no citizen shall be denied the right to vote in any Federal, State, or local election because of his failure to comply with any test or device in any State....

    (c) The phrase "test or device" shall mean any requirement that a person as a prerequisite for voting or registration for voting (1) demonstrate the ability to read, write, understand, or interpret any matter, (2) demonstrate any educational achievement or his knowledge of any particular subject, (3) possess good moral character, or (4) prove his qualifications by the voucher of registered voters or members of any other class.

Source: ourdocuments.gov

4. Describe the historical context that led to the passage of the Voting Rights Act.

_____

_____

_____

_____

Document #5

from "Supreme Court Invalidates Key Part of Voting Rights Act," New York Times, June 25, 2013

The Supreme Court on Tuesday effectively struck down the heart of the Voting Rights Act of 1965 by a 5-to-4 vote, freeing nine states, mostly in the South, to change their election laws without advance federal approval. . . .

"Our country has changed," Chief Justice John G. Roberts Jr. wrote for the majority. "While any racial discrimination in voting is too much, Congress must ensure that the legislation it passes to remedy that problem speaks to current conditions."

The decision will have immediate practical consequences. Texas announced shortly after the decision that a voter identification law that had been blocked would go into effect immediately, and that redistricting maps there would no longer need federal approval. Changes in voting procedures in the places that had been covered by the law, including ones concerning restrictions on early voting, will now be subject only to after-the-fact litigation. . . .

Justice Ruth Bader Ginsburg summarized her dissent from the bench, an unusual move and a sign of deep disagreement. She cited the words of the Rev. Dr. Martin Luther King Jr. and said his legacy and the nation's commitment to justice had been "disserved by today's decision."

She said the focus of the Voting Rights Act had properly changed from "first-generation barriers to ballot access" to "second-generation barriers" like racial gerrymandering and laws requiring at-large voting in places with a sizable Black minority. She said the law had been effective in thwarting such efforts.

Source: "Supreme Court Invalidates Key Part of Voting Rights Act," New York Times, June 25, 2013

5. Describe in your own words the arguments made for and against the rollback of voting protections put into place by this Supreme Court decision.

_____

_____

_____

_____

Document #6

Commentary by Jelani Cobb October 21, 2018 in The New Yorker Magazine

According to the Brennan Center for Justice, ninety-nine bills designed to diminish voter access were introduced last year in thirty-one state legislatures. Many of the recent Republican-led efforts stem from the Supreme Court's 2013 decision in Shelby v. Holder. In an opinion that eviscerated the Voting Rights Act of 1965, Chief Justice John Roberts wrote that discrimination still exists, but not sufficiently to warrant the "extraordinary" remediation measures that the act imposed on the states of the former Confederacy. That argument is roughly equivalent to saying that a decline in the prevalence of an infectious disease means that we should stop vaccinating against it. Within hours of the decision, Texas announced a strict new voter-I.D. law. Mississippi and Alabama shortly afterward began enforcing similar laws that previously had been barred.

Source: Cobb, Jelani, The New Yorker, "Voter-Suppression Tactics in the Age of Trump," October 29, 2018

6. What is Mr. Cobb's main concern with the new bills introduced in 2017?

_____

_____

_____

_____

7. **Document-Based Essay:** Select two examples of groups or individuals that have attempted to extend or limit voting rights and for each example (1) describe the historical circumstances surrounding the attempt, (2) discuss the actions taken and (3) evaluate the successfulness of the actions in reaching the group or individual's goal.

_____

_____

_____

_____

_____

_____

_____

_____

_____

_____

_____

_____

_____

Index

A

Abolitionist movement, 84
Abolitionist's creed, 103
Adams, Abigail, 49
Adams, John, 39, 40, 49
Adams, Samuel, 40, 53
  speech on rights of the American Colonists, 71
Addams, Jane, 170
  need, for social settlements, 166
Affordable Care Act, 354
Agrarian issues and movements
  election of 1896, 161
  Grange Movement, 160
  cooperatives, formation of, 160
  Populist Party, birth of, 160
Aldrin, Buzz, 300
Allied victory and Wilson's defeat
  Fourteen Points, 197
  negotiation, for peace, 198
  League of Nations and United States Senate, 199
  Treaty of Versailles, 198
Al-Qaeda, 373
American Federation of Labor, 162–163
American Indian Movement, 342
American Railway Union, 163
American Recovery and Reinvestment Act, 352
American women's movement. *See also* Women
  constitutional amendment, 124
  Declaration of Sentiments, 123
  demands, for voting and property rights, 123
  Married Women's Property Act, 125
  suffrage movement, 123
Annan, Kofi
  speech, by, 371
Anthony, Susan B.
  American Equal Rights Association, 126
  born in, 125
  Declaration of Sentiments, 125
  emancipation of enslaved people, fought for, 125
  fight, for equal rights, 126
  The Revolution, 126
  Stanton, Elizabeth Cady and, 126
  woman suffrage, fight for, 126
Antifederalists, 52
  bill of rights, 53
Anti-Imperialist League, 184
Armstrong, Louis, 233
Armstrong, Neil, 300
Articles of Confederation
  amendments, 52
  drafting, 51
  rules and structure, 51
  successes of government under, 51
  weaknesses of government under, 51
Attucks, Crispus, 39
Automobile revolution
  credit, offer, 238
  growth of other industries, 237
  ideas of mass-production, 237

B

Baghdad, 393
Baltimore, Lord, 29
Barrin, Roland-Michel, 6
Battle of Antietam, 92–93
Battle of Lexington, 43
Begin, Menachem, 307

The Berlin Wall
  Commonwealth of Independent States, 313
  end of the Cold War, 313
Bessemer process, 151
Beverly, Robert, 28
Bill of Rights
  excluded rights, 56
  included rights, 55–56
  rights and protections, 55
  sovereignty, of the people, 56
Birmingham protest, 335
Black Codes, 117–118
Black Congressman
  testimony of, 121
Black nationalism, 233–234
Black Power movement, 337
Boston Massacre, 38–39
  effect of, 39
Boston Tea Party, 40
Brezhnev, Leonid, 302
British control over colonies
  Coercive Acts, 40
  initial colonial reaction
    Boston Massacre, 38–39
    Boston Tea Party, 40
    boycott, 38
    Stamp Act riots, 38
  letter, from Cadwallader Colden, 41
  Proclamation of 1763, 37
  Stamp Act, 37
  Tea Act, 38
  Townshend Acts, 38
Brown, John, 88
Burr, Aaron, 62
Bush, George W., 63
Business regulation
  freight rates, of railroad companies, 154
  Interstate Commerce Act, 154
  Sherman Antitrust Act, 154
  Trust-Busting, Court Cases, 154

C

Cabble, Samuel
  letter from, 97
Calvert, Cecil, 29
Carmichael, Stokely, 337
  what we want, 363
Carnegie, Andrew, 153
  Gospel of Wealth, 150
Carson, Rachel
  Silent Spring, 347
Cash crops
  meaning of, 15
Castro, Fidel, 301
Chávez, César, 343
Chicago Defender, 207
Chicano Movement, 343
Chief Canassateego
  speech, by, 30
China's economic and strategic rise
  crackdown in Tiananmen Square, 383
  gradual evolution, 383
  growth and maturity, 383–384
  relations between the United States and, 389
  trade deficit, 384
  United States and, 384
Chinese contribution and exclusion
  central Pacific railroad, 137

Chinese Exclusion Act, 138
    discrimination against Chinese, 137
    immigration of, 137
    nativist, 138
Chinese Exclusion Act, 138, 147
Chinese Merchant
    appeals to Congress, 146
Churchill, Winston, 264
Citizenship question, 101
Civil Rights Act, 118–119, 338
Civil rights movements
    assassinations, 337
    Birmingham protest, 335
    black power, 337
    Brown v. Board of Education of Topeka, 333
    civil disobedience, 333
    Defense of Marriage Act, 345
    Don't Ask, Don't Tell policy, 345
    equal rights for women, 361
    Freedom Summer, 336
    gay rights and the LGBT movement, 344
    immigration, 344
        Immigration Reform and Control Act, 344
    Little Rock School desegregation, 334
    march on Washington, 335
    Montgomery bus boycott, 333
    organizations, 334
    Racial Unrest, 336–337
    segregation and education, 339
    Selma, 336
    Stonewall Inn riots, 345
    students' rights, 346
        free speech rights, 357–358
Civil War
    African American participation, in, 95
    Battle of Antietam, 92–93
    battle of Gettysburg
        loss of life, at, 93
    captured over Vicksburg, 93
    election of Lincoln, 91
    engraving, of Fort Sumter in Charleston harbor, 91
    impacts of, 96
    North and South, in, 92
    secession, 91
        Southern States, 91
    Southern victories, 92
    Union and the Confederacy, 92
Clean Air Act, 346
Clean Water Act, 346
Code Talkers, 281
Coercive Acts, 40
Cold War
    Berlin Airlift, 293
    cause of, 291
    communism and McCarthyism, 293
    containment policy of U.S., 292
    Marshall Plan, 293
    North Atlantic Treaty Organization (NATO), 293
    Truman Doctrine, 292
Collins, Michael, 300
Colonial development
    influencing factors
        geographic factors
            climates and weather conditions, 15–16
            colonial economic systems, development of, 16
            patterns of settlement, 16
        slavery
            colonial economic system, 18
            development as racial institution, 19
            indentured servitude and, 19
            transatlantic slave trade, 17
            triangle trade, 18–19
    social structures and labor systems, 17
        free black people and slaves, 17
        indentured servants, 17
        women and, 17
    letter, from indentured servant, 14
    tobacco Farming, 16
Columbus, Christopher, 31
Connecticut
    conflicts with Native Americans, 10
    Fundamental Orders of, 10
Constitutional reforms
    amendment, for
        right for vote, 116
        rights of American citizenship, 115
    congressional reconstruction, 115
    initial plans, 115
    thirteenth amendment (1865)
        illegal, slavery, 115
Constitution, of the United States, 50
    bill of rights, 54
    Cherokee nation, of, 57
    debated issues
        foreign commerce, 52
        number of representatives, 52
        slave trade, 52
    Great Compromise, 52
    proper size for republic, 53
Council of Censors of Pennsylvania
    petition of the Philadelphia Synagogue, to, 68
Cuba
    and the Spanish-American War, 186–187, 212
    missiles in, by Soviet, 301
        hot line, 301
        nuclear test ban treaties, 301
Curtis, Carl, 254

D

Dachau concentration camp, 286
Debs, Eugene V.
    How I Became a Socialist, 176
Declaration of Independence
    British troop movements, monitoring of, 43
    Common Sense, impact, 43
    gunfire, at Lexington and Concord, 43
    ideas in, 44
    impacts of, 44
    purpose of, 44
    united action, to defend rights, 43
Declaration of Sentiments, 85, 103
Declaration of the Rights of Man, 285
Defense of Marriage Act (DOMA), 345
de Las Casas, Bartolomé, 31
Democratic Party Platform, 201
Diary of Elizabeth De Hart Bleecker, 64
Dodd-Frank Wall Street Reform and Consumer Protection Act, 352
Dollar diplomacy, 190
Douglass, Frederick, 84
    To My Old Master, 89
Du Bois, W.E.B., 224
Dust Bowl, 243

E

Economic growth
    demand, for enslaved labor, 79
    domestic industries, growth of, 78
    free black people, status of, 79
    market revolution, 77
    mill life, 78–79
    technology, 77
    transportation
        construction, of the Erie Canal, 77
    women, change in roles, for, 79

Education for All Handicapped Children Act, 343
Eichmann, Adolph, 276
Eisenhower doctrine, 305
Eisenhower, Dwight D., 304
Ellington, Duke, 233
Emancipation Proclamation, 94
Endangered Species Act, 346
English in America, 7
        conflict, 8
        Powhatans and the Colonists, 8
        rescue, 8
        Virginia Company, establishment of, 8
English–Native American relations, 8
Environmental Protection Agency (EPA), 346
Equal Pay Act, 341
Equal Rights Amendment (ERA), 342
European colonization of the Americas, 6–12
        French Colonies, praise for, 6
European Influences
        British traditions, 23–24
                Common Law and Civil Law, difference, 24
        colonial experience, effect on colonial institutions, 24
        colonial institutions, 24–25
        enlightenment ideas, 23
        New England town meetings, 25

F
Fascism
        characteristics of, 255
        Nazi Party, 255
Faubus, Orval, 334
FDR and the New Deal. *See* Roosevelt, Franklin D.
Federalists, 52
        federal plan, of government, 52
Federal Meat Inspection Act of 1906, 179
Federal Power Expansion
        civil liberties, 93
        Emancipation Proclamation, 94
        National Bank Act, 93
        suspension of habeas corpus, 94
Fireside Chat, 259
First Amendment Rights
        Supreme Court, 209
First Continental Congress, 40
Flapperhood, 245
Ford, Henry, 237
        automobiles, 153
        The First Assembly Line, 177
Fourteenth Amendment, 115
Free black people, 17
Freedmen's Bureau, 116
Freedoms and tolerance
        action, in the Red Scare, 206
        Ku Klux Klan, 206
        Schenck v. United States, 205–206
        Sedition Act, 205
        xenophobia, 206
Freedom Summer, 336
French and Indian war, 12
French Colonies
        alliances with Indian Nations, 6
        France's colonial venture
                alliances with Native Americans, 12
                French and Indian war, 12
French monarchy
        revolution, 59
Frethorne, Richard, 19
Fulgencio Batista, 301
Fur trade, 11

G
Garrison, William Lloyd
        abolitionist movement, 84

Garvey, Marcus, 233–234
Gelb, Leslie H., 323
Gettysburg Address, 93
Gilman, Charlotte Perkins
        Is America Too Hospitable?, 229
Glasnost, 311
Glenn, John, 300
Globalization
        advances in technology, 381
        corporate Influence on
                other countries, 382
                the United States, 382
        free trade and, 380
        multinational corporations, 380
        NAFTA, 380
        negative consequences, 381
        overview, 380
        positive consequences, 381
        rise of multinationals, 382
Gompers, Samuel, 156
Gorbachev, Mikhail, 311
Gore, Al, 63
Governmental reforms
        Federal Reserve System, 167
        income tax, 167
        senators, direct election of, 167
        Susan B. Anthony Amendment, 168
Grain deal, 302
Great Compromise, 52
Great Depression
        agriculture stagnation, 238
        buying stocks, on margin, 238
        consumption and income issues, 238
        FDR and The New Deal
                Agricultural Adjustment Act, 241
                banking and stock market reforms, 241
                Brain Trust, 240
                business and labor, 242
                direct federal assistance programs, 241
                Dust Bowl, 242
                New Deal programs/agencies, 242
                resistance and court challenges, 243
                Social Security Act, 243
        Hoover administration's response
                betting on business and banks, 239
                Hoovervilles, 240
                unemployment, 240
        immediate and devastating economic consequences, 239
        international consequences, 239
Great Migration
        African Americans Postwar, 204
        pull factors, 205
        push factors, 204
        reception, of African Americans in the North, 205
Great recession. *See also* Great Depression
        banks to foreclose, 351
        Consumer Financial Protection Bureau, 352
        Economic Stimulus Act, 351
        Emergency Economic Stabilization Act, 351–352
        Financial Services Oversight Council, 352
The Great Society
        Economic Opportunity Act, 349
        gross domestic product, 350
        Lyndon Johnson and, 349
        reaganomics, 350
        supply-side economics, 350
        Tax Reform Act, 350
        war on poverty, 349
Grimké, Angelina, 82, 85
Grimké, Sarah, 85

H
Hallock, Joseph, 260

Hamilton, Alexander, 45, 52
Hamilton's economic plan
    areas of, 60
    conflict over, 60
    Democratic-Republicans
        strict construction of constitution, 60–61
    federalists and loose construction, 60
Harlem Renaissance, 205, 230, 231
    cause of, 231
Henry, Patrick, 26, 53
Hidalgo, Guadalupe
    treaty of, 134
Hiroshima, 267
Hitler, Adolf, 255
Hitler, Adolph, 275
Holocaust, 275
Homestead Act, 129
Hoover, Herbert, 239
    economic crisis, 239
        bets on business and banks, 239
        policies to improve crisis, 239
    unemployment and Hoovervilles, 240
Hoovervilles, 240
How the Other Half Lives, 173
Hughes, Langston, 231
Humanitarian intervention
    debate, 387
    defending human rights, 369
    ethnic cleansing, 370
    Genocide in Rwanda, 370
    North Atlantic Treaty Organization (NATO), 370
    Vietnam syndrome, 369
    war in Kosovo, 370
    Yugoslavia disintegrates, 369
Hurston, Zora Neale, 231
    Art and Such, 251
    The Crisis, 251

I

Immigration
    Americanization process, 158
    European immigrants, 158
    new immigration
        reactions, to, 158
    patterns of immigration, 157
    public education, 157
    push-pull factors, 157
    search for jobs, 157
Immigration Reform and Control Act, 344
Imperialism
    acquisition of Hawaii, 185
        plea, from the Queen of Hawaii, 191
    annexation of Samoa, 185
    arguments
        against expansion, 185
        for expansion, 185
    social Darwinism, 185
    in the Western Hemisphere
        dollar diplomacy, 190
        Panama Canal, 185
        Roosevelt Corollary, 189
        U.S. policy of intervention, 190
IIndian Removal Act, 80
Individual reformers
    African American rights, movement for, 172
    early fight for birth control, 170–171
    Henry Street Settlement, 170
    muckrakers, 170
    Settlement House Movement, 170
    tenement reform, 171
Industrialization, after the Civil War
    automobiles, 153

Bessemer process, 151
communications, 152
energy sources, 152
finance for, 153–154
oil-refining company, 152–153
regulation of companies, 154
Second Industrial Revolution, 151
steel works, 153
transportation, 151
Industrial Workers of the World, 164
International Ladies' Garment Workers' Union, 163
Interstate Commerce Act, 154
Intolerable Acts, 40
Iran Hostage Crisis, 308
Iran-Iraq War, 367
Iraq
    competing groups in, 375
    new Iraqi government, 377
    operation Iraqi freedom, 376
    possible preemptive strike, 376
    postwar problems, 376–377
    U.S. policy of regime change, 394
    weapons of mass destruction, 376
Islamic extremism, 373

J

Jackson, Andrew, 76
    Indian Removal Act, 80
    rise of political democracy, 80
    spoils system, 80
    Trail of Tears, 80
    Worcester v. Georgia, 80
Jackson, Helen Hunt, 128
Japanese relocation, 280
Jazz, 233
Jefferson, Thomas, 52, 60, 62
Jinping, Xi, 384
Johnson, James Weldon
    Race Prejudice and the Negro Artist, 235
Johnson, Lyndon, 294–295, 297
    signing of the medicare bill, 356
Joint-stock company, 8

K

Kansas-Nebraska act, 87
Kennan, George, 292
Kennedy, John F., 299
Kerry, John
    speech on behalf of Vietnam Veterans against the war, 322
Khomeini, Ayatollah, 308
Khrushchev, Nikita, 299
King, Martin Luther, 333, 334,
    and Crispus Attucks, 39
    assassination, 337
    Birmingham Protest, 335
    "I Have a Dream" speech, 332
    letter from Birmingham jail, 362
    march to Selma, 336
King Philip's War, 10
Kissinger, Henry, 301
Knights of Labor, 162
Knights of the White Camellia, 118
Ku Klux Klan (KKK), 118, 246
    returns, 226
    Texas Minister Defends, 246

L

Labor Movements
    American Federation of Labor, 162–163
    American Railway Union, 163
    farmers speak, 165
    Industrial Workers of the World, 164

International Ladies' Garment Workers' Union, 163
Knights of Labor, 162
strikes, reactions to, 164
Laden, Osama bin, 373
Lebanon tragedy, 308
LGBT movement, 344
Lincoln, Abraham
Civil War and, 105
election of, 91
Southern reaction, to, 91
Emancipation Proclamation, 94
expansion of federal power, 93
fight for human equality, 93
Gettysburg address, 90
With Malice toward none, 96
suspension of habeas corpus, 94
thirteenth amendment (1865), 115
Little, Malcolm, 333 *see* Malcolm X
Locke, John, 44
natural rights, on, 71
Louisiana Purchase
nationalism and, 75
Lynching, 180
announcements, of public lynching, 181

M

Malcolm X, 333, 334
assassination, 337
Manhattan Project, 266
Manifest destiny, 86
description of, 100
Married Women's Property Act, 125
Marshall Plan, 293
Marshall, Thurgood, 333
Maryland Toleration Act of 1649, 25
Massachusetts Bay Colony, 10
Mayflower Compact, 24–25
McCarthy Cries Again, 321
McCarthyism, 293
McCarthy, Joseph, 293, 320
McClure's magazine, 170
McKinley, William, 185
Means, Russell, 342
Mexican Americans
anti-Latino discrimination, 136
Chicano Movement, 343
effects, of the treaty, 136
fight against Anglo settlers, 136
Mexican-American war, 86
Middle East
Eisenhower Doctrine, 305
Israel wars with Arab neighbors, 305
oil crises, 306
peace in, search for, 318
U.S. foreign policy, 305
Modern Women's Movement. *See also* Civil Rights Movement
American Indian Movement, 342
Bureau of Indian Affairs, 342
Chicano Movement, 343
Civil Rights Act, 341
Equal Pay Act, 341
Equal Rights Amendment, 342
The Feminine Mystique, 341
gender discrimination, 342
National Organization for Women (NOW), 341
Native Americans Rights
National Congress of American Indians (NCAI), 342
Roe v. Wade, 342
Self-Determination and Education Assistance Act, 343
Title IX, 342
United Farm Workers (UFW), 343
Monroe Doctrine, 76–77

Theodore Roosevelt's Corollary to, 208
Morgan, John Pierpont, 153
Morrill Act, 120, 129
Mott, Lucretia
antislavery society, foundation of, 85
women's rights, reform movements for, 85

N

Nagasaki, 267
National Aeronautics and Space Administration (NASA), 300
National Association for the Advancement of Colored People
(NAACP), 172, 222, 226, 233, 234, 333, 334, 337
National Congress of American Indians, 342
Nationalism
Louisiana Purchase, 75
Monroe Doctrine, 76–77
overview, 75
Tecumseh's rebellion, 75
tensions with Britain, 75–76
war of 1812, 76
National Organization for Women (NOW), 341
purpose of, 360
National Recovery Administration (NRA), 242
Nation, Carry, 169
Native Americans, consequences for
account , of signing treaty, 142
arrival of white settlers, 131
Dawes Act, 132
forced assimilation, 132
legal status, 131
people, of plains, 130
reservation system, 132
treaties, 131
war against white settlers, 131
Nat Turner's rebellion, 84
contemporary account of, 98
Nazi Party, 255
New Deal
Agricultural Adjustment Act, 241
banking and stock market reforms, 241
Brain Trust, 240
business and labor, 242
direct federal assistance programs, 241
Dust Bowl, 242
New Deal programs/agencies, 242
resistance and court challenges, 243
Social Security Act, 242
New England
Connecticut River, 10
Massachusetts Bay Colony, 10
Plymouth colonists, 9
Puritan movement, 9
town meetings, 25
direct government, 25
War between Colonists and Native Americans, in, 10
New Federal Government
creation of checks and balances, 55
federal/state division of power, 54
judicial independence, 55
separation of powers, 55
New immigrants, 157
New Netherland
English control, 11
fur trade, 11
law passed, by the Council of, 27
right of petition in, 26
Nixon, Richard, 302
televised address to the Soviet people, 303
North Atlantic Treaty Organization (NATO), 293, 370
Nuclear arms race
atoms-for-peace plan, 299
The Berlin Wall, 299

hydrogen bomb, 299
nuclear scientists, on the dangers of, 316
satellite launching, 300
Sputnik and the space race, 300
U-2 Incident, 299
use of atomic weapons at Hiroshima and Nagasaki, 299
Nuclear test ban, 301
Nullification
abolitionist movement, 84
Alien and Sedition Acts, 81
Virginia and Kentucky resolutions against, 83
Nat Turner's rebellion, 84
Ordinance of, 83
Sojourner Truth, 84
Nuremburg trials, 276
Opening Statement, 287

O

Obama, Barack, 352
Obamacare, 354
Oil crises, 306
Old immigrants, 157
Organization of Petroleum Exporting Countries (OPEC), 306

P

Pacific Railroad Act, 129
Pacific Railway Act, 141
Paine, Thomas
The American Crisis, 67
Palestine Liberation Organization (PLO), 308
Parks, Rosa, 333
Parliament of Great Britain
plan, to unite thirteen colonies, 70
Patriot Act, 374
impact of, 375
Penn, William
colony of Pennsylvania, foundation of, 33
letter to the Colonists of Pennsylvania, 32
treaty with the Lenni Lanape, singing, 32
Pequot War, 10
Perestroika, 311
Persian Gulf War
Iran-Iraq War, 367
Iraqi invasion to Kuwait, 367
objection, by Bush, 367
negative consequences of, 369
Operation Desert Storm, 368
positive consequences of, 369
U.S. Ambassador Glaspie, 393
use of economic sanctions, 368
Pilgrims, 9
Podesta, John, 392
Policies spur expansion
building of transcontinental railroad, 129
closing, of the frontier, 130
Homestead Act, 129
Morrill Act, 129
Pacific Railroad Act, 129
Policy of détente, 302
Postwar recession, 203
Potsdam Conferences, 291
Powhatan, 9
Presidential election of 1800 vs. 2000, 62–63
Proclamation of 1763, 37
Progressive Era. See Governmental reforms
Pull factors, 157
Puritan movement, 9
Push factors, 157

Q

Queen Liliuokalani, 185
Quota Acts of the 1920s, 227

R

Reagan and the Russians, 314
Reagan, Ronald, 308, 311, 314, 330, 358–359, 369
and the EPA, 346
INF Treaty, 312
vs. Lyndon Johnson, 349–350
Reaganomics, 350
Realpolitik, 302
Reconstruction
African American Abolitionist, 145
African American hopes, 120
Black Colleges, 120
economic realities, 120
election of 1876, 118
end of, 117
Freedmen's Bureau, 116
Morrill Acts, 120
policies
African Americans, in government, 117
Black Codes, 117
Civil Rights Act, 118
compromise of 1877, 118
the Ku Klux Klan, 118
radical republican congressman, on, 144
republicans, in the South, 117
voting rights, 119
methods used to prevent African Americans, from, 119
Red scare, 211
Reparations, 198
Return to normalcy, after World War I
flappers and freud, 225
Prohibition and the Volstead Act, 226
congressman on the failure of, 247
rise in women power, 225
Revolutionary War
George Washington and, 44
impacts on
African Americans, 46
Native Americans, 47
women, 46
workers, 45–46
letter from Abigail Adams, to Her Husband John Adams, 48
Native American Tribes, in, 47
turning points, 45
victory, at Yorktown, 47
Reza Pahlavi, Shah Mohammad, 308
Rights of the disabled
Americans with Disabilities Act, 344
Education for All Handicapped Children Act, 343–344
rights of the accused, 344
Robeson, Paul, 232
Robinson, Harriet
autobiography of, 74
Rockefeller, John D.
oil-refining company, 152
Standard Oil Company, 153
trust, 152
Roosevelt Corollary, 189
Roosevelt, Eleanor, 278
Speech to the United Nations, 279
Roosevelt, Franklin D., 138, 236, 240, 254, 258, 272, 284
death, 266
Fireside Chat, 259
Japanese internment, 269
letter, from C.B.S., Rural Supervisor of Schools, 244
New Deal, 236
Quarantine Speech, 257
solving economic crisis
banking and stock market reforms, 241
Brain Trust, 236
direct federal assistance programs, 241
Dust Bowl, 242

speech, at the Democratic Convention, 236
Supreme Court packing scheme, 243
wartime leadership, 263, 270
Roosevelt, Theodore, 171, 172, 188
"muckrakers," 170
New York State Tenement Housing Commission, 171
Panama Canal, 188
Roosevelt Corollary, 189, 208
Rough Riders, 187
trust busting, 154
Ross, John
protest, treaty of New Echota, 81
Rough Riders, 187

S

Sadat, Anwar, 307
Sausage factory
conditions, in, 178
Scopes Monkey Trial, 227–228
Scott, Dred, 88
Seabed Agreement, 302
Secession, 91
Second war for independence, 76
Self-Determination and Education Assistance Act, 343
Selma, 336
Seneca Falls convention, 85
Separation of powers, 55
September 11 attacks, 373
act's effects on civil liberties, 375
Afghanistan after Taliban rule, 374
Americans reactions, to, 374
attackers, 373
electronic surveillance programs, 376
invasion of Afghanistan, 374
Muslims Denounce, 378
Patriot Act, 374
roots of islamic extremism, 373
Shepard, Alan, 300
Sherman Antitrust Act, 154
Sinclair, Upton
Appeal to Reason, 170
The Jungle, 170
Slavery
development, as racial institution, 19
indentured servitude, 19
transatlantic slave trade, 17
triangle trade, 18–19
Slavery's expansion, fight over
Compromise of 1850, 87
Dred Scott decision, 88
John Brown's raid, 88
Kansas-Nebraska act, 87
manifest destiny, 86
Mexican-American war, 86
Missouri Compromise, 85
Texas, as independent nation, 86
Social Darwinism, 185
Social welfare programs
cost-of-living adjustment (COLA), 353
health care reform, 353–354
medicare, 353
percentage, of Americans without health insurance, 354
retirement of baby boomers, 353
social security, 353
Sojourner Truth, 79, 84
Southern Christian Leadership Conference (SCLC), 333
Spanish-American War
causes of, 186
decision for, 186
historical society, of Pennsylvania, 186
results of, 187
anti-imperialist argument, 187
imperialist argument, 187

Insular Cases, 188
revolt, in the Philippines, 188
Treaty of Paris, 187
Treaty of Paris, 212
Spanish colonization, 7
Caribbean islands, 7
North American Mainland, 7
Spoils system
spoils system, 80
Stalin, Joseph, 264
Molotov-Ribbentrop Pact with Hitler, 256
Stamp Act, 37
arguments over, 37
New York Merchants response, to, 66
riots, 38
tax on colonial newspapers and legal documents, 37
Standing bear, testimony of, 133
Stanton, Elizabeth Cady, 123
States' rights. *See* Nullification
Statue of Mercy Otis, 53
Stonewall Inn riots, 345
Stowe, Harriet Beecher, 84
Strategic Arms Limitation Treaty (SALT I), 302
anti-ballistic missiles, 311
Intermediaterange Nuclear Forces Treaty, 312
SALT II, 311
Strategic Defense Initiative, 311
Student Nonviolent Coordinating Committee (SNCC), 334
Subsistence farmers, 15
Suffrage movement
constitutional amendment, 124
demands for voting, 123
property rights, demand for, 125
suffragists, 123
Suffrage parade, 168
Suffragists
Anthony, Susan B., 123
Catt, Carrie Chapman, 124
Paul, Alice, 124
Stanton, Elizabeth Cady, 123
Stone, Lucy, 123
Summit conference, 299
Supreme Court, impact of
Gibbons v. Ogden, 62
Marbury v. Madison, 61–62
McCulloch v. Maryland, 62
powers of the Federal Government, 62
principle of judicial review, 62

T

Taliban, 374
Tarbell, Ida
History of the Standard Oil Company, 170
Tariff, 60
Tea Act, 38
Tecumseh's Rebellion
tensions with Britain, 75–76
Tehran Conferences, 291
Temperance movement
Anti-Saloon League, 169
congressman, on the failure of, 169
National Prohibition Act, 169
prohibition laws, 168
temperance crusaders, 169
Tet Offensive, 295
The 9/11 Commission Report, 391
The Four Freedoms, 284
The History and Present State of Virginia, 1705, 28
Tonkin Gulf Resolution, 295
Too big to fail, 355
Townshend Acts, 38
Transfer of power
Presidential election of 1800

roles, of Electoral College and Congress, 62
Presidential election of 2000
  roles, of Electoral College and the Supreme Court, 63
Treaty of Paris, 187
Treaty of Versailles, 198, 255
Truman Doctrine, 292
Truman, Harry, 290
Truman, Harry S., 266
  Press release about the atomic bomb, 267
Truman's War in Korea
  causes of, 293
  China involvement, 294
  military casualties, 294
Twain, Mark
  imperialism, 213

U

Uncle Tom's Cabin, 84
Union prevails
  13th amendment, 96
  African American participation, 95
  Richmond and Appomattox, 95
  Sherman's march, to the Sea, 95
United Nations Climate Conference, 385
United Nations (UN)
  League of Nations, 277
  permanent members of, 277
  purpose of, 276
  universal declaration of human rights, 277–278
United States
  domestic impacts of World War II
    African Americans, 271
    effects of mobilization, 269
    entertainers, 271
    rationing, 271
    womanpower, 270–271
  globalization in, 280–382
  involvement in World War I
    opposition to involvement, 196
    short-term causes of, 196
    troops, to Europe, 197
    War Industries Board, set up of, 197
  Japan and
    attack, on the Pearl Harbor, 258
    declaration of war against Japan, 258
    Japanese policies toward China, 258
  Japanese Internment, 269–270
  Mexico clash and
    American expansion, 135
    decision for, 197
    treaty of Guadalupe Hidalgo, 135
  Middle East policy of, 307–308
  Wartime Conferences, 291
Universal Negro Improvement Association (UNIA), 233

V

Vietnamization, 295
Vietnam War
  causes, 294
  Johnson, Lyndon, 294–295
  Nixon and, 295
  student protests, 295
  Tet Offensive, 295
  Tonkin Gulf Resolution, 295
  Vietnamization, 295
  War Powers Act, 296
  Watergate crisis, 296
Virginia House of Burgesses, 26
Voting Rights Act, 338

W

War of 1812
  spirit of nationalism, 76
War Powers Act, 296, 317
War's effect, on the economy
  new jobs, for women and minorities, 203
  postwar recession, 203
Washington, Booker T., 114
Washington, George, 44
  death of, 65
  Presidency
    Cabinet, 59
    farewell address, 58, 59
    taxation and rebellion, 59
    transfer of power, 59
  soul and sword of the American Revolution, as, 45
  Valley Forge, at, 45
Watergate crisis, 296
Wells, Ida B., 172
  Lynch Law in America, 180
West, Benjamin, 32
Wiesel, Elie
  Nobel Prize acceptance speech, 309
Willard, Frances, 169
  20th Annual Conference of the WCTU in Chicago, 174
Wilson, Woodrow, 190, 192
Woman's Christian Temperance Union (WCTU), 169
Woman suffrage, 127
Women
  antislavery society, 85
  declaration of rights, 85
    suffragist, on women's rights, 140
  demands, for voting and property rights
    constitutional amendment, 124
    Married Women's Property Act, 125
    suffrage movement, 123
  fights for the abolition of slavery, 84
  Grimké sisters, 85
  new opportunities, for, 123
  Seneca Falls convention, 85
  Sojourner Truth, on equal rights for, 122
  in War Industry, 283
World War I
  allied powers, 193
  central powers, 193
  European military alliances, 193
  involvement, of United States, 195
  long-term causes of, 193
  short-term causes of, 194
  United States, as neutral country, 194
  U.S. Army Air Service Recruiting Poster, 215
World War II
  air war, 263
  Allied Leader in, 264
  atomic bomb, use of, 266
  cause of, 255–256
  Europe, 261
  Hitler's rising aggression, 255
  Molotov-Ribbentrop Pact with Hitler, 256
  Operation Overlord, 261
  in the Pacific, 264–266
  Pearl Harbor, 258
  policy of appeasement, 256
  sea war, 262
  Treaty of Versailles, 255
  U.S. involvement in
    Lend-Lease Act, 257
    Neutrality Act, 257
    tension with Japan, 258
  Yalta Conference, 264

Y

Yalta Conference, 264, 291